Managerial Economics

Managerial Economics

Samuel C. Webb

Wichita State University

HOUGHTON MIFFLIN COMPANY Boston
Atlanta Dallas Geneva, Illinois Hopewell, New Jersey
Palo Alto London

This book is dedicated with love
to my optimal family

Jane

Bronson

Jennifer

Mark

Holly

who patiently sacrificed
and persevered with me during
a protracted intellectual pregnancy

Much of the material in Chapter 29 has been condensed and adapted from *The American Idea of Success* by Richard M. Huber. Copyright 1971 by McGraw-Hill Book Company. Used with permission of McGraw-Hill Book Company.

Printed in the U.S.A.

Library of Congress Catalog Card Number: 75-31039

ISBN: 0-395-20589-1   81-5440

Contents

Preface

The discipline of managerial economics covers a broad range of topics of growing popularity in academic colleges of business throughout the United States. Many institutions are transforming standard courses in microeconomic theory into those that have more immediate use to modern business people. At present, there is no universally accepted body of knowledge to be included in such courses, but they all try to convey to students the usefulness of economics in solving business problems. Such diversity is not bad, because the field is rich with topics of interest and use to those in business, and too much standardization of course material can discourage innovation and creativity among faculty and students. However, this diversity does make text selection difficult.

Another problem faced by professors teaching managerial economics is the lack of uniform prerequisites. In some schools, adequate mathematical backgrounds are assured at a fairly advanced level, enabling the instructor to assign material that is uniformly challenging to all students in the course. In others, managerial economics courses provide the student's only required exposure to analytical-quantitative techniques. Where the course is optional, prerequisites are kept minimal to maintain enrollment and to encourage all students to take at least one mathematically analytical course. Such heterogeneity precludes adoption of more advanced material that professors in many schools of business would like to teach. Too often, also, the text does not provide the necessary review of the basic mathematical tools, and professors hesitate to impose on their students the additional financial burden of purchasing a supplementary mathematics text.

Finally, available texts in this field generally provide a disproportionate treatment of topics, with chapters ranging in length from less than twelve pages to more than fifty. Such variation makes it difficult to assign chapters from one class period to the next. Moreover, students dislike long chapters and are somewhat dismayed by those that they cannot read thoroughly in a single sitting. Most tend to prefer relatively short chapters followed by interesting problems that review the material, explore its implications, and extend key concepts just introduced. Working out problems helps them take an active part in the learning process instead of becoming passive intellectual vacuum sweepers. Most classroom instructors also like good problems and questions because they too can learn from the ensuing discussions.

To deal with these various problems, this book was written with an eye to providing a comprehensive, balanced coverage of the topics of managerial economics in concise chapters of approximately fifteen pages each, except where the material is more descriptive and easier to read. Flexibility is provided by a broad choice of topics; innovation, by including some topics that have not yet appeared in competing texts. Sufficient material is included so that some chapters may be omitted if the topics are sufficiently covered in other courses or are of lesser interest to the instructor, without exhausting the supply of ideas and concepts that can be covered in a course of three credit hours. Few instructors will cover in depth all the chapters in a single semester or quarter. While this text was designed primarily for use in Master of Business Administration programs, it also has enough flexibility to be used in undergraduate courses in managerial economics and microeconomics. Moreover, it could be used for a two-course sequence in programs designed to introduce students with minimal backgrounds to such material. Where this book is to be used by undergraduates, Chapters 1–3, 6–9, 12, 14, 15, 20, 21, 26, and 27 (as listed below) are recommended, leaving the remaining, more advanced chapters for graduate study. Part One is optional where only a portion of the class needs a review of basic mathematics, but some instructors will have to devote a large portion of their courses to this section. Those instructors who wish to give their courses a greater social emphasis may pass lightly over Part One and proceed to the later chapters of the book. Suggested chapter assignments are provided for convenient reference at the end of this preface for a standard MBA course, an undergraduate one, and a more advanced graduate one.

Managerial Economics includes concepts and ideas from the literature of microeconomics that I have found over the past decade to have the greatest appeal and potential use to practical-minded business people and engineers. Traditional and modern theory at the intermediate level is outlined very briefly and supplemented with many real-world examples to help capture the students' immediate interest. Although the presentation of each topic is brief, the intellectual challenge is preserved. Students with single courses in calculus, economic theory, and statistics should find the material quite meaty. Those with more than one course in these subjects should find this book useful for reviewing and integrating their past work and for learning much that is new and challenging to them.

As to my motivations for writing this book, the first was a desire to teach more and different material than was available in current texts. The second stemmed from a desire similar to that of Alfred Marshall's: to teach economic theory for the useful purpose of interpreting current economic life.[1] I hope the student will gain intellectually in other ways as well from reading this book. I certainly have from writing it.

I wish to acknowledge my indebtedness to the multitude of writers referred to in the text and at the end of each chapter, who have obviously helped make this book possible. Acknowledgments must also be given to my colleagues and administrators at Wichita State University who helped create a conducive atmosphere. In the

[1]John Maynard Keynes, *Essays in Biography* (New York: W. W. Norton, 1951), p. 170. Indeed, managerial economics owes much to Marshall, "the founder of modern diagrammatic economics," (p. 157) and to his dedication to "the study of the causes of poverty" (p. 136). His work and his desire to be read by business people (p. 160) establish him as a foremost managerial economist. See especially Marshall's *Principles of Economics* (London: MacMillan, 1890–1920), which was given much of his attention over a period of four decades and published in eight editions, and which is used to this day as a ready reference by economists the world over.

early stages, my prolific business historian colleague Jimmy Skaggs made detailed constructive criticims of at least a half dozen manuscript chapters; I owe much to him for helping me improve my writing skills, and this undoubtedly improved the readability of the rest of the book as well. To my economist colleagues Randall B. Haydon, Maurice Pfannestiel, Dennis C. Duell, Dale S. Drum, and Bernard J. Marks, I am indebted for their encouragement and critical comments of individual chapters related to their specialties. The first of numerous drafts of Chapter 17 on learning curves was written by one of my graduate students, Ronald Lee (now deceased), who had taught the subject at both the Boeing and Cessna Companies and who first impressed me with its wide-spread usefulness in industry. Numerous other students over the years have played a significant role in detecting errors and in making many chapters more understandable. Valuable comments and suggestions were received from the following reviewers: Albert S. King of Kansas State University, Leonard A. White of the University of Arkansas, John R. Moore of the University of Tennessee, Guy Black of George Washington University, and Thomas Calmus of the University of Oregon. Typing assistance was obtained from numerous persons, the largest portions of which were provided by Jo Stockton, Ann Vyers, Debby Hartung, Mary Berry, and Jennifer Brown. The staff at Houghton Mifflin Company performed admirably in the painstaking task of converting the manuscript to a bound book. While all of the above should be given credit for their contributions, none should be held responsible for any of the book's remaining defects.

Samuel C. Webb

Suggested Chapters

A. MBA Course

*Optional math review for students who need it.

**Instructor's option depending upon student backgrounds, interest, length of the course, and supplementary material used.

B. Undergraduate Course

1. Introduction
2. Elementary Mathematics and Marginal Analysis
3. Linear Programming
6. The Motivation and Ability to Consume
7. The Concept of Demand
8. Other Uses of the Elasticity Concept
9. Consumer Demand Theory I
12. Production Theory
14. Production and Linear Programming
15. Cost Concepts in Economics and Business
20. Market Structure and Price Determination
21. Pricing Analysis
26. Antitrust and Antimerger Constraint on American Industry
27. Ecology, Economics, and Ecoethics

C. Graduate Course (for students with exposure to B above or equivalent)

1. Introduction
4. Dual Linear Programming
5. Nonlinear Programming
10. Consumer Demand Theory II
11. Demand Estimation
13. Some Technical Aspects of Continuous Production Functions
16. Reconstruction of the Classical Cost Function and Notes on Empirical Studies
17. The Learning Curve
18. Technological Change and Forecasting
19. Toward an Operational Theory of Economic Production
22. Welfare Analysis
23. Externalities
24. Investment Decisions in Business and Society
25. Knowledge, Risk, and Uncertainty
28. Ecoethics—Social Responsibility in Business
29. The American Idea of Individual Success
30. Summary and Conclusions

1 Introduction

Managerial economics is the study of the firm and how it makes its decisions under constraints imposed by the laws of nature and society. The discipline overlaps microeconomic theory, operations analysis, and various other approaches to studying the activities of the firm. It utilizes the tools of mathematics, programming, and statistics. This chapter discusses the goals, theories, and constraints of the firm—topics that are basic to the study of managerial economics and that provide a linear programming framework for synthesizing the subjects covered throughout the book. For example, profit maximization and share of the market are goals subject to the constraints of adequate price-earnings ratios and growth of sales. Also provided are a brief discussion of the organization of the book, a statement of why economists are becoming more interested in studying the firm, and the author's opinion as to why students, business executives, and government officials need to know managerial economics.

1-1 Goals of the Firm

Critics of economic analysis frequently speak out against the widely held assumption that firms maximize only profits. Impressionable students hearing these criticisms are sometimes diverted from their purpose by the mistaken belief that such an assumption is universally invalid and unwarranted. In the interest of meeting this criticism head-on and dispelling some of the confusion, consider a sample of concerns of the firm suggested by various writers, as surveyed by Fritz Machlup [12, p. 21]:

1. size and growth of profits
2. ratio of profits to investment
3. size and growth of sales
4. share of the market
5. rise in market value of common stock
6. retained earnings or dividends paid out
7. price-earnings ratio of stock
8. size and growth of capital investments

9. size of staff, salary, bonuses, and stock options

10. expense accounts and personal services, including travel expenses, beautiful secretary, chauffeur, and seminars in resort areas

11. leisure, recreation, and length and number of vacations

12. education and health expenses

13. budgets for public relations, advertising, research and development

14. lead in wage increases and industrial relations

15. contribute to humanitarian and patriotic causes

16. influence decisions of government, industry, and society

A poll of business executives of large corporations would undoubtedly confirm that each of these concerns is considered important by the firm and should be given some weight—how much weight, however, is a matter of judgment among different companies and frequently a bone of contention among the managers of an individual firm. Indeed, the firm's character and public image is a product of such collective judgments.

It is important to recognize that all of these concerns are related either as complements or substitutes to the making of profits. Pursuit of short-run goals that increase costs or reduce revenues serve, by definition, to reduce short-run profits. On the other hand, money spent to expand markets, improve and develop new products, make the company a more desirable place for employees to work, and produce a positive public image may be very important in increasing the firm's long-run profits, as implied by the old saying "It takes money to make money." However, excessive expenditures on any of these activities can, because of diminishing returns, serve to reduce long-run profits. Even if analysis is restricted to the short run, the self-sustaining firm must be capable of generating some minimum amount of profits to be able to provide funds to advance other goals. The managers of the firm must, first and foremost, insure their continued control by convincing stockholders that sufficient profits are forthcoming. If this is not accomplished, managers are replaced and funds may be denied and capital diverted to other uses. Once stockholders are pacified, it is possible for managers to give their attention to worthwhile competing goals. But if cutbacks in expenses are required because of a recession or some other more specific decline in demand for the product, attempts are often made to preserve profits at the expense of other goals.

Competitive pressures also play a significant role. When domestic competitors attempt to expand their market shares, when there is danger of new competitors entering the field, or when imports from abroad begin to rise, the firm is said to be subject to *effective competition*. Effective competition compels the firm to react to potential or real sales losses and dictates that goals other than profit maximization must eventually be set aside. Otherwise, profit rates would be regarded as below normal at the time. If competition forces profits below the acceptable rate, maximization of managerial incomes, which is often mentioned as a competing goal, then becomes synonymous with maximization of profits. For these reasons economists accord a dominant role to the profit goal, at least up to some minimum level.

Where competition is not effective, managerial discretion as distinguished from ownership prerogative comes into play. Managers are then free to maximize their own utility functions based upon their feelings of self-esteem, pride,

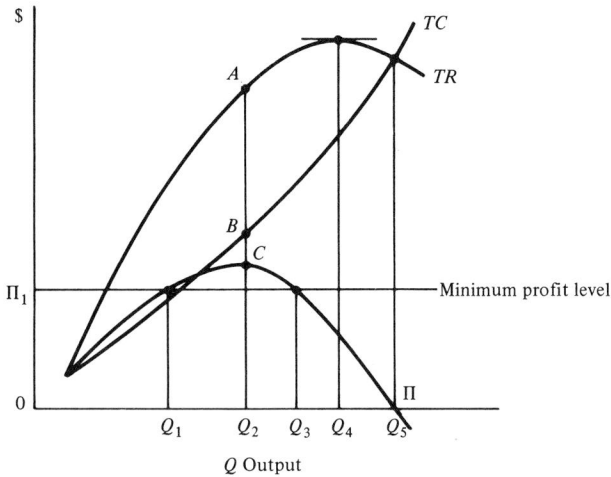

Figure 1-1

prestige, accomplishment, present or anticipated consumption of material goods, leisure, pleasure, and conscience. These feelings may be associated with advancing the national interest, indulging in luxuries, and pursuing other goals previously listed [12, p. 21].

A famous model of revenue maximization invented by William J. Baumol [2, pp. 45–55] is useful in illustrating how multiple goals can influence a firm's decision as to the size of its output. A graphical version is given in Figure 1-1. Professor Baumol assumes that as long as some minimum level of profits is earned to satisfy stockholders, the firm will devote its attention to increasing total revenue. Managers are believed to behave in this manner because their salaries and bonuses are typically tied to their sales performance; also, certain competitive advantages are thought to be associated with greater size and growth, such as greater ease in recruiting employees and distributors, lower interest rates and credit terms on loans obtained from commercial banks, and improvements in the firm's overall public image and political clout. The profit curve shown in Figure 1-1 is derived by measuring the vertical distance between the total revenue and total cost curves; for example, the maximum vertical distance is equal to AB, which is also equal to CQ_2 at output Q_2, and profits are zero where TR and TC intersect at output Q_5. If the firm were a profit maximizer, it would produce and sell at output Q_2 because the profit curve reaches its peak at point C. If the managers chose to maximize sales revenue without regard to profits, they would produce Q_4 units. In the event that leisure time was judged to be more important than sales after attainment of the minimum profit level, output Q_1 would be preferred; this assumes, of course, that lower levels of output require less effort and provide more leisure, an assumption that is not necessarily valid in all cases.

In addition to the desires of management for leisure and greater individual monetary rewards, other considerations not specifically mentioned as goals prevent profit maximization. They include (1) the desire of managers and sub-ordinates to avoid resentment and disruption of routines by rigid enforcement of profit-maximizing rules, (2) preference for greater-than-optimal liquidity and security of assets, (3) screening and distortion of information flowing through various levels of management, (4) maintaining control by the present group against corporate raiders, (5) strivings by individuals and groups for status, power, and prestige, (6) instincts of workmanship, professional excellence, and aesthet-ics, (7) compromises among executives with different interests, such as pro-duction, marketing, finance, research, personnel relations, and public relations, and (8) external influences from suppliers, labor organizations, affirmative action groups, consumer groups, bankers, and government agencies. There is no doubt that these considerations exist to greater or lesser degree. All may be important in guiding the firm along the path to greater long-run profits.

If the firm's managers could agree upon the relative weightings to be given to some array of formal and informal goals, they could construct an index of goals referred to by economists as a *utility* (or preference) *function*, which could be used in plotting the firm's performance. Trade-off ratios could be calculated to guide the firm to optimal resource usage. Training programs, seminars, and rules for rewards and penalties would have to be devised to insure employee compliance with the designated objectives—whether or not they personally agreed with the multiple goals and their relative importance. Also, it must be assumed that the contributions of each goal to the composite utility function remain constant, or change in some predictable manner, during the relevant period; otherwise, the calculated trade-off ratios would soon become inappropriate. Provision must therefore be made for adjustment of priorities in response to changes in, say, profits. An increase in tax rates would encourage greater discretionary expenses relative to profits. A change in staff salaries would change the cost of prestige accruing from having a larger staff. Also, if the utility functions of other firms in the same or related industries were known, trade-off ratios between firms could be constructed to facilitate cooperation and competition.

It may be argued (perhaps unconvincingly) that in a practical world it is not possible to deal with a multitude of goals and interrelationships. What we need in business and economic decision making are fewer goals, preferably one. This argument has some intuitive appeal, since personal experience sometimes teaches us that attention to too many goals results in confusion and distraction from the most important. Moreover, exceptional success in achieving *one* goal may lead to success in furthering other goals, as in Adam Smith's "invisible hand" concept where the individual is said to advance the interests of society by pursuing his own best interest. Such reasoning is also sometimes offered in defense of profit maximization when firms are exposed to vigorous competition.

In spite of these arguments, some observers remain unconvinced about the appropriateness of the profit maximization assumption. Support for this assumption is given by a recent study [11] of the compensation of the highest-paid executives of 50 of the largest industrial corporations in the United States in 1968. It concluded that executive compensation was closely related to profits (and equity values) and unrelated to sales. Accordingly, the interests of managers and stockholders are thought to be much the same. Additional research is underway on this still controversial subject, however, by various critics.

If the arguments for assuming profit maximization under conditions of effective competition are quite compelling, why are criticisms still made? A major reason is that not everyone asks the same questions and that different conceptions (models) of the firm are required to obtain the answers. No single model of the firm is appropriate for dealing with all problems.

1-2 Theories of the Firm

Although economists tend to refer to *the* theory of the firm, it should be made clear that they are generally discussing the neoclassical theory of pure competition. They do not mean to imply that there is only one theory capable of giving valid answers to all conceivable questions. Consider briefly some of the major theories and the roles of the firm they characterize [12, pp. 27–28]:

1. In competitive price and allocation theory the firm is purely a theoretical construct (one without a necessary empirical counterpart) that reacts to changing conditions in puppet fashion. The firm is thus "an imaginary reactor to environmental changes."

2. In innovation and growth theory the entrepreneur initiates or invents new items or methods. In this context the firm is "an imaginary or a typical reactor or initiator."

3. In welfare economics knowledge of environmental conditions is assumed to be accurate, so that a change in price and output may be judged to increase or reduce welfare. Here the firm is "an imaginary or a typical reactor or initiator with accurate knowledge of his opportunities."

4. In oligopoly and monopoly theory there are a few (or one) sellers who are influenced in some materialistic way by the actions of others in their group. In such a circumstance the firm is "a typical reactor and initiator in a small (or zero) interacting group."

5. In organization theory the firm is said to be "a typical cooperative system with authoritative coordination."

6. In management science business decisions are guided by the use of operations research tools in problems of inventories, replacement, search, queueing, and routing. In this "art of business management," the firm is "a functional information system and decision-making system for typical business operations."

7. In business consultation emphasis is given to particular projects rather than to techniques and theoretical principles. Here the firm is "an actual or potential client for advice on optimal performance."

8. In accounting theory the concept of the firm is one of "a collection of assets and liabilities."

9. In legal theory and practice a business organization is treated as an artificial person. The firm may be said to be "a juridical person with property, claims, and obligations."

10. In statistical descriptions as employed by the United States Census, a manufacturing firm is defined as "a business organization under a single management or a self-employed person with one or more employees or with an established place of business."

Which of these definitions of the firm is best? This question cannot be answered *except with reference to the purpose at hand*. Each theory and corresponding definition was devised for a different purpose. None is applicable for all circumstances. Different goals or sets of goals may be appropriate for different problems. Some critics of the neoclassical theory of the firm seek to gain more from the model than it was constructed to provide. Some inquirers wish to know future prices of particular commodities and the reactions of single firms to changing economic events. They mistakenly look to the traditional competitive model and turn away frustrated. As Fritz Machlup explains,

> The model of the firm in that [traditional price] theory is not, as so many writers believe, designed to serve to explain and predict the behavior of real firms; instead, it is designed to explain and predict changes in observed prices (quoted, paid, received) as effects of particular changes in conditions (wage rates, interest rates, import duties, excise taxes, technology, etc.). In this causal connection the firm is only a theoretical link, a mental construct helping to explain how one gets from the cause to the effect. This is altogether different from explaining the behavior of a firm. As the philosopher of science warns, we ought not to confuse the *explanans* with the *explanandum* [12, p. 9].

To confuse a theoretical construct designed as a guide to thinking with real organizations and institutions is to commit the "fallacy of misplaced concreteness," that is, to attribute concrete meaning to abstract symbols [12, p. 9], and to mistake "a thought-object for an object of sense perception" [12, p. 26].

Another kind of confusion sometimes leads observers to reject entirely any deductions obtained from a model that assumes firms can actually maximize profits. They reason that this is futile in bureaucratic organizations where information required to make the necessary decisions is deficient and defective, especially when it must pass through many hands in the hierarchy of management. The error in reasoning made here has to do with *which questions are being asked*. In determining competitive prices and the allocation of resources, the correctness of the firm's information concerning the conditions of demand, supply, and production is not as important as the firm's *response* to any *change in such conditions*. Previous stores of information before changes in wage or tax rates are not important for determining the direction of change in prices. It is only required that managers take notice of the *change* and react correctly. Confusion in the above reasoning is similar to that of shifting a curve versus moving along the curve. The direction of change in variables that causes the curve to shift is usually independent of the shape and location of the original curve. If only the direction of change, and not the magnitude, is sought, the original location of the curve, corresponding to given accurate information, is irrelevant.

In managerial models of the internal workings of the firm—the most efficient production process, optimal inventory, and the like—usable information is not so difficult to obtain. These models can prove quite helpful to the firm in pursuing its goals.

In short, it may be concluded that the traditional economic theory of the firm based upon the assumption of maximization of profits is suitable for predicting the general movement of prices and resources in response to economic change in the presence of substantial competition. This theory is not appropriate (1) for describing the behavior or actions of any particular firm, (2) for predicting results in markets where competition is not great, and (3) for developing numerical values of the extent of change anticipated. In the complex world of reality the ambitious goal of predicting the *direction of change* in market price and allocation of resources under effective competition is all that price theory aspires to attain. Such information in itself can be most useful to the business person. However, if more realism is desired in the model, a different preference function can be assumed and more complex and specialized models developed. The methodology of model building is applicable to setting up any number of models in which business executives may be interested.

1-3   Constraints of the Firm

Some of the most interesting topics in the domain of managerial economics are associated with several types of constraints on the activities and decisions of the firm.[1] The first type has to do with the freedom of people and organizations in a free enterprise system to act independently of, and even contrary to, the firm's objectives. In a free society the firm must persuade and bargain for the cooperation of its employees, suppliers, competitors, and customers.

In the market for *resources* the firm is free to purchase materials and supplies at prices equal to or greater than the minimum demanded by sellers. It would appear foolish to pay a price higher than necessary, but a free enterprise system allows its participants to incur losses and failures. To the extent that the firm cannot obtain its required inputs at prices below the sellers' minimum, the firm is constrained by the sellers' freedom to charge that price. The firm may also refuse the sellers' price. One group's freedom is another's constraint. Similarly, in some labor markets employees are free to refuse to work for a wage below some minimum rate, thus establishing a minimum wage constraint on the employer; the employer, in turn, is free to refuse to hire workers at rates above some maximum, which establishes a maximum wage constraint on employees.

In the market for *goods and services* the firm is free to sell below the going price and consumers are free to pay more if they wish. The market price is a maximum constraint for the seller and a minimum one for the buyer.

When one or more competing or complementary firms are powerful enough to exert some control over the market price, their actions and reactions must also serve as constraints on the original firm's freedom and behavior—just as the firm's behavior may act as a constraint on theirs.

In a slave society freedom of all people, except perhaps for those in authority, is reduced. Behavior space may be said to be more confined by a closing in of the constraining walls.

A second type of constraint is technological, having to do with the physical-biological properties of matter and man's physiological-psychological-intel-

---

[1] A categorization of constraints similar to that presented here is given by Irvin M. Grossack and David D. Martin [8, pp. 49–62].

lectual ability to organize, manipulate, and control his world. Regardless of how well the firm organizes production, there is some crucial minimum amount of each input required to produce a given amount of output. The firm strives through research to find the most efficient and least costly way of combining the essential ingredients. The different recipes according to which the inputs are combined are referred to in production economics as *processes*. Difficulties arise because some inputs are not perfectly divisible in the way gases, liquids, powders, and grains are divisible; they are often available only in lumps or other discrete units, such as a tool, generator, building, and worker. Sometimes problems of indivisibility can be overcome by renting the part-time use of people and things that come in units and sizes too large to be fully utilized. There are supporting firms organized for the purpose of renting equipment, trucks, typists, and management consultants to other firms that cannot justify their purchase for full-time use. In the world of business it is frequently neces-sary to purchase some minimum number of units in order to obtain a suffi-ciently low price, as by the dozen, gross, ton, carload, and crop. This may require purchasing more than is currently needed, causing problems of inventory, storage, preservation of perishables, and security. Outputs are subject, all the more, to problems of indivisibility; they must be matched with the widely differing needs of diverse consumers.

Biological properties of matter are important constraints in farm industries, where production is limited by the growing season, hours of daylight, rainfall, basic mineral content of the soil, pests, fungi, and diseases. Commercial and industrial firms are not exempt from the problems of insects, allergies, humidity, dust, and disease. All firms, with the possible exception of those that are com-pletely mechanized, are operated by people with physiological and psychological problems that constrain them from realizing their full productive capability. Potentially profitable ventures are often destroyed or simply not undertaken because of the presence or threat of the common cold, Asian flu, malaria, personality conflicts, sex problems, family problems, deficient nutrition, in-adequate physical exercise, alcoholism, and a host of unproductive attitudes and mental problems. All these and other factors can be considered constraints to the firm's technical ability to produce. Many writers tend to ignore the human and biological aspects of technical production, but any experienced business person can testify to their importance.

A third type of constraint has to do with the inability of the firm to acquire all the inputs it needs because of shortages of some key ingredients and budget limitations. These so-called fixities may be temporary, as when stocks are peri-odically depleted, or permanent, as when the earth's remaining exhaustible resources are carefully rationed for critical uses. When the fixities are too severe, they cease to be fixities, because the firm either substitutes other inputs in their place or ceases to produce the product requiring them.

A fourth category of constraints is a lack of knowledge of future resource availabilities, prices, markets, technologies, product interdependencies, and actions of competitors. Ignorance of coming events accounts in large measure for the fickleness of fate for men and institutions. Omniscience would remove the guesswork, risk taking, and uncertainty, but such a God-like quality does not exist in the world of business. The firm can gain knowledge through time-consuming research efforts, but much ignorance remains as a constraint. This helps to explain the perpetually high premium on good managerial judgment.[2]

Another category deals with legally imposed constraints. Government makes laws establishing the rules of business. Corporations are required to obtain charters, pay taxes, fulfill contracts, bargain with labor unions, pay minimum wages, provide safe working conditions for employees, observe quality standards, restrict pollution, engage in ethical practices, and conform to antitrust laws. Public utilities are in addition subject to output and price controls of regulatory commissions. Firms are protected against unfair business practices and from foreign competition by tariffs and quotas. Inventors, authors, and artists are protected by patents and copyrights; consumers, by pure food and drug laws, rent ceilings, labeling laws, building codes, traffic regulations, safety laws (such as against defects in automobiles and appliances, for seat belts and nonflammable textiles), and truth in lending. These rules enhance the freedom of the protected and constrain the activities of others.

The sixth type of constraint has to do with self-imposed standards of performance, morality, and fair dealing with employees, competitors, and customers. The character of the firm often reflects the personality and convictions of the founder. The engineer-manager, architect, or writer yielding to perfectionist instincts may insist upon standards of quality that satisfy some inner craving although they may unduly narrow the market for his services. The heirs of a deceased head of an enterprise may choose to preserve the firm "just as he would have wanted it." Glorification of the family farm, store, or other business organization sometimes leads to inefficient commitment of resources. Keeping unneeded employees on the payroll, unwillingness to take advantage of competitors' oversights, and refusal to conceal latent product defects from unsuspecting consumers are all examples of short-run self-imposed constraints. The reader should not infer from this discussion that the author believes all uneconomic decisions to be unwise. Personal needs of the owner should be given careful consideration as long as the owner is aware of the costs of his actions and others are not subjected to injury or undue hardship. Such discretionary standards are sometimes useful in reconciling other conflicting goals of the firm.

A seventh and final type of constraint may be referred to as acts of God or acts of nature, which include injury and other forms of loss from earthquakes, tornados, lightning, storms, and supernatural causes. Actually, these events are not properly termed constraints if the behavior of the firm is uninfluenced by the possibility of their occurrence. And they are not entirely unpredictable. A firm located in a region noted for one or more of these recurring events can take precautionary steps in locating the plant on high ground, placing facilities underground, installing lightning rods, and heeding storm and earthquake warnings. Perhaps wars, revolutions, and riots should also be included here. The wary business person can sometimes limit losses by being better informed, building stronger structures, relocating or covering equipment on first warning, and purchasing insurance. This type of constraint should not be attributed wholly

---

[2] The reader with an interest in the philosophy of knowledge should read Kenneth Boulding's 1965 Richard T. Ely Lecture, titled "The Economics of Knowledge and the Knowledge of Economics" [4].

to chance. Some unfortunate souls go through life being surprised time and again by "chance" events, that is, they are not constrained by an awareness of the probability of their occurrence. Acting upon such information could have helped them reduce or avoid their losses and even opportunistically turn misfortune into gain. Such awareness of external events is also useful in giving decision makers humbleness and understanding that sustains them psychologically over bad times.

It should be helpful for students when reading through this book to keep in mind the goals and constraints outlined here. This programming approach of optimizing goals subject to multiple constraints is quite useful as a theoretical construct in maintaining perspective and synthesizing the interdisciplinary study of managerial economics. This statement should become more meaningful to readers as they progress through the book.

1-4   Organization of the Book

This text is divided into five parts. The first provides a review of mathematical tools commonly used in the literature; such background is essential for a full appreciation of this text and as a stepping stone to comprehending more advanced writings. Part Two presents the analysis of demand, building gradually from a very elementary to a fairly sophisticated level. Part Three treats the analysis of production and cost, again beginning with the most basic material and progressing to that having greater challenge. Part Four covers the analysis of price, output, investment, and welfare. Part Five deals with some broader problems of the environment within which executives of firms must operate.

1-5   Why Economists Have a Growing Interest in Studying the Firm

Traditionally, economists have been more interested in understanding and explaining the operation of the economic system than of the firm. Their interest in the firm derived largely from the expectation that such study might lead them to a better understanding of the overall allocation of scarce resources. Today, firms are no longer exclusively viewed as being so numerous, small, and competitive that individually they can exert little, if any, influence on economic activity. Many have grown so large and powerful that few observers would deny their actions have important economic and social implications. The transformation to big, multiproduct, international business has been aided by the burgeoning computer technology and use of linear programming to which many economists have been important contributors. The past 20 years have also brought an increase in mergers, conglomerates, holding companies, and international corporations, the impacts of which may require decades to discover. It is inevitable that economists must turn more and more to the behavior of the firm in seeking answers to national and worldwide economic problems. At the same time, it is also inevitable that managers of business firms will turn to economists for assessing the implications of their actions for their own and for society's good. There is also a growing awareness at all levels of government that available stocks of exhaustible natural resources must be employed in the wisest way in pursuit of social goals. Politicians, statesmen, and administrators, because of a greater public awareness of the complexities of social problems and their solutions, will have to base their decisions upon the analysis of economists and other scientific investigators. Rapidly changing institutions and the mutual interests of economists, business managers, and government administrators promise to continue to make managerial economics an exciting area of study.

1-6   The Need for Managerial Economics

Students and business executives with a penchant for the practical aspects of life should have little fear that exposure to the abstract reasoning of economic theory will in some way corrupt their minds and leave them the worse for the experience. Theoretical models at the very least provide a way of organizing thought that is vastly superior to the simple models of the mind that (perhaps unknowingly) dictate much of our behavior. Once mental models are put down on paper, they are immediately subject to a critical analysis, which helps to reveal mistakes in reasoning. It is admittedly a challenge—an especially difficult one for the novice—to reduce thought to words, numbers, curves, and equations on paper. Those who shun the task and give precedence in business decisions to overall impressions, gut feelings, and hunches are forgoing an opportunity to gain a higher degree of understanding of the problem at hand and perhaps to increase profits as well.

Knowledgeable people are often suspicious, in some cases justifiably so, of decisions made by those in authority who are unable to explain why they made them. An air of mystery hides ignorance and wisdom alike. If a person is truly unable to convey his thoughts to others, it is probably fair to judge that he doesn't really understand them himself and is in a position demanding more ability than he possesses. If he conveys to others that he does understand his own thoughts but is unwilling to share them with others, he creates the impression of deceiving, which also could disqualify him for his job. In any case, exposure to theory and model building cannot increase one's ignorance—one's awareness of this unfortunate state, perhaps, but not in the absolute—and the potential rewards in terms of intellect and materialism are enormous.

Managerial economics provides the analytical tools and perspective for understanding the functions and contributions of business institutions. Modern scientific management requires more than superficial comprehension of the functional activities of firms, traditionally classified as accounting, production, marketing, finance, and personnel management. Penetrating and sophisticated treatments of these subjects today make use of mathematical models as aids to human thought. Models of the mind can thereby be extended by use of linear programming, econometrics, behavioral analysis, industrial dynamics, and corporate simulation to encompass a much larger number of variables and complex relations. While many business decisions cannot be quantified, a surprisingly large and increasing number can be estimated quite accurately and tested for logical consistency. Where facts are made apparent, the extent of judgment and guesswork is reduced and the probability of success increased. In those cases where decisions cannot be reduced to mechanical calculations, judgments must somehow be made. Perhaps they are made on the basis of fuzzy comprehension of random and limited personal experience. Perhaps they are made consciously with reference to well-thought-out company and personal goals. Perhaps they stem from unconscious reference to philosophies inherited from parents, childhood playmates, comic books, the football coach, a favorite teacher, a film hero, a popular novel, a former boss, a political leader, and maybe even a radio or television commercial. John Maynard Keynes expressed an awareness of such influences when he made his oft-quoted observation:

> Practical men, who believe themselves to be quite exempt from any intellectual influences, are usually the slaves of some defunct economist. Madmen in authority, who hear voices in the air, are distilling their frenzy from some academic scribbler of a few years back. [*General Theory of Employment, Interest, and Money* (New York: Harcourt, 1962), p. 383. First published in 1936.]

It cannot be overemphasized at this stage that a study of economic analysis and models should be very useful to the business executive in giving him an awareness of how his company and its activities relate to the economy and society as a whole. Discussion of the objectives of firms subject to limitations imposed by the laws of nature and society cannot fail to provide a meaningful framework within which the business person can make important decisions.

Questions and Problems

1-1. Is managerial economics really a discipline? or is it interdisciplinary?

1-2. Which of the goals of the firm mentioned in the text other than profits seem most reasonable to you? Are there any others not mentioned that you believe are important? How are these dependent upon or related to profit optimization?

1-3. In reference to Figure 1-1, which output level would you personally prefer if you owned the firm? What would be your answer if you only managed the firm for others? for your parents? for people you disliked?

1-4. What is your reaction to the statement "The economists' theory of the firm is at best irrelevant and at worst all bad"?

1-5. What types of constraints restrict the behavior of the firm? Can you think of any others than those given in the text?

1-6. How might you reply to the following advice of a fellow student: "There is no real need to know detailed problem-solving techniques, because when you get to be boss you can hire someone else to do it, if necessary"?

1-7. What is realistic and unrealistic about a model?

1-8. Comment on the statement "If we had a model that perfectly portrayed reality, we probably wouldn't recognize it."

References

1. William L. Baldwin. "The Motives of Managers, Environmental Restraints, and the Theory of Managerial Enterprise." *Quarterly Journal of Economics* 78 (May 1964): 238–256. Reprinted in Haynes, Coyne, and Osborne [9, pp. 18–31].

2. William J. Baumol. *Business Behavior, Value and Growth.* Rev. ed. (New York: Harcourt, Brace and World, 1967), ch. 1, 6–7.

3. ———. "What Can Economic Theory Contribute to Managerial Economics?" *American Economic Review* 51 (May 1961): 142–146. Reprinted in Haynes, Coyne, and Osborne [9, pp. 3–7].

4. Kenneth E. Boulding. "The Economics of Knowledge and the Knowledge of Economics." *American Economic Review* 56 (May 1966): 1–13.

5. ———. "The Ethics of Rational Decision." *Management Science* 12 (February 1966): B-161–B-169. Reprinted in Haynes, Coyne, and Osborne [9, pp. 8–17].

6. Milton Friedman. "The Methodology of Positive Economics." In *Essays in Positive Economics* (Chicago: University of Chicago Press, 1953), pp. 3–43. See also the later discussion by Paul A. Samuelson, Earnest Nagel, and Herbert A. Simon in the *American Economic Review* 53 (May 1963): 211–219, 229–236.

7. Gerald Garb. "The Problem of Causality in Economics." *Kyklos* 17 (January 4, 1964): 594–609. Reprinted in Neel [14, pp. 21–32].

8. Irvin M. Grossack and David D. Martin. *Managerial Economics—Microtheory and the Firm's Decision* (Boston: Little, Brown, 1973), ch. 1–3, 12.

9. W. Warren Haynes, Thomas J. Coyne, and Dale K. Osborne. *Readings in Managerial Economics* (Dallas, Tex.: Business Publications, 1973).

10. Oscar Lange. "The Scope and Method of Economics." *Review of Economic Studies* 13 (1945–1946): 19–32. Reprinted in Neel [14, pp. 3–20].

11. Wilber G. Lewellen and Blaine Huntsman. "Managerial Pay and Corporate Performance." *American Economic Review* 60 (September 1970): 710–770. Reprinted in Kristian S. Palda. *Readings in Managerial Economics* (Englewood Cliffs, N.J.: Prentice-Hall, 1973), pp. 4–14.

12. Fritz Machlup. "Theories of the Firm: Marginalist, Behavioral, Managerial." *American Economic Review* 57 (March 1967): 1–33.

13. Jacques Melitz. "Friedman and Machlup on the Significance of Testing Economic Assumptions." *Journal of Political Economy* 73 (February 1965): 37–60. Reprinted in Neel [14, pp. 33–60].

14. Richard E. Neel. *Readings in Price Theory* (Cincinnati: South-Western Publishing Co., 1973).

15. Eugene Rotwein. "On 'The Methodology of Positive Economics.'" *Quarterly Journal of Economics* 73 (November 1959): 554–575.

16. Herbert A. Simon. "Theories of Decision Making in Economics and Behavioral Science." *American Economic Review* 49 (June 1959): 253–280. Reprinted in Haynes, Coyne, and Osborne [9, pp. 32–57].

17. Phillip H. Wicksteed. "The Scope and Method of Political Economy." *Economic Journal* 24 (1914): 1–23. Reprinted in American Economics Association, *Readings in Price Theory* (Homewood, Ill.: Richard D. Irwin, 1952), pp. 3–26.

PART ONE

Review of Mathematical Tools

I *will study and get ready and some day my chance will come.*

Abraham Lincoln

Greek Alphabet

Letters		Names	Letters		Names	Letters		Names
A	α	Alpha	I	ι	Iota	P	ρ	Rho
B	β	Beta	K	κ	Kappa	Σ	σ	Sigma
Γ	γ	Gamma	Λ	λ	Lambda	T	τ	Tau
Δ	δ	Delta	M	μ	Mu	Υ	υ	Upsilon
E	ε	Epsilon	N	ν	Nu	Φ	ϕ	Phi
Z	ζ	Zeta	Ξ	ξ	Xi	X	χ	Chi
H	η	Eta	O	o	Omicron	Ψ	ψ	Psi
Θ	θ	Theta	Π	π	Pi	Ω	ω	Omega

2 Elementary Mathematics and Marginal Analysis

This chapter reviews briefly some elementary mathematics used in managerial economics. The treatment is insufficient for those with no previous training. It is designed mostly as a ready refresher and reference for those whose tools have become rusty through lack of use. Discussion begins with some basic algebra and curve construction and moves quickly into a review of differential calculus, Lagrange multipliers, and optimization theory. All have their place in the modern economic manager's repertoire.

2-1 The Equation for a Straight Line

A straight line, defined as the shortest distance between two points, is typically written in equation form as

$$Y = a + bX \tag{1}$$

If the Y variable is plotted along the vertical axis and the X variable along the horizontal, the constant term a indicates the vertical intercept; that is, the value of Y equals a when X has the value of zero. The other constant, b, denotes the slope of the line, defined between any two points on the curve as the ratio of the vertical to the horizontal distances, or simply as the rise over the run. Figure 2-1 shows several straight lines with various values assigned to a and b. In the equation $Y = 2 + 0.2X$, $a = 2$ and $b = 0.2$. The graph for this equation intersects that for $Y = 4 - 0.2X$, where $X = 5$ and $Y = 3$, the point being indicated by the coordinates (5, 3).

Note that a and b can assume both positive and negative values; keeping track of the sign is critical. For example, if the minus sign of the equation $Y = 4 - 0.2X$ were ignored, its graph would be parallel to that for $Y = 2 + 0.2X$ and there would be no intersection of the two lines for any values of X and Y.

Suppose for the moment that the line with the positive slope (where $b = +0.2$) represents a supply curve and the one with the negative slope ($b = -0.2$) is a demand curve. The intersection of the two lines shows the quantity (X value) and price (Y value) of the product exchanged. Finding the intersection is a

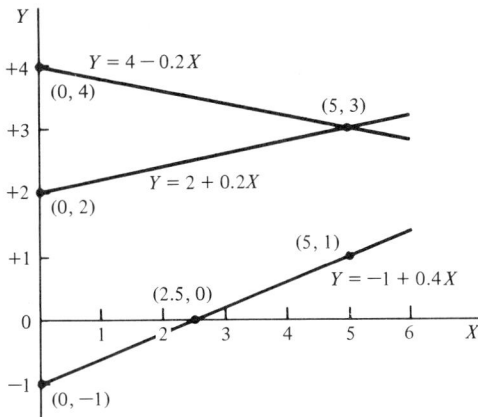

Figure 2-1

simple matter once it is recognized that the price must be the same for both sellers (supply curve) and buyers (demand curve). If

$$Y_S = Y_D \tag{2}$$

then the values for Y_S and Y_D can be substituted into equation (1):

$$2 + 0.2X = 4 - 0.2X \tag{3}$$

Solving for X, transfer the terms containing X to one side,

$$0.4X = 2 \tag{4}$$

and divide both sides by 0.4:

$$X = \frac{2}{0.4} = 5 \tag{5}$$

The value of Y is found by inserting $X = 5$ into either the supply or demand equation:

$$Y = 2 + 0.2(5) = 2 + 1 = 3 \tag{6}$$

Thus the intersection is at point (5, 3).

This discussion of supply and demand curves implies a three-equation model of the firm:

$$
\begin{array}{ll}
Y_S = 2 + 0.2X & \text{(supply)} \\
Y_D = 4 - 0.2X & \text{(demand)} \\
Y_S = Y_D & \text{(equilibrium)}
\end{array} \tag{7}
$$

If some event caused any one of the a's or b's to change, a shock to the system of equations is said to have occurred, which changes the equilibrium solution. If only the a value changes, the curve shifts upward or downward in parallel fashion; Figure 2-2a shows the impact of a fall from $a = 2$ to $a = 1$. If, instead,

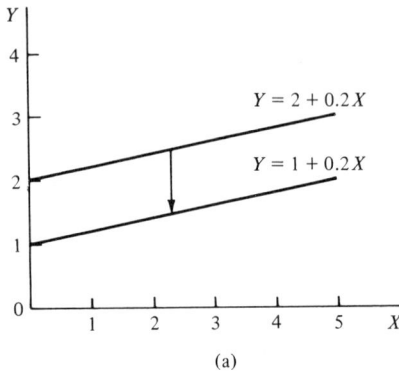

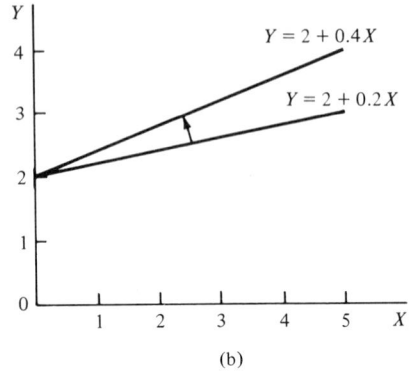

Figure 2-2

the b value shifts from $b = 0.2$ to $b = 0.4$, the slope is increased and the curve rotates counterclockwise as shown in Figure 2-2b. The student should verify (by solving the equations and plotting the curves) that the new equilibrium points corresponding to the intersections of these two new supply curves to the given demand curve are $(7\frac{1}{2}, 2\frac{1}{2})$ and $(3\frac{1}{3}, 3\frac{1}{3})$, respectively.

A linear equation may also exist if there are more than two variables and two dimensions. For example, Y in the equation

$$Y = a + bX + cZ \tag{8}$$

is a linear function of both X and Z and can be graphed in three-dimensional (rather than two-dimensional) space. When Y is a function of more than two, say some finite number n, variables, the equation is typically written

$$Y = a + b_1 X_1 + b_2 X_2 + \cdots + b_n X_n \tag{9}$$

which cannot be graphed in two dimensions when n exceeds 1 in $(n + 1)$-dimensional space.

2-2   Equations for Curved Lines

Equations that are nonlinear take many forms, the most common types of which are shown in Figure 2-3. All are algebraic, except for the one shown in Figure 2-3g, since they involve sums, products, quotients, and constant powers and roots. Transcendental functions include exponential, logarithmic, and trigonometric functions. The curves shown are sometimes used in economics for establishing and examining relations between variables. Note that the slope changes in each of these curves as one moves along them to the right. Quadratic curves, shown in Figures 2-3a to 2-3c, have a squared term, that is, X^2; change direction once; and have only one peak or one trough. Cubic curves, like the one in Figure 2-3d, on the other hand, have two reversals and both a peak and a trough. The quartic curve in Figure 2-3e has three reversals and three bumps. Curves can have no more peaks and troughs than the power of the

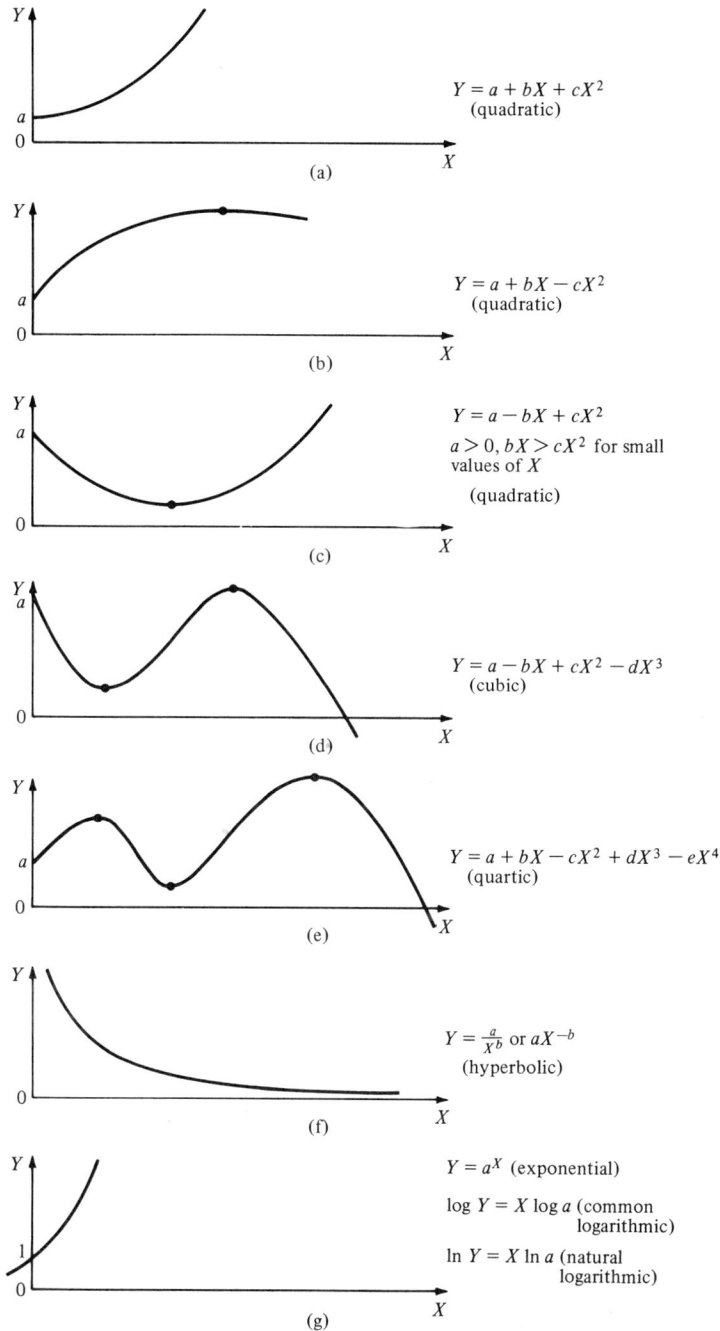

$$Y = a + bX + cX^2$$
(quadratic)

(a)

$$Y = a + bX - cX^2$$
(quadratic)

(b)

$$Y = a - bX + cX^2$$

$a > 0, bX > cX^2$ for small values of X

(quadratic)

(c)

$$Y = a - bX + cX^2 - dX^3$$
(cubic)

(d)

$$Y = a + bX - cX^2 + dX^3 - eX^4$$
(quartic)

(e)

$$Y = \frac{a}{X^b} \text{ or } aX^{-b}$$
(hyperbolic)

(f)

$Y = a^X$ (exponential)

$\log Y = X \log a$ (common logarithmic)

$\ln Y = X \ln a$ (natural logarithmic)

(g)

Figure 2-3

variable minus 1; for instance, a cubic has an X to the third power and two points where slope is equal to zero.

Figure 2-3f shows a frequently encountered case where values of X and Y are approached asymptotically, that is, the curve comes ever closer but never quite touches the axes. The special case illustrated, for $b = 1$, is a rectangular hyperbola where both axes are approached asymptotically. Figure 2-3g shows the explosive exponential function, where values of Y become progressively larger for larger values of X (assuming $a > 1$); it is often used in its logarithmic form. If a relation is specified by logarithmic functions, it may be plotted as a straight line on log graph paper—semilog paper for exponential functions and double-log paper for power functions. Differentiation is also sometimes made easier by using logarithmic functions, as shown in the next section.

2-3   Manipulation of Exponents and Logarithms

A variable X raised to the nth power is simply the variable multiplied by itself $(n - 1)$ times. For example, if $n = 4$, then

$$X^n = X \cdot X \cdot X \cdot X = X^4$$

Also, if $n = 1$, $X^1 = X$, because $X \cdot X^{n-1} = X \cdot X^0 = X \cdot 1 = X$. This follows from Rules 1 and 3:

Rule 1. Multiplication. Two otherwise identical terms raised to different powers may be multiplied by summing the powers of the terms:

$$X^a \cdot X^b = X^{a+b}.$$

If $a = 2$ and $b = 3$, then $X^2 \cdot X^3 = X^5$.

Rule 2. Division. Two otherwise identical terms raised to different powers may be divided by subtracting the exponents of the term in the denominator from that of the term in the numerator:

$$\frac{X^a}{X^b} = X^{a-b}$$

If $a = 5$ and $b = 2$, then $X^5/X^2 = X^3$.

Rule 3. Zero Exponents. Any term raised to the zero power is equal to 1:

$$X^0 = 1$$

This follows from Rule 2, where $b = a$:

$$\frac{X^a}{X^a} = X^{a-a} = X^0 = 1$$

which must be so because $X^a/X^a = 1$.

Rule 4. Reciprocal Exponents. A term may be moved from the denominator to the numerator by changing the sign of its exponents:

$$\frac{1}{X^a} = X^{-a}$$

Rule 5. Powers. The exponent of a term X^a raised to the bth power is the product of the a and b exponent:

$$(X^a)^b = X^{ab}$$

If $a = 2$ and $b = 3$, then $(X^2)^3 = X^{2 \cdot 3} = X^6$.

Rule 6. Roots. The bth root of the term X^a is X raised to the a/b power:

$$\sqrt[b]{X^a} = X^{a/b}$$

If $a = 6$ and $b = 2$, then $\sqrt{X^6} = X^{6/2} = X^3$.

Rule 7. Multiplication by Use of Logarithms. The logarithm Y of a number i to the base j is defined as the power to which j must be raised to equal i; that is, if $Y = \log_j i$, then $i = j^Y$. *Common* (Briggsian) *logarithms*, those to the base 10 and denoted by log without a subscript or by $\log_{10}$, are most useful in numerical computation. *Natural* (Napierian) *logarithms*, those to the base $e = 2.71828$ and denoted by ln or by $\log_e$, are most convenient in problems involving differentiation and integration. To find the product of two numbers, say a and b, find (by use of log tables or slide rule) the number whose logarithm is equal to the sum of the logarithms of a and b; that is, if $Y = a \cdot b$, then

$$\log Y = \log a + \log b$$

Rule 8. Division by Use of Logarithms. To find the quotient of two numbers, say a and b, find the number whose logarithm is equal to the logarithm of the numerator minus the logarithm of the denominator; that is, if $Y = a/b$, then

$$\log Y = \log a - \log b$$

Rule 9. Powers by Use of Logarithms. To find the value of a number a raised to a power b, find the logarithm of the product of b times the logarithm of a; that is, if $Y = a^b$, then

$$\log Y = b \log a$$

Rule 10. Roots by Use of Logarithms. To find the bth root of a number a, find the number whose logarithm is the product of the inverse of b times the logarithm of a; that is, if $Y = \sqrt[b]{a}$, then

$$\log Y = \frac{1}{b} \log a$$

Consider the savings in computation time by using logarithms to obtain the value of $100(1.07)^{20}$, the value in 20 years of a \$100 investment yielding 7 per cent compounded annually:

$$Y = 100(1.07)^{20}$$
$$\log Y = \log 100 + 20 \log 1.07$$
$$= 2 + 20(0.02938)$$
$$= 2 + 0.5876$$
$$= 2.5876$$
$$Y = \text{antilog of } 2.5876$$
$$= \$387$$

2-4   Differentiation

The slope of a curve at a point is given by the first derivative of its equation. This is the foundation for marginal analysis, to be discussed in greater detail later. If one wishes to determine from an equation relating profits to advertising how much additional profit to expect from a unit increase in advertising outlay (perhaps in thousands of dollars), one need only look at the slope of the associated curve at the current level of advertising. Alternatively, one could look at the first derivative of profits (Π) with respect to advertising A. For example, if the relation is given by the linear equation

$$\Pi = 15 + 1.7A \tag{10}$$

we know immediately from the slope of the line ($= 1.7$) that Π will rise by 1.7 units for every unit increase in A. Stated otherwise, we want to know the value of $\Delta\Pi/\Delta A$, where Δ denotes an incremental change, which can be obtained as follows: The new profit level is

$$\Pi + \Delta\Pi = 15 + 1.7(A + \Delta A)$$

from which the change in profits ($\Delta\Pi$) is obtained by subtracting the original level of profits (Π):

$$(\Pi + \Delta\Pi) - \Pi = [15 + 1.7(A + \Delta A)] - (15 + 1.7A)$$
$$\Delta\Pi = 1.7 \, \Delta A$$

$$\frac{\Delta\Pi}{\Delta A} = 1.7$$

This is clear enough for linear relations but not necessarily for nonlinear ones. Suppose the equation were

$$\Pi = 15 + 1.7A^2 \tag{11}$$

Obtaining $\Delta\Pi/\Delta A$ by the previous procedure, we find

$$\Pi + \Delta\Pi = 15 + 1.7(A + \Delta A)^2$$
$$= 15 + 1.7[A^2 + 2A(\Delta A) + \Delta A^2]$$
$$(\Pi + \Delta\Pi) - \Pi = [15 + 1.7A^2 + 3.4A(\Delta A) + 1.7(\Delta A)^2] - (15 + 1.7A^2)$$
$$\Pi\Delta = 3.4A(\Delta A) + 1.7(\Delta A)^2$$

$$\frac{\Delta\Pi}{\Delta A} = 3.4A + 1.7 \, \Delta A \tag{12}$$

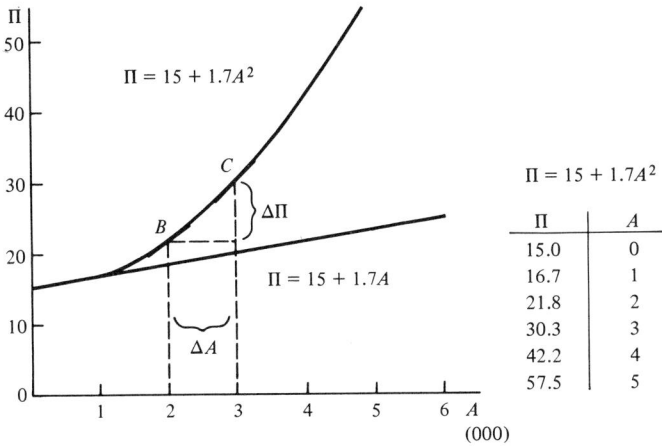

The table shown in the figure:

Π	A
15.0	0
16.7	1
21.8	2
30.3	3
42.2	4
57.5	5

$\Pi = 15 + 1.7A^2$

Figure 2-4

The change in Π with respect to an incremental change in A is not a constant as in the linear case but depends upon the level of A and its amount of change (ΔA). This is to be expected, since the relation is specified as curved rather than linear, as shown in Figure 2-4.

For the progressively rising curve of Figure 2-4, the slope increases as one moves along the quadratic curve from any point B to another point C. (A useful technique for plotting curves is preparing a table like that in Figure 2-4, which shows the various values of Π calculated for assumed values of A.) Two slopes are therefore involved when there is an incremental change in A. Calculus deals with this problem by reducing the change in A to ever smaller amounts until points B and C coincide. By causing ΔA to approach a limiting value of zero, the slope at a point, indicated by $d\Pi/dA$, comes to depend only on the value of A:

$$\frac{d\Pi}{dA} = \lim_{\Delta A \to 0} \frac{\Delta \Pi}{\Delta A} = \lim_{\Delta A \to 0} (3.4A + 1.7\,\Delta A) = 3.4A \qquad (13)$$

This information is very useful in determining if and where a curve has maximum or minimum points. Since the slope of any curve is zero at maximum and minimum points, those points can be located by simply setting up the equation $d\Pi/dA = 0$ and solving for the respective values of A. In the problem at hand,

$$\frac{d\Pi}{dA} = 3.4A = 0$$

$$A = 0$$

In this case, there are no maximum or minimum points on the curve except where $A = 0$. From such a result the business person infers that as much money as possible should be allocated to advertising, because profits will rise by increasingly larger amounts as additional amounts are spent on advertising. Such advice may be warranted for a relevant range up to some undetermined level of advertising. That is, equation (11) holds only for a given range of values of A.

Let us apply the same technique to find the level of A that maximizes Π for still another relation, given by

$$\Pi = 15 + 4A - A^2 \tag{14}$$

Proceed as follows:

$$\begin{aligned}
\Pi + \Delta\Pi &= 15 + 4(A + \Delta A) - (A + \Delta A)^2 \\
&= 15 + 4A + 4(\Delta A) - A^2 - 2A(\Delta A) - (\Delta A)^2 \quad (15)
\end{aligned}$$
$$\Delta\Pi = (\Pi + \Delta\Pi) - \Pi = 4(\Delta A) - 2A(\Delta A) - (\Delta A)^2$$

$$\frac{\Delta\Pi}{\Delta A} = 4 - 2A - \Delta A \tag{16}$$

$$\frac{d\Pi}{dA} = \lim_{\Delta A \to 0} (4 - 2A - \Delta A) = 4 - 2A \tag{17}$$

Set up the equation $d\Pi/dA = 0$:

$$\frac{d\Pi}{dA} = 4 - 2A = 0 \tag{18}$$

Solve for A:

$$2A = 4$$
$$A = 2 \tag{19}$$

Accordingly, the curve of the profit equation has a zero slope at the point where $A = 2$, which in this case is a maximum, as shown in Figure 2-5.

Fortunately, there is a shortcut for determining the first derivatives (slopes or $d\Pi/dA$'s) for these and more complex equations. One need only apply the rules listed in the next section, which have been obtained by using the procedure just discussed.

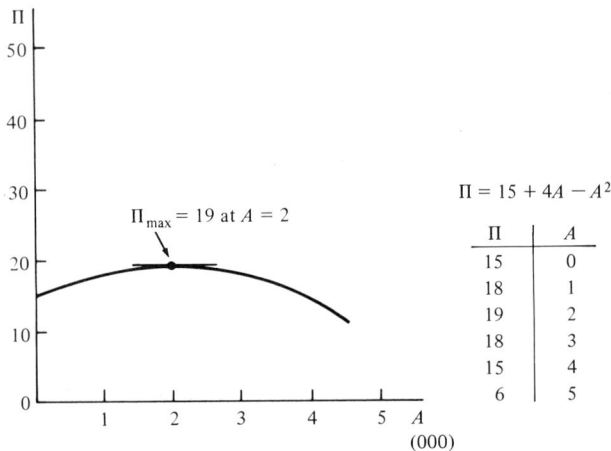

$\Pi_{max} = 19$ at $A = 2$

$\Pi = 15 + 4A - A^2$

Π	A
15	0
18	1
19	2
18	3
15	4
6	5

Figure 2-5

2-5 Rules for Differentiation

The most important rules for differentiation are given here for easy reference:

Rule 1. Constants. If $Y = a$, $\dfrac{dY}{dX} = 0$.

Rule 2. First-Degree. If $Y = aX$, $\dfrac{dY}{dX} = a$.

Rule 3. Powers. If $Y = aX^n$, $\dfrac{dY}{dX} = anX^{n-1}$.

Rule 4. Sums. If $Y = U + V$, $\dfrac{dY}{dX} = \dfrac{dU}{dX} + \dfrac{dV}{dX}$ (where U and V are functions of X).

Rule 5. Products. If $Y = UV$, $\dfrac{dY}{dX} = U\dfrac{dV}{dX} + V\dfrac{dU}{dX}$, and if $Y = aV$, $\dfrac{dY}{dX} = a\dfrac{dV}{dX}$.

Rule 6. Quotients. If $Y = \dfrac{U}{V}$, $\dfrac{dY}{dX} = \dfrac{V\dfrac{dU}{dX} - U\dfrac{dV}{dX}}{V^2}$.

Rule 7. Function of a Function. If $Y = f(U)$ and $U = f(X)$, $\dfrac{dY}{dX} = \dfrac{dY}{dU}\dfrac{dU}{dX}$.

Rule 8. Logarithms. If $Y = a \ln U$, $\dfrac{dY}{dX} = \dfrac{a}{U}\dfrac{dU}{dX}$.   Note also if $Y = \log_{10}U = \ln U \log_{10} e$, then $\dfrac{dY}{dX} = \dfrac{1}{U}\dfrac{dU}{dX}\log_{10} e = \dfrac{1}{U}\dfrac{dU}{dX}(0.434)$.

Rule 9. Exponents. If $Y = a^U$, $\dfrac{dY}{dX} = a^U \ln a \dfrac{dU}{dX}$. Special cases: When $U = X$ and $Y = a^X$, $\dfrac{dY}{dX} = a^X \ln a$. When $a = e$ and $Y = e^U$, $\dfrac{dY}{dX} = e^U\dfrac{dU}{dX}$ (since $\ln a = 1$). When $a = e$ and $U = X$ and $Y = e^X$, $\dfrac{dY}{dX} = e^X$ (the only expression to equal its own derivative).

Rule 10. Partials.[1] If $Y = f(X, Z)$ (where X and Z are independent),

$dY = \dfrac{\partial Y}{\partial X}dX + \dfrac{\partial Y}{\partial Z}dZ$, where $\dfrac{\partial Y}{\partial X}$ is the partial derivative of Y with respect to X (Z remains constant); $\dfrac{\partial Y}{\partial Z}$ is the partial derivative of Y with respect

[1] The partial derivative sign (∂) was introduced by the mathematician Jacobi (1804–1851). It is not a Greek letter.

to Z (X remains constant); dX and dZ are differentials of the independent variables X and Z; and dY is the total differential of the dependent variable Y.

The following examples show how derivatives can be obtained by these rules. The reader should verify each solution.

<table>
<tr><td align="center">Example</td><td align="center">Solution</td></tr>
<tr><td>$Y = 5X$</td><td>$\dfrac{dY}{dX} = 5$</td></tr>
<tr><td>$Y = 3X^2$</td><td>$\dfrac{dY}{dX} = 6X$</td></tr>
<tr><td>$Y = 5X^6$</td><td>$\dfrac{dY}{dX} = 30X^5$</td></tr>
<tr><td>$Y = 1 + 3X + 4X^3$</td><td>$\dfrac{dY}{dX} = 3 + 12X^2$</td></tr>
<tr><td>$Y = (2X + 3)(X^2 - 2)$</td><td>$\dfrac{dY}{dX} = (2X + 3)(2X) + (X^2 - 2)2$</td></tr>
</table>

$$= 4X^2 + 6X + 2X^2 - 4$$

$$= 6X^2 + 6X - 4$$

$$Y = \frac{X^2 + 1}{X^3} \qquad \frac{dY}{dX} = \frac{X^3(2X) - (X^2 + 1)(3X^2)}{X^6}$$

$$= \frac{2X^4 - 3X^4 - 3X^2}{X^6}$$

$$= \frac{-X^4 - 3X^2}{X^6} = \frac{-X^2 - 3}{X^4}$$

$$Y = U^{1/2} \text{ and } U = X^2 + 2X \qquad \frac{dY}{dU} = \tfrac{1}{2}U^{-1/2} \text{ and } \frac{dU}{dX} = 2X + 2$$

$$\frac{dY}{dX} = (\tfrac{1}{2}U^{-1/2})(2X + 2)$$

$$= \frac{(2X + 2)}{2U^{1/2}} = \frac{X + 1}{U^{1/2}}$$

$$= \frac{X + 1}{(X^2 + 2X)^{1/2}}$$

$$Y = \ln\left(\frac{X^3}{\sqrt{3 - 4X}}\right) \qquad \frac{dY}{dX} = \frac{3}{X} - \frac{1}{2}\frac{-4}{(3 - 4X)}$$

$$= 3 \ln X - \tfrac{1}{2} \ln(3 - 4X) \qquad = \frac{3}{X} + \frac{2}{3 - 4X} = \frac{9 - 10x}{X(3 - 4X)}$$

Example	*Solution*

$Y = X^2 \ln(1 + 3X)$

$$\frac{dY}{dX} = X^2 \frac{d}{dX}\ln(1 + 3X) + \ln(1 + 3X)$$
$$\frac{d}{dX}X^2$$
$$= \frac{3X^2}{1 + 3X} + 2X\ln(1 + 3X)$$

$Y = \dfrac{\sqrt{X^2 + 1}}{(X - 3)(3 - X^2)}$

$$\ln Y = \tfrac{1}{2}\ln(X^2 + 1) - \ln(X - 3)$$
$$- \ln(3 - X^2)$$
$$\frac{1}{Y}\frac{dY}{dX} = \frac{1}{2}\frac{2X}{X^2 + 1} - \frac{1}{X - 3} + \frac{2X}{3 - X^2}$$
$$= \frac{X}{X^2 + 1} - \frac{1}{X - 3} + \frac{2X}{3 - X^2}$$
$$\frac{dY}{dX} = \frac{\sqrt{X^2 + 1}}{(X - 3)(3 - X^2)}\left(\frac{X}{X^2 + 1}\right.$$
$$\left. - \frac{1}{X - 3} + \frac{2X}{3 - X^2}\right)$$
$$= \frac{\sqrt{X^2 + 1}}{(X - 3)(3 - X^2)} \times$$
$$\left[\frac{2X^4 - 3X^3 + 3X^2 - 15X - 3}{(X^2 + 1)(X - 3)(3 - X^2)}\right]$$
$$= \frac{2X^4 - 3X^3 + 3X^2 - 15X - 3}{\sqrt{X^2 + 1}(X - 3)^2(3 - X^2)^2}$$

$Y = e^X$

$$\frac{dY}{dX} = e^X$$

$Y = e^{\sqrt{X}}$

$$\frac{dY}{dX} = e^{\sqrt{X}}\frac{d\sqrt{X}}{dX} = e^{\sqrt{X}}(\tfrac{1}{2}X^{-1/2})$$
$$= \frac{e^{\sqrt{X}}}{2\sqrt{X}}$$

$Y = X^X$

$$\ln Y = X\ln X$$
$$\frac{1}{Y}\frac{dY}{dX} = X\frac{d}{dX}\ln X + \ln X\frac{dX}{dX}$$
$$= 1 + \ln X$$
$$\frac{dY}{dX} = (1 + \ln X)X^X$$

$Y = X^3 + 2X^2Z + Z^2$

$$\frac{\partial Y}{\partial X} = 3X^2 + 4ZX$$
$$\frac{\partial Y}{\partial Z} = 2X^2 + 2Z$$

2-6   First- and Second-Order Conditions

For a curve representing an equation in which Y is a continuous function of X to have a maximum (peak of the hill) or a minimum (bottom of the valley), it must have at least one point at which the slope is flat or equal to zero. Since the first derivative gives a value for slope, the points on the curve having zero slopes can be determined by setting the first derivative equal to zero and solving for X. For example, the curve of the equation

$$Y = 2X^2 - 8X + 10 \tag{20}$$

has a zero slope where $dY/dX = 0$, that is, where

$$\frac{dY}{dX} = 4X - 8 = 0$$

$$X = 2 \tag{21}$$

Knowing that the curve has a zero slope at $X = 2$ does not help us to determine whether there is a hill (a maximum value for Y) or a valley (a minimum value for Y). This could be determined for this two-variable equation by plotting the curve as shown in Figure 2-6a. Clearly, Y is a minimum at $X = 2$. If the equation were too difficult to graph or if more than two variables were involved, the decisions about maximum or minimum could be made on the basis of a second differentiation. The second derivative is positive if the slope is increasing, as it does when the curve goes through a minimum in passing from negative values of slope to positive ones. Hence, a positive second derivative indicates a minimum. Similarly, a negative second derivative indicates a maximum. For example,

$$\frac{dY^2}{d^2X} = 4 \quad \text{(a positive value, therefore a minimum)} \tag{22}$$

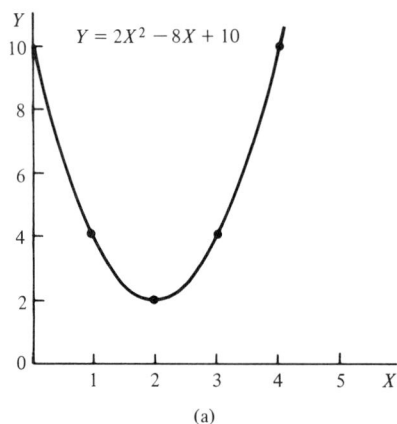

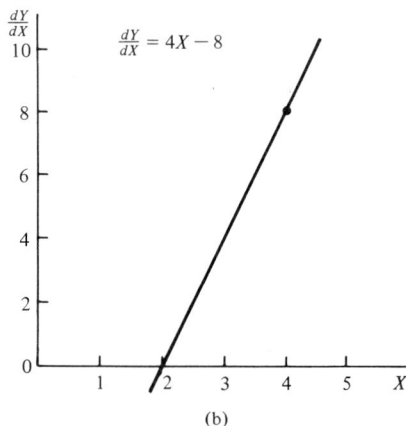

Figure 2-6

A useful device for remembering the significance of the sign of the second derivative is to relate the valley to a bowl filled with water; if the bowl holds water, the sign is plus; if the bowl is upside down, water spills out and the sign is negative. Note also from Figure 2-6b that the slope of the graph of the first derivative is positive. This is the case when the original curve moves progressively upward from the horizontal axis for values of X both larger and smaller than at the point of zero slope. The curve is said to be *convex* to the horizontal axis when the change in the slope is positive, that is, $dY^2/d^2X > 0$. Similarly, if the curve contains a maximum, that is, $dY/dX = 0$ and $dY^2/dX^2 < 0$, it is cupped downward to the horizontal axis, or *concave*, and the curve for the second derivative has a negative slope. These points are illustrated in Figure 2-7, based upon the following calculations:

$$Y = -X^3 + 4X^2 - 4X + 8 = 0 \tag{23}$$

$$\frac{dY}{dX} = -3X^2 + 8X - 4 = 0 \tag{24}$$

Solve for the values of X using the quadratic formula[2]:

$$X = \frac{-8 \pm \sqrt{(8)^2 - 4(-3)(-4)}}{2(-3)}$$

$$= \frac{-8 \pm \sqrt{16}}{-6} = \frac{-8 \pm 4}{-6} = \tfrac{2}{3}, 2 \tag{25}$$

To determine which of these values of X give maximums and which give minimums, the sign of the second derivative must be checked for each:

$$\frac{d^2Y}{dX^2} = -6X + 8 \tag{26}$$

$$= -6(\tfrac{2}{3}) + 8 = 4 \quad \text{(positive sign indicates } Y \text{ is a minimum at}$$
$$X = \tfrac{2}{3})$$
$$= -6(2) + 8 = -4 \quad \text{(negative sign indicates } Y \text{ is a maximum at}$$
$$X = 2)$$

These points are consistent with the curve plotted in Figure 2-7a. In graphing the equation for the second derivative, it is useful to know also where this curve has zero slope, which can be found by setting its derivative (the second derivative of the first equation) equal to zero:

$$\frac{d^2Y}{dX^2} = -6X + 8 = 0$$
$$X = 1\tfrac{1}{3} \tag{27}$$

[2] The well-known quadratic formula is

$$x = \frac{-b \pm \sqrt{b^2 - 4ac}}{2a}$$

when the equation to be solved for x is in the form $ax^2 + bx + c = 0$.

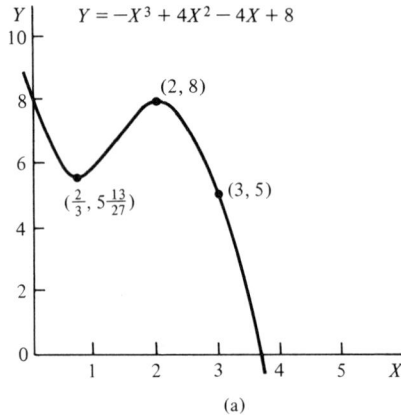

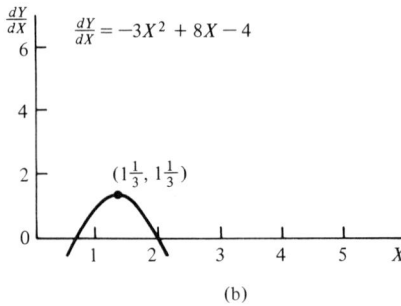

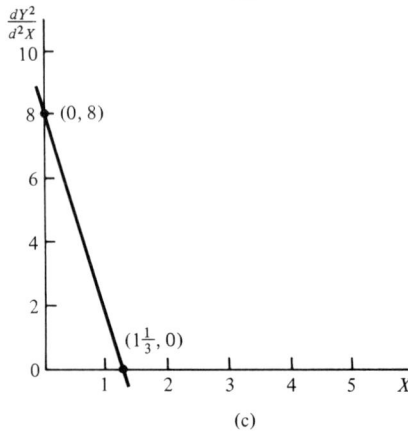

$$Y = -X^3 + 4X^2 - 4X + 8$$

(2, 8)

$(\frac{2}{3}, 5\frac{13}{27})$

(3, 5)

(a)

$$\frac{dY}{dX} = -3X^2 + 8X - 4$$

$(1\frac{1}{3}, 1\frac{1}{3})$

(b)

(0, 8)

$(1\frac{1}{3}, 0)$

(c)

Figure 2-7

To determine if this value gives a maximum or minimum, observe the sign of the third derivative (the second derivative of $dY/dX = -3X^2 + 8X - 4$):

$$\frac{d^3Y}{dX^3} = -6 \quad \text{(negative sign indicates a maximum, as shown} \qquad (28)$$
in Figure 2-7b).

The main points of this section can be summarized briefly. For a continuous equation to have a maximum, it must satisfy the first-order condition of having a zero first derivative and a second-order condition of having a negative second derivative. This is expressed more succinctly in mathematical notation as $dY/dX = 0$ and $d^2 Y/dX^2 < 0$, or $y' = 0$ and $y'' < 0$. Similarly, for there to be a minimum, the first- and second-order conditions are $dY/dX = 0$ and $d^2 Y/dX^2 > 0$, or $y' = 0$ and $y'' > 0$. If $d^2 Y/dX^2 = 0$, there is neither a maximum nor a minimum, but a point of inflection.

2-7   Constrained Optimization and Lagrange Multipliers

An important characteristic of problems requiring executive decisions is that most of the items considered in their models are in limited supply. Constraint conditions are said to be imposed on the model. For example, assume that output Q of some product is to be maximized by the judicious use of labor L and capital C according to the hypothetical production function

$$Q = 6LC \qquad (29)$$

Furthermore, assume (1) that capital services, for instance, the output per unit of time derived from the use of capital, cost $3,000 per unit, (2) that labor services cost $1,000 (each on a monthly basis), and (3) that the firm has available only $900,000 it can spend each month on combined labor and capital. The firm's budget constraint can be constructed as

$$(1)L + (3)C = 900 \qquad (30)$$

This equation simply states that total expenditures on the two inputs (the sum of the dollars per unit times the number of units of labor and capital employed) equal 900 (thousand dollars). The budget limitation is imposed upon the production function as follows.

Put all the terms of the equation on the left side of the equal sign to form what is known as a budget constraint equation:

$$L + 3C - 900 = 0 \qquad (31)$$

Now form a function composed of the original production function and the budget constraint function:

$$Q_\lambda = 6LC + \lambda(L + 3C - 900) \qquad (32)$$

The Greek letter λ (lambda), when used as a subscript, indicates the output is constrained; when used as a variable, it is called *the Lagrange multiplier*. In its latter use, it is an artificial variable added to the model so the the number of variables (L, C, λ) will be the same as the number of equations in the next step (equation (33).)

The next step is to take the partial derivatives of Q_λ with respect to each of the three variables, set them equal to zero, and solve the three simultaneous equations for the unknowns:

1. $\dfrac{\partial Q_\lambda}{dL} = 6C + \lambda = 0$

2. $\dfrac{\partial Q_\lambda}{\partial C} = 6L + 3\lambda = 0$ (33)

3. $\dfrac{\partial Q_\lambda}{\partial \lambda} = 3C + L - 900 = 0$

Multiply equation 1 by -3 and add the result to equation 2:

$$-18C \qquad - 3\lambda = 0$$
$$6L + 3\lambda = 0$$
$$\overline{}$$

4. $-18C + 6L \qquad = 0$

Multiply equation 3 by -6 and add to equation 4:

$$-18C + 6L \qquad\quad = 0$$
$$-18C - 6L + 5{,}400 = 0$$
$$\overline{}$$
$$-36C \qquad + 5{,}400 = 0$$
$$C = \frac{5{,}400}{36} = 150$$

Putting $C = 150$ into equations 1 and 3, we obtain

$$\lambda = -900 \quad \text{and} \quad L = 450$$

These values should produce a maximum value of Q_λ (assuming the second-order conditions are also met). Putting them into equation (32), we find

$$Q_\lambda = 6(450)(150) + (-900)[450 + 3(150) - 900]$$
$$= 405{,}000 \text{ units}$$

Note that the bracketed value is zero, which will always be the case if Q_λ is a maximum, since constraint equation (31) is satisfied. Note additionally, when this is true, that $Q_\lambda = Q$, so that when Q_λ is maximized, Q is too. This is the rationale of the Lagrangian technique. This method is explained further in other chapters of the text.

2-8 Marginal Analysis, or Optimization Theory

The previous discussion of derivatives and Lagrange multipliers provides the basic elements of marginal analysis, or optimization theory. When some variable like profits is to be maximized, marginal analysis supports the recommendation that operations must be expanded to the point where profits on one additional unit of output (that is, marginal profits) are zero. This is easily seen with reference to Figure 2-8, which is the same as Figures 2-7a and 2-7b, reproduced here for more convenient reference.

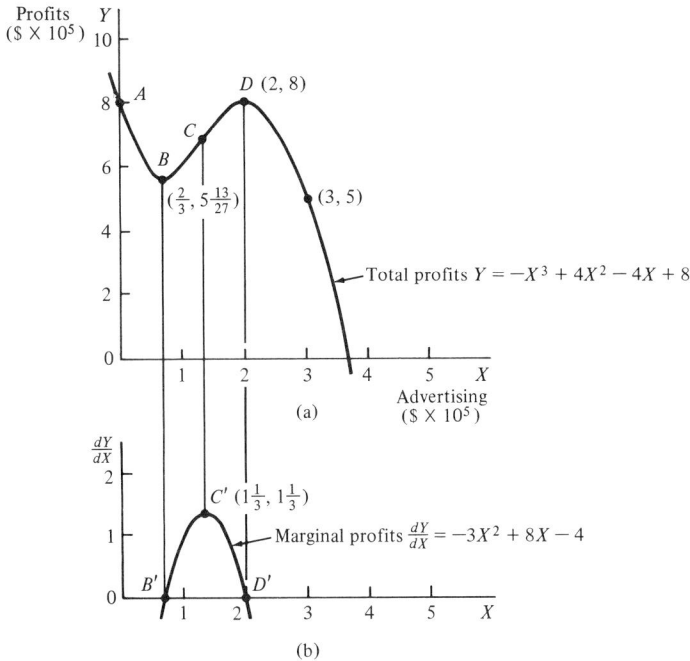

Profits Y
($ × 10⁵)

D (2, 8)

Total profits $Y = -X^3 + 4X^2 - 4X + 8$

$(\frac{2}{3}, 5\frac{13}{27})$

(3, 5)

Advertising
($ × 10⁵)

(a)

$\frac{dY}{dX}$

$C'(1\frac{1}{3}, 1\frac{1}{3})$

Marginal profits $\frac{dY}{dX} = -3X^2 + 8X - 4$

(b)

Figure 2-8

Assume that Y represents the total dollar value of profits, which are related to dollars spent on advertising by the curve of Figure 2-8a. Marginal profits—those accruing to additional dollars spent on advertising—are given by the slope of the total profit curve as shown in Figure 2-8b. When advertising expenditures are zero, profits are $\$8 \times 10^5$ or \$800,000. Profits fall with the initial, relatively small amounts spent on advertising, as shown by the negative slope of the upper curve, and negative marginal profits are shown by the negative values of dY/dX in the lower curve. Profits fall at a decreasing rate as the slope diminishes to zero at point B, where $X = \frac{2}{3}$; marginal profits are necessarily also zero at B', where $X = \frac{2}{3}$, and the lower curve intersects the horizontal axis. With additional expenditures, profits rise at an increasing rate up to point C, then at a decreasing rate to point D. Slope reaches a positive maximum at the inflection point C, as shown by the maximum at C' on the marginal profit curve. For values of X greater than two units, profits decline, because every additional dollar spent on advertising increases costs more than revenues, and marginal profits are negative. From this analysis the manager could conclude that the firm should spend no money on advertising because the best one can hope for is to raise profits back to their original level without advertisment. This situation may not always prevail; at another time the relation could be quite different. In any case, this is the sort of discussion associated with marginal analysis.

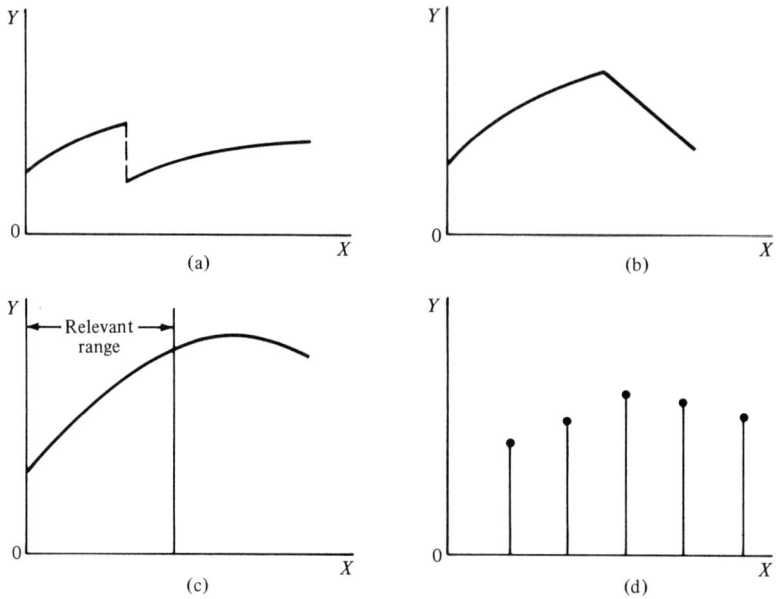

Figure 2-9

2-9 Concluding Comments

The techniques of differential calculus used in maximization and optimization work quite well when the relations are known to be smooth and continuous. Troubles are encountered where there are (1) discontinuities (gaps), as in Figure 2-9a, (2) kinks, as in Figure 2-9b, (3) restrictions on values of X such that the maximum or minimum falls outside the relevant range, as in Figure 2-9c, and (4) indivisibilities where values of X come only in discrete units so that there is no curve but only a series of points, as in Figure 2-9d. Mathematical programming is a powerful assortment of tools for dealing with some of these problems. So widespread is its use in solving problems of the firm and resource allocation that it is given substantial attention in this text.

Questions and Problems

2-1. Determine the slopes for the following functions:

a. $Y = 3X + 2$ c. $3X = 5Y - 1$
b. $2Y = 4X + 1$ d. $Y + 6X = 3$

2-2. Find the first derivative of Y with respect to X:

a. $Y = 10X - 7$ f. $Y = 6U^{1/2}$ and $U = X^2 + 3$
b. $Y = 2X^2 - 5X + 5$ g. $X^2 + Y^2 = 4^2$ (circle)
c. $Y = 4X^4 - 16X$ h. $(X - 2)^2 + (Y - 3)^2 = 16$ (circle)
d. $Y = (X - 15)(X^2 + 3)$ i. $9X^2 - 16Y^2 = 25$ (hyperbola)
                                      j. $Y^2 = 6X$ (parabola)
e. $Y = \dfrac{X^4}{X - 3}$ k. $2XY = 36$ (equilateral hyperbola)
                                      l. $Y = 8X^3$ (cubical parabola)

m. $Y = 2X^2 + X + 3$ (parabola)

n. $Y = \dfrac{8}{X^2 + 4}$ (witch)

o. $Y^3 = X^2$ (semicubical parabola)

p. $X^{2/3} + Y^{2/3} = 8^{2/3}$ (hypocycloid of four cusps)

q. $Y = \ln\left(\dfrac{X^2}{\sqrt{4 - 3X}}\right)$

r. $Y = X^2 \ln(X^2 - 1)$

s. $Y = 15^x$

t. $Y = 2^{-x^2}$

u. $Y = e^{x - 2/3}$

v. $Y = \log X$

2-3. Find the first partial derivatives:

a. $Y = X^3 + 3X^2Z + Z^2$

b. $Y = \dfrac{X}{X - Z}$

c. $Y = XZe^{xz}$

2-4. Find the first and second derivatives:

a. $Y = 3X^3 - 2X + 5$
b. $Y = X^4 + X^3 - 3X^2$
c. $Y = 5X^2 - X + 2$
d. $Y = e^x$

2-5. Find the value of X for which Y is a maximum:

a. $Y = -2X^3 + 6X^2 - 3X$
b. $Y = X^3 - 3X^2 + X$

2-6. The firm's industrial engineer estimates the firm's production function to be $Y = X^2 - 12XZ + 3Z^2$, where inputs X and Z have constant prices of $P_X = 2$ and $P_Z = 1$.

a. How much of X and Z will be purchased to produce the most Y if only $100 can be spent on inputs?
b. How much Y can be produced?
c. The next day the industrial engineer called to report a typographical error in the production function, which should now read $Y = X^2 - 2XZ + 3Z^2$. Recalculate parts *a* and *b*.

2-7. If profits are related to advertising expenditures by the function $Y = -X^3 + 6X^2 - 2X + 5$, determine the following:

a. optimum advertising expenses to maximize profits
b. maximum profits

2-8. In problem 2-7, what would be your response to the suggestion that the firm adopt a more conservative approach of spending only $1 million rather than $3.5 million, and if this proves profitable then doubling the amount?

2-9. Given the firm's total revenue (R) and total profit (Π) functions below, determine the level of output (Q) (see Fig. 1-1):

a. when revenue is maximized
b. when profit is maximized
c. when revenue is maximized subject to a minimum profit constraint of

$$\Pi \geq 10, \quad R = 25Q - Q^2, \quad \Pi = -2Q^2 + 14Q - 2$$

References

1. Clark Lee Allen. *Elementary Mathematics of Price Theory* (Belmont, Calif.: Wadsworth, 1962).
2. R. G. D. Allen. *Mathematical Analysis for Economists* (New York: Macmillan, 1964).
3. William J. Baumol. *Economic Theory and Operations Analysis.* 3d ed. (Englewood Cliffs, N.J.: Prentice-Hall, 1972), ch. 1–4.
4. Paul H. Daus and William M. Whyburn. *Introduction to Mathematical Analysis— With Applications To Problems of Economics* (Reading, Mass.: Addison-Wesley, 1958).
5. Thomas K. Kim and James P. Godfrey. *Introductory Mathematics for Economic Analysis* (Glenview, Ill.: Scott, Foresman, 1971).
6. William R. Longley, Percey F. Smith, and Wallace A. Wilson. *Analytic Geometry and Calculus* (Boston: Ginn, 1951).
7. Lyman C. Peck. *Basic Mathematics for Management and Economics* (Glenview, Ill.: Scott, Foresman, 1970), ch. 6–7, Appendix A.
8. Daniel Teichrow. *An Introduction to Management Science—Deterministic Models* (New York: Wiley, 1964).
9. George B. Thomas, Jr. *Calculus and Analytic Geometry.* 3d ed. (Reading, Mass.: Addison-Wesley, 1960).
10. Taro Yamane. *Mathematics for Economists—An Elementary Survey.* 2d ed. (Englewood Cliffs, N.J.: Prentice-Hall, 1968).
11. Bevan K. Youse and Ashford W. Stalnaker. *Calculus for Students of Business and Management* (Scranton, Pa.: International Textbook Co., 1967).

3 Linear Programming

Linear programming (LP) is a mathematical technique used in business and economics to solve a broad range of practical and theoretical problems.[1] It is suited to optimization problems where the relation between variables can be assumed to be linear over the relevant range and where the range of feasible solutions is limited by inequality, or side conditions.

3-1 Types of Linear Programming Problems

Applications of linear programming are so numerous that only a brief listing of major categories can be given here:[2]

1. Agricultural applications dealing with farm economics (regional or national in scope) and farm management (individual farms) to determine optimal allocation of crops, food costs, methods of production, crop rotation, and cash return.

2. Contract awards as applied to procurement and competitive cash bidding.

3. Industrial applications categorized by type of industry: chemical, coal, airlines, communications, iron and steel, paper, petroleum, railroad. The types of problem are production, inventory, scheduling, pricing, routing, waste reduction, and blending.

---

[1] While calculus has been available for use in obtaining maximum and minimum solutions to many types of problems for roughly 300 years, LP has been in use in the United States only since 1947, when George B. Dantzig, while working with the Air Force, presented a general formulation of the problem and the simplex method for its systematic solution [6, p. ix]. For his contributions, he has been called the father of programming [1, p. 70, fn. 1]. It was not until January 1952 that a successful solution of an LP problem was obtained by use of a high-speed electronic computer, on the SECA machine of the National Bureau of Standards [6, p. x]. In *Linear Programming and Extensions* [3, ch. 2] Dantzig discusses the origins and influences of LP.

[2] A comprehensive bibliography of LP applications containing more than 1,000 items was prepared in 1958 by Vera Riley and Saul I. Gass [7]. A shorter but more current version was provided by Gass in 1969 [6, pp. 325–337], from which the classification scheme of this section was taken. [See also 6, pp. 11–18.]

4. Economic analysis applied to the Leontief interindustry model, theory of the firm interpretation, investment portfolio selection, optimum diet for population, theory of plant location, and utility analysis.

5. Military applications to airlifting tonnage at least cost, aircraft deployment to combat or training to maximize total aircraft months, estimation of spare-engine requirements, least-cost defense against a given attack, and numerous others.

6. Personnel assignment of people with different abilities, training, and experience matched against jobs with various requirements to maximize total value to the firm.

7. Production scheduling and inventory control in which production is smoothed to meet requirements at minimum storage costs. Warehouse space is allocated optimally among multiple products with varying prices. Idle time of assembly line operation is minimized as items pass through the various stages of production.

8. Structural design of least-cost plastic structures and airplane frames to withstand certain types of load.

9. Traffic analysis applied to scheduling traffic signals to move the maximum number of vehicles at various speeds with the fewest delays while moving along roads through a network of intersections.

10. Transportation problems and network theory, where the basic problem involves shipping m units to n destinations over all routes to minimize the total transportation cost. Extensions have been made to include switching between several modes of transportation at intermediate links along the way.

11. Routing sales people to their appointments on a swing through various cities and back home.

12. Other applications include efficient operation of a system of dams to maximize total electricity generated, design of optical filters, and solution of many theoretical problems in mathematics.

3-2 Common Characteristics of Linear Programming Problems

In listing the characteristics common to each of the problems mentioned, it is appropriate to begin with the most basic of all assumptions: All relations between variables are linear. Where such an assumption is not warranted, recommendations based upon linear programming analysis should be viewed with skepticism. For example, it is typically assumed that unit profitabilities of a firm's products are constant regardless of the number sold; if price must be reduced to sell greater amounts, profits are a declining, rather than a constant, function of output. In such a case, the LP solution could be grossly misleading.

A second characteristic of LP problems is that something is to be optimized subject to one or more specified *side conditions*. A side condition in programming is typically the setting of minimum or maximum, rather than precise, requirements, that is, the constraint is not initially an equality but an inequality. For example, it is not required that a quantity must be 100 but only that it be no less than 100.

A third characteristic. is that the system of equations in LP problems is typically underdetermined, that is, it has more variables than equations.

Linear programming deals with this problem by converting the underdetermined system to a determined one by setting some of the variables equal to zero. To obtain an optimum solution, one must be sure that the appropriate variables (those with the least profitability) are the ones assigned a value of zero. Such a procedure, of course, reduces the number of nonzero-valued variables in the optimum solution to equal the number of constraint equations. This outcome may appear surprising to the managers of a firm, since it implies that some of their products are unprofitable and should not be produced, even though the managers "know" they are making a profit on such items. The confusion is attributable to the use of two different concepts of profit. When the optimum LP solution assigns a zero value to an output, it should not necessarily be inferred that the firm cannot sell the product at a price more than sufficient to cover its out-of-pocket cost. It is implied only that scarce resources may be allocated more appropriately to the production of another product—this is an alternative rather than a business cost concept.

A fourth characteristic is that the variables must have nonnegative values. Clearly, it is not possible in the real world to use negative amounts of inputs or outputs, but such information must be fed into electronic computers if realistic answers are to be obtained.

Finally, the method of computation used in programming is iterative, that is, the procedure is one of trial and error—a systematic groping toward the best solution. A mechanical rule prescribes the next step to be taken based upon results of the previous trial. This rule, fed into a computer, makes electronic computation possible and minimizes human judgment where many variables and interrelations are present. The rule also insures that each trial will produce values that progressively approach the correct answer. This feature guides the computer in the right direction, saving time and avoiding unnecessary operations; otherwise, successive steps may move away from the best solution. Several different linear programming techniques are in use today, but only the simplex method will be discussed in this book.

3-3 A Typical Linear Programming Problem

A firm wishes to maximize profits from producing and selling outputs X_1, X_2, and X_3, which have known unit profits of 4, 3, and 2, respectively. The profit function to be maximized, called the *objective function*, will therefore be

$$\Pi = 4X_1 + 3X_2 + 2X_3$$

If the firm is limited to warehouse space W of only 10,000 square feet and space required for units of each output is given as 1, 3, and 2, respectively, the side condition is given by the inequality

$$X_1 + 3X_2 + 2X_3 \leq 10,000 \text{ sq ft}$$

Similarly, if machine time M is limited to 8,000 hours for the three products requiring 2, 1, and 3 hours per unit, respectively, the second constraint is

$$2X_1 + X_2 + 3X_3 \leq 8,000 \text{ machine hours}$$

With the addition of the nonnegativity requirements, the programming problem may be put in the standard form:

    1. Objective function:
        Maximize profits $\Pi = 4X_1 + 3X_2 + 2X_3$
    2. Structural constraints:
        Space limitations $X_1 + 3X_2 + 2X_3 \leq 10{,}000$
        Machine capacity $2X_1 + X_2 + 3X_3 \leq 8{,}000$ (1)
    3. Nonnegativity conditions:

$$X_1 \geq 0 \qquad X_2 \geq 0 \qquad X_3 \geq 0$$

The problem is recognized as linear, since the variables are confined to the numerator, are raised only to the first power, and are multiplied only by constants. It was assumed that input and output prices are fixed and returns to scale are constant—this is implicit in the assumptions of constant unit profits, for example, \$4 profit per unit of X_1 in the profit function, and of constant input proportions. The latter may be recognized from the coefficients of X_1 in the inequalities; it is found that 1 square foot of warehouse space and 2 machine hours are required to produce each unit of item X_1.

If there were only two products, X_1 and X_2 (asssuming for the moment that $X_3 = 0$) requiring both warehouse space and machine time, the problem could be represented graphically as in Figure 3-1a. The warehouse would be completely filled with either 10,000 units of $X_1 (= 10{,}000/1)$ or 3,333 of $X_2 (= 10{,}000/3)$. These two values indicate where the linear warehouse constraint line AB cuts the axes. Similarly, machines would be fully utilized by producing 4,000 units of X_1 or 8,000 units of X_2; the machine constraint can now be plotted as CD. Since combinations above and to the right of AB and CD cannot be produced, the shaded area under both curves indicates the feasible values. Which combination of X_1 and X_2 on or within the boundary of the feasible region will be selected depends upon the relative profitabilities of X_1 and X_2 indicated by their coefficients in the profit function, that is, 4 and 3, respectively. Since fewer

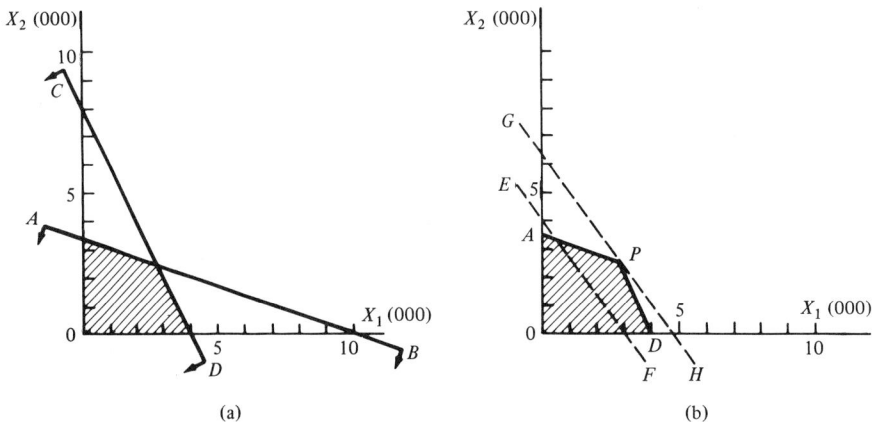

(a)   (b)

Figure 3-1

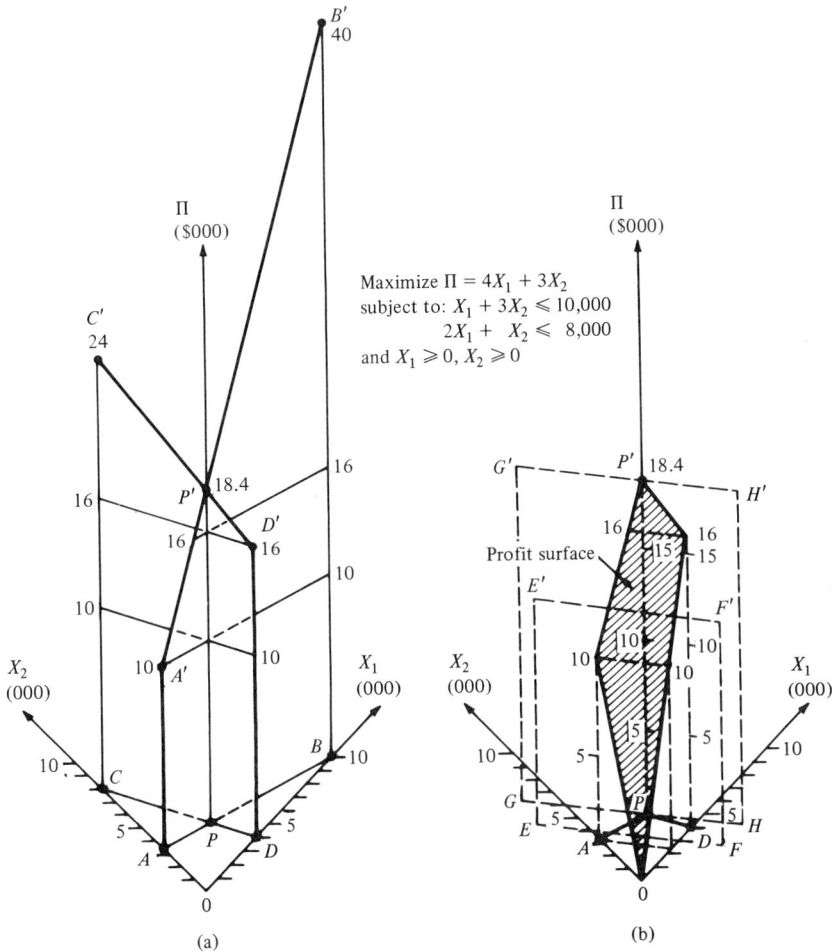

Maximize $\Pi = 4X_1 + 3X_2$
subject to: $X_1 + 3X_2 \leqslant 10{,}000$
$2X_1 + X_2 \leqslant 8{,}000$
and $X_1 \geqslant 0, X_2 \geqslant 0$

Figure 3-2

units of X_1 are required to produce the same profits as a given number of units of X_2, a line of equal profits will have a slope greater than unity. Specifically, the slope will be $-(4/3)$, as for the line EF in Figure 3-1b. (Slope may be obtained by converting $R = 4X_1 + 3X_2$ to $X_2 = -(4/3)X_1 + R/3$ and recalling that the coefficient of X_1 is the slope.) Since profits will be greater for such isoprofit lines that are above and to the right, we wish to know the highest one having the same slope as EF, say line GH, which barely touches the feasible region. The point of tangency at point P indicates that a combination of 2,800 units of X_1 and 2,400 units of X_2 produces maximum profits.

Profits may be represented as a third dimension appended to Figure 3-1, as shown in Figure 3-2. In Figure 3-2a the warehouse constraint line AB may be projected upward from the X_1X_2 plane producing the plane $AA'B'B$. The line $A'B'$ indicates the profits that would be generated by the production and sale of alternative combinations of X_1 and X_2 on AB. Similarly, $C'D'$ shows the profits associated with combinations of X_1 and X_2 along the machine-time constraint line CD. Maximum profits of \$18,400 subject to the two constraints occur at P' where $A'B'$ and $C'D'$ intersect. The shaded area of Figure 3-2b shows the profit surface; note that it begins at the origin and slopes away from the viewer. Lines of equal profits, called isoprofit lines, appear as parallel straight lines on the profit surface. Projection of two of these contour lines onto the $X_1 X_2$ plane yields the same isoprofit lines EF and GH of Figure 3-1b. Maximum constrained profits occur at point P on the highest attainable isoprofit line GH.

In linear programming, optimal solutions will generally occur at one of the corner points $O, A, P,$ or D. This is not necessarily true when the linear isoprofit line has the same slope as, or coincides with, one of the edges of the feasible region, such as AP. Here, the optimal solution would be at A or P or at any point on a straight line between A and P. When such is the case, the manager is indifferent to the output combinations yielding the same optimal level of profits but is free to choose from among these combinations based upon knowledge of variables not taken into account in the model.

Knowing that the optimal solution lies on the boundary of the feasible region, and probably at one of the corner points, is very helpful in simplifying computations—so much so that it provides the rationale for what is designated later as the *basic theorem of linear programming*. All the points within the boundary can be ignored and attention directed to the corner points. In real-world problems with a hundred or more constraints, the number of corner points is quite large. This requires the use of a powerful computational technique, described in succeeding sections.

3-4 Removing the Inequality Signs

To continue with the problem introduced in the previous section, the inequality signs may be removed to facilitate computations by introducing slack variables S_1 and S_2 to represent unused warehouse space and machine time, respectively. The problem can then be rewritten in *equality form* containing both *structural or ordinary variables* and *slack variables*:

Maximize $\Pi = 4X_1 + 3X_2 + 2X_3$

subject to the constraints

$$X_1 + 3X_2 + 2X_3 + S_1 = 10{,}000$$
$$2X_1 + X_2 + 3X_3 + S_2 = 8{,}000 \tag{2}$$

and the nonnegativity condition

$X_1, X_2, X_3, S_1,$ and S_2 each ≥ 0

Except for the nonnegativity requirements, all the inequality signs have been removed. Knowledge of the optimal values of the slack variables may also prove useful. Positive values indicate the extent of unused capacity to be expected, and values close to zero may signal potential bottlenecks for increased production. Such information is important for decision making.

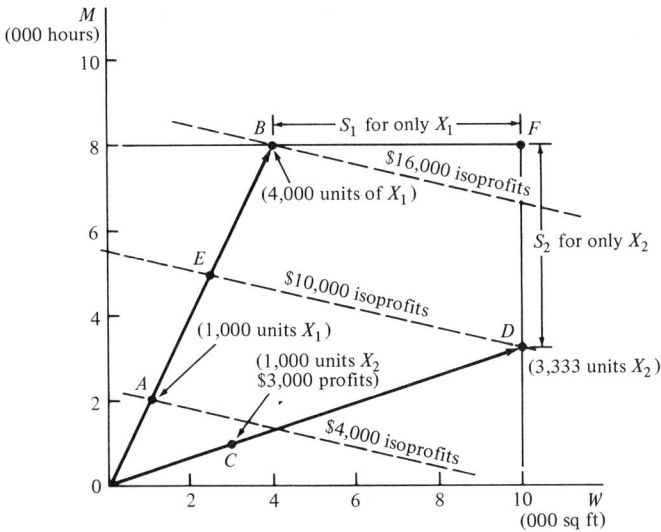

Figure 3-3

In the condensed version of this problem, where production was narrowed to two products X_1 and X_2, slack variables may be shown by a graph with the inputs (rather than outputs) on the axes. From the coefficients of X_1 in constraint equations (2), we know that 1 square foot of warehouse space and 2 machine hours are required to produce one unit of X_1, which will yield $4 of profit according to the coefficient of X_1 in the objective function. Since constant returns to scale and constant profitability per unit of output are assumed by the linearity of the problem, it follows that 1,000 units of warehouse space and 2,000 units of machine time will produce 1,000 units of X_1 at a profitability of $4,000; this is point A in Figure 3-3. Similarly, $4,000W$ and $8,000M$ will produce $4,000X_1$ and $16,000 profit at point B. It is impossible to produce more of X_1 because of the capacity limitations on machine hours; unused machine capacity, S_2, is zero only when X_1 is being produced to its maximum. Warehouse capacity at point B, however, is not fully used, since $S_1 = 6,000$ sq. ft.

In a similar manner, we find that if only X_2 is produced, 1,000 units of X_2 can be manufactured by using 3,000 units of W and 1,000 of M, yielding profits of $3,000 at point C. This means $10,000W$ and $3,333M$ will permit production of 3,333 units of X_2 and $10,000 profit; this is point D in Figure 3-3. Here $S_1 = 0$ and $S_2 = 4,667$.

A $10,000 isoprofit line can be drawn from point D to a point E ten-sixteenths of the distance OB from point O. The slope of ED indicates the relative profitabilities of producing X_1 and X_2, calculated to be $2/9$ $[= (5,000 - 3,333)/(10,000 - 2,500)]$. It is now clear that if production is devoted exclusively to only one of the two products, there will be unused capacity and profits will not be maximized. Full utilization of capacity would push production to point F, the point of maximum profits. A geometric explanation of how point F may be reached will be deferred to Chapter 14 on linear production. For now, it is sufficient to know that the optimal profit solution requires the production of both X_1 and X_2.

3-5   Forming the Programming Matrix and Obtaining Solutions That Are Both Feasible and Basic

Putting the equations in tableau form facilitates solution. We need only adjust equations (2) by putting the slack variables in the constraint equations on the left of the equal signs:

$$\text{Maximize } \Pi = 0 + 4X_1 + 3X_2 + 2X_3$$

$$\text{subject to } S_1 = 10{,}000 - X_1 - 3X_2 - 2X_3$$
$$S_2 = 8{,}000 - 2X_1 - X_2 - 3X_3$$

$$\text{where all } X_1 \text{ and } S_1 \text{ are } \geq 0$$

(3)

From equations (3) the tableau can be formed:

	1	X_1	X_2	X_3
Π	0	4	3	2
S_1	10,000	-1	-3	-2
S_2	8,000	-2*	-1	-3

(4)

Maximum Π will be given by the optimal feasible and basic solutions. Any combination of values of the X's and S's that meets the conditions imposed by the constraint equations and nonnegativity requirement is said to be a feasible solution. Any set of values in which the number of nonzero-valued variables equals the number of constraint equations is a basic solution. For example, if the X's are assumed to be zero, then S_1 and S_2 are 10,000 and 8,000, respectively; this solution is both feasible and basic—feasible because it meets the conditions (may be solved from the equations) of the problem and basic because only two variables (excluding Π), S_1 and S_2, have nonzero values and there are also only two constraint equations.

Consider the possible solutions:

	X_1	X_2	X_3	S_1	S_2
1.	0	3,333	0	0	4,667
2.	0	0	2,000	6,000	2,000
3.	0	0	0	10,000	20,000

Solution 1 is both feasible and basic; solution 2 is feasible but not basic, because the number of nonzero-valued variables exceeds the number of constraint equations; solution 3 is basic but not feasible, because the value of S_2 does not satisfy the constraint equations.

The observation that the optimal solution to any linear programming problem is a basic one, in which the number of nonzero-valued variables equals the number of constraints, is so important that it is called the basic theorem of linear programming. This result may seem surprising, since it implies that a firm using a total of 10 fixed-capacity inputs to produce 50 items is losing profits on 40 of the 50 products, that is, profits will be maximized by the firm's concentrating its attention on only 10 products. Such a conclusion is valid only where the assumptions of linearity are realistic. Where diminishing returns to scale in production or falling prices of inputs or outputs with increased sales are the rule, a different conclusion will probably apply.

The basic theorem's rationale may be grasped by observing that if only one fixed input is used, it should be employed on the product yielding the greatest returns. Where there are two such inputs, it is likely that one can be used more efficiently in producing one product while the other is more efficient in producing a second, causing the sharing of inputs to be more profitable. This reasoning may be extended to n additional inputs and constraints. Thus, it will generally be true that additional kinds of products should be produced only as the number of scarce inputs are increased.

In graphical terms, a basic solution is simply a corner point on the boundary of the feasible region. One of the corner points will give an optimal solution to the problem. A technique for searching for this particular point is the simplex method.

3-6   The Simplex Method

The simplex method begins with picking a solution that is both feasible and basic, that is, selecting a corner point, computing profits for this solution, and checking to see if adjacent corners promise greater profits [1]. If adjacent corners appear more profitable, the one with the most profits is given the same treatment as the previous corner. This procedure is repeated until adjacent points are observed to be less profitable; then the optimal solution has been found.

Now let us apply this technique to solving the problem shown in tableau (4). The easiest point at which to begin is the origin, where the structural variables (X_i's) are zero and the slack variables (S_i's) have positive values equal to the input capacities. We can keep track of the variables given zero values by placing them above the matrix rectangle at the top of the column; this leaves the variables arranged on the left equal to the adjacent values found in the first column. That is, $\Pi = 0$, $S_1 = 10,000$, and $S_2 = 8,000$. Solutions are feasible if every element in this first column is positive. This being the case, all feasible solutions appearing in the matrix must also be basic, because room is provided for only two nonzero variables (or rows) below the objective.

The feasible, basic solution indicated in tableau (4) is not an optimal solution as long as any of the coefficients of the objective function (the first row of the matrix) are positive. This may be understood by recognizing that the coefficients are also marginal contributions to profits from the production and sale of additional outputs, that is, the partial derivatives of profit with respect to outputs. Which product should be produced, that is, which X_i should be given a nonzero value, is determined by the magnitude of the coefficients in row 1. The largest positive value is 4, for X_1; therefore, X_1 should be interchanged with one of the slack variables. Which slack variable to be selected, S_1 or S_2, is determined by the fraction having the smallest absolute value, obtained by dividing the corresponding element in column 1 by the element in column X_1: $|10{,}000/-1| = 10{,}000 > |8{,}000/-2| = 4{,}000$, so X_1 is interchanged with S_2. This step, in essence, is the same as moving to another corner point that gives a closer to optimal solution; it is described as pivoting on the element -2 designated by an asterisk in tableau (4).

In order to switch X_1 and S_2 in matrix (4), some of the elements must be given different values. They may be calculated in two ways; the first is longer but more useful in explaining what is being done, while the second is more expedient. Begin with the equation

$$S_2 = 8{,}000 - 2^*X_1 - X_2 - 3X_3$$

taken from row 3 in tableau (4). Divide through by -2^* and solve for X_1:

$$X_1 = \frac{-8{,}000}{-2^*} + \frac{1}{-2^*} S_2 + \frac{1}{-2^*} X_2 + \frac{3}{-2^*} X_3 \tag{5}$$

Equation (5) coefficients may now be put in a revised tableau:

	1	S_2	X_2	X_3
Π				
S_1				
X_1	4,000	$-\frac{1}{2}$	$-\frac{1}{2}$	$-\frac{3}{2}$

$$(6)$$

Other elements in the new tableau (6) may be obtained by substituting the value of X_1 into the other equations:

$$\Pi = 0 + 4\left(\frac{-8{,}000}{-2^*} + \frac{1}{-2^*} S_2 + \frac{1}{-2^*} X_2 + \frac{3}{-2^*} X_3\right) + 3X_2 + 2X_3$$

$$S_1 = 10{,}000 - 1\left(\frac{-8{,}000}{-2^*} + \frac{1}{-2^*} S_2 + \frac{1}{-2^*} X_2 + \frac{3}{-2^*} X_3\right)$$

$$- 3X_2 - 2X_3$$

Collecting terms:

$$\Pi = \left[0 - \frac{(4)(8{,}000)}{-2^*}\right] + \frac{4}{-2^*} S_2 + \left[3 - \frac{(4)(-1)}{-2^*}\right] X_2$$

$$+ \left[2 - \frac{(4)(-3)}{-2^*}\right] X_3$$

$$\tag{7}$$

$$S_1 = \left[10{,}000 - \frac{(-1)(8{,}000)}{-2^*}\right] + \frac{-1}{-2^*} S_2 + \left[-3 - \frac{(-1)(-1)}{-2^*}\right] X_2$$

$$+ \left[-2 - \frac{(-1)(-3)}{-2^*}\right] X_3$$

One may wonder why the minus signs were distributed as they were and not canceled out. The reason is that this form lends itself to prescribing mechanical rules, which permit quicker solution. We will return to this shortly.

Equations (7) may be simplified to

$$\Pi = 16{,}000 - 2S_2 + X_2 - 4X_3$$
$$S_1 = 6{,}000 + \tfrac{1}{2}S_2 - \tfrac{5}{2}X_2 - \tfrac{1}{2}X_3$$

(8)

The coefficients of the variables may now be put into tableau (6) to form tableau (9):

	1	S_2	X_2	X_3
Π	16,000	-2	1	-4
S_1	6,000	$\tfrac{1}{2}$	$-\tfrac{5}{2}$	$-\tfrac{1}{2}$
X_1	4,000	$-\tfrac{1}{2}$	$-\tfrac{1}{2}$	$-\tfrac{3}{2}$

(9)

The solution

$$S_1 = 6{,}000 \qquad X_1 = 4{,}000 \qquad S_2 = X_2 = X_3 = 0$$

is feasible because the values of S_1 and X_1 are positive, and basic because the number of nonzero-valued variables (two) equals the number of constraint equations (two). $\Pi = 16{,}000$ is not optimal, however, because one of the elements found in row 1 (other than 16,000) is positive, indicating a positive marginal profitability from producing some of product X_2. This means we must move to the next corner point by repeating the steps just taken to interchange the column variable X_1 with a row variable. But before repeating the iteration, several mechanical rules will be explained that will save a great deal of work in hand computations and can aid in writing a computer program for electronic computation.

3-7 Mechanical Rules for Pivoting

As mentioned before, the interchanging of column and row variables involves pivoting about a common element found in the tableau. The column variable was selected by Rule 1.

> *Rule 1.* The pivot column is the one with the largest positive element in the first row (excluding the element in column 1).

The row variable to interchange with the column variable was selected by Rule 2.

> *Rule 2.* The pivot row is the one with the smallest number (disregarding the sign) obtained by dividing each element in column 1 by the corresponding *negative* element in the pivot column.

The pivot element is the one common to the pivot column and the pivot row. It is flagged by an asterisk for future reference. After the column and row variables have been interchanged for a new tableau, new elements must be computed by the following rules.

> *Rule 3.* The new pivot element is simply the reciprocal of the old pivot element.

Rule 3 may be verified by comparing tableau (4) with equation (5) and tableau (6). Note that $-2*$ becomes $-\frac{1}{2}$ in the new tableau.

Rule 4. Other elements in the pivot column are obtained by dividing the old element by the pivot element, for instance, $4 \div (-2*) = -2$ for the first element in column X_1.

Rule 4, as well as the other remaining rules, may be verified by following elements from tableau (4) through equations (7) and (8) to tableau (9).

Rule 5. Other elements in the pivot row are obtained by dividing the old element by the pivot element and changing the sign, for instance, $(-3) \div (-2*) = \frac{3}{2} \rightarrow -\frac{3}{2}$.

Rule 6. Elements not in the pivot coulmn or row may be found by forming a rectangle around the pivot element and the element to be replaced, as illustrated in dashed lines below for the upper left element, 0:

	1	X_1	X_2	X_3	
Π	0	4	3	2	
S_1	10,000	-1	-3	-2	(10)
S_2	8,000	$-2*$	-1	-3	

The new element to replace 0 is found by subtracting from 0 the product of elements found in the adjacent corners (8,000 and 4), divided by the old pivot element:

$$0 - \frac{(4)(8,000)}{-2*} = 16,000$$

Observe the same calculation in the first part of equations (7).

Similarly, the new element to replace the second one in column X_3 may be obtained by constructing the box as shown in tableau (11):

	1	X_1	X_2	X_3	
Π	0	4	3	2	
S_1	10,000	-1	-3	-2	(11)
S_2	8,000	$-2*$	-1	-3	

Then calculate

$$-2 - \left[\frac{(-1)(-3)}{-2*} \right] = -2 + \frac{3}{2} = -\frac{1}{2}$$

which is found in equations (7) and (8) and tableau (9).

3-8 Repeating the Iteration to Move Toward the Optimal Solution

Now that the mechanical rules have been discussed, they can be used, instead of the longer technique employed in the first iteration, to perform the second iteration. Let us direct our attention back to tableau (9). Rules 1 and 2 may be applied to obtain the new pivot element. Column and row variables X_2 and S_1 are selected to be interchanged, because column X_2 has the largest (only one in this case) positive element in the first row (excluding column 1), and the smallest absolute value obtained by dividing elements in column 1 by those in column X_2 is found to be in row S_1:

$$\text{row } S_1: \ |6{,}000 \div (-\tfrac{5}{2})| = |-2{,}400| = 2{,}400$$
$$\text{row } X_1: \ |4{,}000 \div (-\tfrac{1}{2})| = |-8{,}000| = 8{,}000$$

Since $2{,}400 < 8{,}000$, element $-\tfrac{5}{2}$ in row S_1 is the new pivot element; it may be designated with an asterisk as shown in matrix (12). Rules 3–6 may now be applied to matrix (12) to obtain the values in matrix (13).

	1	S_2	X_2	X_3	
Π	16,000	-2	1	-4	
S_1	6,000	$\tfrac{1}{2}$	$-\tfrac{5}{2}*$	$-\tfrac{1}{2}$	(12)
X_1	4,000	$-\tfrac{1}{2}$	$-\tfrac{1}{2}$	$-\tfrac{3}{2}$	

	1	S_2	S_1	X_3	
Π	18,400	$-\tfrac{9}{5}$	$-\tfrac{2}{5}$	$-\tfrac{21}{5}$	
X_2	2,400	$\tfrac{1}{5}$	$-\tfrac{2}{5}$	$-\tfrac{1}{5}$	(13)
X_1	2,800		$\tfrac{1}{5}$		

Since there are no remaining positive values in row Π of matrix (13) (other than in the first column) and all values in the first column are positive, the optimal solution is $X_2 = 2{,}400$, $X_1 = 2{,}800$, $S_2 = S_1 = X_3 = 0$, yielding maximum profits of $18,400. It is unnecessary at this time to calculate the elements left blank.

3-9 Concluding Comments

The simple method of solving linear programming problems described in this chapter works well when the objective function is to be maximized and where the origin represents one of the basic feasible solutions. If these two conditions are not met, the method must be modified. The first condition is not met when the objective function is to be minimized rather than maximized. This would be the case when the problem is formulated in terms of minimizing cost instead of maximizing profits. A well-known example is the minimum-cost diet problem specifying minimal amounts of calories (b_1), proteins (b_2), vitamins (b_3), and minerals (b_4) required from use of two feeds, such as hay (X_1) and cottonseed cake (X_2), which also have different unit costs (c_1 and c_2). This LP problem may be formulated as follows:

$$\text{Minimize } C = c_1 X_1 + c_2 X_2$$

$$
\begin{aligned}
\text{subject to } a_{11}X_{11} + a_{12}X_2 &\geq b_1 \text{ (calorie requirement)}\\
a_{21}X_1 + a_{22}X_2 &\geq b_2 \text{ (protein requirement)}\\
a_{31}X_1 + a_{32}X_2 &\geq b_3 \text{ (vitamin requirement)}\\
a_{41}X_1 + a_{42}X_2 &\geq b_4 \text{ (mineral requirement)}
\end{aligned}
\tag{14}
$$

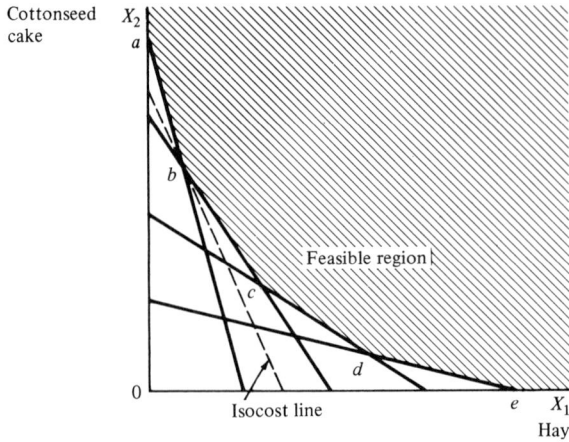

Figure 3-4

where all the X's and b's ≥ 0
and a_{11} = amount of calories in a unit of hay
$\quad a_{21}$ = amount of protein in a unit of hay
$\quad a_{31}$ = amount of vitamins in a unit of hay
$\quad a_{41}$ = amount of minerals in a unit of hay
$\quad a_{12}$ = amount of calories in a unit of cottonseed cake
and so on

The problem is presented graphically in Figure 3-4. The feasible region now lies above the constraint lines. Minimum cost of satisfying all of the four nutritional requirements will involve purchasing the combination of X_1 and X_2 where the boundary of the feasible region just touches the isocost line closest to the origin. If cottonseed cake costs half as much per unit as hay, the slope of the isocost lines will be -2, and the optimum combination of X_1 and X_2 will be at point b. This problem may be solved using the dual technique explained in Chapter 4. The method for solving problems with a nonfeasible solution at the origin for both the primal and dual will also be described.

Questions and Problems

3-1. Maximize $Z = 2X_1 + 4X_2 + 3X_3$
$\quad$ subject to $\quad X_1 + 2X_2 + X_3 \leq 7$
$\qquad\qquad\qquad X_1 + X_2 + X_3 \leq 4$
$\quad$ where $X_1, X_2,$ and $X_3 \geq 0$
3-2. Maximize $Z = 6X_1 + 5X_2$
$\quad$ subject to $2X_1 + 7X_2 \leq 10$
$\qquad\qquad\quad X_1 + 2X_2 \leq 8$
$\qquad\qquad\quad X_1 + X_2 \leq 6$
$\quad$ where X_1 and $X_2 \geq 0$

3-3. Maximize $Z = 4X_1 + 6X_2$
    subject to $X_1 + 2X_2 \leq 7$
               $2X_1 + X_2 \leq 8$
               $3X_1 + X_2 \leq 3$
    where X_1 and $X_2 \geq 0$

3-4. Maximize $Z = 5X_1 + 3X_2$
    subject to $X_1 + 2X_2 \leq 6$
               $3X_1 + 2X_2 \leq 5$
    where X_1 and $X_2 \geq 0$

3-5. Maximize $Z = X_1 + 3X_2 + 2X_3 + 5X_4$
    subject to $2X_1 + 5X_2 + 2X_3 + 4X_4 \leq 20$
               $3X_1 + X_2 + 4X_3 + 7X_4 \leq 30$
    where $X_1, X_2, X_3,$ and $X_4 \geq 0$

References

1. William J. Baumol. *Economic Theory and Operations Analysis*. 3d ed. (Englewood Cliffs, N.J.: Prentice-Hall, 1972), ch. 5.
2. Robert W. Clower and John F. Due. *Microeconomics* (Homewood, Ill.: Richard D. Irwin, 1972), Appendix A, pp. 359–380.
3. George B. Dantzig. *Linear Programming and Extensions* (Princeton, N.J.: Princeton University Press, 1963), ch. 1–5.
4. G. M. Ferrero di Roccaferrera. *Introduction to Linear Programming Processes* (Cincinnati: South-Western Publishing Co., 1967), ch. 7.
5. Robert Dorfman, Paul A. Samuelson, and Robert M. Solow. *Linear Programming and Economic Analysis* (New York: McGraw-Hill, 1958), ch. 2–4.
6. Saul I. Gass. *Linear Programming*. 3d ed. (New York: McGraw-Hill, 1969), ch. 3, 4.
7. Vera Riley and Saul I. Gass. *Bibliography on Linear Programming and Related Techniques* (Baltimore: Johns Hopkins Press, 1958).
8. Daniel Teichrow. *An Introduction to Management Science—Deterministic Models* (New York: Wiley, 1964), ch. 15, 16.
9. Daniel C. Vandermeulen. *Linear Economic Theory* (Englewood Cliffs, N.J.: Prentice-Hall, 1971), ch. 3.

4 Dual Linear Programming

Duality refers to the fact that every linear programming problem may be expressed in terms of obtaining either a maximum or a minimum solution. Some problems are more easily solved by using the *dual* rather than the original, *primal* form, and the dual solution provides additional information about the problem variables. Examination of the dual problem is also helpful for gaining a better understanding of the nature of linear programming.[1]

The first part of this chapter outlines the operations necessary to convert the profit maximization problem of Chapter 3 to one of minimizing the value (or imputed costs) of the inputs. Then a minimum-cost diet problem is solved, and a technique for solving problems without feasible solutions at the origin is described.

4-1 Converting a Primal Problem to the Dual

The general linear programming problem of Chapter 3 may be taken as the primal problem:

Maximize $\Pi = p_1 X_1 + p_2 X_2 + \cdots + p_n X_n$

subject to
$$
\begin{aligned}
a_{11} X_1 + a_{12} X_2 + \cdots + a_{1n} X_n &\le b_1 \\
a_{21} X_1 + a_{22} X_2 + \cdots + a_{2n} X_n &\le b_2 \\
&\cdots\cdots\cdots\cdots\cdots\cdots\cdots\cdots \\
a_{m1} X_1 + a_{m2} X_2 + \cdots + a_{mn} X_n &\le b_m
\end{aligned}
\tag{1}
$$

where $X_1, X_2, \ldots, X_n \ge 0$

This primal problem (1) may be converted to its dual, problem (2) by
    1. switching the direction of the inequality signs, that is, changing $\le$ to $\ge$ (without changing the nonnegativity signs)

---

[1] Duality theory was suggested first by John von Neumann and rigorously developed by three others: David Gale, H. W. Kuhn, and A. W. Tucker. The dual simplex method is attributed to E. C. Lemke [1, pp. 103, 120].

2. switching the p's and the b's

3. replacing the objective variable, say Π with Z (or vice versa when problem (2) is taken as the primal problem to be converted to problem (1), its dual)

4. replacing the X's with Y's (or vice versa when problem (1) is the dual)

5. transposing the a's, that is, replacing each a_{ik} with a_{ki}

$$\text{Minimize } Z = b_1 Y_1 + b_2 Y_2 + \cdots + b_m Y_m$$

$$\text{subject to} \quad a_{11} Y_1 + a_{21} Y_2 + \cdots + a_{m1} Y_m \geq p_1$$
$$a_{12} Y_1 + a_{22} Y_2 + \cdots + a_{m2} Y_m \geq p_2 \qquad (2)$$
$$\dots\dots\dots\dots\dots\dots\dots\dots\dots\dots\dots\dots$$
$$a_{1n} Y_1 + a_{2n} Y_2 + \cdots + a_{mn} Y_m \geq p_n$$

$$\text{where } Y_1, Y_2, \ldots, Y_m \geq 0$$

The dual variable Z may be interpreted as the minimum total cost of all inputs (the b's) valued at imputed unit costs (the Y's) sufficiently great to exhaust all profits. Additional interpretations of the variables are given in section 4-3.

Note that if the same operations were applied again to problem (2), its form would return to that of problem (1). This is why the problems are said to be duals of each other; the dual of the maximization problem is one of minimization, and vice versa. The dual of the dual problem is the original problem. It is therefore arbitrary which is called the primal and which the dual. When the simplex tableau is a square matrix, solution of one yields an explicit solution of the other.

The inequality signs may be removed by adding the primal and dual slack variables, $S_1, S_2, \ldots, S_n$, and $W_1, W_2, \ldots, W_n$, respectively, giving the programs marked (3). Observe that the W's are preceded by minus signs, since some zero or positive value must be taken away from the left side of the $\geq$ sign to make both sides equal.

Primal Problem	*Dual Problem*
Maximize	Minimize
$\Pi = p_1 X_1 + \cdots + p_n X_n$	$Z = b_1 Y_1 + \cdots + b_m Y_m$
subject to	subject to
$a_{11} X_1 + \cdots + a_{1n} X_n + S_1 = b_1$	$a_{11} Y_1 + \cdots + a_{m1} Y_m - W_1 = p_1$
$\dots\dots\dots\dots\dots\dots\dots\dots$	$\dots\dots\dots\dots\dots\dots\dots\dots$ (3)
$a_{m1} X_1 + \cdots + a_{mn} X_n + S_m = b_m$	$a_{1n} Y_1 + \cdots + a_{mn} Y_m - W_n = p_n$
where $X_1, X_2, \ldots, X_n \geq 0$	where $Y_1, Y_2, \ldots, Y_m \geq 0$
$S_1, S_2, \ldots, S_m \geq 0$	$W_1, W_2, \ldots, W_n \geq 0$

The problem of Chapter 3 may now be written as follows.

Primal Problem   Dual Problem

Maximize $\Pi = 4X_1 + 3X_2 + 2X_3$ Minimize $Z = 10{,}000\,Y_1 + 8{,}000\,Y_2$

subject to   subject to

$$X_1 + 3X_2 + 2X_3 + S_1 = 10{,}000 \qquad Y_1 + 2Y_2 - W_1 = 4$$
$$2X_1 + X_2 + 2X_3 + S_2 = 8{,}000 \qquad 3Y_1 + Y_2 - W_2 = 3$$
$$2Y_1 + 2Y_2 - W_3 = 2 \qquad (4)$$

where   where

X_1, X_2, X_3, S_1, S_2 each ≥ 0 Y_1, Y_2, W_1, W_2, W_3 each ≥ 0

It may also be written in tableau form as follows.

Primal Tableau   Dual Tableau

	1	X_1	X_2	X_3			1	Y_1	Y_2
Π	0	4	3	2		Z	0	10,000	8,000
S_1	10,000	-1	-3	-2		W_1	-4	1	2
S_2	8,000	-2	-1	-3		W_2	-3	3	1
						W_3	-2	2	3

(5)

Except for the difference in signs, the dual tableau may be recognized as being a flipped-over version of the primal tableau, where the lower left and the upper right corners have been interchanged. This being the case, both may be merged in a *combined tableau*:

	1	X_1	X_2	X_3	
Π	0	4	3	2	1
S_1	10,000	-1	-3	-2	Y_1
S_2	8,000	-2	-1	-3	Y_2
	Z	$-W_1$	$-W_2$	$-W_3$	

(6)

Or in the more general form:

	1	X_1	X_2	X_3	
Π	0	p_1	p_2	p_3	1
S_1	b_1	$-a_{11}$	$-a_{12}$	$-a_{13}$	Y_1
S_2	b_2	$-a_{21}$	$-a_{22}$	$-a_{23}$	Y_2
	Z	$-W_1$	$-W_2$	$-W_3$	

(7)

Several observations may be made with regard to the combined tableau. First, the primal structural variables are paired with their corresponding dual slack variables, that is, the X's and W's are written opposite each other, as are the Y's and S's. The primal and dual variables are always paired in this manner. Second, while the zero-valued variables of the primal problem are arranged on top of the tableau, those of the dual problem are on the right-hand side. Similarly, the nonzero-valued variables of the primal are on the left and those of the dual are on the bottom. This is because the dual tableau was flipped over for use in the combined matrix. The values of Z and the W's are given by the elements in the first row; the signs of the W's (or any other variable interchanged with the W's) must, of course, be reversed, as indicated by the negative signs preceding the W's below the tableau.

The pivoting rules of Chapter 3 may be applied to the combined tableau in the same manner as for the primal tableau. Care must be taken to interchange the row and column variables of the dual problem at the same time they are interchanged for the primal. The technique may be illustrated by following the preceding problem through to solution.

First Tableau

	1	X_1	X_2	X_3	
Π	0	4	3	2	1
S_1	10,000	-1	-3	-2	Y_1
S_2	8,000	-2^*	-1	-3	Y_2

$$Z \quad -W_1 \ -W_2 \ -W_3$$

Second Tableau

	1	S_2	X_2	X_3	
Π	16,000	-2	1	-4	1
S_1	6,000	$\frac{1}{2}$	$-\frac{5}{2}^*$	$-\frac{1}{2}$	Y_1
X_1	4,000	$-\frac{1}{2}$	$-\frac{1}{2}$	$-\frac{3}{2}$	W_1

$$Z \quad -Y_2 \ -W_2 \ -W_3$$

Third Tableau

	1	S_2	S_1	X_3	
Π	18,400	$-\frac{2}{5}$	$-\frac{2}{5}$	$-\frac{13}{5}$	1
X_2	2,400	$\frac{1}{5}$	$-\frac{2}{5}$	$-\frac{1}{5}$	W_2
X_1	2,800		$\frac{1}{5}$		W_1

(8)

$$Z \quad -Y_2 \ -Y_1 \ -W_3$$

From the tableau (8), the solution is:

Primal Problem	*Dual Problem*
$\Pi = 18,400$	$Z = 18,400$
$X_2 = 2,400$	$Y_2 = \frac{2}{5}$
$X_1 = 2,800$	$Y_1 = \frac{2}{5}$
$S_2 = S_1 = X_3 = 0$	$W_3 = \frac{13}{5}$
	$W_2 = W_1 = 0$

4-2 Optimality and Feasibility Criteria

It is known from Chapter 3 that the solution to the primal maximization problem is optimal if all elements in the first row (except the first one) are negative, indicating that no positive marginal contribution to profits can be made by substituting a zero-valued variable on the top of the tableau for one of the positive-valued variables on the left. With the dual minimization problem, however, one must look for positive elements in the first column rather than negative ones in the first row. If the problem is viewed as one of cost minimization, it is easy to see that the variables with positive coefficients (those in the first column), indicating increased costs, should be set equal to zero while those with negative values (found in the first row) should be employed to reduce costs. The *dual optimality criterion*, assuming the solution is also feasible, is therefore that all elements in the first column, except for the first row, be positive.

The feasibility criterion for the minimization problem is also different from that for the maximization problem. In maximization, it will be recalled, elements in the first column had to be positive for the solution to be feasible. But for the minimization problem, elements in the first row (except for the first) must be negative for the solution to be feasible. This *dual feasibility criterion* must be so, because when their signs are changed by applying the negative signs at the bottom of the tableau, positive values of the variables are obtained—a necessary condition for feasibility that coefficients of the variables used be nonnegative.

In short, the optimality and feasibility criteria for the maximization problem are the feasibility and optimality criteria, respectively, for the dual minimization problem, and vice versa.

It is important to keep in mind at all times that the X's and S's of the primal problem refer to physical quantities measured in units such as square feet, gallons, tons, and kilowatt hours, while the Y's and W's refer to monetary units measured in dollars and cents per unit. Also, the X's and W's are related to outputs, while the S's and Y's are related to inputs.

Figure 4-1, resembling a saddle or perhaps a Pringle's new-fangled potato chip, is helpful in visualizing the dual problem, although the curved lines are appropriate for a nonlinear rather than a linear program. Vertical planes passed through the figure perpendicular to the Y axis will cut sections such as ABC, DEF, and GHI. These sections show the various dollar profits that can be realized from various combinations of outputs produced and sold. Points B, E, and

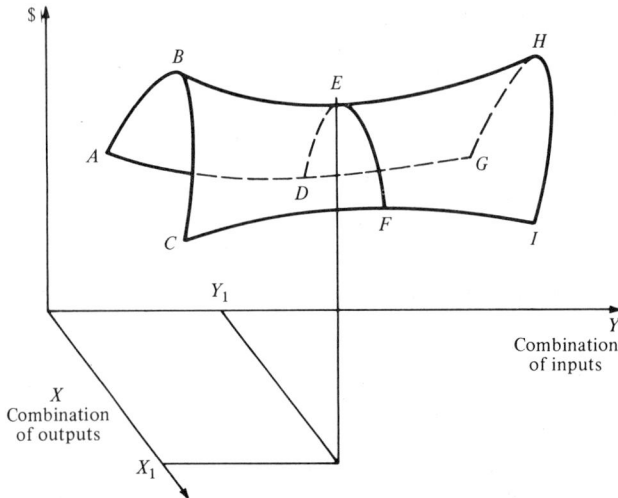

Figure 4-1

H indicate maximum profits to be obtained consistent with available inputs. Similarly, if horizontal planes were passed through the figure perpendicular to the X axis, sections such as ADG, BEH, and CFI would be traced. Point E along BEH represents the least-cost combination of inputs to produce the given outputs.

4-3 Economic Explanation of the Dual

In the problem labeled (3), in section 4-1, the variable Z to be minimized may be considered to be the total value or cost attributable to the n inputs, that is, $b_1, b_2, \ldots, b_n$. The Y's are the imputed costs, or *shadow prices* (also called *accounting prices* or *fictitious prices*), of the inputs; they indicate the marginal contributions to profits of additional units of inputs and are equivalent to partial derivatives of the objective function of the primal problem with respect to the input constraints. The imputed values assigned to the Y's have the effect of spreading all the firm's profits over the employed inputs.

In the primal problem the a_{11} coefficient of X_1 represents the number of units of input b_1 required to produce one unit of output X_1. Similarly, a_{21} units of b_2 are also needed to produce that unit of X_1, as are a_{m1} units of b_m. Since these coefficients retain their identities in the dual problem, the left side of the first constraint equation of the dual problem, $a_{11}Y_1 + \cdots + a_{m1}Y_m - W_1$, gives the total value of inputs required to produce one unit of output X_1. Similarly, the coefficients a_{ij} of X_2 in the constraints in the primal problem are the input requirements in the dual constraint equation for one unit of output X_2, and so on for each X_i up to X_n. Since the X's are the number of units of output produced and the p's are their unit profitabilities, it is clear that Π will give total profits. What interpretation, however, can be given to Z in the dual problem? It simply is the total value of the inputs under the firm's control $(= \sum_{i=1}^{m} b_i Y_i)$; it is to be minimized to find the smallest value of the inputs that accounts for the profits.

The dual slack variables, the W's, may be interpreted as relative losses attributable to the resources having more value than when employed to produce outputs. For instance, from the dual problem (3), we see that

$$W_1 = (a_{11}Y_1 + a_{21}Y_2 + \cdots + a_{m1}Y_m) - p_1$$

where the parenthesis contains the imputed value of the resources used in producing the unit of X_1, and p_1 is the unit profit of X_1.

4-4 Duality Theorems

Several duality theorems are useful in understanding the nature of dual linear programming. They have application in theoretical work, where actual solutions are not so important as the knowledge that solutions actually exist. Two theorems are given here.

Theorem I. Maximum Π exactly equals minimum Z, and this equality insures optimality for any pair of feasible solutions.

Theorem II. Optimal solutions require the use of only those commodities with zero values of the W's, and the employed inputs (those having nonzero shadow costs) must be used to capacity. This theorem may be written as a set of equations described as the *complementary slackness conditions*: Optimality requires $X_j W_j = 0$ for each commodity j and $S_i Y_i = 0$ for each input i.

Rigorous proof of these theorems is not provided here, but reference to the combined tableaus of this chapter should convince the reader of their validity. Values of Π and Z are both equal to the number in the upper left corner and are therefore equal at all times. When they are not optimal, one or more of the elements in the first column must be negative (indicating the Π is not feasible), or the first row must be positive (indicating the Z is not feasible).

The second duality theorem must also be true, since the commodities used (the X's on the left of the tableau) are associated with the dual slack variables (W's) that are set equal to zero (those on the right side), and the slack output variables (the S's) that are set equal to zero (those on the top) face the nonzero-valued input shadow prices (the Y's on the bottom). Since one of the two variables, either X_j or W_j in the first case, and S_i or Y_i in the second, must equal zero, it follows that $X_j W_j = 0$ and $S_i Y_i = 0$ for all j's and i's.

4-5 The Least-Cost Diet Problem

The problem of this section is to find the least-cost combination of hay (X_1) and cottonseed cake (X_2) that will fatten cattle at an appropriate rate; unit costs are given as c_1 and c_2, respectively. The two feeds contain the required nutrients in different proportions. The nutrients are calories (b_1), proteins (b_2), vitamins (b_3), and minerals (b_4), and their proportions are given by the a_{ij} coefficients. This information may be arranged as in Table 4-1. Note that this is linear programming problem (14) formulated in section 3-9 of Chapter 3.

Table 4-1

Nutrients	Feeds (units)		Minimum requirements
	X_1	X_2	
Calories	a_{11}	a_{21}	b_1
Proteins	a_{12}	a_{22}	b_2
Vitamins	a_{13}	a_{23}	b_3
Minerals	a_{14}	a_{24}	b_4
Unit costs	c_1	c_2	

Table 4-2

Nutrients	Feeds (units)		Minimum requirements (milligrams)
	X_1	X_2	
Calories	0.50	0.25	2
Proteins	1.50	0.30	3
Vitamins	0.10	0.60	1
Minerals	0.60	0.50	3
Unit costs	$0.50	$0.30	

Suppose the values of the a's, b's, and c's are given as in Table 4-2. The problem may be formulated as follows.

Minimize $C = 0.50X_1 + 0.30X_2$

subject to $0.5X_1 + 0.25X_2 \geq 2$

$\qquad 1.5X_1 + 0.3X_2 \geq 3$

$\qquad 0.1X_1 + 0.6X_2 \geq 1$

$\qquad 0.6X_1 + 0.5X_2 \geq 3$

(9

where X_1 and $X_2 \geq 0$

It is shown graphically in Figure 4-2.

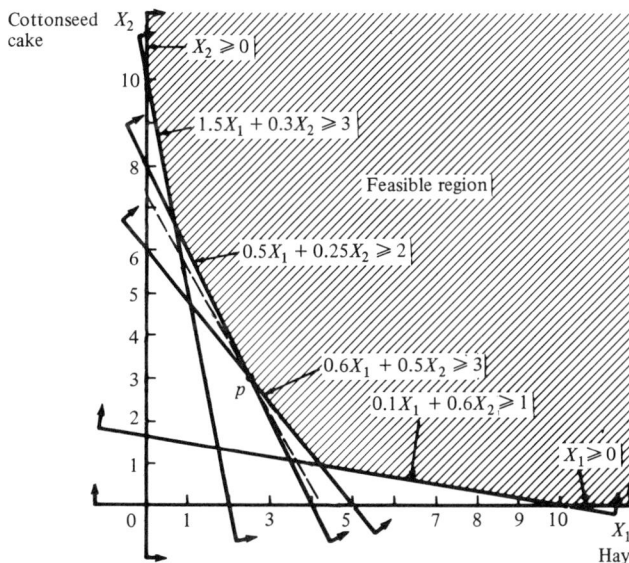

Figure 4-2

To obtain the dual simplex solution, the inequality signs must be removed by adding the slack variables to the constraint equations.

$$0.5X_1 + 0.25X_2 - S_1 = 2$$
$$1.5X_1 + 0.3X_2 - S_2 = 3$$
$$0.1X_1 + 0.6X_2 - S_3 = 1 \tag{10}$$
$$0.6X_1 + 0.5X_2 - S_4 = 3$$

Then solve for the S's.

$$S_1 = -2 + 0.5X_1 + 0.25X_2$$
$$S_2 = -3 + 1.5X_1 + 0.3X_2$$
$$S_3 = -1 + 0.1X_1 + 0.6X_2 \tag{11}$$
$$S_4 = -3 + 0.6X_1 + 0.5X_2$$

These equations may now be put in the dual simplex tableau (12), which may be solved by applying the simple rules of Chapter 3.

First Tableau

	1	Y_1	Y_2	Y_3	Y_4		
Π	0	2	3	1	3	1	
W_1	0.5	-0.5	-1.5^*	-0.1	-0.6	X_1	(12)
W_2	0.3	-0.25	-0.3	-0.6	-0.5	X_2	
	C	$-S_1$	$-S_2$	$-S_3$	$-S_4$		

Second Tableau

	1	Y_1	W_1	Y_3	Y_4		
Π	1	1	-2	$\frac{4}{5}$	$\frac{9}{5}$	1	
Y_2	$\frac{1}{3}$	$-\frac{1}{3}$	$-\frac{2}{3}$	$-\frac{1}{15}$	$-\frac{2}{5}$	S_2	(13)
W_2	$\frac{1}{5}$	$-\frac{3}{20}$	$\frac{1}{5}$	$-\frac{29}{50}$	$-\frac{19}{50}^*$	X_2	
	C	$-S_1$	$-X_1$	$-S_3$	$-S_4$		

Third Tableau

	1	Y_1	W_1	Y_3	W_2		
Π	$\frac{37}{19}$	$\frac{11}{38}$	$-\frac{20}{19}$	$-\frac{33}{19}$	$-\frac{90}{19}$	1	
Y_2	$\frac{7}{57}$	$-\frac{10}{57}^*$	$-\frac{50}{57}$	$\frac{31}{57}$	$\frac{20}{19}$	S_2	(14)
Y_4	$\frac{10}{19}$	$-\frac{15}{38}$	$\frac{10}{19}$	$-\frac{29}{19}$	$-\frac{50}{19}$	S_4	
	C	$-S_1$	$-X_1$	$-S_3$	$-X_2$		

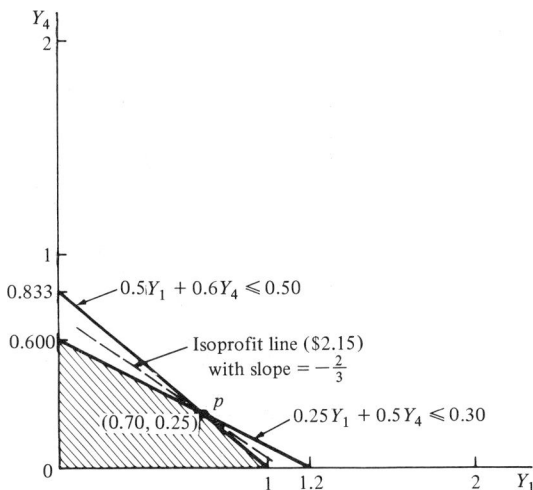

Figure 4-3

Fourth Tableau

$$
\begin{array}{c|ccccc|c}
 & 1 & Y_2 & W_1 & Y_3 & W_2 & \\
\hline
\Pi & 2\frac{3}{20} & -\frac{33}{20} & -\frac{5}{2} & -\frac{319}{380} & -3 & 1 \\
Y_1 & \frac{7}{10} & & & & & S_1 \\
Y_4 & \frac{1}{4} & & & & & S_4 \\
\hline
 & C & -S_2 & -X_1 & -S_3 & -X_2 &
\end{array}
\qquad (15)
$$

The solution taken from the fourth tableau (15),

$$C = 2\tfrac{3}{20} \qquad X_1 = 2\tfrac{1}{2} \qquad X_2 = 3 \qquad S_2 = 1\tfrac{13}{20},$$

$$S_3 = \tfrac{319}{380} \qquad S_1 = S_4 = 0$$

is consistent with Figure 4-2 at the intersection of the heavy dashed line (minimum-cost line) and the corner point P.

The primal (minimization) problem was treated here as the dual because it had no feasible solution at the origin, as may be observed from Figure 4-2. The dual (maximization) problem, however, does have a feasible solution at the origin, as shown in Figure 4-3, which fits the mechanical scheme set up in Chapter 3 for solving this type of problem. Section 4-6 shows how LP problems without feasible solutions at the origin for either the primal or dual may be solved.

4-6 The Feasibility Program

In the event that neither the primal nor the dual problem has a feasible solution at the origin, all is not lost. The feasibility program has been developed to deal with such cases in which not all b_j in maximization problems similar to problem

(a) Primal   (b) Dual

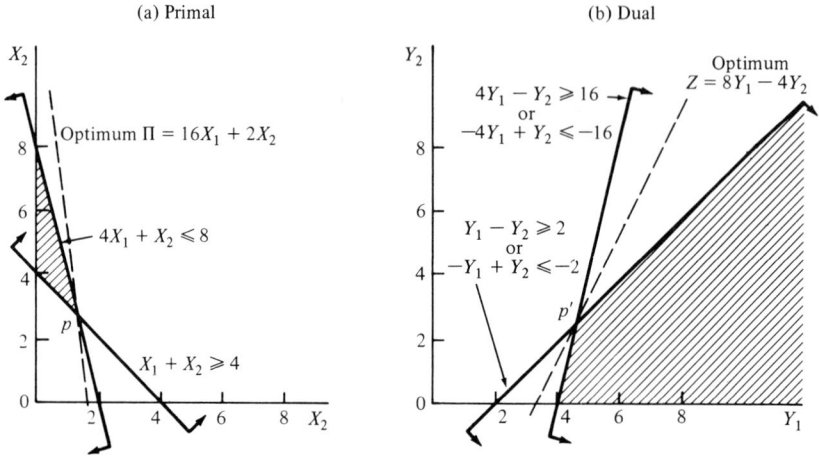

Figure 4-4

(3) in section 4-1 are ≥ 0 and not all p_i in the dual minimization problems are ≤ 0. Initial explanation is most easily given by use of a simple example.

Suppose profits are to be maximized in the objective function $\Pi = 16X_1 + 2X_2$, where the outputs X_1 and X_2 are constrained by machine capacity such that $4X_1 + X_2 \leq 8$ and by a contractual agreement of a minimum delivery of four units of either, that is, $X_1 + X_2 \geq 4$. The primal and dual problems are as shown in Figure 4-4. (A useful rule for determining on which side of a linear inequality the feasible solution lies is to substitute a fixed point, say the origin $(0, 0)$, into the inequality. If the inequality is satisfied, the fixed point is contained in the feasible solution; if not, the side of the inequality away from the fixed point satisfies the inequality. Note also that the direction of the inequality sign may be reversed by changing the sign of each term.) It is clear from the graphs that the origin provides no feasible solution to either the primal or dual programs. This is also evident in dual simplex tableau (16) in this section, since the -4 in the first column indicates an unfeasible solution to the primal program when X_1 and $X_2 = 0$. Similarly, the positive elements in the first row indicate an unfeasible dual solution.

$$
\begin{array}{c|ccc|c}
 & 1 & X_1 & X_2 & \\
\hline
\Pi & 0 & 16 & 2 & 1 \\
S_1 & 8 & -4 & -1 & Y_1 \\
S_2 & -4 & 1 & 1 & Y_2 \\
\hline
 & Z & -W_1 & -W_2 &
\end{array}
\tag{16}
$$

The program invented by George Dantzig can be adjusted to permit the solution of the problem in the usual manner, by setting all structural variables equal to zero. The problem is written as follows.

Maximize $\Pi = 16X_1 + 2X_2$

subject to $4X_1 + X_2 + S_1 = 8$ (17)

$X_1 + X_2 - S_2 = 4$

where the X's and S's are ≥ 0

(Notice the $-S_2$, because of the $\geq$ in the second constraint.) The problem may be converted to a feasibility program in two steps: (1) add a new artificial variable, R, to the left side of each constraint having a slack variable with a minus sign, and (2) subtract kR from the original objective function, where k is a co-efficient selected arbitrarily of sufficient size to permit solution. Applying these steps to program (17) gives

Maximize $\Pi R = 16X_1 + 2X_2 - kR$

subject to $4X_1 + X_2 + S_1 = 8$

$X_1 + X_2 - S_2 + R_2 = 4$ (18)

where the X's, S's, and R_2 are ≥ 0

This permits an initial basic solution of

$$S_1 = 8 \qquad R_2 = 4 \qquad X_1 = X_2 = S_2 = 0$$

since S_2 can now be treated as a structural variable and put with the X's on the top of the tableau. Solution of this feasibility program proceeds as with other problems, and its optimal solution will also be that of the original problem. The constraints become

$$S_1 = 8 - 4X_1 - X_2$$
$$R_2 = 4 - X_1 - X_2 + S_2$$

and the objective function becomes

$$\begin{aligned}
\Pi R &= 16X_1 + 2X_2 - k_2 R_2 \\
&= 16X_1 + 2X_2 - k_2(4 - X_1 - X_2 + S_2) \\
&= -4k_2 + (16 + k_2)X_1 + (2 + k_2)X_2 - k_2 S_2
\end{aligned}$$

Now k_2 must be set equal to a number sufficiently large so that $k_2 R_2$ in the objective function will be so large that R_2 will always be set equal to zero. That is, R_2 must be made so expensive in taking $k_2 R_2$ dollars away from "profits" that we will be sure to set $R_2 = 0$ to maximize profits. (Where the problem is one of minimization, the $k_i R_i$ must be *added* (rather than subtracted) to the objective function, so that r will have the effect of adding sufficiently to accounting costs and will be set equal to zero.) In this problem k_2 may be set equal to, say, 100. The objective function then becomes

$$\Pi R = -400 + 116X_1 + 102X_2 - 100S_2$$

The initial tableau for the feasibility program will be

	1	X_1	X_2	S_2		
ΠR	-400	116	102	-100	1	
S_1	8	-4	-1	0		Y_1
R_2	4	-1	-1	1		Y_2

$$\qquad\qquad Z \quad -W_1 \quad -W_2 \quad -W_3$$

(19)

Now that the elements in the first column are nonnegative (except for the first row), a solution at the origin to the primal problem is feasible. This problem may now be solved using the standard dual simplex method.

Questions and Problems

4-1. *a.* Write out the dual for this primal problem:

Maximize $\Pi = 5X_1 + 3X_2$

subject to $4X_1 + 2X_2 \leq 6$
$\qquad\qquad 3X_1 + \ X_2 \leq 5$
$\qquad\qquad 2X_1 + 2X_2 \leq 7$

where X_1, X_2 each ≥ 0

b. Show that the dual of the dual is the original problem.
c. Write the dual program in slack variable form.
d. How many iterations are required to solve the primal problem? how many for the dual?

4-2. Minimize $Z = 500\,Y_1 + 300\,Y_2$

subject to $\ Y_1 + Y_2 \ \geq 25$
$\qquad\qquad 2\,Y_1 + Y_2 \ \geq 30$
$\qquad\qquad 2\,Y_1 + 3\,Y_2 \geq 50$

where Y_1, Y_2 each ≥ 0

4-3. Minimize $Z = 15\,Y_1 + 20\,Y_2$

subject to $\ Y_1 + 2\,Y_2 \geq 5$
$\qquad\qquad 3\,Y_1 + \ Y_2 \ \geq 6$
$\qquad\qquad Y_1 + 4\,Y_2 \geq 8$

where Y_1, Y_2 each ≥ 0

4-4. Minimize $Z = 16\,Y_1 + 10\,Y_2 + 12\,Y_3$

subject to $\ Y_1 + 2\,Y_2 + 3\,Y_3 \geq 30$
$\qquad\qquad 4\,Y_1 + 5\,Y_2 + 2\,Y_3 \geq 40$

where Y_1, Y_2, Y_3 each ≥ 0

4-5. Set up the primal and dual forms of LP problems (1) and (2) in section 4-1. Instead of using notation like X, Y, a, and b, however, set up the objective functions and constraint inequalities in terms of the units that the letters symbolize, that is, in terms of value where dollars are involved, value/output or value/input where unit costs are involved, and so on.

4-6. *a.* Given the following information, find the least-cost combination of corn (X_1), beans (X_2), and meat (X_3) to provide 120 calories and 60 units of protein.

	Corn	Beans	Meat
Calories/unit	10	6	1
Protein/unit	3	5	1
Cost/unit	3	2	5

    b. Find the shadow prices of the nutrients (outputs) derived from beans and meat in the preceding problem.

    c. Write out the dual problem and define in words the meaning of each type of symbol and number

4-7. Given the following nutrition problem minimizing the cost of a diet that fulfills minimum requirements,

    a. reconstruct the problem in terms of the units employed

    b. construct the dual both in terms of symbols (Y's, p's, b's) and units (outputs, inputs, values)

Minimize $C = c_1 X_1 + c_2 X_2 + c_3 X_3$

subject to $a_{11}X_1 + a_{12}X_2 + a_{13}X_3 \geq p_1$
$$a_{21}X_1 + a_{22}X_2 + a_{23}X_3 \geq p_2$$
$$a_{31}X_1 + a_{32}X_2 + a_{33}X_3 \geq p_3$$

where X_1, X_2, X_3 each ≥ 0

and C = food budget in dollars

$c_{1,2,3}$ = food cost per pound of corn, beans, and meat, respectively

$X_{1,2,3}$ = pounds of corn, beans, meat, respectively

$p_{1,2,3}$ = specified minimum nutrient requirements of calories, protein, and calcium, respectively

    a_{ij} = nutrients (outputs) per pound of food (inputs), for example, calories per pound of corn for a_{11}

4-8. Minimize $Z = 8Y_1 - 4Y_2$

subject to $4Y_1 - Y_2 \geq 16$
$$Y_1 - Y_2 \geq 2$$

where Y_1, Y_2 each ≥ 0

4-9. Minimize $Z = 10Y_1 - 3Y_2$

subject to $3Y_1 - Y_2 \geq 15$
$$2Y_1 - Y_2 \geq 4$$

where Y_1, Y_2 each ≥ 0

4-10. Suppose a firm has $1,000 to invest in bonds that pay interest at the following rates. Also at least 30 percent of the total investment portfolio must be in type A while no more than 50 percent can be invested in only B or C. How much should be invested in each type to yield the greatest return? Set up a simplex tableau and solve.

Bonds	Interest Rate
A_1	4.0
A_2	3.5
B_1	4.5
B_2	5.0
C_1	5.5
C_2	6.0

References

1. William J. Baumol. *Economic Theory and Operations Analysis*. 3d ed. (Englewood Cliffs, N.J.: Prentice-Hall, 1972), ch. 6.
2. George B. Dantzig. *Linear Programming and Extensions* (Princeton, N.J.: Princeton University Press, 1963), ch. 6, 11, 27.
3. G. M. Ferrero di Roccaferrera. *Introduction to Linear Programming Processes* (Cincinnati: South-Western Publishing Co., 1967), ch. 8, 23.
4. Robert Dorfman, Paul A. Samuelson, and Robert M. Solow. *Linear Programming and Economic Analysis* (New York: McGraw-Hill, 1958), ch. 7.
5. Saul I. Gass. *Linear Programming*. 3d ed. (New York: McGraw-Hill, 1969), ch. 5, 11.
6. Jati K. Sengupta and Karl A. Fox. *Economic Analysis and Operations Research: Optimization Techniques in Quantitative Economic Models* (Amsterdam: North-Holland Publishing Co., 1969), ch. 2.
7. George J. Stigler. "The Cost of Subsistence." *Journal of Farm Economics* 27 (May 1945): 303–314.
8. Daniel C. Teichrow. *Linear Economic Theory* (Englewood Cliffs, N.J.: Prentice-Hall, 1964), ch. 16, 17.

5 Nonlinear Programming

While the linear programming techniques described in the previous chapters have many applications in business and economics, the linearity assumptions are quite restrictive and inappropriate in many cases. A familiarity with the difficulties encountered when either the objective function or the constraints contain nonlinear terms is a good basis for understanding the nature of assumptions sometimes left implicit in LP studies. This chapter discusses nonlinear functions and regions, the well-known Kuhn-Tucker conditions, and a simple method for calculating integer solutions to LP problems.[1]

5-1 General Statement of the Programming Problem

Where the variable to be optimized (Π) is a nonlinear function of one or more variables, such as

$$\Pi = a_1 X_1^2 = a_2 X_2 X_3 + a_3 X_4^3$$
$$\Pi = a_1 \log X_1 + a_2 \log X_2 + a_3 \log X_3^2 \qquad (1)$$
$$\Pi = a_1 \sin X_1 - a_2 \cos X_2$$

the mathematical programming problem is often stated in the more general form using functional notation:

$$\Pi = f(X_1, X_2, X_3, X_4) \qquad (2)$$

Functional equation (2) simply states that Π depends in some way upon the variables X_1, X_2, X_3, and X_4. Problems are often conceptualized in this manner when the precise relations are not yet known and in the early stages of attempting to build a model of some business or economic situation.

The general nonlinear programming problem can be expressed in the three-part form:

---

[1] Much of this chapter is based upon Baumol's chapters 7 and 8 [1].

1. Objective function:
   Maximize (or minimize) $\Pi = f(X_1, X_2, \ldots, X_n)$

2. Constraints:
   $$g_1 (X_1, X_2, \ldots, X_n) \geq p_1$$
   $$g_2 (X_1, X_2, \ldots, X_n) \geq p_2 \qquad\qquad (3)$$
   $$\cdots\cdots\cdots\cdots\cdots\cdots\cdots\cdots$$
   $$g_m (X_1, X_2, \ldots, X_n) \geq p_m$$

3. Nonnegativity conditions:
   $$X_1, X_2, \ldots, X_n \geq 0$$

Nonlinearities can creep into economic analysis where total profits are assumed to be a linear function of the X_1, X_2, X_3 products sold times their respective a_1, a_2, a_3 unit profitabilities:

$$\Pi = a_1 X_1 + a_2 X_2 + a_3 X_3 \qquad\qquad (4)$$

All that is needed to destroy linearity is the additional assumption that the unit profitability, a_3, of X_3 is a decreasing function of the number of units sold, which is the case for all downward-sloping demand curves with sufficiently small price elasticities; in algebraic terms,

$$a_3 = a_4 - a_5 X_3 \qquad\qquad (5)$$

The profit function then becomes

$$\begin{aligned} \Pi' &= a_1 X_1 + a_2 X_2 + (a_4 - a_5 X_3) X_3 \\ &= a_1 X_1 + a_2 X_2 + a_4 X_3 - a_5 X_3^2 \end{aligned} \qquad (6)$$

Notice that the X_3^2 term makes the function nonlinear in spite of the fact that both equations (4) and (5) were linear [1, p. 137].

5-2 Geometric Representations of Nonlinear Functions and Constraints

The surface of a nonlinear objective function is curved and perhaps irregular. Profits may be an ever-increasing function of some variables; for example, if marginal profits are diminishing, the profit surface is shaped as shown in Figure 5-1a; if increasing, as in Figure 5-1c. Figures 5-1b and 5-1d show the corresponding profit contours or isoprofit lines in two dimensions; these are simply projections onto the $X_1 X_2$ plane of the intersection of horizontal planes passed through the profit surfaces. The isoprofit lines located farther away from the origin in Figures 5-1b and 5-1d indicate higher profit levels.

An objective function surface may also form a conical shell, as in Figure 5-2a, and have closed lines representing a given level of the maximized variable, as in Figure 5-2b. In this case, the peak of the hill at point A corresponds to the highest profits at point A'. Profits measured in any direction away from A' in the $X_1 X_2$ plane are lower. One must be careful, however, not to assume this will always be so; Figures 5-2c and 5-2d illustrate a case where it is not. Figure 5-2c is shaped like a symmetrical vase or volcano, with its maximum vertical values found on

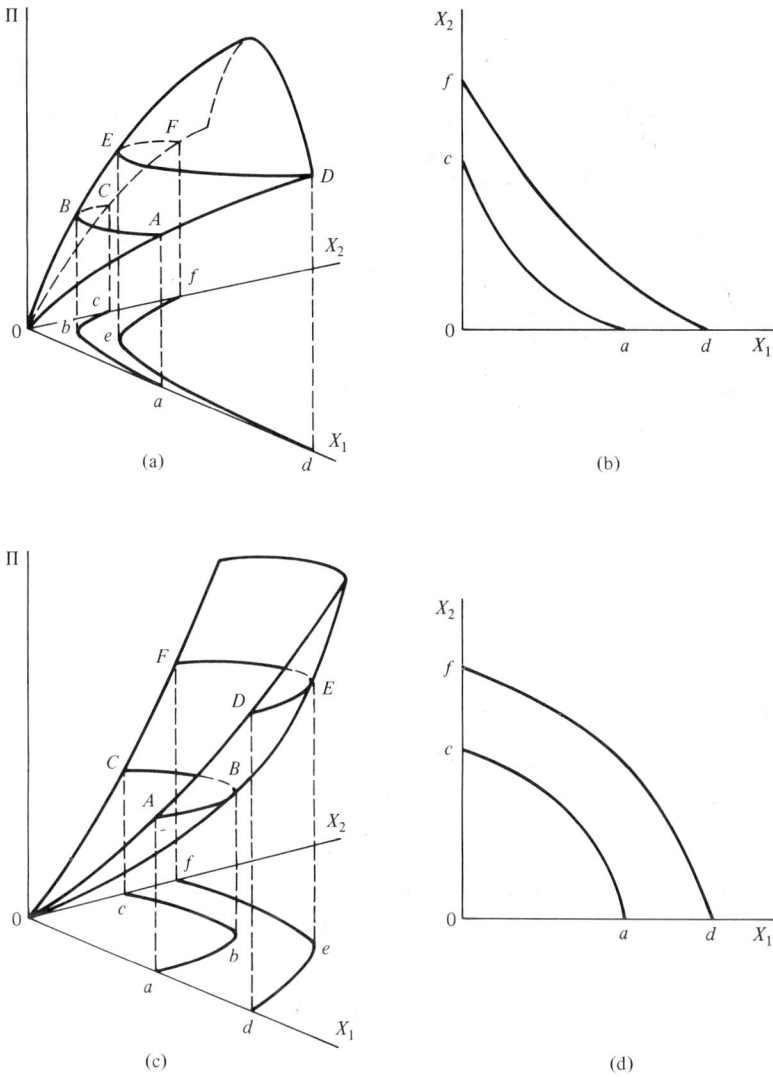

Figure 5-1

the rim denoted by C. The highest isoprofit line corresponds to C', which is not the center of all the circumferential rings. In this case, the center point is associated with zero profits and profits are lower, and progressively so, for contours on both sides of C'. Contours B' and D' represent equal profit levels, but both are lower than that of C'.

When the objective function is regular and continuous, solution is somewhat facilitated by the presence of linear constraints, but the optimum point is not necessarily an extreme point in the feasible region. An example of this is given in

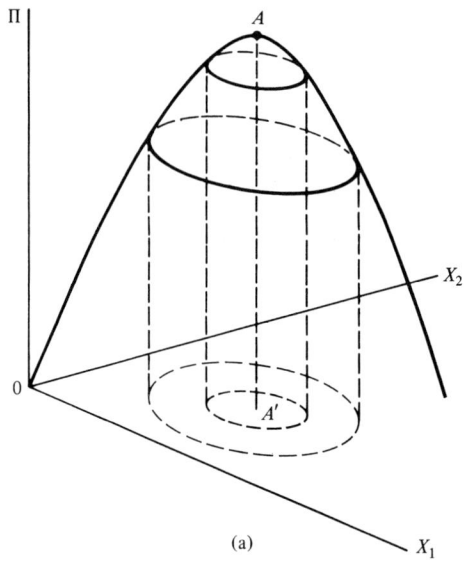

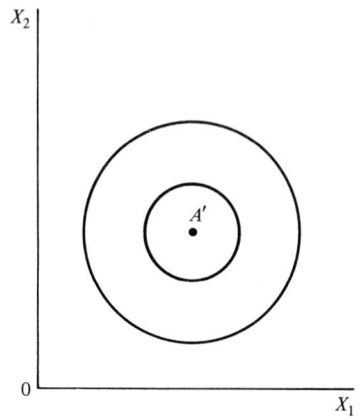

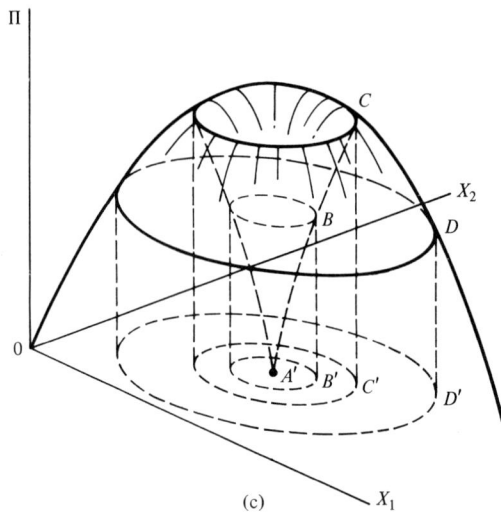

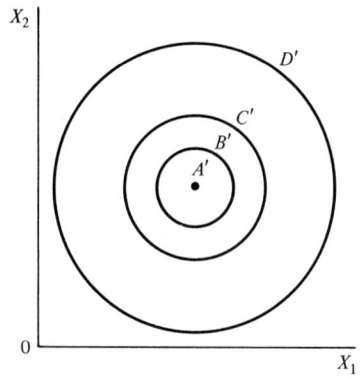

Figure 5-2

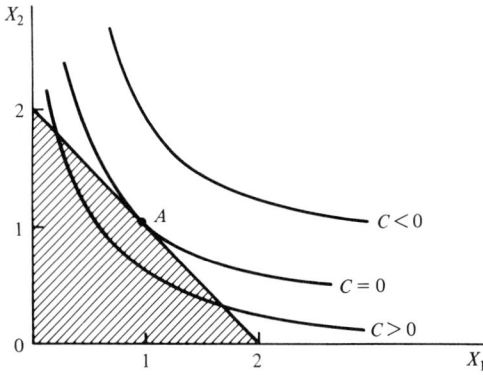

Figure 5-3

a simple program used by Dorn [4, p. 412] and also by Gass [7, pp. 293–294]:

Minimize $C = -\log X_1 - \log X_2$
subject to $X_1 + X_2 \leq 2$
where X_1 and $X_2 \geq 0$

which is graphed in Figure 5-3. Here the solution is at point A, which *is not at a corner point* of the feasible, shaded, triangular region. Furthermore, if the constraint line were shifted to the right, for example, by increasing the 2 in the above constraint equation to 3 or 4, the optimum solution would be *inside* the feasible zone. This clearly conflicts with the basic theorem of linear programming mentioned in section 3-3, which holds that when an optimal solution is found the number of positive variables will ordinarily equal the number of constraints. Stated in geometrical terms, this means that an optimal solution is always found at a corner point of the feasible region. Thus, in linear programming, only the

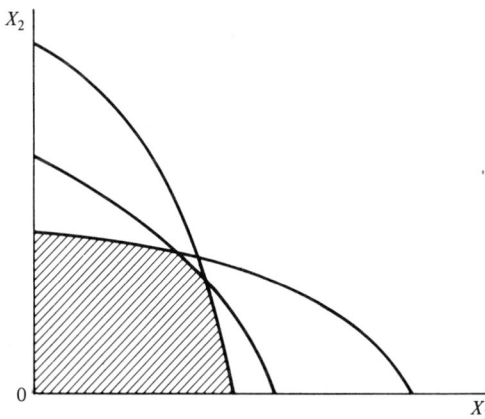

Figure 5-4

corners need be examined; this gives LP a large computational advantage over nonlinear programming, where the remaining infinite set of points in the feasible region cannot be ignored.

When the constraints are not linear, feasible regions may appear as shown in Figure 5-4. The boundaries are no longer straight lines except where the axes come into play. The constraints of Figure 5-4 correspond to quadratic equations of the general form $aX_1^2 + bX_2^2 \le c$.

5-3   Convex and Nonconvex Regions and Functions

A convex region is one in which a straight line between any two points in the region (or on its boundary) lies entirely within the region [1, pp. 140–145]. The shaded area of Figure 5-5a is an example of a convex region, since any straight lines such as AB, AC, and AD lie entirely within (or on) the shaded area. The region of Figure 5-5b is not convex, since straight lines drawn between points E and G, F and H, and G and H do not lie entirely within the shaded area.

Programming problems with nonconvex regions are generally more difficult to solve than those with convex regions because the optimal point may be harder to find, and once found, the point may be difficult to recognize as being optimal. For example, if a linear objective function is assumed, so that the isoprofit lines are straight, then maximum profits will be Π_2 at tangency point D in Figure 5-5a. This must be so, because a movement along the boundary of the convex feasible region away from D in either direction reduces profits. Such reasoning does not necessarily hold for nonconvex regions, however. In Figure 5-5b four different profit levels are found at corner or tangency points, from which a small movement along the boundary reduces profits. Points H, E, and I are said to be local optimums, because they produce greatest profits only in their immediate vicinities. The greatest optimum, called the *global optimum*, exists at point G with profits Π_4.

The presence of local maximums makes iterative procedures like the LP

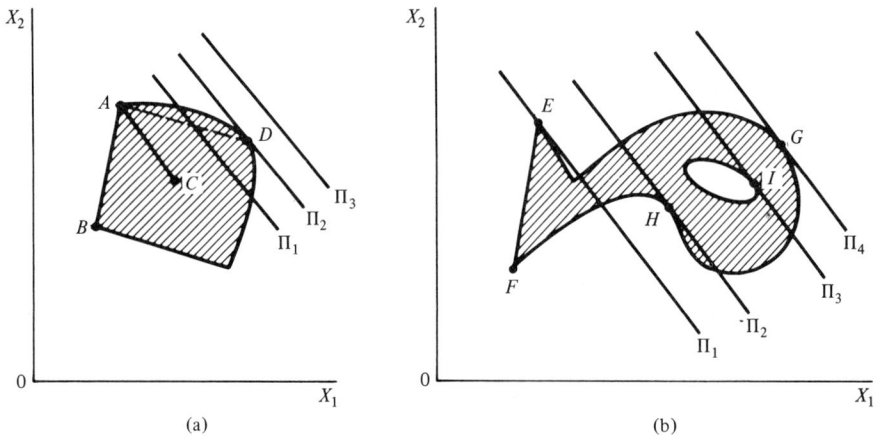

Figure 5-5

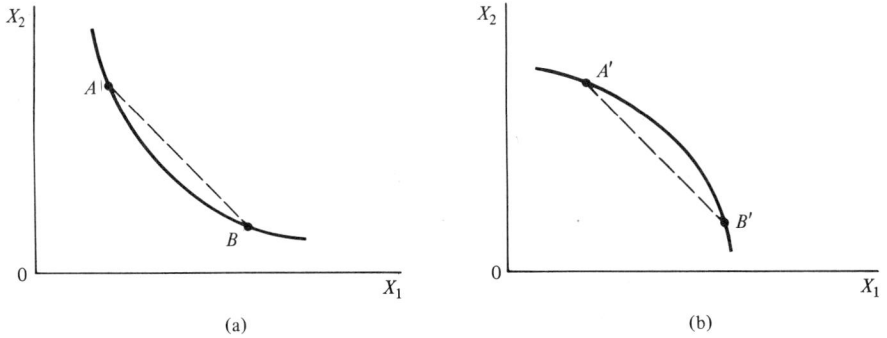

Figure 5-6

simplex method (where mechanical steps are repeated until solution is found) inappropriate. Professor Baumol refers to the normal simplex technique as being "near-sighted," since it will accept the first local optimum it reaches as the true optimum. This is satisfactory for LP problems, because their feasible regions are always convex. But where regions are not convex, other approaches (two of which are described in more advanced literature as "creeping" and "hopping" techniques) must be used.

An objective function is said to be strictly *convex* with respect to the horizontal axis if all points of an arc of the curve (excluding the end points) lie below a straight line connecting two points on the curve. This is illustrated in Figure 5-6a. If the arc lies entirely above the straight line, the curve is said to be *strictly concave* in that range, as shown in Figure 5-6b. If the curve happens to be a straight line coinciding with a line drawn between two points on the curve, the curve is *both* convex and concave. Linear functions whose graphs are planes or hyperplanes (where there are more than three dimensions) are also considered to be both convex and concave. A difficulty with nonlinear objective functions is that they will on occasion, when used with "near-sighted" procedures, produce local rather than global solutions.

5-4 Decreasing and Increasing Returns

If profit functions have the characteristics of the concave curves of Figures 5-1a and 5-2a, decreasing marginal returns are present. As more of either X_1 or X_2 is sold, profits on the upward-sloping surface expand by diminishing additional amounts. If the same curves are taken to represent cost functions instead of profit functions, the problem would be one of increasing returns, that is, marginal costs decrease as output expands. Similarly, the convex function of Figure 5-1c could represent either a profit function with increasing returns or a cost function with decreasing returns. It follows that diminishing returns are present when either concave functions are to be maximized or convex functions are minimized.

Difficulties arise when objective functions are not of the appropriate shape relative to the feasible region. For example, if the graph of an objective function in a maximization problem is convex, as in Figure 5-7, one cannot be sure that a

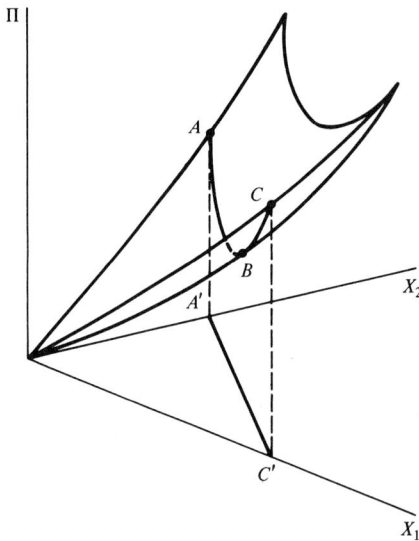

Figure 5-7

movement upwards, as with linear programs, will always lead to a global maximum. The simplex technique may lead us to point C, a local maximum, rather
than to point A. Such a convex function is representative of the case of increasing returns—as more of X_1 or X_2 is employed, profits rise by increasingly
larger amounts. Note that with this and other convex functions, there is a
tendency to specialize in either X_1 or X_2, leaving the other unused. In such cases,
the number of nonzero-valued variables tends to be less than the number of
constraints—a violation of the basic theorem of linear programming, which
requires that they be equal. Therefore, if LP techniques are used where increasing
returns are present, the answer will have too few positive variables. Similarly, if
LP techniques are used with decreasing returns (concave maximization problems),
the answer will have too many positive variables.

   These conclusions are intuitively evident in the case of a firm producing 100
products. A linear program with 15 constraints would recommend reducing the
product line to 15 and discontinuing 85 items. This is based upon the implicit
assumption that the firm may sell as many of the 15 produced items as it desires
without having to lower price. However, many firms attract additional customers
through the breadth of the product line. If this assumption is not valid and prices
would have to fall to enable the firm to sell the recommended amount, then
decreasing returns are present and production of more than 15 items would
probably be more profitable. If demand and prices rise as more and more of a
product is sold, exhibiting the bandwagon effect of some fads in their early stages,
increasing returns are present; here the firm might do well to specialize for a
time in the production of only that single product. Knowing these rules should
help the decision maker and researcher in adjusting the results of linear approximations and in maintaining an awareness of the dangers of using LP where nonlinearities are present.

5-5   Kuhn-Tucker Conditions

Some problems are of such complexity that it is important to learn at the start if a solution actually exists before much effort is spent trying to crank out an answer. The Kuhn-Tucker (K-T) conditions are a widely used set of criteria that, when satisfied, guarantee that the problem at hand has a theoretical solution.

Simply stated, the K-T conditions for a constrained maximization problem are (1) that the first partial derivatives of its Lagrangian expression be less than or equal to zero for the structural variables and more than or equal to zero for the dual (Lagrange) variables; and (2) that the product of each partial derivative and the value of the variable with respect to which the derivative is taken equal zero. In mathematical terms, if

$$\Pi_\lambda = f(Q, \lambda) \tag{7}$$

is differentiable, then a solution exists

1. if $\dfrac{\partial \Pi_\lambda}{\partial Q} \le 0$ and $\dfrac{\partial \Pi_\lambda}{\partial \lambda} \ge 0$ and

2. if $Q\dfrac{\partial \Pi_\lambda}{\partial Q} = 0$ and $\lambda\dfrac{\partial \Pi_\lambda}{\partial \lambda} = 0$

These conditions must hold for all Q_i, where $i = 1, 2, \ldots, n$ and for all λ_j, where $j = 1, 2, \ldots, n$. For a minimization problem, the inequality signs are reversed. An example of how the K-T conditions are used will help the reader to comprehend the procedure. The program

$$\begin{aligned} &\text{Maximize } \Pi = Q_1^2 + Q_1Q_2 + Q_2^3 \\ &\text{subject to } Q_1 - 20 \quad \le -Q_2^4 \\ &\qquad\qquad Q_1^2 + 3Q_2 \ge 10 \\ &\text{where } Q_1 \text{ and } Q_2 \ge 0 \end{aligned} \tag{8}$$

can be written in the Lagrangian form

$$\Pi_\lambda = Q_1^2 + Q_1Q_2 + Q_2^3 + \lambda_1(20 - Q_1 - Q_2^4) + \lambda_2(-10 + Q_1^2 + 3Q_2) \tag{9}$$

subject only to the constraints that $Q_1, Q_2, \lambda_1, \lambda_2 \ge 0$. Note that in a maximization problem, the variables of the constraint equation are placed on the left side of the $\ge$ sign before being put in the Lagrangian expression. If a minimum solution is sought, the constraint equation variables are placed on the other side.

K-T conditions require the following:

1. $\dfrac{\partial \Pi_\lambda}{\partial Q_1} = 2Q_1 + Q_2 - \lambda_1 + 2\lambda_2 Q_1 \le 0$

$\dfrac{\partial \Pi_\lambda}{\partial Q_2} = Q_1 + 3Q_2^2 - 4\lambda_1 Q_2^3 + 3\lambda_2 \le 0$

2. $Q_1 \dfrac{\partial \Pi_\lambda}{\partial Q_1} = Q_1(2Q_1 + Q_2 - \lambda_1 + 2\lambda_2 Q_1) = 0$

$Q_2 \dfrac{\partial \Pi_\lambda}{\partial \lambda_2} = Q_2(Q_1 + 3Q_2^2 - 4\lambda_1 Q_2^3 + 3\lambda_2) = 0$

3. $\dfrac{\partial \Pi_\lambda}{\partial \lambda_1} = 20 - Q_1 - Q_2^4 \geq 0$

$\dfrac{\partial \Pi_\lambda}{\partial \lambda_2} = -10 + Q_1^2 + 3Q_2 \geq 0$

4. $\lambda_1 \dfrac{\partial \Pi_\lambda}{\partial \lambda_1} = \lambda_1(20 - Q_1 - Q_2^4) = 0$

$\lambda_2 \dfrac{\partial \Pi_\lambda}{\partial \lambda_2} = \lambda_2(-10 + Q_1^2 + 3Q_2) = 0$

5. $Q_1, Q_2, \lambda_1, \lambda_2$ each ≥ 0

If all these conditions are met, a solution is theoretically possible. In practice, a problem may be so complicated that an actual solution may be impractical to obtain, but the K-T conditions indicate whether the problem has a solution without actually computing it. For some problems in theoretical analysis, this information may be all that is needed.

The K-T conditions may be considered extensions of the first-order conditions of calculus for obtaining a maximum to cases where the solution may lie at a corner point rather than at some interior point. Figure 5-8 illustrates corner and interior maximums. K-T conditions work for both corner and interior maximums. K-T conditions 2 and 4 determine if corner maximums are present and hold only because of the limitations of Q_i to positive or zero values. Suppose the problem is to be examined for a corner maximum. This means that $\partial \Pi_\lambda / \partial Q_1 \leq 0$ at $Q_1 = 0$, as at points A and B, respectively, in Figure 5-8. There is no possibility that $\partial \Pi_\lambda / \partial Q_1 > 0$ at $Q_1 = 0$ can produce a maximum, since Π_λ cannot be increased by raising Q_1. Condition 2 requires that either or both $Q_1 = 0$ and $\partial \Pi_\lambda / \partial Q_1 = 0$. If Q_1 is positive and a maximum exists, it must be an interior

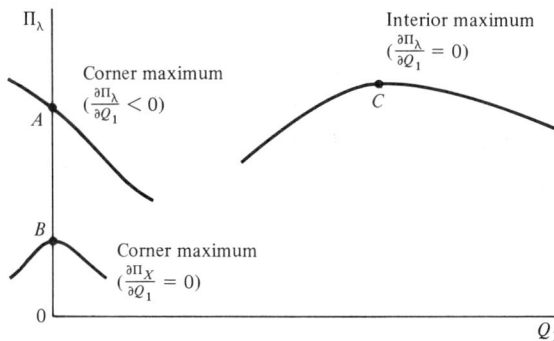

Figure 5-8

one where $\partial \Pi_\lambda / \partial Q_1 = 0$. If the corner maximum occurs at the vertical axis where $Q_1 = 0$, then $\partial \Pi_\lambda / \partial Q_1$ must be ≤ 0.

Similar reasoning may be used to validate condition 4. It should be recognized that in the Lagrange problem, when a maximum value of Π is obtained, the problem is simultaneously being solved (as with its dual) for the minimum value of Z. A *saddle point solution* (as in Figure 4-1) is obtained, where $\Pi = Z$; optimal values of Q_i yield maximum Π, and optimal values of λ_j yield minimum Z. Since Z is minimized with respect to λ, the inequality sign is reversed from that of condition 4. Corner minimums thus require $\partial \Pi_\lambda / \partial \lambda_j \geq 0$, where $\lambda_j = 0$. Where an extremum is present, the K-T conditions provide a test to see if an optimum exists, which is more information than can be obtained only from first-order calculus conditions.

This section assumes, of course, that second-order conditions are also satisfied, guaranteeing that the feasible region is convex and that the objective function is concave in the vicinity of the maximum point and convex near the minimum point. It is possible, however, that a solution satisfying the K-T conditions is not the maximum maximorum (or global maximum).[2]

5-6   Integer Programming

Integer programming is a form of nonlinear programming used where answers to problems must be whole numbers, free from fractional parts. Integer solutions may be required where units are indivisible, as with a blast furnace, locomotive, dam, or general manager, where the item must be whole and intact. In some cases, as with workers, part-time employment may be a possibility for getting around indivisibilities; in others, as with typewriters, automobiles, electronic computers, and some kinds of tools, part-time use is often possible through rentals. Sometimes ordinary linear programming solutions are sufficiently accurate so that rounding off the answer is all that is needed. This might be true where LP analysis recommends production of 634,021.3 electric saws. Inaccuracies in the data and omission of some relevant variables from the model could permit us reasonably to ignore the .3 and likely the 21 as well, making the recommendation an even 634,000 units. In many other cases, however, it is critical that solutions be integers without the help of rounding. An example would be a transportation problem where goods are to be delivered according to a least-cost route between a group of cities. Little help is gained from a recommendation to proceed next to city number 5.735 when only cities numbered 5 and 6 exist. Another example is where a harmonious team of workers is to be assembled for a task. Individual members must be either accepted or rejected, which may be expressed mathematically as $X_i = 1$ (accepted) or $X_i = 0$ (rejected). If candidates i and j cannot function together because of a personality conflict, this fact can be included in the problem by adding the constraint equation $X_i + X_j = 1$, making the selection of i and j mutually exclusive. Fractional solutions in this context also have no meaning.

The method of obtaining integer solutions is easily understood by reference to Figure 5-9. A noninteger solution to the problem

---

[2] On this point the reader is referred to Dorfman, Samuelson, and Solow [3, pp. 194–196].

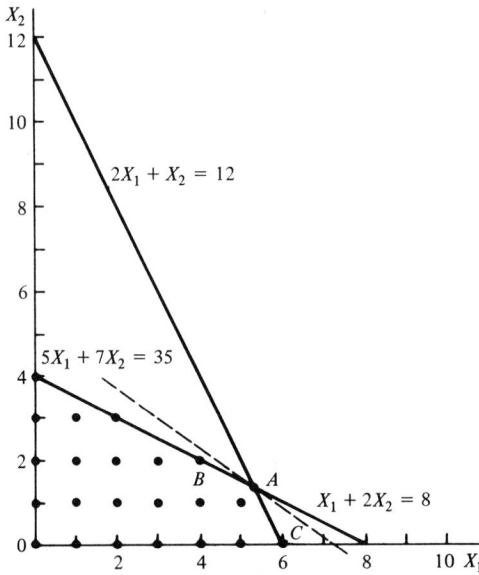

Figure 5-9

$$\text{Maximize } \Pi = 5X_1 + 7X_2$$
$$\text{subject to } X_1 + 2X_2 \leq 8$$
$$2X_1 + X_2 \leq 12 \tag{10}$$
$$\text{where } X_1 \text{ and } X_2 \geq 0$$

is found by the technique of Chapter 4 to be at point A. Since the optimum values of X_1 and X_2 have fractional parts, which for this problem are assumed to be inappropriate, the feasible region must be reduced so that the corner-point solution will have integer coordinates. Points where both coordinates are integers are shown as dots, called *integer lattice points*. The region may be reduced so that corner-point solutions will be at lattice points by adding a new constraint line through points B and C. The optimal solution is then found to be at point B, the point on the boundary of the feasible region that touches the highest iso-profit line with slope $-(5/7)$. When the feasible region is reduced to the smallest possible convex region containing all the lattice points, it is referred to as a *convex hull*.

The procedure for deriving the required additional constraint equation, called a *Gomory constraint* after Ralph E. Gomory, who developed the method, will now be described. The first step is to obtain the optimal noninteger solution by the usual procedure, producing the following tableaus:

	1	X_1	X_2
Π	0	5	7
S_1	8	-1	-2^*
S_2	12	-2	-1

$$(11)$$

	1	X_1	S_1
Π	28	$\frac{3}{2}$	$-\frac{7}{2}$
X_2	4	$-\frac{1}{2}$	$-\frac{1}{2}$
S_2	8	$-\frac{3}{2}*$	$\frac{1}{2}$

$$(12)$$

	1	S_2	S_1
Π	36	-1	-3
X_2	$1\frac{1}{3}$	$\frac{1}{3}$	$-\frac{2}{3}$
X_1	$5\frac{1}{3}$	$-\frac{2}{3}$	$\frac{1}{3}$

$$(13)$$

The second step is to select the row with the largest fractional part in the first column. In this problem, either row 2 or 3 may be chosen, since fractional parts are $\frac{1}{3}$ for both. If row 2 is selected, the corresponding equation is

$$X_2 = 1\tfrac{1}{3} + \tfrac{1}{3}S_2 - \tfrac{2}{3}S_1 \tag{14}$$

The third step is to change the sign of the coefficients, except the first on the right-hand side of the equal sign, in accordance with the equation

$$g_i = a_{io} + \sum_{j=1}^{n} (-a_{ij}X_j) \tag{15}$$

where the a's are the constants, thus obtaining

$$X_2 = 1\tfrac{1}{3} - \tfrac{1}{3}S_2 + \tfrac{2}{3}S_1 \tag{16}$$

The fourth step is to obtain the *nonnegative* fractional parts, which are

$$\tfrac{1}{3}, \tfrac{2}{3}, \tfrac{2}{3},$$

The nonnegative fractional part of $-\frac{1}{3}$, for example, is $\frac{2}{3}$, obtained from knowing that $-\frac{1}{3} = -1 + \frac{2}{3}$. If the coefficients are unity (or any other whole number), there is no fraction, and the nonnegative fractional part is therefore zero. The fractions are then inserted into the Gomory constraint equation:

$$S_i^g = -f_{io} + \sum_{j=1}^{n} f_{ij}X_j \tag{17}$$

corresponding to some straight line through point B in Figure 5-9, where the f_{ij} are the nonnegative fractions corresponding to the a_{ij} constants of equation (15).

The fifth step thus requires changing the sign of the constant term (f_{io}) and inserting it and the coefficients into equation (17) with the integers omitted:

$$S_3^g = -\tfrac{1}{3} + \tfrac{2}{3}S_2 + \tfrac{2}{3}S_1 \tag{18}$$

This equation is added to the bottom of tableau (13), which is solved using the now familiar mechanical rules:

	1	S_2	S_1
Π	36	-1	-3
X_2	$1\frac{1}{3}$	$\frac{1}{3}$	$-\frac{2}{3}$
X_1	$5\frac{1}{3}$	$-\frac{2}{3}$	$\frac{1}{3}$
S_3^g	$-\frac{1}{3}$	$\frac{2}{3}*$	$\frac{2}{3}$

$$(19)$$

A complication exists, because none of the first-row elements, ignoring the first column, is positive. The negative element in the fourth row of the first column, however, indicates the present solution is, with the addition of the new constraint, no longer feasible. This obstacle may be overcome by applying the dual simplex method, reversing the rows and columns, and in effect changing the sign of the first and last column elements. In fact, the only real difference between the dual and the ordinary simplex computation is in the selection of the pivot element.

The dual simplex pivot element is selected from the row having the largest negative number in the first column. It is selected from that column among the positive row elements that have the smallest ratio (ignoring the sign) obtained by dividing the corresponding element in the first row by the element in the pivot row, (a_{oj}/a_{ij}). In the preceding example the last row is selected as the pivot row, because the $-\frac{1}{3}$ is the largest (only in this example) negative number in the first column. The element in the second column of this row, $\frac{2}{3}$, is chosen because the value of $-(-1 \div \frac{2}{3})$ is less than the value of $-(-3 \div \frac{2}{3})$. A new tableau is formed by pivoting on the starred element and following the usual rules:

	1	S_3^g	S_1
Π	$35\frac{1}{2}$	$-\frac{3}{2}$	-2
X_2	$1\frac{1}{2}$	$\frac{1}{2}$	-1
X_1	5	-1	1
S_2	$\frac{1}{2}$	$\frac{3}{2}$	-1

$$(20)$$

Since fractions remain, the procedure is repeated and a new Gomory constraint added:

	1	S_3^g	S_1
Π	$35\frac{1}{2}$	$-\frac{3}{2}$	-2
X_2	$1\frac{1}{2}$	$\frac{1}{2}$	-1
X_1	5	-1	1
S_2	$\frac{1}{2}$	$\frac{3}{2}$	-1
S_4^g	$-\frac{1}{2}$	$\frac{1}{2}*$	0

$$(21)$$

	1	S_4^g	S_1
Π	34	-3	-2
X_2	2		
X_1	4		
S_2	2		
S_3^g	1		

$$(22)$$

This final tableau (22) gives the integer solution: $X_1 = 4$, $X_2 = 2$, $\Pi = 34$ corresponding to point B of Figure 5-7.

Questions and Problems

5-1. Given the constraint equation $X^2 + Y^2 = 1$, prove by the use of calculus that the curve is concave to the origin.

5-2. Find the Kuhn-Tucker conditions:

    a. Maximize $\Pi = Q_1 - 3Q_1Q_2 + Q_2^2$

        subject to $Q_1 + Q_2 \leq 300$

                     $Q_1Q_2 \geq 200$

    b. Minimize Π in part a.

    c. Maximize $\Pi = 5Q_1^2 Q_2$

        subject to $3Q_1 + Q_2^2 \geq 100$

                     $Q_1 \leq 15$

    d. Minimize Π in part *c.*

5-3. Find maximum noninteger and integer solutions:

    a. $\Pi = 14X_1 + 4X_2$

        subject to $X_1 + X_2 \leq 7$

                  $4X_1 + X_2 \leq 9$

    b. $\Pi = 10X_1 + 7X_2$

        subject to $4X_1 + X_2 \leq 8$

                  $5X_1 + 4X_2 \leq 18$

References

1. William J. Baumol. *Economic Theory and Operations Analysis.* 3d ed. (Englewood Cliffs, N.J.: Prentice-Hall, 1972), ch. 7, 8.
2. George B. Dantzig. *Linear Programming and Extensions* (Princeton, N.J.: Princeton University Press, 1963), ch. 24, 26.
3. Robert Dorfman, Paul A. Samuelson, and Robert M. Solow. *Linear Programming and Economic Analysis* (New York: McGraw-Hill, 1958), ch. 8.
4. W. S. Dorn. "A Duality Theorem for Convex Programs." *IBM Journal of Research and Development* 4 (October 1960): 407–413.
5. ———. "Duality in Quadratic Programming." *Quarterly Journal of Applied Mathematics* 18 (1960): 155–162
6. ———. "Nonlinear Programming—A Survey." *Management Science* 9 (January 1963): 171–208.
7. Saul I. Gass. *Linear Programming.* 3d ed. (New York: McGraw-Hill, 1969), ch. 9, 13.

PART TWO

Analysis of Consumer Demand

The ideas of economists and political philosophers, both when they are right and when they are wrong, are more powerful than is commonly understood. Indeed the world is ruled by little else. Practical men, who believe themselves to be quite exempt from any intellectual influences, are usually the slaves of some defunct economist. Madmen in authority, who hear voices in the air, are distilling their frenzy from some academic scribbler of a few years back.

John Maynard Keynes, *The General Theory of Employment, Interest, and Money* (1936)

6 The Motivation and the Ability to Consume

The analysis of consumer demand is of critical importance to business people in pursuing the firm's goals of augmenting profits, sales, the value of the firm, earnings per share, share of the market, or some combination (called a utility or preference function) of these and others mentioned in Chapter 1. Part Two of this text is devoted to demand considerations. It discusses many factors believed to influence consumers' motivation and ability to purchase what the firm has to sell and explains the important concepts of the demand curve, elasticity, indifference, and estimation.

A useful way of viewing these topics and of connecting them to others in managerial economics is to consider them in relation to a programming model in which the firm produces and markets n different products (X_1, X_2, X_3, ..., X_n) so as to maximize its set of goals subject to various demand and supply considerations. This multiproduct, multigoal model of the firm can be expressed symbolically as follows:

Maximize z (that is, optimize the firm's goals) $= f(\pi_1 X_1, \pi_2 X_2, ..., \pi_n X_n)$

subject to
demand considerations X_1, X_2, X_3, ..., $X_n = f(p_i, D_i)$ (for instance, consumer motivation and ability to consume, extent of the market)
supply considerations X_1, X_2, X_3, ..., $X_n = f(c_i, S_i)$ (for instance, technology, costs, scarcities)

where all $X_i \geq 0$

and π_i = unit profits (unit price minus unit cost) of the firm's ith product
X_i = units of the firm's products sold during a unit of time
p_i = unit price of products
c_i = unit cost of products

The first constraint, demand considerations, is the part of the model discussed in Part Two. The objective function states that the firm's combination of goals is a function of the quantities of products sold times their unit profitabilities. Stating

84

in this way that the firm's success depends on the profit contributions of each of its different products does not necessarily imply that each product is profitable (that $\pi_i > 0$) nor that unit profitabilities are constant (that $\pi_i = k$) or independent of each other (an increase in the profitability of one product may have a favorable or adverse effect on others the firm sells). D_i refers to a multitude of demand considerations to be discussed in this and the following chapters. S_i refers to the supply considerations, examined in Part Three.

6-1 Satisfaction of Human Needs and Wants

Each individual or family seeks satisfaction of basic human needs: food, heat, shelter, security, health. Superimposed upon these human needs are many less tangible human desires, including the satisfaction of tastes and preferences, variety, additional comfort, sexual satisfaction, power, understanding, purpose in life, love, success, travel, privacy, independence, and leisure. Each consuming unit establishes priorities or hierarchies that indicate the order in which the needs and desires, in various amounts, are to be met.[1] The human mind matches these ranked preferences against the alternative methods of satisfying them. Those that can be fulfilled, at least in part, by using commodities purchased from others are obtained by the exchange of a valued physical possession (money, in modern societies) or by a promise to pay.

Economist philosophers have abstracted from such observations the existence of something called *utility* to represent the satisfaction derived by people from their various endeavors or commodities purchased and consumed. Moreover, a *law of diminishing marginal utility* has been postulated from the observation that after a certain amount of a commodity has been consumed, additional units will yield diminishing increments of utility. Assuming further the use of money (say, dollars), a given amount of money to spend, and a constant utility of money, the consumer will maximize satisfaction by exchanging money for commodities that yield greater utility than holding onto his money would, so that the additional utility per dollar spent is equal for each of the commodities purchased. In symbolic notation, this concept may be shown as follows:[2]

$$\frac{MU_1}{P_1} = \frac{MU_2}{P_2} = \frac{MU_3}{P_3} = \cdots = \frac{MU_n}{P_n}$$

[1] A well-known hierarchy of human needs frequently cited in the literature of industrial psychology and business management is given by Abraham H. Maslow [16]. See also the contribution of Douglas M. McGregor [17], reprinted in James V. Clark's article [4], which in turn was reprinted in Kolb, Rubin, and McIntyre [11]. In Maslow's scheme, needs are ordered from lower to higher levels in the following sequence: (1) physiological (hunger, thirst), (2) safety (security, health), (3) belonging and love (identification, affection), (4) esteem (prestige, success, self-respect), (5) self-actualization (self-fulfillment, personal growth, worthwhile accomplishments). As a need level is satisfied, one moves to higher-level needs, and a new behavior pattern emerges. Industrial studies based upon the hierarchy model are discussed in Maier [13, ch. 14]. If satisfaction of the next level cannot be provided by society, there is thought to be danger that much human energy and motivation for work is lost. See Chris Argyris [1, esp. p. 32] and [2].

[2] This relation may be derived by the use of calculus and the Lagrangian multiplier method as follows. If the utility function is given by

$$U = f(q_1, q_2, q_3, \ldots, q_n) \tag{1}$$

where MU_i is the marginal utility derived from an additional unit of commodity i ($i = 1, 2, 3, \ldots, n$); and P_i is the price per unit paid for an additional unit of commodity i ($i = 1, 2, 3, \ldots, n$). While utility is very difficult, if not impossible, to measure, this concept is useful in showing that rational behavior for a utility maximizer may be to purchase a variety of goods and services, some of which may be substitutable in part for others, the amounts of each commodity depending upon its price and contribution to the consumer's total utility.

It is difficult to measure utility objectively because the concept is wholly a subjective, psychological matter. It cannot be verified with certainty that any two people derive equal satisfaction from consumption of identical commodities. One person's pleasure may be another one's poison. The only objective gauge of utility available is the price measure—the amount of money, labor, or other commodity an individual is willing to sacrifice to obtain something. This may be crudely illustrated by use of Figure 6-1, which shows the equilibrium of two forces: the marginal utility of the good and the marginal disutility of labor (the price). In the case of Robinson Crusoe fishing for food to eat, there is a rising disutility of labor and a falling utility of fish. The first few fish caught yield a large consumer surplus (vertical distance between the two curves for one unit, or area for more than one, indicating the difference between the amount of utility received

---

where U is the total utility obtained from the purchase and consumption of commodities $q_1, q_2, q_3, \ldots, q_n$, subject to the budget limitation, or side condition,

$$M = p_1 q_1 + p_2 q_2 + p_3 q_3 + \cdots + p_n q_n \tag{2}$$

then the Langrangian function can be formed:

$$U_\lambda = f(q_1, q_2, q_3, \ldots, q_n) + \lambda(M - p_1 q_1 - p_2 q_2 - p_3 q_3 - \cdots - p_n q_n)$$

where λ (interpreted as the marginal utility of money) is the Langrangian multiplier, an unknown variable added so that there would be an equal number of equations and variables.

If the function is continuous, differentiable, and meets the necessary second-order conditions, the ratios of marginal utilities to prices that maximize the constrained total utility, U_λ, may be obtained by differentiating U_λ with respect to $q_1, q_2, q_3, \ldots, q_n$ and setting the partial derivatives equal to zero:

$$\frac{\partial U_\lambda}{\partial q_1} = \frac{\partial U_\lambda}{\partial q_1} - \lambda p_1 = 0$$

$$\frac{\partial U_\lambda}{\partial q_2} = \frac{\partial U_\lambda}{\partial q_2} - \lambda p_2 = 0$$

$$\frac{\partial U_\lambda}{\partial q_3} = \frac{\partial U_\lambda}{\partial q_3} - \lambda p_3 = 0$$

Thus

$$\lambda = \frac{\dfrac{\partial U}{\partial q_1}}{P_1} = \frac{\dfrac{\partial U}{\partial q_2}}{P_2} = \frac{\dfrac{\partial U}{\partial q_3}}{P_3} = \cdots = \frac{\dfrac{\partial U}{\partial q_n}}{P_n}$$

$$= \frac{MU_1}{P_1} = \frac{MU_2}{P_2} = \frac{MU_3}{P_3} = \cdots = \frac{MU_n}{P_n}$$

This necessary condition for the maximization of utility is sometimes called the *law of equimarginal utilities* [20, p. 201].

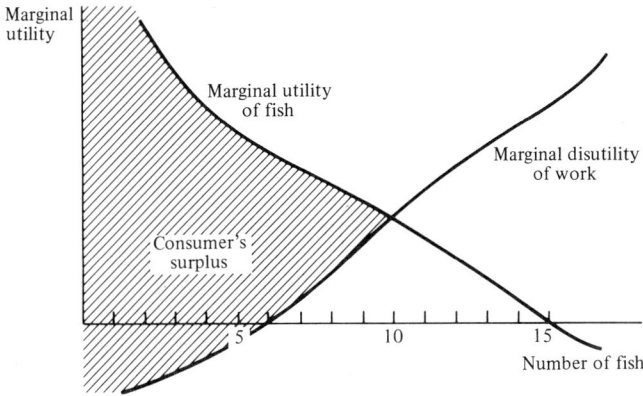

Figure 6-1

and the amount to be given up) because he is hungry. With the hooking of each successive fish, the initial joy of labor erodes until it is fatiguing and monotonous, and the utility derived from having additional fish declines. With 10 fish, the utility of the fish equals the disutility of getting the fish. At 10 units of fish, utility (satisfaction) equals the price (sacrifice).

Of course, price may not be a very accurate yardstick, because the purchase price may represent an amount of money that is more easily atttainable for some people than others and because people may not even know how much utility to associate with a particular item. And even if people had perfect knowledge and understood their own minds, there is little assurance that they would provide perfectly honest answers to questions concerning their utilities.[3]

The problem of predicting the amounts of a commodity that will be purchased by consumers in a particular market during a selected period of time and at different prices is studied by economists through the concept of consumer demand. The rest of this chapter discusses the many factors from which the abstraction is made.

6-2   The Demand for a Commodity

The consumer demand for a particular commodity is the schedule of amounts that consumers would purchase at various unit prices. The amounts depend upon

---

[3] John Ise in his *Economics* provides a colorful insight, true as much of some men as it is of the women he writes about: " With all its inadequacies, the price measure of utility is more accurate than what people say, for most people are surprisingly careless—not to say dishonest—in what they say. A woman says she would 'just give anything to be able to play the piano,' by which she really means that she would give anything but the time and effort necessary to learn; she may say that she 'just loves to read Shakespeare' but cannot find time, which means that she really prefers to do something else with her time; ... Most people fool themselves easily and often about such things; but we may assume that they usually do the things they want to do, subject to the limitations imposed by their necessary work, and buy the things they want, subject to the limitations imposed by their incomes " [10, p. 130].

a host of factors that may be categorized under two necessary and sufficient conditions: the *will* and the *ability* to buy.

6-2-1   *The will to buy a commodity*

The basic needs and desires, as discussed in section 6-1, are sufficient to establish the will to purchase commodities that promise to satisfy them, but it has not yet been shown which commodities or products, most of which are to some degree substitutes for one another, will actually be selected. The priority and amount of a particular product a consumer would select with a given amount of purchasing power is determined by knowledge of the commodity, the intensity of desire for it, the number of different uses of the commodity, tastes and preferences, expectations as to future income, prices, scarcities, and interest rates, the spending habits of neighbors and associates, association of price with quality, the amount of advertising to which the consumer and family members are subjected, whether the seller is liked or not, and irrationality.

Knowledge of the commodity

For consumers to have the will to buy a commodity, they must know of its existence and be able to associate its possession with the satisfaction of some basic desire. Business people have discovered, upon attempting to exploit the natural resources of remote backwoods areas of the world, that laborers in primitive societies are willing to work (if at all) only until a sufficient absolute amount of compensation is obtained that apparently will satisfy all of their immediate needs and desires. An explanation sometimes given is that they are naively unaware of available products and do not associate possessing them with improving their well-being. Business managers have been known to bridge this gap in knowledge by distributing Sears catalogs to families of potential workers. Even in advanced societies, of course, consumer ignorance of certain commodities continues to exist.

Intensity of desire

In attempting to satisfy various needs and desires, the economizing person will select from the available, known commodities those which have the greatest personal importance. The highest priority is generally attached to these basic commodities of life (food, clothing, shelter) and lower significance to those providing degrees of pleasure, the degrees being defined in terms of intensity and duration of the satisfaction anticipated. Carl Menger illustrated these thoughts [18, pp. 122–128] in 1871, by a numerical example similar to Table 6-1, whereby an ascending scale from 1 to 10 indicates the importance of personal satisfaction anticipated from the expenditure of, say, $1 for the different commodities.

Suppose column I represents food. The anticipated satisfaction derived from the purchase and consumption of $1 worth of food is given the highest degree of satisfaction, a rank of 10. As additional dollars are spent on food, smaller degrees of satisfaction are attached to these additional morsels of food. The second dollar spent on food will yield 9 units of satisfaction, the third dollar will yield 8, and so forth until additional dollars spent on food will yield no additional

Table 6-1 Commodities

	I	II	III	IV	V	VI	VII	VIII	IX	X
Additional satisfaction anticipated from the ex-penditure of additional dollars	10	9	8	7	6	5	4	3	2	1
	9	8	7	6	5	4	3	2	1	0
	8	7	6	5	4	3	2	1	0	
	7	6	5	4	3	2	1	0		
	6	5	4	3	2	1	0			
Sixth additional dollar	5	4	3	2	1	0				
	4	3	2	1	0					
Eighth additional dollar	3	2	1	0						
	2	1	0							
Tenth additional dollar	1	0								
	0									

satisfaction. Suppose that column V shows the satisfaction anticipated from the purchase and consumption of an additional dollar's worth of tobacco. The highest degree of satisfaction the individual can derive from $1 worth of tobacco is a rank of 6, for the first unit. It is therefore evident that this individual will not purchase any tobacco until he or she has previously purchased at least $4 worth of food, $3 worth of II, $2 worth of III, and $1 worth of IV. Thus, the maximizing individual will allocate dollars among commodities to derive the greatest personal satisfaction. It is apparent that some needs will remain unsatisfied so long as financial resources are limited and higher degrees of satisfaction are obtainable from additional units of other commodities.[4]

[4] This illustration implies the following assumptions:
1. The maximizing individual can measure his satisfactions cardinally (assign numbers to) as well as ordinally (assign rank to).
2. The satisfaction derived from the consumption of each commodity is independent of the amount of consumption of other commodities.
3. Successive additions to total satisfaction in each column result from successive equal additions to the amount of the commodity consumed.
4. Additional amounts of the different commodities are all obtained with an equal expenditure of some other resource (say, dollars, which could be considered as one of the columns in Table 6-1).
5. The intensity of desire for the commodity depends upon a subjective valuation of the need and the quantities of commodities that are available to meet that need.

Number of uses

The different uses of a commodity, say wheat, could be substituted in the preceding discussion for the alternative products. Under column I could be symbolized the satisfaction derived from an additional unit of wheat being used personally by the farmer. Column II may show the satisfactions he derives from nourishing his wife and children. Column III may be for his farm animals. Column IV may be for making luxury beverages. Column V may be for poor neighbors who live down the road. As long as there is an abundance of wheat, all needs can be met.

However, if for some reason there is a scarcity of wheat, the grain will not be allocated to uses of least importance. The farmer will begin to economize in the use of his wheat, reserving portions to provide for his highest priorities. Thus, the consumer's will to buy a unit of a commodity depends also upon the ways he can utilize it.

Tastes and preferences

Tastes and preferences is a category under which economists have lumped the motivations to consume attributable to customs, folkways, religion, habit, inclination, and sometimes all things that do not conveniently fit under the other enumerated categories. History indicates that over time these factors change, and these shifts may exert a considerable impact upon the quantities of commodities that consumers are willing to buy. There is great uncertainty, however, as to which direction and to what extent the net of these factors will tend to move. The manager who can foresee the future direction of consumer tastes and preferences, whether because of a sixth sense for such matters, useful research, or just plain good fortune, has one of the major requisites for becoming an overwhelming success.

Expectations

Expectations undoubtedly play a great role in influencing the will of consumers in the short run to purchase or not to purchase certain commodities. If the *price* is expected to rise in the near future, consumers will speed up at least some purchases in the current period; alternatively, if price is expected to fall, they will decrease inventory in the current period so that they can buy later at a lower price. If consumers anticipate a rise in *income* because of wage increases, bonuses, inheritances, windfalls, or whatever, they may purchase greater quantities in the current period than normally; if a fall is expected, as with retirement, current consumption may be smaller. Anticipated *scarcities*, such as those associated with the rationing of critical commodities in wartime, will in the absence of selfless patriotism cause hoarding and accentuation of scarcities and, in the case of opportunistic nonpatriots, blackmarket and spiraling, clandestine príces. For those loyal countrymen who refuse to hoard, the glow of patriotism is a consumer good of equal value to what might have been gained by buying ahead. Expectations of rising *interest rates* will cause lenders to postpone making loans at the current rate, especially loans of longer maturities; home buyers will attempt to obtain long-term mortgages before rates rise; bond speculators will sell now with the expectation of buying back later at lower prices. In some short-run periods expectations may well be the most important factor in determining the will of consumers to purchase a given commodity or group of commodities.

Spending habits of neighbors and associates

Self-sufficient indeed is the family that is unmoved by envy the day a new car is found parked in the neighbor's driveway. Or, if it is unaffected by new cars, what about the neighbor's new garbage disposal, color TV, shrubs, air-conditioning, house painting, bicycle, fur coat, brick barbeque, swimming pool, Chippendale furniture, camper, vacation trip to Hawaii, baby, pet, water bed, or whatever? How many husbands have not been rebuked by their wives with "How come we have as much income as the Joneses, but they always seem to have more than we do?" How many families with children have not heard the sobbing pleas for a new tricycle like Johnnie has? In addition to feelings of envy or jealousy, there is a desire to be accepted into a peer group that consumes at a certain level. When the desire of the individual for a commodity *increases* because others are purchasing the same item, this is called keeping up with the Joneses, or the bandwagon effect. An association is made between the desire to be one of the group and to consume in the manner of the in-crowd. When the desire *decreases* because others are buying the same commodity, this is called the snob effect. Which tendency is dominant depends upon the nature of the commodity and the subjective values and needs of the consumer [see 12, pp. 12–30]. Indeed, views of the state of well-being and wills to purchase are substantially influenced by the purchasing habits of our acquaintances.

Association of price with quality

Occasionally the desirability of a commodity may be diminished if the price is too low. The man receiving a gift from his girlfriend, say a tie, may be quite pleased until he later discovers its price to be $2. Somehow, a tie costing $2 is deemed inappropriate for the well-dressed man, and he may associate the price paid for the gift with the level of esteem in which he is held. However, a similar tie at a price of $10 may be quite satisfying. The association of the desire to consume with the price of a commodity is called the *Veblen effect* after the economist Thorstein Veblen (1857–1929) and his concept of conspicuous consumption. Similar biases may be held, if not about clothes, then about cars, records, wines, cologne, appliances, and so on.

Advertising

Advertising is the process through which the seller informs and motivates the buyer to consider and purchase a product. There is little doubt that advertising in newspapers, periodicals, television, radio, billboards, and elsewhere can influence consumers to buy. They may view much of the advertising they see and hear with mixed feelings. Some commercials may be enjoyed, others detested. Some may be considered a waste of time, others an insult to the intelligence. Individual consumers may even be harmed by certain commercials, especially when the will to buy has been stimulated but the economic wherewithal is lacking. Still, this is the manner in which consumers may first come to know of the availability of a new or improved product. Some knowledge of available goods is essential for a transaction eventually to take place. Without it, many desirable products and the firms producing them might fall by the wayside.[5]

Benevolent or malevolent feelings toward the seller

Kenneth E. Boulding [3] has recently emphasized the importance of a feeling of benevolence (goodwill) toward the seller, without which exchange would not be as great or, in some cases, exist at all. No one wants to trade with a hated enemy unless a distinct advantage can be obtained. People would rather not purchase products from a person or firm they detest. Perhaps they have been alienated by previous experience, a distasteful television commercial, a difference in politics or religion, or advice from a friend. Such feelings of malevolence inhibit or restrict trade and should be avoided whenever possible by ambitious business managers. The sensitive manager is quick to emphasize in the training of employees who have contact with the public that the customer is always right. A happy, comfortable customer listening, perhaps unconsciously, to conducive background music is apt to buy more items than a disgruntled, uncomfortable one.

Irrationality

When struck with sudden whims or urges to buy something that serves no other rational purpose, consumers may be said to be acting irrationally. The rational acts of an economic person would dictate that purchases be planned and calculated to maximize utility. Satisfaction of a passing fancy that is later regretted would indicate impetuousness. Still, most consumers have a lack of knowledge or foresight and are occasionally guilty of making such purchases. This is one reason why retail store managers locate impulse items near the cash register. Consumer irrationality is evident in cases of *overindulgence* in the consumption of almost anything.[6] Rationality would require weighing the delayed pain of a hangover or stomachache against the initial but temporary pleasure and comparing the net balance against the other costs associated with the purchase of the commodity. Irrationality occurs when there is a delay in the pleasure-pain-regret chain of events, for instance, the consumer may fail to anticipate fully the delayed pain following the immediate pleasure. Rationality may develop, however, when there are several repetitions of the sequence of events. This would not be true, of course, where the experience is addictive, as with drugs, tobacco, and liquor.

A second source of irrationality may result from a *conflict between instinct and pleasure.* Instinct may tell one to eat, drink, or make love at the slightest pang of hunger, thirst, or eroticism. It prompts people to avoid the cold of outdoors and

---

[5] Associated with the influence of advertising on consumers and other sales promotion is what John Kenneth Galbraith [8] calls the *dependence effect.* According to Professor Galbraith, desires of consumers to purchase are created by producers through advertising the products they have already produced. This is in contrast to the position that producers respond to the independent needs of consumers. Friedrich A. Hayek [9] rejects Galbraith's contentions as being exaggerated, because Professor Hayek feels that the wants of consumers are shaped by many other factors in the environment besides advertising and that Galbraith is attempting to justify a socialist argument for coercing minorities to buy commodities selected by the political authority.

[6] The remainder of this section draws heavily upon Scitovsky [19, pp. 243–247].

the fatigue of long work or active sports when the first degree of discomfort appears. In the process of trying to remove the first degree of discomfort, individuals may be depriving themselves of the infinitely greater pleasures associated with eating a meal when hunger peaks, enjoying warmth after longer exposure to cold, and realizing the satisfactions of a difficult job well done, a hard game won. In short, higher degrees of satisfaction depend upon willingness to endure greater degrees of discomfort. Deprivation may be essential to gratification. Pleasure may require sophistication of forethought and discipline, but instinct, advertising, and social pressures are biased in favor of comfort as the easy alternative.

A third source of irrationality arises where the *enjoyment* of a certain consumer good *requires a skill*. As in the preceding cases, the pleasure of using a commodity versus the pain of acquiring the skill are weighed against each other, and the net weighed against the cost. But here the time sequence is reversed—the pain of acquiring the skill precedes enjoyment of its use. This explains why consumption in this case may not be pushed far enough, rather than too far as in the case of overindulgence. Also, there is no opportunity for a learning experience to aid rational consumption. The pain of acquiring the skill will not be assumed because the pain is immediate and certain, and the rewarding pleasures to be derived from skilled consumption are remote, uncertain, and perhaps unknown. No accumulation of experience is obtained with which to correct future behavior. Lack of knowledge may account for the fact that most, if not all, people to some degree are deprived of many pleasures of life where training and skill are prerequisites. While a lack of funds or opportunity may account for the failure of poor people to acquire the skills of consumption, the barrier of inadequate knowledge that can be negotiated only through pain may account for the failure of rich people to acquire them. Most who acquire the requisite aptitudes do so early in life in their general education, under compulsion of curriculum requirements or parental guidance. Once the tools are acquired, people have greater ability to enjoy music, art, reading, and active sports and generally regard their initial investment of time, effort, and discipline as well spent. Failure to capitalize upon opportunities to learn to appreciate acquired tastes often must be regarded as an irrational decision.

Other sources of consumer irrationality are attributable to ignorance of the existence, nature, quality, and availability of commodities.[7]

---

[7] Since consumer irrationality is based at least in part on ignorance, there may be justification of public policies to offset the bias of irrationality. This has been done with curbs on advertising and special taxes on tobacco and alcoholic beverages to discourage their consumption by consumers not fully realizing their dangers. Obstacles have been erected to obtaining dangerous and addictive drugs. Other items thought to be underconsumed due to irrationality have received public subsidy, such as concerts, operas, museums, and public education in the arts and crafts. Such taxes and subsidies can help the consumer obtain a better life than he has the knowledge to seek. Education and experience required for enlightened formulation of wants is just as important as the freedom to select the means to satisfy wants. The consumer can be gently induced or nudged by taxes and subsidies in the hope of educating him. But if the taxes or subsidies are too great, the nudge becomes less gentle. Too great a nudge may cause an arbitrary imposition of behavior norms that is unjust and contribute to an inappropriate disruption of resource allocation relative to consumer preferences, a disruption of the equality between producers' marginal costs and consumers' marginal benefits.

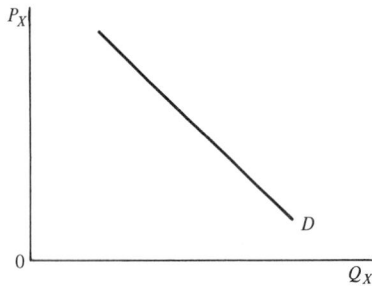

P_X

D

0   Q_X

Figure 6-2

6-2-2   *The ability to buy a commodity*

In order for a commodity demand to exist, the consumer's will to buy must be supplemented by a corresponding ability to buy (sufficient means). Ability to purchase is influenced by many factors, including the price of the commodity, convenience, the rate of interest, and consumer income, wealth, and access to credit.

Price

For those commodities that consumers do not have to purchase, price is undoubtedly one of the most important factors influencing the ultimate decision about which products to buy and in what amounts. Economists traditionally have focused on price as the primary determinant of quantities purchased because of its central role in resource allocation through the market mechanism. Thus, in the most fundamental two-dimensional graph used in demand analysis, unit price, in preference to all other factors, is placed on the vertical axis, as in Figure 6-2. Initially, all other factors bearing on the decision as to how much to purchase are held constant; this is the assumption of "other things being equal." For consumers with limited funds to spend on a particular commodity, the unit price may be so high as to exceed their budgets. In this case, they cannot purchase any amount of the commodity and are said to not be in the market. If the price declines to within their means, they can then enter the market. As the price declines further, they are financially able to purchase more units. For this reason, coupled with the assumption of diminishing marginal utility, the demand curve for the individual consumer is typically drawn downward-sloping to the right.[8]

Convenience

Closely associated with the price of a commodity is the convenience with which a purchase can be made. Included in this category would be proximity to a retail store having the desired commodity, availability of nearby parking if driving is necessary, ease of access to the store (many large doors in the best locations),

---

[8] It has been shown in more advanced works that the assumption of diminishing marginal utility is unnecessary to justify a downward-sloping demand curve when the utility of X depends also upon the quantities purchased of another commodity.

ease of moving to the location where the goods are displayed (wide aisles un-cluttered and uncrowded with other shoppers), and ease of finding the correct size, color, and brand (visible shelves of well-organized merchandise). Once the desired goods have been located, the problems have not yet ended. Customers may have to stand in line to pay for purchases, have them packaged, load them into the car, unload them at home, carry them inside, and unpackage them. The time and bother associated with these actions are sometimes discussed under the headings of search, queues, transportation, ordering, delivery, and handling, but may be summarized under the broader term *convenience*. Inconvenience involves a cost that must be added to the purchase price in determining the salability of the commodity. Some potential customers may not have the ability to purchase certain items because of some handicap—age, a lack of mobility, or a lack of physical health. In such cases, inconvenience may be translated into inability to purchase.

Interest rates

The level of interest rates may be a large factor in determining consumer decisions to purchase expensive items. Note in Table 6-2 that the monthly payment re-quired to amortize a $20,000 purchase over a 20-year period increases more than $11 per month for each increase of 1 percentage point in interest rates above 5 percent and up to 8 percent. The monthly payment on a home at

Table 6-2   Monthly Payment to Amortize a $20,000 Loan in 20 Years

Rate of interest	Monthly payment	Increase in monthly payment (percent)
5%	$131.99	—
6%	143.29	$11.30 (8.56)
7%	155.06	11.77 (8.21)
8%	167.29	12.23 (7.89)

SOURCE: Figures in column two calculated from equation (23) of Chapter 24.

higher rates of interest may be out of reach for low-income families living on tight budgets. These families may alternatively rent a home, rent an apartment, or even purchase a mobile home (even though the annual interest rates on loans for mobile homes may be twice as high). The person who has not previously discovered the significance of interest rates is usually staggered to learn that the interest payments on a 20-year, 8 percent loan add up to an amount exceeding the principal. Changes in interest rates undoubtedly have an impact upon the ability of consumers to purchase large items on credit. Lower interest charges permit consumers to spend a greater proportion of their yearly incomes on con-sumer goods and services. The interest payment itself, however, can be considered a payment for the service of having present rather than future consumption. When relatively inexpensive items are purchased on credit, the size of monthly payment generally takes priority over the annual interest rate.

Income

It is evident that consumers with larger *current* incomes have the ability to purchase more commodities at a given price, other things being equal, than consumers with smaller current incomes. In some cases, the mere anticipation of a higher income will be sufficient to invoke consumption, as in the case of the student nearing graduation or where someone is expecting an inheritance, dowry, reward, or bonus. In addition to *expected* income, the amount spent on consumption of commodities has been shown to be influenced by the *relative* incomes and consumption habits of neighbors and others to be impressed with levels of affluence. James Duesenberry argues [5] that consumers attempt to maintain their peak levels of previous purchases as their current incomes fail. Milton Friedman suggests [7; see also 11] that people will purchase according to what they believe their permanent levels of income to be.[9] It is generally agreed that income has a substantial influence on the quantities of commodities purchased.

Wealth

Consumers with stocks of real or financial assets may choose to spend a greater proportion of their current incomes on consumer goods than would people with the same levels of income who had smaller stocks of wealth.[10] Assets may have been accumulated from past incomes for the very purpose of increased consumption in later periods. It is possible for those with no current income to enjoy high levels of consumption merely by diminishing their stores of wealth. An example would be a holder of high-growth common stocks that pay no current dividends selling a few shares to pay for consumption goods. Obviously, other things being equal, wealthier consumers generally have a greater *ability* to consume than poorer consumers do.

Access to credit

Consumers who know they can borrow funds when needed and who can use credit cards to obtain necessary commodities have the ability to purchase greater amounts than consumers who cannot borrow and who must pay cash for purchases. A good credit rating is generally recognized as important in our society, because it permits individuals to borrow at lower rates of interest, even at zero rates where balances are paid within the allotted time.

The position people hold in their communities may have a great deal to do with the determination of their credit ratings and therefore their access to credit. It helps to be born to "proper" parents, "proper" meaning in some cases affluent white Anglo-Saxon Protestants who are members of the establishment. Deficiencies in heredity can be overcome at times if the credit seeker shows promise by

---

[9] While most of this literature is listed under the category of macroeconomics, many of the suggested theories used to explain aggregate statistics are also of interest on the microeconomics level.

[10] The term *wealth* as used in economics generally refers to real goods and resources, including the skills and abilities of labor and managers. Financial assets are excluded, since their "real" value is the value of the paper upon which the markings are made. In a broader sense, however, the concept of personal wealth typically includes financial assets. The broader definition of wealth is used here.

having some recent successes, good character, motivation, persuasiveness, education, unique abilities, personal contacts, or a prestigious position. Whatever the logic, access to credit enhances a consumer's ability to buy commodities over short periods of time and perhaps over long periods as well.

6-3 Summary

Many factors influence the motivation and ability of the individual consumer (or the spending unit, such as a family) to purchase a particular commodity. The many human needs and wants of a consumer are typically subsumed in economics under the concept of utility. The economic laws of diminishing marginal utility and equimarginal utilities were introduced in this chapter. The demand for a commodity depends upon two necessary and sufficient conditions: the *will* and the *ability* to purchase. Will is determined by knowledge, intensity of desire, number of uses, tastes and preferences, expectations, neighbors, associations of price and quality, advertising, likes and dislikes, and irrationality. Ability depends upon price, convenience, interest, income, wealth, and access to credit. In Chapter 7 the discussion is extended to the market demand curve.

Questions and Problems

6-1. Identify and explain:

a. utility	*j.* irrationality
b. diminishing marginal utility	*k.* pleasure-pain-regret sequence
c. equimarginal utility	*l.* pain-pleasure sequence
d. expectations	*m.* demand
e. tastes and preferences	*n.* income
f. snob effect	*o.* wealth
g. bandwagon effect	*p.* price
h. Veblen effect	*q.* amortize
i. malevolence	*r.* a good credit rating

6-2. Which of the items listed in section 6-2-1 under the will to buy a commodity can be subsumed under the concept of utility?

6-3. What economic concepts are being revealed by the following?

   a. the children of poor people playing ball with oranges obtained through the food subsidy program

   b. the failure of carpenters to pick up the nails they drop on the ground while building a house

   c. the giving of old clothes to Goodwill or the Salvation Army

   d. the corporation executive untangling and saving the string from a package received in the mail

   e. the practice of a timber cutter stripping the ground bare without regard to conservation practices

6-4. Suppose Table 6-1 refers to the additional or marginal satisfaction derived from additional gallons of water by Crusoe on an isolated island from the different uses for a limited quantity of fresh water. The uses may range from column I for drinking to column X for washing his dog. If he has 10 gallons, how many will be used for each of the different uses from I to X?

6-5. Suppose the shipmates on a sailing ship each have 10 pounds of biscuits, which are just sufficient to keep each shipmate alive for the required 20 days of sailing to reach land. Assume that the lives of the voyagers can be maintained only if each consumes a half pound of biscuits daily.

    a. Would a rich traveler on the boat be able to purchase for a pound of gold a pound of biscuits to alleviate his hunger pangs from the scant rations?

    b. If one shipmate had 11 pounds of biscuits, one more than absolutely required to maintain his life, would he necessarily be willing to part with the extra biscuits in exchange for a pound of gold?

    c. Assume the galley has no food, voyagers have no food of their own, and the ship has a cargo of 100 tons of biscuits, of which the captain will permit the voyagers to take as much as they can eat. Under these conditions, how much would a voyager be willing to pay for an additional pound of biscuits?

    d. Explain why a pound of biscuits has diminished importance in moving from part a to b to c [18, pp. 136–139].

References

1. Chris Argyris. *Integrating the Individual and the Organization* (New York: Wiley, 1964).
2. ———. *Management and Organizational Development* (New York: McGraw-Hill, 1971).
3. Kenneth E. Boulding. "Economics as a Moral Science." In *Economics as a Science* (New York: McGraw-Hill, 1970), pp. 117–138.
4. James V. Clark. "Motivation in Work Groups: A Tentative View." *Human Organization* 19 (Winter 1960–1961): 199–208.
5. James S. Duesenberry. *Income, Employment, and Public Policy* (New York: W. W. Norton, 1948), pp. 54–81. Reprinted in M. G. Mueller. *Readings in Macroeconomics* (New York: Holt, Rinehart and Winston, 1966), pp. 61–76.
6. M. J. Farrell. "The New Theories of the Consumption Function." *Economic Journal* 69 (December 1959): 678–696. Reprinted in M. G. Mueller. *Readings in Macroeconomics*, pp. 77–92.
7. Milton Friedman. *A Theory of the Consumption Function.* National Bureau of Economic Research (Princeton, N. J.: Princeton University Press, 1957), pp. 20–37. Reprinted in Harold R. Williams and John D. Huffnagle. *Macroeconomic Theory—Selected Readings* (New York: Appleton-Century-Crofts, 1969), pp. 141–158.
8. John Kenneth Galbraith. *The Affluent Society* (New York: New American Library, 1958), ch. 11. Reprinted in Edwin Mansfield. *Microeconomics—Selected Readings* (New York: W. W. Norton, 1971), pp. 3–6.
9. Friedrich A. Hayek. "The Non Sequitur of the Dependence Effect." *Southern Economic Journal* (1961). Reprinted in Edwin Mansfield. *Microeconomics—Selected Readings*, pp. 7–11.
10. John Ise. *Economics.* Rev. ed. (New York: Harper, 1950).
11. David A. Kolb, Irwin M. Rubin, and James M. McIntyre. *Organizational Psychology—A Book of Readings* (Englewood Cliffs, N.J.: Prentice-Hall, 1971), pp. 93–109.

12. Harvey Leibenstein. "Bandwagon, Snob, and Veblen Effects in the Theory of Consumers' Demand." *Quarterly Journal of Economics* (1950). Reprinted in Edwin Mansfield. *Microeconomics—Selected Readings*, pp. 12–30.
13. Norman R. F. Maier. *Psychology in Industrial Organizations.* 4th ed. (Boston: Houghton Mifflin, 1973).
14. Alfred Marshall. *Principles of Economics.* 8th ed. (London: Macmillan, 1920; reprinted 1962). The first edition was published in 1890.
15. Abraham H. Maslow. *Eupsychian Management—A Journal* (Homewood, Ill.: Richard D. Irwin, 1965).
16. ———. *Motivation and Personality* (New York: Harper, 1954).
17. Douglas M. McGregor. Fifth Anniversary Convocation. School of Industrial Management. M.I.T. Cambridge, Mass. Quoted by Clark [4, p. 200].
18. Carl Menger. *Principles of Economics* (Glencoe, Ill.: Free Press, 1950). This is a translation of the first edition of *Grundsatze* published in Vienna in 1871.
19. Tibor Scitovsky. *Welfare and Competition.* Rev. ed. (Homewood, Ill.: Richard D. Irwin, 1971).
20. Taro Yamane. *Mathematics for Economists—An Elementary Survey.* 2d ed. (Englewood Cliffs, N.J.: Prentice-Hall, 1968).

7 The Concept of Demand

This chapter is the second of six dealing with demand considerations which may be viewed as constraints in the programming model of the firm outlined briefly at the beginning of Chapter 6. Several considerations are discussed in this chapter that are inherent in attempts to utilize the concept of demand as a measure of the responsiveness of the quantity taken to small changes in price. Individual and market demand curves are described. Some conceptual difficulties of determining demand and of explaining why the demand curve shifts in response to changes in significant variables are examined. The concept of elasticity—price elasticity of demand in particular—is emphasized. These rather technical matters should be thoroughly understood by business managers if they are to utilize wisely the information provided by market research studies.

7-1 The Individual and Market Demand Curves

While economists are generally aware that the amount of a product a typical consumer will purchase at a given price is determined by many factors, like those discussed in Chapter 6, they believe that the problem of analyzing consumer demand requires a number of simplifying assumptions. Demand analysis begins with the assumption that all factors except price are held constant and that as price changes, so too will the quantity of that commodity a consumer will purchase. It is further assumed that a person's will and ability to purchase remain fixed during the period of analysis. The schedule of quantities that will be purchased at various prices is plotted as shown in Figure 6-2 or Figure 7-1a to form the demand curve. The reason most commonly given for the curve sloping downward and to the right is the assumption of diminishing utility associated with additional units of the commodity. Notice that the dependent variable (quantity) rather than the independent variable (price), is plotted on the horizontal axis, contrary to mathematical convention. Perhaps the only explanation for this is tradition. Economist Alfred Marshall popularized this usage, but he did not invent it.

Notice that the demand curve is shown as a smooth and continuous relation between quantity and price. There are no discontinuities (gaps) in it. While this

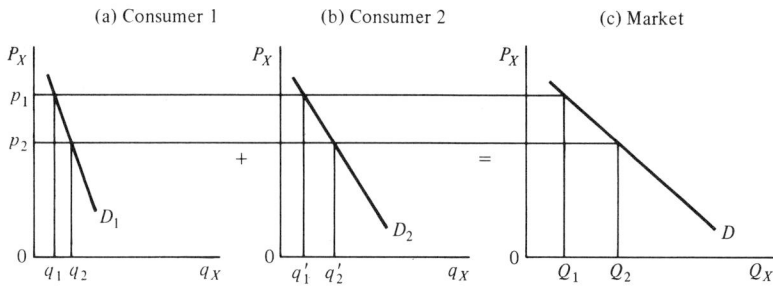

Figure 7-1

relation may hold true for many small items, it surely would not exist for commodities not in constant use. As Marshall succinctly noted, "There are many classes' of things the need for which on the part of any individual is inconstant, fitful, and irregular. There can be no list of individual demand prices for wedding cakes, or the services of an expert surgeon" [10, p. 83]. Problems of discontinuities disappear however, as the concept is extended to large groups of consumers and as the demands of individuals—D_1 and D_2 in Figures 7-1a and 7-1b—are summed horizontally to obtain a composite market demand curve, Figure 7-1c.

> In large markets, then—where rich and poor, old and young, men and women, persons of all varieties of tastes, temperaments and occupations are mingled together,—the peculiarities in the wants of individuals will compensate one another in a comparatively regular gradation of total demand. Every fall, however slight in the price of a commodity in general use, will, other things being equal, increase the total sales of it; just as an unhealthy autumn increases the mortality of a large town, though many persons were uninjured by it... [10, p. 83].

Note that $Oq_1 + Oq_1' = OQ_1$ and $Oq_2 + Oq_2' = OQ_2$. The market demand curve D will be less downward-sloping than most consumer demand curves similar to D_1 and D_2, because at lower prices more consumers are in the market than at higher prices. Those with more limited budgets become excluded from the market as prices rise.

7-2   Conceptual Problems of Determining Demand

For the concept of demand to be meaningful, it must first be specified in terms of product, relevant market, and period of time, discussed in the following subsections.

7-2-1   *Appropriate definition of product*

It is not always clear in application how commodities (outputs of industries) and products (outputs of firms) should be defined. As used in antitrust cases, the choice between a broad or narrow definition may be critical for the future of the

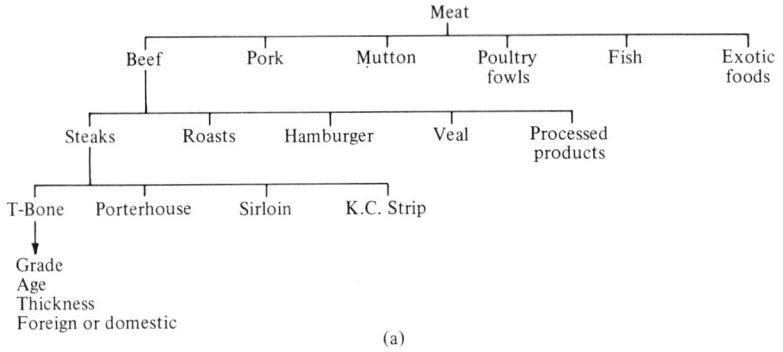

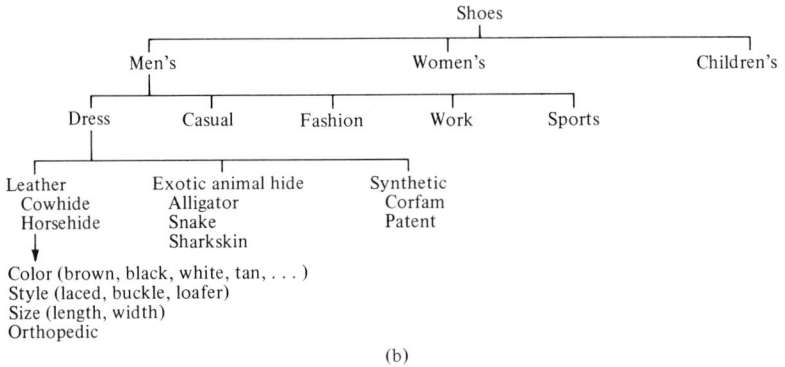

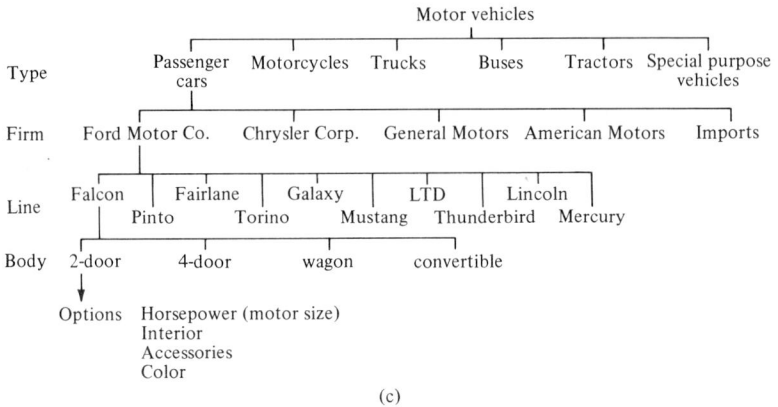

Meat
- Beef
- Pork
- Mutton
- Poultry fowls
- Fish
- Exotic foods

Beef
- Steaks
- Roasts
- Hamburger
- Veal
- Processed products

Steaks
- T-Bone
- Porterhouse
- Sirloin
- K.C. Strip

T-Bone
↓
Grade
Age
Thickness
Foreign or domestic

(a)

Shoes
- Men's
- Women's
- Children's

Men's
- Dress
- Casual
- Fashion
- Work
- Sports

Dress
- Leather
  Cowhide
  Horsehide
- Exotic animal hide
  Alligator
  Snake
  Sharkskin
- Synthetic
  Corfam
  Patent

↓
Color (brown, black, white, tan, . . .)
Style (laced, buckle, loafer)
Size (length, width)
Orthopedic

(b)

Motor vehicles

Type
- Passenger cars
- Motorcycles
- Trucks
- Buses
- Tractors
- Special purpose vehicles

Firm
- Ford Motor Co.
- Chrysler Corp.
- General Motors
- American Motors
- Imports

Line
- Falcon
- Fairlane
- Galaxy
- LTD
- Lincoln
- Pinto
- Torino
- Mustang
- Thunderbird
- Mercury

Body
- 2-door
- 4-door
- wagon
- convertible

↓
Options   Horsepower (motor size)
           Interior
           Accessories
           Color

(c)

Figure 7-2

firm. For example, take the meat, shoe, or motor vehicle industries, which are themselves subdivisions of the food, clothing, and transportation industries. They may be subdivided as shown in Figure 7-2.

A merger of two firms that produced predominant amounts of beef, men's shoes, or passenger cars would more likely be judged to lessen competition substantially and therefore be in restraint of trade than if the two firms were producing amounts of foreign produced T-bone steaks, men's orthopedic sharkskin shoes, or Ford Falcons. It is clear that Ford Motor Company has a monopoly position in the production of Falcons, but not of passenger cars. If the court ruled that Falcons were the relevant economic good, it could be concluded that in order to eliminate a monopoly two-door Falcons should be produced by one firm, four-door Falcons by another, and Falcon wagons by a third. Thus, the existence of monopoly depends upon the definition of the commodity and product.

For the internal use of Ford Motor Company, it is clearly important to know the overall demand for its line of cars, but it may be more crucial to gauge the demand for each of its individual cars, the body styles and the options of each. Such information could reveal that profits could be increased by, say, raising the price of Mustangs by $300 and lowering the price of Falcons by $200.

In general, the more narrowly defined the commodity, the fewer substitutes there will be and therefore the more inelastic the demand for the commodity with respect to price. In the case of meat, there are many substitutes, but for T-bone steaks sold by the local grocery store at 6:30 P.M. Saturday evening, there may be no close substitutes immediately available. The demand (as well as supply) for the relevant period (that evening) may be quite inelastic. The consumer, faced with taking what is available, or as an alternative doing without, may be willing to pay a larger price or even accept inferior cuts (which is equivalent in principle, if not in fact, as long as inferior cuts are judged to be steaks) than he would if a truer buyer's market prevailed at that moment.

7-2-2 Market

The word *market* also has a flexible meaning and can be subdivided into different sets of contracts between buyers and sellers. Markets may be geographical (local, regional, national, and international) or not confined within such boundaries (as with the market for university professors). Markets may be defined in terms of age groups, sex, military status, race, income levels, membership in clubs, unions, and other organizations. In any case, the relevant market for the product must be specified and selected with care. The presence of a monopoly position may be attributable entirely to such a narrowly defined market.

7-2-3 Time

Demand for a product must be specified for a period of time, such as a day, a week, a month, or a year. The period selected should be short enough to provide information of current value but also long enough to be useful in planning for longer periods.

If the demand is the same for every day of the 7-day week, it is clear that demand for a week should be 7 times as great as demand for a single day, and if this constant demand continued for a month, it would be 30 times the daily demand, as Table 7-1 and Figure 7-3 demonstrate. It should be noted as a strictly technical point that the demand curves for the different time periods are not

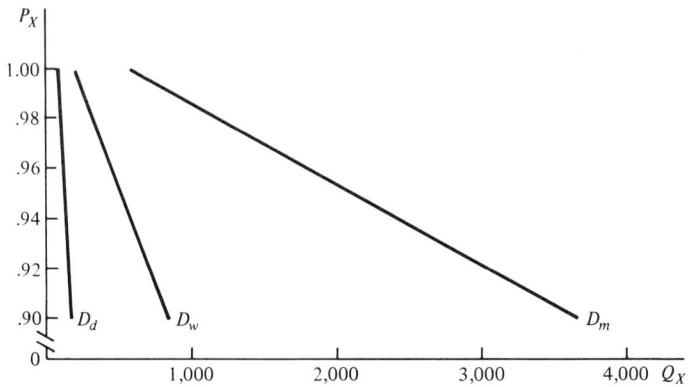

Figure 7-3   **Daily (D_d), Weekly (D_w), and Monthly (D_m) Demand**
for Product X

Table 7-1

| | Quantity of X demanded (Q_x) | | |
Price of X (P_x)	Day	Week	Month
$1.00	20	140	600
.98	40	280	1,200
.96	60	420	1,800
.94	80	560	2,400
.92	100	700	3,000
.90	120	840	3,600

parallel to each other when the quantities for longer periods are simply multiples of the daily demands. D_d has a steeper slope than D_w and D_m.

It is likely that quantities demanded will not be uniformly constant from day to day. When this is the case, a demand curve obtained from single-day observations may be of limited usefulness in estimating demand for other days or for longer periods; for instance, it may not be representative of the days in a month. Aside from this, however, adjustments to a change in price may not be immediate. It may be necessary for a period of time to pass before all potential consumers are aware of the price change, have a need to replenish their stocks, give consideration to making substitutes in their purchases, obtain the required cash or credit, travel to seller's place of business, otherwise communicate to the seller that the buyers wish to buy, and make the actual purchase. Adjustment to changes in income level is another factor. Delayed response of consumers to a change in the price by the seller means that there will be diminutions in the slope of demand curves for longer periods, as shown in Figure 7-4.

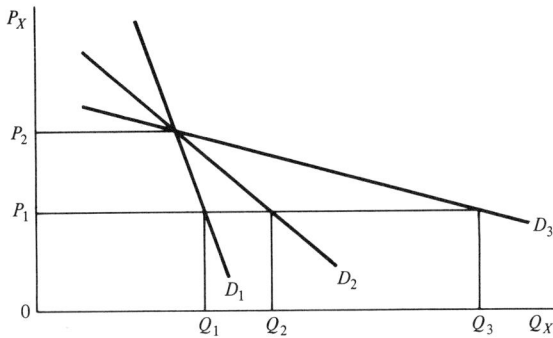

Figure 7-4   Response Through Time to Fall in Price

Suppose, for example, that D_1, D_2, and D_3 represent demand curves for T-bone steaks at a local grocery store for successively longer periods of time, say 1, 2, and 3 days. Now suppose a person notices while shopping that the price of T-bone steaks has fallen from $1.20 to $1.00 per pound. To take advantage of this opportunity to buy at a price that is lower than usual, he buys more than he initially anticipated and plans to store the additional steaks in his home freezer. This increased the quantity demanded to OQ_1 in Figure 7-4. As he unloads his groceries from his car, he sees a neighbor working in his garden and mentions that the price of T-bones steaks at the grocery store has fallen 20 cents. While this information is of some value, it alone probably will not suffice to cause the neighbor to rush to the store. He may well mention it to his wife at supper, who will look for the bargain at the store the next day and may purchase T-bone steaks rather than some other cut of meat and may stock up the family freezer. This means that the quantity demanded over a 2-day period may rise to OQ_2. A buyer may inform friends and neighbors of the bargain, and they may increase their purchases the following day, thereby expanding the quantity demanded in the 3-day period to OQ_3. In such a manner the quantity demanded rises as greater time is allowed for consumers to gain knowledge of a change in price, make adjustments in their purchasing habits, and actually complete their purchases. The time lag can be diminished by a seller through sales promotion, choosing a convenient location for his store or making home deliveries, maintaining convenient store hours for his customers, and providing credit or check-cashing services.

7-3   Shifting the Demand Curve

After decisions have been made as to specification of the product, the relevant market in which it is to be sold, and the specific time period, the market researcher can turn his or her attention to the examination of factors that might cause the demand curve to shift. A shift in the curve could be to the right, as from curve D in Figure 7-5 to D', or to the left, as from D to D''. This is in contrast to a movement along the curve, as from 1 to 2, which is described as a change in the *quantity demanded* and is attributable to a change in price. A shift in the curve is

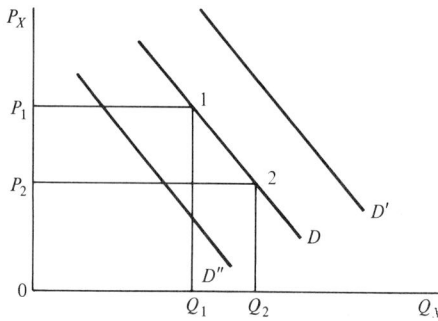

Figure 7-5

described as a change in *demand.* The student should be very careful to use these terms appropriately to avoid confusion in thought as well as in communication with others.

The demand curve may be shifted by changes in any factors that determine the amount consumers will purchase, *except for a change in the price of the product.* These factors, discussed in Chapter 6, are described as the determinants of demand and summarized under the following major categories:

1. tastes and preferences (T)
2. income or budget of consumer (Y)
3. prices of related goods (Pr)
4. expectations (E)
5. informative advertising (A)
6. benevolence (B)
7. irrationality (I)

Demand is said to be a function of these major variables, or in functional notation,

$$D = f(T, Y, Pr, E, A, B, I) \tag{1}$$

The theoretically correct demand curve is one that is obtained when all the determinants of demand remain unchanged; or, if some of the determinants have changed, their alterations have been removed over the period of analysis.

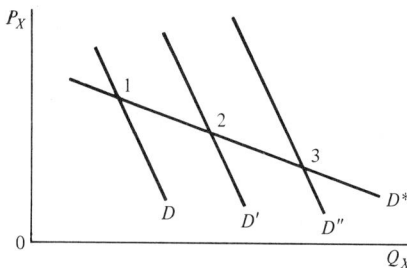

Figure 7-6

This is essential, for observations of different quantities sold at different prices over successive months may be quite misleading. For example, suppose in Figure 7-6 that combinations of price and quantities indicated at points 1, 2, and 3 were observed in January, February, and March. If we were not aware that rising incomes, or perhaps inflationary expectations, were shifting the demand curve to the right from D to D' to D'', we might jump to the conclusion that the statistically derived demand curve D^* is the true demand curve, which is not the case. Sophisticated statistical techniques have been developed for dealing with this so-called *identification problem* and are taught in courses in econometrics. It is enough to say here that the true demand curve is the focus of attention, since it is required for calculating the optimal price-output relation.

7-4 Price Elasticity of Demand

The concept of price elasticity of demand was devised by Alfred Marshall for measuring the responsiveness of quantity taken to small changes in price. Upon reflection it is clear to most observers that the slope of the demand curve is insufficient for measuring such responsiveness, since it can be changed simply by changing the units or scales on the axes. For example, if price and quantity of wheat are measured in terms of dollars and bushels, as in Figure 7-7a, the slope is $1/600$. But if pecks are used on the quantity axis, the slope diminishes to $1/2,400$. Similarly, if price was measured in cents rather than dollars, the slope would increase. Elasticity was used to overcome the scale difficulties inherent in the use of slope as a measure of the responsiveness of quantity taken to a small change in price.

Price elasticity of demand is defined as the percentage of change in quantity taken divided by the percentage of change in price, when the price change is small. Symbolically, for discrete changes in price,

$$E_D = \frac{\Delta Q/Q}{\Delta P/P} = \frac{\Delta Q}{\Delta P} \cdot \frac{P}{Q} \tag{2}$$

or for infinitely small changes in price, the corresponding derivative can be used:

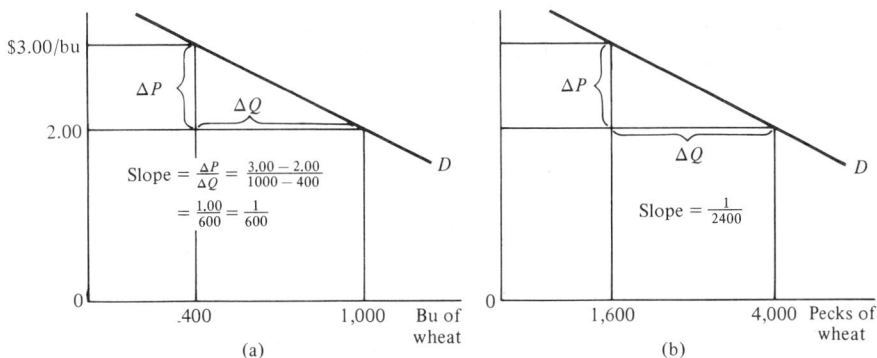

Figure 7-7

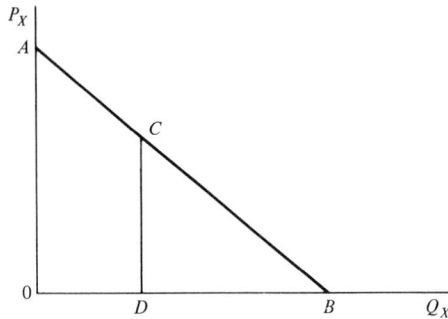

Figure 7-8

$$E_D = \lim_{\Delta P \to 0} \frac{\Delta Q}{\Delta P} \cdot \frac{P}{Q} = \frac{dQ}{dP} \cdot \frac{P}{Q} \tag{3}$$

The scale problem has been removed, since elasticity, the ratio of two percentages, is a pure number independent of the units selected for price and quantity. A minus sign is sometimes shown following the equal sign to render the elasticity coefficient positive. Other sources use it simply to indicate an inverse relation between price and quantity—a demand curve downward-sloping to the right.

Note that elasticity depends upon the reciprocal of the slope, $\Delta P/\Delta Q$ (or dP/dQ), so that when P and Q are constant the demand curve will be flatter for greater elasticities and steeper for lower elasticities. Where the slope is constant, however, elasticity is greater for points higher up the curve. For example, in Figure 7-8, assume that the demand curve is a straight line AB and we wish to obtain the price elasticity of demand at point C. This can be obtained by putting values into formula (2), recognizing that the reciprocal of the slope of a straight line, $\Delta Q/\Delta P$, equals the ratio of the horizontal and vertical components, say DB/CD, between any two points on the curve, say B and C:

$$E_D = \frac{\Delta Q}{\Delta P} \cdot \frac{P}{Q} = \frac{DB}{CD} \cdot \frac{CD}{OD} = \frac{DB}{OD} \tag{4}$$

Also, since a line CD drawn parallel to AO cuts a diagonal line AB proportionally (AC is to OD as CB is to DB), elasticity is also equal to CB/AC. This relation is useful in visually estimating elasticity for any point on a demand curve.

At the risk of redundancy, it is probably worth emphasizing that slope and elasticity are not the same. While it is true that a horizontal demand curve like that shown in Figure 7-9a has an elasticity approaching infinity and that a vertical demand curve like that shown in Figure 7-9b has zero elasticity, it is not correct to assume that the flatter the demand curve the more elastic it will be and that the steeper the demand curve the less elastic it will be. This point may be clarified by referring to Figure 7-10a, which shows two demand curves with a common x-intercept at B. From the discussion, it is evident that the elasticity of AB at point C is equal to DB/OD; but this is also true at C' for the demand curve EB. This indicates that all downward-sloping linear demand curves with a

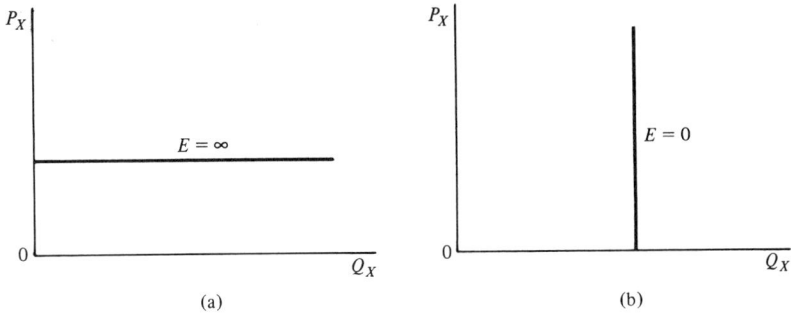

Figure 7-9

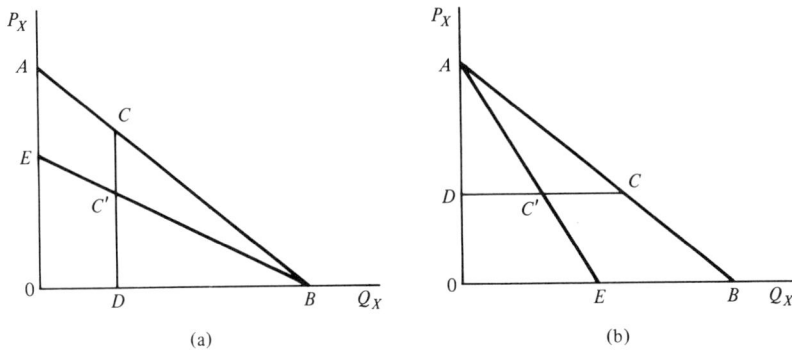

Figure 7-10

common x-intercept will have the same elasticity at any given quantity OD regardless of the slopes of the curves. Similarly, for all downward-sloping linear demand curves with a common vertical axis intercept as in Figure 7-10b elasticity at any given price OD is the same (at C and $C' = OD/DA$) regardless of the slopes of the curves.

For a demand curve that is not perfectly vertical or perfectly horizontal, it is not strictly correct to refer to the curves as being inelastic or elastic. It is correct to refer to demand at a point on the curve as being inelastic or elastic. Also, a nonlinear demand curve may have a constant elasticity over a range.

For any demand curve that is not a straight line, like D in Figure 7-11a, the elasticity at any point C can be obtained by drawing a line tangent to D at C and extending the tangent line to the axes at points A and B. Elasticity is then obtained by simply dividing the distance CB by AC. It is evident that where C bisects AB, $CB = AC$ and the elasticity coefficient is equal to unity. It follows that points along AB that lie above the midpoint (C) have elasticity greater than unity (ignoring the minus sign) and those below less than unity, as indicated in Figure

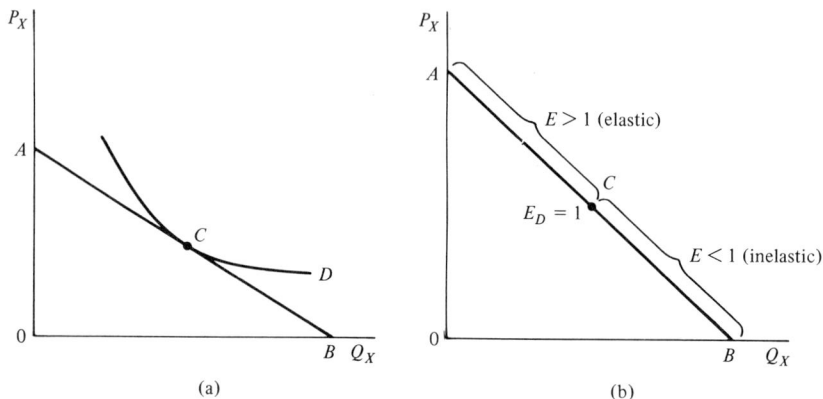

Figure 7-11

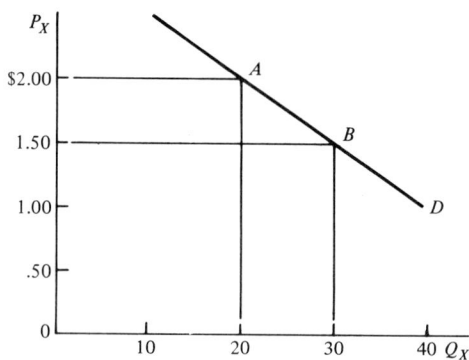

Figure 7-12

7-11b. Where the absolute value of the coefficient is greater than unity, demand is said to be elastic. Where it is less than unity, demand is inelastic. The demand curve as shown in Figure 7-12 may approach the vertical axis at a point where the consumer runs out of money to spend on X and will cut the horizontal axis at the consumer's point of satiety.

7-5   Difficulties in Applying the Elasticity Formula

In section 7-4 it was shown that price elasticity of demand can be obtained precisely for any single point on the demand curve. This gives an unambiguous measure of the responsiveness of quantity taken to an infinitely small change in price. A problem arises in attempting to apply the point elasticity formula to a real-world problem, because prices must be changed, if at all, by more than an infinitely small amount. An example can illustrate this point. Suppose we wish to compute the elasticity of demand between points A and B of Figure 7-12. If we apply the elasticity formula in moving from A to B, we obtain

$$E_D = \frac{\Delta Q}{\Delta P} \cdot \frac{P}{Q}$$

$$= \frac{30 - 20}{1.50 - 2.00} \cdot \frac{2.00}{20} = \frac{10}{-0.50} \cdot \frac{1}{10} = -2$$

But if we move from B to A, we obtain a different value for the elasticity coefficient:

$$E_D = \frac{20 - 30}{2.00 - 1.50} \cdot \frac{1.50}{30} = \frac{-10}{0.50} \cdot \frac{1}{20} = -1$$

To overcome this difficulty, *arc* elasticity of demand can be measured by picking an average price and quantity

$$(arc)E_D = \frac{\Delta Q}{\Delta P} \cdot \frac{(P_1 + P_2)/2}{(Q_1 + Q_2)/2} = \frac{\Delta Q}{\Delta P} \cdot \frac{P_1 + P_2}{Q_1 + Q_2}$$

$$= \frac{10}{-0.50} \cdot \frac{3.50}{50} = -1.4$$

or by always using the lower prices and quantities

$$(arc)E_D = \frac{\Delta Q}{\Delta P} \cdot \frac{P_B}{Q_A} = -\frac{10}{0.50} \cdot \frac{1.50}{20} = -1.5$$

While these two arc elasticity formulas give different answers, either would probably be better than blind application of the point elasticity formula. Also, most practical problems will not involve large relative changes in price. For smaller price changes, the concept of elasticity is more accurate and the difference in coefficients obtained by the two arc formulas will be smaller.

7-6 Significance of Price Elasticity of Demand

The business manager is very interested (whether consciously or not) in knowing the price elasticity of demand for a product, because it yields valuable information as to what pricing policy should be. If additions to revenue are greater than additions to costs, profits can be increased. Some businesses (especially the airline and the telephone industries) have been criticized for not recognizing that their profits actually could be increased if they would only lower their prices. The critics are assuming (or they know) that the elasticity coefficient is sufficiently great. Henry Ford may have recognized a high elasticity of demand for Model T automobiles when he priced his car low enough for the mass market.

If the coefficient is less than unity, the business manager can enhance his total revenue (or sales volume) by increasing price. This surely means that profits will be greater, because it costs less to produce fewer goods. The manager with power to set price can therefore profit from raising prices of goods and services that are necessities. Users of medical services want them when the need arises, regardless of the price, since health and life may depend upon obtaining treatment. They and their possessions are at the mercy of the physician, hospital, and drug firm.

If the coefficient is equal to unity, total revenue will remain unaffected by a change in price. In this case, an increase in price will probably increase profits.

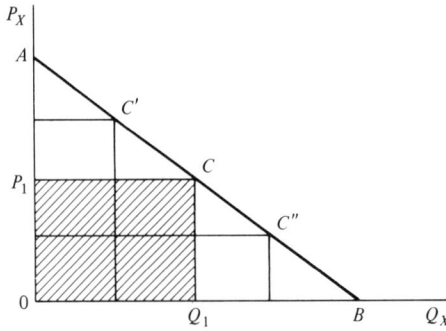

Figure 7-13

The effects of a price change on total revenue with various elasticity coefficients may be seen from Figure 7-13. If C is the midpoint of AB, the coefficient is equal to unity and total revenue is maximized where price is P_1 and output Q_1:

$$\text{Total revenue} = P \cdot Q = (OP_1)(OQ_1) \quad \text{(shaded area)}$$

For any other points C' or C'' on AB, elasticity is not equal to unity, and the rectangular area under the point is less than maximum. If this is not immediately evident, the reader should undertake to prove it true.

Figure 7-14 shows how total revenue (TR) varies as the price-quantity combinations change along the demand curve. Notice that total revenue reaches a maximum where the elasticity of the linear demand curve equals unity at point C.

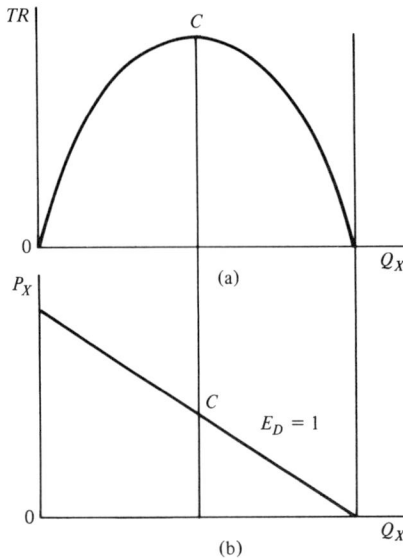

Figure 7-14

7-7   A Note on Empirical Studies of Price Elasticity of Demand

Studies of the elasticity of demand for individual products are routinely made in market research departments but are seldom made public for fear that such information could be used in some way against the firm by competitors, stock-holders, unions, consumer groups, and government bodies. Industry studies do sometimes appear in periodical literature, and these results are relevant here.

Julian L. Simon estimated the price elasticity of demand for cigarettes to be about −0.64 for the year after a price change [11]. This indicates that higher excise taxes can decrease cigarette smoking, but Simon cautions that this could cause people to smoke their cigarettes closer to the butt end, causing increasingly greater amounts of toxic materials to be released into their lungs. He also estimates the elasticity of per capita consumption with respect to advertising at +0.05; thus government abolition of cigarette advertising could reduce consumption of 5 percent each year. Simon also studied the price elasticity of liquor consumed in 28 states; −0.79 was the median [12].

In 1958 the Kefauver committee found that −1.2 and −1.5 was the range of the price elasticity of demand for automobiles and +2.5 to +3.9 was the range of the income elasticity [15]. It used this information to encourage the auto-mobile industry to lower its prices in its own interest as well as that of the pub-lic. See also the studies by Chow [4] and Suits [14].

A classic study of the demand for steel made by Theodore O. Yntema esti-mated the price elasticity to be −0.3 to −0.4. Accordingly, a 10 percent cut in price would increase the amount of steel sold by only 3 to 4 percent. The inelastic demand for steel indicates that revenues are increased by raising, rather than lowering, steel prices [18].

H. S. Houthakker reported estimates of demand elasticities for food, clothing, rent, durables, and miscellaneous commodities for 13 countries including the United States ([7]; see also [8]).

Questions and Problems

7-1. Referring to Figure 7-15, find the following:

      a. slope of the demand curve *AB*

      b. *y*-intercept of *AB*

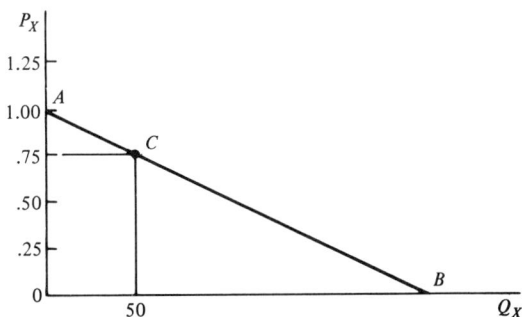

Figure 7-15

c. x-intercept of AB
d. equation for AB
e. elasticity at point C
f. elasticity at $Q_X = 100$
g. elasticity at $P_X = 0.25$
h. Q_X where elasticity of demand is $-\frac{1}{4}$
i. P_X where elasticity of demand is $-\frac{1}{4}$
j. Q_X where elasticity of demand is -4
k. P_X where elasticity of demand is -4

7-2. Which point, C or C', has the greater elasticity in Figure 7-16?

7-3. Prove that elasticity of the demand curves AB and DE at C and C', respectively, are equal in Figure 7-17.

7-4. What will be the shape of a demand curve that has unitary elasticity for all points on the curve?

7-5. For a demand curve given by the equation $Q = k/P^a$, or kP^{-a}, can you show by the use of calculus that price elasticity $E_D = -a$?

7-6. Comment on the following statement: "The price of a commodity cannot fall permanently, because if price fell, the demand for the good would increase, causing the price to rise again."

7-7. Prove that the relation between arc elasticity (E_D) and total revenue (R) for a linear demand curve is given by the equation $E_D = (\Delta R/Q\Delta P) - 1$.

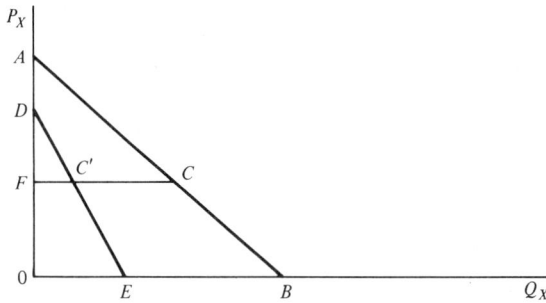

Figure 7-16

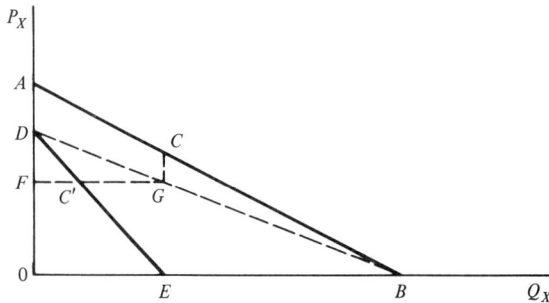

Figure 7-17

7-8. For the following nonlinear demand functions, determine the price elasticity of demand at $P_X = 4$:

a. $Q_X = 30 + 3P_X - 2P_X^2$

b. $Q_X = 100 - 4P_X + 10P_X^2 - 2P_X^3$

c. $Q_X = 50 - P_X^2$

References

1. Clark Lee Allen. *The Framework of Price Theory* (Belmont, Calif.: Wadsworth, 1967), ch. 2–4.

2. William J. Baumol. *Economic Theory and Operations Analysis.* 3d ed. (Englewood Cliffs, N.J.: Prentice-Hall, 1972), ch. 9.

3. Richard A. Bilas. *Microeconomic Theory: A Graphical Analysis.* 2d ed. (New York: McGraw-Hill, 1971), ch. 2.

4. Gregory C. Chow. *Demand for Automobiles in the United States* (Amsterdam: North-Holland Publishing Co., 1957). See also Harberger [5, pp. 149–178].

5. Arnold C. Harberger (ed.). *The Demand for Durable Goods* (Chicago: University of Chicago Press, 1960).

6. W. Warren Haynes, Thomas J. Coyne, and Dale K. Osborne. *Readings in Managerial Economics* (Dallas: Business Publications, 1973), pp. 59–123.

7. H. S. Houthakker. "New Evidence on Demand Elasticities." *Econometrica* 33 (April 1965): 277–288. Reprinted in Haynes, Coyne, and Osborne [6, pp. 74–84].

8. ——— and Lester D. Taylor. *Consumer Demand in the United States: Analyses and Projections.* 2d ed. (Cambridge, Mass.: Harvard University Press, 1970).

9. Richard H. Leftwich. *The Price System and Resource Allocation.* 5th ed. (Hinsdale, Ill.: Dryden Press, 1973), ch. 3.

10. Alfred Marshall. *Principles of Economics.* 8th ed. (London: Macmillan, 1920; reprinted 1962), III, ch. 1–5.

11. Julian L. Simon. "The Health Economics of Cigarette Consumption." *Journal of Human Resources* 3 (Winter 1968): 111–114. Adapted in Watson [16, pp. 19–21].

12. ———. "The Price Elasticity of Liquor in the U.S. and a Simple Method of Determination." *Econometrica* 34 (January 1966): 193–205. Reprinted in Haynes, Coyne, and Osborne [6, pp. 113–123].

13. George J. Stigler. *The Theory of Price.* 3d ed. (New York: Macmillan, 1966), ch. 3.

14. Daniel B. Suits. "The Demand for New Automobiles in the United States, 1929–1956." *Review of Economics and Statistics* 40 (August 1958): 273–280.

15. U.S. Congress, Senate, Subcommittee on Antitrust and Monopoly, Committee on the Judiciary. "Ch. 6: The Demand for Automobiles." *Administered Prices: Automobiles.* 85th Cong. 2d sess. 1 November 1958. Pp. 130–148. Adapted in Watson [16, pp. 26–36]. See also Edwin Mansfield. *Microeconomics— Selected Readings* (New York: W. W. Norton, 1971], pp. 73–81.

16. Donald S. Watson. *Price Theory and Its Uses.* 3d ed. (Boston: Houghton Mifflin, 1968), ch. 2–3.

17. ———. *Price Theory in Action.* 3d ed. (Boston: Houghton Mifflin, 1973), pp. 1–55.

18. Theodore O. Yntema. "The Price Elasticity of Demand for Steel." *Investigation of Concentration of Economic Power* (January 1940). Congressional hearings adapted in Watson [16, pp. 40–42].

8 Other Uses of the Elasticity Concept

This is the third of six chapters dealing with demand considerations that serve as constraints on the firm's goal-optimizing activities. The concept of elasticity is shown to have been extended from its use as price elasticity of demand to a number of other applications of interest to business researchers and managers. The principal of elasticity is noted as useful in sorting out the influence on the quantity demanded of changes in the prices of related products, in income levels, in advertising expenditures, and in price expectations. The price elasticity of supply is also introduced. These are all fundamental economic tools.

8-1 Cross-Elasticity of Demand

Most of the needs and desires of consumers in a free enterprise economy can be met to some degree by a variety of commodities and products. The quantities of each product actually purchased depend partly upon the relative prices of alternative products. If the relative price of a substitute product rises, other things being equal, consumers will purchase fewer units of the substitute product and more of the one whose price did not rise. Suppose, for example, that a new law requires the processors of hot dogs to install pollution control devices or to

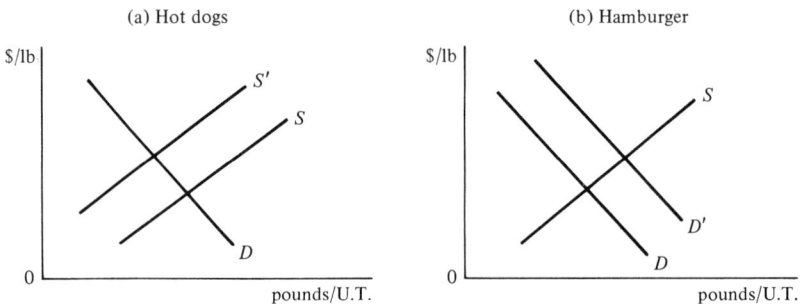

Figure 8-1

decrease the amount of fat content, and an upward shift in the production supply curve occurs, as in Figure 8-1a. The increased price of hot dogs may cause some consumers to shift to hamburger—a shift to the right in the demand curve for hamburger from D to D' in Figure 8-1b.

The extent of the responsiveness of the relative increase in the quantity of hamburger $\Delta Q_A/Q_A$ taken to a small relative increase in the price of hot dogs $\Delta P_B/P_B$ is reflected in the coefficient of cross-elasticity of demand as given by the formula

$$E_{A,\,B} = \frac{\Delta Q_A/Q_A}{\Delta P_B/P_B} = \frac{\Delta Q_A}{\Delta P_B} \cdot \frac{P_B}{Q_A} \tag{1}$$

or for continuous functions,

$$E_{A,\,B} = \lim_{\Delta P \to 0} \frac{\Delta Q_A}{\Delta P_B} \cdot \frac{P_B}{Q_A} = \frac{dQ_A}{dP_B} \cdot \frac{P_B}{Q_A} \tag{2}$$

For substitute products, such as hamburger and hot dogs, $E_{A,\,B}$ will be positive, because the prices and quantities are assumed to be positive and the changes in each are in the same direction. For example, if the price of hot dogs (P_B) rises, the quantity of hamburger (Q_A) also rises. Note that the slope of a curve plotting P_B and Q_A is also positive, as in Figure 8-2. The larger the positive coefficient of cross-elasticity, the greater the degree of substitutability between the products. Sometimes a high coefficient is said to indicate that the products, and the firms that produce them, are in the same industry. This inference is open to question, however, since there may be disagreement as to how high is "high," and the industry designation may not be truly relevant to the problem investigated. For example, one might wish to study the compact-car industry even though there might be a high cross-elasticity between compact cars and large cars.

If the coefficient of cross-elasticity is negative, the products are said to be complements. Continuing the example, it may be found that the increased demand for hamburger may cause an increased demand for hamburger buns, as illustrated in Figure 8-3. In this case, where an increase in the quantity of buns is caused by the greater demand for hamburger meat, a blind application of the cross-elasticity formula would yield a positive coefficient, indicating a substitute rather than a complementary relation. This would not be correct, because the "other things being equal" assumption would be violated, that is, other things,

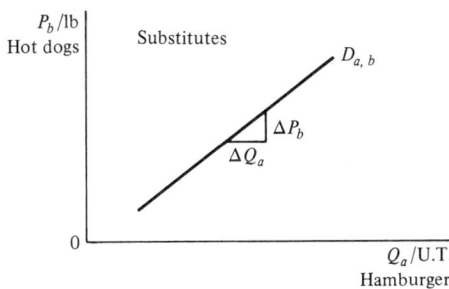

Figure 8-2

(a) Hamburger   (b) Hamburger buns

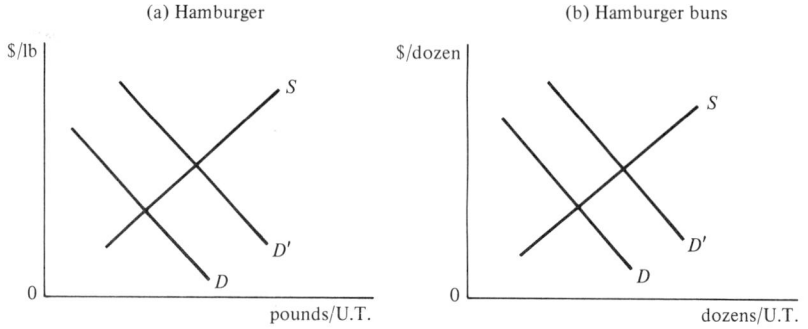

Figure 8-3

such as the location of the demand curve and level of income, are no longer the same when the demand curve shifts. A rise in price of hamburger, other things being equal, means that there must be a movement along the demand curve without a shift in the curve. When there is a movement along the curve, as there would be with a shift in the supply curve, the formula can be used to measure the responsiveness of the quantity of buns taken to a change in the price of hamburger. The slope of a curve obtained by plotting the price of hamburger (P_A) and the quantity buns (Q_C) must be negative, as shown in Figure 8-4.

In summary, it may be said that the significance of cross-elasticity is that the sign of the coefficient indicates whether the commodities are substitutes or complements. The larger the absolute value of the coefficient, the stronger is the relation. If the coefficient is zero, the commodities are said to be independent.

8-2 Partial Elasticities of Demand

If the quantity demanded of commodity A (hamburger) depends simultaneously upon the price of A and the price of some related commodity B (hot dogs), this may be indicated by the functional notation

$$Q_A = f(P_A, P_B)$$

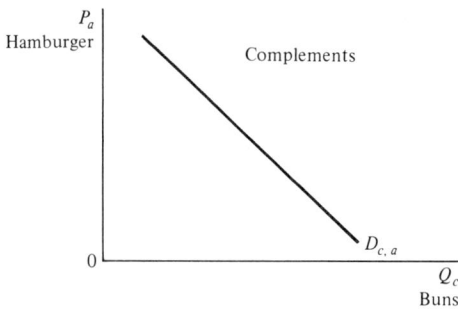

Figure 8-4

The partial elasticity of demand for A with respect to its price is defined, when the relation is continuous, as the limit of the ratio of the relative change in quantity demanded to the relative change in its price, as the change in price approaches zero and the price of B remains fixed:

$$E_{A,A} = \lim_{\Delta P_A \to 0} \frac{\Delta Q_A/Q_A}{\Delta P_A/P_A} = \frac{\partial Q_A}{\partial P_A} \cdot \frac{P_A}{Q_A} \qquad (3)$$

The partial cross-elasticity of demand for A with respect to P_B may be defined similarly by letting ΔP_B approach zero and holding P_A constant:

$$E_{A,B} = \lim_{\Delta P_B \to 0} \frac{\Delta Q_A/Q_A}{\Delta P_B/P_B} = \frac{\partial Q_A}{\partial P_B} \cdot \frac{P_B}{Q_A} \qquad (4)$$

Exercise. Suppose that the demand function for commodity A is known to be

$$Q_A = 40 - 4P_A + 2P_B$$

The partial elasticities of demand for A with respect to P_A and P_B, respectively, are

$$E_{A,A} = \frac{\partial Q_A}{\partial P_A} \cdot \frac{P_A}{Q_A} = (-4)\frac{P_A}{40 - 4P_A + 2P_B} = \frac{-4P_A}{40 - 4P_A + 2P_B} \quad \text{and}$$

$$E_{A,B} = \frac{\partial Q_A}{\partial P_B} \cdot \frac{P_B}{Q_A} = (2)\frac{P_B}{40 - 4P_A + 2P_B} = \frac{2P_B}{40 - 4P_A + 2P_B}$$

At $P_A = 8$ and $P_B = 4$,

$$E_{A,A} = \frac{-4(8)}{40 - 4(8) + 2(4)} = \frac{-32}{16} = -2 \quad \text{and}$$

$$E_{A,B} = \frac{2(4)}{40 - 4(8) + 2(4)} = \frac{8}{16} = \frac{1}{2}$$

8-3 Income Elasticity of Demand

As income rises, the demand for normal goods rises, because there is more money to spend. This, of course, assumes that the additional income is not held idle and that other factors remain unchanged, which is the "other things being equal" assumption. The responsiveness of the quantity demanded of a product to a change in income is given by the income elasticity of demand formula:

$$E_Y = \frac{\Delta Q/Q}{\Delta Y/Y} = \frac{\Delta Q}{\Delta Y} \cdot \frac{Y}{Q} \qquad (5)$$

Normal goods are defined as those for which E_Y is positive. If the coefficient has a value greater than unity, income elasticity is said to be high; if less than unity, it is said to be low. For inferior goods, those purchased in smaller amounts as income rises, E_Y is negative.

Business people should be aware of the sign and approximate value of the coefficient of income elasticity for their products, because the profitability of their businesses may depend upon the actions resulting from such knowledge. Knowing the value of E_Y will help in estimating the pattern of sales over the business cycle. The demand for luxury goods, those with high income elasticities, purchased in greater amounts as income rises, such as swimming pools, color television sets, expensive cars, and some vacation trips, will be brisk during periods of economic expansion and full employment. If good times are expected, producers of luxury goods who anticipate high sales will have more confidence in investing their money in equipment, labor, and inventories. However, if they expect a recession within the year, they will cut investment plans to avoid losses or may switch to producing a product considered to be an inexpensive necessity —those with low income elasticities, such as toothpicks, gum, salt, cigarettes, and basic foods. Obviously, a knowledge of trends in income levels and their impacts should also be of value to stock market investors and speculators. Income distribution changes and patterns are of similar importance, for instance, income related to demand in a country or region with lower levels or very unequal distributions.

8-4 Price Elasticity of Supply

Price elasticity of supply is similar to price elasticity of demand except that it pertains to the supply curve rather than to the demand curve:

$$E_S = \frac{\Delta Q/Q}{\Delta P/P} = \frac{\Delta Q}{\Delta P} \cdot \frac{P}{Q} \qquad (6)$$

The value of the coefficient will be positive for supply curves sloping upward to the right. The relation between price and quantity is said to be direct, since price and quantity are assumed to change in the same direction.

For linear supply curves with positive slopes passing through the origin, the coefficient will equal unity *at all points* on the curve. This may be proved by taking the first derivative of the linear curve $P = a + bQ$, where a is zero, and substituting dP/dQ for $\Delta P/\Delta Q$ in the elasticity formula:

$$\frac{dP}{dQ} = b$$

$$E_S = \frac{dQ}{dP} \cdot \frac{P}{Q} = \frac{1}{b} \cdot \frac{bQ}{Q} = 1$$

A geometric proof may also be given by referring to Figure 8-5a and substituting appropriate values into the elasticity formula. Elasticity of supply at any point B on the curve is given by

$$E_S = \frac{\Delta Q}{\Delta P} \cdot \frac{P}{Q} = \frac{OA}{AB} \cdot \frac{AB}{OA} = 1$$

If the linear supply curve were to intersect the quantity axis at some positive value, as in Figure 8-5b, elasticity would be less than unity. This follows directly from substitutions into the elasticity formula:

$$E_S = \frac{\Delta Q}{\Delta P} \cdot \frac{P}{Q} = \frac{CA}{AB} \cdot \frac{AB}{OA} = \frac{CA}{OA} < 1$$

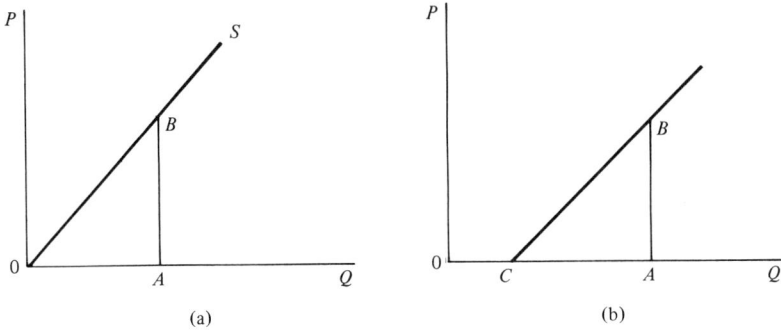

Figure 8-5

It may be shown similarly that the coefficient will be positive for all points on a linear supply curve intersecting the price axis above the origin.

If the supply curve is not linear, the coefficient could range between values of zero and infinity, as indicated in Figure 8-6. The elasticity at any point on the curved portion of the supply curve may be obtained by drawing a straight line tangent to the curve at that point. If the tangent line cuts the P axis, supply is elastic; if it cuts the Q axis, supply is inelastic. The value of the coefficient is given by CA/OA in Figure 8-5b.

8-5 Elasticity of Price Expectations

The quantity demanded of a product is sometimes predominantly influenced by people's price expectations, which may shift with political events, economic forecasts, stock market fluctuations, emotions of the times, and experience with past trends in prices. J. R. Hicks devised a concept in 1939 for relating price experience with expectations of future prices. His elasticity of price expectations is given by the formula

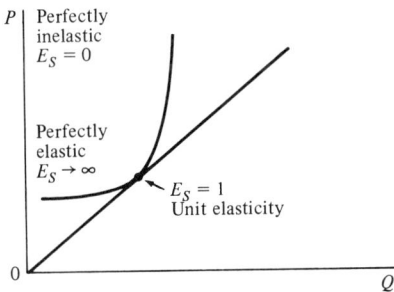

Figure 8-6

$$E_P = \frac{\Delta P_f/P_f}{\Delta P_c/P_c} = \frac{\Delta P_f}{\Delta P_c} \cdot \frac{P_c}{P_f} \tag{7}$$

where P_f refers to future prices and P_c to current prices.

The coefficient obtained indicates the extent to which buyers feel future prices will change as a result of a change in present prices. If the coefficient is greater than unity, buyers expect future prices will rise by a greater percentage than current prices and elasticity is said to be high. A coefficient of unity means that buyers expect future prices to change proportionally to present prices. A coefficient between unity and zero is considered low, since buyers expect future prices to change proportionally less than current prices. A zero coefficient indicates no influence of current prices on future prices. A negative coefficient indicates that buyers expect that a change in current prices will be followed by a change in prices in the opposite direction.

The business manager may conclude from the knowledge that elasticity of price expectations is greater than unity that a rise in current prices will provoke a shift in his demand curve to the right. This means he should be able to sell a greater quantity at the same or possibly higher prices, depending upon his competitors' reactions.

8-6   Advertising Elasticity of Sales

Managers often wish to know the responsiveness of their sales to additional expenditures on advertising. Such information permits them to estimate appropriate budget outlays and to schedule production, purchasing, and manpower needs. Advertising elasticity of sales is defined as the percent change in sales divided by the percent change in advertising:

$$E_A = \frac{\Delta S/S}{\Delta A/A} = \frac{\Delta S}{\Delta A} \cdot \frac{A}{S} \tag{8}$$

where both sales (S) and advertising (A) are measured in dollars.

The slope of a curve relating sales to advertising is described as the marginal sales productivity of an advertising dollar.

8-7   Elasticity of Substitution

The degree of substitution between commodities X and Y is sometimes measured by the concept elasticity of substitution, which is defined as

$$E_{sub} = \frac{\Delta \frac{X}{Y} \Big/ \frac{X}{Y}}{\Delta MRS/MRS} \tag{9}$$

where MRS, as will be explained in Chapter 9, is the marginal rate of substitution of X for Y—the slope of the consumer's indifference curve. The MRS indicates the change in units of Y consumed that will exactly offset a unit change in X, leaving the consumer at the same level of satisfaction.

In consumer equilibrium, which will also be explained in Chapter 9,

$$MRS = \frac{Y}{X} = \frac{P_X}{P_Y}$$

Substitution into equation (9) gives

$$E_{sub} = \frac{\Delta \frac{X}{Y} / \frac{X}{Y}}{\Delta \frac{P_X}{P_Y} / \frac{P_X}{P_Y}} \tag{10}$$

which is more easily employed in empirical work, since prices are objectively determined, while MRS is subjective. Where changes are finite, the arc measure must be used:

$$E_{sub} = \frac{\left[\left(\frac{X}{Y}\right)_2 - \left(\frac{X}{Y}\right)_1\right] / \left[\left(\frac{X}{Y}\right)_2 + \left(\frac{X}{Y}\right)_1\right]}{\left[\left(\frac{P_X}{P_Y}\right)_2 - \left(\frac{P_X}{P_Y}\right)_1\right] / \left[\left(\frac{P_X}{P_Y}\right)_2 + \left(\frac{P_X}{P_Y}\right)_1\right]} \tag{11}$$

An elasticity coefficient of zero would indicate that products are being used in fixed proportions regardless of changes in their relative prices. A negative coefficient would indicate that the relatively cheaper commodity is being substituted for the now relatively higher-priced commodity. If the negative coefficient is greater than (less than) unity, the substitution of X for Y responds more than (less than) proportionally to price changes. Knowledge of such relations may serve as a useful guide for determining pricing policies for the firm. This concept is also used in production theory in measuring the substitutability of two factors in the production of a given level of output.

8-8 Price, Income, and Substitution Elasticities

The relationship of price, income, and substitution elasticities for a single consumer faced with goods X and Y is given by the single equation

$$E_D = k_X E_Y + (1 - k_X)E_{sub} \tag{12}$$

where E_D is the price elasticity of demand, E_Y the income elasticity of demand, E_{sub} the elasticity of substitution, k_X the proportion of the consumer's income spent on X, and $(1 - k_X)$ the proportion of the consumer's income not spent on X [7]. It is clear from this equation that the quantity of X demanded in response to a change in its price depends upon the proportion of one's income spent on X as well as upon one's income and substitution elasticities. This appears reasonable, since, for example, if the price of X falls, a proportionately larger amount of income is available for spending now that X is cheaper—and some of the additional spending will go for X if it is not inferior. Also, more of X is substituted when possible for the relatively more expensive good Y. The term $k_X E_Y$ shows the income effect on price elasticity of demand, while $(1 - k_X)E_{sub}$ shows the substitution effect; these effects will be discussed more fully in Chapter 9.

Numerical illustrations may help to make the meaning of the formula clearer. If there are no close substitutes for X, E_{sub} will be close to zero and E_D will depend largely upon the amount spent on X and E_Y. If X is a necessity good that is relatively independent of income, E_Y will be close to zero and E_D will depend upon the amount not spent on X and the degree of substitutability of X for Y. Alternatively, if E_Y and E_{sub} are both equal to unity, E_D will also equal unity, because $k_X + (1 - k_X)$ is always unity and $k_X \cdot 1 + (1 - k_X) \cdot 1$ also equals unity. As a third case, suppose $E_Y = 3$, $E_{sub} = 2$ and the consumer spends $\frac{1}{10}$ of his income on X. Then

$$E_D = \tfrac{1}{10} \cdot 3 + \tfrac{9}{10} \cdot 2 = \tfrac{3}{10} + \tfrac{18}{10} = \tfrac{21}{10}$$

Formula (12) helps to explain why elasticity of demand for a good is high or low. The demand for a necessity like salt is known to be inelastic. This is attributable in part to the knowledge that the income effect of a fall in the price of salt is small because a small proportion of income is spent on salt. Also, the demand for salt is inelastic partly because of a low substitution effect, since there are no close substitutes for salt. The inelastic demand for medical services is attributable more to the lack of a substitute for them than to their cheapness (income effect is not relevant when life hangs in the balance or when pain is severe).

8-9   Use of Logarithms in Defining Elasticity

Since elasticity measures the percentage change in one variable with respect to the percentage change in another variable, it may also be described as the ratio of change in logarithms, for instance, sales elasticity of advertising is given by

$$E_A = \frac{\Delta \log S}{\Delta \log A} \tag{13}$$

If sales and advertising data are plotted on a double-log graph as in Figure 8-7, elasticity may be obtained by simply measuring the slope of a straight line fitted to the points. More on the topic of curve fitting will be said in Chapter 11.

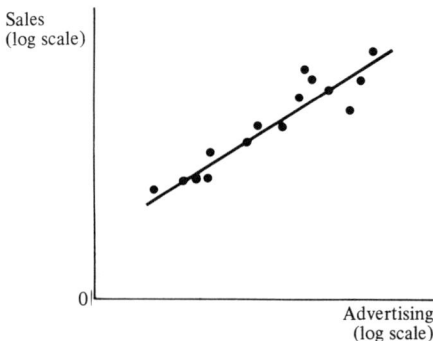

Figure 8-7

Questions and Problems

8-1. Write out the formulas for the following:
  a. cross-elasticity of demand
  b. own elasticity of demand
  c. income elasticity of demand
  d. price elasticity of supply
  e. elasticity of price expectations
  f. advertising elasticity of sales
  g. elasticity of substitution

8-2. Which of the elasticities in problem 8-1 is used to determine if goods are
  a. luxury goods
  b. complementary
  c. inferior
  d. price elastic
  e. substitutes
  f. susceptible to advertising
  g. influenced by expected price changes

8-3. Compute the partial elasticities of demand for A given the following demand function and prices:
  a. $Q_A = 10 - 3P_A + 6P_B; P_A = 2; P_B = 1.5$
  b. $Q_A = 58 - 0.6P_A + 3P_B; P_A = 15; P_B = 0.9$
  c. $Q_A = 20 - 0.4P_A P_B + 2P_B; P_A = 3; P_B = 2$
  d. $Q_A = 5 - 2P_A/P_B + 4P_B; P_A = 1; P_B = 0.8$

8-4. Compute the price elasticity of demand given an income elasticity of $+1.5$, elasticity of substitution of -1.3, and that 10 percent of the consumer's income is spent on the commodity.

8-5. Prove that all points on an upward-sloping linear supply curve intersecting the price axis above the origin will have an elasticity coefficient greater than unity.

8-6. In Figure 8-8 what is the value of the elasticity coefficient at point B? at B'?

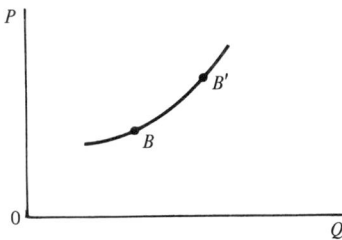

Figure 8-8

References

1. Clark Lee Allen. *Elementary Mathematics of Price Theory* (Belmont, Calif.: Wadsworth, 1962), ch. 11, 16, 17.

2. R. G. D. Allen. *Mathematical Analysis for Economists* (New York: Macmillan, 1964), pp. 251–257, 300, 340–345.
3. William J. Baumol. *Economic Theory and Operations Analysis*. 3d ed. (Englewood Cliffs, N.J.: Prentice-Hall, 1972), pp. 196–204.
4. Richard H. Leftwich. *The Price System and Resource Allocation*. 5th ed. (Hinsdale, Ill.: Dryden Press, 1973), pp. 38–51.
5. Alfred Marshall. *Principles of Economics*. 8th ed. (London: Macmillan, 1920; reprinted 1962), III, ch. 4.
6. Milton H. Spencer. *Managerial Economics*. 3d ed. (Homewood, Ill.: Richard D. Irwin, 1968), ch. 5.
7. Alfred W. Stonier and Douglas C. Hague. *A Textbook of Economic Theory* (London: Longmans, Green, 1953), ch. 3.
8. Donald S. Watson. *Price Theory and Its Uses*. 3d ed. (Boston: Houghton Mifflin, 1972), ch. 3; ch. 5, pp. 88–89; ch. 6.

9 Consumer Demand Theory—I

This chapter summarizes the fundamentals of indifference curve analysis as they are invariably covered in courses in intermediate microeconomic theory. The student as well as the business executive should be familiar with this body of knowledge for the insights it evokes and for the essential background it provides for understanding why certain assumptions are made in economic research studies of consumer behavior.

9-1 The Concept of the Indifference Curve[1]

Modern demand theory is based upon the concept that there can be alternative combinations of commodities to which the consumer will be indifferent. A graphic illustration of this, as it is typically drawn, is shown in Figure 9-1. The

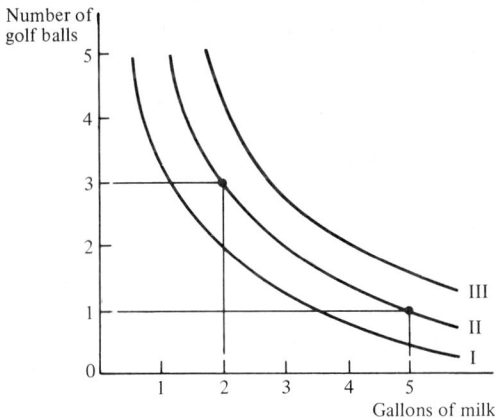

Figure 9-1

[1] Humorously called by Professor Kenneth Boulding the "Immaculate Conception of the Indifference Curve," emphasizing that tastes are simply given without adequate explanation of their origin [4, p. 2].

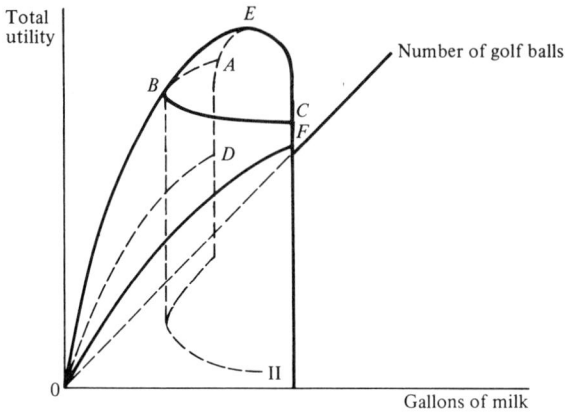

Figure 9-2

consumer presumably would be indifferent between having various combinations of golf balls and gallons of milk in the ratios of 5 to 1 and 2 to 3. Either
combination would therefore satisfy him equally well. When faced with having
to choose one or the other, he is able to select one combination without having
feelings of regret or elation. Regardless of which selection he makes, however,
he would prefer to have more of either or both; that is, he would want to be on
a higher indifference curve—one that lies above and to the right of II, say III.
Similarly, he would interpret his position as being worse off on lower indifference curves such as I. An indifference curve may thus be defined as the locus
of combinations of commodities from which the consumer derives the same level
of satisfaction. An indifference map is a collection of indifference curves having
different levels of satisfaction.

9-2   Indifference and Utility

Indifference curves may be considered projections onto the horizontal plane of
contour lines of equal utility, as shown in Figure 9-2. The equal-utility contour
ABC on the utility surface *ODEF* is projected onto the horizontal plane as curve
II, which is also curve II in Figure 9-1. It is clear from the surface drawn that
contours of higher (lower) utility will be farther from (closer to) the origin. Such
association of utility and indifference curves may be objectionable to some
theorists, since it may be thought to imply that utility is cardinally measurable—
a feat not yet accomplished. But as long as no numbers are used for utility,
cardinal measurability is not implied, and the three-dimensional graph is helpful
in visualizing the relation between the indifference curves and utility.

Economists have turned from cardinal utility to relative utility (indifference
analysis) primarily because less heroic assumptions are required.[2] The older

[2] Francis Y. Edgeworth's *Mathematical Psychics* (1881) is cited by George Stigler
[9, p. 46] as being the greatest work supporting the existence and use of cardinal utility.

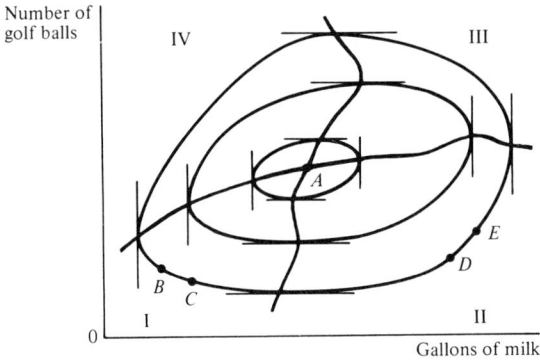

Figure 9-3

utility analysis assumed that utility could be measured cardinally (by numbers), whereas indifference analysis assumes preferences can be measured ordinally (by ranking). The literature of economics shows that all the fundamental theorems in consumer economics can be proved as adequately with the indifference approach as with cardinal-utility analysis.

9-3 Major Assumptions

Before it is demonstrated how indifference curves are used in analysis, it is essential that the major assumptions of this technique be made explicit.

9-3-1 *Nonsatiety*

It is typically assumed that the consumer values additional units of the commodities considered; that is, there is positive utility associated with additional amounts of the commodities. This is implicit in the statement that combinations indicated by curves above and to the right are preferred. This point may be secured by reference to Figure 9-3, showing four quadrants, or four possible relations between two commodities. Quadrant I is where both milk and golf balls have positive utility associated with additional units of either. In moving from point *B* to point *C*, the consumer would be willing to give up golf balls to get more milk, More of either or both will move the consumer to a higher indifference curve until the boundaries of other quadrants are touched and satiety is reached. In quadrant II additional units of milk have disutility to the consumer—milk has become a nuisance commodity [9, p. 50] or a discommodity [3, p. 61].[3] Perhaps he has no additional use for milk, no place to keep it without spoiling, and no opportunity to trade it for a profit. In this case, in order to get the consumer willingly to take more milk that he does not want, as in moving from *D* to *E*, he must be compensated with additional golf balls that

---

[3] A nuisance commodity can be dealt with by alternatively considering its desirable converse or complement. For example, garbage removal may be used in place of garbage, and leisure may be substituted for work [9, p. 50, fn. 2].

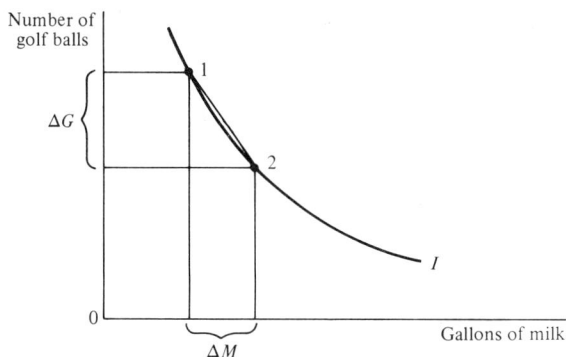

Number of golf balls

Gallons of milk

Figure 9-4

still have positive marginal utility. Quadrant IV is symmetrical to quadrant II in that the roles of milk and golf balls are reversed—milk now has positive marginal utility, while golf balls have negative. Quadrant III is where both have marginal disutilities. Point *A* signifies the blissful state of providing the combination of commodities that has maximum possible satisfaction. It should be clear now that the downward-sloping indifference curves in quadrant I generally imply the consumer has not yet attained satiety in the commodities considered. Those in quadrant III also have negative slopes but represent commodities with negative marginal utility.[4]

9-3-2 *Diminishing (marginal) rate of substitution*

According to this assumption, the more units of a commodity the consumer has, the less he values additional units of the commodity relative to others. Specifically, as he moves downward and to the right along an indifference curve, he is willing to give up fewer and fewer golf balls in exchange for additional units of milk. The amount of one commodity (golf balls) the consumer would forgo to obtain an additional unit of another (milk) while remaining on the same level of indifference is defined as the marginal rate of substitution (MRS_{MG}). The MRS is also the slope of the indifference curve. With reference to Figure 9-4, the MRS of milk for golf balls is equal to the change in number of golf balls (ΔG) given up to obtain an additional gallon of milk (ΔM)

$$MRS_{MG} = \frac{\Delta G}{\Delta M}$$

or for continuous functions,

$$MRS_{MG} = \frac{dG}{dM} \tag{1}$$

[4] An additional assumption is also being made here—that a consumer finding himself in quadrants II, III, or IV does not have a zero disposal cost nor disposal costs so low that he can reach a higher indifference curve by getting rid of one commodity [10, p. 1179].

Note that an indifference curve that is convex toward the origin has a slope that diminishes as one moves along the curve downward to the right—the characteristic indication of diminishing *MRS*.

The assumption of convexity implies that if a consumer is to remain on his indifference curve, his gains must be equally offset by losses; the *MRS* is therefore equal to the ratio of incremental utilities:

$$MRS_{MG} = \frac{\Delta G}{\Delta M} = \frac{\Delta U_M}{\Delta U_G} \tag{2}$$

As he moves from point 1 to 2 in Figure 9-4, the loss of utility from golf balls forgone (ΔU_G) must be equal to the gain of utility from the additional milk (ΔU_M). When ΔM is 1 gallon, incremental utility equals the marginal utility for milk, that is,

$$\Delta U_M = MU_M \cdot \Delta M = MU_M \cdot 1 = MU_M$$

It could be said for golf balls that

$$\Delta U_G = MU_G \cdot \Delta G$$

Only if ΔG were also unity—which probably would not be the case, since unity is only one of a multitude of possibilities—would incremental utility equal marginal utility for golf balls. For small increments, however, it is substantially correct to state (as do many microeconomic texts) that

$$MU_G \cdot \Delta G = MU_M \cdot \Delta M \quad \text{or}$$

$$MRS_{MG} = \frac{\Delta G}{\Delta M} = \frac{MU_M}{MU_G} \tag{3}$$

This discussion of convexity is based upon the assumptions of diminishing marginal utility and independence of utilities between the two commodities. It may be shown, however, that diminishing marginal utility is not required for convexity, and vice versa, if there is dependence, that is, if a decrease in commodity X increases the marginal utility of an amount of commodity Y. This can be shown mathematically. If utility is a continuous function of commodities X and Y,

$$U = f(X, Y) \tag{4}$$

$$f_X = \frac{\partial U}{\partial X} = MU_X$$

$$f_Y = \frac{\partial U}{\partial Y} = MU_Y \tag{5}$$

The equation for indifference curves is

$$U = \text{constant} \tag{6}$$

Total differentiation gives

$$dU = f_X \, dX + f_Y \, dY = 0 \quad \text{or}$$

$$MRS_{XY} = \frac{-dY}{dX} = \frac{f_X}{f_Y} \tag{7}$$

Diminishing MU requires

$$f_{XX} = \frac{\partial^2 U}{\partial X^2} < 0$$

$$f_{YY} = \frac{\partial^2 U}{\partial X^2} < 0$$

(8)

But the condition for convexity of indifference curves is

$$\frac{d(MRS_{XY})}{dX} < 0 \quad \text{or}$$

$$\frac{d(f_X/f_Y)}{dX} = \frac{f_Y f_{XX} + f_Y f_{XY}(dY/dX) - f_X f_{XY} - f_X f_{YY}(dY/dX)}{f_Y^2} < 0$$

(9)

Substituting $-(f_X/f_Y)$ for dY/dX,

$$\frac{d(f_X/f_Y)}{dX} = \frac{f_Y f_{XX} + f_Y f_{XY}[-(f_X/f_Y)] - f_X f_{XY} - f_X f_{YY}[-(f_X/f_Y)]}{f_Y^2} < 0$$

$$= \frac{f_Y f_{XX} - (f_X f_Y f_{XY})/f_Y - f_X f_{XY} + (f_X^2 f_{YY})/f_Y}{f_Y^2} < 0$$

$$= \frac{f_Y^2 f_{XX} - 2f_X f_Y f_{XY} + f_X^2 f_{YY}}{f_Y^3} < 0$$

(10)

It may be concluded that diminishing MU (satisfying equation (8)) does not imply convexity, because f_{XY} may be negative (making condition of equation (9) unfulfilled), and that convexity does not imply diminishing MU, because f_{XY} may be positive (fulfilling condition (9)) when MU is increasing (when f_{XX} and f_{YY} are positive) [9, p. 341].

Additional support for the assumption of convexity is provided by revealed preference theory (see section 10-1) based upon observable behavior. Indifference curves must be convex if the consumer buys some of each commodity, because linear or concave ones would generally imply that some commodities would not be purchased.

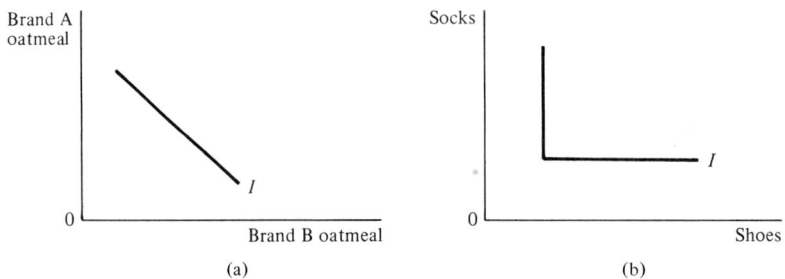

(a)   (b)

Figure 9-5

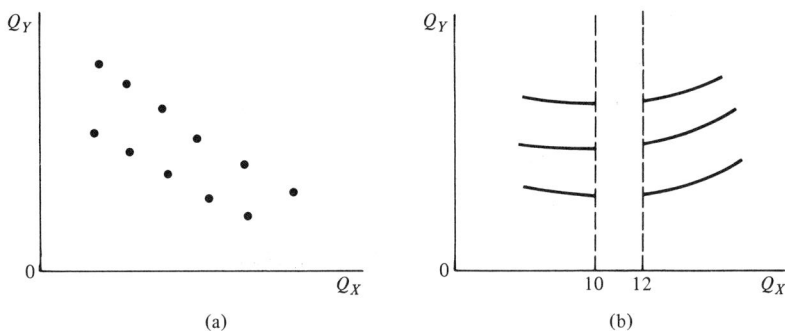

Figure 9-6

The degree of substitution between the commodities is indicated inversely by the degree of curvature of the indifference curve. If there is no curvature, as in the case of the downward-sloping linear indifference curve in Figure 9-5a, the commodities are described as perfect substitutes. An indifference curve for perfect complements would appear as in Figure 9-5b; this would be the limiting case of maximum curvature.

9-3-3 *Divisibility*

To be able to draw smooth and continuous indifference curves, we must assume that the commodities are infinitely divisible. This assumption is most nearly met by commodities in the form of grain, granules, pellets, or liquids, but not necessarily if they must be purchased by ton or carload units. Figure 9-6 shows two cases that do not satisfy the divisibility assumption: Figure 9-6a is simply a collection of discrete points; in Figure 9-6b units of X between 10 and 12 are not acceptable, possibly because of poisonous qualities or explosive oscillations in materials associated with these specific quantities. Perhaps a better example to explain the gap in Figure 9-6b would be where O_X is in thousands of square feet of warehouse space and requirements must exceed 12,000 square feet before a building addition or a new building is warranted. Also, continuity requires that the consumer be able to discriminate between combinations that differ by infinitesimal amounts.

9-3-4 *Transitivity*

This assumption is that the consumer is consistent in his choice between different combinations of commodities. If he is indifferent between combinations A and B and between B and C, then he must be indifferent between A and C. This consistency is essential for indifference analysis because if it did not hold, indifference curves could intersect, and it would be unclear whether a shift to another curve was an improvement or not. This is illustrated in Figure 9-7. The first two conditions are met if there is indifference between A and B, and between B and C. But the third condition fails; transitivity must be assumed in order to avoid intersecting indifference curves.

Number of
golf balls

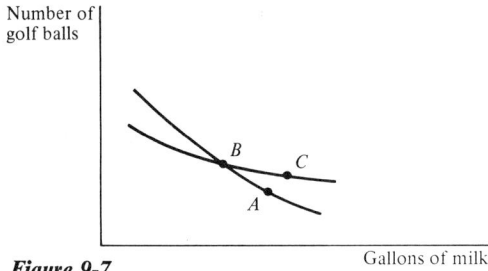

Gallons of milk

Figure 9-7

It should be noted that indifference analysis never specifies the amount by which one level of indifference is preferred over another, because this requires cardinality. The size of the gap between adjacent indifference curves has no significance, since the gap cannot be measured. Note that some indifference curves will pass through every point on the graph; it is therefore true that a graph contains an infinitely large number of indifference curves.

9-4 Optimal Allocation of Limited Funds

Indifference curves are useful in helping one to visualize fundamental principles of how the most value can be obtained by judicious spending of a consumer's budget. Suppose the consumer has a limited amount of income (R) which he or she will spend on some combination of two infinitely divisible commodities X and Y. This budget may be represented by the line AB in Figure 9-8a. Note that the maximum amounts of X or Y that could be purchased are indicated by the points where AB intersects the Q_X or Q_Y axis; such points are derived by dividing income (R) by the known prices of X and Y. It is true, of course, that if the entire budget is spent on either X or Y, then none will be left to spend on the other—which is the case at A and B. At any point P on AB, the consumer will buy OD of X and OC of Y. It is also true that

$$R = P_X Q_X + P_Y Q_Y \qquad (11)$$

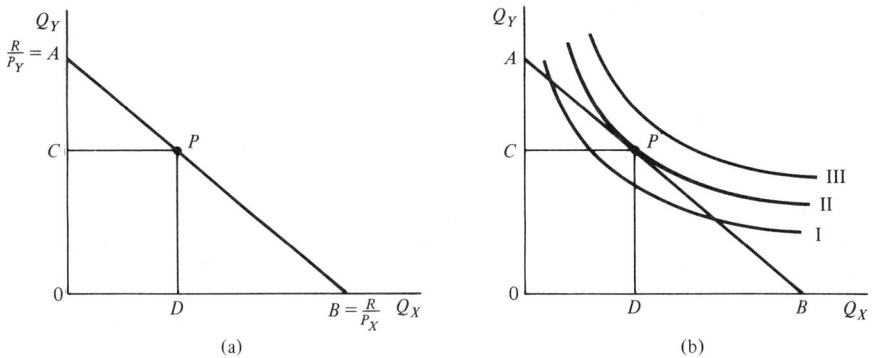

(a)   (b)

Figure 9-8

that is, the amount spent equals the sum of expenditures on both commodities. When equation (11) is solved for Q_Y, we obtain

$$Q_Y = \frac{R}{P_Y} - \frac{P_X}{P_Y} Q_X \tag{12}$$

which may be recognized as the equation of a straight line with a vertical intercept of R/P_Y and a slope of $-(R_X/P_Y)$, the budget line AB.

The optimal combination of X and Y to be purchased is obtained by superimposing the budget line on an indifference map, as shown in Figure 9-8b. The budget line AB is just barely touching the highest indifference curve attainable, II, at the tangency point P. Thus, OD of X and OC of Y will yield maximum satisfaction for a given outlay R. Point P necessarily provides maximum satisfaction, because all other points on AB are on lower indifference curves. At point P the slopes of the budget line and of indifference curve II are equal, that is,

$$\frac{OA}{OB} = \frac{\Delta Q_Y}{\Delta Q_X} = MRS_{XY} \tag{13}$$

From Figure 9-8a we know that $OA = R/P_Y$ and $OB = R/P_X$. Then

$$\frac{OA}{OB} = \frac{R/P_Y}{R/P_X} = \frac{P_X}{P_Y} \tag{14}$$

In summary, satisfaction obtained from a given expenditure on X and Y is given by the rule

$$MRS_{XY} = \frac{\Delta Q_Y}{\Delta Q_X} = \frac{P_X}{P_Y} \tag{15}$$

In words, the marginal rate of substitution of X for Y is equal to the ratio of the change in the quantity of Y to the change in the quantity of X, which is equal to the ratio of the price of X to the price of Y.

Equation (15) is said to express the condition of consumer equilibrium, because point P in Figure 9-8b indicates the combination of X and Y that provides maximum consumer satisfaction from the given expenditure—a point the consumer will move toward and, having reached it, will not voluntarily move away from. Since $MRS_{XY} = \dfrac{MU_X}{MU_Y}$ from equation (3) and $MRS_{XY} = P_X/P_Y$ from equation (15), it is also true that at equilibrium

$$\frac{MU_X}{MU_Y} = \frac{P_X}{P_Y} \quad \text{or}$$

$$\frac{MU_X}{P_X} = \frac{MU_Y}{P_Y} \tag{16}$$

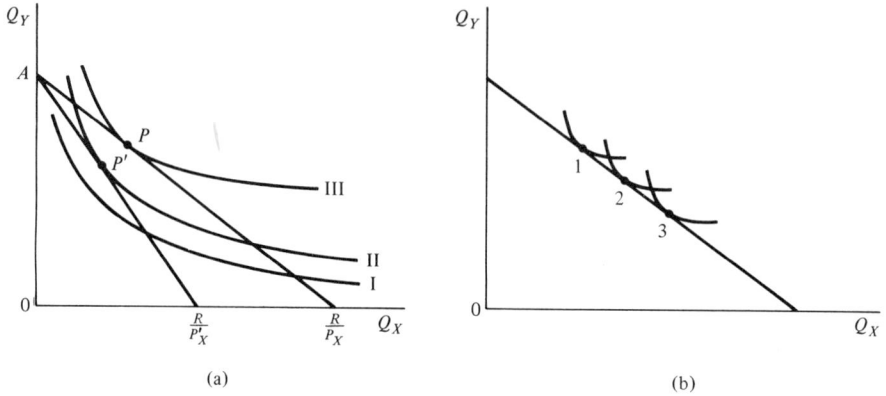

(a)   (b)

Figure 9-9

which is the law of equimarginal utilities from Chapter 6.[5] If this condition were violated, the consumer could increase her or his total utility by shifting dollars to the commodity providing greater marginal utility per dollar until equality of the ratios is restored.

Example. Suppose that the equilibrium condition given by equation (16) is disturbed by a rise in P_X from \$4 per unit to \$5 per unit and P_Y remains constant. Now, $MU_X/P_X < MU_Y/P_Y$. One dollar will now purchase only

[5] Incidentally, it is not necessary to assume diminishing marginal utility to obtain a negatively sloped demand curve if X and Y are interdependent. This may be demonstrated by use of the Lagrangian techniques. Consider the utility function

$$U = X^2 Y^2$$

Then

$$\frac{\partial U}{\partial X} = 2XY^2 = MU_X \quad \text{and} \quad \frac{\partial U}{\partial Y} = 2X^2 Y = MU_Y$$

As either or both X and Y increase, MU_X and MU_Y increase. From equation (16), equilibrium is where

$$\frac{MU_X}{P_X} = \frac{MU_Y}{P_Y}$$

$$\frac{2XY^2}{P_X} = \frac{2X^2 Y}{P_Y}$$

$$\frac{Y}{P_X} = \frac{X}{P_Y} \quad \text{or} \quad XP_X = YP_Y$$

Substituting into equation (11),

$$R = P_X X + P_Y Y$$

$$= 2P_X X \quad \text{or} \quad X = \frac{R}{2P_X}$$

which is a negatively sloped demand curve with a price elasticity of unity throughout.

$\frac{1}{5}$ unit of X rather than $\frac{1}{4}$, and utility per dollar spent on X is thereby reduced. To achieve maximum utility for her or his money, the consumer would divert dollars from X to Y until equality of the ratios is restored.

In this example the consumer's equilibrium position shifted from some point P in Figure 9-9a to some point P' by the rise in the price of X. The shape of the indifference curves, of course, will determine the precise location of the equilibrium point on the appropriate budget line. Any violation of the assumptions of the previous section will prevent equilibrium from occurring at a point of tangency. If the consumer were satiated with both commodities as in quadrant III of Figure 9-3, she or he would prefer lesser, rather than greater, quantities; if she or he were satiated with only one, there would be no diminishing MRS, indifference curves would be either straight or concave lines, and the highest indifference curve would intersect the budget line at one of the axes, causing the consumer to purchase only one commodity; the tangency point with a concave indifference curve would be a point of minimum satisfaction. Also, if the slope of the budget line is everywhere greater or less than the slopes of the indifference curves, corner solutions again exist. Furthermore, if the consumer were not consistent in choosing, a number of points of tangency might occur, as in Figure 9-9b.

9-5 Responses to Price and Income Changes

If the relative price of X changes, then the slope of the budget line will rotate. In Figure 9-10a a fall in the price of X while holding money income, prices of all other commodities, and tastes constant, will cause a counterclockwise rotation of the budget line. This is clear, because the intersection of the price line with the horizontal axis is progressively farther to the right when a given money income R is divided by increasingly lower prices. The vertical axis may be interpreted as the second commodity in a two-commodity model, as all commodities other than X, or as purchasing power in terms of dollars or some other exchangeable commodity also called income (R). It is assumed that all of the budget must

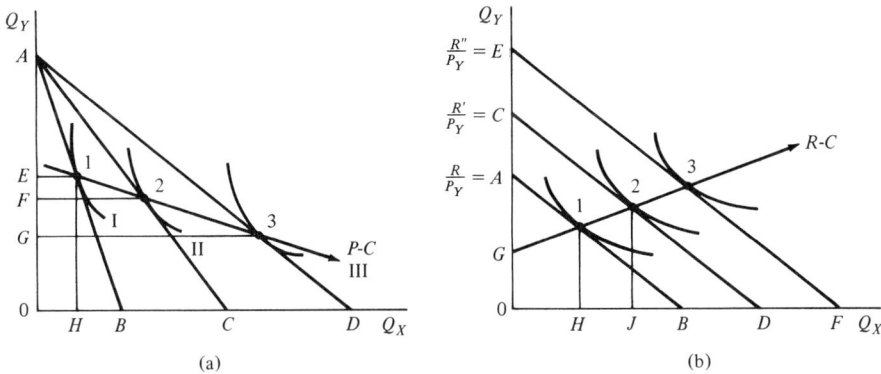

Figure 9-10

be spent in the given time period. At price P_X, AE of income is spent on OH units of X, as indicated by the tangency point of budget line AB with indifference curve I. At a lower price P'_X more income is spent on X (that is, $AF > AE$), as indicated at point 2. Point 3 is obtained similarly. By connecting tangency points 1, 2, and 3 by a continuous line, a price-consumption curve is derived that indicates the influence of changes in price on quantity purchased. When P-C slopes downward, price elasticity of demand is greater than 1—because the amount spent on X increases ($AE \rightarrow AF \rightarrow AG$) as price falls. If P-C is a straight horizontal line, elasticity is unitary throughout—the demand curve is a rectangular hyperbola. For an upward-sloping P-C curve, demand is inelastic.

If income changes while the relative prices of X and Y remain constant, the budget line will shift parallel to itself, as in Figure 9-10b. If the points of tangency with indifference curves are connected, an income consumption curve (R-C) is traced. If R-C is a straight upward-sloping line with a vertical intercept, income elasticity of demand is greater than 1; if a straight line passing through the origin, income elasticity is unitary; if a straight line with a positive horizontal intercept, income is inelastic; if sloping upward to the left, elasticity is negative. In Figure 9-10b it may be shown that income elasticity between points 1 and 2 equals OA/GA:

$$
\begin{aligned}
E_R &= \frac{\Delta Q_X}{Q_X} \div \frac{\Delta R}{R} = \frac{\Delta Q_X}{Q_X} \div \frac{\Delta Q_Y}{Q_Y} \\[2mm]
&= \frac{HJ}{OH} \div \frac{AC}{OA} = \frac{HJ}{OH} \cdot \frac{OA}{AC} \\[2mm]
&= \frac{1\text{-}2}{G\text{-}1} \cdot \frac{OA}{AC} = \frac{AC}{GA} \cdot \frac{OA}{AC} = \frac{OA}{GA}
\end{aligned}
\tag{17}
$$

9-6 Substitution and Income Effects of a Change in Commodity Price

When the price of a commodity declines (rises), real income is affected because the consumer can now purchase a greater (smaller) quantity of all goods than before. This effect, of course, will not be great for small changes in price nor for commodities that occupy a minor role in the consumer's budget. For example, if the price of hamburger falls from 60 to 50 cents per pound and the consumer normally purchases only 1 pound per week, his or her weekly income has risen 10 cents—a relatively insignificant amount compared to a salary of, say, $150 per week. For expensive commodities, and those purchased in large amounts, a 17 percent fall in price may be a quite important change in real income. Also, the "all others" on the vertical axis can be used to show the effect of inflation. In any case, the income effect of a price change may be found theoretically by shifting the budget line parallel to itself from a point of tangency on one in-difference curve to that on another, as in Figure 9-11a. As the price of X falls, the budget line rotates from AB to AC, and consumer equilibrium shifts from point 1 to point 3. The income effect may be obtained by shifting AC parallel to itself to DE, tangent to indifference curve I at point 2. This shift may be described as the money transfer necessary to maintain the consumer's welfare at its *original*

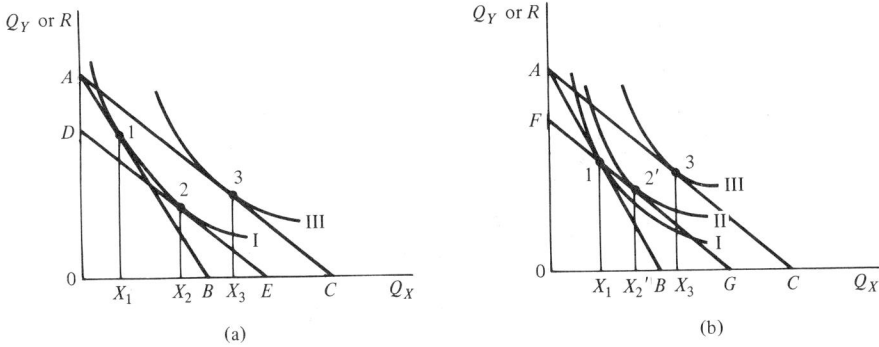

Figure 9-11

level. Either AD or EC is the cash equivalent of the subjective gain obtained from the price drop.[6] In terms of commodity X, the income effect is $X_2 X_3$ and the substitution effect—a movement along the indifference curve—is $X_1 X_2$. The total effect of the price change is $X_1 X_3$.

A problem arises in attempting to apply this Hicksian approach in a real-world situation, since the shape of the indifference curve I must be known to locate point 2. An alternative approach attributed to Eugen Slutsky may be used to obtain an approximate solution. By the Slutsky approach, shown in Figure 9-11b, budget line FG is drawn through point 1 rather than tangent to indifference curve I. This is the equivalent to taking away from the consumer an amount of cash (purchasing power of AF of Q_Y) that will permit him or her to buy the same combination (market basket) of X and Y as he or she could before P_X fell. It is clear, however, that the consumer will not actually buy combination 1, since he or she can purchase combination 2', which is on a higher indifference curve, II. In terms of X, the Slutsky income effect is $X_2' X_3$ and substitution effect is $X_1 X_2'$.

The distinction between the two approaches is revealed by the different location of point 2. According to Hicks, real income is said to be held constant, since the consumer is held to indifference curve I. By the Slutsky approach, however, *apparent* real income is said to be held constant, since the consumer retains the ability to purchase the same combination as before the price decrease. The Slutsky measure can be computed directly from observable market data (prices and quantities purchased under controlled experiments) whereas the Hicks measure cannot. For small changes in price, the total effect is less and the difference between points 2 and 2' is less significant. Perhaps it should be emphasized that the income effect will generally be much smaller than the substitution effect; the opposite impression may have been given from the figures that were

---

[6] This convention of transferring money to return the individual to the original level is not the only one that could be used. The consumer could have been given (or taxed) sufficient cash to permit him or her to rise (fall) to the level they would have obtained following some economic change. The money transfer in the former case is defined as the compensating variation (CV) and in the latter as the equivalent variation (EV). See Hicks [7] or Mishan [8, ch. 18].

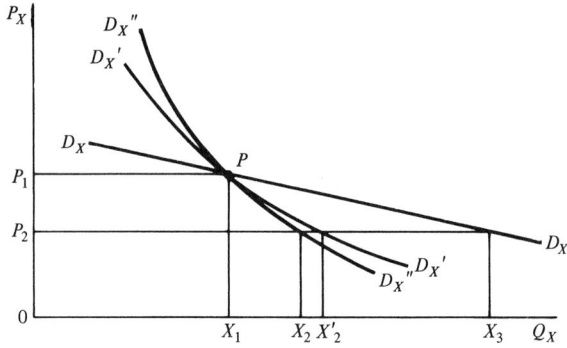

Figure 9-12

exaggerated to make the distinctions visually clear. Also, Figures 9-11a and 9-11b were drawn for normal (or superior) goods and would not apply for inferior goods. A special case of inferior goods, where the substitution effect is more than offset by a negative income effect, is called the *Giffen effect*; point 3 lies left of 1, since less of X is bought as the price of X falls.

A significant point of this section is that income effects may be important in some cases and must therefore be taken into account when attempting to derive a demand curve. In Figure 9-12 D_X shows an ordinary demand curve before adjustments are made for changes in real income stemming from the price changes; all other prices and money income are held constant for all points on the curve. Curve D'_X is the demand curve where real income is held constant by maintaining the consumer on the same indifference curve and making adjustments in money income. Curve D''_X is the demand curve where apparent real income is held constant and the consumer is always able to buy the original market basket of commodities.

For price decreases from P_1 to P_2 in Figure 9-12, it is clear that greater quantities can be purchased at higher incomes. The ordinary demand curve, D_X, along which real income changes, will be located to right of the other curves that incorporate real-income adjustments. Curve D'_X will be farther left from D_X than will D''_X because of more complete adjustments for changes in real income than for apparent real income. The consumer would prefer income adjustments under the Slutsky approach to those under the Hicks, since he or she can accordingly have more X and attain a higher level of indifference. Thus, X'_2 lies to the right of X_2. For price increases, however, for normal goods, the sequencing of the demand curves is reversed between D_X and the other two, since the reduction in real income that is allowed to vary with price along D_X will reduce the amount that can be purchased. The sequencing of D'_X and D''_X is also reversed, because the Slutsky compensation again permits the consumer to have more X and a higher level of indifference than does the Hicks compensation.[7]

---

[7] The student should draw the graphs for the various effects for both increases and decreases in prices and make comparisons to demonstrate the validity of Figure 9-12. See Richard A. Bilas [3, pp. 78–84].

9-7   The Slutsky Equation

The substitution and income effects of the previous section can be written as

$$\frac{\partial Q_X}{\partial P_X} = \left(\frac{\partial Q_X}{\partial P_X}\right)_{U=\text{constant}} - Q_X\left(\frac{\partial Q_X}{\partial R}\right)_{P=\text{constant}} \tag{18}$$

where total effect is the substitution effect (movement along indifference curve) minus the income effect (shift in budget line) and where Q_X and P_X are the quantity and price of commodity X whose price is permitted to change, and R is money income. Equation (18), known as the Slutsky equation, is not an exact representation of Figure 9-12 (and vice versa), because the rates of change in the equation correspond to discrete changes in the figures; otherwise, the relation holds true [9, p. 343].

The Slutsky equation may also be expressed in terms of determinants as

$$\frac{\partial Q_X}{\partial P_X} = \frac{D_{11}\lambda}{D} + \frac{Q_X D_{31}}{D} \tag{19}$$

and in terms of elasticities as

$$E_{Dx} = E_{DU=\text{constant}} - a_X E_R \tag{20}$$

The derivations and notations of these last two equations will be explained in Section 9-7-1.[8]

9-7-1   *Derivation of Equations (19) and (20)*

Assuming that a consumer derives utility from his consumption of two commodities Q_X and Q_Y, his utility function is

$$U = f(Q_X, Q_Y) \tag{21}$$

where Q_X and Q_Y are the quantities of Q_x and Q_y that he consumes. The function is assumed to be continuous and to have first- and second-order partial derivatives. The period of analysis is taken as so short that desire for variety and change in tastes cannot take place. U will be constant for a given level of utility, as on an indifference curve. The consumer's problem is viewed as one of maximizing his satisfaction by selecting the most desirable combination of Q_x and Q_y with his limited budget of

$$R = P_X Q_X + P_Y Q_Y \tag{22}$$

To maximize U subject to the budget constraint R, the Lagrangian function may be used:

$$U_\lambda + f(Q_X, Q_Y) + \lambda(R - P_X Q_X - P_Y Q_Y) \tag{23}$$

---

[8] This section is included for the benefit of students with an inclination for mathematics. It may be skipped by those who are not so inclined without loss in understanding of the material that follows.

To maximize U_λ, partial derivatives must be taken with respect to the three variables and set equal to zero:

$$\frac{\partial U_\lambda}{Q_X} = f_X - \lambda P_X = 0$$

$$\frac{\partial U_\lambda}{Q_Y} = f_Y - \lambda P_Y = 0 \qquad (24)$$

$$\frac{\partial U_\lambda}{\partial \lambda} = R - P_X Q_X - P_Y Q_Y = 0$$

where $f_X = \partial f(Q_X, Q_Y)/\partial Q_X$ and $f_Y = \partial f(Q_X, Q_Y)/\partial Q_Y$. By transferring P_X and P_Y to the right side of the first two equations of (24) and dividing the first by the second, the first-order condition—that the ratio of marginal utilities must equal the ratio of prices—is obtained:

$$\frac{f_X}{f_Y} = \frac{P_X}{P_Y} \qquad (25)$$

To determine the magnitude of the effect of price and income changes on the consumer's purchases, all the variables are allowed to vary simultaneously. This is accomplished by total differentiation of equations (24):[9]

$$f_{XX} dQ_X + f_{XY} dQ_Y - P_X d_\lambda = \lambda\, dP_X$$
$$f_{YX} dQ_X + f_{YY} dQ_Y - P_X d_\lambda = \lambda\, dP_Y \qquad (26)$$
$$-P_X dQ_X - P_Y dQ_Y \qquad\quad = dR + Q_X dP_X + Q_Y dP_Y$$

If we regard the terms on the right of the equal signs as constants, this system of equations may be solved for dQ_X, dQ_Y, and $d\lambda$ by the use of determinants. Solving equations (26) by Cramer's rule,

$$dQ_X = \frac{\lambda D_{11} dP_X + D_{21} dP_Y + D_{31}(-dY + Q_X dP_X + Q_Y dP_Y)}{D} \qquad (27)$$

$$dQ_Y = \frac{\lambda D_{12} dP_X + \lambda D_{22} dP_Y + D_{32}(-dY + Q_X dP_X + Q_Y dP_Y)}{D} \qquad (28)$$

where the bordered Hessian determinant,

$$D = \begin{vmatrix} f_{XX} & f_{XY} & -P_X \\ f_{YX} & f_{YY} & -P_Y \\ -P_X & -P_Y & 0 \end{vmatrix}$$

The cofactor of the element in the first row and the first column is denoted by D_{11}, the cofactor of the element in the first row and second column by D_{12}, and so on.

The second-order condition for a constrained maximum is that $D > 0$, or the same thing in different form

$$2 f_{XY} f_X f_Y - f_{XX} f_Y^2 - f_{YY} f_X^2 > 0$$

[9] See James M. Henderson [6, pp. 31–37].

By dividing both sides of (27) by dP_X and assuming that P_Y and R do not change, that is, $dP_Y = dR = 0$, we obtain the rate of change of purchases of Q_X with respect to changes in P_X:

$$\frac{\partial Q_X}{\partial P_X} = \frac{D_{11}\lambda}{D} + \frac{Q_X D_{31}}{D} \tag{29}$$

which is the same as equation (19). $D_{11}\lambda/D$ is the rate of change of consumer purchases of Q_X holding income and P_Y constant, and $-D_{31}/D$ is the rate of change with respect to income holding P_X and P_Y constant. Equation (29) thus becomes equation (18):

$$\frac{\partial Q_X}{\partial P_X} = \left(\frac{\partial Q_X}{\partial P_X}\right)_{U=\text{constant}} - Q_X\left(\frac{\partial Q_X}{\partial R}\right)_{P=\text{constant}}$$

Multiplying through by P_X/Q_X and the last term on the right by R/R,

$$\frac{\partial Q_X}{\partial P_X}\cdot\frac{P_X}{Q_X} = \left(\frac{\partial Q_X}{\partial P_X}\right)_{U=\text{constant}}\cdot\frac{P_X}{Q_X} - Q_X\frac{\partial Q_X}{\partial R}\cdot\frac{P_X}{Q_X}\cdot\frac{R}{R}$$

$$E_{D_X} = E_{D_{U=\text{constant}}} - \frac{Q_X P_X}{R}\cdot\frac{\partial Q_X}{\partial R}\cdot\frac{R}{Q_X}$$

$$= E_{D_{U=\text{constant}}} - a_X E_R \tag{30}$$

where E_{D_X} is the own (as opposed to cross-) price elasticity of demand for X, $E_{D_{U=\text{constant}}}$ is the own price elasticity of the compensated demand function (where the consumer is compensated by changes in his income to maintain his utility constant when the price of X changes), a_X is the proportion of the total spent on commodity X, and E_R is the income elasticity of demand. It follows that the ordinary demand curve will have an elasticity (E_{D_X}) greater than the compensated demand curve $E_{D_{U=\text{constant}}}$ if the income elasticity of demand (E_R) is positive. This is consistent with Figure 9-12.

Questions and Problems

9-1. If the diminishing slope of the indifference curve in the first quadrant of Figure 9-3 indicates a diminishing *MRS*, how can the curvatures in the other quadrants be explained?

9-2. Prove that income elasticity in Figure 9-13 is OA/AT for a rise in income of AC

9-3. Prove that price elasticity of demand is greater than unity when a price consumption curve slopes downward to the right.

9-4. Given a consumer's indifference map, level of money income, various prices at which commodity X is sold, and constant prices of all other commodities, construct the consumer's demand curve.

9-5. Given the utility function $U = Q_X^3 Q_Y^3$ and the budget equation $R = P_X Q_X + P_Y Q_Y$, demonstrate that the demand curve must be downward-sloping. Is the demand curve linear?

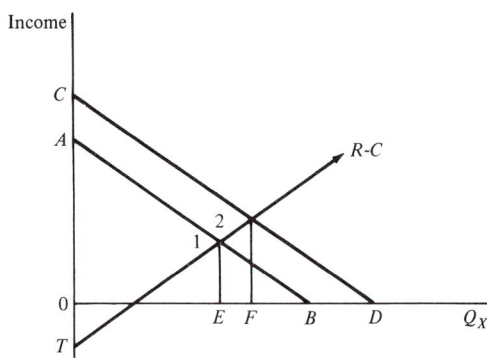

Figure 9-13

9-6. Derive the demand function for commodity X, given the following:

    a. $U = 5Q_X Q_Y$, $P_Y = \$a$, $R = \$50$

    b. $U = 5 \log Q_X + 2 \log Q_Y$, $P_Y = \$10$, $R = \$70$

    c. $U = Q_X + 2Q_X^2 + 3Q_Y - 4Q_Y^2 + 80$, $P_Y = \$2$, $R = \$30$

    d. $U = 3Q_X - 6Q_X^2 + 2Q_Y - Q_Y^2 = 60$, $P_Y = \$3$, $R = \$60$

9-7. Draw a diagram illustrating the Hicksian substitution and income effects for the following:

    a. a rise in the price of a normal good

    b. a rise in the price of an inferior good, but where the substitution effect dominates the negative income effect

    c. a fall in the price of a Giffen good (one where the negative income effect dominates the substitution effect)

References

1. Clark Lee Allen. *The Framework of Price Theory* (Belmont, Calif.: Wadsworth, 1967), ch. 6.
2. William J. Baumol. *Economic Theory and Operations Analysis.* 3d ed. (Englewood Cliffs, N.J.: Prentice-Hall, 1972), ch. 9.
3. Richard A. Bilas. *Microeconomic Theory: A Graphical Analysis.* 2d ed. (New York: McGraw-Hill, 1971), ch. 4.
4. Kenneth E. Boulding. "Economics as a Moral Science." *American Economic Review* 59 (March 1969): 1–12.
5. Milton Friedman. *Price Theory—A Provisional Text.* Rev. ed. (Chicago: Aldine, 1962), ch. 2.
6. James M. Henderson and Richard E. Quandt. *Microeconomic Theory: A Mathematical Approach.* 2d ed. (New York: McGraw-Hill, 1971), ch. 2.
7. J. R. Hicks. "The Four Consumers' Surpluses." *Review of Economic Studies* 11 (1944): 31–41.
8. E. J. Mishan. *Cost-Benefit Analysis* (London: Allen & Unwin, 1971), ch. 18.
9. George J. Stigler. *The Theory of Price.* 3d ed. (New York: Macmillan, 1966), ch. 4.
10. Oscar Von Morgenstern. "Thirteen Critical Points in Contemporary Economic Theory: An Interpretation." *Journal of Economic Literature* 10 (December 1972): 1163–1189.

10 Consumer Demand Theory—II

Building upon the fundamentals of indifference curve analysis presented in Chapter 9, this chapter shows first how it is theoretically possibly to construct an indifference curve and then how the concept has been employed to shed light upon the nature of income and excise taxes, subsidies, and indexes. The latter topics are important real-world problems often faced by business executives and government officials, and they have a profound influence on the lives of many people.

10-1 Revealed Preference

The technique of revealed preference, invented by Paul Samuelson, permits a researcher to construct an indifference curve for a consumer by simply observing his market behavior—that is, what he buys at different prices. It is assumed (1) that the consumer's taste and preference patterns remain constant during the experiment, (2) that his choice is consistent, (3) that his choice is transitive, and (4) that he can be induced to buy a given basket of commodities at some price and given amount of money to spend. The consistency assumption means that if he chooses combination A over B, he will not switch to B unless its relative price has fallen. An example of inconsistency would be where a Chrysler buyer shifts to a Ford because the price of the Ford was raised to $15,000; this change in preference might have resulted from snob appeal and judging quality by price. Transitivity, as explained in section 9-3-4, is satisfied if A is revealed to be preferred to B, and B is revealed preferred to C, then A is revealed preferred to C.

The idea of revealed preference theory is that a consumer will buy a particular basket of commodities because he likes it more than other baskets or thinks it is a better buy than other baskets. If he selects basket A rather than B and there is no other basket C of equal or lower price that he prefers to A, then A by its selection has been revealed preferred to B.

An indifference curve may be constructed in the following manner. The consumer is given an amount of money, R, as indicated by AB in Figure 10-1a and observed to spend it on the combination at point P, which is revealed preferred to every point on or below AB. Also, all points, such as C, that are above and

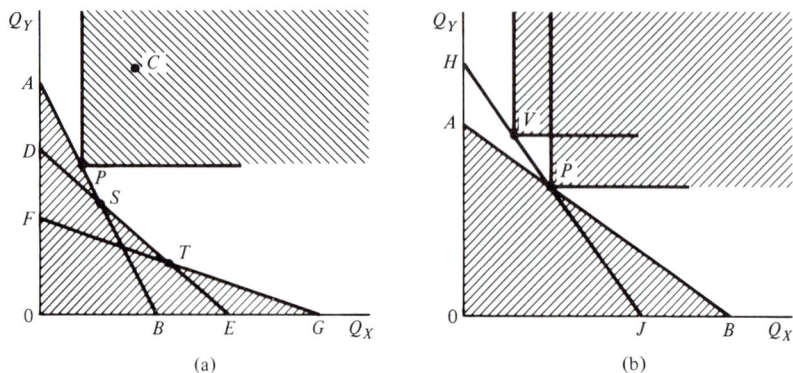

Figure 10-1

to the right of *P* are revealed preferred to *P*, because they are combinations having more of at least one commodity (and no less of the other) and require a larger expenditure. This indicates at once that near *P* the indifference curve must have a negative slope, since it does not penetrate the upper shaded region, and cannot be concave to the origin, since it does not penetrate the lower. The unshaded *zone of ignorance* can be chipped away by varying the amount of money the consumer has to spend and the prices he must pay until he is observed to purchase some combination *S* on his previous budget line *AB*. This is possible under assumption 4. Since *S* has been revealed inferior to *P* and preferred to all other points on or under *DE*, *P* is also preferred to all points in or on the triangle *BSE*. This is permitted under assumption 3. The zone of ignorance may be reduced by this area. The process may be repeated as many times as desired to eliminate other triangles above or below *P*. Also, one may take points on one of the added price lines, such as *T* on *DE*, and observe the relative prices as indicated by the line *FG* at which *T* is bought. Triangle *ETG* may also be removed, since it is revealed inferior to *T*, which is inferior to *S*, which is inferior to *P*. In this manner, the indifference curve is approached closer and closer from below.

The upper portion of the zone of ignorance may also be chipped away by drawing any new price line *HJ* through *P*, as in Figure 10-1b. The consumer is observed to purchase some combination *V* when his income and prices correspond to *HJ*. All the area above and to the right of *V* is revealed preferred to *P*, because *V* costs no more than *P* but was selected over *P*. This procedure can be repeated with additional price lines through *P*, yielding points similar to *V* and revealed preferred to *P*. The locus of all such points, shown as *Z* in Figure 10-2, is called an *offer curve*. It indicates the various combinations, such as *V*, that would be bought at different prices with an amount of money equal to that spent on combination *P*. All points on or above *Z* are revealed preferred to *P* and may be subtracted from the zone of ignorance. Furthermore, additional areas of ignorance may be eliminated by picking any point *V* on offer curve *Z* and observing the consumer's purchases with various price lines through *V* and thereby constructing the offer curve *Z* through *V*. The point on or above *Z'* is revealed preferred to *V*, which is preferred to *P*; therefore, the additional area may be taken

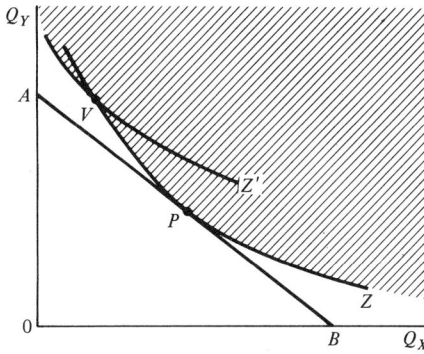

Figure 10-2

from the zone of ignorance. These procedures may be repeated until the region containing the indifference curve is narrowed as far as desired. It has been shown elsewhere by use of differential equations that the zone of ignorance can be reduced by the upper and lower chopping sequences to a single indifference curve.[1]

10-2   The Income Tax Versus the Excise Tax

One of the most popular applications of indifference curve analysis to real-world problems is in comparing the economic burdens of the excise tax and the income tax. Analysis is based upon the following assumptions:

  1. Two commodities X and Y (where Y could be all other commodities) are purchased by one individual.
  2. Initial real income is indicated by AB in Figure 10-3.
  3. There are given tastes and preferences (indifference map).
  4. Money income is held constant at OA during the period of analysis except when the income tax is levied.
  5. Prices of all commodities are held constant except for the impact of the excise tax on X.
  6. Taxpayer will not stop buying X because of its higher price due to the tax.

An excise tax imposed on commodity X will shift the budget line from AB to AC, because the unit tax effectively raises the price of that commodity. Consumer equilibrium shifts from point 1 to 2, from indifference curve III to I. The amount of the excise tax paid on quantity OH of Q_X is the vertical distance $F2$ in terms of the amount of Q_Y forgone. Alternatively, if an income tax were imposed that would yield an identical amount of tax revenue to the government, it could be represented by a parallel shift in the budget line from AB to DE through

[1] See H. S. Houthakker [5]. It is also shown in his article that the assumptions of revealed preference theory are not sufficient to deal with the problem of integrability. This has to do with attempting to derive a utility surface when more than two commodities are involved. The problem of integrability arises when differential equations describing indifference curves cannot be integrated to form any conceivable utility surface [1, p. 223, fn. 14].

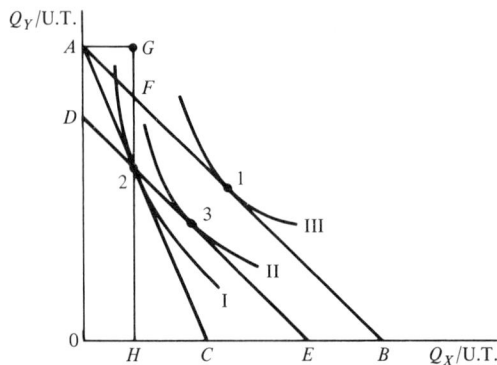

Figure 10-3

point 2 (as with the Slutsky income effect). The tax yield under either tax is $F2$ or AD, and amount spent on X is $G2$. The consumer prefers the income tax, because he can substitute combination 3 for 2 along budget line DE to reach the higher indifference curve II, while under the excise tax he must remain on I. This conclusion must follow as long as the indifference curves are downward-sloping, smooth, continuous, and convex to the origin. But there is no indication of the degree to which the income tax is preferred—only that it is preferred.

A common-sense explanation for this conclusion is that the excise tax distorts the existing price relations and forces the consumer to adjust around the higher price of one commodity. He cannot spread the decrease in his purchasing power as advantageously over many commodities as he could under the income tax.

This line of reasoning is generally accepted by economists as it applies to an individual consumer but not to the community as a whole. It cannot be con-cluded, according to Milton Friedman [3, pp. 59–67], that everyone would be better off under the income tax, because individuals are not all alike in their tastes, preferences, and resource holdings; nothing is said about the use of the tax proceeds to maintain employment, incomes, and prices, or to subsidize X or Y; and no account is taken of the initial conditions in which there may be monopolies or other market imperfections. Friedman would replace the "alleged proof of the superiority of an income tax" with "a 'correct' analysis." Assume a community of individuals identical in their tastes, preferences, and resource holdings (equal incomes and identical bundles of goods). The position of the community could now be represented by the position of any one individual. Available resources can be used to produce combinations of X and Y as indicated by a production possibility curve CD in Figure 10-4. At full employment of society's resources, each individual would be at point P, where there is equality of the rate of substitution in consumption (slope of III), purchase in the market (slope of price line AB), and production (slope of CD, also called marginal rate of technical transformation).

If the proceeds of a proportional income tax were impounded or returned to individuals as per capita subsidies, Figure 10-4a could represent the situations both before and after the tax for purposes of comparison with an excise tax.

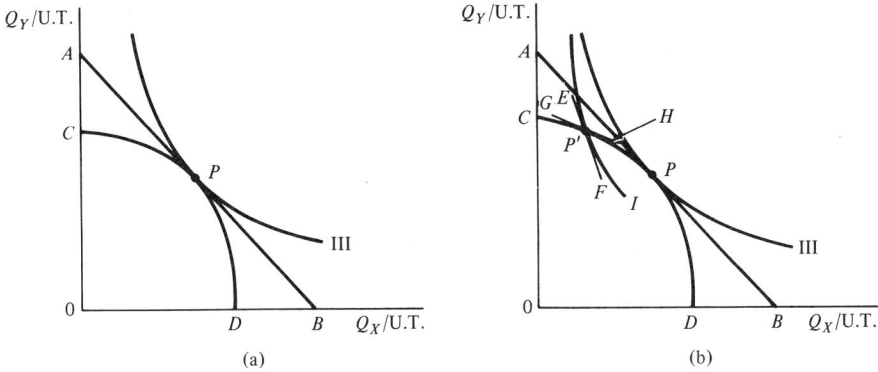

Figure 10-4

That is, the budget line *AB* would be shifted parallel toward the origin when the income tax is imposed and then restored to its original position when the subsidy is received.

Under the excise tax there will be a divergence between the price paid (including the tax) by the consumer (reflected in the slope of *EF*) and the price paid (excluding the tax) by the producer (slope of *GH*).[2] The price ratio cannot be calculated simply from the initial price ratio and the tax rate as in Figure 10-4a, because production considerations must be taken into account. The divergent wedge *GP′E* in Figure 10-4b is driven between consumers and producers, causing a shift from *P* to *P′*, thus placing consumers on a lower indifference curve.

If the initial position *P* were one of competitive equilibrium with no taxes or subsidies, it could be agreed that the excise tax is inferior to the income tax because of its reducing the consumer to a lower indifference curve. But if the initial position had been *P′*, because, say, of monopoly production of *X* having the same impact as the excise tax under competitive conditions, an excise tax on *Y*, offsetting some of the inefficient distribution of resources caused by the monopoly and causing a movement toward *P*, would improve the consumer's position. The initial conditions are therefore critical in determining the desirability of the excise tax.

10-3   Housing Versus Cash Subsidy

In a society where government subsidizes practically every sector of the economy, it is in the interest of business managers to be aware of a pertinent theorem proved by indifference analysis. The theorem is that the receivers of government aid prefer cash to subsidies in kind. Analysis is based upon the following assumptions:

---

[2] One might ask why the line *EF* cannot be extended to the vertical axis at point *A*. This would be true if the amount of the excise tax were diverted by the government to uses other than returning them to the consumer. When the consumer receives the rebate, his budget line shifts outward parallel to itself.

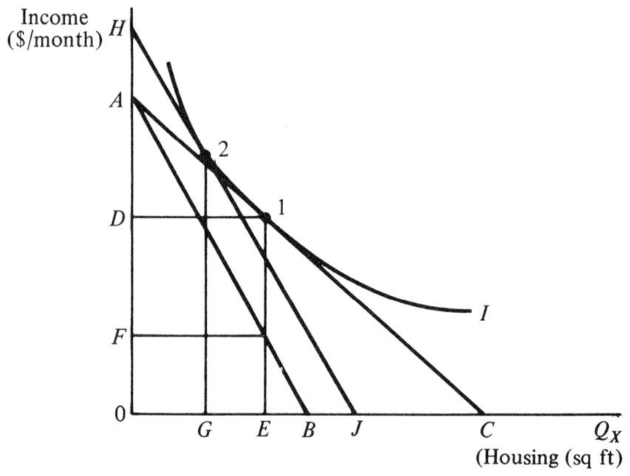

Figure 10-5

1. Two commodities X and Y, the latter of which may be considered in terms of money income, are both purchased by one consuming unit, say a family.

2. Initial real income is indicated by AB in Figure 10-5.

3. There are given tastes and preferences (indifference map).

4. Money and income are held constant at OA during the period of analysis except when the cash subsidy is given.

5. Prices of commodities are held constant except for the effective cost of housing being reduced because of subsidy in kind being given.

If, for example, X is housing measured in terms of square feet, a 50 percent housing subsidy would shift the family's budget line from AB to AC. The family would spend AD of its income on OE of housing, which without the subsidy would have cost AF. The difference between the old and new rent levels is DF, the cost of the subsidy to the government. The consumer would have been just as happy, to the extent that he is on the same indifference curve I, with a cash subsidy HA obtained by a parallel shift from AB to a point of tangency on I at point 2. Since $DF > HA$, the cost to the government is greater than the subjective gain to the family. This conclusion must follow as long as the indifference curves are downward sloping, continuous, smooth, and convex.

It does not follow, however, that subsidies in kind should not be given. Where considerations of etiquette, sentiment, and social costs or benefits enter, subsidies may be appropriate. Such would be the case where OE is judged by society to be the minimum standard of housing and where a large portion of a cash subsidy would be spent in a socially objectionable way (on alcohol or other drugs). Without a housing subsidy, the intended recipients of most such welfare payments, the disadvantaged children whom society wishes to shelter adequately, might not have a reasonable chance to become useful, productive citizens.

10-4 Cost-of-Living Indexes

Indifference curves indicate a constant level of living. Cost-of-living indexes may conceptually be said to measure the cost over time of remaining at the same point on one indifference curve. The index most commonly referred to as a measure of changes in the cost of living in the United States is the Consumer Price Index, which is an application of the Laspeyres index defined as

$$L = \frac{\sum P_2 Q_1}{\sum P_1 Q_1} \tag{1}$$

where Q_1 represents the quantities of items contained in a collection of commodities purchased by a representative consuming unit (a family) during some base period of time, say 1970; P_1 is the price of commodities purchased in the base period; and P_2 is the current, say 1978, price of Q_1 commodities, and the summation signs indicate addition over all commodities purchased.

For example, suppose in the base year the average family buys OX_1 units of commodity X and OY_1 of commodity Y. The family spends $R_1 = (OX_1)P_{X1} + (OY_1)P_{Y1}$, which is the budget line in Figure 10-6a tangent to indifference curve I at Q_1. Suppose in some following year prices change in unequal proportions (as indicated by a different slope in the budget line) and income rises (a shifting of the budget line to the right). The family could now purchase combination Q_2 on III for an amount $R_2 = (OX_2)P_{X2} + (OY_2)P_{Y2}$. To isolate the price effect, take away enough income so that the family could purchase the original basket Q_1—that is, draw a new budget line R_2' parallel to R_2 through Q_1. This shows the combinations of Q_X and Q_Y the family could buy in period 1 with period 2 prices, spending $R_2' = (OX_1)P_{X2} + (OY_1)P_{Y2}$. Thus, it can be said that the cost of living rose from period 1 to period 2 *at most* in the proportion

$$\frac{R_2'}{R_1} = \frac{(OX_1)P_{X2} + (OY_1)P_{Y2}}{(OX_1)P_{X1} + (OY_1)P_{Y1}} \tag{2}$$

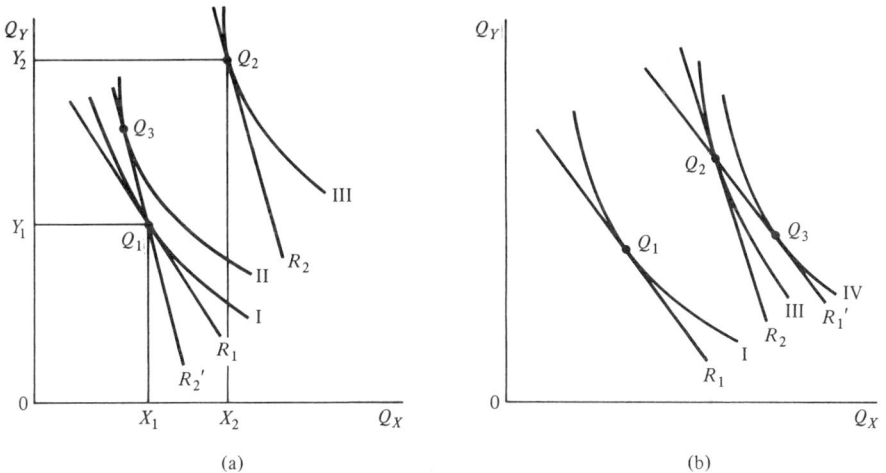

(a)   (b)

Figure 10-6

which is the same as equation (1). But the real cost of living did not rise by the full amount indicated by the price index, because the consumer can shift from Q_1 to Q_3 on a higher indifference curve II by substituting lower- for higher-priced goods. This means that an income level that would permit the family to purchase Q_1 with period 2 prices would give the family a purchasing power that would make it better off than in period 1. This means, in terms of satisfaction, that Q_1 is too high to be used as a true base in period 2—that is, if Q_1 in equation (1) is too high, L is too high. The L index is therefore said to overstate the change in the cost of living due to a rise in prices. To be entirely accurate, the price line R_2' should have been drawn tangent to I, not through Q_1.

While the Laspeyres index measures the change in the cost of living at the same level as in the base period, another index could be made to measure the change in the cost of living using quantities of some later base period. This could be illustrated in Figure 10-6b by shifting R_1 parallel to itself through Q_2. The cost of living in the base year relative to a later period may be said to have risen at most in the proportion

$$\frac{R_1'}{R_2} = \frac{(OX_2)P_{X1} + (OY_2)P_{Y1}}{(OX_2)P_{X2} + (OY_2)P_{Y2}} = \frac{\sum P_1 Q_2}{\sum P_2 Q_2} \tag{3}$$

If reckoned forward in time, the reciprocal must be used:

$$P = \frac{\sum P_2 Q_2}{\sum P_1 Q_2} \tag{4}$$

Where equation (3) gives the maximum relative change in cost of living from periods 2 to 1, equation (4) gives the minimum relative rise from periods 1 to 2. The latter formula has been labeled P to designate it as the Paasche index. It would yield the same change as the Laspeyres index if the same quantities were purchased in both years, but then the prices would not have changed. This, of course, assumes that tastes have not changed from one period to the next. No measure of change in cost of living can be made for a family switching from TV dinners in period 1 to health foods in period 2, because there was no quantity of health foods consumed in period 1. The family and its consumption habits are different in the two periods, and its satisfactions cannot be compared. An attempt might be made to find the money income that provides equal satisfaction in the two periods, but this is similar to postulating money incomes that provide equal real incomes for ranch hands, artists, ministers, and general managers—a task most economists would judge impossible to accomplish other than in pure theory.

Questions and Problems

10-1. Under what conditions is it correct to conclude that the income tax is superior to the excise tax?

10-2. In regard to the housing versus cash subsidy analysis, answer the following questions:

  a. What assumptions were made?

  b. Trace the step-by-step analysis.

   c. Is the analysis valid on strictly economic reasoning? Discuss.

   d. Is there some similarity between this analysis and that used in the income versus the excise tax analysis? Explain.

   e. Does the analysis apply also to other kinds of subsidies, such as to farmers, military suppliers, researchers, bankers, and educators?

10-3. a. In what way is the Laspeyres index upward-biased as a measure of change in the cost of living?

   b. Can you see any implications of this discussion that are of practical value to the business executive?

References

1. William J. Baumol. *Economic Theory and Operations Analysis*. 3d ed. (Englewood Cliffs, N.J.: Prentice-Hall, 1972), ch. 9.

2. Richard A. Bilas. *Microeconomic Theory: A Graphical Analysis*. 2d ed. (New York: McGraw-Hill, 1971), ch. 5.

3. Milton Friedman. *Price Theory—A Provisional Text*. Rev. ed. (Chicago: Aldine, 1962), ch. 3.

4. Malcolm Galatin. "A True Price Index When the Consumer Saves." *American Economic Review* (March 1973): 185–194.

5. H. S. Houthakker. "Revealed Preference and the Utility Function." *Economica* 17 (May 1950).

6. George J. Stigler. *The Theory of Price*. 3d ed. (New York: Macmillan, 1966), ch. 4.

11 Demand Estimation

The economic theory of demand summarized in previous chapters provides a framework for organizing knowledge and thought about the problem of estimating how many units of a product can be sold in a market at alternative prices [4, p. 36]. Attention is now directed toward the problems of quantifying demand for use by business managers in forecasting sales and profits, estimating the need for or impact of marketing effort, and adjusting production and inventory to predicted sales. Discussion is presented in the following order: sources of data, statistical estimation, pitfalls to consider, power functions, explanation of the error term, and regression analysis.

11-1 A Note to the Skeptic

Experienced teachers are aware that the demand functions of economic theory are viewed with skepticism by practical-minded executives and engineers. The abstraction and hypothetical assumptions create an air of unreality. It is true, for instance, that only one point on a demand curve can be observed directly with much confidence, because with the passage of time required to gather the data to plot another point, conditions may have changed so much that the whole curve has shifted. The assumption of "other things being equal" appears only to cover up rather than deal with the difficulties. Many students of human behavior are well aware, through their contacts with the public, that tastes and desires of consumers may not remain constant for very long. It is little wonder that the theorist's demand function is viewed with suspicion.

It may be of some consolation to students to learn that much of their skepticism is shared by the theorists and that a cautious or suspicious attitude is one of the most important lessons the professor wishes to teach. Skepticism, however, is not sufficient ground for rejecting a concept. The problem is that there is no acceptable substitute available for the demand function in probing the market-decision process. The concept may not completely satisfy anyone, but it is the best at hand and must be used until a better one is invented. A problem related to demand estimation is that of determining the appropriate number of sales people, for this, too, depends upon a knowledge of how consumer purchases vary with alternative sales-force sizes. This is the same sort of hypothetical information used in the demand function. There is just no way of getting around the problem. The techniques employed in this chapter should be understood with a knowledge of all their limitations, however, so that they will not be accepted with undue confidence and misapplied.

11-2   Sources of Data

Three different approaches have been used by practitioners to obtain data for use in demand determination: (1) direct interview, (2) market experiment, and (3) analysis of available statistics [1, pp. 235–238]. Which one is appropriate for a given situation depends upon the need for accuracy, the relative cost, the availability of resources, and the judgment of the researcher as to the appropriateness of the approach for the products considered.

11-2-1   *Direct interview*

The direct interview is sometimes tempting to use because of its simplicity and directness. *Why not* ask potential customers how much of a given product they would be willing to buy at several alternative prices? Who should know more about consumer behavior than consumers themselves? While this method may be useful in some cases, it is at best an unreliable procedure. Consumers are asked to predict their behavior in situations in which they may have had no experience. Their snap judgments in a hypothetical situation, even if honestly given, may be useful only for the moment. If confronted with a concrete situation —of "putting your money where your mouth is," so to speak—they may respond differently from even their own expectations. With the passage of time and additional thought, tastes and desires may change. Exposure to advertising may also make a difference.

Sometimes an indirect question may be more revealing than a direct one. If, for example, consumers were asked the difference in price between two competing products, it may be discovered they have no knowledge of the matter. Where knowledge of the existence of the product or its substitutes is slight, it might be inferred that a slightly higher price would have little influence on the quantity purchased—indicating an inelastic demand. Careful planning of interview questions should aid in discovering information through indirect questions that may remain hidden by use of direct ones.

Simulated market situations or "consumer clinics" have also been used in seeking information about consumer preferences. For example, selected groups of consumers are given small amounts of money to be spent on items on display. Posted prices of, say, six brands of toothpaste are varied from group to group, and the purchases are recorded. In this manner, information is obtained with which to estimate price and cross-elasticities.

In using these interview techniques, one must be careful not to attribute greater reliability to the information received than is warranted, keeping in mind the limitations of small samples, the artificiality of such experiments, and the problems of interpreting and quantifying answers to subtle and indirect questions.

11-2-2   *Direct market experiment*

Demand information is sometimes sought by first conducting direct market experiments. This involves selecting representative markets, say three cities with similar population mixes, income levels, and so on, typical of the national market, and charging different prices or varying the promotional schemes in each market. The percentage change in sales in response to a percentage change in price or advertising outlay may provide real answers to the hypothetical questions of the direct interview without the artificiality of the consumer clinic.

The researcher using direct experimentation must, however, be aware of the associated limitations:

1. Tinkering with price increases may cause a permanent loss of customers to competitive brands that might otherwise have never been tried.

2. The expenses of obtaining information in this way may run larger than estimated because of factors that cannot be controlled. Observations in different markets, even when conducted simultaneously, may be distorted by local events, variation in weather, and advertising programs of competitors. This may require beginning the experiment again in a different set of markets.

3. It may be prohibitively expensive and physically impossible to obtain a satisfactory number of observations. This may be true where a firm would like to know the different effects of variations in size and layout of periodical advertising. Different ads cannot be run in different cities in a national magazine that does not have regional editions. In such a case, management is faced with a choice of using or not using an advertisement that may have unfortunate results if consumers react adversely. Where uncertainty prevails and results are crucial, feedback may be gained by initial use of local periodicals and newspapers.

4. Direct experimentation is typically of brief duration because of its expense. Results obtained are therefore impact effects that may prove unreliable for longer periods. Resistance to increases in price may only be temporary, but this could not be determined from brief experiments. Consumers may need time to think about making changes in their consumption habits.

While the limitations of market experiments are great, such experiments have been profitably used as a check on results obtained from statistical studies and as a source of information on critical points with which the firm had has no past experience.

11-2-3   *Analysis of available statistics*

Perhaps the most attractive approach to determining a demand function for products that are not new is to extract information from accumulated records for previous years (time-series data) and/or comparisons of performance of different products in the market (cross-section data). As an example of the use of time-series data, assume the data of Table 11-1 have been accumulated.[1]   A

---

[1] A good first source to consult is the *Statistical Abstract of the United States*, because it collects data from many sources to which it gives reference. The U. S. Department of Agriculture publishes annually *Agricultural Statistics*, a useful general source of data relating to agricultural products. *Business Statistics*, published biannually by the U. S. Department of Commerce, is another general volume of statistical data available in college libraries.

Table 11-1

	1966	1967	1968	1969	1970	1971	1972	1973	1974
Units sold (millions)	1.80	2.90	5.02	4.83	4.11	4.60	2.08	2.22	4.05
Price (cents)	27	15	16	17	16	19	22	21	23

straight line or regression curve is fitted to the data if they appear to form a pattern.[2] If only a crude estimate is desired, a line may be drawn freehand or by use of a straightedge. Values of the vertical intercept and the slope of the line can then be read directly from the graph. A limitation of this sight-judgment method is that different people will draw different curves for the same data and it will not be possible to evaluate from sample data the precision of any prediction based on this judgment curve—that is, to set confidence limits on such predictions. A superior technique most commonly used is the method of least squares, whereby the sum of squared vertical distances from the data to the fitted line (such as *AB*, *CD*, and *EF* in Figure 11-1) is made as small as possible. It is clear that the smaller the deviations from the line, the better the line represents the dots. The deviations are squared, of course, because without squaring, the plusses and minuses will cancel out, leaving zero for the sum of deviations. The sum of squared deviations will never yield a small number unless the line closely fits the data. The line obtained by the method of least squares, which indicates the expected value of *P* for any given value of *Q*, is referred to as a

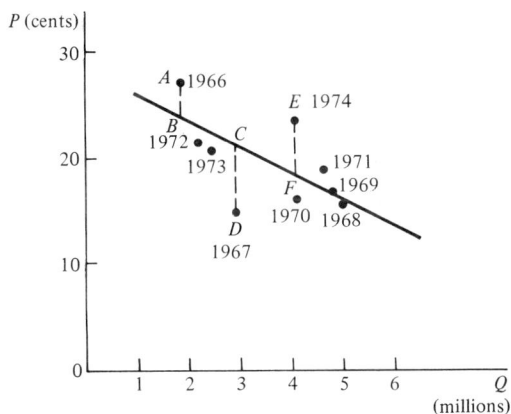

Figure 11-1

[2] Simple regression analysis assumes there is a cause and effect relation between one dependent variable plotted on the vertical axis and one independent variable plotted on the horizontal axis. In multiple regression analysis there are two or more independent variables.

regression curve. When the regression curve is a straight line, the equation for the curve will take the linear form

$$P = a + bQ \tag{1}$$

where P is taken as the dependent variable, Q as the independent variable, a as the vertical intercept and b as the slope of the curve. Parameters a and b are to be estimated from the observed data. The manner in which values for a and b are obtained is explained in section 11-3.

11-3   Estimating the Parameters by the Technique of Least Squares

Statistical derivation of equation (1) requires estimating the values of parameters a and b. This is done by solving simultaneously two normal equations for a and b. The first normal equation, I, is obtained by multiplying each term in equation (1) by the coefficient of a and summing like terms. The coefficient of a is, of course, 1. Normal equation I is simply the summation of like terms for each observation of P and Q:

$$P_1 = a + bQ_1$$
$$P_2 = a + bQ_2$$
$$\dots\dots\dots\dots$$
$$P_n = a + bQ_n$$

I. $$\sum P = Na + b \sum Q$$

Subscripts indicate successive observations. The coefficient of b is Q.

The second normal equation, II, is obtained by multiplying each term in equation (1) by Q and summing the equations for each observation of P and Q:[3]

$$P_1 Q_1 = aQ_1 + bQ_1^2$$
$$P_2 Q_2 = aQ_2 + bQ_2^2$$
$$\dots\dots\dots\dots\dots$$
$$P_n Q_n = aQ_n + bQ_n^2$$

II. $$\sum (PQ) = a \sum Q + b \sum Q^2$$

[3] Normal equations I and II may also be derived by the use of calculus. Given the equation of the straight line to be fitted to the dots as $P = a + bQ_t$ and observation P_t and Q_t for the different years $t = 1966, 1967, \dots, 1974$, proceed with the following steps:

1. Define a deviation from the line as

$$P_t - P = P_t - (a + bQ_t) = P_t - a - bQ_t$$

2. Square the deviation.

$$(P_t - P)^2 = P_t^2 + a^2 + b^2 Q_t^2 - 2aP_t - 2bP_t Q_t + 2abQ_t$$

3. Sum the squared deviations.

$$\Sigma(P_t - P)^2 = \Sigma P_t^2 + Na^2 + b^2 \Sigma Q_t^2 - 2a \Sigma P_t - 2b \Sigma P_t Q_t + 2ab \Sigma Q_t$$

4. To minimize the sum of the squared deviations, take partial derivatives with

The next step is to solve normal equations I and II for a, by solving I for b and putting its value into equation II:

$$b = \frac{\sum P - Na}{\sum Q}$$

I'. $$\sum (PQ) = a \sum Q + \frac{\sum P - Na}{\sum Q} \sum Q^2$$

Multiplying both sides by $\sum Q$ and grouping the coefficients of a,

$$\sum Q \sum (PQ) = a(\sum Q)^2 + (\sum P - Na) \sum Q^2$$
$$= a(\sum Q)^2 + \sum P \sum Q^2 - Na \sum Q^2$$
$$= a[(\sum Q)^2 - N \sum Q^2] + \sum P \sum Q^2$$
$$a = \frac{\sum Q \sum (PQ) - \sum P \sum Q^2}{(\sum Q)^2 - N \sum Q^2} \qquad (2)$$

Similarly, the expression for b may be found by solving equation I for a and putting its value into equation II:

$$a = \frac{\sum P - b \sum Q}{N}$$

II'. $$\sum (PQ) = \frac{\sum P - b \sum Q}{N} \sum Q + b \sum Q^2$$

Solving for b,

$$N \sum (PQ) = \sum P - b \left(\sum Q\right) \sum Q + bN \sum Q^2$$
$$= \sum P \sum Q - b(\sum Q)^2 + bN \sum Q^2$$
$$= \sum P \sum Q + b[N \sum Q^2 - (\sum Q)^2]$$
$$b = \frac{N \sum (PQ) - \sum P \sum Q}{N \sum Q^2 - (\sum Q)^2} \qquad (3)$$

---

respect to a and b and set the equations equal to zero.

$$\frac{\partial \sum (P_t - P)^2}{\partial a} = 2Na - 2 \sum P_t + 2b \sum Q_t = 0 \quad \text{or} \qquad (I)$$

$$\sum P_t = Na + b \sum Q_t$$

$$\frac{\partial \sum (P_t - P)^2}{\partial b} = 2b \sum Q_t^2 - 2 \sum P_t Q_t + 2a \sum Q_t = 0 \quad \text{or} \qquad (II)$$

$$\sum P_t Q_t = a \sum Q_t + b \sum Q_t^2$$

This procedure may be extended to deal with equations having more than two variables and to curvilinear equations.

**Table 11-2   Computations for Linear Regression Analysis of
Price-Quantity Data for Table 11-1**

(1) Date	(2) P	(3) Q	(4) PQ	(5) P^2	(6) Q^2
1966	27	1.80	48.60	729	3.24
1967	15	2.90	43.50	225	8.41
1968	16	5.02	80.32	256	25.20
1969	17	4.83	82.11	289	23.33
1970	16	4.11	65.76	256	16.89
1971	19	4.60	87.40	361	21.16
1972	22	2.08	45.76	484	4.33
1973	21	2.22	46.62	441	4.93
1974	23	4.05	93.15	529	16.40
Totals (9 years)	176	31.61	593.22	3,570	123.89

Equations (2) and (3) provide least-squares regression estimates of the parameters a and b in terms of observations of P and Q. In actual calculations, either (2) or (3) only need be used, since once the value of either a or b is determined, its value may be inserted into either I' or II' (whichever is appropriate) to determine the value of the other. A calculation of the parameters for the observations of Table 11-1 will serve to illustrate the procedure. First a new table like Table 11-2 is set up to facilitate the calculations. These numbers are then put into equation (3) to obtain the estimator b:

$$b = \frac{9(593.22) - (176)(31.61)}{9(123.89) - (31.61)^2}$$

$$= \frac{-224.38}{115.82}$$

$$= -1.937$$

From equation (2) the estimator a may be obtained:

$$a = \frac{(31.61)(593.22) - (176)(123.89)}{(31.61)^2 - 9(123.89)}$$

$$= \frac{-3,052.96}{-115.82} = 26.36$$

The same result could have been more easily obtained from equation II':

$$a = \frac{176 - (-1.937)(31.61)}{9} = \frac{176 + 61.23}{9}$$

$$= \frac{237.23}{9} = 26.36$$

11-4   Pitfalls in Estimating Demand

The investigator may encounter many pitfalls in attempting to derive the demand curve for a product. The purpose of this section is to summarize briefly some of the well-known problems that have been encountered.

11-4-1   *Omitting important variables*

Two-variable equations are tempting to use because of their inherent simplicity and small research cost, but the information they provide may be grossly misleading. Consider the data given in Table 11-3. The data fit perfectly the equation

$$Q = 4{,}210 - 7{,}500P + 0.02\,Y \tag{4}$$

and also the two-variable equation

$$Q = 8{,}104 - 15{,}000P \tag{5}$$

If the Y data were ignored, one would have the impression that the number of units sold (Q) could be increased by 150 for every cent drop in price. This, of course, is not correct, since only 75 units are attributable in equation (4) to a 1-cent price decrease, whereas the other 75 are attributable in part to rising income (Y) of the consumers in the relevant market.

Similarly, if analysis had begun with the relation between Q and Y to the exclusion of P, the two-variable equation would have been found to be

$$Q = 316 + 0.04\,Y \tag{6}$$

An inference that sales could be increased by 40 units for every \$1,000 increase in income would also be incorrect, since part of the change in Q is, according to equation (4), attributable to price changes not taken into account in equation (6).

Just as income proved to be an important variable in the preceding example, other variables may also be important, such as growth of population, new uses of the product, sales promotion effort, and actions taken by competitors. Changes in government regulations may also be critical in regard to tariffs, subsidies, expansion of trade markets with foreign countries, environmental control laws, and food and drug standards. Statisticians, however, are limited in the number of variables they can include in their analyses by the amount of marketing data

Table 11-3

Year	1970	1971	1972	1973
P	0.50	0.49	0.48	0.47
Q	604	754	904	1,054
Y	7,200	10,950	14,700	18,450

they have available to disentangle the influences of each variable. Time and expense frequently dictate the use of skimpy figures and few variables in spite of the hazards involved.

11-4-2   *Including mutually correlated variables*

Occasions may arise when some of the relevant variables are themselves significantly interrelated. For example, advertising effectiveness studies sometimes will include both income and years of education as independent variables. Income and education are closely related because wealthier families can afford more education and people with more education often qualify for jobs with higher incomes. The implications of these two variables for advertising effectiveness may, however, be quite different. A rise in income with no change in education may cause a person to be more susceptible to advertising, whereas more education with income constant could have the opposite effect. Which effect is most important may not be detectable from the model, because for the population in general, income and education increase simultaneously. One may be forced to conclude from the directions of variations of the statistics that when sales increased so did both income and education; there may be no unarbitrary way of ascribing sales increases to either income or education individually.

When there is an unacceptable degree of mutual correlation, as in the example just given, the mechanics of curve fitting may produce nonsensical results. This is because there is no common-sense way of imputing changes in sales to the separate influences of changes in income and education.

Since standard computational procedures may not be able to separate the influences of mutually correlated variables, the wisest procedure may be to omit all except one of such variables (see section 11-7-4).

11-4-3   *Simultaneous relations*

A more complete and sophisticated treatment of data than discussed in preceding sections is frequently discussed under the heading of simultaneous relations. Close correlation between variables may indicate a dependent relation. This means that another equation must be added to the single demand equation (recall section 11-4-1). Taking into account such relations may require a system of equations with interacting variables to be solved simultaneously. This is typical of economic relations; price determination by use of demand and supply equations is a standard example, as is IS-LM analysis in macroeconomics. The several simultaneous relations must be separated before the data are suitable for estimation by employing regression equations. Until this is done, any results obtained from manipulation will be riddled with distortions, the nature of which are briefly considered in section 11-4-4. Further discussion of this topic is deferred until after the necessary statistical terminology has been introduced (see section 11-7-4).

11-4-4   *The identification problem*

When the simultaneous relations cannot be unscrambled from the statistics, they are unidentifiable. Several mathematical tests (discussed later in the chapter) have

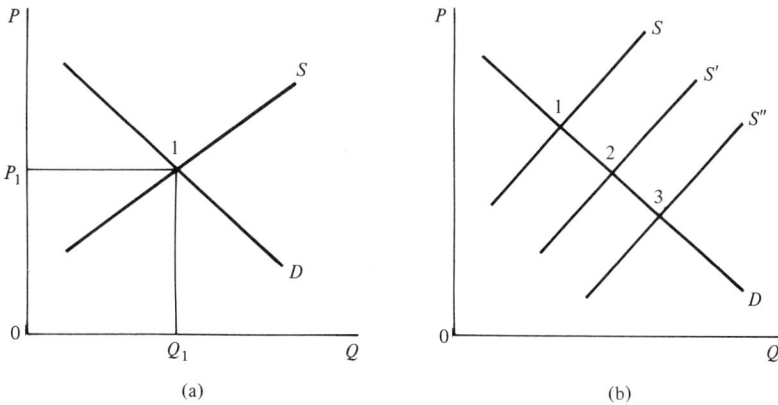

Figure 11-2

been devised to determine if an equation is identified. This important step should not be omitted by the researcher when attempting a statistical investigation. If the structural equation does not pass the tests, it is impossible to determine from the data if the hypothesized relation really exists, and other approaches must be used.

The identification problem is said to exist (1) when neither the demand or supply curves (or any other curves examined) are identified, because neither of them ever *shifted* through time; (2) when one curve is identified and the other is not, because only one curve shifted; and (3) when both curves can be identified, since both of the curves have shifted. The first case is the worst possible situation in terms of plotting a curve, since a single point of intersection cannot be a curve, as shown in Figure 11-2a where only point 1 is observable. Statistically, however, the situation is ideal, since the observed point 1 is also the predicted point as long as neither curve shifts.

The second case is useful for the statistician if the relation (curve) sought is not the one shifting; for example, if the supply curve only is shifting, the observed points 1, 2, 3 in Figure 11-2b will describe the demand curve. A problem sometimes remains, however, of ascertaining which of the curves shifted and which did not.

The third case, illustrated in Figure 11-3, presents the challenging problem of unscrambling the relations. A plotting of points 1, 2, 3 generates the curve *AB*, which remotely resembles neither the demand or supply relation. These points are simply intersections of the two curves as they shifted through time. Standard curve-fitting techniques will yield spurious results when blindly applied to cases involving such simultaneous relations. Information so obtained may be worse than no information at all, because it misrepresents the true relations.

An attempt could be made to untangle the curves by searching for variables that will account for the shift in one of the curves but not the other. Perhaps demand was influenced by changes in the consumer's disposable income (Y). If Y is judged to be the only significant variable influencing demand, then the

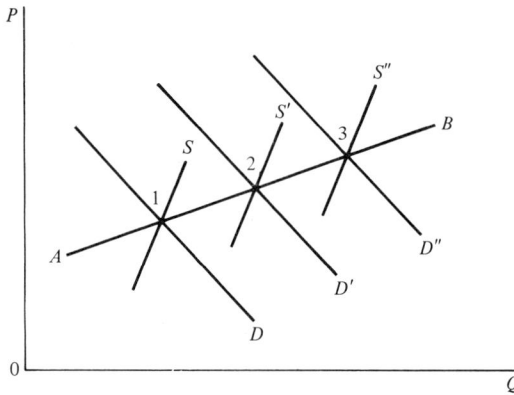

Figure 11-3

relation $Q = f(P)$ may be changed to $Q = f(P, Y)$. Once the effect of changes in Y have been removed from the demand curve, statistical curves D, D', and D'' of Figure 11-3 should coincide, producing a situation similar to that shown in Figure 11-2b. Thus, the demand curve is said to be identified. If there were periods in which income did not change, observations for those periods only (excluding observations where income changed) could be used to approximate the demand relation. Similarly, if the supply curve were to be identified, the significant variables causing only the supply curves to shift must be found and their influence removed from the statistics.

Sometimes in demand studies of agricultural products, perhaps the most common example of which is beef, population (along with income) is taken as an important variable determining demand. An attempt is made to remove the influence of population changes by dividing quantity sold by the relevant population and dividing price by disposable income per capita. Beef consumption per capita is then regressed on the price of beef divided by disposable income per capita, as shown in Figure 11-4 [10, p. 128]. This example is mentioned here as one way in which a simultaneous-equation model can be replaced by a single-equation model that reflects (indirectly, of course) the presence of another influence. Which model is most appropriate depends upon the case in hand and the questions to be answered.

Another example of the use of statistical techniques in business situations where simultaneous relations exist is that of deriving an advertising-demand curve. The number of units sold, Q, may be known to be affected by advertising, $Q = f(A)$. But the advertising budget may in turn be affected by a rule of thumb fixing advertising expenditure as a percentage of total revenues; with the assumption of constant prices, it may be hypothesized that $A = g(Q)$. Information provided by the first relation should aid the business person in determining optimal advertising expenditure, while that of the second, if gathered from industry records, should reveal something about the behavior patterns of competitors. The two relations are shown in Figure 11-5a. If the available data were

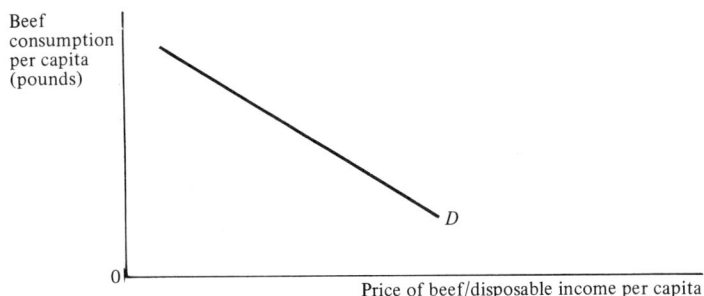

Figure 11-4

plotted and a curve such as AB in Figure 11-5b were fitted to the points, the curve might have no resemblance to either the budget or advertising demand curves. Shifts in the curves can be accounted for only by introducing variables known to shift only one of the curves and not the other. For instance, if the consumer's disposable income is known to affect sales from advertising but the firm's budget only indirectly through increased sales, the relation could be changed to

$$Q = f(A, Y) \tag{7}$$

Also, if the firm's advertising budget is thought to be influenced by dividends, where the budget is related to the amount left over from revenues after dividends and expenses have been paid, the advertising budget equation could be modified to

$$A = g(Q, D) \tag{8}$$

Thus, changes in Y would shift the advertising demand curve, while changes in D would shift the advertising budget curve.

11-5   Power Functions

Where quantity demanded is thought to be a function of two or more interrelated variables and constant elasticities can be assumed, power functions[4] can be of use, such as

$$Q = aP^b Y^c A^d \tag{9}$$

This popular multiplicative form has intuitive appeal, since it reflects the notion that the marginal effects of each of the independent variables depend upon the values of the other variables in the function. For example, the marginal impact of a change in price on the quantity demanded will be different for different levels of disposable income and advertising expenditures. The quantity of lobster

---

[4] Most of the rest of this chapter draws heavily on the exceptionally clear presentation of Eugene Brigham and James Pappas [2, ch. 5]. The same topics, however, are treated in greater detail in some of the other references listed at the end of this chapter.

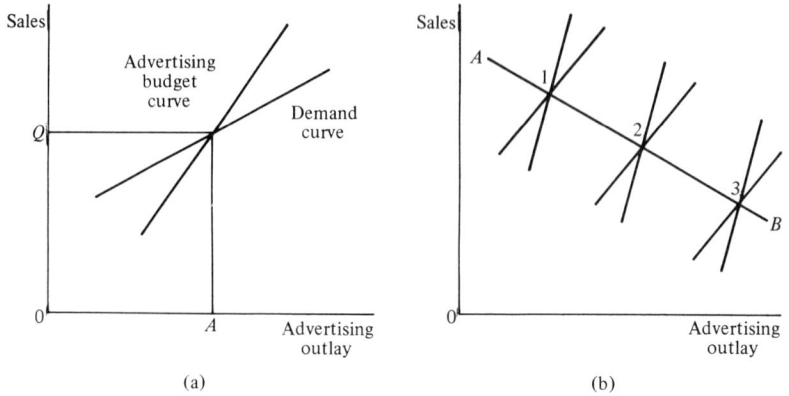

Figure 11-5

demanded may not increase at a constant rate as income rises; it may rise by large amounts at lower income levels, but taper off as income moves to higher levels. The multiplicative approach is generally thought to be more realistic than assuming, as with linear functions, that the marginal impact of the independent variables is constant.

The power function is also used for the technical reason that it can easily be transformed into a linear relation by use of logarithms. Equation (9) is the equivalent of

$$\log Q = \log a + b \log P + c \log Y + d \log A \tag{10}$$

This equation is said to be linear in logarithms and permits the use of least-squares regression analysis in estimating the parameters a, b, c, and d. Another useful feature is that b, c, and d are constant elasticity coefficients. This may be demonstrated by recalling that price elasticity is given by the formula

$$E_P = \frac{\partial Q}{\partial P} \cdot \frac{P}{Q} \tag{11}$$

The partial derivative of Q with respect to P from equation (9) is

$$\frac{\partial Q}{\partial P} = abP^{b-1} Y^c A^d \tag{12}$$

Substituting values from equations (12) and (9) into (11) gives

$$E_P = (abP^{b-1} Y^c A^d) \frac{P}{aP^b Y^c A^d}$$

$$= \left(\frac{abP^b Y^c A^d}{P} \right) \frac{P}{aP^b Y^c A^d}$$

$$= b$$

Income and advertising elasticities of demand can be similarly shown to be *c* and *d*, respectively. These elasticities are said to be constant elasticities, because their values are not functions of the values of the variables, for instance, *b* does not change with changes in *P*, *Q*, *Y*, or *A*.

The constant elasticity feature is useful where the applications are appropriate. For instance, if income elasticity is thought to be constant for window glass, then its demand can be expected to rise proportionately with income regardless of the level of income. If constant income elasticity does not hold, then the decision maker must judge which way, and how much, the elasticity will change as income moves from one range to another. Perhaps it should be stressed that constant elasticity does not imply the curve is linear; recall that elasticity changes from one point to another along a linear demand curve when arithmetic scales are used. Opportunities in which to employ constant elasticities may not be frequent, but where they do fit the data, analysis is greatly simplified.

11-6 Equations Containing an Error Term

In actual situations the data will seldom fit perfectly any single equation, as the hypothetical data did for equation (4). Other variables not taken into account may have influenced the data. Errors in reporting, collecting, and handling the data may have crept in. The effects of all omitted determinants and errors (stochastic or random elements) are summarized in an error term, or residual μ, added to the equation:

$$A = a + bP + cY + \mu \tag{13}$$

The error term measures the vertical deviation of each data point from the fitted regression line.

11-6-1 *Four conditions the residuals should meet for full validity of the least-squares method*

The residuals must meet the conditions of (1) being randomly distributed, (2) following a normal distribution, (3) having an expected value of zero, and (4) having a constant variance. If any one of these conditions is not met, the validity of the least-squares regression technique is reduced. The residuals obtained as part of the computer printouts may be put in graphical form to aid in detecting violations of the four conditions.

Random distribution may be checked by plotting the time-series residuals in sequence as shown in Figure 11-6. Ideally, they should be randomly distributed within a horizontal band centered on the horizontal axis as in Figure 11-6a. If the sequenced plots conform to a systematic pattern as in Figure 11-6b, the residuals are dependent on each other. This problem of serial correlation (called autocorrelation in time-series regression) is often present and is sometimes difficult to determine by simple observation of the plotted residuals. In such cases, the Durbin-Watson statistic is calculated as a measure of the problem, a value

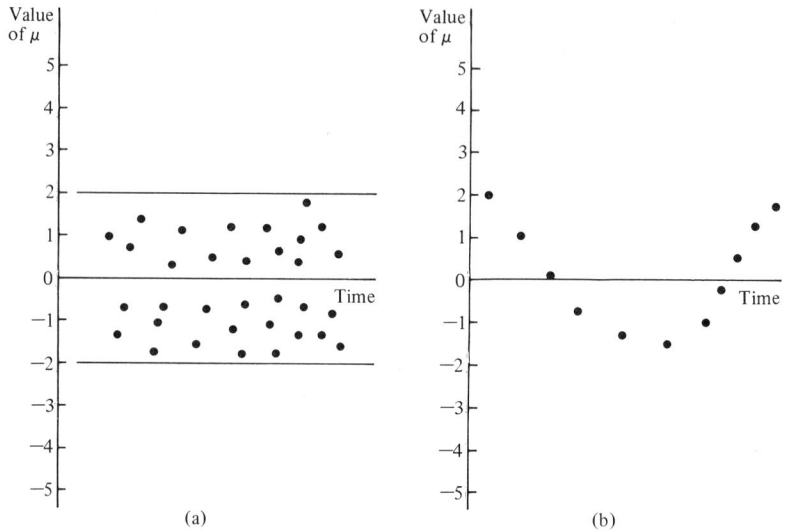

Figure 11-6 Plot of Residuals

of 2 indicating absence of serial correlation, and deviation in either direction indicating a nonrandom distribution of residuals.[5]

Positive serial correlation may often be removed by transforming the data to first differences (using incremental changes in variables rather than absolute amounts). This may be important where product demand is subject to influences that for some reason cannot be measured and specifically incorporated into the statistical analysis. Examples would be tastes slowly changing or new related products being put on the market.

The second condition, that the residuals be normally distributed, may be judged by plotting a frequency distribution similar to that of Figure 11-7. If the frequency plots approximate a bell-shaped curve, normal distribution is assumed to hold.

[5] The Durbin-Watson statistic is obtained by dividing the sum of squared first differences by the sum of the squared residuals:

$$d = \frac{\sum_{i=2}^{N} (\mu_i - \mu_{i-1})^2}{\sum_{i=1}^{N} \mu_i^2}$$

It can be written as

$$d = \frac{2\sum_{i=1}^{N} \mu_i^2 - 2\sum_{i=2}^{N} \mu_i \mu_{i-1}}{\sum_{i=1}^{N} \mu_i^2} = 2(1 - \rho)$$

which relates the Durbin-Watson statistic to the correlation coefficient between successive residuals ρ (rho). Put in this form, it is easy to see that d will equal 2 when $\rho = 0$; 0 when $\rho = +1$; and $+4$ when $\rho = -1$. Most results will lie between these extremes of perfect positive or negative serial correlation.

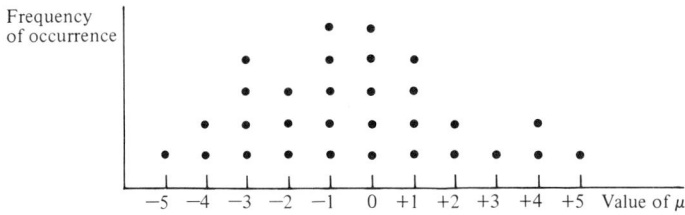

Figure 11-7

If the points are distributed on both sides of zero such that the mean of residuals is approximately zero, the third condition is met.

The fourth condition, constant variance, is met if the points fall randomly within a horizontal band as in Figure 11-6a or within the bands of Figures 11-8a and 11-8b. If the bands of sequence plots tend to conform to the shapes of Figure 11-8c, variance is not constant. Figure 11-8a may indicate changes in consumer tastes or habits over time. If the trend is not constant, Figure 11-8b may be more representative. These problems can be dealt with by including time as one of the independent variables in the multiple regression equation. In the second case, Figure 11-8b, quadratic terms can be used for the time variable.

The megaphone plot of Figure 11-8c presents a more serious problem that requires the use of the weighted least-squares technique, which is beyond the scope of this text.

11-6-2 *Plots of residuals against regression variables*

Further plots of residuals against regression variables are useful in detecting problems other than variance of the error term. If the band has positive or negative slope, an error has been made in the regression calculations, since proper account has not been taken of the variable's linear effect. If the slope is found with regard to the dependent variable, the error may be one of calculation, omission of an important variable, or suppression of the intercept term. If the band is curved, power terms are needed in the equation. If the band of residuals is curved with respect to the dependent variable, a squared term is probably needed, such as $Q = a + bX - cX^2$ in the model. If curved with respect to an independent variable, a quadratic term is needed in the same variable. If the band is megaphone-shaped, the weighted least-squares regression method may be used or the dependent variable data may be transformed to a logarithm or ratio before the regression parameters are estimated.

11-7 Regression Statistics

It is important for the business executive to be familiar with at least three more key terms that are used to help judge the validity of the results obtained from regression models: (1) coefficient of determination, (2) standard error of the estimate, and (3) standard error of the coefficient.

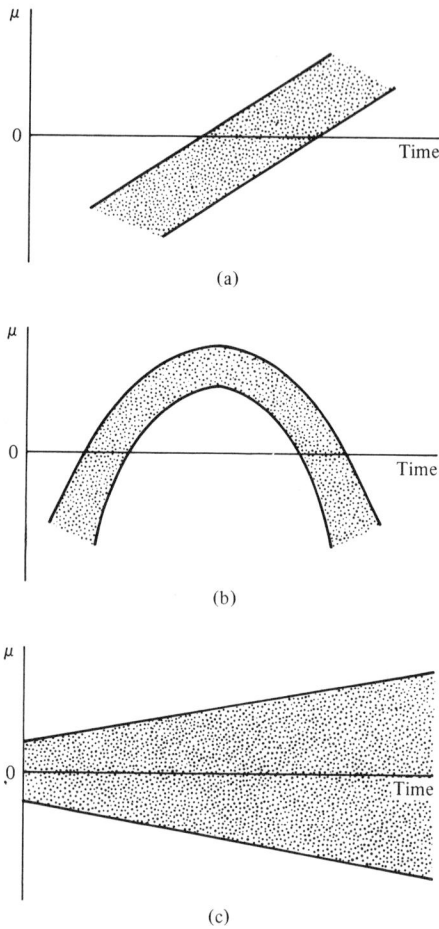

(a)

(b)

(c)

Figure 11-8

11-7-1   *Coefficient of determination*

The coefficient of determination, R^2, indicates how well the variations in the dependent variable are explained by the multiple regression model.[6] "It is defined as the proportion of the total variation in the dependent variable that is explained by the full set of independent variables included in the model"

[6] In simple regression models (with only a single independent variable) goodness of fit of the data to the linear regression curve is measured by the square of the correlation coefficient

$$r = \frac{\sum x_i y_i}{\sqrt{(\sum x_i^2)(\sum y_i^2)}}$$

In multiple regression the square of the coefficient of multiple correlation, R, is used similarly.

[2, p. 130]. Values of R^2 can range from 1.0, indicating complete explanation of the variation of the dependent by the independent variable, to 0, indicating failure to provide explanation. Values close to 1.0 are associated with observations found close to the regression line and small residuals.

Total variation of the dependent variable Q is simply the sum of the squared deviations of observed values of Q from its mean value:

$$\text{Total variation of } Q = \sum (Q_t - \bar{Q})^2 \tag{14}$$

Deviations are squared to avoid the canceling out of plus and minus deviations. If all observed points lay on the regression line or, what is the same thing, conformed to the conditional mean values, variation would be zero. The larger the variability in Q, the larger the total variation given by equation (14).

Total variation of Q is composed of two parts: that which can be explained by changes in the independent variable and that which cannot.

$$\text{Explained variation} = \sum (\hat{Q}_t - \bar{Q})^2 \tag{15}$$

$$\text{Unexplained variation} = \sum (Q_t - \hat{Q}_t)^2$$

$$= \sum \mu_t^2 \tag{16}$$

where $\hat{Q}_t$ is the predicted value of Q as calculated from the equation fitted to the data: $\hat{Q}_t = a - bP + cY$. Equation (14) is the sum of equations (15) and (16):

$$\sum (Q_t - \bar{Q})^2 = \sum (\hat{Q}_t - \bar{Q})^2 + \sum \mu_t^2 \tag{17}$$

Since the coefficient of determination is defined as the proportion of the total variation explained by the model,

$$R^2 = \frac{\sum (\hat{Q}_t - \bar{Q})^2}{\sum (Q_t - \bar{Q})^2} \tag{18}$$

When all variation has been explained, R^2 will be equal to 1.0, $\sum (\hat{Q}_t - \bar{Q})^2 = \sum (Q_t - \bar{Q})^2$, and for each observation $\hat{Q}_t = Q_t$. Each data point lies on the regression curve and $\mu_t = 0$ for every point in time, t. When deviations increase, R^2 falls, because $(Q_t - \hat{Q}_t)$ grows larger until the numerator of (18) becomes equal to zero and no changes in the dependent variable can be explained by the regression equation. In actual demand studies high R^2 values of 0.80 are considered quite acceptable, while those below 0.30 are generally rejected.

11-7-2   Standard error of the estimate

The standard error of the estimate, S_e, is a statistic that defines the confidence limits for predictions of values for the dependent variable based upon given values for independent variables. Assuming a normal distribution of error terms about the regression equation, estimates will fall within 1 S_e with a 68 percent probability, within 2 S_e with a 95.45 percent probability, and within 3 S_e with a 98 percent probability.

Figure 11-9 illustrates the confidence limits located a distance of 2 S_e from the

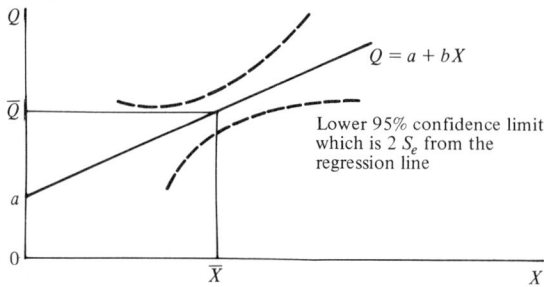

**Figure 11-9　Confidence Limits Defined by Standard Errors
of the Estimate**

regression line. Ninety-five percent of the data points will fall within this interval. Notice that the confidence limits are closer to the regression line near the mean values of Q and X. Less confidence can be put in values predicted some distance from the mean values, and very little where predicted values are beyond the range of the observed values.

11-7-3　*Standard error of the coefficient*

The standard error of the coefficient, S_c, indicates the degree of confidence that can be placed in the estimated parameter of an independent variable. For example, if the regression coefficient c in equation (13) is more than double its standard error, we can be 95 percent confident in the hypothesis that there is a relation between Q and X. The greater the regression coefficient relative to its standard error, the greater the confidence placed in the relation.

11-7-4　*Multicollinearity*

At this point, the discussion of section 11-4-2 concerning mutually correlated variables may be resumed. When the independent variables are themselves significantly interrelated, a problem of multicollinearity is said to exist. This may be detected directly by observing the correlation among the independent variables. The problem may also be uncovered indirectly by comparison of other statistics already discussed. For example, if the regression model provides a value of R^2 near 1.0, indicating that most of the variation in the dependent variable is explained but S_c is large relative to the coefficient, little confidence can be placed in the predictive value of any single independent variable. This information indicates that the group of independent variables is significant but that the specific individual relations with the dependent variable have not been separated properly. The independent variables are said to be jointly determined. In such cases, regression analysis may assign arbitrary values to the coefficients. One variable may be assigned a high coefficient and the other a low one, while neither may correspond to the true relation. To avoid this problem, all but one of the mutually correlated variables must be removed from the single-equation regression model, and this variable represents the combined influence of the mutually correlated variables on the dependent variable. While this representative variable may be used for forecasting purposes, it does not really explain the demand relation.

11-8   An Example of the Use of Regression Analysis

An apparently successful application of multiple linear regression analysis [2, pp. 138–140] involved an analysis of the demand for the frozen fruit pies of Wisco Foods in 1970.

The demand for Wisco pies was hypothesized to be a function of price (P), advertising effort (A), competitor's price (PX), income per capita (Y), marketing area population (Pop), and a trend factor (T) to account for possible changes in preferences by the public for prepared foods and increased awareness of the product. Quarterly data were obtained for the preceding 2 years for each of the variables. Results of the regression analysis were as follows:

$$Q = -500 - 275P + 5A + 150PX + 7.25\,Y + 0.25\text{Pop} + 875T \qquad (19)$$
$$\quad\;\; (52)\quad (1.1)\quad (66)\qquad (3.2)\qquad (0.09)\qquad (230)$$

where the coefficient of determination (R^2) = 0.92; standard error of the estimate = 775; standard errors of the coefficients are given in the parentheses; and assumptions regarding residuals were found to be met.

Interpretation of the regression equation is as follows. No economic meaning can be given to the intercept term, -500, since $Q = -500$ requires values of zero for all the independent variables and lies outside the range of the observed data. The coefficients, or slope values, preceding each of the independent variables indicate the marginal effect of a unit change in an independent variable on the number of pies that can be sold in one quarter of a year, holding all the other independent variables constant. For example, the coefficient of A, $+5$, indicates that a dollar increase in advertising expenditure increases quarterly sales by 5 pies. Similarly, every dollar increase in income augments sales by 7.25 pies.

The $R^2 = 0.92$ indicates that the regression model explains 92 percent of the variation in pie sales. This fortunate result for the model as a whole is reinforced by finding that each of the coefficients is more than twice its standard error (found in parentheses below the coefficients), indicating that all estimates are significant at the 95 percent level of confidence. Note the very small standard errors relative to the coefficients for the most important (controllable) variables P and A.

Demand may be estimated for the following quarter by inserting assumed values into the regression equation:

$$Q = -500 - 275(150) + 5(900) + 150(140) + 7.25(6,000)$$
$$\qquad\qquad\;\; \text{cents}\qquad\qquad\qquad \text{cents}$$
$$\quad + 0.25(50,000) + 875(8)$$
$$= 46,750$$

While 46,750 is the best point estimate of demand, a confidence interval of sales can be obtained from the standard error of the estimate found to be 775. Projected sales may be anticipated to fall within 2 standard errors of the estimate with a confidence level of 95 percent. Two standard errors will be $2 \times 775 = 1,550$. Therefore, sales are expected to fall in the range of 45,200–48,300 pies. A similar analysis could be done for each marketing area and summed to obtain total product demand for the firm.

11-9   Summary

This chapter dealt with the problems of assessing the impact of various factors on product demand. Interviews and market experiments are sometimes used to obtain pertinent information but often entail more expense than they are worth. Greater reliance is generally placed on statistical analysis by use of linear regression techniques. Therefore, a major portion of the chapter was devoted to explaining the terms, pitfalls, and interpretation of commonly used statistics employed in this technique, so that the business executive would be able to understand statistical economic research studies and to ask knowledgeable questions when required. The chapter concluded with an example of an actual study in which the results appeared promising. Similar statistical techniques are sometimes used in cost studies, discussed in Chapter 16.

A limitation of this short discussion of demand estimation is that the data used were either hypothetical, for industries rather than firms, or omitted. Actual data used by firms are jealously guarded and therefore difficult to obtain. The problems of data collection for demand studies for a firm or product must be left to on-the-job encounters. The techniques and terms used in this chapter can be applied equally well to data relevant to a particular firm. Where detailed data are prohibitively expensive to gather, some researchers will use industry data to obtain industry demand and then estimate the firm's demand as a certain proportion of the industry's.

Questions and Problems

11-1. Define and explain:
    a. direct interview
    b. direct market experiment
    c. omission of important variables
    d. inclusion of mutually correlated variables
    e. indentification problem
    f. serial correlation
    g. coefficient of determination
    h. standard error of the estimate
    i. standard error of the coefficient
    j. multicollinearity

11-2. Under what conditions are power functions useful?

11-3. Given the power function $Q = aP^b Y^c A^d$, demonstrate that the elasticity of demand with respect to advertising (A) is given by d.

11-4. Given the data below and the equation $Q = a + bP$, solve for a and b, using the least-squares regression technique.

P	Q
0.50	604
0.48	754
0.46	904
0.44	1,054

11-5. Given the data below and the equation $Q = a + bP = cY$, solve for a, b, and c, using the least-squares regression technique.

	P	Q	Y
1970	0.50	604	7,200
1971	0.48	754	7,600
1972	0.46	904	8,000
1973	0.44	1,054	8,400

11-6. Calculate the price and income point elasticities for equation (4) using the data for 1973.

References

1. William J. Baumol. *Economic Theory and Operations Analysis*. 3d ed. (Englewood Cliffs, N.J.: Prentice-Hall, 1972), ch. 10.
2. Eugene F. Brigham and James L. Pappas. *Managerial Economics* (Hinsdale, Ill.: Dryden Press, 1972), ch. 5.
3. W. R. Draper and H. Smith. *Applied Regression Analysis* (New York: Wiley, 1966).
4. Milton Friedman. *Price Theory—A Provisional Text*. Rev. ed. (Chicago: Aldine, 1962), pp. 31–36.
5. J. Johnston. *Econometric Methods* (New York: McGraw-Hill, 1963).
6. ———. *Statistical Cost Analysis* (New York: McGraw-Hill, 1963).
7. Edward J. Kane. *Economic Statistics and Econometrics—An Introduction to Quantitative Economics* (New York: Harper & Row, 1968).
8. Lawrence R. Klein. *An Introduction to Econometrics* (Englewood Cliffs, N.J.: Prentice-Hall, 1962).
9. Leroy H. Mantell. *Economics for Business Decisions* (New York: McGraw-Hill, 1972), ch. 6.
10. Milton H. Spencer. *Managerial Economics*. 3d ed. (Homewood, Ill.: Richard D. Irwin, 1968), ch. 5.

PART THREE

Analysis of Production and Cost

To take an example . . . from a very trifling manufacture; but one in which the division of labor has been very often taken notice of, the trade of the pin-maker; a workman not educated to this business . . . nor acquainted with the use of the machinery employed in it . . . could scarce, perhaps, with his utmost industry, make one pin in a day, and certainly could not make twenty. But in the way in which this business is now carried on . . . one man draws out the wire, another straights it, a third cuts it, a fourth points it, a fifth grinds it at the top for receiving the head; to make the head requires two or three distinct operations; to put it on is a peculiar business, to whiten the pins is another; it is even a trade by itself to put them into the paper; and the important business of making a pin is, in this manner, divided into about eighteen distinct operations, which, in some manufactories, are all performed by distinct hands. . . . I have seen a small manufactory of this kind where ten men . . . could, when they exerted themselves, make among them . . . upwards of forty-eight thousand pins in a day. . . . But if they had all wrought separately and independently, and without any of them having been educated to this peculiar business, they certainly could not each of them have made twenty, perhaps not one pin in a day.

Adam Smith, *An Inquiry into the Nature and Causes of the Wealth of Nations* (1776)

12 Production Theory

Part Three is devoted to production and cost analysis. Such analysis within the overall scheme of managerial economics falls in the category of supply considerations mentioned in Chapter 6 as the second constraint condition in the general programming model of the firm:

Maximize Z (that is, optimize the firm's goals) $= f(\pi_1 X_1, \pi_2 X_2, \ldots, \pi_n X_n)$
subject to
demand considerations $X_1, X_2, \ldots, X_n = f(P_i, D_i)$ (for instance, consumer motivation and ability to consume, extent of the market)
supply considerations $X_1, X_2, \ldots, X_n = f(C_i, S_i)$ (for instance, technology, costs, scarcities)
where all $X_i > 0$.

In this chapter the reader is introduced to basic production theory, which examines the manner in which resources (factors, inputs) are combined to create commodities (products, outputs). In broadest terms, production satisfies human wants through the provision of commodities, including services. This implies that production encompasses even simple exchange, since each person obtains something he values more highly than the item he gave up. A major objective of production theory is to discover rules for determining the optimum proportions of inputs so that waste and cost will be minimized. Discussion in this chapter is largely concerned with a simple continuous process whereby two factors are used to construct a single product. Returns to the variable factor and to scale are emphasized, followed by discussions of the least-cost criteria and the expansion path. Chapters 12 and 15, which deal with cost concepts in business and economics, are the basic ones of Part Three; the others consider more advanced topics. All of Part Three should be of interest to business executives, however, for attaining a thorough understanding of the nature of production and cost analysis.

12-1 The Production Function

The firm's production function employing two inputs is typically represented by the expression

$$Q = f(a, b) \tag{1}$$

where Q represents the physical units of product that can be produced in a unit of time and where the a and b are the minimum amounts of two different inputs employed. In most of the analysis that follows, these assumptions are made:

1. The function is continuous and smooth, implying a perfect divisibility of inputs and outputs.

2. The quantity of output given by the production function represents the maximum amount that can be produced from the inputs used.

3. Variable factors are available in unlimited supply in the short run, as are fixed factors in the long run.[1]

4. Factors are to some degree substitutable for each other in production, given sufficient time for adjustment to take place.

5. The level of technology is known and held constant during the period of analysis. This means the various input-output combinations are all known but are not permitted to change because of new factor-saving inventions.

Figure 12-1 illustrates the relation between the two inputs and the single output. The vertical distance from the ab plane to the surface of the production "mountain" indicates the number of units of the product produced with a given combination of inputs. With a given state of technology, the maximum number is $A'A$, employing Oa^* of factor a and Ob^* of factor b.

The most fundamental relation between inputs and outputs, attributable to T. R. Malthus and Edward West in 1815 [11, p. 122], is designated the *law*

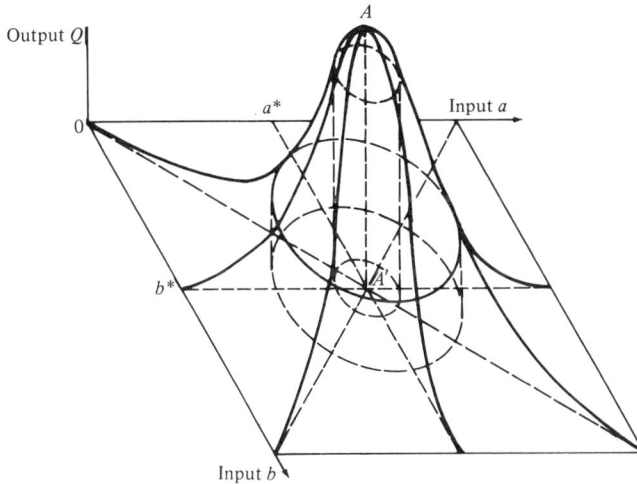

Figure 12-1

[1] In economic analysis three periods of time are assumed: (1) *very short run*, in which all factors are fixed and only products held in inventory are available for sale; (2) *short run*, in which the variable factors (say labor and materials) may be increased or decreased but fixed factors (say plant capacity) cannot; and (3) *long run*, where all factors are variable (plant capacity may be changed and firms may enter and leave the industry).

of diminishing returns: As equal amounts of an input are added to given amounts of other inputs, output will increase up to a point and then begin to decrease.

The point referred to is commonly known as the point of diminishing total returns to the variable factor and is indicated by the top of the production "mountain" in Figure 12-1 and by point C in Figure 12-2a. Other ways of expressing the concept refer to the average- and marginal-product curves of Figure 12-2b. Modern interpretation typically includes all three curves (total, average, and marginal) and their explanations to give a relatively complete

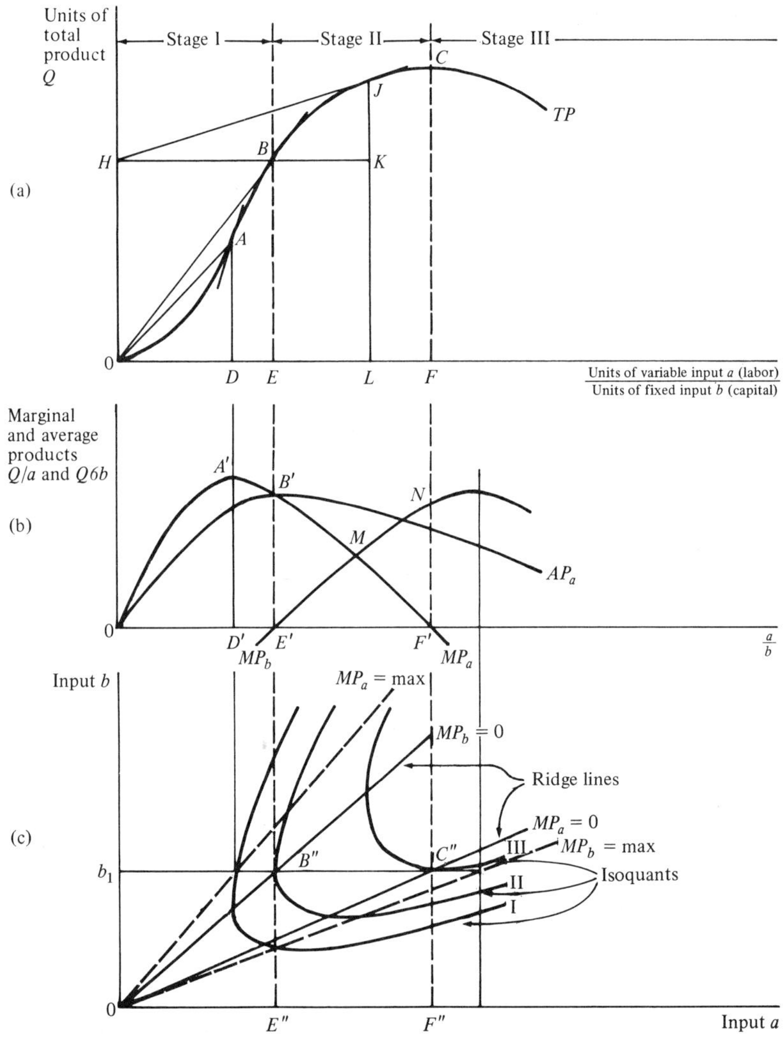

Figure 12-2

description. Total product rises from zero at an increasing rate for greater ratios of *a* to *b* up to a point—the inflection point at *A*, which is also the maximum point on the marginal curve. Thereafter, product climbs at a decreasing rate until it reaches a maximum at point *C*, where the marginal product of factor *a* is zero. Average productivity is maximized at point *B*, where, as will be explained later, the marginal product of factor *b* is zero.

One must be careful when discussing *the* point of diminishing returns, because there are three such points: (1) diminishing *total* returns, (2) diminishing *average* returns, and (3) diminishing *marginal* returns. The average and marginal curves shown in Figure 12-2b may be obtained from the total-product curve in the following manner. Points on the average product of factor *a* curve for a given *a/b* ratio are found from the slope of a straight line drawn from points on the total-product curve to the origin. For example, the AP_a at point *A* (equal to the vertical distance $A'D'$) is simply the slope of *OA* in Figure 12-2a. Maximum AP_a will be at point *B*, because *OB* drawn tangent to *TP* has greater slope than any other straight line drawn from *TP* to the origin. Other points on AP_a are derived similarly.

The MP_a curve is a plotting of the slope of *TP* for the different *a/b* ratios. Notice that the MP_a curve rises as *TP* increases at an increasing rate up to point *A*, where the slope of *TP* and the value of the MP_a are maximums. Beyond point *A*, *TP* increases for a time at a decreasing rate up to its maximum at point *C*, and MP_a falls to zero. *TP* then begins to decrease and it necessarily follows that as long as *TP* is falling, MP_a must be negative.

12-2   The Nature of Diminishing Physical Outputs

In a general way, farmers have always recognized that production of corn cannot be indefinitely increased by applying ever-increasing amounts of seed, fertilizer, and labor to a given plot of farm land. If it could, it has been said, enough food for the world's population could be grown in a flower pot. Similarly, shoe manufacturers are aware that attempts to fill increasing orders by working more and more people in one plant will reach a point where output increases by a lesser proportion than labor. One who polishes furniture and floors reaches a point where more rubbing adds little if any gloss to the finish. Sales managers find they can increase sales by adding more sales people up to a certain point, after which there is insufficient increase. Each of these cases exemplify diminishing returns [3, p. 275].

Decreasing returns result from the relative scarcity of other factors required in greater and greater proportions. Increasing returns, however, are attributable to phenomena other than scarcities—such as economies of large scale operations, division of labor, specialized machinery, utilization of by-products, and improvements in organization and skills evolving from greater experience and repetition of tasks. Changes in the state of technology are dynamic rather than static and therefore must be held constant while distinguishing the effects of changes in factor proportions. This assumption is necessary for the use of homogeneous production functions in which a doubling or trebling of all factors will double or treble outputs [5, pp. 224–225].

12-3 Homogeneous Production Functions

Homogeneous functions are often mentioned in the literature of production economics, so a precise understanding of their nature is desirable. Figures like 12-2 have traditionally been used to represent a firm's production function, which is usually assumed to be homogeneous of degree 1, that is *linearly homogeneous*.

A homogeneous function is one in which some arbitrarily chosen constant k, multiplied by each of the input variables, can be entirely factored out. The function $f(a, b)$ is said to be homogeneous of degree n in a and b if

$$f(ka, ky) = k^n f(a, b) \quad \text{if } k \neq 0 \tag{2}$$

For example, if

$$z = 3a + 2b$$

then

$$k^n z = f(ka, kb)$$
$$= 3(ka) + 2(kb)$$
$$= k(3a + 2b)$$

Thus, if a and b are each multiplied by k, z also has been multiplied by k. Since k is to the first power ($n = 1$), the function is homogeneous to degree 1, that is, linearly homogeneous.

Similarly, if

$$z = \frac{3a + 2b}{5a - 3b}$$

then

$$k^n z = f(ka, kb)$$
$$= \frac{3(ka) + 2(kb)}{5(ka) - 3(kb)} = k^0 \left(\frac{3a + 2b}{5a - 3b}\right)$$

The function is homogeneous to degree zero, since $n = 0$. (Recall $k^0 = 1$.) Increased use of inputs a and b in this case yields no change in output. The function is neither linear nor linearly homogeneous.

If

$$z = \frac{3a^3 + 2b^3}{5a^2 - 3b^2}$$

then

$$k^n z = f(ka, kb) = \frac{3(ka)^3 + 2(kb)^3}{5(ka)^2 - 3(kb)^2}$$
$$= k \left(\frac{3a^3 + 2b^3}{5a^2 - 3b^2}\right)$$

The function is *not linear* but is *linearly homogeneous*, since $n = 1$.

The degree of homogeneity is useful to know, because it indicates the extent to which output changes when proportional changes are made in all inputs; for example, when the degree of homogeneity, n, is 1, a doubling of every input causes a doubling of outputs and *returns to scale* are said to be constant. When $n > 1$, returns to scale are increasing; when $0 < n < 1$, returns to scale are decreasing; when $n < 0$, returns to scale are negative. Mathematical properties and other examples of linear homogeneous functions are given in Chapter 13.

12-4 Variable Proportions and Symmetry

In many production processes factor b can be changed as readily as factor a. It is therefore preferable to call the law of diminishing returns (also called the law of diminishing productivity and the principle of diminishing physical outputs) the *law of variable proportions*. The latter wording calls attention to the fact that with the passing of sufficient time, factor b could be allowed to change while holding factor a constant. This would be moving from right to left along the horizontal axes of Figure 12-2. This can be seen more clearly in Figure 12-3, which is a quarter section of Figure 12-1; the total product curve for input a while holding input b constant at b_1 is b_1PE, and that for b while holding a constant at a_1 is a_1PD. Notice also in Figure 12-2b that the MP_b

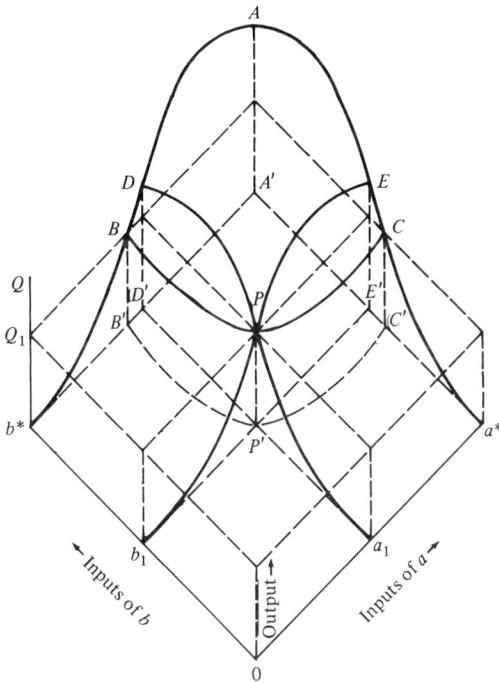

Figure 12-3

curve cuts the horizontal axis at point E'; this will be the case for any production function that is linearly homogeneous.

The range of values of a/b between E' and F' in Figure 12-2 designated as stage II is said to be the relevant range for economic uses of the factors. This *economic region* lies between the points where the marginal products are zero and the average products are maximums. These two conditions represent the same input points when the production function is homogeneous of degree 1. Otherwise they do not. Outside of stage II, one of the inputs is being used so excessively that its marginal contribution to the total product is negative. Only in stage II are the *MP* of both inputs positive. Stages I and III are called symmetrical, since the factor proportions are counterproductive with respect to one and then the other input.

Symmetry of stages I and III is easily seen by use of equal-product curves, called isoquants, in Figure 12-2c. The two solid rays rising from the origin are particular isoclines called ridge lines. They pass through the vertical and horizontal points on the isoquants. These special isoclines indicate, as will be shown in the next section, points on the isoquants where the marginal products of one factor or the other are zero. Returns to factor a while holding factor b fixed at b_1 are found by moving to the right along the horizontal line from b_1; the range along this line between the isoclines coincides with stage II, while stages I and III lie on the left and right, respectively.

The diagrams of Figure 12-2 may be derived from the three-dimensional, smoothly contoured hill of Figures 12-1 and 12-3. Total product curves may be obtained by slicing vertical sections parallel to the Qa plane, and isoquants may be obtained by taking horizontal slices parallel to the ab plane. Viewed in this manner, the isoquants are seen as closed lines, but this is not the case for all functions.

12-5   Substitute and Complementary Inputs

In production processes where exact amounts of two or more inputs are required to produce given units of output, the inputs are said to be perfect complements. A classic example is the primitive case where one man plus one shovel can produce a hole in the ground in a given amount of time; this is point

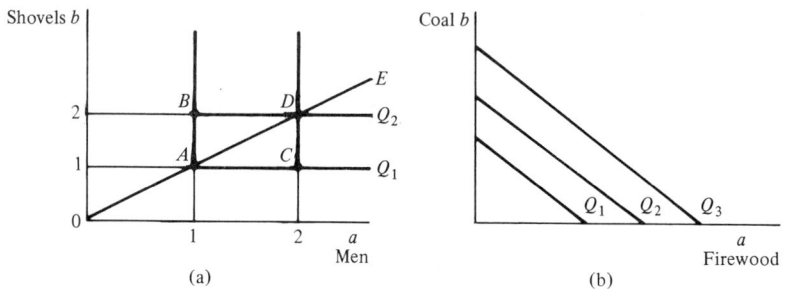

Figure 12-4

A on isoquant Q_1 in Figure 12-4a. An additional shovel, at point B, is of no value to a man who can use only one at a time. Similarly, an additional man where there is only one shovel at point C can produce no more holes, assuming shovels are essential for digging and that a man can work continuously without relief. As shown in the diagram, isoquants for perfect complements take the shape of right angles. Other examples would include component parts, such as frames and wheels for vehicles, leather and buckles for leather belts, handles and blades for knives, foundations and roofs for houses, and ingredients specified in receipts for gourmet foods and prescription drugs.

Some products can be produced by inputs that can be readily substituted for each other. Coal and firewood might be perfect substitutes for each other in the production of heat. Two nickels will work as well as one dime in operating many vending machines. Alternative foods may fulfill minimum nutrient requirements equally well; for instance, peanut butter and corn meal are both rich in protein, while potatoes and spinach are good sources of ascorbic acid. Shipments may be made as quickly by river barge as by rail. Isoquants for such examples are given in Figure 12-4b.

Between the extreme cases of perfect complements and perfect substitutes are the more common cases where inputs are substitutable for each other in differing degrees. Clothes can be made with less wastage of cloth if more man-hours are spent in fitting patterns and cutting more carefully. More fertilizer and herbicide can be substituted for hand labor in maintaining a crop yield. More intensive advertising in a market territory may maintain revenue with a reduced sales force. Saturation bombing of military targets may accomplish the objective with fewer casualties to friendly infantrymen. Figure 12-5a illustrates these cases with isoquants convex to the origin.

Figure 12-5a shows that a unit increase of labor from a_1 to a_2 permits a reduction in cloth used by an amount b_3b_2. Further unit increases of labor from a_2 to a_3 permit a much smaller reduction of cloth than before, equal to b_2b_1.

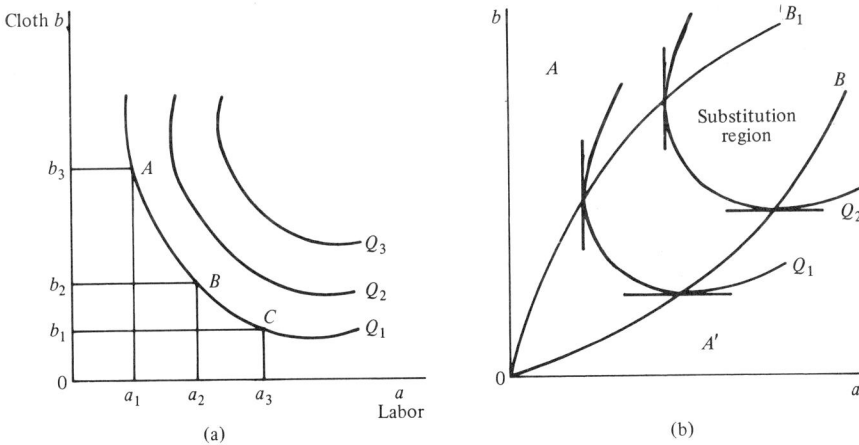

Figure 12-5

This indicates a diminishing marginal rate of technical substitution of input a for input b ($MRTS_{ab}$). Similarly, if one moves up and to the left along the isoquant Q_1 in equal increments of input b, diminishing $MRTS_{ba}$ would also be observed. Consequently, a downward-sloping isoquant convex to the origin indicates a diminishing $MRTS$ for both a and b. At any point on isoquant Q_1 the $MRTS_{ab}$ is given by its slope and first derivative at that point:

$$MRTS_{ab} = \text{slope} = -\frac{db}{da} \tag{3}$$

The slope of the isoquant obviously diminishes from A to B to C, verifying that $MRTS_{ab}$ diminishes.

The equation for an isoquant may be obtained by taking the total differential of the continuous production function $Q = f(a, b)$:

$$dQ = \frac{dQ}{da}\,da + \frac{dQ}{db}\,db \quad \text{or} \quad f_a\,da + f_b\,db \tag{4}$$

where f_a and f_b are the marginal products of a and b, respectively. Along an isoquant, Q is constant, necessitating a first derivative equal to zero:

$$dQ = f_a\,da + f_b\,db = 0 \tag{5}$$

The slope of the isoquant is therefore given by

$$\frac{db}{da} = -\frac{f_a}{f_b} \tag{6}$$

Substitution of equation (6) into (3) reveals that the $MRTS$ also equals the ratio of the marginal products:

$$MRTS_{ab} = -\frac{db}{da} = \frac{f_a}{f_b} \tag{7}$$

This result assumes the input variation is confined to the substitution range lying between the ridge lines that correspond to zero and infinite $MRTS$. Between the ridge lines the marginal products of both inputs are positive. Furthermore, the $MRTS$ is seen as diminishing as long as the isoquant is convex to the origin. Convexity, of course, depends upon the derivative of the slope:

$$\frac{d^2b}{da^2} = \frac{-(f_a/f_b)}{da} = -\frac{f_b[f_{aa} + f_{ab}(db/da)] - f_a[f_{ab} + f_{bb}(db/da)]}{f_b^2} \tag{8}$$

Substituting equation (6) into (8) gives

$$\frac{d^2b}{da^2} = -\frac{1}{f_b^3}(f_b^2 f_{aa} - 2f_a f_b f_{ab} + f_a^2 f_{bb}) \tag{9}$$

The isoquant is convex if the right side of (9) is positive and concave if negative.

12-6   Input Proportions, Limitational and Limitative Inputs

Inputs are said to be *limitational* when their increased use is a necessary but insufficient condition for increased output [7, pp. 8–11]. By this definition, both inputs at points A and D in Figure 12-4a are limitational. No such points are found in Figures 12-4b or 12-5 nor in any other production function characterized by variable proportions. Limitational restrictions on production functions imply that for every output level a factor combination exists where no increase in a single input can expand output. If the function is also homogeneous, it is defined by a single process and represented by the ray OE in Figure 12-4a.

The term *limitative* refers to an input whose increased use is necessary *and* sufficient for increased output. In Figure 12-4a factor a is limitative at point B and all other points on vertical segments of the isoquants. In the same manner, b is limitative at point C and all other points on horizontal portions of the isoquants. In the function given in Figure 12-5b the region of limitativeness for factor a is given by the domain designated by A between OB_1 and the vertical axis. In this region factor b is superfluous. Similarly, in domain A' factor b is limitative and factor a is superfluous. In Figure 12-4a b is superfluous at point B or any other point within the cone bOE, as is factor a at C or any other point within aOE. Both inputs along the common boundary OE are limitational rather than limitative.

These two terms are useful in pointing out a technological characteristic distinguishing functions having fixed and variable proportions. A function having fixed proportions, as in Figure 12-4a, has a common boundary of input limitativeness; there is no opprtunity for input substitution. A function like that in Figure 12-5b with a cone[2] (not necessarily a curvilinear cone) of mutual limitativeness separating regions of single-factor limitativeness is required for the existence of an economic region (stage II) within which input proportions can be varied. This contrasts with the fixed-proportions case, where the region of mutual limitativeness degenerates to an *economic ray*.

12-7 Returns to Scale Versus Returns to the Variable Factor

While returns to the variable factor involve changes in one input while holding the others constant, returns to scale require proportional changes in all inputs. This is most easily seen by reference to Figure 12-6. Returns to the variable factor a are deduced from the spacing of isoquants along the horizontal line from b_1. Successive isoquants represent equal increases in output for those above and to the right. Increasing returns to labor are observed over the range a_1–a_4 along b_1, where spaces between isoquants are becoming smaller. This follows from the fact that smaller and smaller increments of labor are required to produce equal increases in output. Returns are constant over the range a_4–a_5 and decreasing over a_5–a_7.

Returns to scale may be observed from the spacing of isoquants along any ray from the origin. Movement up and to the right along the ray OC requires that inputs be employed in fixed proportions to each other. If the spacing of isoquants becomes progressively less along OC, outputs are increasing in greater proportion than inputs and returns to scale are said to be increasing.

---

[2] The cone is closed if the function has an absolute maximum for variations in input combinations in all directions. Otherwise it is open, as is the case with linearly homogeneous functions.

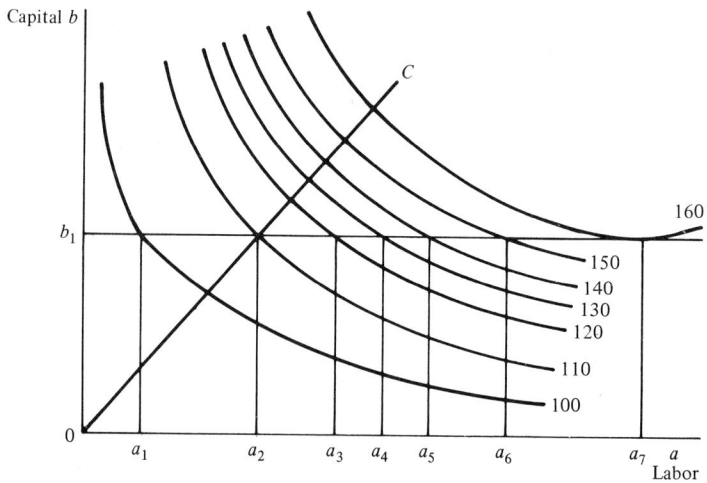

Figure 12-6

Where they are spaced evenly along OC, returns to scale are constant, and where progressively farther apart, returns to scale are decreasing.

Returns to scale may be interpreted in terms of total product curves by shifting them upward for proportional increases in both inputs a and b, as in Figure 12-7. Notice that the maximum average products are the same for each scale of production as long as the ratio of a/b is held constant. This is evident from their tangencies to the ray OB. The marginal products are also constant for B_1, B_2, and B_3, as well as for C_1, C_2, and C_3, since the slopes are the same. Moreover, the AP and MP will remain the same for successive intersections of any ray with the TP curves. This follows from the knowledge that the marginal and average products are homogeneous of degree zero for a total function homogeneous of degree 1. One may easily convince oneself that this is true. The marginal function, being the first derivative of the total function, is typically reduced to one power less. The average function, obtained by dividing the total function by output Q, is also reduced by one power. Since the power of the function is reduced by 1, the degree of homogeneity is also reduced by 1—in this case from 1 to zero. Functions with zero homogeneity yield no change in value for proportional changes in inputs and therefore remain the same along any straight line from the origin. Marginal and average products are therefore seen to be affected only by the input ratio and are independent of the scale of input use [7, pp. 112–113].

12-8 Least-Cost Criteria and the Expansion Path

Up to this point, no mention has been made in this chapter about prices of inputs or outputs. Nothing has been said about how the decision is to be made as to the precise input combinations that will be employed to produce a given quantity of output at least cost. One way of treating the problem may be to maximize output subject to budget constraints on inputs. As long as the functions

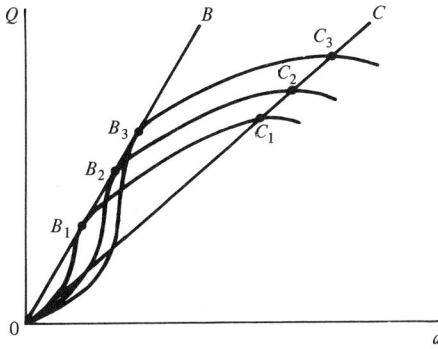

Figure 12-7

are known, continuous, and smooth, the maximizing criteria may be easily derived by use of calculus. The production function $Q = f(x, y)$ may be converted to the Lagrangian expression

$$Q_\lambda = f(x, y) + \lambda(p_x x + p_y y - M) \tag{10}$$

where x and y are inputs, p_x and p_y are their respective unit prices, and M is the amount of money that can be spent on x and y. The expression in parentheses on the extreme right following the Lagrange multiplier lambda sign is obtained by placing all of the terms of the budget equation, $M = P_x x + P_y y$, on the right hand side of the equal sign.

Taking the partial derivatives with respect to x, y, and λ, and setting them equal to zero,

$$\frac{\partial Q_\lambda}{\partial x} = \frac{\partial f}{\partial x} + \lambda p_x = 0$$

$$\frac{\partial Q_\lambda}{\partial y} = \frac{\partial f}{\partial y} + \lambda p_y = 0 \tag{11}$$

$$\frac{\partial Q_\lambda}{\partial \lambda} = p_x x + p_y y - M = 0$$

Rewrite the first two partial derivative equations as

$$p_x = -\lambda \frac{\partial f}{\partial x} \quad \text{and} \quad p_y = -\lambda \frac{\partial f}{\partial y} \tag{12}$$

whose ratio is

$$\frac{p_x}{p_y} = \frac{\partial f/\partial x}{\partial f/\partial y} \tag{13}$$

Recognizing the partial derivatives as marginal products and assuming the second-order conditions are met, the production-maximizing criterion for two inputs is that the price ratio equals the ratio of the marginal products,

$$\frac{p_x}{p_y} = \frac{MP_x}{MP_y} \tag{14}$$

or the ratios of MP to price are equal:

$$\frac{MP_x}{p_x} = \frac{MP_y}{p_y} \qquad (15)$$

This last version of the criterion simply states that output will be maximized when inputs are used such that their marginal products per dollar are equal.

A geometrical illustration of this criterion in the form of equation (14) is shown in Figure 12-8. First, the slope of the straight line y_1x_1, called the price line or budget line, represents the price ratio p_x/p_y. As one moves downward to the right, an increase in x, say Δx, requires a decrease in y, say Δy. Since the opportunity cost of using more x is the giving up of some units of y, one may say the price of x is Δy. Similarly, the price of y is Δx. Therefore the slope of the price line is $\Delta x/\Delta y = p_x/p_y$.

Next, the slope of the isoquant Q_1 is known from the identity equation (7) to be the $MRTS_{xy}$. Since Q_1 is the highest isoquant that can be touched with the amount of M dollars given by price line y_1x_1, point A represents the optimum quantities of x and y equal to Ox_0 and Oy_0, respectively.

As additional money is made available for purchasing inputs, the price line shifts away from the origin to y_2x_2 and y_3x_3, permitting the expansion of output to Q_2 and Q_3, respectively. Plotting the tangencies obtained in this manner yields the curve called the *expansion path*, which shows how inputs will be increased for the most economical expansion of output.

> *Example 1.* A mathematical example will help to show how the firm's expansion path can be obtained in terms of available budgets. Suppose output given by the production function
>
> $$Q = 3 \log x + 4 \log y$$
>
> is to be maximized. Assume also that the prices of inputs x and y are given at $p_x = 5$ and $p_y = 10$ with a limitation on total expenditure of M dollars. The Lagrangian expression to be maximized is therefore
>
> $$Q_\lambda = 3 \log x + 4 \log y + \lambda(5x + 10y - M)$$

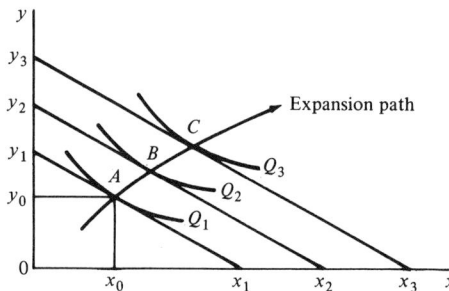

Figure 12-8

whose partial derivatives are

$$\frac{\partial Q_\lambda}{\partial x} = \frac{3}{x} + 5\lambda = 0$$

$$\frac{\partial Q_\lambda}{\partial y} = \frac{4}{y} + 10\lambda = 0$$

$$\frac{\partial Q_\lambda}{\partial \lambda} = 5x + 10y - M = 0$$

Multiplication of the first equation by 2 and subtraction of the second gives

$$\frac{6}{x} - \frac{4}{y} = 0 \quad \text{or} \quad x = \frac{3}{2}y$$

Substitution into the third equation yields

$$5\left(\frac{3}{2}y\right) + 10y - M = 0$$

$$17.5y = M$$

$$y = \frac{M}{17.5}$$

Further substitution gives $x = \frac{3}{35}M$ and $\lambda = -7M$. The values of x and y in terms of M constitute the required relations to produce the expansion path. The values of $-\lambda$ indicates that an additional M dollar spent on inputs will increase output by 7 units.

Example 2. Another example shows how the information of example 1 may be used to derive the firm's supply function and the derived input demand functions. The firm desires to maximize profits

$$\Pi = \text{total revenue} - \text{total cost}$$
$$= PQ - C$$
$$= PQ - (5x + 10y)$$

as constrained by the firm's production function. The Lagrangian function becomes

$$\Pi_\lambda = PQ - 5x - 10y + \lambda(Q - 3\log x - 4\log y)$$

whose partials are zero at maximum profits:

$$\frac{\partial \Pi_\lambda}{\partial Q} = P + \lambda = 0$$

$$\frac{\partial \Pi_\lambda}{\partial x} = -5 - \frac{3\lambda}{x} = 0$$

$$\frac{\partial \Pi_\lambda}{\partial y} = -10 - \frac{4\lambda}{y} = 0$$

$$\frac{\partial \Pi}{\partial \lambda} = Q - 3\log x - 4\log y = 0$$

Simultaneous solution of these four equations gives

$$Q = 3 \log \tfrac{3}{5}P + 4 \log \tfrac{2}{5}P \quad \text{Supply function}$$
$$x = \tfrac{3}{5}P$$
$$y = \tfrac{2}{5}P$$
$$\lambda = -P$$

Derived demand functions for inputs x and y

This indicates the marginal productivity of an additional dollar spent on inputs equals the price of a unit of output.

12-9 Summary and Conclusions

This chapter considered the traditional topics of production theory: the general production function, returns to variable inputs, returns to scale, product curves, isoquants, least-cost criteria, and the expansion path. Chapter 13 extends the discussion to the four most commonly used production elasticity concepts and to several of the most popular mathematical functions.

It should be recognized that until the least-cost criteria and the expansion path were discussed, nothing had been said about prices of inputs and outputs. Analysis dealt first with only the technical efficiency of possible combinations of inputs. Then prices were brought into the picture to determine the input point within the economic region where production is performed most economically.

Questions and Problems

12-1. What assumptions underlie the traditional production function described in this chapter?

12-2. Of what significance is a discussion of returns to variable factor and scale that excludes costs of inputs and prices of outputs?

12-3. Referring to the production function graphed in Figure 12-2, answer the following questions:

a. What factor proportions will be employed if *a* is free? if *b* is free?

b. What is the optimal ratio of factors to minimize the total cost of production?

c. $AP_a = MP_a$ at what point in Figure 12-2a? Why?

d. Which point is the point of diminishing returns?

e. As a production manager striving to minimize cost, would you prefer to operate at the point of diminishing marginal, average, or total returns? Why?

12-4. What exactly is symmetrical about stages I and III in a production function homogeneous of degree 1?

12-5. For Figure 12-9, why would the firm reject using input combinations at points A and B in producing at output level Q_1?

12-6. Assume that a firm produces products Z_i using x_i inputs:

$$Z_1 = 2x_1 + 3x_2 + 6x_3$$
$$Z_2 = 2x_1^{0.3} + 4x_2^{0.4} + 5x_3^{0.4}$$
$$Z_3 = 0.78x_3 + 52$$
$$Z_4 = 5x_1 x_2 x_3$$
$$Z_5 = 4x_1^{0.2} x_2^{0.1} x_3^{0.5}$$

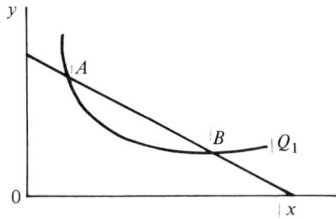

Figure 12-9

    a. Which products should be produced in greater amounts if expansion is most desired?

    b. Which functions are homogeneous?

12-7. Given the following production functions and input prices, determine the expressions in terms of expenditures M for the following:

    a. expansion path

    b. supply function

    c. derived demand for the inputs

$$Q = -6x^2 + 10x + 4xy + 2y - y^2$$
$$p_x = 2 \qquad p_y = 1$$

12-8. Do the same as in problem 12-7 for the following:

$$Q = 6x^{1/2} + 12y^{1/2}$$
$$p_x = 1, \qquad p_y = 3$$

References

1. William J. Baumol. *Economic Theory and Operations Analysis*. 3d ed. (Englewood Cliffs, N.J.: Prentice-Hall, 1972), pp. 274–293.
2. Richard A. Bilas. *Microeconomic Theory*. 2d ed. (New York: McGraw-Hill, 1971), pp. 113–146.
3. John D. Black. *Introduction to Production Economics* (New York: Holt, 1926), ch. 11.
4. Eugene F. Brigham and James L. Pappas. *Managerial Economics* (Hinsdale, Ill.: Dryden Press, 1972), pp. 145–171.
5. John M. Cassals. "On the Law of Variable Proportions." In *Explorations in Economics*, ed. F. W. Taussig (New York: McGraw-Hill, 1936), pp. 223–236.
6. C. E. Ferguson. *Microeconomic Theory*. 3d ed. (Homewood, Ill.: Richard D. Irwin, 1972), pp. 133–206.
7. ———. *The Neoclassical Theory of Production and Distribution* (Cambridge: Cambridge University Press, 1969), ch. 1–3.
8. Richard H. Leftwich. *The Price System and Resource Allocation*. 5th ed. (Hinsdale, Ill.: Dryden Press, 1973), pp. 135–161.
9. Edwin Mansfield. *Microeconomics—Theory and Applications* (New York: W. W. Norton, 1970), pp. 114–147.
10. Milton H. Spencer. *Managerial Economics* (Homewood, Ill.: Richard D. Irwin, 1968), pp. 171–212.
11. George J. Stigler. *The Theory of Price*. 3d ed. (New York: Macmillan, 1966), pp. 121–161.

13 Some Technical Aspects of Continuous Production Functions

This chapter examines the technical aspects of production analysis and discusses four well-known elasticity concepts: (1) output elasticity, (2) elasticity of average product, (3) function coefficient, and (4) elasticity of substitution. Such measures prove useful in comparing homogeneous with nonhomogeneous functions and in comparing various homogeneous functions with each other. A familiarity with the material of this chapter, which is perhaps more specific and tedious than most business students may desire, is essential background for reading the economic and managerial literature of production.

13-1 Mathematical Properties of Linearly Homogeneous Functions

Before discussing production elasticities and specific mathematical functions, it is instructive to introduce some mathematical properties for the general type of most commonly used production functions.

Mathematical properties of all homogeneous functions of degree 1 are given here without proof for easy reference [3, pp. 94–95].[1]

1. $Q = a f_a + b f_b$, where f_a and f_b denote $\partial Q/\partial a$ and $\partial Q/\partial b$, respectively. This property is known as Euler's theorem.

2. The first partial derivatives are homogeneous of degree zero.

3. $f_{bb} = \dfrac{a^2}{b^2} f_{aa}$.

4. $a f_{aa} = -b f_{ab}$ and $b f_{bb} = -a f_{ab}$.

5. When any one of f_{aa}, f_{bb}, or f_{ab} is zero, they all equal zero.

6. $Q^2 = a^2 f_a^2 + 2ab f_a f_b + b^2 f_b^2$.

7. An inflection point indicating a change in direction of concavity exists at $a = a_1$ if $f_{aa} = 0$. If $f_{aa} < 0$, the function changes from convex to concave from the a-axis. If $f_{aa} > 0$, the change is in the opposite direction.

Additional discussion of homogeneous functions is introduced when appropriate in the remainder of the chapter. A specific example of the usefulness of

---

[1] Proofs of all except property 6 are to be found in standard calculus texts. Property 6 is given in C. E. Ferguson [3, p. 95].

such properties is given in section 13-2 to illuminate a point made in Chapter 12 about the symmetry of stages I and III.

13-2   Demonstration of Symmetry by Use of Euler's Theorem

Euler's theorem, given by property 1 for linearly homogeneous functions, which is also valid for homogeneous functions of any degree, is helpful in conveying the symmetrical property of the marginal product curves [11]. Euler's theorem,

$$Q = a\frac{\partial Q}{\partial a} + b\frac{\partial Q}{\partial b} \tag{1}$$

may be rearranged as

$$b\frac{\partial Q}{\partial b} = Q - a\frac{\partial Q}{\partial a} \tag{2}$$

At the beginning of stage II, at point B of Figure 12-2a,

$$MP_a = \frac{\partial Q}{\partial a} = \frac{BE}{OE} \tag{3}$$

Substituting equation (3) into equation (2),

$$b\frac{\partial Q}{\partial b} = Q - BE = BE - BE = 0 \tag{4}$$

Since $b > 0$, $\partial Q/\partial b$ must equal zero. Thus, the marginal product of factor b is zero at points B, B', and B''.

At point C on the boundary between stages II and III, the MP_a is zero and

$$a\frac{\partial Q}{\partial a} = a \cdot 0 = 0 \tag{5}$$

Substituting equation (5) into equation (2),

$$b\frac{\partial Q}{\partial b} = Q - 0 \quad \text{or}$$

$$\frac{Q}{b} = \frac{\partial Q}{\partial b} \tag{6}$$

Thus, the average product of b equals the marginal product of b at the boundary on the right, that is, at points C, N, and C'' in Figure 12-2.

It may be demonstrated that the marginal product of b is also positive in stage II as drawn in Figure 12-2b. Selecting any point J on the total product curve in stage II of Figure 12-2a,

$$MP_a = \frac{\partial Q}{\partial a} = \frac{JK}{HK} \tag{7}$$

Then

$$a\frac{\partial Q}{\partial a} = HK\frac{JK}{HK} = JK \tag{8}$$

Substituting equation (7) into equation (2),

$$b\frac{\partial Q}{\partial b} = Q - JK$$

$$= JL - JK = KL \quad \text{or}$$

$$\frac{\partial Q}{\partial b} = \frac{KL}{b} \tag{9}$$

Since both KL and b are positive, $\partial Q/\partial b$ is positive. Thus, the marginal product of b, as well as that of a, is positive in stage II.

13-3   Output Elasticity, E_i

The first of the commonly used production elasticities is the output elasticity [3, pp. 76–77, 114–116]. It measures the proportional change in output in response to a proportional change in one input while holding other inputs constant. It may be expressed symbolically for input x_i as

$$E_i = \frac{\partial Q}{Q} \div \frac{\partial x_i}{x_i} \tag{10}$$

or as the ratio of marginal and average products

$$E_i = \frac{\partial Q}{\partial x_i} \cdot \frac{x_i}{Q} = \frac{\partial Q}{\partial x_i} \cdot \frac{1}{Q/x_i} = \frac{MP_i}{AP_i} \tag{11}$$

Output elasticity varies as the ratio of inputs, say a/b in Chapter 12, and changes for most production functions. The Cobb-Douglas function is an exception, however, since (as will be shown later) its output elasticity is a constant equal to unity, independent of the factor point.

The change in output elasticity for the function of Figure 12-2 may be observed from the relation of the average and marginal curves. In stage I, $MP_a > AP_a$, indicating a positive value of output elasticity of factor a from unity at the origin, which rises to a maximum in the vicinity of D' and returns to unity at E'. In stage II output elasticity of a is a diminishing fraction, which becomes zero where the marginal product is zero at the boundary of stages II and III. In stage III elasticity is negative. In short, $E_a > 1$ in stage I; $0 < E_a < 1$ in stage II; and $E_a < 0$ in stage III. For most functions that are homogeneous to degree 1, other than the Cobb-Douglas, which is an exception, output elasticity is different for different input ratios. This follows from the fact that the marginal and average products of such functions are homogeneous of degree zero, as is their ratio MP_i/AP_i, and the output of functions of zero homogeneity vary, not with scale but with the input ratio. In graphical form, this means that the output

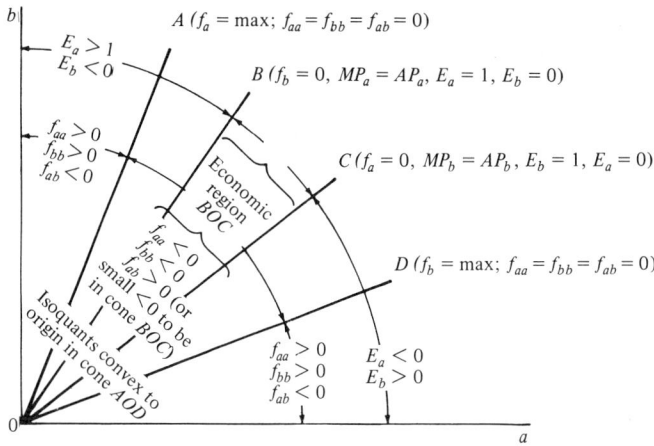

A $(f_a = \max;\ f_{aa} = f_{bb} = f_{ab} = 0)$

$E_a > 1$
$E_b < 0$

B $(f_b = 0,\ MP_a = AP_a,\ E_a = 1,\ E_b = 0)$

$f_{aa} > 0$
$f_{bb} > 0$
$f_{ab} < 0$

C $(f_a = 0,\ MP_b = AP_b,\ E_b = 1,\ E_a = 0)$

Economic
region
BOC

D $(f_b = \max;\ f_{aa} = f_{bb} = f_{ab} = 0)$

$f_{aa} < 0$
$f_{bb} > 0$
$f_{ab} < 0$ (or
small < 0 to be
in cone BOC)

Isoquants convex to
origin in cone AOD

$f_{aa} > 0$
$f_{bb} > 0$
$f_{ab} < 0$

$E_a < 0$
$E_b > 0$

b

0

a

Figure 13-1

elasticities of both inputs are constant along rays from the origin, as in Figure 13-1. Ray OB is constructed for the input ratios such that the marginal and average products of a are equal at all points on the ray; hence, $E_a = 1$. Similarly, OC is constructed such that the marginal and average products of b are equal, and $E_b = 1$.

Since the MP_a, denoted by f_a, is homogeneous to degree zero by property 2 of linearly homogeneous functions listed previously, it remains constant along any ray from the origin. Ray OA was selected so that f_a is a maximum. For f_a to be a maximum, the second derivative of output with respect to a, $\partial^2 Q/\partial a^2$, or f_{aa}, must equal zero. By property 5, f_{bb} and f_{ab} must also be zero when f_{aa} is zero. Ray OD was constructed similarly for b.

In the space above and to the left of the isocline OB for $f_a = 0$, $MP_a > AP_a$ for lower a/b ratios, and $E_a > 1$. Similarly, below and to the right of OC, $E_b > 1$. Since $f_{aa} = 0$ along OA, $f_{aa} > 0$ to the left of OA, and $f_{aa} < 0$ to the right. By properties 4 and 5, $f_{bb} > 0$ and $f_{ab} < 0$ on the left of OA. The conditions $f_{aa} < 0$, $f_{bb} > 0$, $f_{ab} < 0$ do not meet the necessary conditions for the isoquants to be convex to the origin; specifically, convexity requires that the second derivative of b with respect to a in the equation for the isoquant be positive. This rule may be derived as follows: The total differential of

$$Q = f(x_a, x_b) \tag{12}$$

is

$$dQ = f_a\, dx_a + f_b\, dx_b = 0 \tag{13}$$

The slope of the isoquant (or the $MRTS_{ab}$) is, accordingly,

$$\frac{dx_b}{dx_a} = -\frac{f_a}{f_b} \tag{14}$$

The second derivative is

$$\frac{d^2x_b}{dx_a^2} = \frac{d[-(f_a/f_b)]}{dx_a} = -\frac{f_b[f_{aa} + f_{ab}(dx_b/dx_a)] - f_a[f_{ab} + f_{bb}(dx_b/dx_a)]}{f_b^2}$$

$$= -\frac{1}{f_b^3}(f_b^2 f_{aa} - 2f_a f_b f_{ab} + f_a^2 f_{bb}) \tag{15}$$

The isoquant is convex to the origin if equation (15) is positive and concave if negative. If the term within the parentheses is negative, the right-hand side of the equation is positive and the isoquant convex. Within the cone AOD, f_{aa} and f_{bb} are both negative; f_{ab} is typically positive, but if negative it must be sufficiently small to make the term in the parentheses negative. Ratios of a/b within the cone AOD of Figure 13-1 meet the convexity condition, but those outside do not. Ratios within BOC are in the economic range [3, pp. 88–89, 114–116] [12, pp. 156–157].

13-4   Elasticity of Average Product, E_{AP}

An elasticity concept related to output elasticity is the elasticity of average product [3, pp. 76–77]. Its value may be calculated by use of the conventional elasticity formula,

$$E_{AP} = \frac{\partial(Q/x_i)}{\partial x_i} \cdot \frac{x_i}{Q/x_i} = \frac{x_i f_i - Q}{x_i^2} \cdot \frac{x_i^2}{Q}$$

$$= \frac{f_i}{Q/x_i} - 1 = \frac{MP_i}{AP_i} - 1$$

$$= E_i - 1 \tag{16}$$

Elasticity of average product thus equals output elasticity minus 1. Average returns to factor a are therefore increasing, constant, or decreasing as $E_a \gtreqless 1$, respectively.

13-5   Function Coefficient, E_Q

The elasticity of output with respect to a proportional change in all outputs is called the function coefficient, which will be denoted by E_Q [see 3, pp. 79–83]. It measures the proportional change in output relative to proportional changes in inputs while moving along a ray from the origin, as along OC in Figure 13-1.

If $Q = f(\lambda x_a, \lambda x_b, \ldots, \lambda x_n)$ along a ray from the origin,

$$E_Q = \frac{\partial Q}{Q} \div \frac{d\lambda}{\lambda} \tag{17}$$

where λ is a scale factor indicating proportional changes in all inputs. E_Q has several interesting features:

1. Returns to scale are increasing, constant, decreasing, or negative, as $E_Q \gtreqless 1$, $E_Q < 0$. $E_Q = 0$ where TP is a maximum.

2. For homogeneous production functions, E_Q is given by the degree of homogeneity.

3. For nonhomogeneous functions, the value of E_Q depends upon the input proportions (the ray), for instance, x_a/x_b and the scale of inputs used (the point on the ray).

E_Q may be derived for a production function as follows. The total differential of

$$Q = f(x_1, x_2, \ldots, x_n)$$

is

$$\partial Q = f_1 \, dx_1 + f_2 \, dx_2 + \cdots + f_n \, dx_n$$
$$= f_1 \, x_i \frac{dx_1}{x_1} + f_2 \, x_2 \frac{dx_2}{x_2} + \cdots + f_n \, x_n \frac{dx_n}{x_n} \tag{18}$$

When all inputs are changed by the proportion λ,

$$\frac{dx_i}{x_i} = \frac{d\lambda}{\lambda} \tag{19}$$

which, on substitution in equation (18), yields

$$dQ = \left(\sum_{i=1}^{n} f_i \, x_i \right) \frac{d\lambda}{\lambda} \tag{20}$$

Inserting equation (20) into the definition (17) gives the expression for the function coefficient:

$$E_Q = \frac{\sum\limits_{i=1}^{n} f_i \, x_i}{Q} \tag{21}$$

$$= \frac{\partial f}{\partial x_1} \frac{x_1}{Q} + \frac{\partial f}{\partial x_2} \frac{x_2}{Q} + \cdots + \frac{\partial f}{\partial x_n} \frac{x_n}{Q} \tag{22}$$

$$= E_1 + E_2 + \cdots + E_n \tag{23}$$

The final form reveals that the function coefficient equals the sum of the output elasticities. Note that the inputs may be varied one at a time or simultaneously in producing the final proportional change in output; this indicates an independent relation between inputs that may or may not be valid for specific real-world production processes.

A final relation, one between average returns to an input and returns to scale, is of great importance. The elasticity of average product of factor x_i with respect to the scale factor λ is given by the expression

$$E_{AP\lambda} = \frac{\partial(Q/x_i)}{d\lambda} \frac{\lambda x_i}{Q} = \frac{(dQ/d\lambda)x_i - Q(dx_i/d\lambda)}{x_i^2} \frac{\lambda x_i}{Q}$$

$$= \frac{dQ}{d\lambda} \frac{\lambda}{Q} - \frac{dx_i}{d\lambda} \frac{\lambda}{x_i} \tag{24}$$

Recognizing the first expression on the right of the equal sign as E_Q and noting that the elasticity of any input with respect to the scale factor is unity [3, p. 83],

$$E_{AP\lambda} = E_Q - 1 \tag{25}$$

These results indicate that for small movements along an input ray the average products will increase, remain unchanged, or decrease as $E_Q \gtreqless 1$. In other words, as inputs are varied proportionally, average returns for each input are increasing, constant, or diminishing depending upon whether returns to scale are increasing, constant, or decreasing.

13-6   Elasticity of Substitution, E_{sub}

One final elasticity concept treated in this chapter which is very important in neoclassical theory of distribution is the elasticity of substitution [3, pp. 89–92, 95–111]. This is

$$E_{sub} = \frac{d(b/a)}{b/a} \div \frac{dMRTS_{ab}}{MRTS_{ab}} \tag{26}$$

E_{sub} measures the relative change in factor proportions in response to a relative change in the $MRTS$ for a movement along the substitution curve of Figure 13-2b. The substitution curve may be constructed from the isoquant of Figure 13-2a as follows: At point A on the isoquant Q_1 the input ratio b/a is given by the slope of the ray OA, the tangent of the angle θ, and the $MRTS_{ab}$ is given by the slope of the line drawn tangent to the isoquant at A, the slope of Aa_1 or $\tan \eta$. Point A' in Figure 13-2b corresponds to point A in Figure 13-2a. Similarly, at point B the input ratio is given by $\tan \phi$ and $MRTS$ by $\tan \omega$; point B' corresponds to point B. A movement from A to B along the isoquant is thus a movement from A' to B' along the substitution curve. The elasticity of this curve is called the elasticity of substitution.

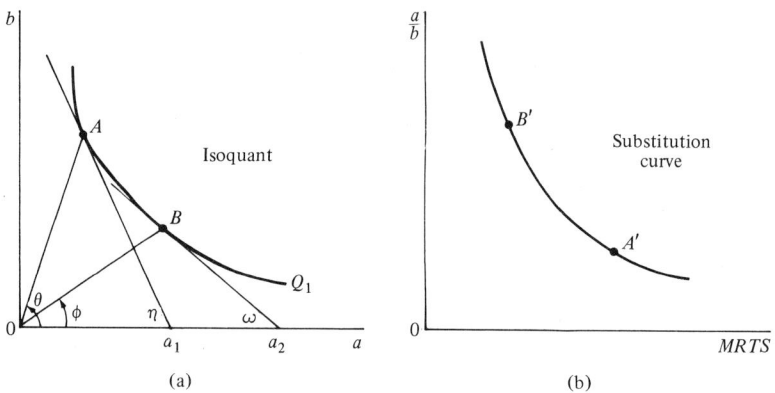

Figure 13-2

An expression for E_{sub} that holds for any production function may be written in terms of partial derivatives of the production function by putting equations (28) to (31) into equation (26). In the following equations $MRTS$ is shortened to s and the negative sign dropped, that is, $s = f_a/f_b$. From equation (14),

$$db = -\frac{f_a}{f_b} da \tag{27}$$

Then we find

$$d\left(\frac{b}{a}\right) = \frac{a\,db - b\,da}{a^2}$$

$$= \frac{a[-(f_a/f_b)da] - b\,da}{a^2} \tag{28}$$

$$= \frac{(-as - b)da}{a^2} = -\frac{as + b}{a^2}\,da$$

$$d(MRTS) = ds = \frac{\partial s}{\partial a}\,da + \frac{\partial s}{\partial b}\,db$$

$$= \frac{\partial s}{\partial a}\,da + \frac{\partial s}{\partial b}[-(f_a/f_b)da] \tag{29}$$

$$= \frac{\partial s}{\partial a}\,da + \frac{\partial s}{\partial b}(-s)da$$

$$= -\left(s\frac{\partial s}{\partial b} - \frac{\partial s}{\partial a}\right)da$$

$$\frac{\partial s}{\partial b} = \frac{\partial(f_a/f_b)}{\partial b} = \frac{f_b f_{ab} - f_a f_{bb}}{f_b^2} \tag{30}$$

$$\frac{\partial s}{\partial a} = \frac{\partial(f_a/f_b)}{\partial a} = \frac{f_b f_{aa} - f_a f_{ab}}{f_a^2} \tag{31}$$

Putting equations (28) to (31) into (26) yields

$$E_{sub} = -\frac{f_a f_b(a f_a + b f_b)}{ab(f_{aa}f_b^2 - 2f_{ab}f_a f_b - f_{bb}f_a^2)} \tag{32}$$

A shorter version of equation (32) may be obtained by using properties 1, 4, and 6 of homogeneous functions of degree 1 [3, pp. 95–96]:

$$E_{sub} = \frac{f_a f_b}{Q f_{ab}} \tag{33}$$

In this form it is easy to see that there is no problem of symmetry, since $E_{ab} = E_{ba}$, that is, the a and b may be interchanged and still yield the same value for E_{sub}.

A second alternative expression provides still more information. Substitute equations (28) and (29) into (26):

$$E_{sub} = \frac{d(b/a)}{b/a} \div \frac{ds}{s}$$

$$= \frac{-\dfrac{as+b}{a^2}\,da}{b/a} \div \frac{-\left(s\dfrac{\partial s}{\partial b} - \dfrac{\partial s}{\partial a}\right)da}{s}$$

$$= \frac{s}{ab}\frac{as+b}{s\left(\dfrac{\partial s}{\partial b} - \dfrac{\partial s}{\partial a}\right)} \tag{34}$$

Recognize that the slope of an isoquant is

$$\frac{d^2b}{da^2} = -\frac{ds}{da} = s\left(\frac{\partial s}{\partial b} - \frac{\partial s}{\partial a}\right) \tag{35}$$

Substitute equation (35) into equation (34):

$$E_{sub} = \frac{s}{ab}\frac{as+b}{(d^2b/da^2)} \tag{36}$$

The following information is obtained from equation (36):

1. Since s, a, and b are positive, E_{sub} is inversely proportional to a change in slope of the isoquant.

2. Since the isoquant must be convex to the origin over the substitution region, $d^2b/da^2 > 0$, and E_{sub} is invariably nonnegative.

3. The limiting values of E_{sub} are

    a. Infinite where a and b are perfect substitutes and isoquants are straight lines; in such a case the second derivative is zero and $E_{sub} \to \infty$.

    b. Zero where a and b are perfect complements that permit no substitution for each other; this is where proportions are fixed between limitational inputs; since isoquants are right angles, $d^2b/da^2 \to \infty$ and $E_{sub} \to 0$.

4. Typically for most production functions, inputs a and b must be mutually limitative (more of an input is necessary and sufficient to increase output) if E_{sub} is to be > 0 and are mutually limitational (more of an input is necessary but not sufficient to increase output) when $E_{sub} = 0$.

In summary, the elasticity of substitution is a nonnegative measure of the relative ease with which one input may be substituted for another while maintaining a constant output. Typically, the elasticity is zero when the inputs are mutually limitational and strictly positive when the inputs are mutually limitative. The elasticity is a pure number independent of the units in which inputs and outputs are measured. Finally, it is a symmetrical relation that is typically a function of the input point at which it is measured [3, p. 92].

13-7 Mathematical Production Functions

Actual production functions employed in business and industry often involve many inputs and jointly produced outputs [3, ch. 4–5]. It is not possible here to deal with all such complex functions. One can only examine a few of the basic types, which may serve as a basis for understanding the more complicated functions in the future. The simplest form, which is the basis for the Leontief input-output model, is

$$Q = \sum_{i=1}^{n} a_i x_i \tag{37}$$

However, this linear function, which is treated in Chapter 14, implies that proportional increases in outputs can be obtained indefinitely from increases in one or more inputs, and there is no nonzero second partial derivative, a requirement necessary for curvilinear marginal product curves and isoquants to exist.

The two best-known curvilinear functions are the Cobb-Douglas,

$$Q = cx^{\alpha}y^{\beta} \quad \text{(where } 0 < \alpha < 1, \ \beta = 1 - \alpha) \tag{38}$$

and the Arrow-Chenery-Minhas-Solow constant elasticity of substitution (*CES*),

$$Q = c[\alpha x^{-\beta} + (1 - \alpha)y^{-\beta}]^{-(1/\beta)} \quad \text{(where } c > 0, 0 < \alpha < 1) \tag{39}$$

Both of these functions are homogeneous of degree 1, but the second can assume constant elasticities of substitution other than unity. These two functions are discussed more fully in the following sections. Other examples of homogeneous functions were given in Chapter 12.

One example of a particular inhomogeneous function having a bell-shaped total product curve has also been carefully examined by C. E. Ferguson [3, ch. 4]:

$$Q = c[x^2y + xy^2 - \tfrac{2}{3}x^4 - \tfrac{2}{3}y^4] \quad \text{(where } c > 0) \tag{40}$$

The total, average, and marginal product curves for this function are given in Figure 13-3. Its precise symmetry is appealing to the eye, perhaps more so than the homogeneous functions approved by Frank Knight, which cut the horizontal axis to the right of the origin and then after reaching maximum cut the horizontal axis again at a finite value.

13-8 The Cobb-Douglas Function

A well-known linearly homogeneous production function is the Cobb-Douglas function[2] of the form $Q = cx^{\alpha}y^{\beta}$, where $\beta = 1 - \alpha$; the x and y are inputs and c, α, and β are constants $(0 < \alpha, \beta < 1)$ [see 3, pp. 99–101]. The degree of homogeneity is given by the sum of $\alpha + \beta$, as indicated by

$$kQ = c(kx)^{\alpha}(ky)^{\beta} = ck^{\alpha+\beta}x^{\alpha}y^{\beta} \tag{41}$$

This function is often used because of the simplicity of reading the output elasticities with respect to the inputs directly from the equation. This may be

---

[2] Notation for inputs was changed from a and b to x and y to avoid confusing a with α.

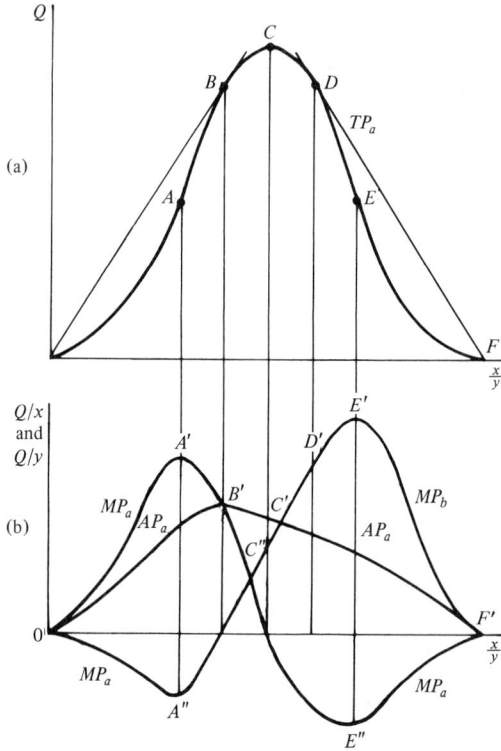

Figure 13-3

shown by substituting the partial derivatives of output Q into the elasticity formulas:

$$\frac{\partial Q}{\partial x} = c\alpha x^{\alpha-1} y^{\beta} \tag{42}$$

$$E_x = \frac{\partial Q}{Q} \div \frac{\partial x}{x} = \frac{\partial Q}{\partial x} \cdot \frac{x}{Q}$$

$$= (c\alpha x^{\alpha-1} y^{\beta}) \frac{x}{cx^{\alpha} y^{\beta}} = \alpha \tag{43}$$

Similarly, $E_y = \beta$. The output elasticities for this particular function are constant and independent of the other inputs. This is generally not the case with other functions.

The parameter c in equation (41) is called the *efficiency parameter*, because larger values mean greater levels of output for every input combination. The α is referred to as the *input intensity parameter*, because input x is required in greater amounts relative to y for larger values of α. This latter point may be demonstrated by examination of the $MRTS_{xy}$ for the equation. From section

13-5, the *MRTS* is defined as the ratio of the marginal products. Thus,

$$MRTS_{xy} = \frac{MP_x}{MP_y} = \frac{\alpha}{1 - \alpha} \frac{y}{x} \tag{44}$$

The expression on the far right is obtained as follows:

$$MP_x = \frac{\partial Q}{\partial x} = \alpha c \left(\frac{x}{y}\right)^{\alpha - 1}$$

$$MP_y = \frac{\partial Q}{\partial y} = (1 - \alpha)c \left(\frac{x}{y}\right)^{\alpha} \tag{45}$$

Therefore,

$$MRTS_{xy} = \frac{\alpha c(x/y)^{\alpha - 1}}{(1 - \alpha)c(x/y)^{\alpha}} = \frac{\alpha}{1 - \alpha} \frac{y}{x} \tag{46}$$

Note that the *MP*'s are always positive and decrease monotonically (marginal curve falls continuously without changing direction) for all positive input values. The latter point may be verified by checking to see if the second partial derivatives,

$$\frac{\partial Q^2}{\partial x^2} = \alpha(\alpha - 1)cx^{\alpha - 2}y^{1 - \alpha}$$

$$\frac{\partial Q^2}{\partial y^2} = -\alpha(1 - \alpha)cx^{\alpha}y^{-\alpha - 1} \tag{47}$$

are always negative, indicating concavity to the origin. Substituting positive values for parameter c and inputs x and y, and recalling that α is a positive fractional value, we find the second partials are indeed negative.

Two other characteristics of the Cobb-Douglas function are that it has a constant elasticity of substitution of unity, and that output expands without limit in stage II as one input is expanded infinitely while holding the others constant ($\alpha > 1$ and $\to \infty$). The second feature is considered mildly undesirable, according to Ferguson, since ideally output would approach some maximum value as the marginal product approaches zero asymptotically [3, pp. 100–101].

13-9 The ACMS *CES* Function

Since the 1961 articles by Arrow, Chenery, Minhas, and Solow (ACMS) [1], their production function has dominated the Cobb-Douglas in statistical studies and theoretical analyses [3, ch. 4–5 esp. pp. 101–107]. Analysis was thereby extended from the crucial limitation of elasticity of substitution of unity to one of any nonnegative constant one might choose to use. Returns to scale were also extended to include cases of increasing and decreasing returns.

In terms of the notation given in equation (39), the parameters are designated as:

c = efficiency constant

α = input intensity constant

β = substitution constant

Table 13-1

	Cobb-Douglas	ACMS CES	Ferguson
Equation for total product	$Q = cx^\alpha y^\beta$ (where $c > 0$, $0 < \alpha < 1$, and $\beta = 1 - \alpha$)	$Q = c[\alpha x^{-\beta} + (1-\alpha)y^{-\beta}]^{-(1/\beta)}$ (where $c > 0, 0 < \alpha < 1$)	$Q = c[x^2y + xy^2 - \tfrac{2}{3}x^4 - \tfrac{8}{3}y^4]$ (where $c > 0$)
Homogeneous	first degree	any degree	no
Function coefficient, E_Q, equals the degree of homogeneity	$E_Q = 1$	E_Q is a constant.	E_Q is a variable depending upon the value of x/y and scales.
Equation for MP	$\dfrac{\partial Q}{\partial x} = \dfrac{\alpha Q}{x}$ $\dfrac{\partial Q}{\partial y} = \dfrac{\beta Q}{y}$	$\dfrac{\partial Q}{\partial x} = c^{-\beta}\alpha\left(\dfrac{Q}{x}\right)^{1+\beta}$ $\dfrac{\partial Q}{\partial y} = c^{-\beta}(1-\alpha)\left(\dfrac{Q}{y}\right)^{1+\beta}$	$\dfrac{\partial Q}{\partial x} = c\left(2xy + y^2 - \tfrac{8}{3}x^3\right)$ $\dfrac{\partial Q}{\partial y} = c\left(x^2 + 2xy - \tfrac{8}{3}y^3\right)$
Homogeneous	(MP always positive for positive levels of inputs.) zero degree	(MP always positive for nonzero levels of inputs.) zero degree	no
Second derivatives	$\dfrac{\partial Q^2}{\partial x^2} = \alpha(\alpha-1)cx^{\alpha-2}y^{1-\alpha}$ $\dfrac{\partial Q^2}{\partial y^2} = -\alpha(1-\alpha)cx^\alpha y^{-\alpha-1}$	$\dfrac{\partial Q^2}{\partial x^2} = \dfrac{1}{E_{sub}}\alpha c^{-\beta}\left(\dfrac{Q}{x}\right)^{(1-E_{sub})/E_{sub}}\left(\dfrac{x\frac{\partial Q}{\partial x}-Q}{x^2}\right)$ $\dfrac{\partial Q^2}{\partial y^2} = \dfrac{1}{E_{sub}}(1-\alpha)c^{-\beta}\left(\dfrac{Q}{y}\right)^{(1-E_{sub})/E_{sub}}\left(\dfrac{y\frac{\partial Q}{\partial y}-Q}{y^2}\right)$	

	(These show the MP decrease monotonically for input values from 0 to ∞.)	(These plus property 1 show the MP decrease monotonically for input values from 0 to ∞.)	
Output elasticity, E_i	$E_x = \alpha$	$E_x = c^{-\beta}\alpha\left(\frac{Q}{x}\right)^{\beta}$	$E_x = \frac{cx}{Q}(2xy + y^2 - \frac{8}{3}x^3)$
	$E_y = \beta$	$E_y = c^{-\beta}(1-\alpha)\left(\frac{Q}{y}\right)^{\beta}$	$E_y = \frac{cx}{Q}(x^2 + 2xy - \frac{8}{3}y^3)$
MRTS, s	$s = \frac{\alpha}{1-\alpha}\left(\frac{y}{x}\right)$	$s = \left(\frac{\alpha}{1-\alpha}\right)\left(\frac{y}{x}\right)^{1/E_{sub}}$	$s = \frac{2xy + y^2 - \frac{8}{3}x^3}{x^2 + 2xy - \frac{8}{3}y^3}$
Elasticity of substitution, E_{sub}	unity	A constant equal to the reciprocal of the exponent of the input ratio in the expression for the $MRTS$. (1) When the constant is unity, $E_{sub} = 1$; the function is the same as the Cobb-Douglas; (2) When $E_{sub} > 1$, TP increases without bound as $a/b \to \infty$; (3) When $E_{sub} < 1$, TP increases to a maximum as $a/b \to \infty$; (4) When $E_{sub} = 0$, the function becomes the same as the Leontief.	

The c plays the same role here as in the Cobb-Douglas function in determining the level of output for every input combination. The α is so designated because from the expression for the $MRTS$ of x for y,

$$s = \frac{dy}{dx} = \frac{dQ}{dx} \div \frac{dQ}{dy}$$

$$= \frac{\alpha c^{-\beta}(Q/x)^{1/E_{sub}}}{(1-\alpha)c^{-\beta}(Q/y)^{1/E_{sub}}} \tag{48}$$

$$= \frac{\alpha}{1-\alpha}\left(\frac{y}{x}\right)^{1/E_{sub}}$$

it may be seen that for given values of s and E_{sub}, greater values of α mean smaller y/x ratios and therefore more intensive use of input x.

The reason for referring to β as the substitution constant follows from the the relation

$$E_{sub} = \frac{1}{1+\beta} \tag{49}$$

which shows E_{sub} is a constant related to the inverse of β.

Other technical aspects of the ACMS function are given in Table 13-1 for easy reference and comparison with other functions.

Questions and Problems

13-1. The following Arrow-Chenery-Minhas-Solow function is one of the best known in production theory [3, pp. 62, 76]:

$$q = \gamma[\delta x^{-p} + (1-\delta)y^{-p}]^{-(1/p)}$$

where γ and δ are > 0.
a. Is the function linear?
b. Is the function homogeneous? Prove it.
c. Find the expressions for the output elasticities.

13-2. Plot the total product curves assuming $b = 5$ for each of the following homogeneous equations of degree 1:

a. $Q = 100\left(\dfrac{2a^3b^2 + a^2b^3}{a^4 + b^4}\right)$ [Ref: Ferguson, 3, pp. 122–124]

b. $Q = 22a^{1/4}b^{3/4} - 20a^{1/3}b^{2/3}$ [Ref: Nutter, 10, and comments by Liebhafski, pp. 739–744; Rowe, pp. 745–746; DeFontenay, p. 750]

c. $Q = \dfrac{a^2b^2}{0.5a^3 + 0.5b^3}$ [Ref: Rowe, p. 746 in Ref. 10]

d. $Q = \dfrac{5a^2}{b} - \dfrac{a^3}{3b^2}$ [Ref: Ferguson, 3, p. 126, representing the class of equations used by Knight, Borts, and Mishan]

13.3. On what grounds might equations in parts *b* and *d* be judged as not realistic production functions?

References

1. Kenneth J. Arrow et al. "Capital-Labor Substitution and Economic Efficiency." *Review of Economics and Statistics* 43 (1961): 225–250.
2. George H. Borts and E. J. Mishan. "Exploring the 'Uneconomic Region' of the Production Function." *Review of Economic Studies* 29 (October 1962): 300–312.
3. C. E. Ferguson. *The Neoclassical Theory of Production and Distribution* (Cambridge: Cambridge University Press, 1969), ch. 4–7.
4. James M. Henderson and Richard E. Quandt. *Microeconomic Theory—A Mathematical Approach.* 2d ed. (New York: McGraw-Hill, 1971), pp. 52–102.
5. Frank H. Knight. *Risk, Uncertainty and Profit* (New York: Harper & Row, 1965), ch. 4, esp. pp. 94–104. First published in 1921.
6. Fritz Machlup. "The Commonsense of the Elasticity of Substitution." *Review of Economic Studies* 2 (1935): 202–213.
7. ———. "Reply." *Review of Economic Studies* 3 (1936): 151–152.
8. Thomas H. Naylor and John M. Vernon. *Microeconomics and Decision Models of the Firm* (New York: Harcourt, Brace & World, 1969), pp. 70–91.
9. G. Warren Nutter. "Diminishing Returns and Linear Homogeneity." *American Economic Review* (December 1963): 1084–1085.
10. ———. "Diminishing Returns and Linear Homogeneity: Reply." *American Economic Review* 59 (September 1964): 751. See also the comments by H. H. Lebhafsky, Ryuzo Sato, John W. Rowe, Jr., Dieter Schneider, and Patrick B. DeFontenay in the same issue, pp. 739–750.
11. Terutomo Ozawa. "A Note on the Three Stages of Production." *Nebraska Journal of Economics and Business* 10 (Spring 1971): 60–63.
12. Taro Yamane. *Mathematics for Economists—An Elementary Survey.* 2d ed. (Englewood Cliffs, N.J.: Prentice-Hall, 1968), ch. 4.

14 Production and Linear Programming

In this third chapter on production analysis it is instructive to re-examine the neoclassical production theory of the two preceding chapters in the context of linear programming.[1] First, while standard economic theory assumes that the optimal technical production process is a given parameter, programming analysis helps explain how it is determined. Second, this will present an opportunity to juxtapose some important concepts introduced previously but separately. While Chapter 3 dealt with the choice of optimum *product line*, that is, which items to produce in what numbers, this chapter focuses attention on the optimum *manufacturing process* by which factors are combined to produce output most efficiently. This difference in application does not, however, destroy the generality of the analysis, which covers both applications.[2] The analysis that follows deals with the simple case in which a single product is produced by more than one process.

14-1 Feasible Region and Process Rays

In contrast to the graphs of Chapter 3 with quantities of outputs X_1 and X_2 on the axes constrained by straight lines reflecting input capacities, the graphs used here have inputs b_1 and b_2 on the axes and production indifference curves reflecting production levels. Such representations focus attention upon *means* rather than *ends* or, in the terminology of Charnes and Cooper [2], upon *requirements space* rather than *solution space*, and are more similar to those of economic theory. While the formulations of Chapter 3 are more appropriate for analysis of a multiproduct firm with products competing for the limited resources, the present conception emphasizes the complementary productive relations between inputs.

To illustrate the concept of process and how linear programming relates to the standard economic theory of production, we will refer here to a simple example

---

[1] Much material in the first four sections of this chapter is based upon Baumol [1, ch. 12].

[2] For example, if the quantity of a commodity, Q_i, is given an additional subscript j to designate the process used, then Q_{ij} can be used to represent the amounts produced with the aid of process j. A single analysis could then be used to determine both the optimal outputs and optimal processes at the same time.

that could apply to a company engaged in manufacturing, say, automobiles, aircraft, residential homes, and most other manufacturing processes. Several alternatives are available to the firm for its use in forming the final product. The first alternative is to purchase all materials and labor necessary to produce all component parts entirely on the plant premises. The second alternative is to sub-contract the construction of some components that because of their specialized nature and relatively greater degree of labor-intensiveness might be produced as economically by a small job shop. The third is to subcontract all component parts to other firms, leaving only final assembly operations for the company itself to perform. After taking into account all costs and revenues, it is determined that constant unit profits under the three alternatives are 120, 110, and 100, res-pectively. The profit function to be maximized is therefore

$$\Pi = 120X_1 + 110X_2 + 100X_3$$

where X_1 is the number of units produced under process alternative 1, X_2 the number of units under process 2, and X_3 the number of units under process 3.

It is clear that process 1 would be the most profitable if there were no labor or plant restrictions. Existing conditions, however, dictate that the company can hire only 600 man-hours per week and must perform all its portion of the work within the confines of its existing plant, which has 800 square feet of floor space. Labor and space requirements for the three processes are, respectively, 100, 200, 300 and 400, 200, 150. The LP problem may be specified as

$$\text{Maximize } \Pi = 120X_1 + 110X_2 + 100X_3$$
$$\text{subject to} \quad 100X_1 + 200X_2 + 300X_3 \leq 600$$
$$400X_1 + 200X_2 + 150X_3 \leq 800 \qquad (1)$$
$$\text{where } X_1, X_2, X_3 \geq 0$$

represented by Figure 14-1.

Labor and space limitations are indicated by the shaded rectangular area.

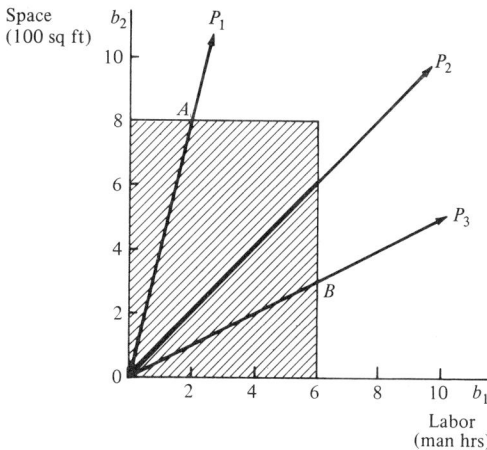

Figure 14-1

Process rays are obtained by drawing straight lines from the origin at slopes determined by the ratios of the coefficients for the particular processes, for instance, the slope of process ray P_1 is obtained by dividing 400 by 100, giving a space-labor ratio of 4 to 1. Fixed input proportions are implied in our definition of process, but we must be careful not to conclude that all processes having the same space-labor ratios are equally profitable. One process may be so much more efficient than another that twice the output can be obtained from a given amount of resources.

One unit of output can be obtained by combining 100 man-hours with 400 square feet of space using process 1. Because of space restrictions, only two units per week can be produced if the company performs all detailed operations. This is evident from the graph, because point A falls on the perimeter of the feasible region; 400 man-hours of the obtainable labor will evidently be unused.

Similarly, process 3 entails using a space-labor ratio of 1 to 2 ($= 150/300$). Labor is the effective constraint for this process, limiting production to two units of product per week at point B; 500 units of available space are unused. Process 2 is intermediate to processes 1 and 3, with a ratio of 1. It is evident from Figure 14-1 that process 2 utilizes available labor time more fully than process 1 and permits production, within the constraints, of one additional unit of output. On this basis, process 2 appears to be superior to process 1. It is clearly superior to process 3 in that output can be increased to three units by spreading plant operations over twice the floor space.

According to Figure 14-1, if choice is limited to using only one process, the second would be selected, since it permits greater output and fullest use of the limited resources. Some space, however, will not be used. If it is possible to use more than one process—producing some units under one and additional units under another—both labor and space can, as will be shown later, be fully employed to increase output. In any case, production is limited to space-labor ratios on, or within, the cone $P_1 O P_3$.

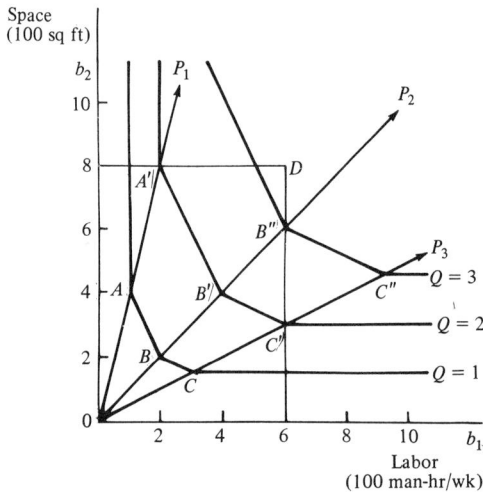

Figure 14-2

14-2   Construction of Isoquants

Isoquants for the LP model of equations (1) may be constructed by connecting points of equal output levels found along the process rays. For example, points A, B, and C in Figure 14-2 are points indicating the different combinations of labor and floor space required by processes 1, 2, and 3, respectively, to produce one unit of output. Points of equal output on adjacent process rays may be connected by straight lines if both processes can be used and no indivisibilities are present.

All points on, say, AB, representing one unit of output, are obtainable by use of various combinations of processes 1 and 2. This may be proved by reference to Figure 14-3. Given that OA and OB represent equal rates of production (Q), pick any point X on line AB. Construct YX parallel to OP_b and ZX parallel to OP_a. Recalling from plane geometry that parallel lines cut transverse lines proportionally, we observe that

$$\frac{OZ}{OB} = \frac{AX}{AB} = k$$

OZ thus represents an output level equal to a fraction k of that at point B produced with process P_b. That is, output at point $Z = kQ$. Similarly,

$$\frac{OY}{OA} = \frac{BX}{AB} = \frac{AB - AX}{AB} = 1 - \frac{AX}{AB} = 1 - k$$

indicating the fraction of Q produced at point Y by process P_a. Output at point $Y = (1 - k)Q$. The sum of outputs at points Y and Z are therefore

$$kQ + (1 - k)Q = Q$$

Output at point X is also the sum of the outputs at Y and Z, since $OY = ZX$ and $OZ = YX$, which follows from the fact that opposite sides of the parallelogram $OYXZ$ are equal.

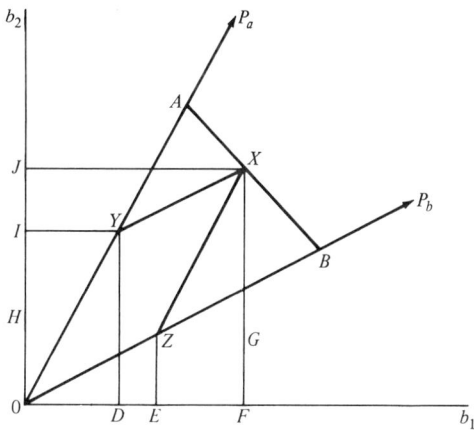

Figure 14-3

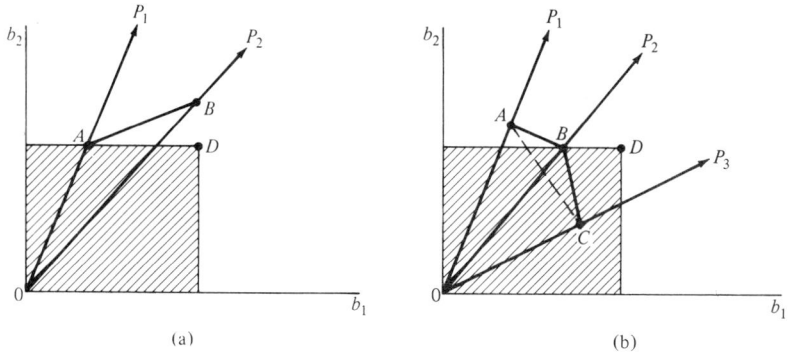

Figure 14-4

Having established that a line segment like AB coincides with the isoquant connecting points A and B, we can use this information to construct other isoquant segments shown in Figure 14-2. If process P_2 were for some reason not available to the company, the isoquant for $Q = 1$ would include segment AC without passing through point B. But as long as process 2 is a viable alternative, all points along AC are inferior to those along ABC, because they require greater amounts of resources to produce equal levels of outputs. The kinked isoquants of Figure 14-2 are characteristic of LP problems: Slopes are nonpositive and relevant segments are convex to the origin, indicating a nonincreasing marginal rate of substitution. If the isoquant had a positive-sloping segment, as shown in Figure 14-4a, all points on AB above point A would require more inputs for the same output level and could be ignored for purposes of efficiency. If the segments were concave, as in Figure 14-4b, consistent with an increasing marginal rate of substitution, process combinations along AC would be more efficient, for reasons just given, than along ABC. Fewer resources are used with AC than with ABC to produce the same level of output, making it the pertinent isoquant for optimal solution.

Isoquants of LP problems have parallel line segments between adjacent process rays, because the coefficients in the constraint equations are constant. This guarantees the isoquants will never intersect. The coefficients are actually output-input ratios; output must therefore rise by a fixed proportion of any increase in inputs. This implies a linearly homogeneous production function—one in which returns to scale are constant.

14-3 Calculation of Maximum Possible Output

In Figure 14-2 it is evident that the maximum possible output under the given constraints is greater than three units, because point D lies on some other isoquant above and to the right of isoquant $Q = 3$. Assuming that fractional units of output are permissible, the problem is reduced to finding the value of the isoquant that just touches the feasible region at point D. This may be determined graphically by drawing a new isoquant parallel to the segments falling between the process rays P_1 and P_2 and noting its intersection with P_2. Output can then

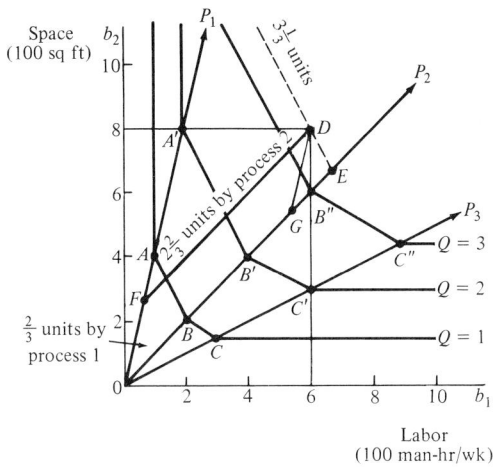

Figure 14-5

be measured by the distance along OP_2 from the origin to a point E shown in Figure 14-5. The distance $B''E$ appears to be about one third the distance between adjacent isoquants. Since the distance between isoquants Q_1, Q_2, and Q_3 represents one unit of output, output at point E must be about $3\frac{1}{3}$ units.

A combination of processes 1 and 2 must be used to obtain point D. How much to produce under each process may be determined by drawing a line parallel to either OP_1 or OP_2 to point D, such as FD or GD, and scaling output from the appropriate rays. The distance $OG\ (=FD)$ indicates about $2\frac{2}{3}$ units by process 2 and $OF\ (=GD)$ indicates about $\frac{2}{3}$ of the distance OA and $\frac{2}{3}$ units. The sum of $2\frac{2}{3}$ and $\frac{2}{3}$ is $3\frac{1}{3}$, which is equal to the number of units scaled from points O to E along OP_2.

The answers could be computed exactly by solving the LP problem of equations (2) using the technique of Chapter 3:

$$\text{Maximize } Q = X_1 + X_2 + X_3$$
$$\text{subject to } 100X_1 + 200X_2 + 300X_3 \le 600 \tag{2}$$
$$400X_1 + 200X_2 + 150X_3 \le 800$$
$$\text{where } X_1, X_2, X_3 \ge 0$$

	1	X_1	X_2	X_3
Q	0	1	1	1
S_1	600	-100	-200	-300
S_2	800	-400^*	-200	-150

(3)

	1	S_2	X_2	X_3
Q	2	$-\frac{1}{400}$	$\frac{1}{2}$	$\frac{5}{8}$
S_1	400	$\frac{1}{4}$	-150	$-\frac{525}{2}^*$
X_1	2	$-\frac{1}{400}$	$-\frac{1}{2}$	$-\frac{3}{8}$

(4)

	1	S_2	X_2	S_1
Q	$2\frac{20}{21}$	$-\frac{1}{525}$	$\frac{1}{7}$	$-\frac{1}{420}$
X_3	$1\frac{11}{21}$	$\frac{1}{1050}$	$-\frac{4}{7}*$	$-\frac{2}{525}$
X_1	$1\frac{3}{7}$	$-\frac{1}{350}$	$-\frac{2}{7}$	$\frac{1}{700}$

$$(5)$$

	1	S_2	X_3	S_1
Q	$3\frac{1}{3}$	$-\frac{1}{600}$	$-\frac{1}{4}$	$-\frac{1}{350}$
X_2	$2\frac{2}{3}$	$\frac{1}{600}$		
X_1	$\frac{2}{3}$			

$$(6)$$

As it turns out in this particular case, the answers are exactly the same as those roughly scaled from the graph.

14-4 Construction of Isoprofit Curves

The quantities found in section 14-3 would also provide maximum profits if unit profits were equal under each of the three processes. In the original problem (1), however, they were different, as indicated by the coefficients 120, 110, and 100, respectively. The tasks of this section are to convert the above isoquants to isoprofit lines and to determine optimum profits.

The isoquant ABC reproduced in Figure 14-6 is transformed into an isoprofit curve LKC as follows. Point C represents one unit of output and also $100 of profit; this will serve as one point on the first isoprofit curve to be plotted. Point B also represents one unit of output, but this unit yields a profit of $110; therefore the point along process ray OP_2 having $100 profits must be $100/110 = 91$ per cent of the distance OB at point K. Similarly, the $100 profit point on ray OP_1 is located $100/120 = 80$ per cent of OA at point L. By connecting the points C, K, and L with straight-line segments, we plot the relevant portion of the $100-isoprofit curve. Drawing upon the parallelism feature of the production function,

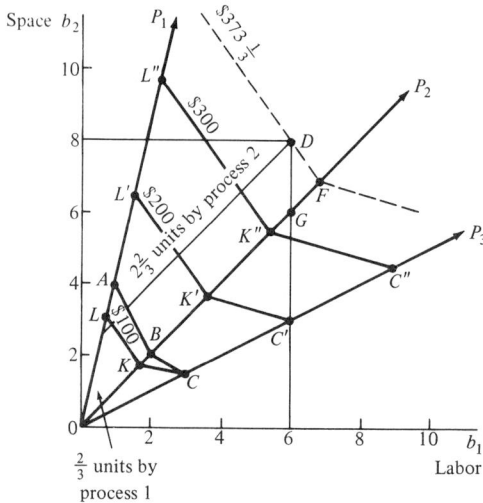

Figure 14-6

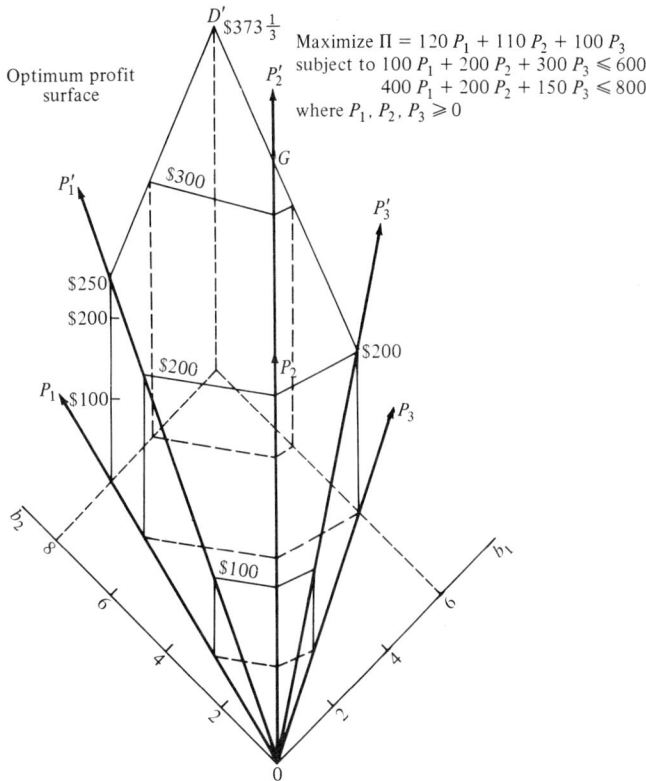

Maximize $\Pi = 120\,P_1 + 110\,P_2 + 100\,P_3$
subject to $100\,P_1 + 200\,P_2 + 300\,P_3 \leqslant 600$
$400\,P_1 + 200\,P_2 + 150\,P_3 \leqslant 800$
where $P_1, P_2, P_3 \geqslant 0$

Figure 14-7

which is homogeneous to degree 1, we can plot segments of higher isoprofit curves parallel to CKL. The spacing between adjacent isoprofit curves in multiples of $100, that is, $100, $200, $300, and so on, must be constant, because of the linearity assumptions of the problem, which imply constant profit returns to scale. Hence, other isoprofit curves such as $C'K'L'$ and $C''K''L''$ can be plotted at constant spacings along the rays.

The highest isoprofit line just touching the feasible region at point D intersects ray OP_2 at point F. Since $K''F$ measures about seven tenths of the distance between adjacent isoprofit lines spaced $100 apart, optimum profits are estimated to be $370. This estimate can be checked by obtaining a simplex solution.

	1	X_1	X_2	X_3	
Π	0	120	110	100	
S_1	600	-100	-200	-300	(7)
S_2	800	$-400*$	-200	-150	

	1	S_2	X_2	X_3	
Π	240	$-\frac{3}{10}$	50	55	
S_1	400	$\frac{1}{4}$	-150	$-\frac{525}{2}*$	(8)
X_1	2	$-\frac{1}{400}$	$-\frac{1}{2}$	$-\frac{3}{8}$	

218 Analysis of Production and Cost

	1	S_2	X_3	S_1
Π	$323\frac{17}{21}$	$-\frac{26}{105}$	$18\frac{4}{7}$	$-\frac{22}{105}$
X_3	$1\frac{11}{21}$	$\frac{1}{1050}$	$-\frac{4}{7}*$	$-\frac{2}{525}$
X_1	$1\frac{3}{7}$	$-\frac{1}{350}$	$-\frac{2}{7}$	$\frac{1}{700}$

(9)

	1	S_2	X_3	S_1
Π	$373\frac{1}{3}$	$-\frac{91}{420}$	$-32\frac{1}{2}$	$-\frac{1}{3}$
X_2	$2\frac{2}{3}$			
X_1	$\frac{2}{3}$			

(10)

The exact solution requires $\frac{2}{3}$ of one unit to be produced each week by process 1 and $2\frac{2}{3}$ units by process 2, yielding profits of $\$373\frac{1}{3}$. Figure 14-7 illustrates the solution in terms of a three-dimensional profit surface.

The fact that two processes are used in the optimal output is consistent with the basic theorem of linear programming, since there are also two constraints. Since optimality occurs at point D, both resources are used fully; slack variables S_1 and S_2 are obviously equal to zero. It is easy to see, however, that if only processes 2 and 3 could be used, b_2 would not be fully utilized. Profits would be greatest at point G, where the slack variable $S_2 = GD = 200$ square feet. Only process 2 would actually be used.

Two rather odd cases can arise, which should be mentioned here. Figure 14-8a shows a case in which the isoprofit line for three processes is a straight line. Here, it makes no difference in terms of profit if three rather than two processes are used, since isoprofit line segments AB and AC coincide at optimal point D. No advantage is gained, however, by using a third process. Figure 14-8b illustrates a phenomenon called *degeneracy*, where the number of processes is less than the number of input constraints. By accident, process 2 alone combines all the variable resources in the right proportion. While the basic theorem of linear programming is violated, computational difficulties may not be serious.

14-5 Sensitivity Analysis

Sensitivity analysis investigates the effects on the optimal solution of a programming problem resulting from actual or assumed changes in one of the con-

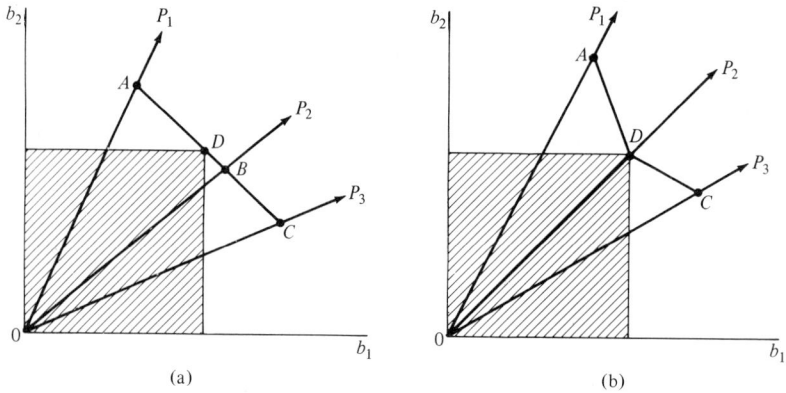

(a)   (b)

Figure 14-8

stants.[3] The information thereby provided may in some cases prove more valuable to the business manager or economist than precise knowledge of the optimal solution itself. This is especially true where the constants are only estimated and in forecasting, where they can change through time.

Consider the LP problem of equations (11).

$$\text{Maximize } \Pi = c_1 X_1 + c_2 X_2$$
$$\text{subject to } a_{11} X_1 + a_{12} X_2 \leq b_1$$
$$a_{21} X_1 + a_{22} X_2 \leq b_2 \tag{11}$$
$$\text{where } X_1,\ X_2 \geq 0$$

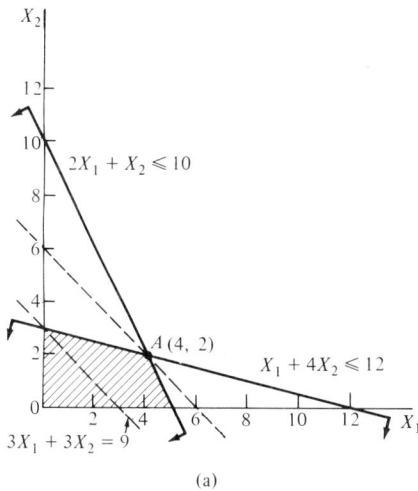

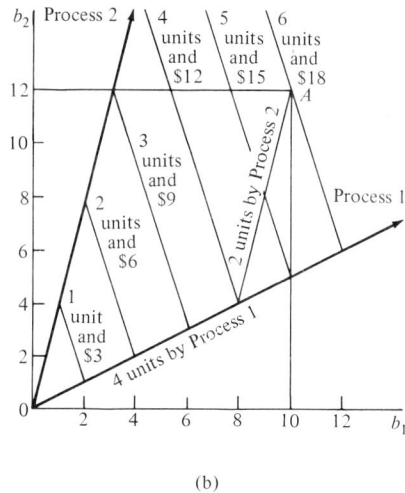

and Π = net revenue, defined as total revenue minus variable costs
    X_i = units of output produced by each process
    c_i = net revenues per unit of output from each process
    b_i = units of each factor available
    a_{11} = units of b_1 used to produce a unit of output by process 1
    a_{12} = units of b_1 used to produce a unit of output by process 2
    a_{21} = units of b_2 used to produce a unit of output by process 1
    a_{22} = units of b_2 used to produce a unit of output by process 2

The values of a_i, b_i, and c_i are given as follows:

$$\text{Maximize } \Pi = 3X_1 + 3X_2$$
$$\text{subject to } 2X_1 + X_2 \leq 10$$
$$X_1 + 4X_2 \leq 12$$
$$\text{where } X_1,\ X_2 \geq 0$$

Figure 14-9

---

[3] Much of this section is based on Thompson [7].

The graphical solution is shown in Figure 14-9. Figure 14-9a plots the constraint inequalities and objective function with X_1 and X_2 taken as the axes. The shaded area represents the feasible region. Four units by process 1 plus two by process 2 yield an optimal solution of six units of output and $18 net revenue. Figure 14-9a shows the solution in terms of process rays and isoquants, with the inputs as axes. Optimum solution is at point A requiring four units by process 1 and two by process 2 with full use of the limited inputs.

The a_i, b_i, and c_i will now be varied one at a time and changes from the original optimal solution noted. First, one of the unit profitabilities, c_i, will be changed, reflecting a possible change in market prices for the outputs or inputs or some combination of both. If output unit prices were to rise from $3 to $4, the optimal output and use of inputs would remain the same. This indicates a perfectly inelastic supply curve. The firm would continue to supply the same amounts for this short-run period but would be attaining total profits of $24 instead of $18.

When many products and processes are involved, it is unlikely that the c_i would change together. This would cause a change in the slope of the objective function and might produce a change in the optimal outputs and programs. Suppose c_1 falls from $3 to $2 because of a rise in costs unique to process 1, perhaps because of some variable factor used in process 1 but not in process 2. Changes in outputs from process 1 will cause changes in the number of variable units required by that process. Such information could be used to derive the firm's demand schedule for the variable factor. Figure 14-10 reflects the decline in c_1. Figure 14-10a shows the reduced slope of the objective function, which when moved out from the origin to the most distant point of the feasible region, has the same corner-point solution as before. Figure 14-10b shows that the isoprofit lines have rotated counterclockwise from their previous positions coincident with the isoquants, which remain unchanged. Maximum net revenue at point

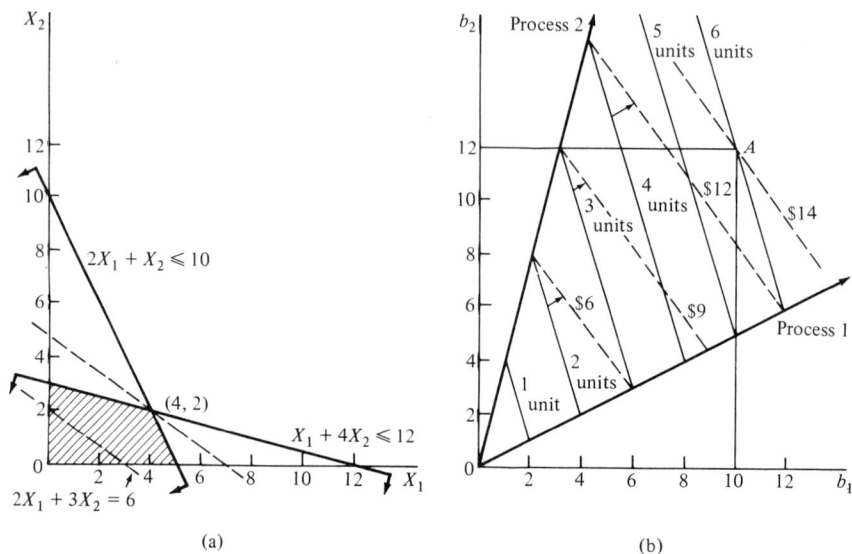

(a)   (b)

Figure 14-10

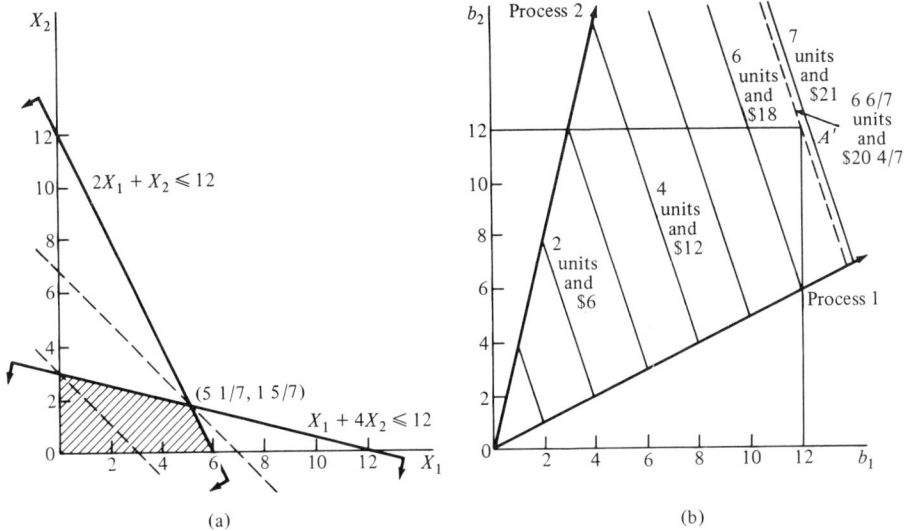

Figure 14-11

A has decreased \$4 to \$14. A fall of unit profits from process 1 by one third (\$3 to \$2) has caused a 22.2 per cent drop in total profits.

By changing the b_i, the effects of changes in resource availabilities can be explored. Figure 14-11a shows a shifting outward of the constraint equation for the first factor from its original position in Figure 14-9a. The new optimum solution requires $5\frac{1}{7}$ units from process 1 and $1\frac{5}{7}$ units from process 2. Figure 14-11b shows a shift in the vertical constraint from $b_1 = 10$ to $b_1 = 12$ and shifting of the optimum from point A in Figure 14-9b to A', with maximum net revenue of \$20$\frac{4}{7}$.

Finally, changes in the a_i mean giving up the assumptions of constant input proportions and rotating the appropriate process rays. The slope of process ray 2 in Figure 14-9b is given by the ratio of a_{22}/a_{12}, or 4/1. Figure 14-12b shows the result of a modification of process 2 whereby a technological change permits a reduction from four to three units of factor b_2 for each unit of output. Note that the slope of process ray 2 is now 3 rather than 4, and the slopes of the isoquants and iso net revenue lines are slightly less. The optimal solution is still at point A, but the maximum units are raised to $6\frac{2}{5}$ units ($3\frac{3}{5}$ produced by process 1 and $2\frac{4}{5}$ by process 2), and the profits are raised to \$19$\frac{1}{5}$. Figure 14-12a shows a clockwise rotation of the second constraint equation, a slightly expanded feasible region, a drop in the units of output produced by process 1 to $3\frac{3}{5}$, and an increase in output by process 2 to $2\frac{4}{5}$.

Several computer manufacturers now have computer programs with efficient solution algorithms[4] for LP problems that permit individual and simultaneous parameter variation of the a_i, b_i, and c_i.

---

[4] An algorithm is a problem-solving technique based upon a series of precise and simple mechanical operations.

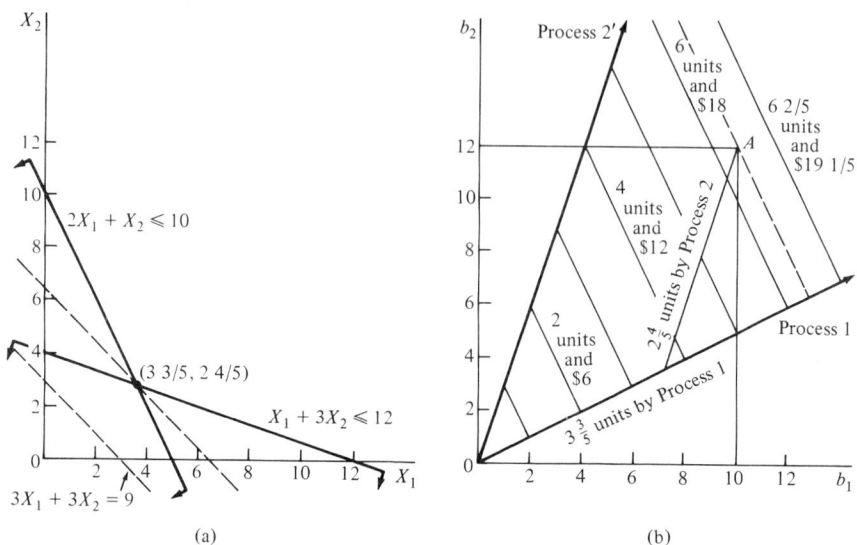

(a)

(b)

Figure 14-12

Questions and Problems

14-1. Answer the following questions with reference to Figure 14-1:
  a. If only process 1 were available to the manufacturer, how much could he produce?
  b. How much labor and space would go unused at point A?
  c. Under the assumptions of the model, does it make any real difference to the manufacturer whether process 1 or 3 is used? Why?
  d. If only one process could be used, which should it be? Why?
  e. Does process ray OP_2 accurately represent process 2?

14-2. Referring to Figure 14-2, answer the following questions:
  a. Explain why it is never efficient to combine processes 1 and 3.
  b. Show numerically by reference to the constraint equations that AB and $A'B'$ are parallel.

14-3. In Figure 14-4a is there any way to use all of the available resource b_1 efficiently by combining processes 1 and 2? Explain.

14-4. In Figure 14-4, which are the optimum output points?

14-5. Plot the isoquants for $Q = 1, 2, 3$ on Figure 14-7.

14-6. Show graphically and calculate using the simplex technique and program the effects produced in Figure 14-9 by each of the following changes:
  a. a_{21} is changed from 1 to 2.   d. b_1 is changed from 10 to 8.
  b. a_{12} is changed from 1 to 4.   e. c_1 is changed from 3 to 4.
  c. b_2 is changed from 12 to 10.   f. c_2 is changed from 3 to 2.

14-7. In problem 14-6, what real-world events could possibly have triggered each of the hypothesized changes?

References

1. William J. Baumol. *Economic Theory and Operations Analysis*. 3d ed. (Englewood Cliffs, N.J.: Prentice-Hall, 1972), ch. 12.
2. A. Charnes, W. W. Cooper, and A. Henderson. *Introduction to Linear Programming* (New York: Wiley, 1953), p. 74.
3. George B. Dantzig. *Linear Programming and Extensions* (Princeton, N.J.: Princeton University Press, 1963), pp. 265–275.
4. Robert Dorfman, Paul A. Samuelson, and Robert M. Solow. *Linear Programming and Economic Analysis* (New York: McGraw-Hill, 1958), ch. 6.
5. Saul I. Gass. *Linear Programming*. 3d ed. (New York: McGraw-Hill, 1969), pp. 144–154.
6. Jati K. Sengupta and Karl A. Fox. *Economic Analysis and Operations Research: Optimization Techniques in Quantitative Economic Models* (Amsterdam: North-Holland Publishing Co., 1969), ch. 4. This is an advanced treatment of sensitivity analysis.
7. Gerald Everett Thompson. "On Varying the Constants in a Linear Programming Model of the Firm." *American Economic Review* (June 1968): 485–495.

15 Cost Concepts in Economics and Business

Two important considerations for the business manager are revenues and the costs of doing business. To be successful today, the business person must have more than a casual understanding of the words of the toastmaster who, with wit and humor, thus condensed the guest professor's 2-hour after-dinner speech: "If your outgo exceeds your intake, then your upkeep will be your downfall." Almost every decision in managerial economics is based upon a cost-benefit comparison of the anticipated results of proposed courses of action. Many cost concepts have been devised over the years to help managers make cost decisions. This chapter presents the major ones. Chapter 16 deals with more advanced topics in cost analysis.

15-1 Relevant Cost

Business managers and economists are most interested in the costs they consider relevant for the problem at hand [3]. Relevant, or "true," costs are not always immediately evident, however. In some situations, accurate identification of relevant cost can be the single most complicated and critical task confronting the decision maker. A few examples will illustrate the point. What is the relevant cost of an item purchased for use at some future time? Should storage and interest costs be included? For purposes of economic analysis, the answer is yes. For income tax purposes, unless the costs are paid to other parties, the answer is no. Similarly, are the costs of building and machinery purchased years ago relevant for current decision making? In general, no, but for purposes of computing income taxes and stockholder reports, historical costs spread over time by one of several techniques (straight-line, sum-of-the-digits, declining balance, amortization) are considered relevant costs. The same building and machinery should, however, be assigned zero costs in decisions to expand facilities or discontinue operations. Also, the relevant cost of a fully depreciated machine may not be zero if it has scrap value and if retention requires maintenance and police protection.

Another kind of problem arises from the treatment of inventories when costs change. Should currently charged prices cover the higher-cost units even though others on hand were produced when materials and labor were cheaper? Accountants are required to adopt and follow consistently some rule for assigning costs of inventory, typically FIFO or LIFO (first-in-first-out or last-in-first-out), but this may be of little relevance to the business person whose price is dictated by the market and by government price controls.

15-2 Alternative Cost

The single most important cost concept for business decision makers and economists is alternative cost. It holds that the value of any resource is determined by its next best use. By this rule, a business person who wishes to buy, say, shares of a corporation on the New York Stock Exchange must pay an amount at least equal to what others will pay. Similarly, a firm must pay its managers sufficient salaries to keep them from being bid away by competitors. This example also provides a hint as to why the term *opportunity cost* is often used synonymously with *alternative cost*. One's opportunity is one's available alternative.

In the event one sells one's resources at a price higher than the next best alternative, one is said to obtain *economic rent*. This is indicated in Figure 15-1a by the shaded area. The stock of resources is indicated by the vertical supply curve. When one sells at a price p_2 greater than the next best alternative p_1, one obtains additional revenue equal to $(p_2 - p_1)q_1$, the shaded rectangular area. In a purely competitive market (discussed in Chapter 20) p_2 and p_1 would be equal and economic rent would equal zero. An example of high economic rent might be the case of a popular \$2,000-a-week rock musician whose next best employment opportunity is as a \$200-a-week truck driver.

In the event that a consumer pays a price lower than he would have paid to obtain a product or service, the difference is called *consumer surplus*. Suppose the consumer's demand curve is shown in Figure 15-1b. For all units up to q_1, he would have paid a higher price, if necessary, to meet his demand. He would have paid a total dollar amount equal to the area of the trapezoid $OABq_1$, but he only paid OP_1Bq_1, leaving a consumer surplus of the shaded area P_1AB. Such concepts are used later in discussing pricing strategy and economic welfare.

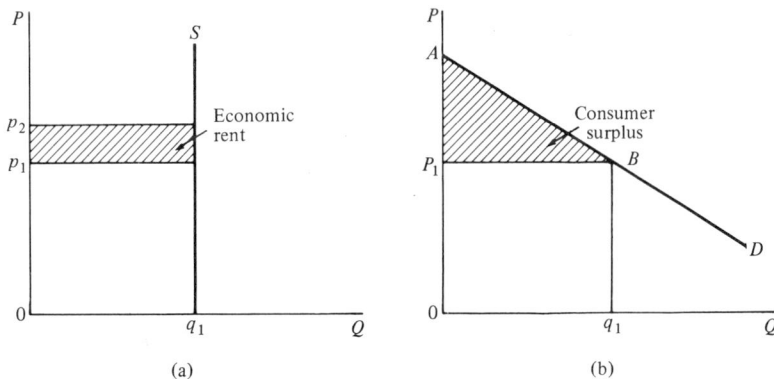

Figure 15-1

15-3   Implicit, Explicit, and Full Costs

Alternative cost calculations require the summation of all costs associated with a proposed action. Even the least knowledgeable business person knows to deduct out-of-pocket expenses paid to others from sales revenue to figure business profits for tax purposes. Such *explicit* costs, however, fail to include his own wages, which he could have obtained by selling his services to another firm, and the use of any of his own capital he may have devoted to the business. The additional, but very real, costs in the form of his wages, interest, and normal profits are *implicit* to the firm's continued operation and must therefore be taken into account. The sum of all implicit and explicit costs is called *full costs*. Why include any costs of land used in a business for which payment has already been made? The reason is that the land can alternatively be rented to someone else. Furthermore, the implicit cost of two managers may not be identical, because one may have superior alternative employment prospects.

15-4   Variable, Fixed, and Total Costs

Variable costs are those over which the manager has control during the relevant time period. Resources such as utilities, supplies, and materials may be purchased at the firm's discretion—these are *variable* costs. On the other hand, some costs may have already been incurred by contractual agreements. Leases may have been signed, land purchased, union employment and wage conditions agreed upon, and advertising space prepaid—none of which can be changed in the short run. Costs of these items are said to be *fixed*. Given sufficient time for adjustments to be made, for instance, plants expanded or sold, all costs are variable. The sum of fixed and variable costs is called *total cost*.

Given the total-cost function

$$C = 500 + 6X_1 + 3X_2 \tag{1}$$

where the X_i represent products or different processes used to produce a single product, fixed costs are $500, since they are incurred regardless of whether a single unit is produced. Variable costs are $6X_1 + 3X_2$; if $X_1 = 30$ and $X_2 = 20$, variable costs equal $6(30) + 3(20) = \$240$. Total cost is therefore $740.

Such variable-cost and fixed-cost concepts play a large role in break-even analysis, discussed briefly in section 15-7. Comments on the limitations of the approach are deferred until then.

15-5   Total, Average, and Marginal Costs

If the firm's total cost of doing business is given by the function

$$TC = 350 + 50Q - 10Q^2 + 20Q^3 \tag{2}$$

then the per unit, or average, cost is

$$AC = \frac{TC}{Q} = \frac{350}{Q} + 50 - 10Q + 20Q^2 \tag{3}$$

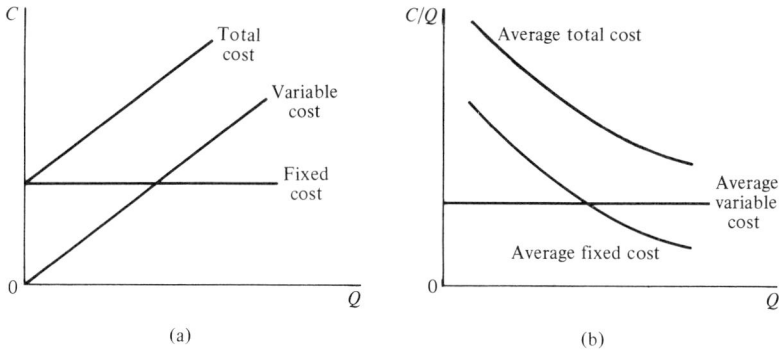

Figure 15-2

Note that average cost, referred to on occasion as average total cost, is the sum of average fixed cost $(350/Q)$ and average variable cost $(50 - 10Q + 20Q^2)$. Marginal cost is defined as the rate of change, or first derivative, of the total-cost function:

$$MC = \frac{d(TC)}{dQ} = 50 - 20Q + 60Q^2 \tag{4}$$

Marginal cost at any point on the marginal-cost curve at a given output is determined by the slope of the total-cost curve.

The variable-cost and fixed-cost curves of Figure 15-2a, used in linear break-even analysis (but not for the preceding equations), may be added vertically to obtain total cost. Total and variable costs are shown to be constant functions of output. This dictates a constant (horizontal) average-variable-cost curve and a continuously falling average-fixed-cost curve, both of which are shown in Figure 15-2b. The horizontal average-variable-cost curve and the hyperbolic average-fixed-cost curve of Figure 15-2b are added vertically to obtain average total cost.

For the average-total-cost and average-variable-cost curves to conform to the traditional saucer shapes, the total assumed in neoclassical economic theory for the variable-cost curve must be shaped not as in Figure 15-2b but with a curvature similar to a reversed S canted to the right, as shown in Figure 15-3a. The average and marginal curves of Figure 15-3b can be derived in a manner similar to that used in deriving the revenue curves of Chapter 2. Points on the AVC curve are plotted to correspond to the slope of a line (tangent of angle θ) drawn from the origin to a point on the variable-cost curve. Points on the ATC curve are drawn similarly with respect to the total-cost curve. Note that the inflection points A and D determine the level of output at minimum marginal cost at point A'. Also, MC equals AVC and ATC at their minimum points C' and B', since the slopes of the total curves are equal to the slopes of lines drawn to the origin.

The inflection points mark the boundary between diminishing and increasing *marginal costs*, which correspond to increasing and diminishing marginal returns to scale. (Recall the discussion in sections 12-3 and 12-7 of Chapter 12.) Points like A and D must not be confused with point B, which marks the boundary

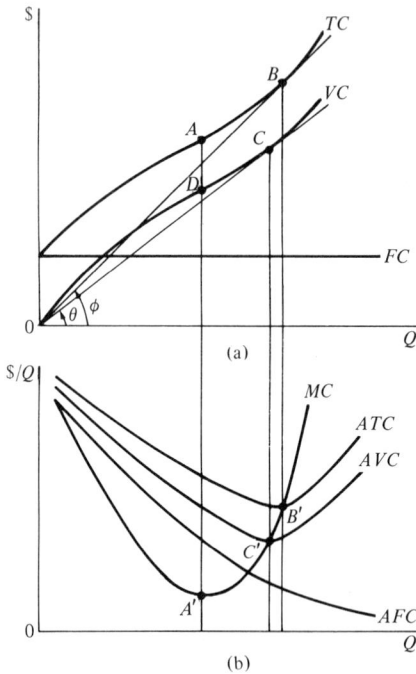

Figure 15-3

between diminishing and increasing *average total cost*, and with point *C* for *average variable cost*. Points *B* and *C* are always at different outputs as long as some costs are fixed, that is, as long as analysis deals with the short run. Omitting the adjective marginal or average from a statement, as many authors do, often results in unnecessary ambiguity.

15-6   Incremental Cost

Incremental cost is closely related to the concept of marginal cost but is less limited in scope. Often in the real world it is not practical to vary output by equal units. Indivisibilities often require production to take place in lumps or batches of different sizes. The additional costs associated with new products, machinery, buildings, and distribution channels typically occur at extended intervals rather than in small amounts added continuously as output is expanded. When the firm reaches the point of needing more floor space, it makes little sense to impute the whole cost of a building addition to the next unit produced. The firm must be sure that the expanded capacity is warranted by the forecasted demand, say, by an increment of 1,000 units. For example, assume that all of the firm's costs come in lumps at various intervals as shown in Figure 15-4. Steps in the total-cost curve in Figure 15-4a represent cost increments of $1 million each, required at the zero, second, third, and fifth 1,000 units of output *Q*. These steps are associated with discontinuities in the average-cost curve shown in Figure 15-4b and with the critical points at which the incremental outlays are made, as indicated by Figure 15-4c.

Once the decision is made to go ahead with an incremental investment and the money is spent, all the preceding costs are *sunk*, that is, they cannot be increased or decreased by varying the rate of production. The profit-maximizing firm should, in the absence of additional costs that vary continuously with the rate of output, endeavor to operate at capacity rates as long as the output can be sold

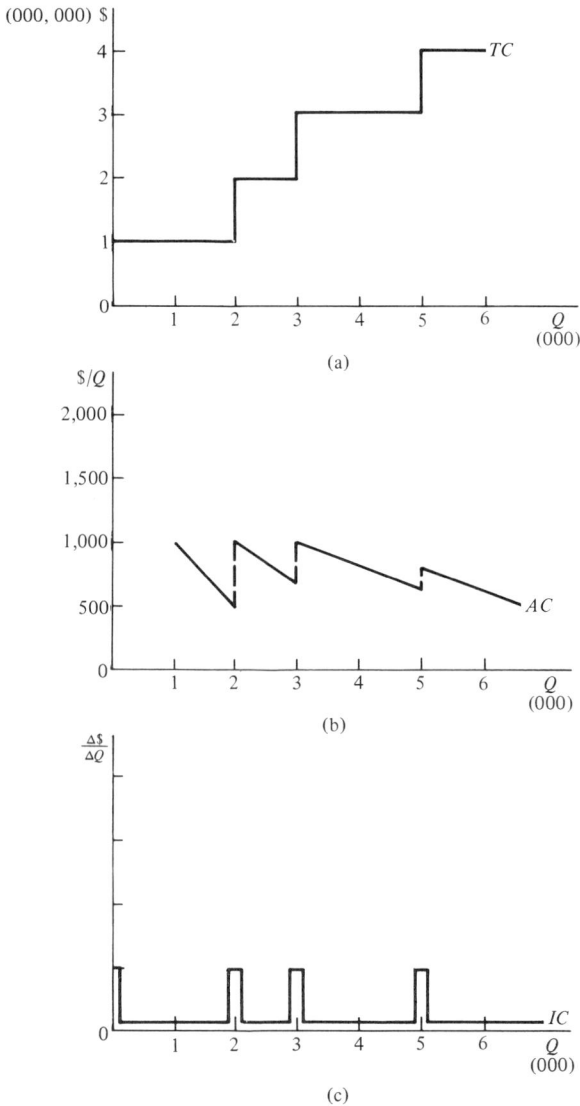

Figure 15-4

at positive prices and without spoiling future sales by selling goods now at below normal prices. Profits are lost when business is turned away if revenues can be brought in with little or no additional outlays.

15-7 Break-Even Analysis

Break-even analysis is of some use in examining costs, revenues, and profits at various output levels. Total revenue and cost curves are plotted on the same graph, as in Figure 15-5. The TC curve is the same as in Figure 15-3a, exhibiting fixed costs of OC_1 and variable costs that initially rise at a decreasing rate and later at an increasing rate. The TR curve depicts, by its diminishing slope, falling revenues attributable to price reductions required to sell greater quantities. Unit prices and costs associated with a given output may be found by noting the slope of a line drawn from the origin to the pertinent points on the TR and TC curves. Profit or loss is measured by the vertical distance between the curves. Profits are present over the range $Q_1 Q_3$, where $TR > TC$, with maximum profits at Q_2, where the vertical distance between the TR and TC curves is greatest. The problem faced by the profit-maximizing business manager is to identify the optimal output Q_2 and do everything possible to hold costs to no higher than the TC curve and sales to no lower than the TR curve.

With this formulation of the problem in mind, the decision maker can find the desired information through simple mathematical calculations. The case at hand will dictate the equations for TR and TC. For example, if they are found to be

$$TR = 200Q - Q^2$$
$$TC = 50 + 50Q + 2Q^2$$

then the break-even points are where

$$TR = TC$$
$$200Q - Q^2 = 50 + 50Q + 2Q^2$$
$$-3Q^2 + 150Q - 50 = 0$$

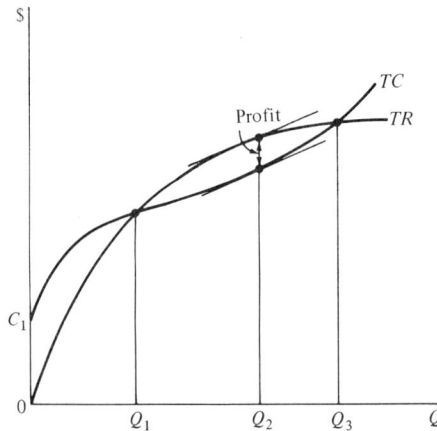

Figure 15-5

By use of the quadratic formula, the break-even values of Q can be calculated:

$$Q = \frac{-150 \pm \sqrt{(150)^2 - 4(-3)(-50)}}{2(-3)}$$

$$Q = \frac{-150 \pm \sqrt{22,500 - 600}}{-6}$$

$$Q = \frac{-150 \pm 148}{-6} = \tfrac{1}{3}, 50$$

Between the break-even points $Q = \tfrac{1}{3}$ and 50, optimum output can be obtained by setting the derivative of the profit function equal to zero and solving for Q:

$$\Pi = TR - TC$$
$$= -3Q^2 + 150Q - 50 = 0$$

$$\frac{d\Pi}{dQ} = -6Q + 150 = 0$$

$$Q = \frac{150}{6} = 25$$

In the simplest application of break-even analysis, linear revenue and cost functions are used. This is appropriate where the relations are approximately linear over the relevant range and where the error introduced is small relative to other uncertainties of the problem. Rough estimates thus obtained are of some value when it is unnecessary to account for more complex variables, such as changes in selling prices, operations of plant other than at capacity, the presence of substitute inputs, or changes in the quality of resources and products. In all cases, good judgment and common sense must prevail over techniques or numerical answers.

In practical matters, the variable–fixed cost analysis is subject to several serious limitations [2, pp. 84–85]. First, data for the study usually come from accounting records, and there is usually no satisfactory way to check the subjective judgment of accountants in their separation of variable and fixed costs. Second, linearity should not be automatically assumed; plots of the data should be made before computing least-squares regression lines to see if linear relations really exist. Synthesis of cost-output relations can also be obtained from engineering data. Third, when output is assumed to be the sole determinant of cost, many other factors are ignored, some of which may be significant. Multiple regression analysis, several examples of which are given in Chapter 16, helps to overcome this problem.

15-8   The Planning Curve

The gap between the short and the long runs is bridged by the use of a graph like Figure 15-6. The long-run average-cost curve, LAC, also called the firm's plan-

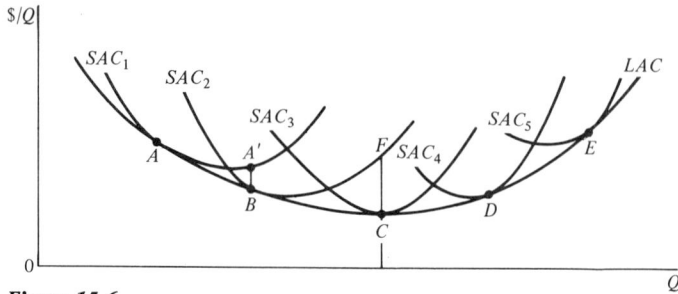

Figure 15-6

ning curve, is portrayed as an envelope of the firm's short-run curves.[1] Each *SAC* curve depicts the unit costs to the firm associated with a limited range of outputs possible when not all factors, such as the size of the assembly line and building, can be changed. Output can be varied by employing different amounts of labor and supply variables. Optimum (least unit cost) output for design size 1 is at point A' on SAC_1. Lower unit costs can be designed for greater outputs by increasing the plant size to SAC_2 and SAC_3. At point C, however, long-run economies of scale turn to diseconomies and unit costs begin to rise.

A curious aspect of this concept is that there is only one plant size and output, point C, where operations will be at minimum unit cost. At plant size given by SAC_1, plant managers will never want to operate at optimum plant capacity A', because even lower unit costs can be obtained by building a larger plant SAC_2. They will choose to operate on the downward-sloping side of SAC_1 at outputs no greater than at point A; beyond point A they would, given time to adjust operations, shift to larger plants. Beyond point C, they will run plants at greater than capacity before building larger ones. In short, they will operate plants at *less than optimum capacity* when long-run *decreasing* costs are present and at *greater than capacity* when long-run *increasing* costs are present.

The bowl shape of the *SAC* curves is attributable to the manner in which the inputs are combined, corresponding to the average-product curves of Chapter 12. This may be explained by reference to Figure 15-8. At successive points along an average-variable-cost (*AVC*) curve, more of factor a is used with a fixed factor b. The *SMC* and *AVC* curves are inverses (flipped-over versions) of the MP_a and AP_a curves, respectively; that is, when *SMC* is falling (rising), MP_a is rising (falling) and the same for *AVC* and AP_a. This may be clarified by examining the definitions of marginal cost and marginal product. The former is simply the

[1] The envelope theorem that the firm's *SAC* curves are indeed circumscribed by a *LAC* envelope curve, attributed to Jacob Viner (1931) [7], may be explained by reference to Figure 15-7. The *LAC* curve of Figure 15-7b corresponds to the expansion path plotted in Figure 15-7a. The *SAC* curve corresponds to a movement along the horizontal line on which capital is fixed at level b_1. When production is at point B in either diagram, short-run and long-run costs are identical. Any variation of short-run output along the horizontal line from b_1 from the optimal input combination at B gives rise to higher short-run costs. For example, if output level Q_1 is produced, the firm operates in the short run at A' rather than at A on isocost line P_2, which is higher than isocost P_1, establishing A' above A in Figure 15-7b. Similarly, production at point C' has a higher total cost, P_5, than at point C with cost P_4. Hence, the *SAC* curve is above the *LAC* except at point B, where a tangency exists. By varying plant size, that is, b_1, the theorem is established [5, pp. 155–156].

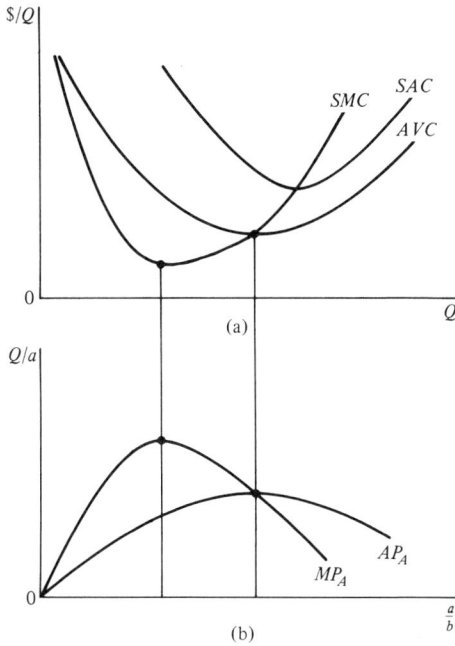

Figure 15-8

additional amount of factor a required to produce an additional unit of output Q times the dollar unit cost of factor a:

$$MC = \frac{da}{dQ} \cdot P_a$$

The latter is the additional amount of output that can be produced by using another unit of factor a while holding all other factors constant:

$$MP_a = \frac{dQ}{da}$$

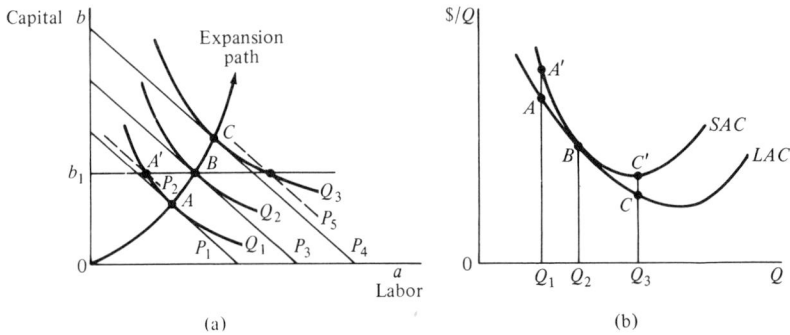

Figure 15-7

For $P_a = 1$, it is obvious that MC and MP_a are inverses:

$$MC = \frac{da}{dQ} = \frac{1}{(dQ/da)} = \frac{1}{MP_a}$$

Moreover, maximum MP occurs at the same output as minimum MC. A similar relation holds for the average-variable-cost and average-product curves.

Observations from American industry suggest that the LAC envelope is actually relatively flat on the bottom over a fairly large range of output, as shown in Figure 15-9. Rather than a single output possessing lowest unit cost, many points C have similar unit costs. Unit costs remain constant as output is expanded from OQ_1 to OQ_2. This could be true for plants operated more hours or work shifts per week where wage differentials are insignificant.

The precise shape of the LAC will vary from firm to firm, but the curve is generally thought to trace the maturity of an industry. In early stages of historical development economies of size prevail, followed by a period of constant unit costs and later by rising costs as resources become more scarce. Many large modern firms in mature industries have experienced an extended life of the middle range, causing observers to believe the curve to be much flatter than typically represented and shaped perhaps more like the letter L than the letter U.

The alleged saucer shape of the LAC curve is believed to result from the presence of economies and diseconomies external to the firm. If spill-overs from the activities of other firms and of consumers serve to decrease the LAC of the firm, such economies account for the downward-sloping portion of the curve. Examples typically given for economies are spreading surplus managerial talents over greater operations and using specialized talent and equipment. If spill-overs result in diseconomies like the bidding up of resource prices and breakdowns in communications within the managerial bureaucracy, these account for the rising portion. Externalities are so important to business executives that Chapter 23 is entirely devoted to explaining their nature and implications. More will be said in Chapter 16 about the rationale for the shapes given to the cost function. But first it may be helpful to tie together the three time periods and the associated cost curves used in standard economic analysis of price and output changes.

15-9 Equilibrium Changes Through Time

Adjustments in output by the production manager to changing demand situations may be traced by following the shifting of the very-short-run-cost ($VSRC$) curves through time in a competitive market [4, 6]. Figure 15-10a shows the initial equilibrium at point 1. In the very short run, production cannot be increased. Since sales can be made only from inventories, the $VSRC$ curve is shown as perfectly inelastic. The curve could be shown with a slight slope to the right to represent more accurately the marketing supply actions of the manager who holds back some of the product for the best customers or to fill emergency orders. The manager may remove such items from the shelves, in the case of a retail outlet, or simply raise the price to ration goods to those who will pay more.

The long-run equilibrium in a very competitive market is one in which price and cost are equal. This is held to be true, since the actual or potential threat of entry of new firms keeps prices so low that there are no *economic* profits. Are

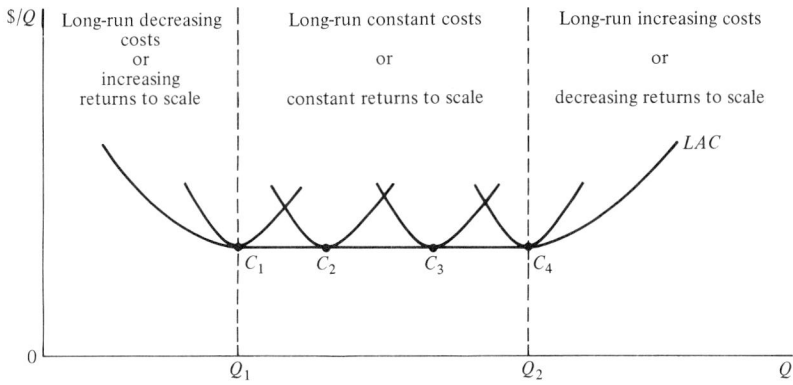

Figure 15-9

there *normal* profits?[2] Yes, because they are considered a cost, but there can be no economic profits. (This is discussed in detail in Chapter 20.) Long-run unit costs are assumed to be constant—hence the horizontal, constant-returns LRC curve. If increasing (decreasing) returns to scale were present, the LRC would be drawn upward (downward).

The short-run cost (SRC) curve is upward-sloping to the right, reflecting the middle ground in which some inputs are held fixed while others can be varied. As additional variable factors are used with other existing factors, there is thought to be some loss of efficiency, reflected by the higher unit cost for greater ouputs.

Figure 15-10b shows an increase in demand for the product from D to D' because of some unforeseen reason such as a favorable shift in consumer tastes. In the very short run, price is bid up to P_2 for the available supply Q_1. Since the unit cost did not rise, profits are obtained. In pursuit of more profits to be earned at prices above P_1, the managers of this and other firms expand production as they can—first by increasing the use of factors that can most readily be increased, such as hiring more man-hours of labor through overtime payments to existing workers and the hiring of new ones. This is reflected by a shifting of the VSRC curve to the right and a movement along the SRC curve, as shown in Figure 15-10c. As expansion takes place in this manner, the market price falls to P_3.

Given sufficient time for all desired adjustments to be made, including adjustments in the size of plant and the entry of new firms, the new long-run equilibrium is established at point 4 in Figure 15-10d. The VSRC and SRC curves continue to shift to the right until economic profits are eliminated. The absence of profits is thought by some economists to be a virtue of a highly competitive market system—a topic considered again in Chapter 20. For the present it is sufficient to note that cost and price have returned to their original levels. This is the case when constant returns to size of output prevail. If the LRC curve were upward-sloping or downward-sloping to the right, this would not be the case. The reader is asked to explain the implications of a rising LAC curve in problem 15-6 at the end of this chapter.

_____

[2] Normal profits are those sufficient to retain the services of the entrepreneur and the capital in the firm.

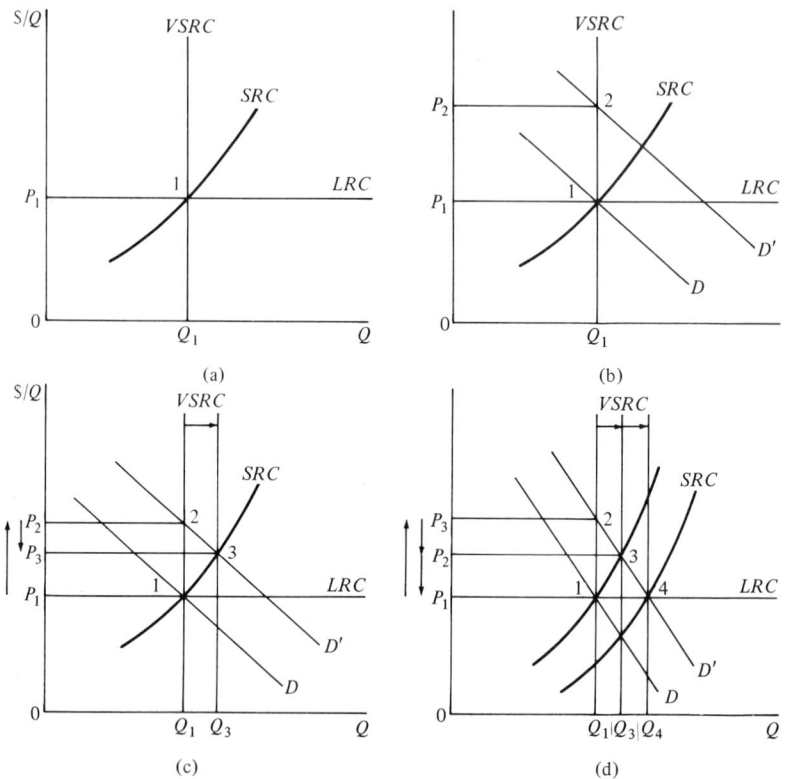

Figure 15-10

Questions and Problems

15-1. Define the following terms:

a. relevant cost
b. alternative cost
c. opportunity cost
d. consumer surplus
e. economic rent
f. implicit costs
g. variable cost
h. average cost

i. marginal cost
j. total cost
k. planning curve
l. envelope curve
m. short-run cost
n. long-run cost
o. normal profits

15-2. The Jenco Jack Company profitably produced custom-made bumper jacks for small automobiles for over a decade. Jim Connors, production manager, was considering replacing the firm's stamping machine with a more efficient one but thought he would not because "the old one will not be fully depreciated for another 10 years and to junk it now would cost too much." Under what conditions should the old stamping machine be replaced? Why?

15-3. Given the following average cost and revenue functions,

$$AC = Q^2 + Q + 1 + \frac{5}{Q}$$

$$AR = Q^2 - 4Q + 4 + \frac{6}{Q}$$

determine the following:
a. the firm's fixed cost at $Q = 3$
b. the firm's variable cost at $Q = 3$
c. the firm's total cost at $Q = 3$
d. the firm's marginal cost at $Q = 3$
e. the firm's break-even output
f. the number of units of Q that will maximize total revenue (sales)
g. the number of units of Q that will maximize profits

15-4. In reference to the planning curve of Figure 15-6, suppose a firm forecasted a quantity demanded next year equal to output at point B and therefore signed for a 2-year base plant of size SAC_2. If the quantity demanded rose, contrary to the forecast, to point C, what would be the firm's unit cost if it attempted to produce that amount with its existing plant?

15-5. Explain why a firm is unlikely to produce at its most efficient plant capacity when long-run average costs are either rising or falling.

15-6. Draw a graph that traces the very-short-run, short-run, and long-run equilibrium points for a firm in a competitive industry responding to an increase in demand for its product. Assume that long-run average costs are rising, and explain each step of adjustment.

References

1. William J. Baumol. *Economic Theory and Operations Analysis.* 3d ed. (Englewood Cliffs, N.J.: Prentice-Hall, 1972), ch. 1, 11.

2. George J. Benston. "Multiple Regression Analysis of Cost Behavior." *Accounting Review* (October 1966), pp. 657–672. Reprinted in Kristian S. Palda. *Readings in Managerial Economics* (Englewood Cliffs, N.J.: Prentice-Hall, 1973), pp. 84–97.

3. Eugene F. Brigham and James L. Pappas. *Managerial Economics* (Hinsdale, Ill.: Dryden Press, 1972), ch. 8.

4. Robert W. Clower and John F. Due. *Microeconomics* (Homewood, Ill.: Dryden Press, 1972), ch. 8.

5. C. E. Ferguson. *The Neoclassical Theory of Production and Distribution* (Cambridge: Cambridge University Press, 1969), ch. 7.

6. Richard H. Leftwich. *The Price System and Resource Allocation.* 5th ed. (Hinsdale, Ill.: Dryden Press, 1973), ch. 8–9.

7. Jacob Viner. "Cost Curves and Supply Curves." *Zeitschrift für Nationalökonomie* 3 (1931): 23–46. Reprinted in American Economics Association. *Readings in Price Theory* (Homewood, Ill.: Richard D. Irwin, 1952).

16 Reconstruction of the Classical Cost Function and Some Empirical Studies

Economic theory teaches that marginal costs rise for the firm having numerous and close competitors because of the law of diminishing marginal returns. Business people, however, claim from experience that their costs usually decline as additional units are produced. This observation is especially true for job shops performing custom work in small runs for a variety of customers, as in the businesses of printing, interior decorating, metalworking, and hauling, where marginal costs fall rapidly for larger orders. Econometric studies frequently fail to reveal rising marginal-cost functions, thus lending support to the business executives' contention. This chapter presents a model that helps to resolve this apparent conflict between traditional economic theory and observations from business practice and explains why the average-cost curve can be flat over a wide range of output.[1]

16-1 The Role of Rate and Volume in Production

According to Professor Armen Alchian, part of the reason for the conflict is the confusion between two dimensions of output: the *rate* of output and the *volume* of output [1]. He hypothesizes marginal cost to be a rising function of the rate of output (a flow) and a falling function of the volume of output (stock). This differs from the standard textbook approach that emphasizes the rate rather than volume of output, assumes the product is homogeneous and produced only for the market to the exclusion of orders by individuals, and implicitly assumes either that the product is to be continuously produced at the present rate, implying that volume is to be infinite, or that volume and rate are changed proportionately to produce a different output level. This last assumption is preferred by Jack Hirshleifer [7], because in the usual case where the length of run is fixed, volume and rate do move proportionately and because it is also useful in showing how the classical U-shaped marginal-cost curve can be derived from Alchian's model.

Alchian assumes that total cost (C) is an inverse function of four major variables: the scheduled volume (or total number of units) of output (V), the rate of

---

[1] Much of this chapter was adapted from Hirshleifer's article [7].

238

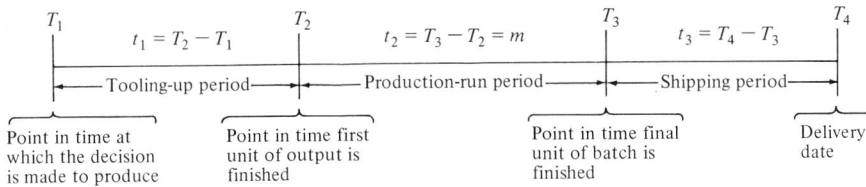

T_1 $t_1 = T_2 - T_1$ T_2 $t_2 = T_3 - T_2 = m$ T_3 $t_3 = T_4 - T_3$ T_4

——Tooling-up period——|——Production-run period——|——Shipping period——

Point in time at   Point in time first   Point in time final   Delivery
which the decision   unit of output is   unit of batch is   date
is made to produce   finished   finished

Figure 16-1

output per unit of time (x), the point in time at which production begins (T), and the length of time over which production takes place (m):

$$C = f(V, x, T, m) \tag{1}$$

Cost is constrained to positive values, that is, $C > 0$.

Alchian's terms and model can be placed in perspective by reference to Figure 16-1. Four points in time are T_1 through T_4, proceeding from the point in time T_1, at which the firm decides to undertake production of some commodity; to the time T_2, when the production line has been primed and the first unit of output has been completed; to time T_3, at which the final unit of the batch contemplated has been produced; to time T_4, when delivery to customers has been completed. The corresponding intervals t_1, t_2, and t_3 are respectively the tooling-up period, in which all steps are taken to prepare for the moment when finished products begin to appear; the production-run period, during which the planned number of units are produced; and the shipping period, during which finished products are transported to places designated by customers. In practice, t_3 could overlap t_2 if shipping were done in parts as goods flowed continuously from the production line.

Alchian's volume V of output, which he further defines as the summation of output rates with respect to time over the period from T to $(T + m)$,

$$V = \int_T^{T+m} X\, dt \quad \text{or} \tag{2}$$

$$V = mX \tag{3}$$

with the additional assumptions of constant production over period m and no advances or delays in T, corresponds to the number of units of output produced in the interval

$$T_2 \rightarrow T_3 = t_2 = m \tag{4}$$

Alchian's output rate x is dX/dt over the m period. Alchian's T corresponds to T_2 in Figure 16-1.

Alchian reasons, in effect, that total cost is a rising function of V and x (that is, $\partial C/\partial V$ and $\partial C/\partial x > 0$) and a declining function of t_1, t_2, and T (that is, $\partial C/\partial t_1$, $\partial C/\partial t_2$, and $\partial C/\partial T < 0$). Furthermore, he asserts that average and marginal costs fall with respect to V, t_1, t_2, and T (that is, $\partial^2 C/\partial V^2$, $\partial(C/V)/\partial V$, $\partial^2 C/\partial t_1^2$, $\partial(C/t_1)/\partial t$, $\partial^2 C/\partial t_2^2$, $\partial(C/t_2)/\partial t_2$, $\partial^2 C/\partial T^2$, and $\partial(C/T)/\partial T < 0$), where T in this

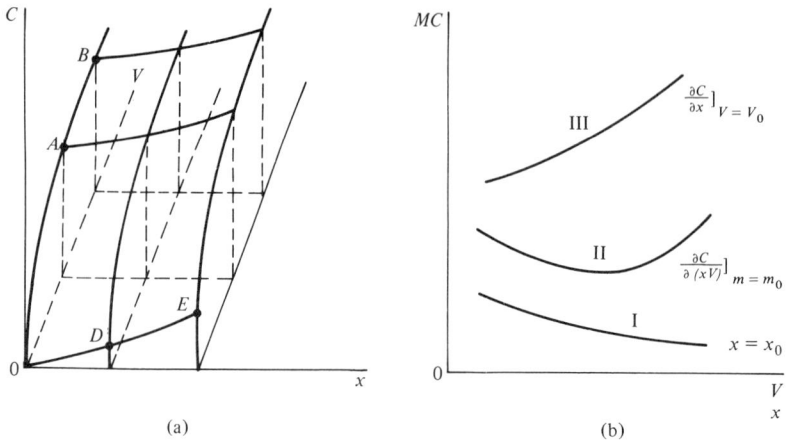

(a)   (b)

Figure 16-2

context refers to the passing of time over which efficiencies from experience and learning take place because of "job familiarization, general improvement in coordination, shop organization and engineering liaison, more efficient subassembly production and more efficient tools" [1, p. 36]. Note that this learning-curve phenomenon has to do with subsequent units of V and changes in production *techniques* rather than simply a larger V for which changes in cost are a matter of changes in *technology*.

Curves exhibiting the preceding properties with respect to V and x are shown in Figure 16-2. Figure 16-2a shows that C rises as either V or x rises; the positive slopes of OAB and ODE indicate positive partials of C with respect to V and x, respectively [1, p. 27]. The diminishing slope of OAB indicates a negative second partial with respect to V. Similarly, the increasing slope of ODE indicates a positive second partial with respect to x. Figure 16-2b plots the marginal costs (first partials) [7, p. 238]. (Note that two scales are required on the horizontal axis for both MC's to be plotted on the same grid.) Curve I holds the rate of output constant at $x = x_0$ while the volume of output is changed; additional units obtained in this manner are continuously less expensive to produce than previous ones. Larger volume of output entails a longer period m when the rate of production is unchanged. This permits a more effective balancing of fixed and variable inputs as the production period is extended and greater use can be made of durable equipment.

Curve III holds the volume of output constant at $V = V_0$ as the rate is allowed to change; additional units obtained in this manner are continuously more expensive.

Curve II shows how marginal cost varies with respect to proportionate changes in V and x when the production period m is held at $m = m_0$. Both V and x vary in moving along curve II (as in the case of classical marginal-cost curves), which encompasses elements of both curves I and III, giving it the characteristic saucer shape.[2] Curve II is thought to be only a special case of Alchian's enriched model. This is discussed further in section 16-4. But first, some examples are considered in which this approach is useful, and some additional terminology is introduced.

16-2 Examples of V and x in Application

A modern example of the classical type of firm that produces a constant stream of output to be sold on the general market is the manufacturer of detergent powders. Here, the V dimension can possibly be ignored without causing confusion in theoretical analysis of firm and market behavior and in measuring statistical cost functions, because the product is quite divisible and homogeneous. On the other hand, production involving short runs to order, such as military aircraft for the government, require consideration of V as well as x, since both greatly influence the firm's profitability over the restricted range of output. A 200-unit order of one model is less costly per unit to fill than two 100-unit orders. In the case of book printing, with its heavy setup costs, an extended printing of a few different works is less costly than a short one of many works; in this case V may be considered to be the number of copies planned per printing. In the telegraph business, messages totaling a given number of words can be transmitted between specified points more cheaply in a few long messages than in many short ones.

A large order may be expected to permit lower unit costs than a short order when production takes place at a constant rate, because more time is available during which learning of more efficient ways can take place. (Chapter 17 examines the observed learning phenomenon in which inexhaustible minor improvements are made as the number of manufactured units rise). Such irreversible increases in knowledge may be treated as improved techniques that shift the traditional cost function. In addition to saving costs this way, the firm may economize by planning and scheduling a larger volume per production run. Prior knowledge permits reduced setup costs. In printing, fewer setups or a better quality of type may result in savings. In the airframe industry, labor-saving specialized machinery can be introduced for stamping and pressing. Cost savings not requiring additional capital outlays are obtainable from a smoother utilization of present machinery, better routinizing of labor tasks, and taking advantage of quantity discounts on materials.

One can, however, emphasize too much the cost reductions to be anticipated from an increased V because of other factors that tend to raise costs. Problems of fatigue or optimum size may come into play. For instance, where much time is required to transport laborers to work sites far below the earth's surface, as in coal mining and deep-sea diving, a production run completing the job in a single trip by a single crew will have a lower cost per unit of output than a larger order requiring a second trip that is not fully used. Similarly, it would be desirable for a chartered flight to avoid a fuel stop by having a load not exceeding a certain tonnage. These are examples of discontinuities in production. Discrete input units must be used to complete the task where only partial ones are desired, causing a rise in unit costs.

---

[2] Admittedly, this is not rigorous proof that curve II has a U-shape. This heuristic argument is pursued in greater depth by Hirshleifer [7, pp. 246–247].

Another cost element that limits the size of some production runs is the application of a rule setting optimum inventory levels at half the shipment size.[3] The regulation of inventory by such a formula is probably superior to a rule of thumb that would raise inventories in proportion to sales, but the business manager should not lose sight of production considerations and the possible creation of inventory problems elsewhere in the organization. Infrequent orders of large size could cause disruptions of plant operations organized to provide a continuous flow of output, and a need for additional storage space at the plant site. To the extent that disruptions occur and additional storage costs are incurred, total costs increase as volume V rises.

16-3 Hirshleifer's "Width" and "Length" in Production

Another consideration bearing upon the analysis, one contributed by Hirshleifer, is the distinction between "width" and "length" of differentiated orders. The horizontal dimension of width corresponds to the characteristics of occupancy

---

[3] One of the well-known formulas making use of this assumption is based upon the total-cost function (see Baumol [2], ch. 1):

$$C = \text{carrying cost} + \text{reorder cost}$$
$$= \frac{aD}{2} + \left(\frac{bQ}{D} + cQ\right) \tag{5}$$

where D is shipment size; $D/2$ is average inventory size, assuming that sales are made at a constant rate and that a new shipment arrives at the moment inventory becomes zero; Q is the units to be sold each year; Q/D is the required number of deliveries per year; a is carrying cost per unit, including interest on the money tied up in inventories; b is reorder costs per delivery not affected by size of shipment, for such items as long-distance telephoning of orders and bookkeeping; c is shipping cost per item by common carrier.

Minimum inventory is determined by setting the first derivative of C with respect to D equal to zero, solving for D, and dividing optimum D by 2:

$$\frac{dC}{D} = \frac{a}{2} + \left(\frac{-bQ}{D^2} + 0\right) = 0$$

$$\frac{a}{2} = \frac{bQ}{D^2} \tag{6}$$

$$D^2 = \frac{2bQ}{a}$$

$$D = \sqrt{\frac{2bQ}{a}}$$

The optimum inventory level, I, where total inventory cost is a minimum, is therefore given by the expression

$$I = \frac{D}{2} = \frac{1}{2}\sqrt{\frac{2bQ}{a}} = \sqrt{\frac{bQ}{2a}} \tag{7}$$

Optimum inventory is thus found to be a function of the *square root* of units of sales and should be increased in size with a fall in carrying cost, a, or a rise in reorder costs per delivery not related to size of shipment, b. Unit shipping cost, c, is dropped from consideration, because it is a fixed cost independent of shipping or inventory considerations. In practice, more inventory than the computed optimal level will be held as a safety factor against unforeseen demands.

in hotel and office-space rental businesses, while the vertical dimension refers to length of stay. For a given occupancy V, cost savings may result from renting several suites and blocks of rooms to, say, a convention gathering. Renting to a few tenants (more units occupied per order, indicating greater width) may be cheaper because of less breakage, policing, and billing than renting to many small ones (less width). Cost savings from greater average length of stay (length) for a given aggregate occupancy rate may also be greater because of less advertising and redecorating for new tenants. In the printing business, width refers to the number and size of pages in a book and length to the number of copies printed, associated with a volume of output V from a planned production run. Output measured as pages per month presumably has a lower cost per page for books with more pages (a width dimension). These examples lead to the proposition that unit costs tend to fall as width and length of production are increased.[4]

16-4   Modifications of Production in Response to Changes in Demand

Suppose a firm plans to produce at a rate of $x = 100$ units per week for $m = 52$ weeks to meet an anticipated market demand. If the firm suddenly becomes aware that the market will absorb 200 units instead, x and V will be increased proportionately, x is shifted from 100 to 200 units per week and V from 5,200 to 10,400 units for the horizon of 1 year. Otherwise stated, x and V have increased while m is unchanged; this, Hirshleifer claims, is an implicit assumption made in obtaining the firm's orthodox U-shaped cost function shown as curve II in Figure 16-2b. Curve II may be said to show the firm's marginal costs associated with proportional changes in x and V in response to *expansions* of demand. In contrast, curve I shows marginal costs reflected by changes in V with x fixed in response to *extensions* of demand. Curve III reflects changes in x with fixed V in response to *accelerations* of demand.

16-5   The Short and the Long Runs

Alchian is critical of conventional statements by economists that in the short run some inputs are fixed. He claims there is no such interval, except for the moment when *all* inputs are fixed. One may choose to hold some factors unchanged in order to hold costs down, but "there are no technological or legal restraints preventing one from varying any of his inputs" [1, p. 33]. *Economic costs* dictate whether inputs will be changed or not. Any distinction between the short and the long runs should provide information about the price and output response of the firm *over time* (dynamically) to a change in demand or supply. Alchian postulates that the marginal-cost derivatives diminish with a lengthening of preparation time T (actually t_1) allowed for planning and initiation of production. The planning and setup period is the crucial determinant of cost—longer t_1 permits lower unit costs. Figure 16-3 contrasts the traditional and the Alchian formulations [7, p. 248].

---

[4] The reader may wish to refer to the discussion by Hirshleifer of other examples taken from the transport and electric power industries [7, pp. 242–244].

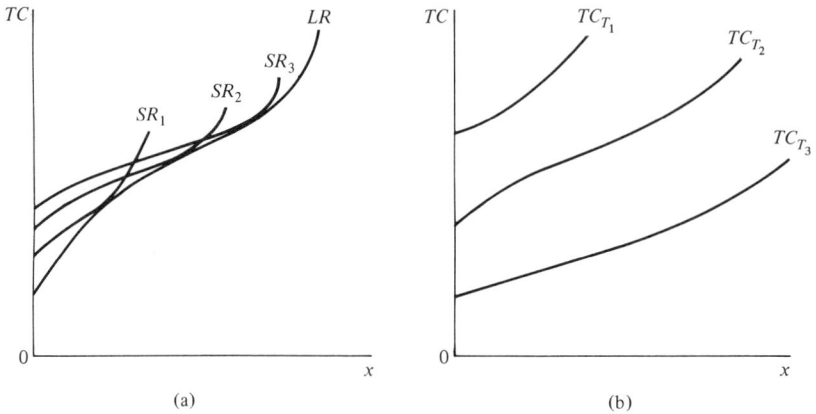

Figure 16-3

In Figure 16-3a, the traditional long-run total-cost curve is shown as an envelope of the short-run curves. Short- and long-run costs are equal at the long-run
equilibrium tangency points. *SMC* (not shown) exceeds (is less than) *LMC* for
outputs greater (less) than equilibrium. Alchian's formulation, dealing only with
curves I and III in Figure 16-2b, is devoid of such implications, since the curves
(their levels and slopes) are merely ordered inversely to time *m*.

Hirshleifer proposed a concept encompassing both approaches. He would define short and long runs not in terms of fixed inputs, but in terms of the relative
length of time, *m*, over which the planned volume of production *V* takes place.
The more chronological time available, the lower the cost. The long-run curve is
still an envelope of curves with shorter *V*'s. The longest of long runs is when *V* is
infinite; that is, when a most efficient size of plant can be planned and set up to
produce an uninterrupted and sustainable flow of output for an indefinitely long
period.

If indeed there is only one cheapest cost of production, why don't producers,
in response to a permanent increase in demand, immediately redesign their plants
for the lowest cost? The reason, Hirshleifer contends, is *uncertainty*. Some firms,
correctly evaluating the demand shift as permanent, will immediately increase
their rates of output and begin plant modifications and additions (long-run
adjustments) to provide a flow of goods to meet the permanent demand. Other
firms, mistakenly evaluating the demand shift as temporary, will schedule costly
short production runs to take advantage of a temporary bulge in demand.
As accumulated evidence dispels uncertainty, surviving firms must shift to long
production runs. Existing machines and facilities might be replaced by larger
and more efficient ones. Permanent, rather than part-time, labor might be hired
to meet a sustained demand of an additional 15,000 units.

Higher salaries for temporary help are justified only if the workers are needed
for a few weeks; while annual salaries are lower per diem, the longer commitment
of employment may be more costly if workers are actually needed for much less
than a full year.

The short run is thus a period in which changes in demand are thought to be temporary, and the long run, a period where changes are thought to be permanent. Empirical propositions that elasticity of supply is greater in the long run thus reflect the passage of time, response to change through accumulated experience, and the fact that longer production runs have lower unit costs.

16-6 Value of the Alchian-Hirshleifer Cost Function to Managerial Economists

The Alchian-Hirshleifer cost function provides an analytical framework for understanding the operations of a business that produces a small number of specialized units in response to orders from different customers. The essentials of economies of scale for these and other firms can be grasped in terms of marginal costs rising with respect to the *rate* of production and declining with respect to scheduled *volume* of production. Furthermore, responses of production managers to changes in demand can be explained with reference to accelerations, extensions, and expansions of demand. Acceleration is increasing the rate of production while holding volume constant; extension, increasing volume while holding the rate constant; and expansion, increasing rate and volume in proportion. In regard to short-run versus long-run decisions, the decision to unfix the fixed factors rests upon the business executive's assessment of the permanence of a change in demand.

Questions may also be answered about discrimination in giving quantity discounts, that is, granting discounts not justified by lower costs to the producer because of the bargaining power of a large customer. Take the historic case of "abuse" by railroads charging more for short hauls than for long ones. According to Alchian's proposition of declining marginal cost with respect to distance hauled ("length" in production, or a vertical dimension of orders), discounts may be justified by reduced costs. The same may be said with regard to size and tonnage of shipment ("width" in production), for which marginal costs also decline. But this ignores any rising marginal costs with respect to providing rapid service to groups of independent customers for whom orders may be bunched.

> If the short-haul order, in contrast, involves an initiating of a terminating point not subject to heavy or regular traffic, it will not be possible to aggregate it with many or possibly any other orders. The cost increment due to the short haul may then be quite large compared to that due to the long haul just described [7, p. 253].

Total cost of the short-haul order may therefore be more costly to the firm than a marginal long-haul order. A lower price for the short haul relative to the long may be unwarranted by cost and judged discriminatory. (Price discrimination is discussed in Chapter 21.)

Awareness of more than one dimension of production, as well as of the different characteristics of aggregate and individual orders, should prove useful in studying and deriving production and cost functions. The "unrealistic" findings of some econometric studies are undoubtedly attributable to overlooking the critical dimensions of the problem for which data might not have been available.

Some magnitudes, such as *planned* rather than actual volume of production, may not be directly observable. For a more thorough discussion of this and applications in the transport industry, the reader is referred to the articles by Alchian and Hirshleifer and the studies they cite.

16-7 Empirical Cost Studies

A summary of statistical cost studies published in leading professional journals over a period of two decades preceding 1960 is provided by John Johnson [8]. While space cannot be allocated here to the details of these studies, a summary can be given by noting the author, date, industry, and equations for each of several studies cited.

　1. Joel Dean (1941), leather belt shop.

$$X_1 = -60,178 + 0.770 X_2 + 70,181.30 X_3$$

where X_1 is total cost, X_2 is output, and X_3 is average weight of belting.

　2. Joel Dean (1941), hosiery mill.

$$X_1 = 2,935.59 + 1.998 X_2$$
$$X_1 = -13,634.83 + 2.068 X_2 + 1,308.039 X_3 - 22.280 X_3^2$$

where X_1 is total cost, X_2 is output, and X_3 is time.

　3. Joel Dean (1942), department store.

$$X_c = -35.440 + 1.052 X_2 - 0.0019 X_2^2 + 0.787 X_4$$
$$X_h = -60.764 + 0.347 X_2 + 1.557 X_4$$
$$X_s = -146.776 + 0.925 X_2 + 0.837 X_4$$

where X_c is total cost in coat department; X_h is total cost in hosiery department; X_s is total cost in shoe department; X_2 is number of transactions; X_4 is average value per transaction.

　4. T. O. Yntema (1940), United States Steel.

$$X_1 = 182,100,000 + 55.73 X_2$$

where X_1 is total cost, and X_2 is weighted output in tons.

　5. E. J. Broster (1938), British Railways.

$$E = 0.5474 P + 1.6564 F + 91,170,000$$
$$E = 0.10000 M_p + 0.3680 M_f + 54,250,000$$

where E is operating costs per unit, adjusted for a falling time trend of 1.17 per cent per annum; P is passenger miles, thousands; F is net ton-miles, thousands; M_p is coaching train miles; M_f is freight train miles.

　6. K. S. Lomax (1952), electricity generation in the United Kingdom.

$$Y = X_1^{-0.12} X_2^{-0.41} \text{ (northwest)}$$
$$Y = X_1^{-0.15} X_2^{-0.70} \text{ (southeast)}$$

where Y is works cost per unit generated; X_1 is capacity of generators, kilowatts; $X_2 = $ load factor.

7. Cecil B. Haver (1956), Iowa grain farms.

$$\log X_1 = 0.165 + 0.061 \log X_2 + 0.475 \log X_3 + 0.566 \log X_4$$
$$(R^2 = 0.72)$$

$$X_1 = 2{,}934 + 0.839 X_2 + 0.644 X_3 + 1.125 X_4 \qquad (R^2 = 0.71)$$

$$X_1 = 1{,}760 + 1.01 X_2 - 0.000022 X_2^2 - 0.098 \times 10^{-8} X_2^3$$
$$+ 2.28 X_3 - 0.000012 X_3^2 - 0.35 \times 10^{-8} + 1.11 X_4$$
$$(R^2 = 0.71)$$

$$X_1 = -2{,}401 + 1.18 X_2 - 0.000053 X_2^2 + 2.66 X_3$$
$$-0.000085 X_3^2 + 1.09 X_4 \qquad (R^2 = 0.71)$$

where X_1 is output in dollars; X_2 is labor input; X_3 is operating expense; X_4 is current fixed expense inputs.

Several types of functions were used in the above studies: linear, power, multiplicative, and logarithmic. A unique feature of the Haver study is that four different production functions were fitted to the same data; curiously, it made little difference which was used, since each "explained" about 70 per cent of the variation in production. More recent studies of cost functions include the following:

8 G. H. Borts (1960), United States railways [4].

$$C = \alpha X_1 + \frac{\beta Z}{X_1} + \delta$$

where C is allocated freight operating expenditure; X_1 is total freight car-miles; Z is total freight carloads. Average- and marginal-cost estimates were made for three geographical regions and for three size classes within each region.

9. Marc Nerlove (1963), United States electric power [11].

$$c = k y^{1/r} p_1^{a_1/r} p_2^{a_2/r} p_3^{a_3/r_v} \quad \text{or}$$

$$C = K + \frac{1}{r} Y + \frac{a_1}{r} P_1 + \frac{a_2}{r} P_2 + \frac{a_3}{r} P_3 + V$$

where capital letters denote logarithms corresponding to the lower-case letters. This equation is only one form of the first of four models used. Here, c is total production cost; y is output (kwh); X_1 is labor input; X_2 is capital input; X_3 is fuel input; p_1 is wage rate; p_2 is "price" of capital; p_3 is price of fuel; V is "a residual expressing neutral variations in efficiency among firms."

16-8 Considerations in Making Cost Studies

Until the advent of computers, simple regression analysis for fitting a straight line to a plotting of cost and output data was considered quite sophisticated. Other related variables were excluded as being computationally infeasible. With the use of multiple regression techniques, the influence of changes in uncontrollable variables such as weather and season on delivery time could be taken into account. Also, relevant weights could be assigned to controllable variables, such as size of batch, size of lots, age of employees, and learning associated with additional experience through time [3, p. 85].

In deciding whether or not to make a cost study, the decision maker must judge that the marginal benefits to be gained from making the study will exceed the marginal costs. The costs of gathering, processing, and presenting information, as well as the opportunity cost of delaying a decision, should be less than the additional revenue obtainable plus an amount to cover any potential loss from otherwise avoidable mistakes. In making such a determination, it is often useful to distinguish between problems that are of a recurring nature and those that are single events. Repetitive problems encompass the setting of catalogue prices, production schedules, performance standards, budgets, and forecasts. Their analysis typically requires the development of a schedule of expected costs associated with the relevant range of activities. Multiple regression analysis is often useful here.

Single events deal with cost-profit-volume decisions to accept a special order, buy or lease equipment, introduce a new product, or discontinue a branch office. Special studies are typically made for each of these one-time decisions, since average-cost information gleaned from generalized past performance may not be sufficiently relevant. Uniqueness and substantial resource commitments may make the average-cost data in the form of regression parameters inapplicable and lead to a high cost of wrong decisions [3, pp. 86–87].

While space limits discussion of problems of collection and use of cost data, a few rules of thumb are offered from the writings of George Benston [3, pp. 89–94]. First, production data observations should be for periods no longer than a month, preferably a week. This will avoid comparisons of data collected in unequal time periods where there are lags in the recording of costs and possible variations in production. Also, the shorter periods insure that the number of observations will be at least one more than the number of independent variables —a requirement for regression analysis. The greater the number of observations than required (called *degrees of freedom*), the greater the confidence that the sample represents the true relation.

Second, data should be sufficiently detailed so that effects of changing conditions of production can be sifted out, such as a change in input prices and production methods during the period analyzed. Values and dates of unusual events should be noted in a journal, such as overtime and unscheduled maintenance.

Third, costs should be recorded in the week in which they affect production. Otherwise, both observations are incorrectly recorded. Similarly, the period of production should also be charged with future costs induced by that production, such as for overtime labor paid the following week and bonuses paid at the end of the year. Production supplies should be omitted from analysis rather than lumped in only one week. Costs that are independent of production, such as rent and insurance premiums, should not be included in the independent variable.

Questions and Problems

16-1. Use the Alchian-Hirshleifer concept of short and long run to explain the entry of new firms into an industry where demand is thought by the established firms to be only temporary.

16-2. Traditional texts often claim, "In the short run the firm may operate at a loss so long as receipts exceed variable costs" or "We are going to operate at a loss in the near future, but operations will be profitable later" (quoted by Hirshleifer [7, p. 251] from Alchian [1, p. 36]). Alchian interprets such statements "as meaning only that cash flows are temporarily negative, to be balanced by future cash surpluses" [7, p. 251] and takes the writers to task for their crude concepts of economic cost. How might considerations of uncertainty be used to preserve meaning for the traditional statements?

References

1. Armen Alchian. "Cost and Outputs." In *The Allocation of Economic Resources*, ed. M. Abramovitz et al. (Stanford: Stanford University Press, 1959), pp. 21–40.
2. William J. Baumol. *Economic Theory and Operations Analysis*. 3d ed. (Englewood Cliffs, N.J.: Prentice-Hall, 1972), ch. 1.
3. George J. Benston. "Multiple Regression Analysis of Cost Behavior." *Accounting Review* (October 1966), pp. 657–672. Reprinted in Kristian S. Palda. *Readings in Managerial Economics* (Englewood Cliffs, N.J.: Prentice-Hall, 1973), pp. 84–97.
4. George H. Borts. "The Estimation of Rail Cost Functions." *Econometrica* 28 (January 1960): 108–131. Reprinted in Arnold Zellner. *Readings in Economic Statistics and Econometrics* (Boston: Little, Brown, 1968), pp. 440–462.
5. Sven Danø. "Diminishing Returns and the Cost Function." *Weltwirtschaftliches Archiv* 2 (1966): 97–107.
6. J. Walter Elliot. *Economics Analysis for Management Decisions* (Homewood, Ill.: Richard D. Irwin, 1973), ch. 8–11.
7. Jack Hirshleifer. "The Firm's Cost Function: A Successful Reconstruction?" *Journal of Business* 35 (July 1962): 235–255. Excerpted in Kristian S. Palda. *Readings in Managerial Economics*, pp. 70–83.
8. John Johnson. *Statistical Cost Analysis* (New York: McGraw-Hill, 1960).
9. Edwin Mansfield. *Microeconomics—Theory and Application* (New York: W. W. Norton, 1970), ch. 6.
10. W. David Maxwell. "Production Theory and Cost Curves." *Applied Economics* 1 (August 1969): 211–224. Reprinted in Richard E. Neel. *Readings in Price Theory* (Cincinnati: South-Western Publishing Co., 1973), pp. 235–253.
11. Marc Nerlove. "Returns to Scale in Electric Supply." In *Measurement in Economics: Studies in Mathematical Economics and Econometrics in Memory of Yehuda Grunfeld*, ed. Carl F. Christ et al. (Stanford: Stanford University Press, 1963). Reprinted in Arnold Zellner. *Readings in Economic Statistics and Econometrics*, pp. 409–439.

17 The Learning Curve

The objective of this chapter is to introduce a very useful tool that has been employed in industry since the 1930s but has as yet received limited attention by academicians.

17-1 Introduction to Learning Curves

The term *learning curve* refers to the phenomenon whereby a decreasing amount of input is required to accomplish a task each time the task is repeated. There are many examples of everyday tasks demonstrating this experience, such as the case where a person may be doing a repair job at home of replacing window screens in a number of windows. He finds that exact measurement, initial fitting, rework, and a repeated fitting take a considerable amount of time on the first window; the second window goes much faster, and third faster still. This effect is known variously as an experience curve, an improvement curve, a progress curve, learning by doing, and, as we call it here, a learning curve. Any industry requiring a repetition of tasks can use the principles outlined in this chapter. The technique has been widely utilized since World War II in the aircraft industry.[1] Since then the application of this empirical law, based on the concept of diminishing returns, has spread to other industries like home appliances, shipbuilding, and construction, and shows promise of being extended to a wide range of problems in forecasting.

17-1-1 *Description of the learning curve*

The learning curve may be described simply as a linear logarithmical curve relating labor requirements to consecutive units of the product produced. It says that some input, say labor requirements, per unit of production diminishes at a constant rate as output expands. In logarithmic terms, the equation $Y = aX^b$ becomes

$$\log Y = \log a + b \log X \tag{1}$$

---

[1] The learning-curve phenomenon was first recognized in 1925 by the commander of Wright-Patterson Air Force Base for use in estimating costs of airplanes. The first published article on the subject was by T. P. Wright [17] in 1936.

250

During World War II an executive of a home-appliance manufacturing company chanced to cross paths with an executive of a large West Coast aircraft firm. The appliance executive mentioned that it had taken his company two years to determine the exact cost of the electric refrigerator which it manufactured.

The aircraft executive pointed out that in many cases his company had been forced to determine costs on similar items in a matter of a few minutes, and said, " I'll bet you a steak dinner that I can predict the cost of your 100,000th refrigerator within 10 per cent accuracy by using a learning curve based on aircraft production."

The manufacturing executive accepted the bet. The only information he furnished was the weight of the refrigerator and the cost of the first unit produced. During the next few minutes he watched while the aircraft executive worked with pencil, ruler, and log-log graph paper.

When he had completed plotting the curve, the aircraft executive stated: "Your 100,000th unit should cost you $162.50."

"Just drop the 50 cents," the appliance executive said. "It was actually $162.00" [2, p. 87].

where Y is man-hour requirements per unit of output; X is units of output; a is the vertical intercept of the theoretical labor requirements for the first unit of output; and b is the slope of the log curve or the rate of reduction in labor requirements—its value is always negative, since the curve is downward-sloping. Figure 17-1 shows three learning curves plotted on both logarithmic and arithmetic scales.

The aircraft industry has found the 80 per cent curve (20 per cent labor reduction) to be an accurate description of its experience in the construction of airframes since the 1930s. In other industries, where machine operations play a greater role in the manufacturing process, a 90 per cent curve has been found more appropriate. This higher percentage, or lower degree of learning, reflects reduced labor efficiencies in the production process. A reduction in the cost of machine operations is limited by the feed and speed of the manufacturing device. Where machinery is automatic, no learning can be expected, other than through improved design or use of more efficient machines. In large volume assembly operations dependent upon sizable amounts of hand labor, opportunity for labor efficiencies are greater and lower-percentage learning curves can be used. It is claimed that learning trends are indicated roughly by the numbers in Table 17-1.

17-1-2   Uses of the learning curve

The learning curve is used to forecast labor requirements more easily, quickly, and accurately than other methods based upon assumptions of level performance and constant costs. Projections of labor needs are necessary in determining

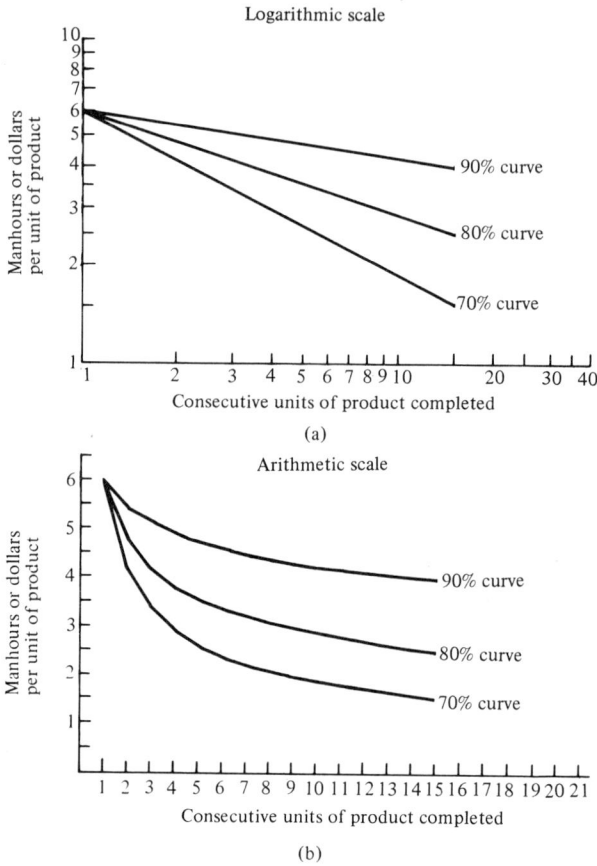

Figure 17-1

Table 17-1

| Per cent of total input | | Per cent |
Assembly labor	Machine labor	learning curve
75	25	80
50	50	85
25	75	90

SOURCE: [13, p. 27].

unit costs of production, shop loads, delivery schedules, capital expenditures, and the reasonableness of contractors' quotations. A learning curve is used to measure the results of
1. improved proficiency of the operator as production increases
2. reductions in manufacturing losses
3. stabilization of design resulting in fewer design changes
4. increases in lot sizes
5. improvement in special tooling
6. an adequate cost reduction and value analysis program
7. changing from a daywork to a piecework system
8. changing from manual to automatic machinery as production warrants [13, p. 27].

17-1-3 *Relating the learning curve to economic analysis*

Economists have long been aware of the existence of economies of mass production and decreasing costs in some industries. Increasing economies are typically said to occur in the early stages of development of an industry followed by a longer (sometimes much longer) period of constant costs that eventually blend, as the industry matures, into a final phase of rising unit costs. When unit costs decrease as output is expanded, the industry is said to be moving along the downward portion of its long-run average-cost curve. This does not mean, however, that the industry will necessarily exhibit a downward-sloping *supply* curve. The supply curve may be simply shifting to the right as economies of large-scale production occur. Decreasing costs attributable to learning may be considered as a dynamic change held separate from other changes in technology.

One of the major reasons given for increasing economies associated with expanded production is that larger production permits the use of more specialized and efficient factors like improved technology. The learning-curve technique concerns primarily the improved use of labor inputs, although it may be applied to other inputs as well. The 80 per cent learning curve is simply based upon the expectation that labor inputs will be reduced to 80 per cent of their previous amounts *whenever production is doubled.* It is recognized today, however, that more than the learning process is involved, for additional capital and improved technology simultaneously enhance potential output. While economists would rather see an allocation of the improvements attributed to the factors involved in order to help remove some of the mystery of the production process, the practitioners (especially the Air Force and aircraft industries) are more impressed with the discovery of a practical tool for predicting improvements in man-hours and dollar costs associated with expanded production.

17-2 Statistical Derivation of the Curve

Statistical derivation of the equation for the learning curve requires estimating the values of parameters log a and b in equation (1). This is accomplished by solving simultaneously two normal equations for a and b. The first normal equation, I, is obtained by multiplying each term in equation (1) by the coefficient of log a and summing like terms. The coefficient of log a is, of course, 1. Normal equation I is simply the summation of like terms for each observation of X and Y:

$$\log Y_1 = \log a + b \log X_1$$
$$\log Y_2 = \log a + b \log X_2$$
$$\cdots\cdots\cdots\cdots\cdots$$
$$\frac{\log Y_n = \log a + b \log X_n}{}$$

I. $\sum \log Y = N \log a + b \sum \log X$

The coefficient of b is log X. Each term in equation (1) is therefore multiplied by log X, and the equations are summed for each observation of X and Y:

$$\log X_1 \log Y_1 = \log X_1 \log a + b(\log X_1)^2$$
$$\log X_2 \log Y_2 = \log X_2 \log a + b(\log X_2)^2$$
$$\cdots\cdots\cdots\cdots\cdots\cdots\cdots\cdots\cdots$$
$$\frac{\log X_n \log Y_n = \log X_n \log a + b(\log X_n)^2}{}$$

II. $\sum(\log X \log Y) = \log a(\sum \log X) + b \sum(\log X)^2$

The next step is to solve normal equations I and II for log a by solving I for b and inserting its value into II:

$$b = \frac{\sum \log Y - N \log a}{\sum \log X}$$

$$\sum (\log X \log Y) = \log a(\sum \log X) + \frac{\sum \log Y - N \log a}{\sum \log X} \sum (\log X)^2$$

Multiplying both sides by $\sum \log X$ and grouping the coefficients of log a,

$$(\sum \log X) \sum(\log X \log Y) = \log a(\sum \log X)^2 + (\sum \log Y - N \log a)$$
$$\times \sum(\log X)^2$$
$$= \log a(\sum \log X)^2 + (\sum \log Y) \sum (\log X)^2$$
$$- N \log a \sum (\log X)^2$$
$$= \log a[(\sum \log X)^2 - N \sum(\log X)^2]$$
$$+ (\sum \log Y) \sum(\log X)^2$$

Thus, log a is found to be

$$\log a = \frac{(\sum \log X) \sum(\log X \cdot \log Y) - (\sum \log Y) \sum(\log X)^2}{(\sum \log X)^2 - N \sum(\log X)^2}$$

$$= \frac{\sum(\log X)^2(\sum \log Y) - (\sum \log X) \sum(\log X \cdot \log Y)}{N \sum(\log X)^2 - (\sum \log X)^2}$$

(2)

Similarly, the expression for b may be found by solving equation I for log a,

$$\log a = \frac{\sum \log Y - b \sum \log X}{N}$$

putting the result into II,

$$\sum(\log X \log Y) = \frac{\sum \log Y - b \sum \log X}{N}(\sum \log X) + b \sum(\log X)^2$$

and solving for b,

$$N \sum(\log X \log Y) = (\sum \log Y)(\sum \log X) - b(\sum \log X)^2 + bN \sum(\log X)^2$$
$$= (\sum \log Y)(\sum \log X) + b[N \sum(\log X)^2 - \sum(\log X)^2]$$

$$b = \frac{N \sum(\log X \log Y) - (\sum \log X)(\sum \log Y)}{N \sum(\log X)^2 - (\sum \log X)^2} \qquad (3)$$

Equations (2) and (3) may be used to obtain estimates, called least-squares regression estimates, of $\log a$ and b in equation (1). Computations are facilitated by use of a table like Table 17-2.

Table 17-2

Number	X	Y	log X	log Y	(log X)²	(log Y)²	(log X)(log Y)
1	2	40	0.30103	1.60206	0.09062	2.56660	0.48227
2	4	20	0.60206	1.30103	0.36248	1.69268	0.78330
3	8	16	0.90309	1.20412	0.81557	1.44990	1.08743
Sum (N) 14		76	1.80618	4.10721	1.26867	5.70918	2.35300

Example 1. Given the three observations of X and Y shown in the second and third columns of Table 17-2, the remaining numbers can be obtained and entered in the table. Insert the appropriate values from the table into equations (2) and (3) to obtain $\log a$ and b:

$$\log a = \frac{(1.26867)(4.10721) - (1.80618)(2.35300)}{3(1.26867) - (1.80618)^2}$$

$$= \frac{0.96075}{0.54372} = 1.76699$$

$$a = 58.5 \quad \text{(from log table)}$$

$$b = \frac{3(2.35300) - (1.80618)(4.10721)}{0.54372}$$

$$= \frac{-0.35936}{0.54372} = -0.66093$$

Equation (1) becomes

$$\log Y = 1.76699 - 0.66093 \log X \qquad (4)$$

which is the log-log least-squares regression equation estimated from the three observations of X and Y. An alternative form of this equation sometimes used is

$$Y = aX^b = 58.5X^{-0.66093} \tag{5}$$

17-3 The Percentage of Learning

It should be pointed out that the value of a is the theoretical amount of time required to do the job the first time. This is the most important number of the learning-curve calculation and is therefore called the *number one* or *#1. It is a theoretical value and has only an indirect relation to an actual first-time value.*

The value of b is the second most important term. This slope of the regression line should not be confused with the percentage of learning, which is defined as the ratio of the values of Y obtained from doubled values of X:

$$\text{Percentage of learning } (P) = \frac{Y_{2X_i}}{Y_{X_i}}(100) \tag{6}$$

Example 2. Using the values of example 1, find the values of Y in equation (4) or (5) for $X = 1$ and $X = 2$; then divide:

$$\log Y_{X=1} = 1.76699 - 0.66093 \log 1$$
$$= 1.76699 - 0.66093(0)$$
$$= 1.76699$$
$$Y_{X=1} = 58.5$$
$$\log Y_{X=2} = 1.76699 - 0.66093 \log 2$$
$$= 1.76699 - 0.66093(0.30103)$$
$$= 1.56803$$
$$Y_{X=2} = 37.0$$

$$P = \frac{Y_{X=2}}{Y_{X=1}}(100) = \frac{37.0}{58.5}(100) = 63.2 \text{ per cent, say 63 per cent}$$

This same percentage could have been found by using any pair of doubled values of X, such as $X = 2$ and 4, 8 and 16, or 50 and 100.

An alternative method of calculating P is to assume a $#1$ of 100 and compute the value of Y for $X = 2$, which is P:[2]

[2] *Proof:*

$$P = \frac{Y_{X=2}}{Y_{X=1}}(100)$$

$$\log P = \log Y_{X=2} - \log Y_{X=1} + \log 100$$
$$= (\log a + b \log X_2) - (\log a + b \log X_1) + \log 100$$
$$= b \log X_2 - b \log X_1 + \log 100$$
$$= b \log 2 - b \log 1 + \log 100$$
$$= \log 100 + b \log 2$$

$$\log P = \log 100 + b \log 2 \qquad (7)$$
$$= 2.00000 - 0.66093(0.30103)$$
$$= 1.80104$$

$$P = 63.2 \text{ per cent curve}$$

There are two major errors, or misunderstandings of concept, frequently made by users of the learning curve. Because these fundamental errors persist even among those who have had training in the use of the curve, it would be well to lay them to rest at this point.

First, it is sometimes said that *the curve must flatten at some future value or it will reach zero*. This cannot be true, because by the nature of the logarithmic function it is impossible to reach zero. It must be remembered that the *rate of improvement is constant between doubled quantities*, not between every time the job is performed. The change between the two millionth (2,000,000) time and the four millionth (4,000,000) time is quite different from the change between the two millionth (2,000,000) and the two millionth and first (2,000,001). It may be helpful to refer again to the arithmetic plotting in Figure 17-1b, where the curves are shown to approach asymptotically, limiting minimum values of the variable on the vertical axis.

A second error sometimes made holds that the *50 per cent curve is impossible*, that a 50 per cent curve would mean that the second half of the job would be done for nothing (see [13, p. 29]). This is not the case. A 50 per cent curve is improbable, but steeper curves for short stretches of time have been observed and accurately used.

17-4   Computation of Unit Values

For ease of calculation, the values of X_i, where i represents the ith trial or the ith time the work was accomplished, will be referred to as the number of units (of output or product from the process). For example, the fifth time the effort was accomplished (X_5) is unit number 5. The simplest problem, and one of the most frequent, is that of finding the value of a specific unit from a given equation for the curve. The procedure is similar to the one used in section 17-3. With a given theoretical number one, a, and the slope of the curve, b, the value of Y may be computed for a specific unit by letting X equal the unit number desired and solving the equation

$$\log Y = \log (\#1) + \text{slope} (\log X)$$
$$= \log a + b \log X \qquad (8)$$
$$\text{antilog } Y = \text{desired value of } Y$$

Also, if the percentage of learning (P), rather than a, is given, b may be found from equation (7) and then Y from equation (8).

Example 3. If we have given a number one of 400 man-hours and a percentage of learning of 80 per cent, b and Y may be computed for

$X_i = X_9$ or for any other value of X desired. From equation (7),

$$b = \frac{\log P - \log 100}{\log 2}$$

$$= \frac{\log 80 - \log 100}{\log 2}$$

$$= \frac{1.90309 - 2.0000}{0.30103} = -\frac{0.09691}{0.30103} = -0.32193$$

From equation (8),

$$\log Y = \log 400 + b \log 9$$
$$= 2.60206 - 0.32193(0.95424)$$
$$= 2.29486$$

$$Y = 197 \text{ man-hours for unit } 9$$

For convenience, Appendix Tables B and C have been provided to simplify these calculations. One can select a given curve, for instance, one with $P = 80$ per cent, and multiply the table value by the theoretical number one to obtain the Y value directly. The computation used in constructing these tables assumes a value of 100 as a number one, and by following the formula, a percentage of the number one is obtained for each unit value.[3] A running total of these percentages is also compiled in order to compute cumulative totals, such as the total value of units 10 through 110. Use of Appendix tables with the following formulas makes the calculation quite simple.

For the unit value of Y,

$$Y = \frac{a(\text{table value for the } X\text{th unit for a given curve})}{100} \qquad (9)$$

For the cumulative value of Y,

$$Y_c = \frac{a\left(\begin{array}{cc}\text{cumulative table} & \text{cumulative table}\\ \text{value for } X_k & \text{value for } X_j - 1\end{array}\right)}{100} \qquad (10)$$

where X_j is the first unit of a series and X_k is the last unit of the series.[4]

Example 4. Using the table in Appendix B, we find the value for X_9 with a number one of 400 man-hours on an 80 per cent curve has been simplified to the calculation:

$$Y = \frac{(400)(49.2950)}{100} = 197.2 \text{ man-hours}$$

---

[3] Some tables use the value of 1 rather than 100, as a number one, eliminating the need for dividing by 100 in equations (9) and (10). See also the explanation given preceding the tables in Appendixes B and C.

[4] Note that in equation (10) if $X_j = a$, then $(a - 1)$ must be defined as equal to 1 rather than zero, because a is the vertical intercept of the learning curve.

If one wishes to know the total value for units 6 through 9, one could simply use the cumulative table:

$$\sum_{i=6}^{9} Y_i = \frac{a(X_9 - X_5)}{100} = \frac{400(583.886 - 373.774)}{100} = 840.4 \text{ man-hours}$$

In some cases, the slopes of curves are not given in the tables because of an extraordinary degree of steepness for large numbers of units. In this event, the following formula gives an approximation of the required cumulative value (slope = b):

$$\sum_{i=1}^{X_n} Y_i \simeq \int_{0.5}^{X_n+0.5} Y \, dX \simeq \int_{0.5}^{X_n+0.5} aX^b \, dX$$

$$\simeq \frac{a}{1+b} [(X_n + 0.5)^{1+b} - (0.5)^{1+b}] \tag{11}$$

where X_n is the last unit of X in the cumulative series. Formula (11) is used to obtain any series of units, that is, to obtain the answer in example 4 for units 6 through 9, use

$$\sum_{X=6}^{9} Y_i = \sum_{n=1}^{9} Y_i - \sum_{n=1}^{5} Y_i$$

$$\simeq \frac{a}{1+b} [(X_9 + 0.5)^{1+b} - (X_5 + 0.5)^{1+b}]$$

$$= \frac{400}{1 - 0.32191} [(9.5)^{1-0.32193} - (5.5)^{1-0.32193}]$$

$$= \frac{400}{0.67807} [(9.5)^{0.67807} - (5.5)^{0.67807}]$$

$$= \frac{400}{0.67807} (4.6021 - 2.1770)$$

$$= 400 \frac{1.4251}{0.67807} = 400(2.1017)$$

$$= 840.7$$

Note that the approximate value of 840.7 is only slightly greater than the exact 840.4 obtained from use of the tables. The source of this error is attributable to the substitution of the integral for a summation sign and a change in limits:

$$\int_{0.5}^{X_n+0.5} Y \, dX \quad \text{for} \quad \sum_{1}^{X_n} Y \tag{12}$$

In Figure 17-2 the area under the smooth curve obtained by use of the integral is obviously larger than the area under the step function (rectangles). The error introduced by use of the integral and revised limits equals the shaded minus the crosshatched areas [8, pp. 183–184].

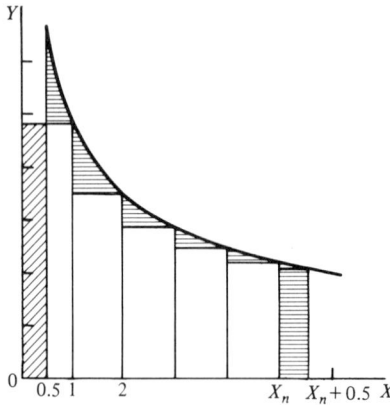

Figure 17-2

17-4-1   *Computation of revised number one*

In analytical work with the learning curve, one must calculate the effects of various changes to the work shop on the number one unit. If the least-squares regression technique is used, a gives the number one value. However, as the slope of the curve changes or new projections are required, one must recalculate this value. It can be found by using estimated or computed values for a given unit or block of units and then solving the proper equation for the number one.

If tables are used and a given slope and single unit value exist, equation (13) gives the required value.

$$\text{Number one} = \frac{\text{table value for } X}{\text{value of unit } Y}(100) \tag{13}$$

If we know the value of a block of units, the cumulative table value can be used in equation (13) instead of the unit table value.

The number one has important theoretical interest. In making estimates of a given job, one should attempt to estimate either the number one or the total cost of the project. The shape of the function depends upon many things as it relates to a given industry and product. There are scallop curves, straight lines, or hump curves, depending on these factors. The reasons for the nonlinear curves will be discussed later, but in general these curved lines make projection difficult and in order to project them properly, the theoretical number one is adjusted so that the ensuing calculation can be based on straight-line projections, and the results are added together to give the desired shape of the curve.

17-4-2   *Average-cost calculations and midpoints*

In production problems man-hours and costs are typically recorded for lots, blocks, or contract quantities of units, as shown in the first three columns of Table 17-3, rather than for each production unit. The average man-hours per unit for each lot, shown in column 4, is obtained by dividing man-hours per

Table 17-3

| | | Man-hours or dollars | |
Lot (1)	Units (2)	per lot (3)	Unit man-hours (4) (3) ÷ (2)
1	1–10	5,800	580
2	11–20	4,400	440
3	21–40	7,500	375
4	41–70	9,800	327
5	71–100	9,300	310

lot by the number of units in the lot. These values may be used for the Y coordinates of points to plot a unit curve. The X coordinate for each lot, however, is not simply the arithmetic midpoint of the lot, for example, for lot 1 of $10/2 = 5$, because the learning curve is not a straight line, except approximately for lots preceded by a large number of units. In Figure 17-3 it is clear that the true midpoint for an initial block of 1 through 299 units is less than $(1 + 299)/2 = 150$. The cumulative man-hours of units 1–299 is given by the area under either the learning curve or within the rectangle drawn at a height $(Y_m = 15.9)$ such that approximately the same area is circumscribed between the same limits of X. If X_m is the true midpoint, the two shaded areas must be equal. This is the appropriate X coordinate for the lot to be used in plotting the unit curve [7, pp. 7–13].

The tables in Appendixes B and C can be used to calculate the unit values, given the average cost of a lot and the slope of the curve. The theoretical number one is first obtained by the formula

$$a = \text{number one} = \frac{(\text{average cost})(n)(100)}{\text{cumulative table value for units included}} \tag{14}$$

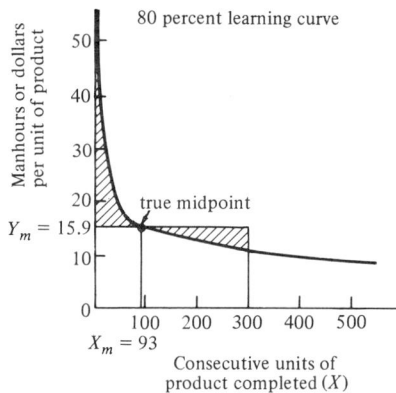

Figure 17-3

where n is the number of units in the lot. Then the unit value is a times the table value:

$$\text{Unit value} = a(\text{unit table value}) \tag{15}$$

Points on the cumulative curve are obtained similarly:

$$\text{Cumulative value} = a(\text{cumulative table value}) \tag{16}$$

The midpoint value of X may be obtained by solving for X_m in the equation

$$Y_m = aX_m^b \tag{17}$$

For example, if a project of 120 units is estimated to require an average of 60 man-hours per unit, the midpoint unit value of X_m may be computed as follows, assuming the 80 per cent learning curve is appropriate: From equation (14),

$$a = \frac{(\text{average cost})(n)(100)}{\text{cumulative table value}}$$

$$= \frac{60(120)(100)}{3705.106} = 194.326$$

Then solve $Y = aX^b$ for X:

$$60 = 194.326X^{-0.32193}$$

$$\log 60 = \log 194.326 - 0.32193 \log X$$

$$1.77815 = 2.28854 - 0.32193 \log X$$

$$\log X = \frac{2.28854 - 1.77815}{0.32193} = \frac{0.51039}{0.32193} = 1.58541$$

$$X_m = 38.49$$

This checks with the Rand Corporation tables [7]. The extensive learning-curve tables provided by the Rand Corporation provide convenient midpoints for log-linear curves and also for log-linear cumulative average curves (discussed later).

This calculation of the midpoints enables researchers to find the break-even unit at which a firm would begin to recoup expenses incurred during the first part of production. Such information is valuable for computing the financial outlay required before the project is self-sustaining or returning a profit.

Other calculations can be derived easily from these formulas. Average value of a group of units can be found by computing the cumulative value of the group and then dividing by the number of units. Note that the value of these units refers to the measurement in which the work is being accomplished, such as man-hours. Cost curves, which include allowance for inflation, price rises, and other factors not associated with the accomplishment of the task, must be adjusted to isolate the learning portion before using these formulas. In general, these cost curves show when plotted in monetary terms a scallop effect, with the actual dollar rising above 100 per cent after a few years because of inflationary trends.

17-5   Log-Linear Unit Versus Log-Linear Cumulative Average

Up to this point, the log-linear curve has been applied to a *unit* of output, that is, the Y in the equation

$$Y = aX^b \tag{18}$$

refers to the cost of the Xth unit of output [7, pp. 1–13]. An alternative relation sometimes used applies the log-linear curve to the *cumulative average* of a block of output, that is, the Y in the same form of equation (18) refers to the average cost of the first X units of output (see [8, p. 194], [10, pp. 90–104], [7, pp. 1–17]). Where confusion is a possibility, subscripts i and c are useful:

$$\text{Log-linear unit} \quad Y_i = aX_i^b \tag{19}$$

$$\text{Log-linear cumulative average} \quad Y_c = aX_c^b \tag{20}$$

The distinction between the unit and cumulative average approaches may also be seen with reference to Figure 17-4. In Figure 17-4a the lower downward-sloping line shows the unit curve, from which the unit cost of producing an additional unit of output can be read. This is analogous to the marginal curves considered in previous chapters. The numbers in Table 17-4 were derived from an 80 per cent learning curve. Note that the unit curve of Figure 17-4a is a plotting of columns 1 and 2 of Table 17-4, while the cumulative average curve is a plotting of columns 1 and 4. As long as the unit (marginal) curve falls to the right, the average curve must lie above it. For a log-linear unit curve, the cumulative average curve is a nonlinear curve for the first unit but approaches asymptotically a line parallel to the unit curve with the value

$$\frac{a}{b+1} X^b \tag{21}$$

which is identical to the unit curve shifted vertically by the constant $1/(b + 1)$. Recognition of this fact permits one to estimate the cumulative average cost by multiplying the unit measure by $1/(b + 1)$ when the number of units is large. For example, for a quantity of 100 units and an 80 per cent curve ($b = 0.32193$), cumulative average man-hours may be estimated by multiplying the unit value of 2,270 from Table 17-4 by $1/(b + 1)$:

$$\hat{Y}_c = (\text{unit value}) \frac{1}{b+1}$$

$$= 2{,}270 \left(\frac{1}{1 - 0.32193} \right)$$

$$= \frac{2{,}270}{0.67807} = 3{,}348$$

Comparing this approximation with the more precise one of 3,265 from Table 17-4, we find a percentage error of

$$\frac{3{,}348 - 3{,}265}{3{,}265} = \frac{83}{3{,}265} = 0.025, \text{ or } 2.5 \text{ per cent}$$

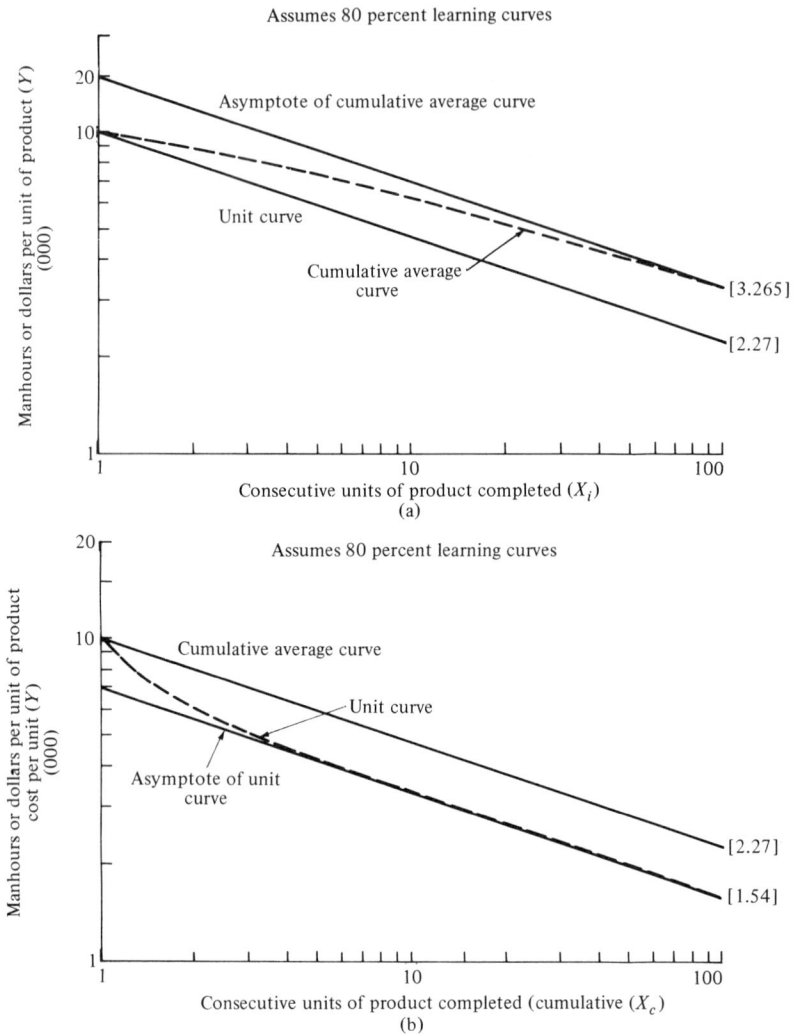

Figure 17-4

The error produced would have been about 1 per cent if a 90 per cent curve were used and almost 5 per cent for a 75 per cent curve. Thus a greater number of units is required for lower percentage curves to maintain the relative accuracy of the asymptote approximation [7, pp. 4–5].

Figure 17-4b illustrates the alternative approach in which the log-linear curve is applied to the cumulative average of a block of output (rather than to units of output) as given in equation (20). Here, the cumulative average curve is a straight line below which the nonlinear unit curve approaches asymptotically another straight line that is parallel to the cumulative average curve. The

Table 17-4

Unit number (X_i) (1)	Unit man-hours or dollars (Y_i) (2)	Cumulative man-hours (3) Σ(2)	Cumulative average man-hours (Y_c) (4) (3) ÷ (1)
1	10,000	10,000	10,000
2	8,000	18,000	9,000
4	6,400	31,421	7,855
8	5,120	53,459	6,682
16	4,096	89,201	5,575
32	3,277	146,786	4,587
64	2,621	239,245	3,738
100	2,270	326,509	3,265

asymptote of the unit curve has a value

$$a(b + 1)X^b \tag{22}$$

which is the log-linear cumulative average curve shifted downward by the constant $(b + 1)$. This approach is employed by researchers where observations indicate a better fit than could be obtained with the log-linear unit curve.

17-6 Application of the Curve

These techniques and observations are applicable to any situation in which progress is observable. The learning curve is therefore called the progress curve. To apply learning curve techniques properly, one must evaluate effectively the portion subject to analysis. One must consider proper pricing, scheduling, prior experience on similar work, size and weight of the job, engineering, process technology, possible disruptive influences, and any other thing that might alter the progress of a given job.

17-6-1 *Scheduling*

Scheduling plays an important part in the actual completion of any project. As Parkinson's law states, work expands to fit the available time, and if budgets allow a given length of time for a project (greater than or equal to sufficient time for the project), this will be the amount of time recorded to the project. Some critics have claimed that the learning curve is simply the result of budgeting and scheduling. Others have demonstrated "progress by serendipity," which shows a level of learning when no pains were taken to insure continued improvement.[5] But any projection based solely on actual experience may be so

[5] Model-T production for the years 1909–1926 for over 15 million automobiles shows an 86 per cent curve.

dominated by the scheduling effect that accurate observations about the theoretical behavior of learning curves may be impossible to prove.

The application of the learning curve in scheduling may be shown by taking as an example a company making farm machinery. Assume the firm wishes to make one machine a week. It is known that the first machine would take 400 man-hours and that the firm has previously been able to produce on an 80 percent improvement level. Therefore, the company must budget ten men for the first 40-hour week, eight men for the second week, and so on. From this example, one can see the effect of scheduling. Could the task have been done with a 300 man-hour number one and improved at a 70 percent rate? In any case, proper coordination within a company of scheduling and budgeting efforts should lead to the best solution of problems and completion of the task. This coordination will furnish the firm's salesmen with the proposed average cost of the product, the resulting margin of each unit, and total sales.

17-6-2 *Pricing*

The two important phases of a firm's production are buying inputs and producing outputs. In section 17-6-1 the effect of the learning curve was discussed in the production of output and the resulting sale price. To evaluate the prices suppliers charge the company and the preparation of a proposal or bid for contract work to be performed, the same procedure is followed, the only difference being the type of conclusion one comes to: One will result in a *price paid* for work performed, and the other will result in a *price received* for work performed. The final price paid for a negotiated contract often depends on the skill and integrity of the negotiators in evaluating the slope of a learning curve and other factors involved in its projections. A number of influences may affect the shape of a learning curve. The significant items, as they affect a given firm's production, must be considered in order to determine the best price.

17-6-3 *Weight*

Many companies use a function involving structural weight as a parameter in order to determine the number one unit value. In order to determine structural weight, subtract major purchased items such as electrical systems, wheels, or other parts that affect the weight significantly but are not actually involved in the construction process. Then take prior number one experience based on various weights of projects, compute a number one man-hour for this project, and proceed with the value calculation as previously outlined.

17-6-4 *Experience*

Prior experience on similar work gives a definite shape to a learning curve. Work done by the Stanford Institute indicates a value can be used to evaluate prior work experience. This factor is known as a *B* factor, which gives a humped-curve effect when plotted. The curve is calculated by assuming that prior experience gives an advantage of a certain number of units, so that the company is actually starting production farther out on the curve than the number one.

For example, assume company A has a *B* factor of 4. Its unit number one will actually be calculated by using unit number five. This implies that through previous experience on this type of work the firm has gained four units of experience. This factor will allow companies with previous experience to submit a low bid on an initial contract but then possibly a higher one than concerns with no experience on a succeeding contract.

An effect opposite to the *B* factor is also observable in some types of production, associated primarily with a new company, labor force, product, or design. This is a scallop effect showing an extremely high number one; as work progresses, rapidly improved items drop significantly and the curve levels off to a more reasonable slope. The theory involved here is actually one of two separate tasks and is also commonly observed in an area where there is mixed assembly-type work and machine work. Where there is machine work, the major portion of time required is for the machine to do its job. It will, perhaps, cut metal at a certain rate and no faster. As the more rapidly improving setup or assembly time progresses, this effort takes less and less of a percentage of total effort, and the resulting curve appears to flatten, but is actually only an outgrowth of a combination of tasks. To evaluate these problems accurately, one must adjust the number of units and correctly break down the task in order to make straight-line projections. The important thing is that learning curves do not flatten, and if one appears to do so, careful analysis can pay big dividends in pricing a similar proposal.

A machinist skilled in the operation of a machine can set up a part for production much faster than an unskilled employee. When evaluating a new contract, one must consider the experience level of the workers who will be performing the work. There could be as many as three learning curves at work on a single piece of machined work: (1) the amount of time it takes a machinist to set up the part for the first time—this effort is a function of familiarity with the machine and the number of parts the worker has set up previously; (2) the setup time required for this given part—this setup time will not only have the machinist number one value but will also improve each time it is set up, based on engineering and the number of setups required for that part; (3) the run time required for the part—the run time is a function of machine efficiency and number of parts made during the run as well as of the machinist's efficiency in running the machine. Improvement is made in quality, product design, special tooling, value engineering, and points of automation. All in all, a combination of setup and run time for a given lot of parts can greatly improve in the longer run.

Disruption can cause unlearning. Studies have been made to determine the amount of learning that can be transferred from one person to another. This disruption can occur with changes in machinery or simply by allowing a span of time to elapse between production runs. It can generally be concluded that there are two phases to the learning process, one involving motor responses, the other involving intellectual decision process. The intellectual portion can be transferred by retaining a few experienced people at key positions. They can tell the new personnel how to do this job and the little eccentricities of a machine, but when the new people actually do the task it is still a number one physical task. They must do it repetitiously until they have learned it. Naturally, if no

experienced personnel are retained, even the intellectual learning is lost. Understanding this situation can allow a shop manager to place his or her personnel
so as to gain an optimum experience level even in times of severe cutback in
employment or in times of rapid expansion.

Recognizing this transfer of learning is also important when making changes
in technology. A new machine may be much faster than an old one, but the
machinist may have been well along his experience curve on the old machine.
If the new one is significantly different, it may take an unexpected length of
time before the machinist is able to use the new machine efficiently. Management
must recognize this in evaluating new contracts calling for new technology and
suggestions for cost improvements in existing technology.

A machinist becoming more skilled as he continues to work on new parts
and transferring his learning to new personnel have certain economic implications. If the aggregate skill level of all workers is considered, this observation
would imply an increased level of proficiency in industry as a whole. Studies
have been developed, using this hypothesis and the constant elasticity of substitution (CES) production function, that lend support to this theory [3, 15].

17-7 A Final Caution to Users of Learning Curves

When historical manufacturing data fit the learning curve, there may be a
tendency for managers and production workers to establish future points on
the curve as targets or goals to strive to attain [8, pp. 195–196]. This would be
desirable where the learning curve represents a valid standard requiring diligence of all employees. But if the standard is too easily attained, there is a
likelihood that nothing more than that standard will be attained. Conformance
to the curve, then, is no guarantee that the correct curve was previously selected.
Empirical evidence in such a case cannot be used in defense of a selected curve.

The researcher must also guard against the manipulation of accounting data
to conform to the curve. For example, if the curve is defined in terms of direct
labor man-hours, there is a temptation to assign questionable workers only as
indirect labor. This would result as an understatement of the direct man-hours
employed and distort production records in an upward direction. Similarly,
judgment must be used where a design change is introduced as to whether the
improvement stems from the supporters' organization or from the introduction
of a new model. In the latter case, a new learning curve may be more appropriate. Such issues must be considered when applying the learning model.

Questions and Problems

17-1. Given the following values for X and Y, compute the #1 value (a), the slope
(b), and the percentage learning curve (P): $X = 2$, $Y = 44$; $X = 10$, $Y = 25$;
$X = 41$, $Y = 12$; and $X = 200$, $Y = 7$.

17-2. Given the following values for X and Y: $X = 4$, $Y = 75$; $X = 25$, $Y = 52$; and
$X = 90$, $Y = 30$,

a. Compute the logarithmic least-squares best-fit equation.

b. Compute the standard error of estimate, as given by the equation

$$\sigma_{est\,Y} = \sqrt{\frac{(\log\,Y)^2 - (\log\,C)(\log\,Y) + n(\log\,X)(\log\,Y)}{N}}$$

Note: This statistic is sometimes useful in establishing confidence limits. The confidence limits are obtained by taking the antilog of the standard error of the estimate. While a knowledge of confidence limits may be useful in statistical analysis, it is not essential to the concept of the learning curve.

17-3. Given man-hours of 1,000, compute the percentage of learning for the following values of b:

a. -3.3219 d. $+0.0704$
b. -1.0000 e. $+1.0000$
c. -0.1520 f. $+3.3219$

17-4. Given the following percentages of learning, compute the corresponding slopes of the equations.

a. 85 per cent   c. 76 per cent
b. 60 per cent   d. 92 per cent

17-5. Compute the required unit value (Y) for the given #1's and curves:

a. unit 17 with an 85 per cent curve and a #1 $= 325$
b. unit 96 with a 70 per cent curve and a #1 $= 496$
c. unit 25 with a 95 per cent curve and a #1 $= 65$
d. unit 4,396 with a 78 per cent curve and a #1 $= 624$

17-6. Compile a table of unit (Y) and cumulative values (Y_c) for an 82 per cent curve for units 1–20.

17-7. Compute cumulative values (Y_c) for the following series units given a #1 and a curve:

a. units 75–100 with an 80 per cent curve and a #1 $= 246$
b. units 1–16 with an 82 per cent curve and a #1 $= 163$
c. units 2,001–4,000 with a 78 per cent curve and a #1 $= 500$

17-8. Given a unit value (Y) and a curve, compute the #1 unit value (a):

a. unit 34 $= 76$ on an 80 per cent curve
b. average value for units 16–25 $= 46$ on a 75 per cent curve
c. total value for units 8–16 $= 863$ on an 85 per cent curve

17-9. Given an average value of 93 man-hours for the first 20 units of a contract, compute the total value (Y_c) and average ($\overline{Y}$) value for units 21–45 based on an 80 per cent curve.

17-10. Company A estimates that a current project of 100 units will require an average of 75 man-hours per unit. At what unit should the company reach the 75-man-hour level? Assume an 80 per cent learning curve.

17-11. Company B has been operating on a project C for 25 units. At this point, a new invention becomes available that will replace a part requiring 10 man-hours for unit 25. The new part is completely different and the estimate for the first unit is 25 man-hours. Based on a 75 per cent curve for the total operation and an expenditure of 54,960 man-hours to date, what should units 26–50 cost in terms of man-hours?

17-12. Company Z estimates that project A will require 600 man-hours for unit #1. Similar projects in the past have followed an 80 per cent curve. The average rate per hour is $9.26. The project requires 15 units in year 1, 30 units in year 2, 30 units in year 3, and 10 units in year 4. Furthermore, a 6 per cent per year increase is expected in the wage rate.

a. Compute the total man-hours required.
b. Determine total cost of the project.
c. Determine total and average cost for each year.

17-13. Company C wishes to hold its employment at 40 people in its factory. This company produces a machine that requires 800 man-hours to build its #1 unit. How many machines will be produced in each week for the first 15 weeks based on an 80 per cent curve and a 40-hour work week?

17-14. The Adv Company wishes to make 10 per cent profit on each project in the first year of production. The first unit is estimated at $649 cost, and they anticipate sales of 120 units in this year.

   a. What is the desired selling price based on an 85 per cent curve?

   b. At what unit should they reach average cost?

   c. At what unit should they break even at zero profit?

17-15. A material buyer wishing to buy a quantity of 50 units faces the following problem of price breaks:

   Qty 10 @ $5.00 each
   Qty 100 @ $2.00 each
   Qty 1,000 @ $0.50 each

   Assuming the price quoted for the 100-unit lot reflects its average cost and a 55 per cent learning curve, what would be the purchase price that just covers the manufacturer's cost?

17-16. Past experience on a given type of machine shows an 80 per cent curve on #1 of 4 man-hours per pound for 1,000 pounds. Machine Z weighs 5,000. How many man-hours are required for the first unit of machine Z?

17-17. Neue Company is attempting to enter the widget market. Ye Olde Company has been making various types of widgets for several years and is generally assumed to have a *B* factor of 6 in this industry. Gobble Company has a new design of widget that it wishes to have produced. Proposals are submitted by Neue and Ye Olde companies for this work based on 25 units. A 50-unit follow-on contract is expected. The 25-unit initial contract proposals were

   Neue's proposal: 2,600 man-hours $26,000
   Ye Olde's proposal: 2,300 man-hours $23,000

   The Gobble Company, knowing of the 50-unit follow-on, evaluated the proposals and discovered Neue used a 75 per cent curve and Ye Olde used an 85 per cent curve.

   a. Determine the expected 50-unit proposal for each company.

   b. Which company would be chosen for production?

17-18. A new appliance is estimated to require 120 man-hours for its theoretical #1. This #1 appliance is composed of 50 per cent assembly work, which normally works on a 70 per cent curve, and 50 per cent machine work, which is normally on a 95 per cent curve. The assembly shop is assigned a *B* factor of 4. Compute total man-hours for units 1, 2, 5, 10, and 20.

References

1. Armen Alchian. "Reliability of Progress Curves in Airframe Production." *Econometrica* 31 (October 1963): 679–693.

2. Frank J. Andress. "The Learning Curve as a Production Tool." *Harvard Business Review* 32 (January–February 1954): 97–98.

3. K. J. Arrow. "The Economic Implications of Learning by Doing." *Review of Economic Studies* 29 (June 1962): 154–174.

4. Harold Asher. *Cost-Quality Relationships in the Airframe Industry.* Report R-291 (Santa Monica, Calif.: Rand Corporation, 1956).
5. A. B. Berghell. "Learning Curve." In *Production Engineering in the Aircraft Industry* (New York: McGraw-Hill, 1944), pp. 166–198.
6. Boeing Airplane Company. "Improvement Curve." In *Aerospace Division Training Manual* (October 1963).
7. H. E. Boren, Jr. and H. G. Campbell. *Learning-Curve Tables* (Santa Monica, Calif.: Rand Corporation, 1970). Vols. I, II, III.
8. W. J. Fabrycky, P. M. Ghare, and P. E. Torgerson. *Industrial Operations Research* (Englewood Cliffs, N.J.: Prentice-Hall, 1972), ch. 7.
9. William Fellner. "Specific Interpretations of Learning by Doing." *Journal of Economic Theory* 1 (August 1969): 119–140.
10. Leonard Hein. *The Quantitative Approach to Managerial Decision* (Englewood Cliffs, N.J.: Prentice-Hall, 1972), ch. 7.
11. Winfred B. Hirchmann. "Profit from the Learning Curve." *Harvard Business Review* 42 (January-February 1964): 125–139.
12. W. Z. Hirsh. "Manufacturing Progress Functions." *Review of Economics and Statistics* 34 (May 1952): 143–155.
13. Raymond B. Jordan. "Learning How to Use the Learning Curve." *NAA Bulletin* 39 (January 1958): 27–39.
14. Frederick T. Moore. "Economies of Scale: Some Statistical Evidence." *Quarterly Journal of Economics* 73 (1959). Reprinted in Edwin Mansfield. *Microeconomics—Selected Readings* (New York: W. W. Norton, 1971), pp. 125–136.
15. Eytan Sheshinski. "Tests of the 'Learning by Doing' Hypothesis." *Review of Economics and Statistics* 49 (November 1967): 568–578.
16. L. L. Thurstone. *The Learning Curve Equation.* Psychological Monographs. Vol. 26, No. 3 (Princeton, N.J.: Princeton University Press, 1919).
17. T. P. Wright. "Factors Affecting the Cost of Airplanes." *Journal of the Aeronautical Sciences* 3 (February 1936): 122–128.

18 Technological Change and Forecasting

Technological change is one of the most fascinating areas of study in economics and business, because it deals with long-run changes in processes, techniques, and products, and with it lie the hopes of managers for success and of consumers for better standards of living. Although its tremendous importance is recognized, many firms devote few resources to its study because of its great complexity, uncertainty, and long-run nature. Planning for tomorrow is given lower priority than the immediate problems of today. Yet technology continually evolves in modern societies, and the manager who knows a little more than his competitors about its nature should prove to be a superior manager.

The study of technological change is one of the less refined areas of managerial economics and therefore is often omitted from standard texts and courses. But the subject has been given much greater attention in recent years. This chapter introduces a few fundamentals of the economics of technological change and then turns away from theory to consider some aspects of techno-

---

The impact of technical forces today is revealed by the following comments:

"We are in the midst of a new technological revolution that started 20 years ago."

"The number of scientists working today exceeds the total number of previous scientists since the beginning of history."

"Scientific activity is doubling each decade."

"Every 10 years one-half of our technical knowledge becomes obsolete."

"R & D is creating increasing pressures for expansion of capital expenditures to take advantage of new processes, new products, new equipment."

"Technological change is the most powerful force in the business world today, and its power is growing."

"Government research programs are becoming increasingly the major factor in guiding research" [16, p. 13].

272

logical forecasting, which has developed quite rapidly since the early 1960s, largely outside of the academic community.

This chapter rounds out the analysis of production and cost presented in previous chapters of Part Three. Also, it is useful in preparing the way for later discussion of social problems stemming in part from technological change, such as the pollution of our environment, ecological imbalance, a climate in which social irresponsibility is profitable, jobs that are excessively dull and unfulfilling, and a moral climate in which a pleasing personality is encouraged over virtuous character—topics treated in Chapters 23, 27, 28, and 29.

18-1   Some Basic Terminology

Technology may be defined as the available set of techniques for combining inputs to yield a given physical output. While a change in *technique* alters the character of physical equipment, products, and organization, a change in *technology* involves a change in knowledge and the production function and the availability of new products.[1]

Research and development is defined by the National Science Foundation to include

> . . . basic and applied research in the sciences (including medicine) and in engineering, and design and development of prototypes and processes. It does not include quality control, routine product testing, market research, sales promotion, sales service, research in the social sciences or psychology, or other nontechnological activities or technical services [29, p. 124].

Basic research deals with original investigation conducted for the purpose of advancing scientific knowledge rather than for specific commercial objectives. *Applied research* also seeks to discover new scientific knowledge but is devoted to practical applications as well. The term *development* concerns technical activity with nonroutine problems encountered in translating scientific knowledge into processes and products; routine customer services are excluded, together with the previously listed items, from the R & D definition.

Technology differs from science, which is defined as "the objective body of knowledge which has been accumulated and organized by systematic study," in being oriented more toward practicality and immediate usefulness than toward understanding per se [24, p. 20].

An *invention* is a novel combination of existing elements in a new and unique way; in the context of science and economics, it is a creation of new technological knowledge. When this new idea is embodied in the available set of techniques, through technological change, it becomes an *innovation*. The spread to

---

[1] The rate of technological change of an industry is believed by Edwin Mansfield to be a function of the quantity of resources devoted to research and development; the competitive market structure; the attitude of managers, workers, and the public toward change (political and cultural); the legal environment (for instance, patents); the extent to which industries can make use of each other's advances (for instance, external economies); and the organizational skill and management of researchers and developers (for example, good long-range planning). The net effect of these factors determines and is determined by the expected profitability of the required research and development efforts [18, pp. 17–24].

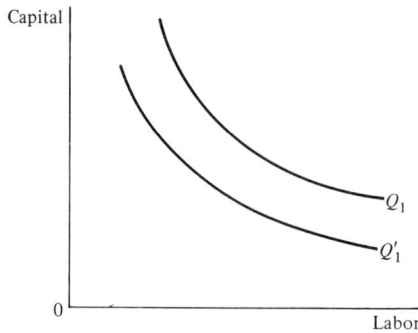

Figure 18-1

other organizations of an innovation beyond its initial use is referred to as diffusion (see [24, pp. 22–23]).

18-2   The Economics of Technological Change

A technological change in the production of an existing product involves a change in the production function. This is illustrated in Figure 18-1 for a hypothetical product requiring inputs of only labor and capital. An individual isoquant, say Q_1, encompasses a given production function that indicates the minimum combination (or techniques) of labor and capital that can be used to produce, say, 100 units of output. Therefore, a shift of Q_1 to Q'_1 closer to the origin represents an improvement in the production function, because an equal level of output now can be obtained with fewer inputs [19, pp. 441–443].

A technological change may be labor-saving, capital-saving, or neutral depending upon which input (neither for neutral change) is required in relatively smaller amounts to produce the same level of output, assuming relative prices and input ratios remain constant. Figure 18-2a illustrates the case of a labor-saving technological change: as isoquant Q_1 shifts to Q'_1, the slope of the isoquant ($MRTS_{LC}$) diminishes in moving along the constant input ratio ray OZ from point 1 to point 2; the MP_C is increased by the change relatively more than the MP_L, causing relatively more capital to be used. In Figure 18-2b the $MRTS_{LC}$ is increased by a move from point 1 to point 2; the MP_C is increased relatively less than the MP_L, causing relatively more labor to be used. In Figure 18-2c the $MRTS_{LC}$ remains the same and the change involves a more efficient use of labor and capital by the same percentages [19, pp. 445–447].

If a technological change requires additional investment in capital equipment, such as a data-processing machine or a new engine, it is said to be capital-embodied. If the change requires adaption of new methods and organization that permit the more efficient use of existing equipment, then the change is referred to as capital-disembodied.

18-3   The Measurement of Productivity and Technological Change

Productivity of an input is defined by the output-input ratio, the most common example of which is the output per man-hour of labor. This is a poor measure

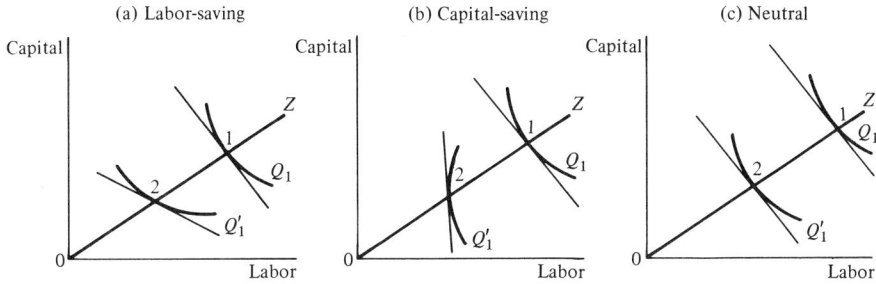

Figure 18-2

of technological change, because it is subject to change through changes in relative prices. For example, if relative prices are given by the slope of the line AB in Figure 18-3, the least-cost units of labor and capital required to produce Q_1 output are OL_1 and OC_1, respectively. A rotation of the price line to DE causes a shift from point 1 to point 2 as the now lower-cost capital is substituted for the relatively expensive labor. Thus, the same output is produced with less labor, and the output per man-hour measure of labor productivity shows an increase, although there has been no change in the production function implicit in the isoquant Q_1.

A better measure of technological change is obtained by relating output to both inputs according to a total productivity index described as follows. Assume the production function is given by the expression

$$Q = a(bL + dC) \tag{1}$$

where Q, L, and C are the same as before, b and d are constants, and a is a time parameter that reflects technological change. To measure the rate of technological change from time 0 to time 1, one need only compute the ratio

$$\frac{a_1}{a_0} = \frac{Q_1}{Q_0} \div \left(R\frac{L_1}{L_0} + S\frac{C_1}{C_0} \right) \tag{2}$$

where

$$R = \frac{bL_0}{bL_0 + dC_0} \quad \text{and} \quad S = \frac{dC_0}{bL_0 + dC_0} \tag{3}$$

The total productivity index a_1/a_0 is therefore the ratio of the relative increase in output to the weighted average of relative increases in labor and capital inputs. A major weakness of applying this index is, of course, that production functions may not be so simple as the very special one assumed here, which is based upon constant returns to scale and fixed input proportions. Attempts to improve the total productivity index have been discussed in the literature but are outside the scope of this chapter (see [19, pp. 448–450], [34], [13]).

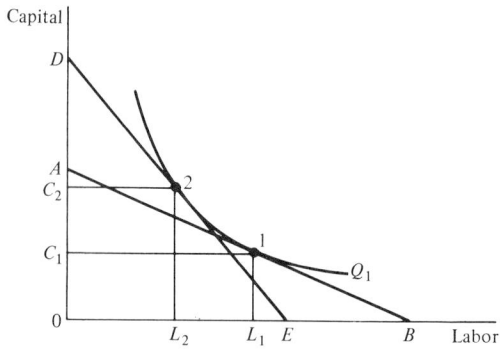

Figure 18-3

18-4 Introduction to Technological Forecasting

Forecasting began with the dawn of history as man began to associate current and historic events with those expected to occur in the future. The sound of falling rock and the roar of a predatory beast served notice to primitive man of a need for action to avoid impending danger. Just as the presence of a dark cloud warned of possible rain, the activities of heavenly bodies were later observed to be of use in predicting seasons and floods. Although the reading of an individual's future from scrambled chicken entrails or dried bones, from palms, crystal balls, and from the relative locations of planets and stars have been discredited by science and practical observation, these and other simple mechanical techniques have retained much of their following and popularity among certain groups and cults. The modern business executive is hardly influenced in making decisions by such primitive approaches but would consider using them *if* convinced that they would actually work with a probability exceeding that of randomness.

Many of the methods used by modern business forecasters, such as the learning curve discussed in Chapter 17 and others mentioned later, are basically mechanical techniques that appear to work even though the precise cause-and-effect relation is little understood. It is right that the practical business person should make use of such techniques, because he or she is by necessity more interested in immediate results than in theoretical understanding.

Technological forecasting, as a subject area about which many books and articles have been written and seminars given, emerged largely in the 1960s as a group of techniques to aid managers in making decisions with regard to resource allocation and priority selection. It is considered a tool for predicting technological achievements believed to occur within a stated period of time. Systematic analysis is applied to technical data so that substantially the same conclusions would be consistently deduced by any competent analyst. The probability of the forecasted event occurring within the stated time should be given in terms of specified levels of resources pledged as support. If the technological forecast influences the actions of planners in terms of resource commitments, then this tool becomes a plan. Indeed, for a forecast to be useful it must be integrated with a system of planning and resource allocation [7, pp. 3–8].

18-5   Outmoded Techniques for Allocating the Firm's Resources

Allocation of the firm's resources among its various departments and activities is not always based upon strictly objective or scientific approaches. Managers confronted with a multitude of alternative input uses frequently find the following methods in use: (1) the *squeaking wheel approach*, whereby resources are cut from all areas, perhaps more from some than others, and the managers wait to hear which areas complain the most, later restoring some funds to the loudest and most insistent until the ceiling budget has been reached; (2) the *level funding approach*, in which the same amounts as last year are allocated this year in order to minimize the noise level and number of squeaks, thereby maintaining the status quo and deferring (or forgoing) opportunities for reassessment and change to better promote the firm's goals; (3) the *glorious past approach*, where resources are diverted to divisions or individuals having the greatest previous success with the idea that "sticking with a winner" is better than analyzing new projects; (4) the *white charger technique*, where a department head with a burst of enthusiasm confronts a somewhat surprised top manager with a well-rehearsed presentation, complete with multicolored graphs, scale models, and handouts; the best speaker or the last one to brief the boss is then rewarded with increased resources; and (5) the *committee approach*, whereby the manager delegates the allocation decision to members who may or may not have his extent of knowledge and experience upon which to base a recommendation [7, pp. 480–481].

Managers should strive to replace such outdated approaches with those in which information can be organized so that objective analysis and sound judgments are more easily derived and each step of the analysis can be considered by other trained researchers.

18-6   The Need for Forecasts and the Role They Should Play in Managerial Decision Making

The need for forecasts and long-range planning is sometimes denied by rationalizations that the environment will remain unchanged, will change in the same manner as in the past, or cannot be anticipated because of a multitude of factors too complex to explain. These attitudes may have disastrous consequences. Expedient remedial action taken *after* the crisis may be too late to avoid failure of the organization and at best is an inefficient approach to realization of company goals. A proper forecast may have permitted a smooth transition and prevented or diminished the severity of a crisis [20, pp. 8–11].

The need for technological forecasting is summarized well by Marvin J. Cetron and Christine A. Ralph:

> Technology is changing so rapidly that it is necessary to be aware of what is going on not only in a specific field of interest, but also in complementary and competitive fields, in the market place, and in the whole social-political-economic environment. Without some formalized method of sifting and weighing all this information, it cannot be used effectively. Additionally, if a decision has been made on an intuitive basis, the rationale or justification for

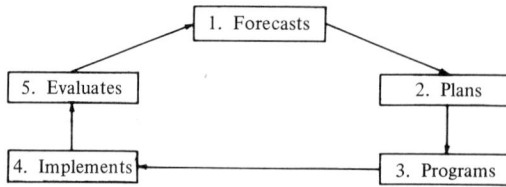

Figure 18-4

it is lost and cannot be repeated or explained. A formalized method provides visibility (projects can be evaluated on the same basis), a dialog can be opened up between the decision makers and the engineers and scientists, and possibly, and more importantly, it can start people thinking about the future, not simply in terms of a bigger, better program of the same sort in which they are currently involved, but functionally in terms of what their work is for. In effect, the techniques provide the tools whereby the technical knowledge and judgment of the forecaster can be applied to logical, systematic thinking about the pattern of development of a particular technology [7, pp. xii–xiii].

They go on to explain that such forecasting describes what the future *could* be, so that long-range planning can reflect, say, the estimated useful life of new investment projects where product obsolescence is a strong possibility.

A figure similar to Figure 18-4 is used by Joseph Martino in explaining the role of forecasting in managerial decision making. As a first step, researchers *forecast* future possibilities and likelihoods, providing the basis for the second step, in which they develop a *plan* prescribing a sequence of activities intended to achieve some goal. The plan is used in the third step of devising a *program*, which specifies the resources to be committed to carry out the plan. Once the necessary resources are acquired and assignment of tasks made, then, in the fourth step, they *implement* the program by expending resources and prescribing activities. After implementation, they *evaluate* the results to determine if the objectives of the plan were attained and to examine any unexpected conditions that might have arisen requiring adjustments in the current forecast. If the forecast is no longer valid, the sequence of steps may be repeated. In practice, the steps may overlap considerably and take place continuously. Revision of the forecast and other phases would be assumed when new information became available [20, pp. 14–15].

Martino stresses that the forecast is an important input for planning and decision making and quotes Ralph Lenz on the role of the forecast:

> The forecast identifies limits beyond which it is not possible to go.
> It establishes feasible rates of progress, so that the plan can be made to take full advantage of such rates; it does not demand an impossible rate of progress.
> It describes the alternatives which are open and can be chosen from.
> It indicates possibilities which might be achieved, if desired.

It provides a reference standard for the plan. The plan can thus be compared with the forecast at any point in time, to determine whether it can still be fulfilled, or whether, because of changes in the forecast, it has to be changed.

It furnishes warning signals, which can alert the decision maker that it will not be possible to continue present activities [20, p. 15].

In a programming context, the forecast may be considered a necessity in updating parameters of all the various demand and supply constraints.

18-7 Truth in Forecasting

Without giving the matter much thought, one might accept without reservation the statement, "A good forecast is one that turns out to be right." A weather forecast, of course, must be correct to be useful, because if the weather is forecasted to be good and plans made on this basis are washed out by rainstorms, then not only was the forecast useless but it prevented its followers from routinely preparing for the inclement conditions. But to judge technological, economic, political, and ecological forecasts by the same standard is inappropriate for two reasons. First, the way in which the forecasts are to be used in decision making is ignored, and second, the definition of good forecasts as those that come true precludes their evaluation prior to the event.

Where decision makers have no control over forecasted events, as in the case of the weather, they must tailor their actions to fit the outcome in order to maximize benefits or minimize losses. Forecasts must be correct to be of value. Where they have absolute control over forecasted events, perhaps as in the case of choice of occupation, they have no need for forecasts; they simply decide to do, or not to do, some act. In the in-between cases where they have some control over the outcome, forecasts can be useful whether or not they eventually prove to be correct.

If the decision responses have an impact on the outcome, forecasts can be self-fulfilling or self-defeating. The seller of a scarce product may announce to the public an expected shortage, knowing full well that this would cause customers to buy more than they currently need thereby bringing about the shortage, as some say occurred in the recent energy crisis. Another business executive might cry to newsmen and congressmen that some resource crucial to the production process will not be available in the future, with the intention of inciting legislators to take remedial measures. Similarly, stock market forecasts may be self-fulfilling or self-defeating, depending upon investors' knowledge that the forecast was made by a Bernard Baruch or an odd-lotter. In many sectors of the business world, information about likely outcomes resulting from given assumptions may indeed provide the necessary stimulus to bring about corrective action.

Knowledge of people's reactions to forecasts has led some forecasters to incorporate this factor in their forecasts, so that the outcome appears to be correct. This approach, like that of a Delphic oracle stating a prophesy in an ambiguous manner to allow different interpretations, makes forecasts useless for decision making. If the outcome is inevitable or believed to be so, there is no guide to appropriate action. Managers must recognize this if they are to continue receiving competent professional forecasting advice, just as fore-casters must understand that their recommendations must be useful even if they turn out wrong. All parties should keep in mind that no one can know the future; the most one can do in forecasting is to apply accepted postulates of logic to extract implications about future events from present information.

18-8 Scientific Techniques Used in Technological Forecasting

Although technological forecasting is in its formative years, some standard terminology and definitions have emerged from the literature. Two general approaches are in use. The first, referred to as *exploratory*, involves projecting technological parameters and capabilities from accumulated knowledge. The second, described as *normative*, begins with an assumption of future goals and an assessment of technological requirements necessary to realize the goals, followed by identification of the various technological deficiencies and barriers to be overcome. Either approach can use one or more of the following catego-ries of forecasting techniques: (1) intuitive methods, (2) analogy, (3) trend extrapolation, (4) growth curves, and (5) analytical models.

18-8-1 *Intuitive methods, including the Delphi technique*

Of the intuitive methods, *expert opinion* is a fundamental technique that depends largely upon an individual's knowledge of specific and related areas of special-ization [20, ch. 2]. An important drawback is that there may be no explicit statement of underlying assumptions and the logic involved that can be sub-jected to critical evaluation by others. In an attempt to offset this shortcoming, managers may solicit the advice of more than one expert by taking a *poll* or structuring a *group project*, panel, or committee. In this way, errors in individual predictions may be discovered and weeded out. However, the committee approach has the disadvantage that the strongest personality may prevail over a group decision even though less forceful contributors may possess better information and judgment.

The *Delphi technique* was developed at the Rand Corporation for obtaining a consensus of expert opinion that would be free of the drawbacks associated with simple polling and face-to-face contacts [10]. The intent of the Rand Corporation study was to map out possible events occurring from 10 to 50 years into the future in six major areas: scientific breakthroughs, population control, automation, space progress, war prevention, and weapons systems. In the pure form of the Delphi technique, a panel of experts is selected, each of whom is assumed to be more knowledgeable than the director of the experiment. The director sends out a sequence of messages and questions called question-naires to the panel members, whose replies remain anonymous to the other members. In this way, panelists can be less hesitant about voicing their beliefs without fear of coercion by members of superior rank or by the sheer weight of a majority opinion or of being embarrassed by later having to reverse a publicly expressed opinion.

In the first round, or Delphi sequence, the questionnaire asks for a list of events to be forecasted that are believed to be relevant to the subject area under study. The wording is open-ended rather than specific, so that the panelists may have the best opportunity to bring into consideration all related events, some of which might initially be unsuspected by the director and other participants. Upon receiving the responses, the director consolidates the lists of events, perhaps by use of a tally where events are mentioned by more than one participant.

In the second round the list is distributed with a request to the panelists to estimate the dates for the occurrence of the expected events and to give reasons in support of their dates. This information is consolidated, and a statistical summary of the group's opinions as to events, dates, and reasons is prepared for the third round. The median date for each event, and also the first and fourth quartile dates, is calculated for the panel. Panelists are asked in the third round to review the arguments and to make new estimates of dates for the events. If the new estimates fall outside the range contained by the two middle quartiles established by the previous round, respondents are asked to justify their views and to respond to opposing comments. Additional arguments and facts also can be cited in support of previous forecasts. The director again summarizes the panel's estimates, calculates new medians and quartiles, and lists the arguments advanced on both sides. If a consensus is not reached and if the director believes there is sufficient merit in attempting to reconcile conflicting views, he can submit his summaries and calculations to the panelists in a fourth round. If events are quite difficult to track because of a variety of important but unmeasured factors, and if the environment is subject to rapid change, additional rounds could be used either to seek a stronger consensus or to update a previous forecast. Figure 18-5a shows a hypothetical experiment in which a Delphi panel converges to the median. In Figure 18-5b three members shifted their estimates to later dates as additional arguments came under consideration.

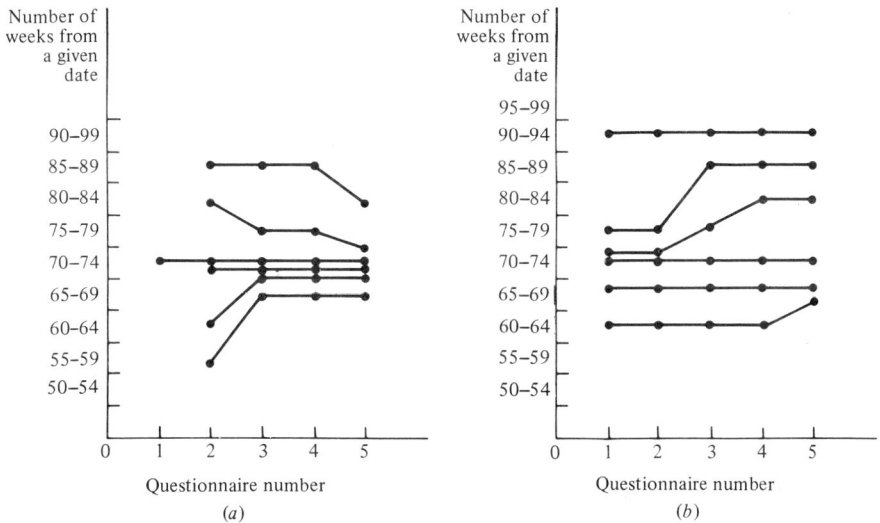

Figure 18-5

Variations of the basic Delphi approach may retain the anonymity, iteration, and statistical response characteristics but make other changes, such as giving the panelists some important information in the initial stage obtained from experts in related fields in which the panelists may not have expertise. Such information might be political, economic, and environmental forecasts that might affect the company's operations. If time is short, the number of rounds may be reduced to two or three. Each panelist may be asked to provide more than one date for each event and to assign probability estimates to them, for instance, to provide dates by which the respondent estimates the probability of occurrence to be 10, 50, and 90 per cent. Another variation has panelists rate themselves on degree of expertise on each question, so that responses may be given appropriate weightings. Some experiments have been made using computers with remote consoles to record responses and provide print-outs at the convenience of each panel member; in this way the current state of the group forecast can be continuously monitored. Murray Turoff claims that a computer-assisted Delphi conference is greatly superior to paper-and-pencil methods in terms of speed, convenience, and capability for interaction with larger groups [33].

18-8-2 *Analogy*

In attempting to predict the implication of some proposed change in technology, one should not fail to consider similar events that have taken place in some previous time or in some other society. In the area of international business, managers and writers frequently refer to the Americanization of Europe, Japan, and many other places. World travelers report seeing in other countries much that is familiar in the United States today and in previous times, the most obvious examples of which are Coca-Cola signs, hamburgers, snarled automobile traffic, and pollution. Many technologies developed in the United States have now spread, or are being spread, to other countries; prominent examples include advances in agriculture, steel, automobile, electronic, and chemical industries, and of course, nuclear weaponry. Marketing executives who attempt to extend the market for their products to foreign countries may find many parallels to draw upon from domestic experience, but they may find to their chagrin, as many others have, that the analogy is less than perfect. Numerous considerations of a political, economic, and cultural nature must be taken into account.

Forecasting by the use of analogy has great intuitive appeal, which undoubtedly accounts for its widespread usage. Analogy is the basis of inductive logic whereby a cause-and-effect relation is established between two events; for example, thunder appears to follow lightning; therefore where one sees lightning one expects to hear thunder shortly thereafter. Analogy is also the basis of empirical science; on a more refined level, the researcher attempts to establish the degree of predictability of the hypothesized relation. A pattern verified as being sufficiently general is termed a scientific law. Then the pattern may be used to forecast many other events, even in cases where some of the events that make up the pattern cannot be observed; an example taken from physics is that the planet Pluto will complete its first orbit around the sun in the year 2178, even though none has been observed since Pluto was discovered in 1930

[20, pp. 65–66]. An example from economics is the use of the law of supply to predict, other things being equal, that sellers will offer more of product if the price is raised.

In technological forecasting a *formal analogy* is defined as "a serious attempt to uncover other similarities (between two events) once some basic resemblances are noted." Formal analogies are of interest to forecasters, while casual ones are not. Problems arise from failing to distinguish between valid (formal) and invalid (casual) analogies; being unable to discern which among several alternative outcomes will be the correct one; being unable to attribute an appropriate weighting of differences between the cases being compared in order to decide which can be ignored and which can invalidate the analogy; and predicting that people involved in the present case will make the same mistakes as those in previous similar cases where they had no historical experience to draw upon, that is, enlightened decision makers will not inevitably make the same choices as unenlightened ones. One may guard against mistaking a casual for a formal analogy by comparing the various dimensions of the analogy; by examining as many analogous cases as possible from different times, places, and cultures; and by asking penetrating questions about the analogies with regard to the desirability of the anticipated outcome, participants' awareness of past experiences, and new techniques and trends that could alter the forecast [20, pp. 66–70].

Joseph P. Martino recommends that analogies be examined broadly with regard to aspects that are technological, political, economic, social, cultural, intellectual, managerial, religious/ethical, and ecological. Important differences in any of these dimensions can invalidate the analogy. As an example of how this approach can be used, he compared the development of American railroads to the space program and found numerous formal analogies. Both programs encountered technological frontiers in design and construction of transportation devices. Both involved significant investment expenditures relative to gross national product: 1.8 per cent for railroads during the period 1842–1901 compared to almost 1 per cent for space programs. Both had high unit costs. Both encountered huge managerial tasks, needs for precise timing, and high potential casualties in the event of mistakes. Both received the support of the government and favorable public attitudes. Few differences were judged to exist in political, social, cultural, religious, and ecological institutions that would significantly influence one but not the other [20, pp. 70–99].

18-8-3 *Trend extrapolation*

Much of economic forecasting makes use of trend extrapolation in the same manner previously discussed in regard to demand estimation in Chapter 11 and learning curves in Chapter 17 [20, ch. 5]. Such projection of events into the future is often used in technological forecasting in cases where there is an absence of known natural limits, such as achieving 100 per cent energy conversion, to prevent the trend from continuing, and where conditions believed to produce the past trend are no longer present in the same form, such as the exhaustion of a critical resource. The idea of approaching a saturation of a functional capability is important in estimating technological change. Consider the task of projecting the speed and altitude capabilities of aircraft through time. Progress was constrained at various points in history while awaiting technological improvements in such diverse areas as the supercharger, pilot's oxygen, metal monoplane, jet propulsion, pressure suit, and rocket propulsion. Without such improvements, advancement could not have overcome the barriers of

Table 18-1   Examples of the Use of Linear Regressions of Technology Through Time (T)

Area of application and years covered	Regression equation	Correlation coefficient	Standard error of regression coefficient
U.S. transport aircraft			
1935–1969	$Y = -226.80282 + 0.12077T,$ where $Y = $ ln of ton mph	0.90087	0.01503
1926–1969	$Y = -242.24943 + 0.12945T,$ where $Y = $ ln of passenger mph	0.96545	0.00713
Illumination			
1850–1960	$Y = -128.71511 + 0.06851T,$ where $Y = $ ln of lm/w	0.94605	0.00830
Electric power			
1945–1966	$Y = -150.14733 + 0.07992T,$ where $Y = $ ln of annual kwh (billions)	0.99594	0.00181
Horsepower (installed)			
1840–1967	$Y = -139.08846 + 0.07919T,$ where $Y = $ ln of hp (thousands)	0.99603	0.00183
	$Y = -123.02909 + 0.06127T,$ where $Y = $ ln of hp (thousands) per capita	0.99009	0.00224
Computers (digital)			
1951–1967	$Y = -1080.81958 + 0.55125T,$ where $Y = $ ratio of memory bits to access time in μsec	0.96053	0.03872
1945–1967	$Y = 740.01219 - 0.37934T,$ where $Y = $ ln of min required to invert a 40×40 matrix	-0.85907	0.05785

sound, heat, need for oxygen, and pressure. Extending a progress line based upon these past achievements is to assume implicitly that additional improvements are forthcoming that will successfully clear any additional barriers. However, to argue that a regular rate of past improvement cannot continue to ever higher levels is to claim that the present level has reached a point of discontinuity and that innovation must come to a halt. Surely the burden of proof falls upon the objector to show why progress must stop rather than upon the forecaster to show why the rate must continue.

Examples of the results of regression analyses of technological advances are given in Table 18-1. Most of the regressions use the natural logarithm of Y, which means that the given equation would plot as a straight line on semilog graph paper. This is another way of saying that Y is subject to exponential growth,[2] often true for many technologies. The equations of Table 18-1 provide empirical evidence that growth in a single technology does tend to take place at a decreasing rate. It is unfortunate, however, that there is no sound theoretical reason other than the presence of diminishing returns to explain why this is so. Indeed, there are empirical examples of other linear and nonlinear technological growths. There are also absolute limits to trends, such as zero pressure for vacuum pumps, absolute zero for technologies dependent upon heat reduction, and 100 per cent as the ultimate in energy conversion. As the limit is approached, forecasts may be adjusted from past trends to approach the limit asymptotically.

The related technique of trend correlation is employed where the change in some technological parameter is believed to be influenced by one or more precursor events. Erich Jantsch cites a case in which the output of plutonium from current thermal reactors was used to forecast the growth of fast-reactor application, which depends on the use of plutonium [11, p. 159]. Ralph Lenz has used maximum speeds of military combat aircraft to forecast similar speeds of commercial aircraft in later years; he found a lag ranging from 6 years in the 1920s to 11 years in 1959 [15, pp. 54–60]. Difficulties in forecasting by analysis of precursor events are that similar levels of performance are seldom realized by the following parameter and the length of the lag often varies by substantial amounts over time [20, p. 152].

---

[2] It may be shown mathematically that the assumption of a constant rate of growth (k) gives rise to exponential growth by rewriting the equation

$$\frac{dY}{dT} = kY \tag{4}$$

as

$$\frac{dY}{Y} = k \, dT \tag{5}$$

which, upon integration, becomes

$$\ln Y = \ln Y_0 + kT \tag{6}$$

where Y_0 is the initial value of Y at the initial time T_0. The antilog of both sides yields

$$Y = Y_0 \, e^{kT} \tag{7}$$

showing that Y indeed grows exponentially [19, p. 142].

18-8-4 *Growth curves*

Some researchers have found it useful to suggest parallels between biological growth and technological growth, using a biological analogy similar to the historical ones mentioned previously. One often finds in nature that the growth of plants and organisms plotted against time progresses along an S-shaped path, rising quickly in earlier stages and then rising at a slower rate in later ones. This is the case with the propagation of fruit flies in a bottle, the spread of contagious diseases, cell increase in white rats, and the growth of a pumpkin, a beanstalk, and yeast cells [15, pp. 40–46], [20, p. 103]. Such growth has been likened to projections of maximum speeds of military aircraft; Ralph Lenz has thereby projected a Mach 6 performance in 1979 and a Mach 12 by 1995 [3, pp. 66–77], [7, pp. 227–231]. S-shaped curves have also been observed for incandescent and fluorescent lamps, maximum speeds of aircraft, and the efficiency of steam engines and commercial electric-power plants [20, pp. 103–108].

Equations based upon S-shaped biological growth include the Pearl curve and the Gompertz curve. The Pearl curve is based upon growth studies of organisms and populations and is given by the equation

$$Y = \frac{L}{1 + ae^{-bt}} \qquad (8)$$

where L is the upper limiting value of Y; a and b are parameters; and t is the time variable. The Gompertz curve is based upon mortality rates and has been used to describe income distributions; its equation takes the form

$$Y = Le^{-be^{-kt}} \qquad (9)$$

Martino shows how these curves have been fitted to the growth of such technologies as steam engine efficiency, power plants, the conversion of merchant marine ships from wooden construction to metal, the percentage of dwellings using electric power, and the number of telephones per capita [20, pp. 111–122]

Figure 18-6 shows how Ralph Lenz made use of the Pearl curve in forecasting maximum speeds of United States combat aircraft. His selection of this growth curve, rather than the exponential trend shown as a straight line plotted on the semilog graph, reveals his judgment that orbital velocity would act as an upper limit of progress toward which advances would be made only asymptotically. This was considered a practical limit for vehicles that were intended to operate within the confines of the Earth's atmosphere, although higher speeds have been attained by ballistic and space vehicles.

The use of equations based upon biological growths for predicting technological events is, of course, a matter of subjective choice in much the same way as the techniques of expert opinion, analogy, and trend extrapolation. While this approach may be superior in some cases, it must be emphasized that there is no adequate theoretical reason to explain why technological growth must follow patterns similar to those of biological growth. The mechanical technique of fitting various equations to observed points adds rigor to the analysis but no guarantee that future performance will really conform to a presumed extension from the past. The product of such exercises may be of little more value than a

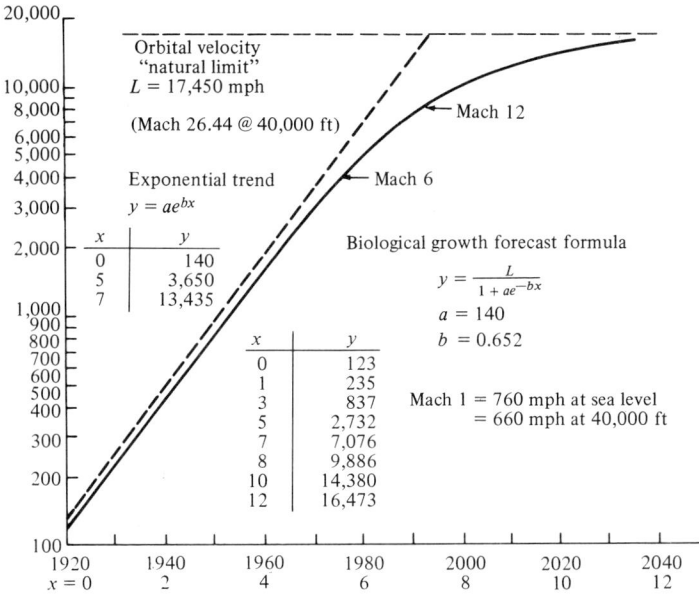

20,000

Orbital velocity
"natural limit"
L = 17,450 mph

(Mach 26.44 @ 40,000 ft)

Mach 12

Exponential trend
$y = ae^{bx}$

Mach 6

x	y
0	140
5	3,650
7	13,435

Biological growth forecast formula

$$y = \frac{L}{1 + ae^{-bx}}$$

$a = 140$
$b = 0.652$

x	y
0	123
1	235
3	837
5	2,732
7	7,076
8	9,886
10	14,380
12	16,473

Mach 1 = 760 mph at sea level
       = 660 mph at 40,000 ft

1920	1940	1960	1980	2000	2020	2040
x = 0	2	4	6	8	10	12

Figure 18-6

best guess based upon more information. However, if a variety of forecasting techniques point to similar expectations, confidence in the projected outcome tends to be greater than if only one had been used.

18-8-5 Analytical models

While trend extrapolation, analogy, and growth curves are more objective approaches to forecasting than intuitive methods, they remain at best "black boxes" whose internal workings are not explained. They simply assume the conditions structuring past behavior will be present and continue producing the same kinds of behavior. Although widely used and very useful, they are subject to at least three shortcomings: (1) They give no warning of changed conditions that can prevent the repetition of past patterns; (2) they are incapable of predicting changes in outcomes even when important changes affecting technological advancement are identified; and (3) they provide no guidance for producing a desired change in technological advance. Analytical models, when they are accurate, are superior to these naive models. The experience of economists with analytical models in predicting large changes in important variables has encouraged technological forecasters to use a similar approach [20, pp. 167–168].

Ideally, causal models of technological advance and their associated theories should pass the qualifying tests of identifying variables that influence technological growth, describing the variables in operational terms that would permit measurement by objective means, and establishing cause-and-effect relations so that predictions can be deduced in a systematic manner. In the words of Joseph Martino,

> We would like to have a model which starts with such items as number of scientists and engineers, number and types of R & D facilities available, predictions of R & D expenditures, description of the current state of the art, etc., and then produce a prediction of the level of some functional capability at a specific time in the future. To be more specific, we might like to take into account all the factors which influence the growth in productivity of, say, commercial transport aircraft, and produce a prediction of transport productivity at a future time [20, pp. 168–169].

The development of a theory that can adequately account for the observed data and permit extrapolation based upon known facts is generally accepted as the most difficult step in designing an analytical model.

At least two suggestions have appeared in the literature as possible theoretical explanations for the use of exponential functions in technological forecasting. The first, attributed by Ralph Lenz to Alan Fusfeld, is identified with the learning-curve function of Chapter 17. His reasoning is that improvement takes place through learning as a similar production process is repeated time and again. Technical progress of the learning variety occurs *because* extended production permits an establishment of routines and improvement in skills of managerial and production employees, and a higher margin of financial return (present under some positive combination of rising demand and falling unit costs) permits greater investment in research and development, which yields even more efficiencies. The second is Robert Seamans's assumption of competitive action and reaction. After competitor A initiates a new product, competitor B begins action to develop a newer version, which is, say, 20 per cent better. The appearance of B's new product, in turn, stimulates A to begin developing another model that will be 20 per cent better than B's. Successive leap-frogging at regular intervals results in an exponential envelope curve of progress in the two-competitor industry illustrated in Figure 18-7. Note that the curves for A and B remain horizontal until the other introduces a new model, and slope upward to the right while efforts to produce a successor are under way. From this concept a model can be developed in which progress is hypothesized to be a function of the number of competitors, timing of responses, length of time required for the development of new models, percentage of advance attempted, and probability of success (which should be made a stochastic function—one that is subject to chance variation) [7, pp. 235–239].

Other theoretical bases have been proposed that yield equations with S-shaped growth curves in the form of the Pearl curve. The Isenson-Hartman model is based upon the concept that the advancement of a specific technology is a process of buying information. The rate of acquisition of such information is expressed in its simplest form by the equation

$$\frac{dI}{dt} = kIN \tag{10}$$

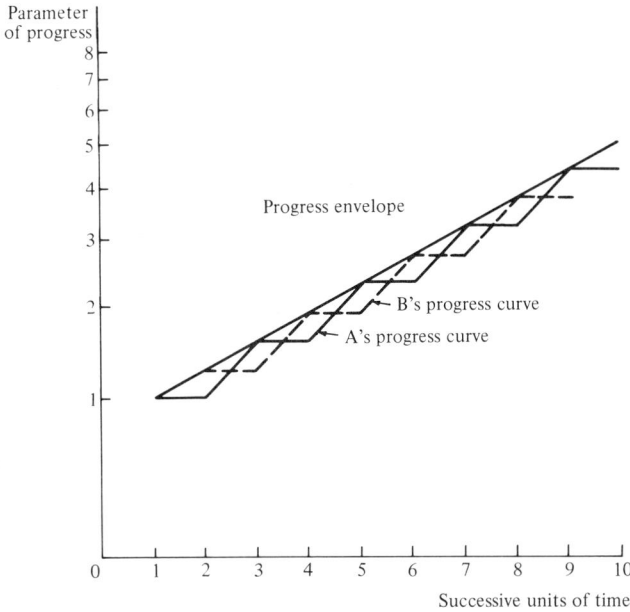

Figure 18-7

where I is the current level of information, N the number of persons active in the field, and k is either a constant or a factor containing additional variables. If an upper limit L of obtainable information is also assumed, equation (10) becomes

$$\frac{dI}{dt} = \left(1 - \frac{I}{L}\right)kIN \tag{11}$$

which can be solved to obtain

$$I = \frac{L}{1 + \left(\dfrac{L}{I_0} - 1\right)e^{kNt}} \tag{12}$$

which may be recognized as equivalent to the Pearl curve (see [20, pp. 170–181]).

Edwin Mansfield's model of diffusion of innovation in an industry also takes the form of the Pearl curve. He hypothesized that the preparation of firms in an industry not using the innovation by some date following its introduction is a function of the relative number of firms already using it, the profitability of adopting the innovation, and the required investment. His model provided a good fit to data on 12 innovations introduced during 1890–1958 in four industries (coal, iron and steel, brewing, and railroad).

18-9   Choice of Forecasting Methods and Possible Problems

Technological forecasters generally agree that no single approach is completely superior to the rest. Success is believed to depend more upon the expertise applied than the method used. A good data bank and conscientious effort contribute a great deal to successful forecasting. Once the forecast has been made, its proper utilization requires a favorable environment, one in which key individuals understand the organization's ultimate objectives and the role forecasting plays in planning. A forecast is self-fulfilling only if appropriate plans are laid to make it so; a 20-year forecast of need for new wood supplies may require current steps to purchase land and to plant seedlings. Several rather obvious but tempting pitfalls in forecasting that must be avoided at all times include failure to update the forecast on a regular basis, substitution of biased narrative for scarce but essential performance data, extrapolation of desires from a single point without regard to past rates of progress, and failure to document the forecast so that it can be constructively criticized, reviewed by others, and revised periodically [7, pp. 23, 241–242].

Questions and Problems

18-1. Define and explain:

a. technological change	*g.* extrapolation
b. technique	*h.* formal analogy
c. research	*i.* growth curves
d. science	*j.* Pearl curve
e. productivity	*k.* Gompertz curve
f. Delphi technique	

18-2.   *a.* Distinguish between a change in technique and technological change using isoquants.

b. Show how a change in technology can take place without causing a change in technique.

c. Show how a change in technique can take place without a change in technology.

18-3. In what ways may a forecast be useful if it proves to be incorrect?

18-4. Relate examples from your own business experience in which resources were allocated according to these approaches:

a. the squeaking wheel	*c.* the white charger
b. the level funding	*d.* the committee

18-5. Discuss the role that forecasts should play in managerial decision making.

18-6. Of what real value is technological forecasting by historical or biological analogy?

References

1. R. V. Arnfield (ed.). *Technological Forecasting* (Edinburgh: Edinburgh University Press, 1969).

2. Robert U. Ayres. *Technological Forecasting and Long-Range Planning* (New York: McGraw-Hill, 1969).

3. James R. Bright (ed.). *Technological Forecasting for Industry and Government* (Englewood Cliffs, N.J.: Prentice-Hall, 1968).

4. ———. *Technological Planning on the Corporate Level* (Boston: Harvard University Graduate School of Business Administration, 1962).

5. ——— and Milton E. F. Schoeman (eds.). *A Guide to Practical Technological Forecasting* (Englewood Cliffs, N.J.: Prentice-Hall, 1973).

6. Marvin J. Cetron. *Technological Forecasting—A Practical Approach* (New York: Technological Forecasting Institute, 1969).

7. ——— and Christine A. Ralph (eds.). *Industrial Applications of Technological Forecasting* (New York: Wiley, 1971).

8. Bela Gold. *Explorations in Managerial Economics—Productivity, Costs, Technology, and Growth* (New York: Basic Books, 1971).

9. Maurice Goldsmith (ed.). *Technological Innovation and the Economy* (New York: Wiley, 1970).

10. T. J. Gordon and Olaf Helmer. *Report on a Long-Range Forecasting Study* P-2982 (Santa Monica, Calif.: Rand Corporation, 1964).

11. Erich Jantsch. *Technological Forecasting in Perspective* (Paris: Organization for Economic Cooperation and Development, 1967).

12. ———. *Technological Planning and Social Futures* (London: Associated Business Programmes, 1972).

13. J. Kendrick. *Productivity Trends in the United States* (Princeton, N.J.: Princeton University Press, 1961).

14. Ralph C. Lenz, Jr. "Forecasts of Exploding Technologies by Trend Extrapolation." In James R. Bright [3].

15. ———. *Technological Forecasting.* 2d ed. Tech. Report ASD–TDR–62-414 (USAF Aeronautical Systems Division, June 1962).

16. Arthur P. Lien, Paul Anton, and Joseph W. Duncan. *Technological Forecasting Goals, Techniques, Applications.* AMA Management Bulletin No. 115 (1968).

17. Edwin Mansfield. *The Economics of Technological Change* (New York: W. W. Norton, 1968).

18. ———. *Industrial Research and Technological Innovation* (New York: W. W. Norton, 1968).

19. ———. *Microeconomics—Theory and Applications* (New York: W. W. Norton, 1970), ch. 16.

20. Joseph P. Martino. *Technological Forecasting for Decision Making* (New York: American Elsevier Publishing Co., 1972).

21. John S. Morgan. *Managing Change* (New York: McGraw-Hill, 1972).

22. Robert Kirk Mueller. *The Innovation Ethic* (American Management Association, 1971).

23. William D. Nordhaus. *Invention, Growth, and Welfare—A Theoretical Treatment of Technological Change* (Cambridge, Mass.: M.I.T. Press, 1969).

24. Keith Norris and John Vaizey. *The Economics of Research and Technology* (London: George Allen & Unwin, 1973).

25. Organization for Economic Cooperation and Development. *The Conditions for Success in Technological Innovation* (Paris, 1971).

26. Edith T. Penrose. *The Theory of the Growth of the Firm* (New York: Wiley, 1959).

27. Nathan Rosenberg. *Technology and American Economic Growth* (New York: Harper & Row, 1972).

28. W. E. G. Salter. *Productivity and Technical Change.* 2d ed. (Cambridge: Cambridge University Press, 1966).

29. K. Sanow. "Development of Statistics Relating to Research and Development Activities in Private Industry." In *Methodology of Statistics on Research and Development* (National Science Foundation, 1959).

30. Jacob Schmookler. *Invention and Economic Growth* (Cambridge, Mass.: Harvard University Press, 1966).

31. Donald A. Schon. *Technology and Change* (New York: Delacorte Press, 1967).

32. Robert A. Solo and Everett M. Rogers (eds.). *Inducing Technological Change for Economic Growth and Development* (East Lansing, Mich.: Michigan State University Press, 1972).

33. Murray Turoff. "Delphi + Computers + Communications = ?" In Marvin J. Cetron and Christine A. Ralph [7, pp. 243–258].

34. U.S. Department of Commerce. "The Measurement of Productivity." *Survey of Current Business*. Vol. 52, no. 5, pt. II (May 1972).

35. B. R. Williams (ed.). *Science and Technology in Economic Growth*. Proceedings. Conference of the International Economic Association (Edinburgh: Macmillan Press, 1973).

36. Gordon Wills, David Ashton, and Bernard Taylor (eds.). *Technological Forecasting and Corporate Strategy* (New York: American Elsevier Publishing Co., 1969).

19 Toward an Operational Theory of Economic Production

Because of widely recognized difficulties of applying traditional production theory to real-world situations, academicians in recent years have increased the search for possible substitutes. A brilliant approach that holds promise of fulfilling this need has been outlined by Professor Nicholas Georgescu-Roegen in his seminal book *The Entropy Law and the Economic Process* [1]. This chapter is a condensation of some of his work, which undoubtedly will gain an increased following with the passing of time.[1]

19-1 The Analytical Process

The term *process* is basic to any useful theory of production. Unfortunately, the term has been used to mean different things by various writers. According to Georgescu, an analytical process requires

    1. the setting of a boundary (or a frontier) in reality between the *partial process* being studied and the *environment* not being studied

    2. a purpose for which the boundary is drawn

    3. a finite duration for which the boundary is drawn

    4. a happening, described as an element crossing the frontier

The term *process* may accordingly be identified broadly with change in the universe. Such change may be studied by carefully slicing the whole, or actuality, into two parts: the partial process of topical interest and its environment. To speak of a partial process without knowing where the boundary should be drawn would surely be an abuse of the term process, since it would have no distinct point of reference.[2] "No analytical boundary, no analytical process" [p. 213]. The boundary is accurately described as the frontier as long as one's thoughts are not restricted to a geographical (spacial) boundary confined within definite space nor

---

[1] The material in this chapter is more advanced and abstract than that of previous chapters and may be skipped without loss of understanding of the rest of the book.

[2] In the rest of this chapter the shorter term *process* will be used synonymously with *partial process*, but it should be recognized throughout that the difference is fundamentally important in helping the researcher maintain his perspective and in emphasizing that no process initiated by man can take place in isolation from the rest of the universe.

to the idea that the process cannot alter the frontier, as in nature when an acorn grows to an oak tree, since both the acorn and tree may on occasion be described as belonging to the same process.

The slicing of actuality admittedly is quite arbitrary, since there are no natural grains, seams, or joints to guide the carving. The boundary must be drawn, however, where it provides some significance for scientific study. For instance, actuality has already been divided into special fields of study, each with its own purpose. One would need to be familiar with the field, say, of chemistry or political science, to know where to draw a particular process boundary. But it should be emphasized that a relevant analytical process must be associated with a purpose.

The third requirement is that the boundary be defined for a length of time beginning at t_0 and ending at t_1, describing the duration of the partial process. If it is not stated when the partial process begins and ends, it cannot be known what has gone into the partial process nor what it has done. An absolutely durationless process, taking place at an instant of time, has been quite appropriately described by the mathematician-philosopher Alfred North Whitehead as nonsense [p. 69].

It should also be noted that drawing a boundary precludes determination of what happens within the boundary. To discover events within the process requires the drawing of another boundary that crosses the process, thereby dividing it into two processes that can be studied separately. Alternatively, if two processes must be combined for some purpose, the frontier separating them must be removed, as well as everything connected with it.

Analysis of a process reduces to observing what has crossed the boundary. If an element crosses from the environment to the process, it is called an input. If an element crosses to the environment, it is called output. If the elements $C_1, C_2, \ldots, C_m$ crossing the frontier are cardinally measurable and finite in number, then $F_i(t)$ can be used to designate the cumulative inputs up to time t, and $G_i(t)$ the cumulative outputs up to time t. The analytical picture may be simplified by designating each element by

$$E_i(t) = G_i(t) - F_i(t) \tag{1}$$

where $G_i(t)$ represents an output element and $F_i(t)$ an input element. $E_i(t)$ then indicates by its sign the net flows out of the process ($+$) or net flows into the process ($-$).

A first category of elements includes those that can be only inputs, such as solar energy for terrestrial processes, or only outputs, such as wastes for nearly all production processes.

A second category includes elements that are inputs for one process and outputs for another. All intermediate products would fit this category, such as seed corn or hammers used to make more hammers.

A third category would be elements, like Ricardian land, which are original and indestructible. For a process of growing corn on land over the duration from 0 to T, the coordinates for an acre of land (a) are

$$\left.\begin{array}{l} F_a(t) = 1 \text{ for } 0 \leq t \leq T \\ G_a(t) = 0 \text{ for } 0 \leq t < T \end{array}\right\} \quad \text{during, or inside, the process}$$

$$G_a(t) = 1 \text{ for } t = T \qquad \text{end of process}$$

Similarly, the coordinates for corn used in the same process, where t' is the seeding time, would be

$$F_c(t) = \ 0 \text{ for } 0 \leq t < t' \quad \text{before planting}$$
$$F_c(t) = \ 1 \text{ for } t' \leq t \leq T \quad \text{growing period}$$
$$G_c(t) = \ 0 \text{ for } 0 \leq t < T \quad \text{growing period}$$
$$G_c(t) = 10 \text{ for } t = T \quad \text{end of process}$$

This recognizes that corn as seed is an input (F_c), but that corn as a crop is an output (G_c). The coordinates shown are for a process where one bag of seed corn yields a crop of ten bags over the process duration 0 to T.

A fourth category includes workers and tools. The worker enters the process *rested* and leaves it *tired*; a tool enters a process *new* (or less than new) and leaves it *used* (or more used than before). These are qualitative changes in inputs that may be acknowledged by assigning a different subscript to tired workers, say j, than is used for rested workers, say k. Thus, a single worker, entering the process at time t' and leaving at t'', may be represented, where $t' < t''$, by both input and output coordinates:

$$E_k(t) = \ \ 0 \text{ for } 0 \leq t < t' \quad \text{before work}$$
$$E_k(t) = -1 \text{ for } t' \leq t \leq T \quad \text{during work}$$
$$E_j(t) = \ \ 0 \text{ for } 0 \leq t < t'' \quad \text{during work}$$
$$E_j(t) = \ \ 1 \text{ for } t'' \leq t \leq T \quad \text{after work}$$

When workers and tools are accounted for in this way, they may be treated in the same manner as the other inputs and outputs previously discussed, such as raw materials, solar energy, Ricardian land, water, and other resources.

A complete analytical description of a process at a point in abstract space may be written symbolically as

$$E_{i_0}^T(t); \quad F_{a_0}^T(t), \quad G_{a_0}^T(t) \tag{2}$$

where the subscript i indicates elements that are either inputs or outputs and a those that are both. This notation emphasizes the fact that every process must have a duration 0 to T and involves wear and tear—factors that are overlooked in models containing only factor inputs and commodity outputs.[3]

19-2 Distinction Between Stocks and Flows

A stock is a physical measure of elements existing within a boundary at a point in time. A flow involves a rate of change in the number of elements over a finite duration of time and may be measured by the number observed crossing the

---

[3] Economics as a discipline is concerned primarily with commodities as they pass between production units or to consumption units. The frontier is drawn to exclude incomplete commodities, such as melted glass used in the production of glassware. But what determines an incomplete commodity depends also upon the nature of human wants and the prevailing technology; half-baked bread and ready-mixed concrete were not until recently considered commodities. Also, the boundary is drawn so as to exclude the using up of tools, the tiring of workers, and the making of waste. To avoid losing track of such items, modes of describing the economic process must be devised to support or qualify the representations of traditional microeconomic analysis.

boundary. When stocks and flows are defined in this way, it is clear that flows may be recorded by an observer at the frontier without his knowing what was happening inside the process. That is, he may have no knowledge of the size of the stock inside (which may be infinite or near exhaustion) or of the efficiency with which it is being used. It would be in error to say that " a process is completely described by its flow coordinates " [p. 219] or that it is completely represented by observing the stock at two points in time. In the latter case, elements perhaps have crossed the boundary in both directions between the times observed, but they would not have been recorded. Models based upon either case tell different parts of the whole story, but one cannot necessarily be deduced from the other.

In the field of finance the distinction between stocks and flows is blurred by the practice of measuring both bank balances (stocks) and incomes (flows) in terms of dollars. To avoid confusion, one must recall the different dimensions of monthly bank balance (dollars, point in time) and monthly income (dollars per unit of time). But the antinomy between stocks and flows involves more than resolving the difference in dimensionality, because the list of elements crossing the boundary as recorded by a mythical census taker will not be the same as that recorded by the customs official standing at a gate. That is, the list of elements will not be the same in the flow and stock representations of the process. In fact, the lists will not even overlap when the census taker records a country's land, roads, dams, and factories but never records any export-import statistics. Conversely, homes may use electricity (a flow), but a census taker may search in vain for its stock of electricity. Within a process, " a flow does not necessarily represent either a decrease or an increase in a stock of the same substance " [p. 223]. Melted glass flowing from a furnace to the rolling machines does not diminish the stock of melted glass, although the stocks of sand and coal may be reduced. Food does not flow from an infinite stock. Time, however, always flows and never exists as stock.

When a flow is discussed, explicit mention must be made of the corresponding stock and duration. A flow of 6 tons of molten steel during 3 hours may be represented by $(S, T) = (6, 3)$, where S is the stock and T the duration. To say that the rate of flow was 2 tons per hour, that is, to replace (S, T) by (S/T), does not provide a complete description.

19-3 Funds and Services

Inputs are employed to create products. Some may be destroyed (consumed) upon entering the process while others may survive but with a few scars. A first category of inputs must enter the process as a flow spread over time; examples include solar energy and rainfall used to complete the process of raising corn, and the paint used by a painter. A second category of inputs is used without being consumed by the process; examples include Ricardian land, tools, and workers. The distinction made here was described many years ago in terms of durable and nondurable factors, the distinction being made relative to the process considered. An input may be termed durable if it retains its identity after being used, as with a painter's ladder, or if it can be identified with the output, as seed corn retains its identity in growing more seed corn. There are difficulties in applying this distinction in some cases because of the problem of recognizing sameness, for instance a consumable space rocket considered expendable today may be replaced by a durable shuttlecraft of tomorrow. But for most applications the distinction is helpful.

A machine (including tools) may be said to provide a *fund of services*. This approach is superior to the alternative of assuming the machine can be spread mechanically over time as it is being used. The machine must be whole and every part functioning to be of use. It cannot be separated into parts that can be used sequentially as inputs until the last is consumed. The use of the machine requires duration; its output must be spread over time. A light bulb may light a room for 500 hours, but it cannot light 500 rooms for 1 hour all at the same time. The machine may therefore be described as a fund of services that, not unlike those of animal labor, can be either used or wasted. These services cannot be stored for use at some future point in time as one might accumulate a flow of resources or products. Flows of materials into a production process may be said to become embodied in the product, but the services of a tool, say a tailor's needle, cannot become embodied in the product (coat) unless left there by mistake by a careless tailor.

The difference between a flow and a service may be noted by reference to their dimensions. An amount of flow is described in numbers of appropriate units, say gallons, tons, or feet. Rate of flow has mixed dimensionality: quantity of a substance per duration of time, say gallons per minute or tons per hour. Services, however, have dimensions described as quantities of a substance times the duration of time, say 6 machine-hours or 5 man-days. In short,

$$\text{Amount of flow} = \text{units of substance}$$

$$\text{Rate of flow} = \frac{\text{units of substance}}{\text{units of time}}$$

$$\text{Amount of service} = \text{units of substance} \times \text{units of time}$$

$$\text{Rate of service} = \text{units of substance}$$

Notice that the rate of service, obtained in a way analogous to obtaining rate of flow, is the amount of service divided by the duration of time. Curiously, the rate of service is the amount of substance, a fund, say six machines or five men. The time factor drops out.

Participation of a fund in a production process by acting upon the flow element may be noted by simplifying representation (2) to

$$[E_{i_0}^T(t); \quad S_{a_0}^T(t)] \tag{3}$$

where $E_i(t)$ continues to represent each flow element and $S_a(t)$ represents the amount of services provided by a fund C_a up to time t, where $0 \le t \le T$. This assumes, of course, that the fund element is left undamaged by its use in the process.

Two additional points should be noted. First, the classification of a factor as a fund or flow element in an actual process depends upon the process duration. The use of an automobile for a short period in a process may require replacement of minor parts (spark plugs, filters, tires), while use for longer intervals may require major repairs (motor, chassis, body parts). Maintenance of the automobile's efficiency requires a flow of replacement parts, but the flow elements are different in the two cases. They could range from zero for very short periods to replacement of all parts for long periods. Ultimately, obsolescence would require replacement of even a perfectly maintained auto. A more lengthy view of life and nature would recognize that all things are eventually destroyed through the workings of entropy (discussed later).

The second point is that an element may appear simultaneously as both a fund and flow, as in the case of producing hammers to produce more hammers. The output flow of hammers is represented by one $E_i(t)$, and the fund services of hammers by one $S_a(t)$.

The fund and flow elements of expression (3) may be expressed more generally by the expanded representation:

$$[R_0^T(t),\ I_0^T(t),\ M_0^T(t),\ Q_0^T(t),\ W_0^T(t);\ L_0^T(t),\ K_0^T(t),\ H_0^T(t)] \qquad (4)$$

$$\underbrace{\hspace{5cm}}_{\text{flow elements}} \qquad \underbrace{\hspace{3cm}}_{\text{fund elements}}$$

where R is natural resources (solar energy, rainfall, oil, iron ore); I is materials coming from other production processes (lumber for a furniture factory, coke for a foundry); M is elements needed to maintain capital equipment (lubricants, paint, replacement parts); Q is output of products; W is waste (unused outputs, pollution); L is Ricardian land (indestructable, the net for catching solar energy and rainfall); K is capital property (buildings, equipment); H is labor power (mental and physical).

19-4 The Role of Entropy

A thesis Georgescu develops throughout his book is that the economic process is ruled by the entropy law, which is identified with the second law of thermodynamics. The first and second laws were formulated by R. Clausius in 1865: the first, "The energy of the universe remains constant," and the second, "The entropy of the universe at all times moves toward a maximum" [p. 129]. In this context, entropy refers to a dispersion or dissipation of heat and other free energy into latent energy—the qualitative degradation of energy. A newer and more controversial interpretation extends the term to cover material order as well as energy. Order and disorder are, of course, subjective terms relative to some human purpose at hand. In any case, entropy describes the shuffling and mixing of elements in the universe. Man, in the most fundamental of economic roles, strives to maintain and improve his existence by sorting out the low entropy (free energy and ordered structures) from his environment and converting it to high entropy (waste) at a rate more rapid than if left to the nonhuman forces in nature [pp. 187–195]. Entropy enters expression (4) above under the symbols M, W, and T.

The ultimate value of the entropy concept may be in creating a general awareness that the length of man's survival on planet Earth depends upon the rate at which he exhausts his limited natural resources. Such an awareness would result in a sooner rise in the price and a more efficient use of such resources, as well as a shifting of technology and preferences to greater use of solar energy. Section 19-5 explains how Georgescu suggests incorporating the use of natural resources and the concept of entropy in the production function.

19-5   The Production Function

The neoclassical representation of the production function is an oversimplification for most real-world applications. The process of production is characterized as a sector in which each coordinate is a number. This overlooks the fact that each coordinate individually is a function of the factors of production $a, b, c, \ldots$, that is, $Q = f(a, b, c, \ldots)$; swift passage has been made from the analytical *function* to the *point function* employed in mathematics. The production recipe of neoclassical economics is merely a listing of ingredients without instructions as to when and how they must be combined.

Description of production should begin with a discussion of the elementary process—the partial process where one unit of output (say, a table) is produced by a particular system of production. This ignores the many varieties of tables that might be produced and the different materials from which they might be constructed. Attention is focused upon the production of only one specific product. Every production process, regardless of type, can be reduced to its elementary process. The most complex systems can be isolated by drawing the appropriate boundary and recording the process's analytical coordinates. A representation of a process that encompasses all the feasible and nonwasteful combinations of ingredients may be given by the functional (mathematical jargon for relating *a set of functions to one function* [p. 236]):

$$Q_0^T(t) = F'[R_0^T(t), I_0^T(t), M_0^T(t), W_0^T(t); L_0^T(t), K_0^T(t), H_0^T(t)] \tag{5}$$

This representation contrasts greatly with the neoclassical production function relating *a set of numbers to one number* [p. 236]. A set of points is obtained in abstract space rather than in Euclidean space.

19-6   The Economics of Production

A common feature of all elementary processes is that the fund factors are unavoidably idle a good deal of the production time. In the production of a table, tools are used by turns: first the saw, then the plane, then the sander, and so on. When not being used, the tools are obviously idle. If the workers are specialists in only one tool, say in operating a saw or applying varnish with a brush, then they also are idle by turns. In fact, all tools and workers are idle while the varnished table is drying, while nature as a silent partner (included in R) provides oxygen from the air, oxidizing the varnish and causing the varnish solvent to evaporate. Idleness is a fact in all elementary processes in farming, mining, manufacturing, construction, or transportation.

If the demand for the product occurs at time intervals equal to or greater than the required production time, the partial processes must be arranged in series, that is, sequentially, with no overlaps of processes in time. Craft shops still produce their products in series. Bridges, canals, large ships, and new factories traditionally are also built in this way. Consequently, long periods of idleness are imposed upon most fund elements by a low intensity of demand. Workers, when idle, can sometimes be shifted to other production lines, as are farm workers who are employed in cities during winter months. In other processes the length of idleness is insufficient to warrant a shift. The craftsman of old was forced by the low intensity of demand to do all the tasks required by his trade or otherwise be idle at times and share his labor revenue with others. Specialization in such a case was to him uneconomical.

Where demand is greater than can be met by a series of elementary processes, production can be increased by arranging elementary processes in parallel or line.

Parallel processes are those in which more than one process ($= n$) is begun and ended at the same time, then successive processes or stages are repeated in unison. A production function composed of three processes or stages, with each successive stage performed in parallel, may be illustrated as follows:

1	Stage 1	Stage 2	Stage 3
2	Stage 1	Stage 2	Stage 3
3	Stage 1	Stage 2	Stage 3
.	.	.	.
.	.	.	.
.	.	.	.
n	Stage 1	Stage 2	Stage 3

The expanded production function for parallel processes is obtained by multiplying each elementary process coordinate by n:

$$[nQ_0^T(t)] = F'\{[nR_0^T(t)], \ldots, [nW_0^T(t)]; [nL_0^T(t)], \ldots\} \tag{6}$$

Little, if any, economic gain is offered by such an arrangement, since idleness of the fund factors is also amplified by n, except where the capacity of a fund factor may be more fully utilized, such as an oven that holds more than one loaf at a time. Even then, the oven would have the same idleness period.

Processes in line involve dividing the elementary process into stages that are assigned equal intervals of time. Then new processes of batches are begun at each time interval in sequence. Thus, a process of 10 stages would constantly contain the makings of 10 batches in successive states of partial completion:

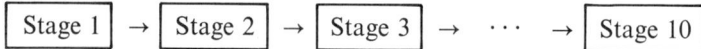

$$\boxed{\text{Stage 1}} \rightarrow \boxed{\text{Stage 2}} \rightarrow \boxed{\text{Stage 3}} \rightarrow \cdots \rightarrow \boxed{\text{Stage 10}}$$

Such a procedure could possibly eliminate the idleness of every fund factor, providing that the product demand is sufficient and that the process can be divided into stages of equal time intervals. This is the factory system in which each tool and worker shifts to the next elementary process after performing service on a process. No funds are idle when the factory is in motion.

19-7   The Production Function for the Factory System

The factory system in operation, with all funds perfectly maintained, may be said to be in a steady state. If an elementary process is begun at each instant, the system is said to have continuity and flow coordinates that can be represented as linear homogeneous functions of t:

$$R(t) = rt, \quad I(t) = it, \quad M(t) = mt, \quad Q(t) = qt, \quad W(t) = wt \tag{7}$$

Capital funds include inventories, S, of the flow elements I, M, Q, W, and goods-in-process, or a process-fund, C, composed of the material inputs within the system under transformation. The producing factory must at all times have a unit or batch of the product being formed at each successive stage of production. These inputs make up the process fund, without which the factory can function no better than an unprimed hand pump. The process fund is essential to the operation of the factory and permits an immediate flow of outputs when activated.

The flow coordinates of equations (7) are visible only from outside the process. For this reason the presence of a process fund makes it appear that production is instantaneous, that is, input materials are fed in one end, outputs emerge at the other. The role of the process fund somewhat resembles an inelastic rod whose tip emerges from a box as its end is pushed into the opposite side. It should not be forgotton that the appearance of instantaneous production requires a duration for preparation of perhaps months or years in which the factory is built and primed.

Fund coordinates for the factory system may be written as

$$L(t) = Lt, \qquad K(t) = Kt, \qquad S(t) = St, \qquad C(t) = Ct, \qquad H(t) = Ht \quad (8)$$

A factory production function can now be represented by the functional

$$(q_0^T t) = G'[(r_0^T t), \ldots, (w_0^T t); (L_0^T t), \ldots, (H_0^T t)] \qquad (9)$$

For an instant of time, the functional degenerates to an ordinary point function:

$$q = F(r, i, m, w; L, K, S, C, H) \qquad (10)$$

For production between two points in time, over a time interval t, the function must be written

$$qt = \phi(rt, \ldots, wt; Lt, \ldots, Ht; t) \qquad (11)$$

where ϕ is a linear homogeneous function of t, as well as the other variables of equation (11), indicating the flows and services in, say, 6 hours are six times those of 1 hour. Hence, the identity $\phi = tF$. In any case, the production function should be appropriately recognized as functionals like (5), (6), or (9), depending upon the system considered, rather than as a point function such as (10), which eliminates the time element. The production function (10) indicates the potential of a system but not what it actually does, just as the label on a light bulb, "60 watts, 110 volts," indicates what the bulb can do, or the M.B.A. degree shows to some extent the potential of a business graduate. Neither description tells us the age and use of the bulb nor the hours worked by the business person.

A factory blueprint should tell us what is required in addition to its technical structure. For instance, capacity output q^* may require L and K in equation (10) to be properly manned with labor, that is, $H^* = H(L, K)$. A variable human element will make q^* unattainable:

$$q = f(L, K, H) \leq q^* \qquad (11)$$

In this function, in contrast to usage in the current literature, q need not fall because of decreases in L and K if H is maintained. Additional interrelations between the variables may also be important. For example, the amount of maintenance (M) may be determined by the manpower used (H) and may in turn determine the extent of waste (W). A doubling of ouput q may require another factory—more L, K, and H— but waste (W) may not be increased proportionally where efficiencies can be made. Also, K, L, and H point functions apply to certain quantities of a given quality. Where qualities are different, substitutions between K, L, and H may not be possible, for instance, a more capital-intensive process may require a different kind of capital; this means that the familiar isoquant map cannot be used in such cases, since concrete capital is not the same as homogeneous abstract capital. Along with the concept of neoclassical substitution, the concept of marginal physical productivity must be considered nonoperational, of value only in pure theory. This may also be said of the neoclassical representation of the production function, because it ignores the time factor, the length of the working day.

19-8   The Advantages and Limitations of the Factory System

According to Professor Georgescu, "The factory system is one of the greatest *economic* inventions in the history of mankind—comparable only to the invention of money" [p. 248]. Independent of technology, it began in old craft shops to meet increased demand prior to the industrial revolution of the eighteenth century and encouraged technological innovations. It should be emphasized that it can be used with any technology of any age in history, but depends predominantly upon the demand for the product. It reigns "superior to all other arrangements of the elementary process. . . because it does away with the idleness of the fund factors [pp. 248–249]. Both the factory system and technological inventions work toward the more efficient utilization of resources and work either hand in hand or competitively in satisfying a growing demand. Greater demand stimulates the breaking down of an elementary process into several distinct tasks, each of which is more specialized than before—this sequence of increased demand to increased specialization is necessary in the development of the factory system. Greater output could alternatively have been provided by replacing one of the funds, say an oven for baking bread, by one of larger size and efficiency—an additional improvement in technology. If demand grows sufficiently, improvements in both the factory system and technology may be employed without increasing the idleness of factors.

Unfortunately perhaps, the factory system is not suited to produce everything man wishes, even when the obstacle of low demand is surmounted. One of man's needs in a changing world is to produce new processes to supplement or replace old ones. Yet, a factory cannot be constructed that will produce new factories of a different type. A third limitation of the factory is that its use is subject to the workings of nature. Production of farms must be started in the proper season of the year and may be interrupted by climatic conditions; thus, production cannot be continuous for all situations. The reproductive pattern of most vegetal and animal species have adapted to the rhythm of seasonality, born in the spring, growing throughout the summer, some reaching maturity in the fall, some lying dormant or dying in winter. Fields must be worked in parallel, since all elementary processes must be begun at about the same time and cannot be arranged in line without being interrupted (unless controlled under greenhouse conditions). Industrial processes are not constrained by nature as agrarian ones are. Manufacturing processes may be initiated at will and carried on without unintended interruption, except for so-called acts of God, disruptive acts of man through human error or sabotage, and resource limitations. They may be arranged in line where agricultural processes cannot, explaining at least in part why technological progress has been greater in manufacturing. Also, idleness is inherent in the parallel processes of agriculture; even if cottage industries could be spliced with agricultural activities to utilize the months of idle human capital on farms, nonhuman capital in both industries would still be idle for sizable time intervals. Overcapitalization is inherent in agricultural economic activity.

In general, agricultural production must be performed in parallel according to functional (6), but there are at least two cases where farm production has been conducted by a system of processes in line. First is the production of rice on the island of Bali, where the climate varies little throughout the year. Buffalo, sickles, plows, flails, and workers could be moved in proper numbers across the fields performing the various tasks of plowing, planting, weeding, and so on, with elementary processes arranged in line, with no agent ever being idle. Production would be instantaneous in the sense that each day rice could be sown in the first stage and harvested in the last. The need for loans for working capital could be eliminated and overcapitalization could be greatly reduced.

A second case would be the American "chicken factory," where incubated crops of chickens are produced in line and available for market almost daily. The price per pound of chicken has fallen so greatly because of reduced cost that chicken is now the lowest priced meat in the United States, while in Europe chicken produced in parallel and by seasons sells at a price so high that it remains "the Sunday dinner."

19-9   Distinctions Between Agricultural and Manufacturing Industries

One of the major differences between agricultural and manufacturing industries lies in the different sources of energy, or as Professor Georgescu refers to it, low entropy. Husbandry draws upon solar radiation, while manufacturing draws more upon mineral resources from beneath the earth's surface. Solar energy cannot be mined at a rate to suit human desires of the moment, but it can for practical purposes be expected to be provided perpetually. In fact, it is estimated that the free energy received by Earth from the sun equals in 4 days the highest estimate of energy from terrestrial resources. The earth's deposits, however, can be mined and used at a rate determined by man and cannot be replaced when exhausted.

Agriculture teaches patience, while manufacturing encourages man to use energy to produce commodities at increasing rates to provide for the most extravagant of wants—all in the name of an efficient allocation of resources. A short time ago we found that man could transport himself to the moon in a matter of days, but it still takes (with some improvements) as long as ever to grow wheat from seed and raise animals to maturity. Progress in husbandry depends upon mutations occurring in natural selection and their duplication under human guidance. Production of artifacts, however, may be accelerated by innovations limited only by human imagination.

Technological progress has been associated with a shift from use of abundant solar radiation to use of the earth's limited mineral resources. Unfortunately, the life of the human species will ultimately be affected more by exhaustion of mineral than of solar energy. The larger the population and its technological progress today, the shorter the life of man on planet Earth. "We can say that every baby born now means one human life less in the future. But also every Cadillac produced at any time means fewer lives in the future" [p. 304]. When this thought becomes widely recognized, the population may be more patient in using mineral resources to produce free energy and synthetic substitute commodities and will have less desire to waste resources. Nevertheless, human nature seems to prefer a brief, exciting, rather than a long, dull, life.

19-10   The Boundaries of Economics

The economic process must not be mistakenly thought of as an isolated system. It exists in a world containing a multitude of other processes: biological, chemical, psychological, sociological, political, and so on. Moreover, the boundaries of objects and events overlap each other in the manner of penumbras that are dialectical as well as analytical. This may be another way of stating that things and events are the result of a multitude of factors that may or may not be measurable. Therefore, abstraction of the field of economics from the total system is fraught with pitfalls.

Economics is intertwined with other fields in many ways. Examples include changes of economic growth of countries with identical resource endowments, and the observation that economic units often do not maximize their economic positions. If economics is defined as the study of how *given* means are used to satisfy *given* ends, it is reduced to "the mechanics of utility and self-interest" [p. 318]. Indeed, any system involving a conservation principle and a maximizing rule reduces to a mechanical problem. It is precisely this identification of economics with a mechanical process in which all elements are given that, according to Professor Georgescu, has caused it to be called dogmatic. This may explain why business students and practitioners familiar with abstractions have criticized standard economic theory—not for its abstraction, but for its dogmatism. It is true that excessive weight has sometimes been given to the information abstracted by standard economics—called by Alfred North Whitehead "the fallacy of misplaced concreteness" [p. 321].

Where should the economic process boundary be drawn? Georgescu sides with Marshall in defining economics: "A study of mankind in the ordinary business of life."

19-11   Concluding Comments

The analytical representations considered in this chapter are for reproductive processes already produced. The process was also assumed to be functioning at a steady rate. No consideration was given to how the process came into existence. Creation of a mechanical system, of course, involves more than simple locomotion; it requires the *production of processes* from commodities already available. Production of additional processes is viewed by Georgescu as *investment*, while the allocation of available commodities to production is viewed as *saving*. Both are required for economic development.

Professor Georgescu's book contains many other things of interest to students of economics and business. Those who have been intrigued by some of the contents of this chapter are encouraged to read the source material. Discussion will end here with one of Georgescu's truly thought-provoking statements.

> It is high time, I believe, for us to recognize that the essence of development consists of the organizational and flexible power to create new processes rather than the power to produce commodities by materially crystallized plants [p. 275].

Questions and Problems

19-1. List Professor Georgescu's four requirements for an analytical process. Are they all really necessary? Are there any others that should be added to the list?

19-2. What is wrong with these statements?

    a. If one accurately examines a process at two points in time, one can accurately describe the process.

    b. An increased flow of elements indicates that the stock must also increase.

    c. Products are simply the embodiment of capital and labor.

    d. Production in a steady-going factory system is instantaneous.

19-3. Production takes place by the proper blending of flow and fund elements. Make a list of each. Where does waste come in?

19-4. Name three limitations of the factory system.

19-5. Contrast the production theory of this chapter with that of Chapter 18.

19-6. What factors distinguish manufacturing from agricultural production?

References

1. Nicholas Georgescu-Roegen. *The Entropy Law and the Economic Process* (Cambridge, Mass.: Harvard University Press, 1971).

    No less than eight reviews of this book have appeared in the periodical literature:

    1. Frank L. Adelman. Review in *Journal of Economic Literature* (June 1972): 459. Reply in December 1972 issue, p. 1268.

    2. Kenneth Boulding. "Search for Time's Arrow." *Science*, March 10, 1972, p. 1099.

    3. Herbert S. Camenson. Review in *Library Journal*, May 15, 1971, p. 1705.

    4–7. Four reviews, by Richard Schlegel, Ralph W. Pfouts, Werner Hochwald, and Glen L. Johnson, in *Journal of Economic Issues* 7 (September 1973).

    8. Samuel C. Webb. Review in *Southern Economic Journal*, October 1973, pp. 336–339.

Analysis of Price and Output

The more I studied economic science, the smaller appeared the knowledge which I had of it, in proportion to the knowledge that I needed; and now, at the end of nearly half a century of almost exclusive study of it, I am conscious of more ignorance of it than I was at the beginning of the study.

Alfred Marshall

20 Market Structure and Price Determination

Part Four deals with various aspects of price and output analysis. Chapters 20 and 24 on market structures and investment decisions are more elementary than the ones immediately following them, 21 and 25, which discuss various topics in pricing and decisions under uncertainty. In between are two chapters, 22 and 23, that examine some of the economic and social implications of business investment decisions. These chapters as a whole should aid the business executive in making price, output, and investment decisions to maximize the firm's preference function subject to the constraints of a market and a social environment. A logical place to begin is with a brief review of the basic market models that are widely used in analysis by economists, legislators, and business people: (1) pure and perfect competition, (2) pure monopoly, (3) monopolistic competition, (4) oligopoly, (5) competition among buyers, (6) monopsony, and (7) bilateral monopoly.

20-1 Pure and Perfect Competition

Pure competition occurs in an abstract world that is idealized in terms of promoting an efficient allocation of resources. It is defined as having four requisites:

1. The market contains many firms, each of which produces an output so small relative to the total of the industry that no single firm acting individually has sufficient market strength to influence the market price by expanding or contracting its production and sales. Thus, no firm will reduce its output or hold its products from the market with the hope that its actions will cause the price to rise; neither will a firm resist expanding its output and sales for fear of spoiling its market in future periods.

2. Products are sufficiently homogeneous with regard to size and qualities so that in the view of the many consumers in the market the products of any firm are perfect substitutes for those of others. Since product differentiation is not possible, there is no need for competitive advertising, which would serve only to raise cost and invoke losses.

3. New firms having the inclination and necessary capital are not restricted in any artificial way (by regulation, exclusion, coercion, or threat) from

entering the market in pursuit of potential economic profits. Existing firms are also free to leave the industry to avoid losses. Note that free entry implies a new firm has equal access to the mobile resources purchased by existing firms.

    4. Each firm acts independently in what it believes to be its best interest in deciding to expand or contract units of output and to enter or leave the industry. There is no collusion among firms, because they are assumed to behave as rivals.

    Perfect competition requires the addition of a fifth assumption.

    5. All buyers and sellers have sufficient knowledge of the offer and bid prices in the market so that none because of ignorance can be taken advantage of by those who might cheat in trade. This assumption is called complete knowledge and may also, perhaps more likely, exist under monopoly.

    To illustrate the flexibility of the term *competition*, it can be noted that George Stigler prefers for modern times the use of the concepts *market competition*, "restricted to meaning the absence of monopoly power in a market" [13, p. 184], *perfect market competition*, whereby many traders with perfect knowledge act independently in the market, and *industrial competition*, in which each resource obtains equal rates of return in all uses. Stigler rejects the traditional distinction between pure and perfect competition, since perfect knowledge is also required in pure competition to prevent pairs of buyers and sellers, a condition that also holds for bilateral monopolies. (A bilateral monopoly is one in which the market is composed of one buyer and one seller. This is discussed later in the chapter.) Stigler's condition of industrial competition requires in each industry that there be market competition, knowledge by resource owners of obtainable returns, free entry and exit, infinite divisibility of resources, and mobility of resources. In the analysis that follows in this section, it is assumed that perfect competition prevails in the market. Elsewhere in this book and throughout most of the literature of economics and business, models that do not meet the conditions of perfect competition are put in the very broad category of *imperfect competition*.

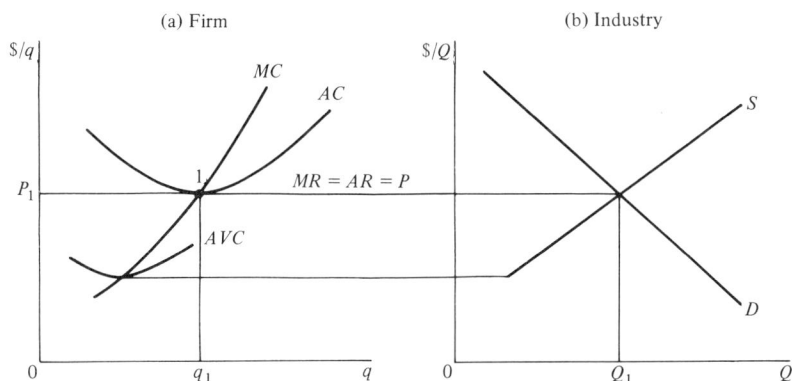

Figure 20-1

Implications of the model of perfect competition are given with reference to Figure 20-1. A representative firm is shown in long-run equilibrium. Price is dictated by the intersection of the industry demand and supply curves. The firm is therefore said to be a price taker rather than a price maker; this is reflected by the horizontal, perfectly elastic marginal and average revenue curves. Output is adjusted by the firm to maximize profits and minimize losses by equating marginal cost with marginal revenue at point 1. The upward-sloping portion of the MC curve, which lies above the average-variable-cost (AVC) curve, is the firm's short-run supply curve, the horizontal summation of which for all firms yields the industry supply curve S, that is, the sum of the q_1's $= Q_1$. The portion of the curve below AVC is considered irrelevant, because at prices below AVC the firm minimizes losses by ceasing production entirely. Long-run equilibrium is said to exist, because no economic profits exist to encourage expansion of production or the entry of new firms and the absence of losses causes no curtailment of production or exit of firms from the industry.

In the short run, profits are a possibility, as shown in Figure 20-2 by a portion of the AC curve lying below the market price. The firm maximizes its profit by setting output at q_1, where $MC = MR$. Short-run profits, indicated by the shaded area, are eliminated in the long run by the entry of new firms, which shifts the industry supply curve to the right from S to S'. This drives down the market price to P_2, eliminating profits and causing the representative firm to reduce its output to q_2. Explanation of the sequence of events whereby losses are eliminated is left for the reader to give in problem 20-4 at the end of this chapter.

This mechanistic model is of value not so much as an accurate description of real-world industries, which is often said to be the case for a variety of farm products, as in providing a mental construct that explains what behavior of firms and course of economic events could logically be anticipated under certain stated conditions. In one sense, it may be considered a stepping stone toward the building of more elaborate models to deal with more complex economic relations between people and institutions. In another, it may be used as a point of reference or standard for comparison against which the merits and implications of other market models can be compared. In any case, the model of pure competition, as well as other markets, should be used without emotion in applica-

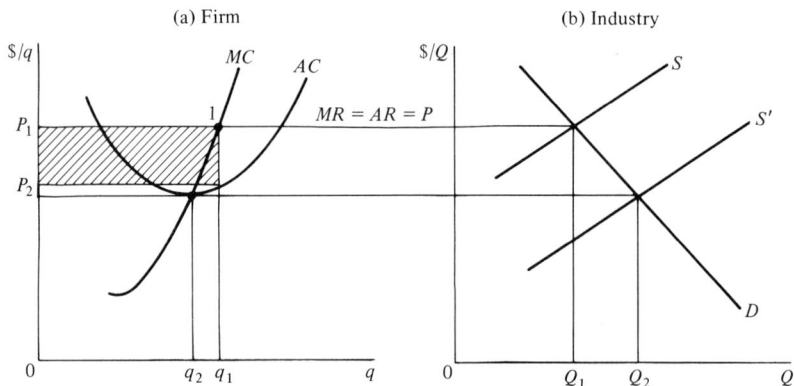

Figure 20-2

tions where it may be useful. Ideological discussions should be avoided as much as possible when objective analysis is the goal. Note that an analytical model is neither inherently good nor bad and should be used only when appropriate for the problem at hand.

20-2 Pure Monopoly

The polar opposite to pure competition is the model of pure monopoly. Here the industry has only one producer of a commodity for which there are no close substitutes as far as the consumer is concerned. An absence of competitors permits the monopoly firm some control over the market price by allowing it to vary the amounts of product offered for sale; this follows from the fact that the firm faces a downward-sloping demand curve. Aware that consumers will pay a higher price if fewer units are placed on the market, the monopoly firm restricts output to increase profits. Figure 20-3a shows on a single graph the short- and long-run equilibriums for both the firm and industry where a single seller faces many independent buyers.

When the firm faces a downward-sloping demand curve, the firm's marginal-revenue curve lies below it and is spaced half the distance toward the vertical axis. This point is easily demonstrated by use of mathematics. Given the linear demand (average-revenue) equation

$$P = a - bQ$$

the total-revenue equation is obtained by multiplying terms on both sides of the equal sign by Q:

$$TR = P \cdot Q = aQ - bQ^2$$

from which the marginal-revenue equation is acquired by taking the first derivative with respect to Q:

$$MR = \frac{d(TR)}{dQ} = a - 2bQ$$

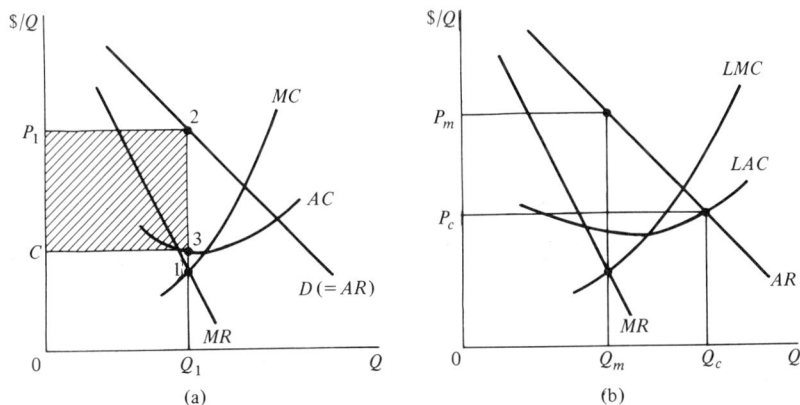

Figure 20-3

Since the slope of the MR curve $(= -2b)$ is half that of the AR curve $(= -b)$, and the vertical intercepts are equal $(= a)$, it follows that the MR curve must be situated half the horizontal distance from the AR curve to the vertical axis.

To maximize profits, the monopoly firm determines output by setting $MC = MR$, at point 1 in Figure 20-3a. For this output $(= Q_1)$, it charges what the market will bear, as indicated by point 2 on the demand curve directly above point 1. A unit price of P_1 is charged for Q_1 units with a unit cost of C, producing unit profits of CP_1 and total profits shown by the shaded area. Since entry of new firms is barred by assumption, there is thought to be no automatic mechanism whereby economic profits are diminished. The monopoly firm is, however, by no means guaranteed a profit when the demand curve lies entirely below the AC curve; this simply means that no one wants widgets for a price at which the firm can afford to sell them.

A comparison of the pure monopoly model with the pure competition model can be made with the aid of Figure 20-3b. The monopoly firm sets output at the intersection of the LMC and MR curves, equal to Q_m, and sets price at P_m. Under pure competition, output Q_c and price P_c are determined by the intersection of the LAC and AR curves, at which there are no long-run profits. Such a comparison leads to the dictum "Monopoly restricts output and raises prices."

Under conditions of constant and rising long-run unit costs, this is undoubtedly true. But when there are efficiencies to be gained from large-scale production, monopolies can have lower unit costs. In the absence of government intervention, the consumer will benefit little from the lower costs, because the monopoly firm will continue to charge a price dictated by market demand. However, if the government imposed a discriminatory property tax on the monopoly, its economic profits could be diverted to tax relief and subsidies to consumers. In taking such a step, the government must be careful to couch the tax in the form of fixed costs, for example, a property tax and a head tax, which will raise the monopoly firm's average-cost curve without moving the marginal curve, as shown in Figure 20-4a. Profits are reduced by the amount of the tax shown by the shaded area. Any form of tax geared to output (such as an excise tax per unit sold and

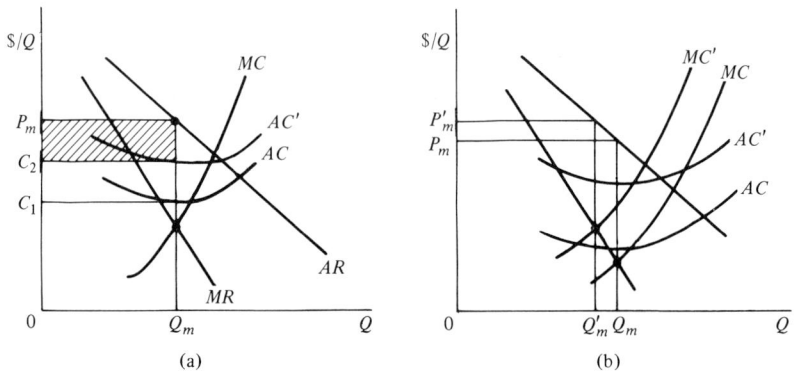

(a)

(b)

Figure 20-4

an income tax) will also raise the *MC* curve, as shown in Figure 20-4b, with the unfortunate result for consumers that even fewer units will be made available.

Between the extremes of pure competition and pure monopoly lies economic reality. Two additional well-known models were formulated in the 1930s to help deal with intermediate cases: *monopolistic competition* and *oligopoly*.

20-3 Monopolistic Competition

Edward Chamberlin's model of monopolistic competition [4] is basically a revision of pure competition that takes into account the fact that most products are not entirely homogeneous. Similar products offered by different sellers are differentiated by consumers with regard to real and alleged differences in size and qualities, and even such nonutilitarian distinctions as brand name and union label. The inclination of consumers to distinguish among products has the effect of permitting them to attach loyalties and habits to the product of certain firms. The firm with devoted customers, gained perhaps through advertising, is thereby endowed with some control over the market price in spite of the fact that there are many other firms producing substantially the same good or service. Locational differences of sellers are a most common form of product differentiation. The selling firm can raise its prices a few pennies (or dollars, depending upon the relative value of the unit) above the going market price without losing all sales. This means that it faces a demand curve that is downward-sloping, similar to that of the monoply firm but with a much smaller slope, as shown in Figure 20-5a. By exploiting its position in the short run, it can capture some economic profits. But, alas, these cannot be sustained into the long run because of the encroachment on the seller's market by new firms desiring to share in the profits. Long-run equilibrium settles at point 1, where the *AR* curve is tangent to the declining side of the *AC* curve.

A comparison of monopolistic competition with pure competition is given in Figure 20-5b. The former is said to be less efficient than the latter because it results in a higher price (P_{mc} rather than P_c) and a smaller output (Q_{mc} rather than

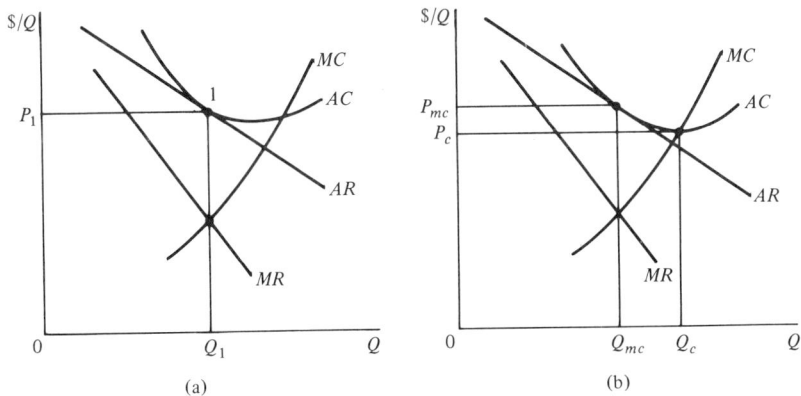

(a)   (b)

Figure 20-5

Q_c). Some observers argue that the resources spent on sales promotion to differentiate the firm's products serves largely to increase costs to the detriment of consumers. Industries characterized by monopolistic competition are believed to include retail clothing stores and gas service stations.

20-4   Oligopoly

Oligopoly is the general category of market models in which there are so few firms that the output and price decisions of one can influence the profits and decisions of others in the industry. Product differentiation may or may not be a factor, since examples from American industry can be cited in support of homogeneous products of the steel and aluminum industries and heterogeneous products of the automobile and tobacco industries. In either case, dependence on decisions of competitors is an important consideration of each firm.

20-4-1   *Kinked demand curve*

The Sweezy *kinked-demand-curve* model [15], illustrated in Figure 20-6, is the best known of the oligopoly models, so much so that it is sometimes incorrectly referred to synonymously with oligopoly. Because of its prominence, it is described first. The firm is assumed to be aware that all other firms in the industry will match any price reductions it initiates but will not follow any price hikes. Demand curves D_1 and D_2 were constructed under these assumptions. The first was drawn relatively flat to reflect a substantial loss of customers and sales to competing firms that did not also raise their prices. For a given rise in price from point 1 and movement along the curve, the decrease in Q is substantial. The second demand curve was drawn relatively steeply to reflect nearly simultaneous reductions of competitors' prices as they strive to preserve their shares of the market. If competitors had failed to follow the firm's unilateral price reductions, the firm could have expected to be able to promote a movement

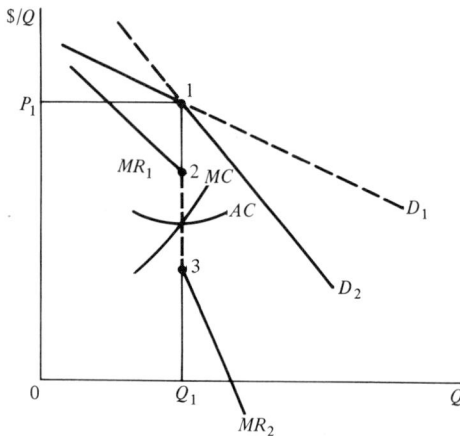

Figure 20-6

to the right along its D_1 (no reactions from competitors) curve rather than along D_2. The firm's demand curve is thus found to be composed of portions of two different curves, which accounts for the kink at the prevailing price and also the discontinuous range between the corresponding marginal-revenue curves from point 2 to point 3. A unique feature of this model is that the profit-maximizing firm will have no incentive to change its price as long as its marginal-cost curve lies in the range of discontinuity, because $MC = MR$ in this range at output Q_1. This phenomenon is said to account for the tendency toward price rigidity in oligopolistic industries. Firms do not raise their prices for fear of losing their customers, and they do not lower their prices for fear of precipitating a price war.

Criticisms of this model are both theoretical and empirical. No adequate explanation is given as to how the initial price was obtained, or if it is changed, how a new one is established. Stigler found that seven oligopoly firms during the 1930s (more recent studies are not available) did not exhibit pricing behavior consistent with the assumptions of the kinked demand curve. Moreover, the prices of monopolies were found to be more rigid than those of oligopolies [14]. Nevertheless, the model has value because of its simplicity in suggesting why rigidities do exist and its clever way of illustrating the need for taking competitors' reactions into account.

20-4-2 *Price leadership*

Price leadership can occur in an oligopolistic industry when one firm has lower unit costs or much greater size than the others. Assume for purposes of simplification that there are only two firms (an industry with two firms is called a *duopoly*), each facing a demand curve d and marginal revenue curve mr shown in Figure 20-7a. The low-cost firm sells output q_1 at price p_1. The high-cost firm desires to sell q_2 at p_2 but cannot obtain this price in competition with the low-cost firm. It must accept the price p_1 of the more efficient firm, thereby recognizing that firm as the price leader [2, pp. 475–482].

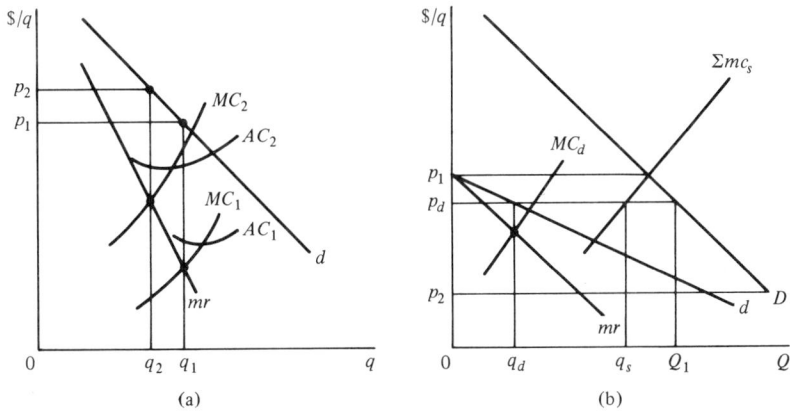

Figure 20-7

Figure 20-7b shows how output is apportioned for a large dominant firm and several small firms in an industry. Assume the dominant firm sets the industry price, lets the small firms sell as much as they wish, and then sells whatever additional amounts the market demands. The small firms tacitly accept the dominant firm's price as if it were set in a perfectly competitive market and produce outputs where their marginal-cost curves intersect their horizontal marginal-revenue curves (neither are shown in Figure 20-7b). The horizontal summation of the small firm's marginal-cost curves is denoted by $\sum mc_s$; this is the short-run supply curve for the group. The demand curve d faced by the dominant firm can now be derived by subtracting the horizontal distances to the $\sum mc_s$ curve from the industry demand curve D, that is, at price p_1 the small firms would supply all of the market, leaving none for the dominant firm, as indicated by the fact that the dominant firm's demand curve touches the vertical axis. Similarly, at price p_d preferred by the dominant firm, the amount sold by the small firms, q_s, subtracted from the market demand, Q_1, leaves the amount q_d to be provided by the dominant firm: $Q_1 = q_s + q_d$. At any price p_2 set below the small firms' variable costs they will leave the whole market to the dominant firm [8, pp. 270-272].

20-4-3   Cartels

A long-familiar and still popular way for oligopolists to avoid competitive price wars and to raise profits is to form a collusive arrangement called a *cartel,* under which the market is divided among the member firms. Industry profits are maximized in the manner of a pure monopolist and distributed according to an agreed-upon formula. Output quotas are assigned to the individual firms on the basis of their individual marginal costs to obtain the lowest industry cost, as shown in Figure 20-8 for two firms. Industry output Q_1 is determined where the sum of the firms' marginal-cost curves, $\sum mc$, intersects the industry marginal-revenue curve. Industry price is set at P_1 by the market demand curve D. Quotas of q_A and q_B are given to firms A and B, respectively, where a horizontal line drawn from the intersection of MR and $\sum mc$ (called the *line of equal marginal costs*) intersects mc_A and mc_B.[1] Notice that a sizeable allocation is given to firm

---

[1] This allocation of quotas in a cartel is the same technique used by a multiplant firm in dividing its output among two or more of its plants. The firm operates each plant at its equal-marginal-cost level, as illustrated in Figure 20-9. Suppose that demand has fallen or not materialized as expected. Reduced output Q_1 is then allocated in amounts Oq to plant A and qQ_1 to plant B, determined by the intersection of the upward-sloping marginal-cost curves. Note that mc_A is measured from the left and mc_B from the right side of the diagram. It is easy to see that this division of output is least costly by recognizing that total variable costs are given by the area below marginal-cost curves. Any other allocation, say at q_1, would cause a rise in costs equal to the shaded area [16, pp. 233-234].

This analysis is valid only if both curves are rising at their intersection. If the *mc* of one plant lies at all points below that of the other, it will produce all the output required, and the other will be closed down if there are no longer-term considerations, such as termination wages and desire to retain the loyalty of a crack labor force should the downturn in demand be only temporary. Other restarting costs can be important, such as the refiring of a blast furnace in steel production.

This two-plant analysis can be extended to many plants by constructing a sum-of-the-marginal-costs curve and noting its intersection with the firm's marginal-revenue curve. This establishes the level of the equal-marginal-cost curve.

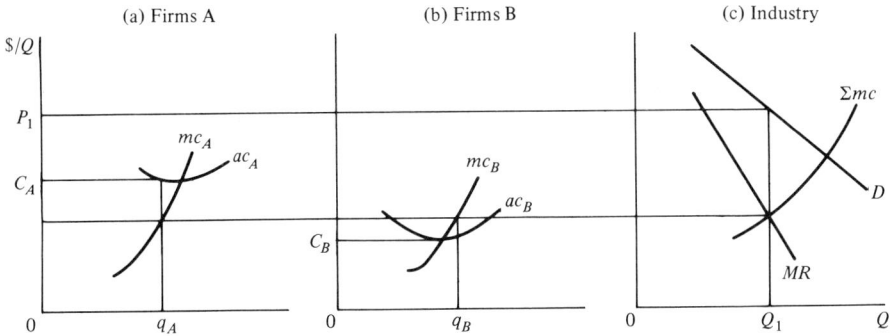

Figure 20-8

A, even though its average costs are substantially higher. The profit contributed by each firm to the cartel is computed by multiplying the number of units produced by the difference between the industry price and the firm's average costs.

There are many situations in which cartels are legal and feasible, as for the Arab oil producers, and other cases where they are subject to severe penalties, as with the well-known price-fixing conspiracy of several major United States producers of electric generators. A problem of maintaining a cartel, even when permitted under law, is maintaining cooperation of the lowest-cost firms eyeing the profits of a market greater than their given share. Disputes concerning the distribution of quotas and profits tend to increase with the passing of time and as the number of members increases. Cartels organized by governments for purposes of international trade, however, have been quite durable in some countries. When the cartel works perfectly, it differs little from pure monopoly.

20-4-4 Price reaction curves

Figure 20-10a shows how a business firm that knows what its competitors' reactions will be determines its price [1, pp. 356–360]. Curve R_B denotes the

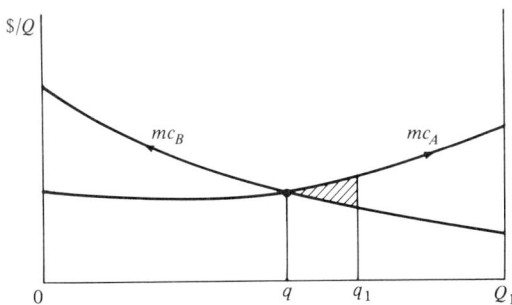

Figure 20-9

reactions of firm B to the pricing decisions of firm A; for instance, if A sets its price at a_1 corresponding to point 1, B will set its price at b_1. Firm A will not charge this price, however, because the price is not on its highest indifference curve (isoprofit curve, if A maximizes profits) of its objective function. Price a_2 tangent to curve I_2 is preferred, where B's price will be b_2 on the assumption that it sticks to this reaction pattern.

Fig. 20-10b shows the situation if firm B is also playing the game of plotting A's reactions. R_B indicates what B believes will be A's pricing reaction to the prices it sets. If both firms remain on their reaction curves and the curves have the appropriate slopes, prices will move toward their intersection at point P. For example, if A's initial price were set at a_1, B would set its price at b_1 on reaction curve R_B. A in turn reacts to B's price by raising its own to a_2, which provokes B to raise its price to b_3, and so on until point P is reached and reactions cease. Suppose, however, that B expects A to react to its optimum price b_5 by setting its own price at point C at the same time that A sets its optimum price at point D, corresponding to point 2 of Figure 20-10a, expecting B to act accordingly. The resulting price in this case would be neither at point C nor at point D but at point 5, where profits are greater or less than expected. Both are now aware that their hypothesized reaction curves were false, since neither reacted as expected. They may set about refiguring their reaction curves, but the eventual outcome is unknown.

A famous old model, perhaps the first oligopoly model, was used by A. A. Cournot in his *Researches into the Mathematical Principles of the Theory of Wealth* (1838), in which he assumed that the other firm does not react to price changes of its competitor. A simple mathematical example can be used to compare the profit-maximizing outcomes under the Cournot assumption with that of collusion. Given the profit functions of each firm in a two-firm industry, where the profits of each depend upon the output of the other,

$$\Pi_A = 15Q_A - Q_A^2 - 2Q_B^2 - 10$$
$$\Pi_B = 20Q_B - 2Q_B^2 - 3Q_A - 8$$

the profit-maximizing output of each acting individually under the Cournot assumption is obtained by setting the partial derivatives equal to zero and solving for Π:

$$\frac{\partial \Pi_A}{\partial Q_A} = 15 - 2Q_A = 0 \quad \text{or} \quad Q_A = 7.5$$

$$\frac{\partial \Pi_B}{\partial Q_B} = 20 - 4Q_B = 0 \quad \text{or} \quad Q_B = 5.0$$

By substitution, the firms' profits are

$$\Pi_A = 15(7.5) - (7.5)^2 - 2(5.0)^2 - 10 = 12.75$$
$$\Pi_B = 20(5.0) - 2(5.0)^2 - 3(7.5)^2 - 8 = 23.25$$

Industry profits are

$$\Pi = \Pi_A + \Pi_B = 36$$

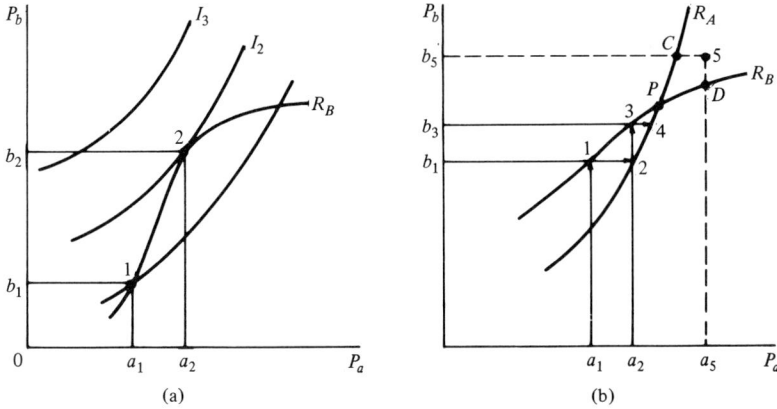

Figure 20-10

Under collusion, optimum combined profits are obtained by maximizing the joint profit function:

$$\Pi = \Pi_A + \Pi_B = 12Q_A - Q_A^2 + 20Q_B - 4Q_B^2 - 18$$

$$\frac{\partial \Pi}{\partial Q_A} = 12 - 2Q_A = 0 \quad \text{or} \quad Q_A = 6$$

$$\frac{\partial \Pi}{\partial Q_B} = 20 - 8Q_B = 0 \quad \text{or} \quad Q_B = 2\tfrac{1}{2}$$

$$\Pi_A = 15(6) - (6)^2 - 2(2\tfrac{1}{2})^2 - 10 = 31.5$$
$$\Pi_B = 20(2\tfrac{1}{2}) - 2(2\tfrac{1}{2})^2 - 3(6) - 8 = 11.5$$
$$\Pi = \Pi_A + \Pi_B = 43$$

Since firm B's profits would be less under collusion, firm A would probably have to pay some of its increase to B to secure the agreement.

20-5 Competition Among Buyers, Monopsony, and Bilateral Monopoly

In the four major market models discussed earlier, we implicitly assumed that sellers sold in a market containing many buyers, who acted individually in their own interests without collusion [10, ch. 17–19]. As perfect competition among sellers requires that the individual firm's demand curve be perfectly elastic, perfect competition among buyers requires a perfectly elastic supply curve. This describes the typical case of buyers walking into a store and being able to purchase as much as they wish from the available supply at current prices; offering less, they could buy none. For such a market to exist, it is sufficient that there be many buyers to whom sellers are indifferent in trading their wares. The latter requirement would not, of course, be met if discounts were given to certain

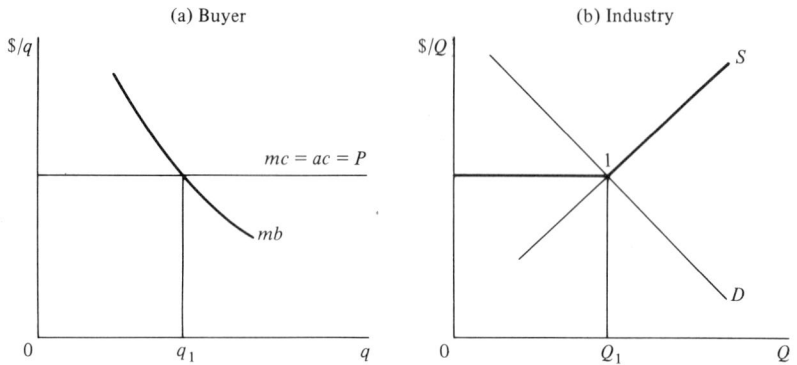

Figure 20-11

groups of customers on the basis of sentiment, familial relationships, gratitude, or hope of gaining favors. Buyers continue to purchase additional units until their expected marginal utility to be derived from the product equals the marginal benefits, as shown at q_1 in Figure 20-11a. The industry demand curve is simply the horizontal summation of the buyers' marginal-benefit curves.

A market in which there is a single buyer for the product of many sellers is called a *monopsony*. This is the case where goods are produced only for the government, such as war materials, and where there is a single buyer for certain resources and intermediate products. Examples of the latter might include the local grain elevator and flour mill for wheat, the local purchaser for a national distributor of hand-crafted items, and a regional steel producer for local scrap and coal. The situation faced by the individual employee in the absence of unions in marketing his or her services to the town factory also comes to mind. (Resource markets are treated in Chapter 21.) Joan Robinson mentions the cases of a socialistic government regulating imports, and "when a certain individual happens to have a taste for some commodity which no one else requires" [10, p. 218].

As long as the supply price remains constant, which will be the case for competitive sellers under conditions of constant average costs, industry price and output are the same as in pure competition. If the AC curve is not flat, however, marginal costs are either greater than average costs, as shown in Figure 20-12a, or less, as shown in Figure 20-12b. These facts are recognized by the monopsony firm that uses them to its advantage. In the case of rising AC, it finds that each additional purchase brings on a higher supply price and will buy Q_1 units at price P_1, both of which are below competitive levels Q_c and P_c. If the industry has a decreasing supply price as evidenced by a falling AC curve, it notes that increased purchases cause lower supply prices and will buy Q_2 units at price P_2, which is a greater quantity and lower price than under perfect competition. In Figure 20-12a the monopsony firm's consumer surplus is greater to the extent that shaded area a exceeds area b, and in Figure 20-12b, greater by area c.

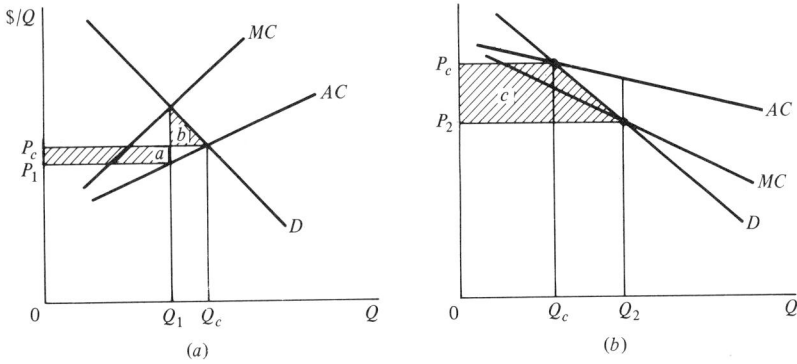

Figure 20-12

The best of all possible worlds from the viewpoint of the firm is to be the sole purchaser of resources (say, labor) and the only seller of its product. Its market power would enable it to extract a lower wage rate *and* a higher product price than if it faced competitors in both markets. Figure 20-13a illustrates the case. The monopoly firm that is also a monopsonist in the labor market will maximize profits by setting output at Q_m, where the marginal cost of labor (wage rate) equals the marginal contribution of labor to producing the product (referred to as the marginal-revenue product of labor) at point 1. Labor is paid W_1, its market supply price as given by the AC curve. Price P_1 is charged for the product, as given by the demand (AR) curve. Profits derived from the use of labor are thus given by the shaded area.

A market in which there is only one buyer and only one seller is called *bilateral monopoly*. This phenomenon is something of a frustration to economists, because no unique price-output solution can be deduced by the same logic used in other models. The outcome depends upon the relative bargaining power or cooperation of the two participants. This conclusion is explained with reference to Figure 20-13b, which assumes limited stocks of product Q and dollars given by the horizontal and vertical dimensions of the box. Person A is indifferent to combinations of Q and dollars at points along each of his A_i indifference curves drawn convex to origin O_A. Indifference curves located farther from O_A, indicating higher preference levels, are given higher numbered subscripts. A similar indifference map is drawn for person B but referenced to the origin O_B in the upper right-hand corner. Initial endowments are assumed at some point 1 within the boundaries of the box, indicating that person A has $O_A Q_1$ units of the product and $O_A D_4$ dollars on indifference level A_3, and person B has the rest ($Q_1 Q_5$ units of product and $D_4 D_5$ dollars) on indifference level B_3.

Analysis begins by noting that person A is indifferent to combinations at points 1 and 2, because both lie on indifference curve A_3, but that person B prefers point 2, because it puts him on a higher indifference curve B_5. Similarly, B is indifferent to combinations at points 1 and 4, but A prefers point 4, because it lies on his higher indifference curve A_5. Movement from point 1 to either points 2 or

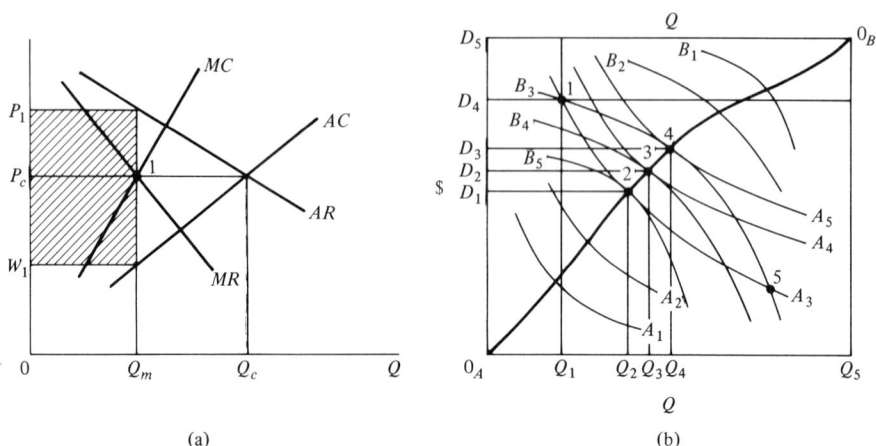

Figure 20-13

4 could be accomplished with no harm done to either person, and either B or A being helped. Person A could buy as few as Q_1Q_2 units for D_1D_4 dollars (at price D_1D_4/Q_1Q_2) without harm, and B could sell as many as Q_1Q_4 units for D_3D_4 dollars (at price $D_3D_4/Q_1Q_4 < D_1D_4/Q_1Q_2$) without harm. A comparison of indifference levels at points 2 and 4, however, indicates that both A and B could improve their positions by moving toward any point between points 2 and 4, that is, at some point 3, both reach higher indifference curves. In fact, the generalization can be made that any movement from either points 1 or 5 toward a line connecting points of tangency of indifference curves, called the *contract curve*, improves the position of both persons. The shaded area thus represents a more desirable distribution of the products and dollars. Once the contract curve has been reached, however, trade cannot take place without making one person lose while the other gains. The point along the contract curve between points 2 and 4 that will be obtained in moving from point 1 must be determined by bargaining. Economic analysis has taken us as far as it can. Several game-theory models have been devised to determine possible alternative solutions; they will not, however, be discussed in this text.

20-6   Concluding Comments

Business executives are often interested in theoretical analysis like that given in this chapter, knowing that many business decisions rest on such a basis. Familiarity with market models and their implications undoubtedly can aid business executives in following high-level discussions in courts of law, before regulatory bodies, in seminars, and in periodical literature. It may help them to organize their own thinking better and to present their views so that they will be given proper consideration. Such tools are also useful for government authorities and for consumer-taxpayers.

Questions and Problems

20-1. Define each of the following terms:

    a. pure competition
    b. perfect competition
    c. complete knowledge
    d. market competition
    e. industrial competition
    f. imperfect competition
    g. pure monopoly
    h. monopolistic competition
    i. oligopoly
    j. kinked demand curve
    k. price leadership
    l. cartel
    m. price reaction curve
    n. competition among buyers
    o. monopsony
    p. bilateral monopoly
    q. box diagram
    r. contract curve

20-2. Define the firm's short-run supply curve in a purely competitive market.

20-3. Why is the downward-sloping portion of the *MC* curve irrelevant to the firm?

20-4. Illustrate graphically and explain in words the sequence of events whereby short-run losses in a purely competitive industry are eliminated.

20-5. Given that total revenue is equal to *PQ*, prove mathematically that marginal revenue is given by the expression

$$MR = P - \frac{P}{E}$$

where *E* is the price elasticity of demand.

20-6. Prove that point 1 in Figure 20-6a lies directly above the intersection of $MC = MR$ and therefore represents the price and output that maximize profits for the firm in monopolistic competition. Use the relation

$$\text{Marginal} = \text{average} + Q\,\frac{d(\text{average})}{dQ}$$

obtained by taking the derivative of the total with respect to *Q*.

20-7. Given the following profit functions, determine the amount by which joint profits can be increased by colluison as compared with individual profit maximization.

    a. $\Pi_a = 6Q_a - Q_a^2 - Q_b$
       $\Pi_b = 8Q_b - Q_b^2 - 2Q_a$

    b. $\Pi_a = 14Q_a - Q_a^2 - 2Q_b - 3$
       $\Pi_b = 7Q_b - Q_b^2 - Q_a$

References

1. William J. Baumol. *Economic Theory and Operations Analysis*. 3d ed. (Englewood Cliffs, N. J.: Prentice-Hall, 1972), ch. 13–14.

2. Kenneth E. Boulding. *Economic Analysis*. Vol. I. *Microeconomics*. 4th ed. (New York: Harper & Row, 1966), ch. 21–23.

3. Hans Brems. *Product Equilibrium Under Monopolistic Competition* (Cambridge, Mass.: Harvard University Press, 1951).

4. Edward H. Chamberlin. *The Theory of Monopolistic Competition*. 7th ed. (Cambridge, Mass.: Harvard University Press, 1956). First published in 1933.

5. Donald Dewey. *The Theory of Imperfect Competition—A Radical Reconstruction* (New York: Columbia University Press, 1969).

6. James M. Henderson and Richard E. Quandt. *Microeconomic Theory—A Mathematical Approach*. 2d ed. (New York: McGraw-Hill, 1971), ch. 6.

7. Robert E. Kuenne. *Monopolistic Competition Theory: Studies in Impact* (New York: Wiley, 1967).

8. Richard H. Leftwich. *The Price System and Resource Allocation*. 5th ed. (Hinsdale, Ill.: Dryden Press, 1973), ch. 3, 10–13.

9. Fritz Machlup. *The Economics of Sellers' Competition—Model Analysis of Sellers' Conduct* (Baltimore: Johns Hopkins Press, 1952).

10. Joan Robinson. *The Economics of Imperfect Competition* (London: Macmillan, 1933).

11. Adam Smith. *An Inquiry Into the Nature and Causes of the Wealth of Nations* (1776). Currently available in a Modern Library edition and as one of Encyclopaedia Britannica's *Great Books of the Western World*.

12. Stanton D. Smith and Walter C. Neale. "The Geometry of Kinky Oligopoly: Marginal Cost, the Gap, and Price Behavior." *Southern Economic Journal* 37 (January 1971): 276–282.

13. George J. Stigler. "Perfect Competition, Historically Contemplated." *Journal of Political Economy* 65 (1957). Reprinted in Edwin Mansfield. *Microeconomics—Selected Readings* (New York: W. W. Norton, 1971), pp. 167–187.

14. ———. "The Kinky Oligopoly Demand Curve and Rigid Prices." *Journal of Political Economy* 55 (October 1947): 432–449. Reprinted in American Economics Association. *Readings in Price Theory* (Homewood, Ill.: Richard D. Irwin, 1952), pp. 410–439.

15. Paul M. Sweezy. "Demand Under Conditions of Oligopoly." *Journal of Political Economy* 47 (August 1939): 568–573. Reprinted in American Economics Association. *Readings in Price Theory* (Homewood, Ill.: Richard D. Irwin, 1952), pp. 404–409.

16. Donald S. Watson. *Price Theory and Its Uses*. 3d ed. (Boston: Houghton Mifflin, 1972), ch. 13, 14, 16–20.

21 Pricing Analysis

Pricing is one of the most interesting and rewarding topics in economics because of its close relation to profits of the firm, its importance in rationing scarce resources among competing uses, and its importance to consumers in determining which of various commodities they can possess within their limited incomes. Rule-of-thumb pricing has given way to scientific pricing as business executives have become more knowledgeable about their products, the inter-dependence of production and demand, and the conditions impinging at the point of sale. This chapter provides an introduction to pricing with regard to discrimination, markups, multiple products, transfer of intermediate products between divisions of the same firm, and new products.

21-1 Price Discrimination

Sellers in imperfectly competitive markets often find that they can increase their revenues and profits by charging more than one price at a time for their products. Different prices are sometimes charged to the same or different individuals on the basis of personal attributes, income, and position; to different groups as distin-guished by sex, age, color, religion, marital status, employer, and geographic location; or to individuals and groups with regard to quantities purchased, qualities of the product, brand name, and time of purchase. Table 21-1 suggests some bases for charging different prices. When such differences in price are not justified by differences in costs, price discrimination is said to exist. Similarly, charging the same price where cost differences are present should also be regarded as discrimination; viewed in this way, discrimination could be the rule rather than the exception for pricing practices. The standard analysis presented in this chapter, however, assumes the absence of cost differences and thereby emphasizes the demand side of the market.

Price discrimination is characterized by three degrees by which the seller is able to capture consumer surplus. Because the first degree is judged to be the simplest in concept and the most advantageous from the standpoint of the seller, it is treated first.[1]

---

[1] A. C. Pigou was the first to discuss degrees of discrimination [17]. His first degree discrimination is identical with Joan Robinson's "perfect discrimination" [18].

Table 21-1   Bases for Charging Different Prices*

Type	Discrimination base	Examples
Individual or personal	Ability to pay in terms of income, wealth, or amount of insurance	Professional fees for services of medical doctors, lawyers, artists, and business consultants.
	Essentiality of the product or service	Drugs in short supply, perhaps sold illegally.
	Relatives, and friends of wealth and fame (this could account for reverse discrimination)	Merchandise sold on account and with free credit. Credit and lower interest rates charged by banks.
	Personal appearance, habits, mannerisms, health, size, weight, skill level	Conditions of purchase requiring a tie, shoes, cleanliness, no swimming or sports attire. Tennis tournament requires women to wear bras. Golf tournament prohibits contestants from wearing shorts or jeans. (Expense of unnecessary purchases raises the effective prices.)
Group	Age, sex, color, religion, marital status, military status, employer, club	Lower admission and transportation charges for children, students, priests, men in the armed forces, government employees. Discounts for employees, stockholders, club members, and new customers. Ladies' day in ball parks and pool rooms. Children's day at the amusement park. Free checking accounts for senior citizens.
	Geographic location	Higher prices for purchasers living outside the country, state, city limits, or zone. Base-point pricing.
	Use of product	Transportation rates based upon size, weight, and value of goods shipped. Utility rates different for homes and factories. Use of milk for drinking, making ice cream, and processing cheese.

Table 21-1—(Cont.)

Type	Discrimination base	Examples
Product	Qualities of product	Relatively higher prices for gourmet foods and drinks, stylish clothes, fine furniture, and deluxe models and accessories.
	Labels and trademarks	Relatively higher prices for branded products of similar quality.
	Quantities of product	Quantity discounts for "the giant economy size"; cheaper by the carload.
Time	Off-peak services	Lower telephone rates for evening calls.
	Season	Off-season rates at resorts. Lower installation prices for storm windows in the summer and air conditioners in the winter.
	Business cycle	Labor and material prices of some items cheaper in periods of depression.

* A similar table is presented by Watson [19, p. 372]. A good classification and discussion is given by Machlup [14].

21-1-1 *First degree*

The imperfectly competitive firm, facing a downward-sloping demand curve for its product, knows when it charges a single price that some of its customers would have paid a higher price if pressed to do so. Figure 21-1a shows the case for an individual consumer who would have paid a higher price on all units up to q_1, where the demand and selling prices are equal. The shaded triangular area under the demand curve and above the selling price represents the additional amount of money the consumer would have paid if necessary to get quantity q_1. The firm may attempt to capture this consumer surplus by initially setting its price very high and then gradually reducing the price over time—a ploy commonly followed in modern merchandising. The buyer who wants the product immediately or believes he must purchase it now if at all may purchase only one unit at the highest price. Having obtained one unit, he may purchase an additional unit only if the price is reduced. By confronting the buyer with successively lower prices, the firm could possibly eliminate all of the consumer surplus. An alternative strategy would be for the firm to confront the buyer with an all-or-nothing or take-it-or-leave-it proposition, offering to sell q_1 units for an amount of money equal to the area $OABq_1$.

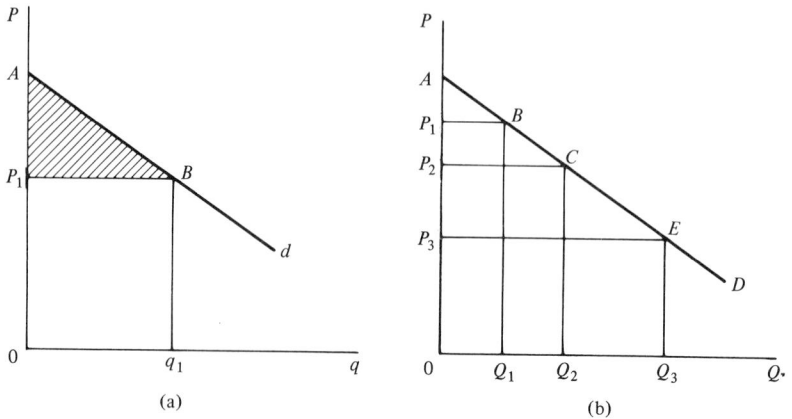

Figure 21-1

This limiting case of first-degree discrimination, whereby all consumer surplus is removed, could occur only where a monopoly firm had a few dispersed or segregated customers whom it could keep apart and for whom it could accurately assess the maximum prices each would pay. The larger the number of buyers, the greater their opportunity to profit from arbitrage and collusion.

21-1-2 *Second degree*

Second-degree price discrimination refers to the case where only part of the consumer surplus is captured by a monopolist. The scheduling of block rates by public utilities according to the number of units purchased by each customer is a good example. A high unit charge, P_1 in Figure 21-1b, is made for the first few gallons of water, cubic feet of natural gas, and kilowatt hours of electricity consumed per month. Then a lower price P_2 is charged for a second block of units $Q_1 Q_2$ used in the same month. Still lower rates are charged for subsequent blocks or steps of typically larger amounts. If a single price P_3 were charged for the Q_3 units, the utility company would (ignoring income effects of consumers having more money to spend at the lower price) receive revenue equal to the area of the rectangle $OP_3 EQ_3$, and consumer surplus would equal the area $P_3 AE$. But with block pricing, revenues equal to the sum of the areas of the three rectangles identified by the diagonal corners OB, $Q_1 C$, and $Q_2 E$ are received, and consumer surplus is reduced to the three shaded triangular areas. Individuals with strong tastes and more money are able to retain some of their surplus.

This type of discrimination is clearly most practical where a single rate or schedule must apply for a large number of buyers and where it is inconvenient, impossible, or not worth the effort for buyers to attempt to cut costs by arbitrage and collusion. It is most useful where inexpensive services are consumed in small amounts by dispersed customers and where they can be metered, recorded, and billed without difficulty.

21-1-3 *Third degree*

Third-degree price discrimination refers to the case where a firm charges a different price in two or more segments of its market. For such a practice to increase the firm's profits, each market segment must have a different price elasticity of demand and must be kept separated from the other segments. The firm maximizes its profits by allocating its output on the basis of equal marginal revenues in each market segment and charging prices commensurate with the respective demand curves. For example, assume that the demand curves for the domestic and foreign markets are as shown in Figures 21-2a and 21-2b. A horizontal summation of these two curves gives the total demand curve of Figure 21-2c, $d_1 + d_2 = D$. The monopoly firm sets output at Q_T, where its marginal-cost and marginal-revenue curves intersect, and allocates output to domestic and foreign markets in amounts Q_1 and Q_2 as dictated by the intersection of the horizontal equal-marginal-revenue (EMR) line and the *mr* curves. Note that $Q_1 + Q_2 = Q_T$. Prices P_1 and P_2 are charged in the two markets as permitted by their demand curves. In this particular example, a higher price is charged in the foreign market and a lower one in the domestic market than if a single price P_3 had been charged in both.

It should be emphasized that price discrimination of this sort requires unequal elasticities in the two markets. This may be demonstrated with reference to the formula

$$MR = P - \frac{P}{E} \tag{1}$$

which is easily derived by taking the first derivative of total revenue (TR) with respect to Q and substituting E for the equation for the price elasticity of demand:

$$TR = PQ$$

$$MR = \frac{d(TR)}{dQ} = P + Q\frac{dP}{dQ} = P\left(1 + \frac{Q}{P}\frac{dP}{dQ}\right) \tag{2}$$

$$= P\left(1 + \frac{1}{-E}\right) = P - \frac{P}{E}$$

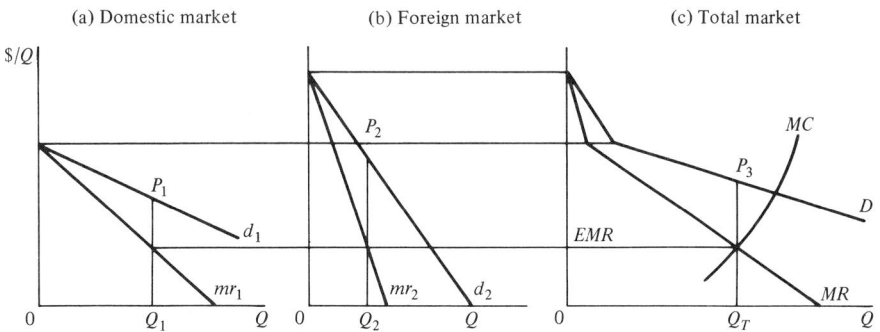

Figure 21-2

Since the marginal revenues of the two markets are set equal, that is, $mr_1 = mr_2$,

$$P_1 - \frac{P_1}{E_1} = P_2 - \frac{P_2}{E_2} \quad \text{or}$$

$$P_1\left(1 - \frac{1}{E_1}\right) = P_2\left(1 - \frac{1}{E_2}\right) \tag{3}$$

Thus, if the elasticities are equal, the prices must also be equal, and if prices are different, the elasticities must also be different.

It is correct to generalize that a higher (lower) price is charged in the market having the relatively lower (higher) *elasticity*, but one must not confuse the elasticity of a *point* on the curve with the *slope* of the curve. It is tempting to refer to a demand curve like d_2 in Figure 21-2b as "obviously" less elastic than another, say d_1 in Figure 21-2a because of its steeper slope. Such comparisons are correct for entire markets but not where particular points on the curves are most important. Consider the curves in Figure 21-3a. Demand curve d_1 is steeper than d_2 but has a lower price; verify that elasticity at point P_1 on d_1 is higher than at point P_2 on d_2 by using the technique described in Chapter 9. Draw the dashed line connecting opposite end points of the demand curves. Elasticities at points P_1, A, and B are equal, and since point B is above P_2 on d_2, indicating a higher elasticity, elasticity at P_1 on d_1 exceeds that of P_2 on d_2. The higher price is indeed associated with the lower elasticity. Consider also Figure 21-3b, where d_1 and d_2 are parallel. By the same reasoning, it is found that point elasticity at P_1 is greater than at P_2. The relevant elasticity concept for price discrimination is point elasticity rather than overall elasticity of the market [15].

Third-degree price discrimination is not limited in application to only domestic and foreign markets; in addition to international trade, it applies to geographic markets between states, regions, cities, neighborhoods, blocks, and even sides of the street. Nongeographical examples of segregated markets also abound in the

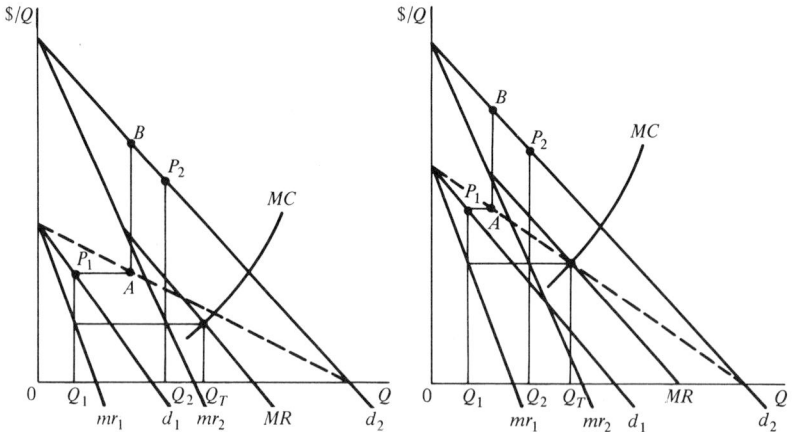

Figure 21-3

form of box, reserved, unreserved, and bleacher seats at baseball games; resident-ial, commercial, and industrial customers of utility companies; milk sold by producers' associations in the form of "fluid" milk for retail markets and of "surplus" milk to producers of butter, cheese, and ice cream; dry-cell batteries used for flashlights, toys, and transistor radios; sports equipment and clothes sold in specialty, department, and discount stores; real estate sold for farm land, residential subdivisions, and commercial-industrial purposes; and human labor allocated for different uses and to different employers on the basis of what the market will bear, especially with regard to moonlighting (holding more than one job). Further discrimination can also take place within each submarket, as with utilities, where second-degree price discrimination is practiced within submarkets. In these examples, and others the reader might cite, monopolistic control may be far from complete, and price differences may be largely attributable to cost differences rather than to discrimination. What is to be gained from consider-ation of these examples is greater awareness of, and potential for, price discrim-ination. The extent of prevailing discrimination is an empirical problem.

21-1-4 *Selective first degree*

Selective first-degree price discrimination is a strategy containing elements of both the first- and third-degree types but can produce profits even greater than under first-degree discrimination [20]. The monopoly firm decides to sell a number of units, say Q_1 units as shown in Figure 21-4a, at an announced price P_1, as when the retail automobile industry issues a manufacturer's list price or an advertised price. Additional units are sold at various bargained prices up to some quantity Q_3, at which the demand price equals marginal cost, where the latter includes any variable costs connected with establishing the discriminatory price. Such costs of price discrimination in the business of retail automobile sales could include additional calls by sales people, advanced delivery dates, better credit terms, and inflated trade-in allowances. Profits on units sold at the announ-ced price are equal to the area $ABFP_1$. Additional profits on those sold by selec-tive discrimination are equal to the triangular area BCF. Total profits are given by the shaded areas.

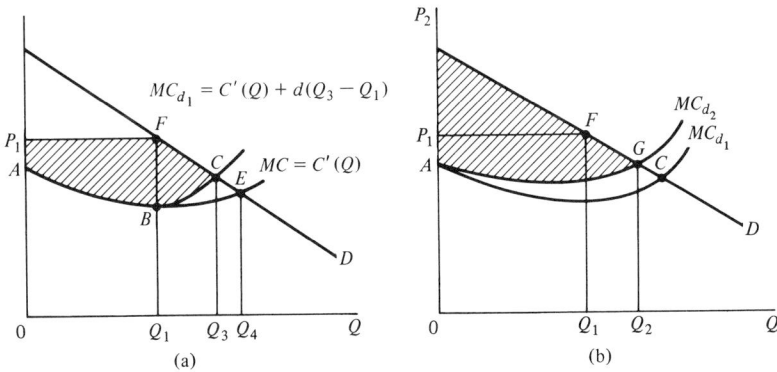

Figure 21-4

Under pure first-degree discrimination, the announced price would be at a level at least as high as P_2 in Figure 21-4b, where no units are sold. Then all units are sold under perfect discrimination, and variable costs of discrimination are greater, as reflected by the higher marginal-cost curve MC_{d_2}. Profits are given by the shaded area AGP_2. It is possible that greater profits can be obtained under selective first-degree discrimination if the shaded area of Figure 21-4a exceeds that of Figure 21-4b. This would be the case where there are sufficient cost savings and revenue gains from selling some units on a nondiscriminatory basis.

A management that wishes to combine two or more of the three degrees of discrimination must consider the associated costs of discrimination and weigh them against changes in expected revenues. Study of the multiple-pricing policies of public utilities could be quite helpful. They practice third-degree discrimination in dividing their market into residential, commercial, and industrial. Each of these in turn is subdivided by time of day and use of service. Furthermore, second-degree discrimination is employed within each submarket by use of block rates, which are lower for larger quantities. Experimenting with the many possible patterns could disclose profitable opportunities to those who understand discriminatory pricing.[2]

21-1-5   The mathematics of price discrimination

Several mathematical examples are provided in this section that are useful in giving the reader a more precise understanding of price discrimination and in comparing solutions under the different types.

First degree

The perfectly discriminating monopoly firm extracts all consumer surplus. Its total revenue is therefore equal to the area under its demand curve, which may be obtained by summing the vertical distances to the demand curve, say D in Figure 21-2c, of all increments in output over the range $Q = 0$ to $Q = Q_T$, or in functional notation,

$$TR = \int_0^{Q_T} D(Q)\,dQ \tag{4}$$

Its profit function is then

$$\Pi = \int_0^{Q_T} D(Q)\,dQ - C(Q) \tag{5}$$

Profits are maximized where the first derivative is set equal to zero

$$\frac{d\Pi}{dQ} = D(Q) - C'(Q) = 0$$

[2] It should be noted that price differences may be justified by service-cost differences. For example, the capacity of electric generators is designed to meet peak-load requirements, but the marginal cost of providing additional services at nonpeak-load periods is relatively low, thereby justifying a lower price.

and   (6)

$$D(Q) = C'(Q)$$

This shows that profit-maximizing output is set where the demand (average-revenue) curve intersects the marginal-cost curve. The second-order condition for profit maximization is that the second derivative be less than zero

$$\frac{d^2\Pi}{dQ^2} = D'(Q) - C''(Q) < 0$$

and   (7)

$$D'(Q) < C''(Q)$$

which means that the slope of the demand curve must be less than the slope of the marginal-cost curve at optimum output.

This information can be used to determine profits under perfect first-degree discrimination from given demand (AR curve) and *total*-cost functions:

$$P = 42 - 5Q$$
$$C = 4 + 2Q$$ (8)

From equation (5) above, the profit function is

$$\Pi = \int_0^Q (42 - 5Q)dQ - (4 + 2Q)$$
$$= 42Q - 2.5Q^2 - 4 - 2Q$$ (9)
$$= 40Q - 2.5Q^2 - 4$$

Therefore,

$$\frac{d\Pi}{dQ} = 40 - 5Q = 0$$

and   (10)

$$Q = 8$$

Then

$$\frac{d^2\Pi}{dQ} = -5 \quad \text{(second-order condition is met)}$$ (11)

Profit under perfect discrimination is therefore

$$\Pi = 40(8) - 2.5(8)^2 - 4$$
$$= 320 - 160 - 4$$ (12)
$$= 156$$

Compare these profits to those of the nondiscriminating monopolist who charges only one price:

$$\Pi = PQ - C$$
$$= 42Q - 5Q^2 - (4 + 2Q) \tag{13}$$
$$= 40Q - 5Q^2 - 4$$

$$\frac{d\Pi}{dQ} = 40 - 10Q = 0 \tag{14}$$

$$Q = 4$$
$$\Pi = 40(4) - 5(4)^2 - 4$$
$$= 160 - 80 - 4 \tag{15}$$
$$= 76$$

Profits gained by perfect discrimination are

$$156 - 76 = 80$$

Consumers also gain to the extent that more units are produced and made available to those who could not pay the single price.

Third degree

Consider now the more realistic case of third-degree price discrimination whereby the monopoly firm divides its market into two parts and charges a different price in each. Assume the demand functions for the two markets are

$$P_1 = 16 - 2Q_1$$
$$P_2 = 24 - 3Q_2 \tag{16}$$

and the total-cost function is

$$C = 4 + 2Q_1 + 2Q_2 \tag{17}$$

The profit function is

$$\Pi = P_1Q_1 + P_2Q_2 - C$$
$$= (16 - 2Q_1)Q_1 + (24 - 3Q_2)Q_2 - (4 + 2Q_1 + 2Q_2)$$
$$= 16Q_1 - 2Q_1^2 + 24Q_2 - 3Q_2^2 - 4 - 2Q_1 - 2Q_2 \tag{18}$$
$$= 14Q_1 - 2Q_1^2 + 22Q_2 - 3Q_2^2 - 4$$

Partial derivatives are

$$\frac{\partial \Pi}{\partial Q_1} = 14 - 4Q_1 = 0$$
$$Q_1 = 3\tfrac{1}{2}$$

$$\frac{\partial \Pi}{\partial Q_2} = 22 - 6Q_2 = 0 \tag{19}$$
$$Q_2 = 3\tfrac{2}{3}$$

By substituting the values of Q_1 and Q_2 into the profit and demand functions (18) and (16), we find

$$\Pi = 60\tfrac{5}{6} \qquad P_1 = 9 \qquad P_2 = 13$$

Marginal revenues are

$$MR_1 = \frac{\partial P_1 Q_1}{\partial Q_1} = 16 - 4Q_1 = 16 - 4(3\tfrac{1}{2}) = 2$$

$$MR_2 = \frac{\partial P_2 Q_2}{\partial Q_2} = 24 - 6Q_2 = 24 - 6(3\tfrac{2}{3}) = 2 \tag{20}$$

Compare these profits, prices, and output with those obtained without discrimination, where $P_1 = P_2$:

$$16 - 2Q_1 = 24 - 3Q_2$$
$$0 = 8 - 3Q_2 + 2Q_1 \tag{21}$$

The Lagrangian expression incorporating this constraint into equation (18) is

$$\Pi_\lambda = 14Q_1 - 2Q_1^2 + 22Q_2 - 3Q_2^2 - 4 + \lambda(8 - 3Q_2 + 2Q_1) \tag{22}$$

Solving for maximum constrained profits by setting the partials equal to zero and solving the equations simultaneously,

$$\frac{\partial \Pi_\lambda}{\partial Q_1} = 14 - 4Q_1 + 2\lambda = 0$$

$$\frac{\partial \Pi_\lambda}{\partial Q_2} = 22 - 6Q_2 - 3\lambda = 0 \tag{23}$$

$$\frac{\partial \Pi_\lambda}{\partial \lambda} = 8 - 3Q_2 + 2Q_1 = 0$$

we obtain $Q_1 = 2.7$, $Q_2 = 4.47$, $\lambda = -1.6$. By substitution into equations (18) and (16), we obtain

$$\Pi_\lambda = 57.66 \qquad P_1 = P_2 = 10.6$$

Marginal revenues were

$$MR_1 = \frac{\partial P_1 Q_1}{\partial Q_1} = 16 - 4Q_1 = 16 - 4(2.7) = 5.20$$

$$MR_2 = \frac{\partial P_2 Q_2}{\partial Q_2} = 24 - 6Q_2 = 24 - 6(4.47) = -2.82 \tag{24}$$

Note that under discrimination, profits were $3\tfrac{1}{6} (= 60\tfrac{5}{6} - 57\tfrac{2}{3})$ greater, while one price was higher and the other lower. Marginal revenues were equal under discrimination, but not under a single price policy where one was actually negative.

Selective first degree

Under selective first-degree price discrimination, shown in Figure 21-4a, the profit function is

$$\Pi = \int_0^{Q_1} [P_1 - C'(Q)] \, dQ + \int_{Q_1}^{Q_3} [D(Q) - C'(Q) - d(Q_3 - Q_1)] \, dQ \tag{25}$$

where P_1 is the announced price, Q_1 is the quantity sold at P_1, and $(Q_3 - Q_1)$ is the additional quantity sold under first-degree discrimination. The value of equation (25) is represented by the shaded area of Figure 21-4a. Given the demand and cost equations

$$D(Q): \quad P = 150 - 10Q$$
$$MC_{d_1}: \quad MC_{d_1} = 86 - 8Q + Q^2 \tag{26}$$

the profit equation is

$$\Pi = \int_0^{Q_1} [P_1 - (86 - 8Q + Q^2)]\, dQ$$
$$+ \int_{Q_1}^{Q_3} [150 - 10Q - (86 - 8Q + Q^2)]\, dQ \tag{27}$$

To simplify the problem, assume that Q_1 is determined by setting $MR = MC_{d_1}$, as a profit-maximizing, nondiscriminating monopolist would do who considers certain discriminating costs as ordinary costs of doing business. Q_1 is thus determined:

$$TR = PQ = 150Q - 10Q^2$$

$$MR = \frac{d(TR)}{dQ} = 150 - 20Q$$

$$MR = MC_{d_1}$$

$$150 - 20Q = 86 - 8Q + Q^2$$

$$-Q^2 - 12Q + 64 = 0$$

$$Q = \frac{12 \pm \sqrt{(12)^2 - 4(-1)(64)}}{2(-1)} = \frac{12 \pm \sqrt{144 + 256}}{-2}$$

$$= \frac{12 \pm 20}{-2} = -16, 4$$

$$\therefore Q_1 = 4$$

Now P_1 can be found from the demand equation:

$$P_1 = 150 - 10(4) = 110$$

Q_3 is where $D(Q) = MC_{d_1}$:

$$150 - 10Q = 86 - 8Q + Q^2$$

$$-Q^2 - 2Q + 64 = 0$$

$$Q = \frac{2 \pm \sqrt{4 - 4(-1)(64)}}{2(-1)} = \frac{2 \pm \sqrt{260}}{-2} = \frac{2 \pm 16.12}{-2} = -9.06, 7.06$$

$$\therefore Q_3 = 7.06$$

The profit equation is now

$$\Pi = \int_0^4 [110 - (86 - 8Q + Q^2)]\,dQ + \int_4^{7.06} (64 - 2Q - Q^2)\,dQ$$

$$= \int_0^4 (24 + 8Q - Q^2)\,dQ + \int_4^{7.06} (64 - 2Q - Q^2)\,dQ$$

$$= [24Q + 4Q^2 - \tfrac{1}{3}Q^3]_0^4 + [64Q - Q^2 - \tfrac{1}{3}Q^3]_4^{7.06}$$

$$= [24(4) + 4(4)^2 - \tfrac{1}{3}(4)^3] - [24(0) + 4(0)^2 - \tfrac{1}{3}(0)^3]$$

$$\quad + [64(7.06) - (7.06)^2 - \tfrac{1}{3}(7.06)^3] - [64(4) - (4)^2 - \tfrac{1}{3}(4)^3]$$

$$= 138\tfrac{2}{3} - 0 + 284.71 - 218\tfrac{2}{3} = 204.71, \text{ say } 205$$

which is the profit under selective discrimination.

Assume now that the monopoly firm wants to compare these results with those of pure first-degree price discrimination and that it estimates a new marginal-cost function that covers the additional costs of discriminating against all customers to be

$$MC_{d_2} = 86 - 3Q + Q^2$$

which intersects the demand curve at

$$150 - 10Q = 86 - 3Q + Q^2$$
$$-Q^2 - 7Q + 64 = 0$$

$$Q = \frac{7 \pm \sqrt{49 - 4(-1)64}}{2(-1)} = \frac{7 \pm \sqrt{305}}{-2} = \frac{7 \pm 17.46}{-2}$$

$$= -12.23, \quad 5.23$$

$$\therefore Q_2 = 5.23 \quad \text{(see Figure 21-4b)}$$

The profit function from equation (5) is

$$\Pi = \int_0^{Q_2} D(Q)\,dQ - C(Q)$$

$$= \int_0^{5.23} (150 - 10Q)\,dQ - \int_0^{5.23} (86 - 3Q + Q^2)\,dQ$$

$$= [150Q - 5Q^2]_0^{5.23} - [86Q - 1.5Q^2 + \tfrac{1}{3}Q^3]_0^{5.23}$$

$$= [64Q - 3.5Q^2 - \tfrac{1}{3}Q^3]_0^{5.23}$$

$$= 64(5.23) - 3.5(5.23)^2 - \tfrac{1}{3}(5.23)^3$$

$$= 334.17 - 95.72 - 47.69$$

$$= 191.30$$

which is the profit under pure first-degree discrimination. Profits and output in this example are greater under selective than under first-degree discrimination because of lower variable costs of discrimination. Consumers are also better off under this example of selective discrimination because of the larger number of goods consumed, the lower average unit price (114.7 versus 123.9), and the presence of some consumer surplus [20].

21-2   Markup Pricing

Many firms price their products by adding a certain percentage of markup to their average variable cost to cover overhead expenses and profit margins. Such practice appears on the surface to be a mechanical rule of thumb that ignores demand considerations and offers little promise of yielding maximum profits. But this is not necessarily the case, as may be shown by use of equation (1) discussed earlier in the chapter. Since profits are maximized at $MR = MC$, MC may be substituted for MR to give

$$MC = P - \frac{P}{E} \tag{28}$$

or

$$P = E(P - MC) \tag{29}$$

or

$$P = E(\text{markup}) \tag{30}$$

or

$$\frac{\text{markup}}{P} = \frac{1}{E} \tag{31}$$

Markup as a percentage of price is thus equal to the reciprocal of the price elasticity coefficient; for example, if $E = 1$, the markup is 100 per cent; if $E = 2$, the markup is 50 per cent; if $E = 3$, the markup is 33 per cent. The higher the elasticity coefficient, the lower the percentage of markup.

Markup as a percentage of *price* is not the same as a percentage of *cost*, but the translation is easily made by dividing equation (30) by E, and again by MC, to obtain

$$\frac{\text{markup}}{MC} = \frac{P}{E(MC)} \tag{32}$$

If MC is constant and therefore equal to average variable cost, it may serve as the cost base for measuring the percentage of markup. If $P = \$20$ and $E = 2$, the cost from equation (28) is $10, and markup as a percentage of cost from equation (32) is 1, or 100 per cent—just double the markup as a percentage of price.[3]

---

[3] Conversion between price and cost markups is easily determined by use of the following relations [3, p. 290]:

$$\text{Price markup} = \frac{\text{cost markup}}{1 + \text{cost markup}}$$

$$\text{Cost markup} = \frac{\text{price markup}}{1 - \text{price markup}}$$

For example, a 40 per cent markup on price is equivalent to a 67 per cent markup on cost:

$$\text{Cost markup} = \frac{0.4}{1 - 0.4} = 0.67$$

When markups are determined with reference to elasticity, they are quite consistent with profit maximization. The fact that multiproduct firms use different markups for their various products provides evidence that competitive pressures and demand elasticities are considered. (See the two studies [7] and [13], and the discussion by Joel Dean against uniform markups [6, pp. 444–457].) Caution must be taken, however, not to accept automatically costs from accounting records as relevant for economic decisions. Recall the discussions in Chapter 15 of relevant, alternative, and implicit costs, and in Chapter 16 of practical considerations in making cost studies.

21-3 Multiple-Product Pricing

Discussion of pricing up to this point has assumed that the firm produces and sells a single homogeneous product. But in this modern age production by the firm of more than one item is the rule rather than the exception. Even very specialized firms have multiple models, styles, and sizes, each of which may be considered a separate product. Much of the analysis for the single-product firm still applies but must be extended to take into account the demand and production interrelations. For example, if the firm has two products that consumers view as complements or substitutes, then the demand for each product is a function of the price charged for the other. That is, if $Q_1 = f(P_1, P_2)$ and $Q_2 = f(P_1, P_2)$, then total revenues derived from the sale of each product are given by $TR_1 = f(Q_1, P_1, P_2)$ and $TR_2 = f(Q_2, P_1, P_2)$, and marginal revenues are

$$MR_1 = \frac{\partial(TR_1)}{\partial Q_1} = \frac{\partial f(Q_1, P_1, P_2)}{\partial Q_1}$$

$$MR_2 = \frac{\partial(TR_2)}{\partial Q_2} = \frac{\partial f(Q_2, P_1, P_2)}{\partial Q_2} \tag{33}$$

If the two products are produced by common production facilities and are entirely interchangeable substitutes in production, their costs are jointly determined. Total revenue (as well as profit) to the firm is therefore maximized where $MR_T = MC$ and where marginal revenues for each product are equal, that is, where $MR_1 = MR_2$. This analysis is identical with that used for a discriminating monopolist selling a single product in two separate markets, and it may be extended to any number of products as long as the assumptions hold.

The assumption of perfect substitution of products in production is approximated in practice when the firm's managers find they have idle, or less than fully utilized, equipment; general-purpose equipment and other facilities; and versatile labor and management [19, p. 379]. Familiarity with the firm's productive capacity and knowhow often leads to discovery of profitable opportunities, as when a firm producing plastic containers finds that it can also produce and sell children's toys and kitchen accessories at prices above their marginal costs. Figure 21-5 is similar to one employed by Eli W. Clemens [4] to illustrate a case where successive products q_2 through q_4 were added to the production line. MR_T is the curve marginal to a composite demand curve that treats the four products as a single product. Intersection of MR_T and MC establishes the common level of marginal revenue used for determining the units of each item to be produced. Amounts are q_1 of product 1, $q_1 q_2$ of 2, $q_2 q_3$ of 3, and $q_3 q_4$ of 4.

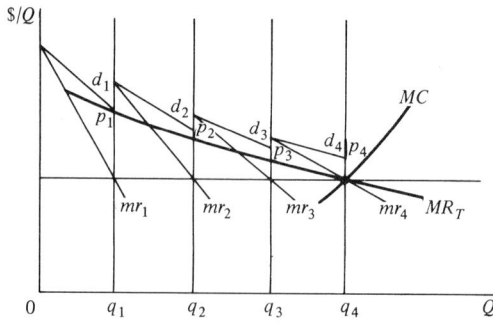

Figure 21-5

Prices charged are dictated by the demand curve for each item, that is, p_1 for product 1, p_2 for 2, p_3 for 3, and p_4 for 4. When estimating the demands, care must be taken to take into account their interdependence as discussed in Chapters 9 and 12.

Another interesting case involves joint products (those produced in fixed proportions), as in the meat-packing industry, where the slaughtering of hogs and cattle produces proportional numbers of sides, livers, hides, and waste used for hot dogs and pet food. Figure 21-6 is similar to those used by Haynes [9, pp. 370–376] and by Brigham and Pappas [3, pp. 304–306], where MR_T is the curve marginal to the total-demand curve D (not shown) obtained by *vertical* addition of the demand curves for the two products jointly produced, say beef hides d_1 and sides of beef d_2. Q may represent the number of cattle slaughtered, hides produced, pairs of beef sides produced, and composite units produced as package outputs containing both hides and sides. The profit-maximizing output Q_1 is where $MR_T = MC$. Optimal product prices are determined by what the market will bear, that is, by the points on the demand curves above Q_1 at p_1 and p_2. The maximum amount of hides that would ever be sold is at Q_2, because greater amounts elicit negative marginal revenues from the hide market.

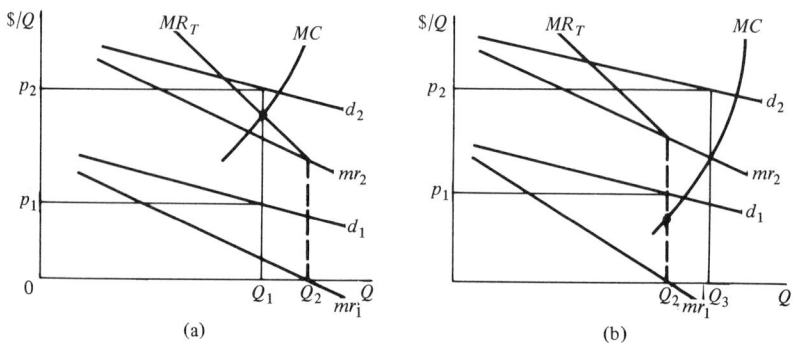

Figure 21-6

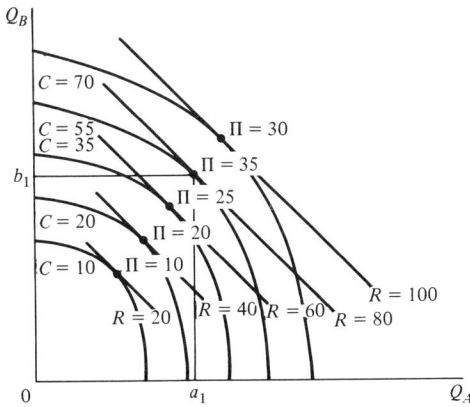

Figure 21-7

If $MR_T = MC$ below the kink in the MR_T curve, say at point 1 in Figure 21-6b, the number of cattle slaughtered, Q_3, is dictated by the intersection of $mr_2 = MC$. Q_3 pairs of sides are sold at p_2. Only Q_2 hides will be sold at p_1; the remaining number, $Q_2 Q_3$, will be destroyed, stored, or used to produce some new product for which there is sufficient demand.

Where products are not substitutable for each other in fixed proportions, the isocost lines are no longer downward-sloping straight lines. If diminishing substitutability is the rule and input prices are relatively constant, the firm's isocost lines, denoted by C's in Figure 21-7, are concave to the origin for products A and B. Assuming constant prices of products A and B, the isorevenue lines, denoted by R's, are linear. The slopes of the C's and R's represent the marginal values associated with the various combinations of products. Tangency points indicate the outputs where marginal costs and revenues are equal for each product and therefore show the optimal product proportions. Profits are maximized where the positive differences between revenues and costs are greatest among the tangent points, which would be at $\Pi = 35$ where $Q_A = a_1$ and $Q_B = b_1$.

Note that in this analysis variable costs can be allocated fairly accurately on economic grounds to the production of A and B. Common costs of production, such as the existing plant and overhead expenses, however, can be allocated only on an arbitrary basis. Use of fully allocated costs for pricing problems of this kind necessarily leads to arbitrary and suboptimal solutions.

21-4 Transfer Pricing

When a large firm separates its operations into divisions or subsidiaries, a problem arises in determining the appropriate price for the intermediate products transferred between them. Setting the values for intrafirm products is referred to as transfer pricing [12]. For example, Western Electric is the manufacturing arm for communications equipment used by the Bell system. Very little of this equipment is sold to other telephone companies, so that a market price cannot be easily ascertained. In the absence of a market price, what is the proper price for products sold to other divisions of the company? The answer is crucial for deciding optimal amounts to be transferred and for determining the overall profits of the firm.

21-4-1 *No external market for the intermediate product*

Consider the case of a firm with two divisions. One arm manufactures an intermediate product that the other modifies and distributes as a final product. Assume for the moment that the distribution division is the sole buyer of the output (intermediate product) of the manufacturing division—a condition that would hold if the product were so specialized that no outside market existed or where a strong technological dependence obtained.[4] The optimum joint output level can be determined with reference to Figure 21-8a. Quantities of both the intermediate and final products are shown on the horizontal axis, with the assumption that the units are commensurate, like pairs of shoes and pounds of copper. Precisely q_1 square feet of specialty shoe material in Figure 21-8a are used to produce q_1 pairs of shoes in Figure 21-8b.

If the *final* product is sold in a competitive market, the distributing division faces a horizontal $AR = MR = P$ curve. Firm profits are maximized at the intersection of this curve with the total-marginal-cost curve MC_T, which was obtained by summing vertically the marginal-cost curves of the manufacturing division MC_m and the additional marginal costs of the distributing division MC_d. Optimum output is at q_1. Profits of the manufacturing division are shown by the upper shaded area and those of the distributing division by the lower.

Centralized management can easily devise a transfer-price rule that would lead

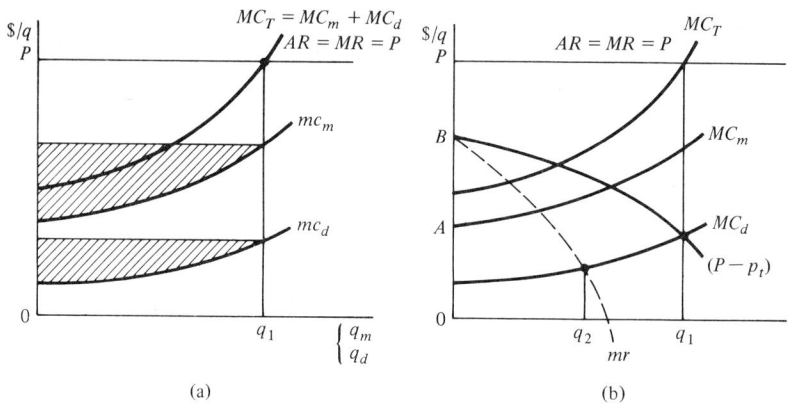

Figure 21-8

[4] An example of technological dependence given by Hirshleifer [12, p. 173] is the exchange of molten iron between two divisions of an integrated steel mill. Here the marginal cost (of cooling, shipping, and reheating the iron) of either division dealing with an outside market is prohibitively high.

each autonomous division to the same solution. The manufacturing division may be required to submit a schedule showing the amounts it would produce for various transfer prices (p_t), which in effect plots out as its MC_m curve. The distributing division can then subtract these values from the corresponding market prices (P) for the final product to obtain an internally derived demand curve $(P - p_t)$ for the services it contributes to the final product, as shown in Figure 21-8b. Note that point B on the new curve is obtained by subtracting the vertical distance OA on the MC_m curve from OP to get PB; other points on $(P - p_t)$ are obtained similarly for other output levels. The output of the distributing division is then set at the intersection of the $(P - p_t)$ curve and its MC_d curve, which is necessarily the same output q_1. Care must be taken, however, to prevent the distributing division from employing a quasi-marginal-revenue curve "MR" in the manner of a monopsonist; this would reduce output to q_2, where the gain in profits of the distributing division is more than offset by losses to the manufacturing division.

If the final product market were not perfectly competitive, the horizontal marginal-revenue curve would be replaced by one with a negative slope. The solution otherwise remains the same, except that overall firm profits are maximized at the output where MC_T is equated with marginal revenue rather than with price.

21-4-2   *Trade with a competitive external market for the intermediate product permitted*

Now turn to the case where each division is free to deal with the outside competitive market for excesses or deficiencies of the intermediate product. In the absence of any technological dependence, both divisions are indifferent to trading within or outside the firm. In Figure 21-9a unit manufacturing costs are measured upward from the horizontal axis, and unit distributing costs are measured downward. If the competitive price for the intermediate product is P_2, then q_2 units should be produced by the manufacturing division; similarly, if the competitive price for the final product is P, the net demand price for the contribution of the distributing division is $(P - P_2)$, at which q_3 units of the final product should be produced. In this case, the distributing division should purchase q_2 units from the manufacturing division and q_2q_3 additional units of the intermediate product from outside suppliers. If a joint output were required, as in the earlier case examined, the output q_1 would prevail where MR_T (equal to the price P in this case) equals the sum of MC_m and MC_d (the vertical distance CE). Joint profits would be lower, since the reduced profits of the distributing division, equal to the lower shaded area, exceeds the increased profits of the manufacturing division, equal to the upper shaded area. This is obviously so since the vertical dimensions of the two areas are equal and the lower area extends farther to the right. If the divisions do not have to produce only a joint output, a transfer price P_2 must be set; otherwise one division (the distribution division in this case) will refuse to trade with the other.

Figure 21-9b shows the solution if the market for the final product is not competitive. The distributing division, facing a sloping demand curve, will simply substitute the lower MR for P in making its output decision. The transfer price

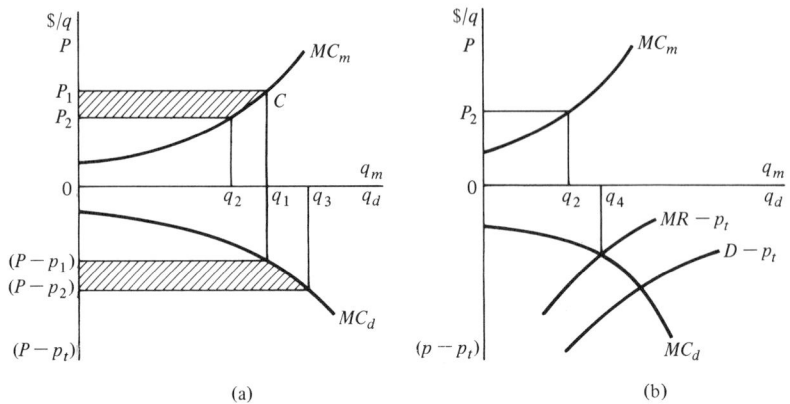

$\$/q$
P
MC_m
P_1
P_2
C
0
q_m
q_2 q_1 q_3 q_d
$(P-p_1)$
$(P-p_2)$
MC_d
$(P-p_t)$

(a)

$\$/q$
P
MC_m
P_2
0
q_m
q_2 q_4 q_d
$MR-p_t$
$D-p_t$
$(p-p_t)$
MC_d

(b)

Figure 21-9

and intermediate units remain the same at P_2 and q_2, respectively, but a smaller quantity equal to q_2q_4 is purchased from external suppliers. Thus, as a general rule, the transfer price should be set equal to the market price when the intermediate market is competitive, regardless of the degree of competitiveness of the market for the final product.

21-4-3   *Transfer under conditions of an imperfect intermediate market*

If the manufacturing division is to some degree a monopolist, it faces a sloping demand curve for sales to outside customers. To simplify the analysis, demand independence is assumed, by which sales of the manufacturing division in either internal or external segments of the market for the intermediate product do not diminish the demand for the distributing division's final product. This would be the case where shoes are sold in the domestic market only through independent distributors and in the foreign market only by the distributing division. Also, a copper manufacturer might use copper in another division to fabricate wire internally but sell copper externally to producers of pots, pans, and toys. With these assumptions, the analysis becomes similar to that employed in third-degree price discrimination.

Figure 21-10a shows the demand and marginal-revenue curves for the intermediate product of the manufacturing division that exists outside the firm. Figure 21-10b shows jointly the demand D and marginal revenue MR_T curves for the final product sold by the distributing division and the net marginal revenue MR_n curve derived by subtracting the marginal-cost curve for the distributing division MC_d from the MR_T curve. Figure 21-10c shows the marginal-cost curve for the manufacturing divison MC_m and the composite marginal-revenue curve for both divisions MR_{m+n}. To be strictly correct, the MR_{m+n} should be derived from a composite demand curve for both divisions, but it is derived in practice with no real error by horizontal summation of the MR_m and MR_n curves. Total output of the manufacturing divisions that maximizes the

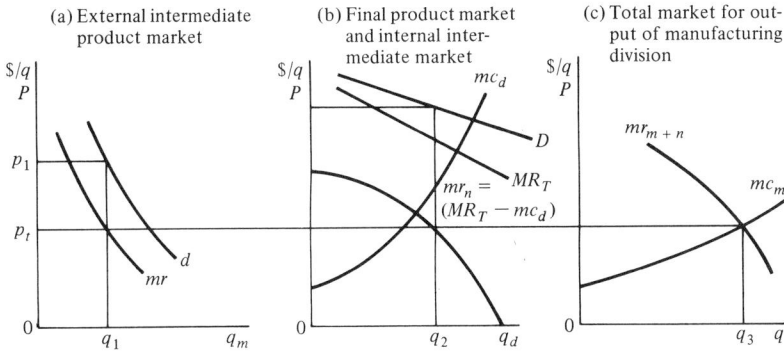

Figure 21-10

firm's overall profits is determined at q_3 by the intersection of the MC_m and MR_{m+n} curves. Output is allocated in amounts q_2 to the distributing divisions and q_1 to the external market for the intermediate product, for which a transfer price of p_t and a market price of P_1 are charged. The distributing division pays p_t for the intermediate product and sells the final product at price P. The general rule is that the firm equates joint marginal cost with marginal revenues in each market.

21-5 Pricing of New Products

When a product is first introduced to the market, there is little information, other than from similar products or uses, by which to judge its demand. Joel Dean [6, pp. 419–424] distinguishes two policies for pioneer pricing: skimming and penetration. Where the product performs a service quite different from accepted ways, a skimming policy of charging a high initial price of three or four times the factory door price, accompanied by large promotional outlays and followed by successive reductions of prices and promotions, is sometimes success-ful. The reasons for success are several. In early stages of market development, price elasticity of demand is usually inelastic because of consumer unfamiliarity with the product, cross-elasticities are usually lower because of an absence of close rivals, and promotional elasticity is high while the newness lasts. Successive price reductions skim more of the cream of consumer surplus as increasingly more elastic segments of the market are tapped. In addition, high introductory prices provide the firm with information useful for determining if the product has the potential of covering production and selling costs, so that products demonstrating little promise of success can be withdrawn before too large an investment has been made. Finally, high initial prices are helpful for recouping development costs and for financing additional expenditures where risks are high and other sources of capital are scarce and expensive.

Penetration pricing follows a reverse policy of charging low initial prices to encourage early penetration of mass markets. Quick sales to customers with relatively low incomes are obtained with an eye to maximizing long-run, rather than short-run, profits. Conditions for success include a high short-run price elasticity of demand; economies of large-scale production where demand elasticity is not high; easy acceptance of the product in consumers' expenditure patterns; and discouragement of potential competitors where entry is easy, the potential market quite large, and early market entrenchment is desirable to establish brand preference.

Numerous examples and practical considerations of business pricing are presented in Joel Dean's pioneering work in the field of managerial economics. They should be studied carefully by business people faced with the responsibility of pricing their firms' products.

Questions and Problems

21-1. Define each of the following terms and list the conditions under which its use can increase the firm's profits:
    a. first-degree price discrimination
    b. second-degree price discrimination
    c. third-degree price discrimination
    d. selective first-degree price discrimination
    e. markup pricing
    f. multiple-product pricing
    g. transfer pricing
    h. skimming
    i. penetration

21-2. Criticize the following statement: "In third-degree price discrimination the higher price will be charged in the market with the lowest overall elasticity."

21-3. Determine prices, outputs, marginal revenues, and profits for a monopolist selling in two markets for the following demand and cost functions under third-degree price discrimination and under a single price charged in both markets.

    a. $P_1 = 16 - 2Q_1, P_2 = 24 - 3Q_2, C = 3 + Q_1 + Q_2$
    b. $P_1 = 4 - Q_1, P_2 = 15 - 5Q_2, C = 2 + Q_1 + Q_2$

21-4. Compare profits, outputs, and prices using the following demand and total-cost functions for the monopolist practicing first-degree price discrimination and selective first-degree price discrimination.

    a. $P = 220 - 10Q, C = 100Q - 5Q^2 + Q^3$ (full discrimination)
                           $C_s = 100Q - 10Q^2 + Q^3$ (selective discrimination)
    b. $P = 50 - 5Q,\quad C = 44Q + 2Q^2 + Q^3$ (full discrimination)
                           $C_s = 44Q - 5Q^2 + Q^3$ (selective discrimination)

References

1. William J. Baumol. *Economic Theory and Operations Analysis.* 3d ed. (Englewood Cliffs, N.J.: Prentice-Hall, 1972), ch. 14.

2. Kenneth Boulding. *Economic Analysis*. Vol. I. *Microeconomics*. 4th ed. (New York: Harper & Row, 1966), pp. 446–453.

3. Eugene F. Brigham and James L. Pappas. *Managerial Economics* (Hinsdale, Ill.: Dryden Press, 1972), ch. 11.

4. Eli W. Clemens. "Price Discrimination and the Multiple-Product Firm." *Review of Economics Studies* 19 (1950–1951): 1–11. Reprinted in American Economic Association. *Readings in Industrial Organization and Public Policy* (Homewood, Ill.: Richard D. Irwin, 1959), pp. 262–276.

5. Robert W. Clower and John F. Due. *Microeconomics* (Homewood, Ill.: Richard D. Irwin, 1972), pp. 189–194.

6. Joel Dean. *Managerial Economics* (New York: Prentice-Hall, 1951), ch. 7–9.

7. James S. Earley. "Managerial Policies of 'Excellently Managed' Companies." *American Economic Review* 96 (March 1956): 44–70. Reprinted in part in Donald S. Watson. *Price Theory in Action*. 3d ed. (Boston: Houghton Mifflin, 1973), pp. 268–273.

8. Edmond S. Harris. *Classified Pricing of Milk—Some Theoretical Aspects*. U.S. Department of Agriculture. Tech. Bull. No. 1184 (1958), pp. 1–106.

9. W. W. Haynes. *Managerial Economics: Analysis and Cases*. Rev. ed. (Austin, Tex.: Business Publications, 1969), ch. 7–8, pp. 319–500. This reference provides more than 100 pages of case studies involving pricing practices.

10. James M. Henderson and Richard E. Quandt. *Microeconomic Theory—A Mathematical Approach*. 2d ed. (New York: McGraw-Hill, 1971), pp. 215–218.

11. Jack Hirshleifer. "Economics of the Divisionalized Firm." *Journal of Business* 30 (January 1957): 96–108.

12. ———. "On the Economics of Transfer Pricing." *Journal of Business* 29 (July 1956): 172–184.

13. A. D. H. Kaplan, Joel B. Dirlam, and Robert F. Lanzillotti. *Pricing in Big Business—A Case Approach* (Washington, D.C.: Brookings Institution, 1958), pp. 1–344.

14. Fritz Machlup. "Characteristics and Types of Price Discrimination." In National Bureau of Economic Research. *Business Concentration and Price Policy* (Princeton, N.J.: Princeton University Press, 1955), pp. 397–435. Followed by comments of Ronald Coase and A. G. Papandreou, pp. 435–440.

15. Terutomo Ozawa. "Intermarket Price Discrimination Under Pure Monopoly: A Supplementary Note." *Nebraska Journal of Economics and Business* 10 (Winter 1971): 55–59.

16. Almarin Phillips and Oliver E. Williamson (eds.). *Prices: Issues in Theory, Practice and Public Policy* (Philadelphia: University of Pennsylvania Press, 1967).

17. A. C. Pigou. *The Economics of Welfare*. 4th ed. (London: Macmillan, 1932), ch. 17.

18. Joan Robinson. *The Economics of Imperfect Competition* (London: Macmillan, 1933), ch. 15–16.

19. Donald S. Watson. *Price Theory and Its Uses*. 3d ed. (Boston: Houghton Mifflin, 1972), ch. 17.

20. Daniel L. White and Michael C. Walker. "First Degree Price Discrimination and Profit Maximization." *Southern Economic Journal* 40 (October 1973): 313–318.

22 Welfare Analysis

Welfare economics is concerned with decisions about which changes in the wealth holdings of individuals and groups are good or bad for society. It tries to identify the optimal production, exchange, and transfer of resources for the betterment of mankind. Ethical decisions are clearly a part of this activity, for assumptions must be made concerning the tastes of every individual involved. Even the assumption of more goods being better than less for the laboring class cannot be taken for granted, especially if this would extend the length of the working day. Since preferences differ from one individual to the next and are interrelated, there is no sure way of knowing that another person will be pleased and better off by a change. It is insufficient to do unto others as you would have them to do unto you, because they may have different tastes. In order to do good for others one must first have a thorough understanding of their value systems. This chapter discusses several well-known criteria used by economists to deal with the complex and unavoidable value judgments that are basic to every economic policy decision; a graphical model of welfare maximization; and some of the problems of group decision making.

22-1 Criteria for Making Welfare Judgments

As individuals, groups, firms, and governments pursue their goals, they make innovations and cause redistributions of wealth and incomes. In attempting to determine when such changes are beneficial to the community as a whole, various writers have proposed that certain criteria be applied.

22-1-1 *Pareto's criterion*

The Italian economist Vilfredo Pareto, writing in the early 1900s, proposed the now standard tool of welfare economics, which is associated with the benefits accruing to a perfectly competitive economy where individuals act to maximize their utilities and firms their profits. Stated in its simplest terms, the Pareto criterion holds that a change produces an improvement in society's welfare as long as someone is made better off and no one else is made worse off in the process.

348

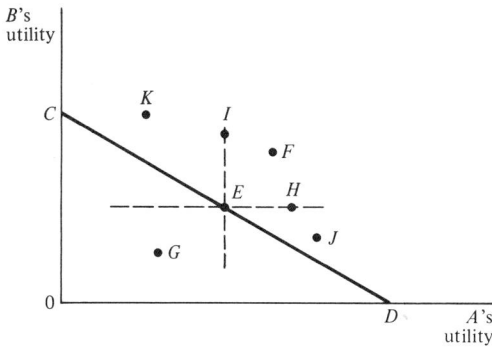

Figure 22-1

Each party is assumed to evaluate his own loss or gain to the best of his ability and to convey this information truthfully to the decision body.

Consider the two-person utility-possibility curve shown in Figure 22-1, in which A's utility is on the horizontal axis and B's on the vertical. The line CD illustrates the different combinations of their utilities associated with various distributions of some given amount of resources. Assuming that A is oblivious to B's wishes, he prefers point D to all others along CD; similarly, B prefers points closest to C. From a given endowment at point E, an economic change causing a movement to some point F above and to the right of point E is an improvement for each person. The change meets the Pareto criterion and therefore should be approved. In cases so clearly defined, there can be no doubt that welfare has been improved. Similar reasoning leads to a rejection of a project causing a movement to some point G below and to the left of point E. Projects causing a movement to points H and I would presumably also be adopted, since one person gains while the other is unharmed, while those causing movements to points J and K would be rejected, since one or the other person is made worse off.

Projects entailing movements to points J and K can possibly be made acceptable by appropriate modification or compensation to gain approval of the potentially harmed person. The gainer might somehow compensate or bribe the loser and still come out ahead; that is, perhaps points J and K could be moved to some point F, or at least to H or I, by compensating the injured person. Points J and K thus have potential for meeting the Pareto criterion but are not acceptable as such.

22-1-2   *The Kaldor-Hicks criterion*

Nicholas Kaldor and John Hicks proposed a criterion for dealing with cases exemplified by points J and K, in which there is only potential improvement under the Pareto criterion. They claimed, in effect, that if those who would gain from a change evaluated their gains at a higher value than those who would lose evaluated their losses, the change should be judged beneficial. There is no requirement that the gainers actually compensate the losers, only that the gainers gain more than the losers lose. Kaldor and Hicks claimed that a change shifting

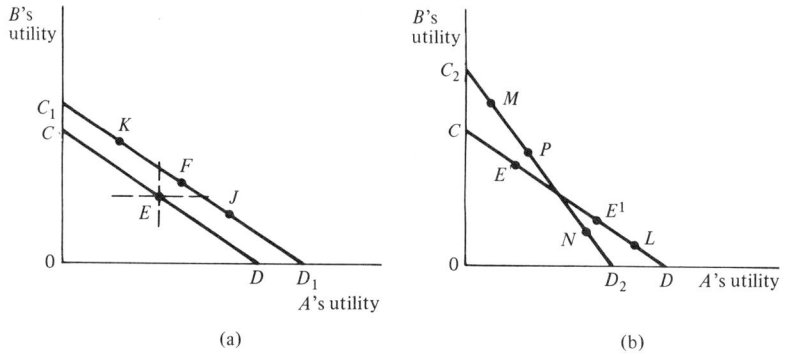

Figure 22-2

the utility-possibility curve outward from the origin from CD to C_1D_1 in Figure 22-2a would produce a gain to society regardless of the point adopted on the new curve. Points F, J, and K meet the criterion. All points on the utility-possibility curve are assumed to be equally desirable. Kaldor's utility-possibility curves are also taken to represent society's indifference curves, and the higher the level the better.

A conflict arises in applying the Kaldor-Hicks criterion when the new utility-possibility curve intersects the old one, as in Figure 22-2b. A movement from point E on the old curve CD to a point M on the new curve C_2D_2 involves an improvement in welfare, since C_2D_2 has some points, like P, that are clearly superior to point E. However, CD also has some points, like E', that are clearly superior to points like N on C_2D_2. Therefore, the situation can arise where a change can be judged to be an improvement and an elimination of the change can also be judged to be an improvement. Stated otherwise, the gainers can bribe the losers to make a change and then the gainers can also bribe the losers to give up the change.

For example, suppose the construction of a new bridge would shift the utility-possibility curve from CD to C_2D_2. If the initial endowment were at point E, then a movement to point M is a potential improvement, because B could compensate A for his loss, causing a movement to point P, which is clearly in their mutual best interests. If the compensation actually took place, there would be no problem; but there is no need for this under the Kaldor-Hicks criterion. It is therefore possible after construction of the bridge that A and B could find themselves at point N (to A's delight and B's dismay if they were previously at point E). However, it is still possible that they would both prefer to have the bridge removed. If destruction of the bridge were judged to produce a movement from point N to point L, A could bribe B to accept point E', which is clearly better for both. The net result of building and tearing down the bridge is a movement from E to E', to A's benefit and B's loss.

22-1-3   *Scitovsky's double criterion*

In an attempt to deal with the potentially conflicting decisions made in applying the Kaldor criterion, Tibor Scitovsky [35] proposed the double criterion that a change is an improvement only if it passes the Kaldor-Hicks criterion and if a change back does not also meet the Kaldor-Hicks criterion. This would prevent one from making a welfare judgment in cases where the old and new utility-possibility curves intersect each other; it would confine welfare decisions to cases depicted by Figure 22-2a. Scitovsky's recommendation is well taken, because under the Kaldor-Hicks construction, intersecting utility-possibility curves also imply intersecting social-difference curves, which violates the transitivity assumption discussed later in this chapter.

22-1-4   *The Bergson-Samuelson criterion*

Bergson suggested that those in the position to make judgments involving the welfare of different parties should form an *explicit* set of value judgments that can be used by analysts in evaluating the situation. Legislators, government authorities, labor leaders, economists, and business executives should make their opinions known, so that others will be able to register approval or opposition. Such information is used to construct an indifference map for the community, shown as U_1, U_2, and U_3 in Figure 22-3 (discussed further later). By using such a map, a judgment can be made as to whether point S lies on a higher social-indifference curve than point R does.

While no kit of instructions is given as to how welfare judgments are to be collected, the Bergson-Samuelson criterion provides a useful frame of reference. Judgments made explicit are more accessible to objective analysis than those left implicit, especially since implicit judgments are often found to be at variance with their originator's intentions. Voters are given an opportunity to accept or reject the statement of a representative presuming to speak for them. Decisions are made consciously and openly, accounting for much of the appeal of this criterion.

All of these criteria, even Pareto's, are considered less than ideal, because they all assume that interpersonal comparisons of utility are possible and that the initial distribution of income and wealth was equitable. In regard to the first, almost everyone is aware that other people's tastes are different from their own.

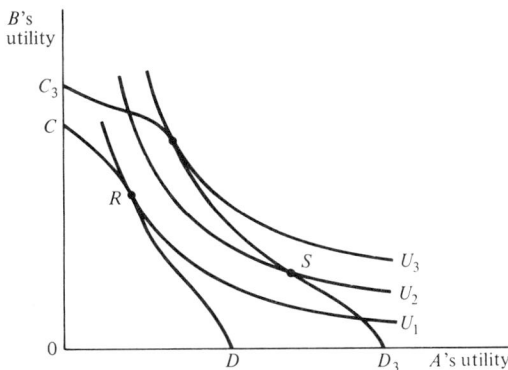

Figure 22-3

The utility one person places upon an item of food, clothing, or recreation may be quite different from another's, as suggested by the modern advice "do whatever turns you on." Income and wealth are commonly referenced not only to one commodity possessing different amounts of utility for different persons but to a composite index of commodities referred to as money. Most economic analysis assumes either a constant or diminishing marginal utility of money. But this is pure conjecture when applied to specific individuals and groups, because no one can fully assume the identity of another. No one can say positively that the utility of an additional dollar is of equal or less value to a rich man than to a poor man. It simply cannot be concluded from unbiased analysis because their tastes and capacities for enjoyment are subject to wide variations.

In regard to an equitable initial distribution of wealth and income, most informed observers would agree that individual endowments result from inheritance, luck, and effort, probably in that order. Few would deny that a person born to intelligent and wealthy parents has a decided advantage over those without. Perhaps no amount of effort by two hypothetical individuals would be sufficient to close the gap in their lifetimes. Analysis that disregards such inequalities simply cannot say with certainty that a change moves toward the ideal for society, especially when it is those with the edge in society who supply the information, make the comparisons, and decide the changes. (In no way are these statements intended as encouragement for a revolution or for turning economic and political decisions of society over to those who happen to be on the least advantageous levels; this would probably by the worst for all concerned.[1] They only caution those who might believe ultimate statements on economic questions can be made where matters of equity are important. Equity considerations are invariably matters of opinion, an awareness of which is useful in helping one avoid making indefensible statements stemming from personal "convictions" based upon incomplete knowledge.)

22-2 A Model of Welfare Maximization

The problem of society in determining the best allocation of resources and distribution of income can be discussed in the skeleton form of two-dimensional diagrams encompassing two inputs, outputs, and persons [2]. More elaborate and rigorous mathematical models are available in the literature that support the general conclusions of this introductory approach, but space limitations prevent discussion of them in this book. In the model presented here, Frank and Hank use their labor and land to produce beans and machines. Frank the farmer works well with the soil, while Hank has a way with gadgets and gimmicks. Both have read Adam Smith's *Wealth of Nations* and are aware of the advantages of specialization according to comparative advantage and trade.

Their first problem, as they see it, is to determine how to use their labor and land resources most efficiently to produce beans (symbolizing food) and machines

---

[1] For those who would like to pursue some fascinating literature on this subject, the works of Frank H. Knight, deceased Chicago economist, are highly recommended. The reader should probably start with Don Patinkin's "Frank Knight as Teacher," *American Economic Review* 63 (December 1973): 787–810, which provides a comprehensive bibliography of Knight's writings.

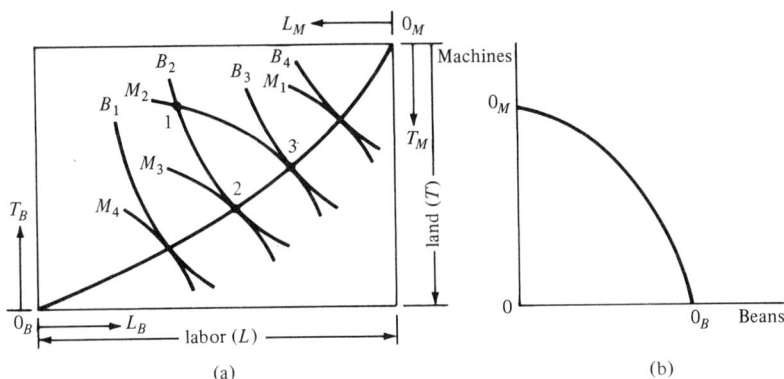

Figure 22-4

(symbolizing all other things they need and want). That is, they wish to find their production efficiency locus of points where increased output of one good requires a cutback in the other. Such a locus is shown in Figure 22-4a as the curve $O_B O_M$, derived by connecting the points of tangency of the bean and machine isoquants. Note that the bean isoquants emanate from, and are convex to, the bean origin in the lower left corner of the Edgeworth-Bowley box diagram, and the machine isoquants are referenced to the machine origin in the upper right corner. The dimensions of the box are given by the sums of their limited resource endowments, with labor (L) on the horizontal side and land (denoted by T for *terra* to avoid confusion with L for labor) on the vertical. Since the slope of the bean isoquants indicates the marginal rate of substitution (MRS) of labor and land in the production of beans, and the machine isoquants show the same MRS for the production of machines, it follows that the MRS are equal where the isoquants are tangent. The production efficiency criterion is that the MRS of labor for land in the production of beans equals the MRS of labor for land in the production of machines:[2]

$$(MRS_{LT})_{\text{beans}} = (MRS_{LT})_{\text{machines}} \tag{1}$$

[2] Points on the production-efficiency curve can also be given in terms of marginal productivities,

$$\left(\frac{MPP_L}{MPP_T}\right)_{\text{beans}} = \left(\frac{MPP_L}{MPP_T}\right)_{\text{machines}}$$

since the slopes of the isoquants are also ratios of marginal products. A third form of the same criterion is sometimes shown in terms of partial derivatives as

$$\frac{\partial L_B}{\partial T_B} = \frac{\partial L_M}{\partial T_M}$$

where

$$\frac{\partial L_B}{\partial T_B} = \frac{\partial B}{\partial T_B} \div \frac{\partial B}{\partial L_B} \quad \text{and} \quad \frac{\partial L_M}{\partial T_M} = \frac{\partial M}{\partial T_M} \div \frac{\partial M}{\partial L_M}$$

The other rules that follow can be similarly shown.

Any point on the production-efficiency curve is efficient because at any point 1 not on the curve in Figure 22-4a, where the isoquant slopes are not equal, more units of one product can be had without giving up units of the other by moving to points toward the efficiency curve in the range between points 2 and 3. For example, movement from point 1 to point 2 along isoquant B_2 would permit the production of machines to be increased from the M_2 to M_3 isoquant levels. Also, once on the curve at some point 2, it is not possible to gain more of one product by moving to any other point, like 3, without giving up some of the other.

Once the production-efficiency curve $O_B O_M$ has been plotted, points on it can be transferred to a grid having products rather than resources on its axes, as shown in Figure 22-4b. The new curve is a *production-possibilities curve* indicating the various maximum combinations of beans and machines that Frank and Hank are capable of creating. Its slope is called the marginal rate of (technical) transformation (MRT), indicating how many fewer machines can be made when land and labor are transferred to the production of one more unit of beans. In short, the slope is the marginal cost in terms of machines forgone of producing another unit (say 100 bushels) of beans.

The next problem Frank and Hank have is to determine which point on the production-possibilities curve is "best." The relative amounts of beans and machines to be produced must somehow be related to relative demands for them as consumer goods. This relation can be established in theory as follows. (Note to the student: Don't be too anxious for the answer to pop out immediately. Have patience to see the answer gradually emerge.) Pick any point C on the productive-possibilities curve reproduced in Figure 22-5. Draw horizontal and vertical lines to the axes, forming another box to be filled with different contents from the one of Figure 22-4a. This time the size of the box is dictated by the amounts of beans and machines that are produced. Within the box are constructed the indifference maps (not isoquants) for Frank, with his origin in the lower left corner and Hank's in the upper right. The exchange-efficiency, or contract, curve is constructed

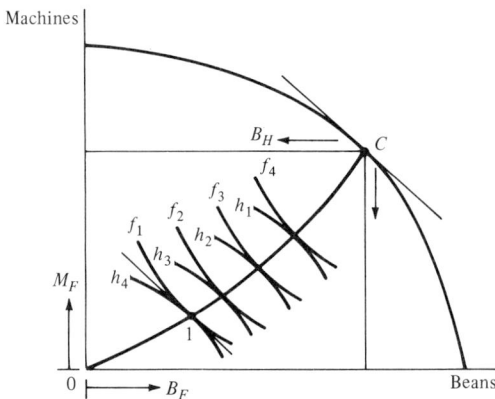

Figure 22-5

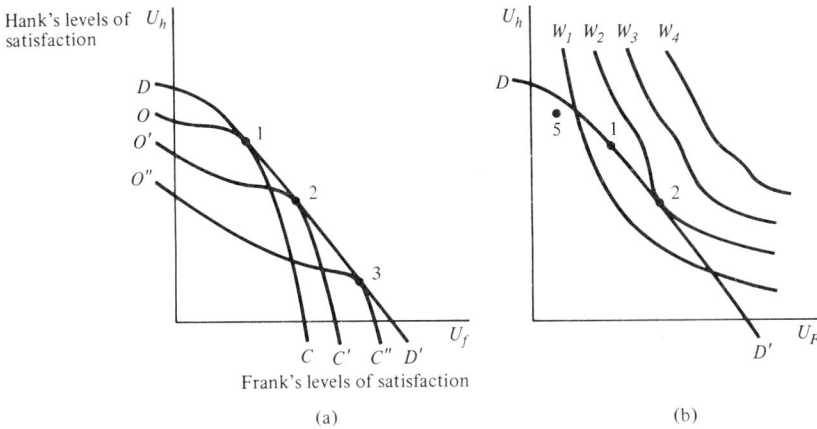

Figure 22-6

by connecting the tangency points of the indifference curves. The curve indicates efficiency in the sense that at points off the curve it is possible, through exchanging goods, for one person to gain in satisfaction without the other being harmed—recall the Pareto criterion. There is, of course, no guarantee that the persons will necessarily move to the contract curve; there is only the potential for mutual gain if they do. Fear of upsetting the existing arrangement and starting a trade war could reasonably prevent their making a trade that would put them on the contract curve.

The levels of satisfaction of Frank and Hank along the contract curve are measured by the levels of their respective indifference curves. Such maximal levels and combinations can be used to plot a utility curve, shown in Figure 22-6a, all points on which are associated only with point C in Figure 22-5. Each *point C* in output space is said to map into a *line* in indifference (or utility) space. (One can also say that each *point* in utility space maps into a *line* found in output space, indicating that many bean-machine combinations can possibly satisfy a specified combination of utilities for Frank and Hank.) The different satisfactions naturally depend upon the manner in which the goods are distributed between Frank and Hank. Other utility-combination lines can be constructed in Figure 22-6a by selecting additional points like C on the production-possibility curve of Figure 22-5, forming other interior box diagrams, constructing new contract curves, and plotting the associated curves also in Figure 22-6a. The envelope curve denoted as DD' of all of the utility-combination curves obtained in this manner is called the *grand utility-possibility frontier*, representing society's maximum set of utility possibilities derived from the most efficient use of its resources.

A shorter way of plotting the frontier would have been to plot only the points on the contract curves at which the slopes of the indifference curves were tangent to the C points on the production-possibilities curve, for instance, point 1 in Figure 22-5, at which the slopes of f_1 and h_4 are equal to that at point C. This establishes another welfare-efficiency rule, that the MRS of beans for machines for each person be equal to the MRT:

$$(MRS_{BM})_{\text{Frank}} = (MRS_{BM})_{\text{Hank}} = MRT_{BM} \tag{2}$$

Point 1 in Figure 22-5 corresponds to point 1 in Figure 22-6a. It should be mentioned, however, that point 1 is not necessarily unique; there may be many such points along the contract curve with equal slopes, requiring that a curve such as OC in Figure 22-6a have multiple tangencies to DD'.

Frank and Hank are now confronted with the complex and unavoidable problem of deciding how to split up the pie; that is, how to determine the distribution of beans and machines that is ideal. Which point (1, 2, or 3) on the Pareto-efficient grand utility-possibility frontier is to be selected? Ultimate value judgments are necessary. Somehow, society must impose its preference, perhaps in the form of a Bergson-Samuelson social welfare (W) function (society's indifference map), which can be superimposed on the grand utility frontier, as shown in Figure 22-6b. Maximum " welfare " is on the highest indifference contour, W_2, touched by the frontier DD' as a unique point 2, referred to as the *point of constrained bliss*. Thus, to attain bliss, it is necessary but not sufficient that the Pareto criterion be met—necessary because production and commodity distribution must be efficient for society to be on its utility-possibility frontier, but not sufficient, because any point on that frontier meets the Pareto criterion. Sufficiency requires a value judgment by society.

Furthermore, it is indefensible to claim that any efficient point on the frontier is better from everyone's point of view than all inefficient points below DD'. For example, Hank would prefer to move in Figure 22-6b from point 1 to point 5 rather than to a point that is on a higher social-indifference curve, because his utility would be greater. In any event, the final rule for welfare maximization to be gleaned from this model is that the slope of society's utility frontier should be equal to the slope of its welfare contour at the point where the curves touch. Otherwise stated, the MRS of Frank's utility for Hank's equals society's MRS welfare judgments as to the relative importance of Frank's and Hank's utilities:

$$MRS_{U_F U_H} = MRS_{W_F W_H} \tag{3}$$

(Although we cannot discuss the implications of this model further here, there is much more of great interest presented in Francis M. Bator's synthesizing article [2], of which we summarized only the first section. Interested students should read the rest of Bator's article.) The simplifying assumptions upon which this model is based are the following:

1. The two inputs are homogeneous, perfectly divisible, and inelastically supplied.

2. The two production functions exhibit diminishing returns to the variable factor, constant returns to scale, and are smooth of curvature.

3. The two ordinal preference functions are smooth indifference curves that are convex to the origin, reflecting consistent and unambiguous preferences in which satiation and externalities are ruled out.

4. A social-welfare function can be constructed having a unique preference ordering based upon individual preferences and establishing the relative "deservingness" for each.

22-3 Group Decisions

In a democratic society, business and economic decisions are typically made by groups [1], [3], [4]. Choices among alternatives are made by boards, committees commissions, legislatures, referendums, and elections. Each member of the decision group presumably considers the available information and votes for the proposed alternative he or she believes is best. The one with the most votes is adopted by the group. When there is a choice between only two alternatives, perhaps an accept or reject proposition, the one with the most votes is unambiguously the will of the majority. When the alternatives are greater than two, the opportunity for inconsistencies is present, as demonstrated by the *paradox of voting*, described as follows.

Suppose three people called John, Jake, and Judy vote on alternatives A, B, and C, as shown in the box in Figure 22-7. They are instructed to write a 3 for their first choice, a 2 for their second, and a 1 for their third. John prefers A to B, and B to C; if John's choices are consistent (transitive), he also prefers A to C. Jake prefers B to C, C to A, and B to A. Judy prefers C to A, A to B, and C to B. To their possible bewilderment, they find a majority (John and Judy) prefer A to B, a majority (John and Jake) prefer B to C, and another majority (Jake and Judy) prefer C to A. Since the group prefers A to B to C, but *also* C to A, their decision is intransitive; a rationally consistent group would have preferred A to C. Thus, we discover that a group of individuals who are transitive in their decision making will not necessarily produce a group decision that is transitive.

In welfare economics an implication of the *paradox of voting* is that statements about the superiority of one social state over another cannot be made unequivocably when based upon the method of majority choice. This is all the more convincing when one recognizes that majority choice itself is a value judgment based upon the concept of one vote per person. Even if individual utilities could be measured and summed to produce a social-welfare function, there is no objective rule of equity that tells how utilities are to be weighted. Perhaps the utility summation should be of products of individual utilities, or of their logarithms, or of sums of two individuals at a time, rather than of simple absolute amounts.

When business decisions are based upon the votes of groups, problems can arise where inconsistent decisions for the firm may not further its stated goals or help its public image among those who look for the same consistency in business (and government) organizations that they regard as virtue in themselves and other individuals. It may be fortunate for this reason that most business organizations do not function as democracies. Most committee decisions are advisory, and the final decision is left to the top executive. In this way the integrity of the

	A	B	C
John	3	2	1
Jake	1	3	2
Judy	2	1	3

Figure 22-7

institution is preserved, assuming he or she is more consistent than groups in making decisions. The boss, upon receiving a committee report displaying the voting paradox or some other tied vote, must make the decision personally; ask the members to reconsider their decision, thereby playing a waiting game until the need for a decision had passed or the member with the least stamina yields to those with more strength or determination; appoint a new member to the committee; or turn the problem over to an entirely different group. Where decisions must be made quickly, dictatorship is to be preferred to democracy.

Kenneth J. Arrow, who won a Nobel Prize in 1972, is credited with elucidating the voting paradox and drawing attention to three other plausible criteria for social decisions. One, which will be called the second criterion, is the *condition of citizens' sovereignty*, which requires that there be no interference or undue influence by outside parties on the members' decision. Arrow's third criterion is that the group's ranking of alternatives remain unchanged as a result of a voter's increased preference (but not ranking) of one of the alternatives. This means that other members of the group would not change their votes in opposition to one of the alternatives just because a member came to like it better. Such a possibility could arise from acts of competitiveness, jealousy, or maliciousness of one voter toward another.

Arrow's fourth criterion, called *the independence of irrelevant alternatives*, comes into play when one of the alternatives is removed (say, a candidate drops out of a race because of death or some other cause). The fact that one of the alternatives is no longer present should have no influence on the group's ranking of the others. The following case would not meet this criterion. Suppose, as a continuation of the previous example, that John, Jake, and Judy rank four alternatives, as shown in Figure 22-8a, giving the higher numbers to preferred candidates; *A* receives the most points and is the undisputed winner over *B*, *C*, and *D*. Now assume that *B* drops out of the running and that another vote is taken, the results of which are shown in Figure 22-8b. This time, with no changes in ordering by the voters, *A* and *C* are tied with seven points each because of elimination of the irrelevant alternative *B*. This criterion appears to hold, in effect, that candidates entering an election with no hope of winning themselves should not be able to influence the election, a requirement that may not be socially desirable, because a third political party derives much of its power in promoting minority interests from such a possibility.

The most immediate objection to Arrow's criteria for democratic decisions is that they fail to take into account the intensity of feelings toward the alternatives. Those who have property near a proposed bridge may intensely desire its con-

	A	B	C	D
John	4	3	2	1
Jake	4	3	2	1
Judy	2	1	4	3
Total points	10	7	8	5

(a)

	A	C	D
John	3	2	1
Jake	3	2	1
Judy	1	3	2
Total points	7	7	4

(b)

Figure 22-8

struction, while large numbers living in other areas are nearly indifferent and may vote against a local government issue of bonds to finance the project. The bridge would not be built under Arrow's criteria because of a lack of votes, but it may be in society's best interest to do so anyway. The same may be said of allocating resources to search for cures for rare but dangerous diseases that would otherwise have been spent on memorial statues and more aesthetic public buildings. Compassion aside, the last two alternatives might receive more votes, but the disease cure could be more important to society, because those who would benefit from it need it so desperately.

Questions and Problems

22-1. Define and explain the following:
- *a.* Pareto's criterion
- *b.* Kaldor-Hicks criterion
- *c.* Scitovsky's criterion
- *d.* Bergson-Samuelson criterion
- *e.* social-welfare function
- *f.* production-possibility curve
- *g.* Edgeworth-Bowley box diagram
- *h.* production-efficiency curve
- *i.* exchange-efficiency curve
- *j.* grand utility-possibility frontier
- *k.* constrained bliss
- *l.* paradox of voting
- *m.* intransitivity
- *n.* condition of citizens' sovereignty
- *o.* malicious voting
- *p.* independence of irrelevant alternatives

22-2. Which welfare criterion was being employed when President John F. Kennedy stated publicly that he felt no one should have to work for less than $1.60 per hour?

22-3. In reference to Figure 22-9, answer the following questions:
- *a.* Why is point 1 thought to be inferior to some points on the exchange-efficiency curve?

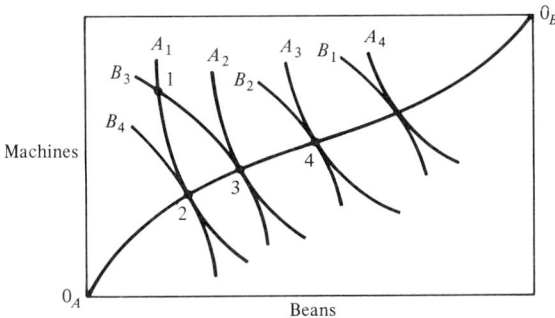

Figure 22-9

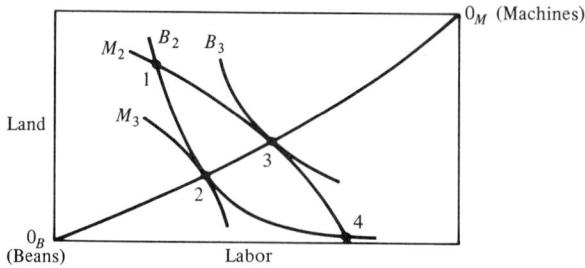

Figure 22-10

b. Would a movement from point 1 to point 2 satisfy the Pareto criterion? from point 2 to point 3? Why?

d. What determines the size of the box?

22-4. In reference to Figure 22-10, answer the following questions:

  a. In moving from point 1 toward the production-efficiency curve $O_B O_M$, is a point half way between points 2 and 3 preferred to both points 2 and 3?

  b. In terms of marginal rates of substitution, what is unique about point 2?

  c. In what way are points 1 and 4 related?

22-5. Matthew, Mark, and Luke are equal partners in a firm. They are trying to decide on one of three towns in which to open a new office: Eureka, El Dorado, and Emporia. On the basis of their votes as recorded in Figure 22-11, which town will be selected? Why?

	Eureka	El Dorado	Emporia
Matthew	3	1	2
Mark	1	2	3
Luke	2	3	1

Figure 22-11

References

1. Kenneth J. Arrow. *Social Choice and Individual Values* (New York: Wiley, 1951; 2d ed., 1963), ch. 1–3. Reprinted in Alfred N. Page [25, pp. 423–454].

2. Francis M. Bator. "The Simple Analytics of Welfare Maximization." *American Economic Review* 47 (March 1957): 22–59.

3. William J. Baumol. *Economic Theory and Operations Analysis.* 3d ed. (Englewood Cliffs, N.J.: Prentice-Hall, 1972), ch. 16.

4. ———. *Welfare Economics and the Theory of the State* (London: Longmans, Green, 1952); 2d ed. (Cambridge, Mass.: Harvard University Press, 1965), ch. 10. Reprinted in Alfred N. Page [25, pp. 363–374].

5. Abram Bergson. "A Reformation of Certain Aspects of Welfare Economics." *Quarterly Journal of Economics* 52 (February 1938): 310–334. A slightly edited version is found in his *Essays in Normative Economics* (Cambridge, Mass.: Harvard University Press, 1966) and also in Alfred N. Page [25, pp. 402–422].

6. Julian H. Blau. "The Existence of Social Welfare Functions." *Econometrica* 25 (April 1957): 302–313.

7. K. E. Boulding. "Welfare Economics." In American Economics Association. *A Survey of Contemporary Economics*. Vol. II. ed. B. F. Haley (Homewood, Ill.: Richard D. Irwin, 1952), pp. 1–34. Followed by comments of Melvin W. Reder and Paul A. Samuelson, pp. 34–38.

8. A. L. Bowley. *The Mathematical Groundwork of Economics* (Oxford: Clarendon Press, 1924).

9. Robert Dorfman, Paul A. Samuelson, and Robert M. Solow. *Linear Programming and Economic Analysis* (New York: McGraw-Hill, 1958), ch. 14.

10. F. Y. Edgeworth. *Mathematical Physics* (London: Kegan Paul, 1881).

11. ———. "Theory of International Values." *Economic Journal* (March, September, December, 1894).

12. Leo A. Goodman and Harry Markowitz. "Social Welfare Functions Based on Individual Rankings." *American Journal of Sociology* 58 (November 1952): 257–262.

13. J. de V. Graff. *Theoretical Welfare Economics* (New York: Cambridge University Press, 1957).

14. John R. Hicks. "Foundations of Welfare Economics." *Economic Journal* 49 (December 1939): 696–712.

15. Clifford Hildreth. "Alternative Conditions for Social Ordering." *Econometrica* 21 (January 1953): 81–94.

16. Robert F. Kahn. "Some Notes on Ideal Output." *Economic Journal* 45 (March 1935): 1–35.

17. Nicholas Kaldor. "A Note on Tariffs and Terms of Trade." *Economica* 7 (November 1940): 377–380. Reprinted in Alfred N. Page [25, pp. 384–387].

18. ———. "Welfare Propositions in Economics and Interpersonal Comparisons of Utility." *Economic Journal* 49 (September 1939): 549–552.

19. Oskar Lange. "The Foundations of Welfare Economics." *Econometrica* 10 (July-October 1942): 215–228.

20. Abba P. Lerner. "Economic Theory and Socialist Economy." *Review of Economics Studies* 2 (October 1934): 51–61.

21. ———. "The Concept of Monopoly and Measurement of Monopoly Power." *Review of Economic Studies* 2 (June 1934): 157–175.

22. ———. *The Economics of Control* (New York: Macmillan, 1946).

23. I. M. D. Little. *A Critique of Welfare Economics*. 2d ed. (New York: Oxford University Press, 1957).

24. E. J. Mishan. *Welfare Economics—Five Introductory Essays* (New York: Random House, 1964), esp. pp. 3–97.

25. Alfred N. Page. *Utility Theory: A Book of Readings* (New York: Wiley, 1968), pp. 297–454.

26. Vilfredo Pareto. *Manuel d'Economie Politique*. 2d ed. (Paris: Girard, 1927). Reprinted in part in Alfred N. Page [25, pp. 375–383].

27. A. C. Pigou. *The Economics of Welfare*. 4th ed. (London: Macmillan, 1932).

28. James Quirk and Rubin Saposnik. *Introduction to General Equilibrium and Welfare Economics* (New York: McGraw-Hill, 1968), ch. 4.

29. Melvin Reader. *Studies in the Theory of Welfare Economics* (New York: Columbia University Press, 1947).

30. Umberto Ricci. "Pareto and Pure Economics." *Review of Economic Studies* 1 (1933): 3–21.

31. Paul A. Samuelson. *Foundations of Economic Analysis* (Cambridge, Mass.: Harvard University Press, 1947), ch. 8. Reprinted in Alfred N. Page [25, pp. 317–362].

32. ———. "Further Commentary on Welfare Economics." *American Economic Review* 33 (September 1943): 604–607.

33. F. M. Scherer. "General Equilibrium and Economic Efficiency." *American Economist* 10 (Spring 1966): 54–70.

34. Tibor Scitovsky. *Welfare and Competition*. Rev. ed. (Homewood, Ill.: Richard D. Irwin, 1971).

35. T. de Scitovszky. "A Note on Welfare Propositions in Economics." *Review of Economic Studies* 9 (November 1941): 77–88. Reprinted in Alfred N. Page [25, pp. 388–401].

36. George J. Stigler. "The New Welfare Economics." *American Economic Review* 33 (June 1943): 355–359.

23 Externalities

Consumption and production activities in an economic society often have unintended effects. They may be beneficial, as when one retailer sees a competitor locate nearby and happily gains from the increase in consumer traffic. Or they may be harmful, like pollution of waterways and the atmosphere or offenses against aesthetic values. Economists call these *externalities*, the incidental effect of people and firms on the utility or profits of others, *without sufficient compensation through the price system.*

It is in the public interest to promote activities having desirable external economies and to discourage those that are undesirable. Awareness of externalities will help the business person to recognize potentially profitable opportunities and to avoid inadvertently antagonizing neighbors and potential customers. Those who lack this kind of social sensitivity and conscience are subject to legal suits from injured parties and adverse publicity from environmental activists. It is thus incumbent upon the executive to understand the nature of externalities.

23-1 Types of Externalities

For purposes of discussion, externalities may be divided into four logical categories and a fifth that must be mentioned but is not conveniently included in any other category: (1) external economies of production, (2) external diseconomies of production, (3) external economies of consumption, (4) external diseconomies of consumption, and (5) pecuniary externalities.

23-1-1 *External economies of production*

In contrast to economies of large-scale production, where internal economies are obtained through lower unit costs of output, external economies of production refer to cases where an increase in the firm's production provides benefits to other producers or to consumers. Remuneration for the benefits conferred upon others may not be collectible within the price system. In such cases, however, it may be in the public interest for these firms to expand their production.

363

Example 1. A firm trains a labor force that is potentially available to competitors, who will not incur the full amount of this training cost. The benefits may be substantial where the training is quite specialized.

Example 2. A firm's expanded operations may permit its suppliers to obtain economies of scale, which in turn would permit lower costs to all firms in the industry. Other firms obtain lower resource costs attributable to competitors' increased production and the suppliers' economies of scale.[1]

Example 3. In the case of private production of public goods for the government, some projects will benefit some firms and individuals more than others, such as a new road or bridge that benefits the owners of land and businesses along the route as well as governments that tax these owners.

23-1-2 *External diseconomies of production*

Increases in a firm's output may also have undesirable effects on other producers or on consumers. The investor in a new activity should be particularly aware of real and potential diseconomies that may have impact on a venture's profitability. Citizens and elected officials should be aware of any disadvantages of attracting new industries to the community. In the public interest it may be necessary to tax or otherwise discourage excessive production by private businesses with large external diseconomies.[2]

Example 4. A trucking firm may crowd the roads, making it more expensive and time-consuming for other firms to ship by truck.

Example 5. A group of fishermen may reduce the supply of fish, making it harder for others to obtain their catch.

Example 6. A Texas rancher using a lot of water may leave an insufficient supply for others.

---

[1] The larger market would be to the suppliers an external economy. Reductions in prices by suppliers resulting from reduced costs would be to competing firms a *pecuniary* external economy, since it is less expensive in *money* terms to produce the same output, but no greater quantities of inputs are required than before. (Pecuniary economies are discussed in section 23-1-5.)

[2] External diseconomies are discussed by Scitovsky [8, pp. 271–282] under the headings (a) *nuisance externalities*, those involving noise, inconvenience, or conflict of tastes; (b) *capacity externalities*, where something with a limited capacity is used beyond its capacity, such as a highway where one additional car will cause a bottleneck or an overcrowded theatre with fixed seating capacity; (c) *supply externalities*, the long-run counterpart to capacity externalities, where resources are fixed in amount, like some minerals, or where current demands exceed the ability to produce more, as with lumber and American bison; and (d) the *environment*, which includes the social-cost problems of pollution, which may be cumulative and irreversible.

Example 7. Firms increasing the pollution of a stream may increase the cost of obtaining pure water needed by firms and communities downstream.

Example 8. A farmer permits Johnson grass or other weeds to grow on his land and spread to other farms, decreasing their production.

Example 9. A factory spews smoke, noise, and offensive odors on the community.

23-1-3 *External economies of consumption*

The consuming activities of some people in society may have desirable effects upon others for which no direct compensation is received. Economizing individuals will take advantage of such situations. The public interest may well call for encouraging such consumption.

Example 10. A family may benefit from buying a home in an area where neighbors are friendly, considerate, responsible, and personable. These neighbors paint their houses, cut their grass, kill their weeds, rear polite children, train their dogs, and invite their neighbors over for a barbecue, card game, or swim. (Note that value judgments enter here.)

Example 11. Parents who procure better education for their children create a benefit for firms (as future employees and managers), for friends (as informed or cultured associates), and for society (as better citizens).

Example 12. A teen-ager obtains a job and buys a private telephone for his room or earphones for his stereo, creating fewer family irritations and arguments.

23-1-4 *External diseconomies of consumption*

In many cases, the private acts of consumers have public disadvantages, as when they bring about deterioration of the environment.

Example 13. Picnickers leave garbage, papers, and tin cans, which spoil the setting for others.

Example 14. The next-door neighbor buys a new car, a mink coat for his wife, or a motorcycle for his son, which you cannot afford to duplicate for yourself and your family.

Example 15. Young people who buy fashionable, stylish clothes may make others feel dowdy and less able to resist the pressure to buy such clothes.

Example 16. Excessive use of drugs causes personal, family, and security problems.

Example 17. Watching late shows on television or taking exhausting vacations may decrease productivity on the job.

23-1-5   *Pecuniary externalities*

Some authors cite additional classification of externalities, distinguishing between *technological* and *pecuniary* externalities. The former would include most of the previous examples in which changes in output by one firm cause changes in the amount of *physical inputs* used by other firms. Pecuniary externalities, on the other hand, result where changes in output by one firm cause changes in the price of its inputs and consequently changes in *money cost*, but not in the quantities, of those inputs to competitors.

> *Example 18.* Firm A purchases enough quantities of goods so that its price is driven up for buyer B. From the standpoint of B's interests, external pecuniary diseconomies have accrued from A's purchases. From the standpoint of the country as a whole (including sellers), the problem is internalized; buyers face the same price, their losses are offset by the seller's gains, and diseconomies disappear.

> *Example 19.* Great Britain during World War II feared that if her private importers were allowed to bid up the prices of food in world markets, rates for food paid by the government would rise and more quickly exhaust the gold and dollar reserves. A British purchasing commission was established in New York through which all imports were channeled. This established a monopsony position to hold down prices on government imports, avoiding pecuniary diseconomies for the Crown [8, p. 283].

> *Example 20.* In example 19 firms are the beneficiaries of pecuniary economies when they receive lower resource costs because of suppliers' economies of scale derived from increased purchases by competitors.

The terms *pecuniary* and *technological* are mentioned here because of their widespread use. Their continued usefulness, however, has been questioned by E. J. Mishan:

> In his classic paper of 1931, "Cost Curves and Supply Curves," Viner introduced some terminological innovations which have since become standard currency despite their being, in my view, superfluous and possibly confusing. The term external *pecuniary* diseconomies was proposed to cover the case of a rising supply price that is the result solely of changes in relative factor prices as output expands. But in the complete absence of external effects, rising supply price is an implication of any interdependent economic model having such familiar features as production functions homogeneous of degree one, imperfectly elastic factor supplies, and factor proportions differing from one product to another. Seen from this perspective there is nothing special about a rising supply curve, and no optimizing correction of equilibrium outputs need be sought under conditions of universal perfect competition. Therefore to invoke the term *pecuniary* external diseconomies to "explain" supply curves that are in fact already explained by this familiar interdependent economic system simply in order to distinguish them from external diseconomies proper—which in the Viner article take on the appel-

lation, external *technological* diseconomies—strikes one today as, perhaps, a verbal extravagance. Moreover, the use of *pecuniary* external *economy* to refer to a reduction in the average cost of industry A as it expands its purchases of materials or services from a falling cost industry B, will surely confuse most readers. . . . We shall, therefore, . . . speak only of external effects proper [7, p. 6].

23-2 Ways of Dealing with Problems of Externalities

23-2-1 *Internalization*

Some diseconomies may be neutralized by internalizing them, for instance by merging firms where the damages of one accrue to the other, where the effluent of an upstream producer, say, pollutes the water used by the downstream producer. Merger will force the enlarged concern to adjust its outputs to deal with the problem [7, p. 3].

Internalization may also be possible where a market comes into being for a new product. An example might be where straw, obtained as a by-product of wheat production, was traditionally used by poorer peasants for fodder or mattress filling. This external economy to peasants would disappear as commercial uses of straw were developed, because the joint products of grain and straw would be intentionally produced and jointly marketed. Profits from wheat production would thus be maximized by equating the demand prices of both grain and straw to the marginal resource cost [7, p. 3].

23-2-2 *Tax or subsidy*

A traditional course for expanding production of a competitive industry that provides significant external benefits to the rest of the economy is for the government to offer manufacturers a subsidy equal to the marginal external economy that would prevail at the optimum output level. Similarly, those producing diseconomies would be assessed an excise tax equal to the value of the marginal external diseconomy prevailing at the optional output. The classic tax or subsidy solution is illustrated by Figure 23-1. The private marginal-cost curve S may be

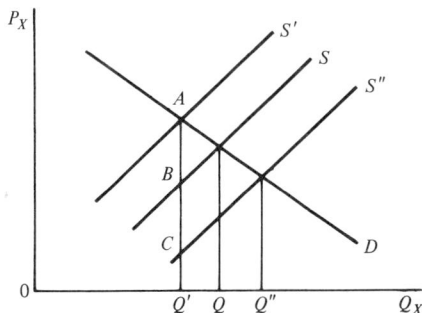

Figure 23-1

shifted to the social marginal-cost curve (including externalities) S' by imposing a unit tax equal to the vertical distance between S and S' (line AB) or by granting a unit subsidy equal to the vertical distance between S and S'' (line BC). The intersection with the market demand curve D determines the prevailing price in a competitive market. A tax equal to the net marginal social cost of diseconomies would determine the socially optimal output OQ'. Where net marginal social benefits are to be exploited, the unit subsidy would expand output to the socially optimal output OQ''.

This approach is of limited practical value except where the costs of collecting the necessary information and supervising the tax or subsidy program are low—which is unlikely for industries with variable demand and supply conditions [7, p. 15]. Also, where the industry producing the external diseconomy is non-competitive and where the monopoly firm equating marginal cost to marginal revenue is producing a smaller output, the unit tax may not be necessary to achieve the socially optimal output OQ'. Where the monopoly produces external benefits, however, greater subsidies may be required to obtain the desired level.

23-2-3   *Voluntary agreement*

Another way of dealing with problems of externalities, which may be superior to government taxes, subsidies, or direct regulation, is to call to the attention of the affected parties the mutual advantages of a voluntary agreement. For example, in Figure 23-2, where S is the private (commercial) marginal-cost curve, there is incentive to deal with the external diseconomies by moving toward the socially optimal output OQ' from the privately optimal output OQ before an excise tax CD is levied. (Assume the tax is levied against only the units $Q'Q$.) This conclusion may be deduced as follows. The area $ABCD$, equal to the vertical distance between S and S' times the number of units of output taxed, represents the incremental tax penalty required to discourage excessive production. It also equals the value of the damage done to the spill-over victims and therefore the amount they would pay to restrict output to the optimum level (assuming a constant utility of money for all parties). The area ABD represents the net benefits to the beneficiaries, otherwise described as the sum of producers' and consumers' surpluses, from the additional output. Under the tax, the loss to all parties equals $ABCD$ (assuming the tax receipts are not returned by the

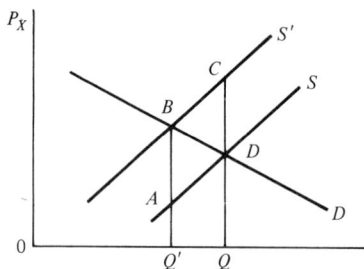

Figure 23-2

government as subsidies or other disproportionate benefits to any of the parties). Under voluntary restriction of output without tax, the loss is only *ABD*, leaving *BCD*, which would be distributed by negotiation between the parties. The expense of the negotiation between individuals, firms, and industries may, however, cause the effort to be impractical—if the negotiation itself is not patently illegal.

23-2-4   *Marginal costs versus marginal benefits*

It should be made clear that the previous approach would not completely eliminate pollution. Only outright prohibition (obtained by civil litigation, zoning regulation, building codes, or specific legislation) could possibly eliminate entirely all traces of pollutants inflicting losses on others. But this would probably be too expensive to enforce. The technical cost of detecting and maintaining control might itself be prohibitive. In any case, a more reasonable goal would be to attempt to remove the discernible or dangerous amounts of pollution and to balance marginal social costs with marginal social benefits. As indicated in Figure 23-3, the value of additional reductions in pollution, as indicated by the marginal-benefit curve *AQ'*, is equal to the additional cost of removing the pollution, as indicated by the marginal-cost curve *OBCD*, at point *B*. This gives an optimal amount of pollution reduction of *OQ*. Complete elimination of pollution at *Q'* would require a unit cost of *Q'D*, which is clearly higher than the zero marginal benefit to be received. Where marginal costs are indicated by *OBCE*, complete elimination of pollution requires an expense approaching infinity. As the concentration of the pollutant becomes greater, perhaps to the point of becoming lethal, the marginal-benefit curve would shift upward, justifying a greater unit expenditure for its removal.

23-3   No Controls Versus Prohibition of Pollution

In the absence of government control and of significant transaction costs, it was generally believed by economists in the early 1960s that it would make little difference in the allocation of resources whether a manufacturer were required to compensate the victims of a diseconomy or the victims bribed the manu-

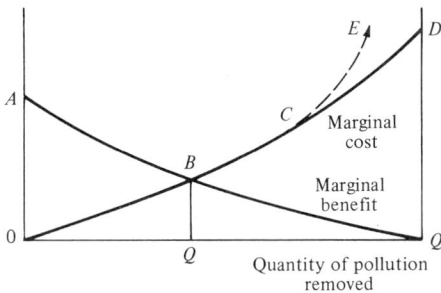

Figure 23-3

facturer.[3] It was also unclear from the standpoint of equity where the interests of the two parties were mutually antagonistic, since the increased cost (for compensation of victims) to the manufacturer was considered to be symmetric to the increased cost suffered by the victims. The question of equity, however, is a question of welfare distribution and not one of the most efficient allocation of resources. It is possible that a movement toward a more optimal allocation could make the poor even poorer. A movement toward an optimal position assured only a *potential* Pareto improvement (where gains would exceed losses), not an *actual* Pareto improvement (where at least some people would gain and nobody else would lose). It was thought that successful mutual agreement implied that the maximum potential shared gains, G, exceeded the transactions cost, T, that a Pareto improvement is possible where $(G - T) > 0$ and not possible where $(G - T) < 0$. In the partial analysis approach of Figure 23-2, G is the area BCD, but T is not treated. Where T is not negligible, the graphical analysis is deficient in that a movement to the "optimal" OQ' output is no longer uniquely determined. When the impact of environmental spill-overs (welfare effects) are also significant, even the $(G - T) > 0$ criterion for net Pareto improvement is not adequate.

23-3-1 *A presumption for the status quo*

Before discussing the nature of transaction costs, it should be understood that a point of mutual agreement may be unattainable regardless of the amounts expended to bring about a transaction. First, take the hypothetical case of a divisible economic arrangement in which an individual, A, is exposed to smoke fumes produced by firm B, which he can escape only by moving his place of residence. Rather than move, however, A would be willing to pay a maximum of $3,000 of his $12,000 annual disposable income to B to eliminate the smoke and thereby avoid moving. He would be willing to pay more if his income were larger but the rest of his current income is required for other purposes. (In Hicksian terminology, the $3,000 is called his *compensating variation*, the amount he would *pay* to restore his welfare to its original level W_o.) If there were a law that compelled the firm to compensate all injured parties, A could claim that he suffered a true loss equivalent to $5,000. (In Hicksian terminology, this is called his *equivalent variation*, the minimum amount he would *accept* to suffer the smoke and maintain his welfare at W_o.) Similarly, firm B would pay a maximum of $3,500 to pollute, but would accept a minimum of $4,000 to refrain from polluting.

The maximum and minimum sums could be associated with the two opposing states of the law where the existing law, L, is tolerant of smoke and another existing law, L', effectively bans all smoke except by mutual agreement. Reading across the first row of Table 23-1 one sees that given the existing law L permitting smoke, A will give $3,000 to have the law changed to L' prohibiting smoke, but firm B must be paid at least $4,000 to agree to the change. The negative $1,000 indicates a deficiency in funds needed to produce the change. Since a change to L' would incur a potential Pareto loss of $1,000, L is deemed Pareto optimal. If,

---

[3] This section draws heavily on Mishan's article [7, pp. 16–24].

Table 23-1

Existing law	Individual A	Firm B	Total
L	+3,000	−4,000	−1,000
L′	−5,000	+3,500	−1,500

however, in row 2, *L′* is taken as the existing law, B will pay up to $3,500 to have the law changed to *L* and A will require $5,000 to agree. The negative $1,500 indicates that the existing *L′* is also Pareto optimal. In either case, the existing law is optimal and agreement for change cannot be obtained.

This analysis may be extended to situations having perfectly divisible external effects by plotting the marginal-benefit and marginal-loss curves as in Figure 23-4. Suppose law *L* is in force before any agreement between individual A and firm B and that the prevailing amount of smoke is measured by OS.[4] SB_L (reading from right to left) shows the minimum compensation B requires for successive reduction of concentrations of smoke. OA_L (reading from left to right) shows the maximum A would pay to avoid successive amounts of smoke. At Q_L, payments by A to B are mutually acceptable. If, however, law *L′* were in effect (no smoke except by mutual consent) before any agreement had been made, the dashed lines would be relevant. The minimum amounts acceptable to A for successive concentrations of smoke (vertical distances to OA_L) are equal to the maximum amounts B is willing to pay for successive amounts of smoke (vertical distances to $B_L′S′$) at $Q_L′$.

It is tempting to conclude that Q_L or $Q_L′$ can be reached by bargaining, depending upon which law prevails at the time. But this is not the case, since reaching agreement means one or both parties are made better off, which causes one or both marginal-valuation curves to shift upwards. The conclusion that *is* warranted is that the optimum smoke obtained by bargaining will be larger when there is no initial law prohibiting smoke.

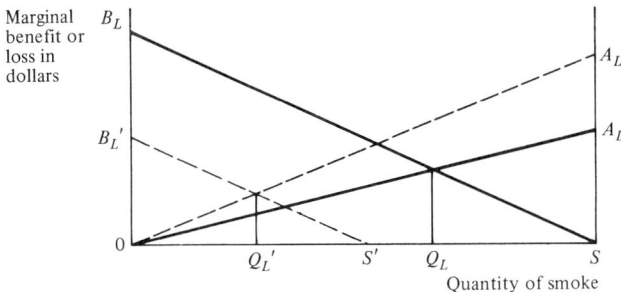

Figure 23-4

[4] Smoke could be measured in cubic feet of a certain level of concentration at the point where it leaves the factory or on the premises of the injured party.

23-3-2   *Transactions costs*

Any movement involving agreements tending to a Pareto improvement involve transactions costs, which include those for negotiations between the two groups, for maintaining and revising the agreement, and for implementing the agreement by any necessary capital expenditure. Costs for negotiations include the costs of identifying members of the group, persuading them to make or accept a joint offer, and reaching agreement within the group on the details of negotiation with the other group. These costs would undoubtedly rise rapidly with increases in the number of members and their dispersion within the two groups [7, p. 21].[5]

Three alternative cases are possible. Movement toward a net potential Pareto improvement where $(G - T) > 0$ will involve a smaller optimum output and pollution under the L' law than under the L law. In comparison with the costless $(T = 0)$ potential optimum equilibrium, output under L will give too much pollution, and zero output under L' will give too little pollution. It is not known, without further assumptions, which condition is apt to be closer to the potential optimum and therefore which law is to be preferred. Where the potential optimum position is closer to the initial L' position than the L position, improvement will take place, as shown in Figure 23-5a only if the L law prevails. This is true because the introduction of transactions costs into consideration will have the effect of raising the minimum amounts A would accept to tolerate smoke, rotating $L'A'_L$ counterclockwise about L'. Also, the maximum amounts B would pay will be reduced by transactions costs incurred, rotating $B'_L L$ counterclockwise about L. Intersection of the curves moves to the left, as indicated by the arrow. Where the potential optimum lies closer to L, improvement may take place only if L' prevails, as shown in Figure 23-5b.

Potential ameliorations can be made by actions other than the mentioned output adjustments based upon voluntary agreements, as by a less costly reloca-

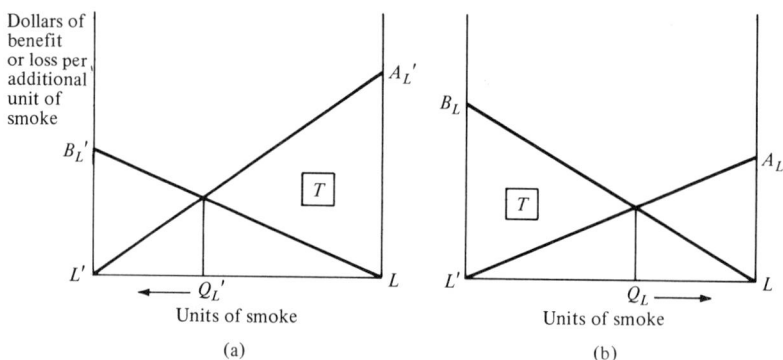

Figure 23-5

---

[5] Dispersion may be geographical, social, cultural, habitual, educational, and other factors that could inhibit the bringing together of the members of, say, the injured group.

tion of plants, installation of pollution prevention devices, or modification of technology to reduce spillovers. Also, government regulation of output through excise taxes or subsidies, discussed previously, could replace voluntary agreements between groups.

23-3-3   *An inclination for prohibition*

No conclusive statements can be made about the implications of transactions costs for the allocation of resources where there is no clear connection between the amount of transactions costs and the type of prevailing law, but other considerations appear to favor law L' (total prohibition of pollution) over law L (complete freedom to pollute). First, if L is in effect, it is less likely that one person in a widely dispersed group injured by pollution will initiate class-action litigation to change the law or to recover damages. The certain loss of time and effort, plus the large risk of substantial and irrecoverable expenses to identify and persuade members of the group, is difficult for an individual to assume. Under L', in contrast, initiative to change the law must come from industry, which is better able to shoulder the task. Executives assume no personal risk in acting on behalf of shareholders. They are unlikely to produce pollution-prone products unless they can meet residual damage claims from generated profits. Also, under L' individuals need incur relatively little expense in making a claim against pollution, since pollution (without prior and explicit permission) is illegal.

Second, under L there is little incentive for industry to invest in pollution-reducing technology. Without penalties for failing to do so, allocation according to the equimarginal principle will mean that resources will be otherwise directed by the firm to sales promotion, product innovations, and cost-reducing technology. But under L' full liability for pollution damage must be included in production costs, and pollution-prevention research is encouraged. Polluting industries will also reduce the social costs of overpollution in some areas by locating some of their plants in more remote areas, redesigning and rerouting highways and air flights over less populated areas, and so on.

23-3-4   *Prohibition of pollution in the interest of equity*

With regard to equity, it appears that under law L the groups having larger incomes will be hurt less by pollution, because it is easier for them to relocate than for those with lower incomes to do so. Also, they tend to own polluting firms, thereby possibly deriving an offsetting monetary gain. The person with an income of $100,000 per year may be willing to give up $20,000 per year to be rid of a noxious spillover but is able to move out of the polluted area for a loss of $10,000 per year. An equally sensitive person earning $10,000 per year may be willing to give up $1,500 per year, but a minimal cost of $2,000 per year for moving out of the polluted area would prevent relocation. In such a case, the distribution effects of welfare would be judged regressive, the burden of pollution falling more heavily on the lower-income recipient.

Under an existing law L and if transactions costs diminish for the public, there may be some incentive for industry to increase the amounts of pollution immediately before any agreement is reached to improve its bargaining position in determining the costs to be shared in reducing pollution.

While the losses to the opposing sides may be Pareto symmetric (the loss to industry from giving up pollution being symmetric to the loss to the injured parties by having pollution), the losses may not be ethically symmetric. The freedom of industry to emit noxious fumes that bother others is not on an equal basis with freedom of individuals to breathe fresh air, which in itself does not harm industry. This may be seen as additional justification for law L', which makes polluters legally liable.

If transactions and regulation costs remain high, the choice between L and L' may mean for society the choice between too much or too little pollution. Since adoption of L' encourages preventive technology more than L, its adoption means that the too little is not as likely to last as long as the too much. Under L, ·a growth of spillovers equal to or exceeding the growth of Gross National Product will lead, where there are increasing marginal disutility of pollution and diminishing marginal utility of GNP, to a zero or negative growth of GNP per capita.

If the damage from some spillovers is virtually irreversible, it may be that the consensus of the groups immediately affected is not in the long-run interest of people on planet Earth. The losses to future generations from the continued destruction of natural beauty and the poisoning of lakes and rivers must be added to the costs carried by the existing population.

If the time lag between the introduction of new products and the knowledge of their long-term effects is extended by the pace of technological innovation, there is a presumption in favor of law L' and public control of the use of new processes and the marketing of any new products, especially chemicals. Even if these steps are taken, there is increased likelihood, as greater numbers of such products are spread over the globe with incredible rapidity, of causing some ecological catastrophe or uncontrollable epidemic.

The problem of pollution is attributable to the population explosion as well as to our improved technology and other interdependent relations. Each link is significant in determining the nature of our environment. In Chapter 27 we will take a broader look at the relation between ecology and economics.

Questions and Problems

23-1. Classify the following as to external economy or diseconomy of production or consumption.
    a. Ford expands production, permitting steel producers to reduce the price of steel to Chrysler Corporation.
    b. IBM trains computer salesmen, who are bid away by Burroughs Computer Sales, Inc.
    c. The United States Army Corps of Engineers constructs a dam that creates a lake where farm land used to be. What is the impact upon suppliers of water-sports equipment? on lake concessions?
    d. A new turnpike of limited access is constructed parallel to an existing highway. What is the impact upon gas stations, restaurants, and other firms along the old route? on trucking firms using the route?

e. You take your friend to a place where other guests provide good entertainment at no expense to you.

f. What are effects of a leak in an off-shore oil well on the fishing industry? on swimmers and surfers?

g. A new color television set, which you cannot afford, is being delivered to the home next door.

h. A beer can is thrown from the car in front of yours.

i. The factory spewing smoke on the community pays most of the taxes, which pay for the public education system.

j. Dope addicts needing money to purchase a fix make night shopping downtown hazardous.

k. Mr. Thirsty, who lives down the street, doesn't kill his dandelions.

l. A factory worker's bones deteriorate from cadmium poisoning received in the production process.

m. A new department store is located in the vicinity of three other department stores.

23-2. What term describes the method of dealing with externalities in the following situations?

a. When a barbershop quartet used to practice their songs in Rico's Tavern, other customers of the tavern would come to enjoy the free entertainment. The crowds became so large that Rico hired the quartet to sing on a regular basis and initiated an entertainment charge.

b. Mrs. Fluffbottom had so many cats in her apartment that they bothered the other tenants, and the apartment manager made a rule that no tenant could have more than one pet.

c. The Latesleeper family agreed to buy an additional quart of orange juice from Caruso, the milkman, if he agreed not to sing while making his deliveries.

d. A toll is imposed on a turnpike to restrict use to avoid overcrowding.

e. A bill was proposed in a state legislature to pay farmers 10 cents a pound to destroy any marijuana found growing on their properties.

23-3. List and discuss the externalities associated with the following case history, which was reported in the *Wall Street Journal*, September 3, 1969, pp. 1, 25.

On Chincha Norte Island, located 15 miles off the coast of Peru, Eduardo Melendez is caretaker for hundreds of tons of bird manure and the huge flocks of birds that produce it. He enjoys the seclusion of his work and has grown accustomed to the foul smell, but he is concerned that the number of Peruvian cormorants, which are longnecked sea birds somewhat larger than gulls, nesting on the islands have fallen from 20 million in 1965 to about 6 million in 1969. This has caused the harvest of guano, a potent and highly prized fertilizer rich in nitrogen, to plummet from 175,000 tons to 35,000 tons. The National Fertilizer Corporation, a state-run monopoly, is, needless to say, quite concerned about the decline of a business which has totaled $3 billion in exports since the mid-19th century—more than the Inca silver and gold yielded to Spanish conquistadors.

The dwindling number of sea birds is attributed by conservationists and guano company officials to starvation caused by the overfishing of Peru's booming fishmeal business. Fishmeal is used in animal feeds and has become one of the nation's leading exports. It is made from anchovies, the basic food of the guano birds. Peruvian anchovy catches have climbed over 4,000% in a dozen years, netting more that 10 million tons of fish in 1968 and producing $200 million of fishmeal.

It is warned that "the day the guano birds disappear, the anchovies will disappear too—and that means the end of our fishmeal industry." The reason supported by marine biologists is that the guano dropped by the cormorants into the sea fertilizes the plankton that anchovies eat.

Fishermen deny that overfishing is hurting the cormorant, claiming that a freak ocean current in 1965 brought unusually warm waters from the North which killed off much of the plankton on the surface, thereby driving anchovies deeper for food and out of reach of the birds. Peru's Marine Institue agrees the freak current caused the death of many birds but feels that since that current has long disappeared the bird population should have bounced back to its former level—thus, there is a correlation between big fishing catches and the decline in birds. An institute official observed, "I'm afraid the guano birds just aren't very efficient producers compared with fishmeal plant."

The impact of reduced guano may, however, be important in other areas. During harvest time, more than 1,000 Indian workers are brought down from Peru's mountain highlands to loosen the handpacked guano with picks and pour it into gunny sacks. An elaborate supply system of food launches and water barges is set up from the mainland. "Guano dust is everywhere, and a sickening ammonia-like odor pervades the air. The workers receive free medical care, food and a bed in a ramshackle dormitory. They're paid as little as 70 cents a day." Guano is almost the only fertilizer used in the highland regions that support half of Peru's 12 million population, since guano, at less than 5 cents a pound, is far cheaper than synthetics. "Hence many economists in Peru fear that if the guano supply continues to decline, it will worsen the nation's already substantial food-production deficit."[6]

23-4. Modern technology has improved the efficiency of strip mining for coal. "Big Muskie," Ohio Power Company's world's largest power shovel, at 220 cubic yards can strip off soil to a depth of more than 160 feet to expose a layer of coal. About 10 miles west of Cumberland where Big Muskie works, devastation is so immense that many students of strip mining are convinced that reclamation of the land being stripped by mammoth machines may be impossible. Richard L. Lancione, a lawyer in Bellaire, Ohio, who heads a group called Citizens Concerned About Strip Mining, claims, "Literally thousands and thousands of acres have been turned upside down, destroyed for all practical purposes" (*Wall Street Journal*, May 24, 1971, pp. 1, 17).

In reference to this situation,

a. should strip mining be stopped to prevent devastation of the countryside?

b. Should strip-mining companies be required by law to spend great sums of money to restore areas where there are few people to observe it?

[6] Reprinted with the permission of *The Wall Street Journal*, © Dow Jones and Company, Inc., 1969.

c. How would you recommend that the advantages and disadvantages of reclamation be weighed?

23-5. Sparks from a railway engine damage crops along the route. Should farmers who can grow crops elsewhere be compensated for the full amount of the damaged crops?

23-6. Where competitive industries *X* and *Y* have reciprocal external economies, will their optimal outputs (where marginal-resource cost is equal to the market price plus the algebraic value of the marginal external effects) exceed their equilibrium outputs without external economies?

23-7. Is it correct to apply the social marginal cost pricing rule to sectors generating externalities when the optimum conditions are not already met in the rest of the economy?

23-8. What reply should be given to the antipollution engineer who states: "We should strive to remove all of the wastes pouring into our streams by whatever amount our technology makes possible"? (Adapted from Robert L. Heilbroner, *The Economic Problem Newsletter*, CP-RH3, vol. 2 (Fall 1970).)

References

1. William J. Baumol. *Economic Theory and Operations Analysis.* 3d ed. (Englewood Cliffs, N.J.: Prentice-Hall, 1972), pp. 392–395.

2. J. M. Buchanan and W. C. Stubblebine. "Externality." *Economica* 29 (November 1962): 371–384.

3. R. H. Coase. "The Problem of Social Costs." *Journal of Law and Economics* 3 (October 1960): 1–44.

4. F. T. Dolbear, Jr. "On the Theory of Optimum Externality." *American Economic Review* 57 (March 1967): 90–103.

5. E. J. Mishan. *Economics for Social Decisions—Elements of Cost-Benefit Analysis* (New York: Praeger, 1972), ch. 15–17.

6. ———. "Reflections on Recent Developments in the Concept of External Effects." In *Welfare Economics—Five Introductory Essays* (New York: Random House, 1964), pp. 98–154.

7. ———. "The Postwar Literature on Externalities: An Interpretative Essay." *Journal of Economic Literature* 9 (March 1971): 1–28.

8. Tibor Scitovsky. *Welfare and Competition.* Rev. ed. (Homewood, Ill.: Richard D. Irwin, 1971), pp. 268–284.

9. R. Turvey. "On Divergencies Between Social Cost and Private Cost." *Economica* 30 (August 1963): 309–313.

24 Investment Decisions in Business and Society

The essence of investment is the sacrifice of present for future benefits. As the term is used by managerial economists, investment refers to the flow of real assets, such as raw materials, labor skills, machines, factories, goods in process, and inventories. Since the stock of such assets is called real capital (C), investment (I) is defined as the rate of change in capital over time:

$$I = \frac{dC}{dI} \tag{1}$$

As the term is used in financial circles, investment also refers to the flow of paper assets, such as money, bonds, and stock certificates.

Real investment involves a social sacrifice of consumption in the present period,[1] whereas financial investment involves only an exchange in ownership of titles to current consumption. The real value of financial assets *to society* is not their face or market values in monetary units but their incidental value in terms of the paper and ink of which they are composed and their tremendous value in terms of the services they render in facilitating exchange, keeping records, storing values, and making contractual arrangements. The distinction between real and financial investment is important in analysis when one is examining economic problems of society as opposed to those of an individual or firm. Since the business executives must consider the implications of decisions at all three levels, they must be aware of the distinction.

This chapter briefly reviews the mechanics of translating the values of assets through time while taking into account the compounding of interest, and also discusses the relative merits of the two most commonly used criteria for making investment decisions: a programming formulation of capital budgeting, and a two-period model of individual investment decisions. More advanced considerations dealing with uncertainty are deferred to Chapter 25.

---

[1] This is not strictly true where some capital inputs can *only* yield benefits over time. Since they are useless in the present, there is no sacrifice, because there is no alternative. However, use of these inputs inevitably requires other inputs, such as labor, which have other uses.

378

24-1   The Use of Compound Interest in Investment Decisions

Basic to any discussion of investment is a knowledge of compound interest. The value of a dollar tomorrow is not necessarily the same as its value today, as any investor, banker, or consumer living in a time of inflation is aware. In order to retain the full value of a dollar saved, one must receive a rate of interest from the investment of that dollar that will at least equal the rate of inflation. Calculations of present and future returns on investments can appear quite complex to one untrained in compound-interest analysis, especially when amounts are received and disbursed at irregular intervals and where interest is compounded at other than annual rates. Other important problems in business involve comparisons of present values and net returns of alternative projects. Such calculations are manageable for persons familiar with the basic ideas of compound interest. A short review of a few tools of most use in investment planning is given in this section.

24-1-1   *Future value of an investment earning compound interest*

Money put in a savings account in a bank for 1 year grows by an amount equal to the annual rate of interest paid. For example, if $100 earns interest at a 4 per cent annual rate, the saver has $104 in her account at the end of the year. More formally, if P dollars are invested at i rate of interest, the nominal value V of the deposit at year's end is given by the expression

$$
\begin{aligned}
V_1 &= P_0 + P_0 i \\
&= P_0(1 + i) \\
&= \$100(1 + 0.04) = \$100(1.04) = \$104
\end{aligned}
\tag{2}
$$

where the subscript 0 denotes the beginning of the first year and 1 the beginning of the second year. If the $104 is left in the account for another year, the amount in the account at the end of 2 years is

$$
\begin{aligned}
V_2 &= V_1 + V_1 i \\
&= (P_0 + P_0 i) + (P_0 + P_0 i)i \\
&= P_0(1 + i) + P_0(1 + i)i \\
&= P_0(1 + i)(1 + i) \\
&= P_0(1 + i)^2 \\
&= \$100(1.04)^2 = \$100(1.0816) = \$108.16
\end{aligned}
\tag{3}
$$

Similarly, the balance at the end of 3 years is

$$
\begin{aligned}
V_3 &= P_0(1 + i)^3 \\
&= \$100(1.04)^3 = \$100(1.1249) = \$112.49
\end{aligned}
\tag{4}
$$

Generally, if interest is left in the account and permitted to compound itself annually, the balance at the end of any given year n is given by the formula

$$
V_n = P_0(1 + i)^n
\tag{5}
$$

Equations (2) to (4) are special cases of equation (5), where $n = 1, 2,$ and 3, respectively. These calculations can be performed by hand, logarithms, or calculator, but compound-interest tables are most useful in shortening the calculations; simply pick the appropriate interest factor equal to $(1 + i)^n$ from any standard set of compound-interest tables and multiply by P_0 to obtain V_n. For example, if \$1,000 can be invested in certificates of deposit for 20 years at a compounded annual rate of 7 per cent, multiply \$1,000 by the factor 3.86968 to obtain a value of \$3,869.68.

When equal investments are made each year on a continuing basis, their total value at some future date may be calculated by use of the well-known formula

$$V_s = P\left[\frac{(1 + i)^n - 1}{i}\right] \tag{6}$$

where V_s is the sum of n annual investments including cumulated compounded interest, and P is the amount invested every year: $P = P_0 = P_1 = P_2 = \cdots = P_n$. The bracketed expression is described as the compounded value of an annuity of 1 (dollar), and its value is provided in compound-interest tables for various values of i and n. For example, if \$100 is invested each year for 20 consecutive years at an interest rate of 7 per cent compounded annually, the dollar amount accumulated at the end of 20 years would be

$$V_s = \$100 \times (40.99549 \text{ from the annuity interest tables}) = \$4,099.55$$

If compounding takes place at intervals other than annually, adjustments must be made in the n and i used. If compounding takes place m times per year, then nm and i/m are substituted into the preceding formulas (except in the denominator of equation (6)) for n and i, respectively:

$$V_1 = P_0\left(1 + \frac{i}{m}\right)^m \qquad \text{replaces equation (2)} \tag{7}$$

$$V_2 = P_0\left(1 + \frac{i}{m}\right)^{2m} \qquad \text{,, \qquad ,, \qquad (3)} \tag{8}$$

$$V_3 = P_0\left(1 + \frac{i}{m}\right)^{3m} \qquad \text{,, \qquad ,, \qquad (4)} \tag{9}$$

$$V_n = P_0\left(1 + \frac{i}{m}\right)^{nm} \qquad \text{,, \qquad ,, \qquad (5)} \tag{10}$$

$$V_s = P\left[\frac{\left(1 + \frac{i}{m}\right)^{nm} - 1}{i}\right] \qquad \text{,, \qquad ,, \qquad (6)} \tag{11}$$

If compounding took place quarterly rather than annually, then $m = 4$, and the preceding examples would have different answers: \$104.06, \$108.29, \$112.68, \$4,006.39, and \$4,294.85. Notice that all answers are greater under more frequent compounding. Use of the compound-interest tables is appropriate and straightforward, except for the last example using equation (11); here the answer obtained from the annuity table for 80 years at 1.75 per cent (171.7938) is divided by $m = 4$, because substituting i/m for i is appropriate only in the numerator.

In recent years, some banks and other savings institutions have begun to compound their savings deposits daily, that is $m = 365$, and even continuously, that is, $m = \infty$, in attempting to get around legal restrictions on the maximum amount of interest they are permitted to pay. Compounding at more rapid intervals is a way of raising the amount of interest paid without actually raising the stated rate. The equation for continuous compounding of a single payment may be obtained by making adjustments to equation (10). Define $k = m/i$, which may be solved for m to give $m = ki$. Then, by substitution,

$$V_n = P_0\left(1 + \frac{i}{m}\right)^{nm}$$

$$= P_0\left(1 + \frac{1}{k}\right)^{kin} \tag{12}$$

$$= P_0\left[\left(1 + \frac{1}{k}\right)^k\right]^{in}$$

$$= P_0 e^{in}$$

where $e = 2.71828$, is the limit of the bracketed quantity as k approaches infinity (which it must do as m approaches infinity).

Although continuous compounding permits the addition of accrued interest to the principal at every moment, total interest amounts in 1 year to only a slightly higher value (only 3 cents on $100 at 7 per cent) than with daily compounding. Over a number of years or where amounts are large, the difference is significant. In the example of $1,000 invested for 20 years at 7 per cent, the value of V_n with continuous compounding is figured as follows:

$$V_{20} = 1,000(2.71828)^{0.07(20)}$$
$$\log V_{20} = \log 1,000 + 1.4 \log 2.71828$$
$$= 3 + 1.4(0.43429) = 3 + 0.608006 = 3.6080$$
$$V_{20} = \$4,055$$

This compares with a daily compounded value of

$$V_{20} = 1,000\left(1 + \frac{0.07}{365}\right)^{365(20)}$$

$$\log V_{20} = \log 1,000 + 7,300 \log 1.000192$$
$$= 3 + 7,300(0.000083) = 3 + 0.6059 = 3.6059$$
$$V_{20} = \$4,036$$

and an annually compounded value of $3,870.

24-1-2   *Present value of a single future amount*

To facilitate comparisons of investment outlays made at different points in time with their revenue returns of various amounts, which are also staggered in time, it has become common practice to calculate their present-value equivalents. Present value may be identified with P_0 in preceding formulas. Equation (2) may be solved for P_0 to give

$$P_0 = \frac{V_1}{1 + i}$$

$$= \frac{\$104}{(1 + 0.04)} = \$100 \tag{13}$$

Thus, $104 at the end of the year, discounted at a 4 per cent interest rate, is the equivalent of having $100 now. By the same reasoning, $108.16 in 2 years and $112.49 in 3 years also have present values of $100, and the general formula for calculating the present value of future amounts is given by

$$P_0 = V_n \frac{1}{(1 + i)^n} \tag{14}$$

The fraction $1/(1 + i)$ is referred to as the *discount factor* or *discount rate* (not to be confused with the interest rate i at which an amount is discounted). Present-value tables provide the discount factors for corresponding values of i and n to facilitate calculations. (They are simply the inverses of the compound-interest factors used in the preceding section.)

For example, suppose a firm has a project requiring an expenditure of $45,000 now and $10,000 at the beginning of each of the next 3 years, and the management wishes to know how much money it would have to set aside today, the remaining balance of which could be invested at 6 per cent compounded annually, when unneeded to cover the outlays. The answer is $45,000 plus the sum of the present values of $10,000 in years 1, 2, and 3, calculated as follows with the aid of standard present-value tables:

$$P_0 = \$45,000 + \$10,000(0.943396) + \$10,000(0.889996)$$
$$+ \$10,000(0.839619)$$
$$= \$45,000 + \$9,434 + \$8,900 + \$8,396$$
$$= \$71,730$$

Suppose that the firm anticipates an income from the project of $20,000 at the end of each of the first 4 years, totaling $80,000, and wants to know if this is sufficient to break even. The present value of the $80,000 discounted at a compounded interest rate of 6 per cent can be calculated as follows:

$$P_0 = \$20,000(0.943396) + \$20,000(0.889996) + \$20,000(0.839619)$$
$$+ \$20,000(0.792094)$$
$$= \$18,868 + \$17,800 + \$16,792 + \$15,842$$
$$= \$69,302$$

The project is clearly not a profitable investment, since the present value of expenditures ($71,730) exceeds the present value of receipts ($69,302) by $2,428. This example, of course, abstracts from the real world of inflation, taxation, risk, and other important considerations.

Similar calculations could have been made for compounding at intervals other than annually by substituting i/m for i, and nm for m in the appropriate equations, as was done in section 24-1-1. The modified equation for the present value of a single amount is thus

$$P_0 = V_n \left[\frac{1}{\left(1 + \dfrac{i}{m}\right)^{nm}} \right] \tag{15}$$

Notice that the bracketed discount factor is the inverse of part of equation (10). If compounding were continuous, the present-value expression would be obtained by solving equation (12) for P_0:

$$P_0 = V_n e^{-in} \tag{16}$$

24-1-3 *Present value of a uniform series of receipts*

The second half of the preceding example is referred to as the *capitalized value of a stream of receipts*, given by the expression

$$P_0 = V_0 + DV_1 + D^2 V_2 + D^3 V_3 + D^4 V_4 + \cdots + D^n V_n \tag{17}$$

where

$$D = \frac{1}{1+i}$$

In the example, $V_0 = 0$, because no revenue was received at the beginning of the first year, and the series ended with $D^4 V_4$ because receipts ended after the fourth year. In the special case where the expected receipts are equal amounts, equation (17) reduces to

$$P_0 = V + DV + D^2 V + \cdots + D^n V$$
$$= V(1 + D + D^2 + \cdots + D^n) \tag{18}$$
$$= V\left(\frac{1 - D^{n+1}}{1 - D}\right)$$

where $V_0 = V_1 = V_2 = \cdots = V_n = V$. Proof that the geometric series $(1 + D + D^2 + \cdots + D^n)$ equals $1 - D^{n+1}/(1 - D)$ is easily given by multiplying and dividing the expression in parentheses by $1 - D$:

$$(1 + D + D^2 + \cdots + D^n)\frac{1 - D}{1 - D}$$
$$= \frac{(1 + D + D^2 + \cdots + D^n) - (D + D^2 + \cdots + D^{n+1})}{1 - D}$$
$$= \frac{1 - D^{n+1}}{1 - D}$$

If the equal receipts are expected to continue indefinitely into the future, as with British consols or as is assumed sometimes with real estate and other business investments, equation (18) reduces to

$$P_0 = V \frac{1}{1 - D} \tag{19}$$

The D^{n+1} approaches zero as n approaches infinity, as long as D is a positive fraction (which it normally is) and therefore can be discarded. If $1/(1 + i)$ is substituted for D in equation (19), another useful relation is obtained:

$$P_0 = V\left(1 + \frac{1}{1}\right) = V + \frac{V}{i} \quad \text{or}$$

$$P_0 = \frac{V}{i} \tag{20}$$

since the value of V (the maturity value) by itself is meaningless for an investment that never matures.

Equation (20) is a commonly used rule of thumb for quickly estimating the market value of long-term bonds and other investments and for recalling that market value (P_0) and market rates of interest (i) tend to move in opposite directions. For example, suppose a 20-year bond costing $1,000 pays $50 per year and yields a 5 per cent return. This may be verified by inserting values into equation (10):

$$\$1,000 = \frac{\$50}{0.05}$$

Now suppose that the market rate of interest on other negotiable bonds of similar risk and maturity is expected to fall to 4 per cent. What would this mean in terms of the market value of the bond? Simply divide $50 by 0.04 to obtain $1,250, the new market value. An opportunity therefore exists for obtaining a capital gain by purchasing long-term bonds now for $1,000 and selling each of them for $1,250 after the interest rate falls.

As another example, suppose you are interested in buying income property on the Chicago loop that you believe will generate net revenues (receipts minus costs of everything but interest) of $40,000 every year into the indefinite future. How much could you pay for the property in order to earn a 10 per cent return? Inserting the values into equation (19), we estimate a price of

$$\frac{\$40,000}{0.10} = \$400,000$$

At any price up to $400,000, the desired return could be earned, assuming estimates of costs and revenues are correct. A more accurate calculation seldom merits the effort because of the many unknown factors, but, if desired, can be obtained by use of equation (18) minus the first payment of $40,000 not received at the beginning of the first year. Inserting $1/(1 + i)$ for D into equation (18),

$$P_0 = V \left[\frac{1 - \left(\frac{1}{1 + i}\right)^{n+1}}{1 - \left(\frac{1}{1 + i}\right)} \right] \tag{21}$$

which can be simplified to

$$P_0 = V\left[1 + \frac{1 - (1 + i)^{-n}}{i}\right] \tag{22}$$

where the first 1 inside the bracket denotes the first \$40,000 payment (upon which no discounting would be necessary), which was not received and therefore can be omitted, giving

$$P_0 = V\left[\frac{1 - (1 + i)^{-n}}{i}\right] \tag{23}$$

The bracketed expression is known as the *present-value-of-annuity factor*, for which standard tables are available. From standard interest tables for $i = 10$ per cent and $n = 25$ years, the bracketed value is found to be 9.07704, yielding a present value of

$$P_0 = \$40,000(9.07704)$$
$$= \$363,082$$

Similarly, for $n = 50$ and 100, the factors are 9.91481 and 9.99927, and present values are \$396,592 and \$399,971, respectively. As the years are extended into the future, the present value approaches \$400,000. Investors in real estate are typically not concerned with holding property beyond their lifetimes but are perfectly willing to use a multiplier of 10 instead of 9 or less, because they believe the selling price will appreciate sufficiently to merit capitalization over an infinite number of years.

24-1-4 *Purchase on credit with equal payments*

An individual may invest in an automobile or home by signing an agreement with a mortgage holder stipulating that he will pay uniform installments until the purchase price plus compounded interest is paid in full. Purchase is thereby extended typically up to 3 years on automobiles and up to 20 or 30 years on homes. Firms may purchase their plant and equipment on a similar basis, while reserving their current funds for use as working capital. Equation (23) can be solved for V and used to figure the amount of annual payment to be made:

$$V = \frac{P_0}{\left[\dfrac{1 - (1 - i)^{-n}}{i}\right]} \tag{24}$$

The annual payment can be found by dividing the amount to be amortized (P_0) by the bracketed value taken from a standard present value of an annuity table.

For a practical example, suppose a firm wishes to purchase a \$2-million building by paying \$500,000 now and spreading the remainder over 20 equal annual payments with interest compounded annually at 7 per cent. The annual payment $V = \$141,585$ is found by dividing \$1.5 million by the factor 10.59401 from the table. Annuity tables are also available that give the reciprocals of the present-value factors, for instance, those providing the inverse of $10.59401 = 0.09439$ directly; in this form they are called capital-recovery factors or annuity whose present value is 1.

24-1-5   *Setting equal amounts aside to provide for a future purpose*

Individuals and firms alike have occasion to save monthly and yearly amounts with the plan of purchasing some expensive item at some future date. Such behavior is admittedly contrary to American practice in this age of buying on credit, but some conservative souls continue by choice to save until they can pay cash in order to avoid paying interest charges; others who are in some way unqualified for credit are forced to pay cash. Corporations set up sinking funds for replacement of deteriorating and obsolescent facilities, if only on paper in the form of depreciation allowances for income-tax purposes. Corporate bonds with sinking-fund clauses require that installments be made into a trust. The annual amount to be set aside drawing compounded interest is calculated from the equation

$$P = V\left[\frac{1}{(1+i)^{n-1}}\right] \tag{25}$$

where P is the equal annual payment and V the future amount required. This equation is the same as equation (6), solved for P rather than V, and the bracketed expression is sometimes referred to as the *sinking-fund deposit factor*.

For example, if \$100,000 is needed after 8 years and interest is compounded annually at 6 per cent, the constant amount to be invested each year for 8 years (payments begin at the end of the first year and the last payment earns no interest) is calculated to be

$$P = \$100,000\left[\frac{0.06}{(1+0.06)^{8}-1}\right] = \$100,000(0.10104)$$

$$= \$10,104 \text{ per year}$$

If payments are made quarterly and interest compounded quarterly, the quarterly payment is

$$P = \$100,000\left[\frac{\dfrac{0.06}{4}}{\left(1+\dfrac{0.06}{4}\right)^{4(8)}-1}\right] = \$2,458$$

If sinking-fund tables are used, the factor found for $i = 0.015$ and $n = 32$ provides the correct answer.

24-2   Acceleration Principle, Retained Earnings, and Marginal Efficiency of Investment

In the literature of business cycle theory it is hypothesized that firms adjust their capital to the demand for their products. Increased demand believed to be permanent is met with increased investment. A doubling of demand leads to a doubling of capital, and this leads to more than doubling of an investment routinely needed only for replacement purposes. Investment is thus thought to be proportional to the rate of change in sales. That is, if capital is a linear function of sales,

$$C = kS \tag{26}$$

where k is the constant of proportionality, then investment must be a function of the rate of change of sales with respect to time,

$$I = \frac{dC}{dT} = k \frac{dS}{dT} \tag{27}$$

The decision to invest therefore depends upon whether sales are rising or falling. When sales are constant, investment will be only for replacement of worn-out machines, buildings, and vehicles. When sales are growing, investment grows proportionately.

The acceleration principle clearly applies only to *capital widening*—that is, the duplication of the same kind of capital. This is only part of the story, however, since firms also tend to purchase capital utilizing progressively more efficient technology and to replace labor with additional capital as labor becomes relatively more expensive. (This is discussed further in section 24–7.)

Another type of investment behavior is that a firm with high and stable sales generates a flow of internal funds in the form of retained earnings, which managers pour into capital expansion. This is sometimes associated with the sales-maximization hypothesis that managers desire to increase sales as long as profits are sufficiently high to pacify the stockholders. Internal funds may provide the cheapest way of financing capital expansion needed to increase sales. But in the absence of diminishing returns, it may also be appropriate for the profit-maximizing firm to expand its plant with funds from other sources, such as bank loans, bonds, and stock.

Expected future profits provide the motivating force for investment, according to John Maynard Keynes in his *General Theory of Employment, Interest, and Money*. Keynes held that firms have an array of investments that have various rates of profitability, the most profitable of which are given higher priority. He referred to this array as the marginal efficiency of capital, more accurately described as the *marginal efficiency of investment* (*MEI*), and defined it as the expected rate of return on new investment expenditures. The *MEI* curve is shown in Figure 24-1. All costs were taken into account in calculating the *MEI* except the

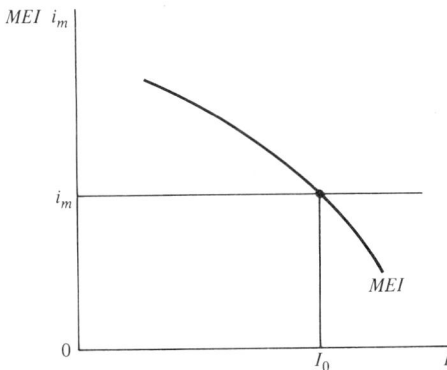

Figure 24-1

cost of financing the investment. Keynes maintained that investments would be undertaken as long as the *MEI* exceeded the cost of capital, referred to as the market rate of interest, denoted by the horizontal line at i_m. Thus, the firm will borrow funds, if necessary, to expand its investments to I_0, because the margin of profits indicated by the vertical distance between the *MEI* curve and the i_m line provides the incentive to do so. Investment will not exceed the equilibrium at I_0, because additional returns are negative. Investment is viewed as a function of expected profit on new investments and the market rate of interest:

$$I = f(MEI, i_m) \tag{28}$$

Investment expands if business people believe new investments will be more profitable (an upward shift in *MEI*) or if interest rates fall (a downward shift in i_m). Investment behavior may at times then be related to sales, retained earnings, and expected profitability according to the above hypothesis, but whether it is profitable for a firm to behave according to one or all of these rules must ultimately rest upon an expected-profit calculation.

24-3 Standard Investment Criteria

The two most commonly used criteria for determining the profitability of investment projects are the *net discounted present value* (abbreviated *NPV*) and the *internal rate of return* (*IRR*). An example of the *NPV* calculation given in section 24-1-2 involved figuring the present value of a stream of cash receipts expected to be generated by the investment and then subtracting the present value of all relevant outlays the investment entails. In short,

$$NPV = \sum_{t=1}^{n} \frac{R_t}{(1+r)^t} - \sum_{t=1}^{n} \frac{C_t}{(1+r)^t} \tag{29}$$

where R_t is cash received in year t, C_t is investment expenditures in year t, and r is rate of return the firm believes it must earn to make the investment worthwhile. If the *NPV* is positive, the investment is profitable under the *NPV* criterion. If a choice is to be made between two or more projects, then the one with the highest *NPV* is given priority. If there is no limit to the amount of funds the firm can borrow at the market rate of interest, all projects with a positive *NPV* would be undertaken.

The *IRR* criterion is basically the same as Keynes's comparison of *MEI* and i_m. It involves calculating the rate of return (r) at which the present values of receipts and expenditures are equal, or where the *NPV* is zero, that is, where equation (29) equals zero. Any r in excess of the firm's alternative cost of capital (plus a percentage added to compensate for any risk and uncertainty surrounding the investment, as discussed in Chapter 25) meets the criterion. If the r is sufficiently high and sufficient funds are obtainable, all such projects should be undertaken.

In most of the cases business people encounter, the calculations are straightforward and either criterion will provide the same advice. There are situations, however, where the criteria give advice that appears conflicting. In the ensuing discussion it is important to recognize that the present value of a stream of net revenue (receipts minus costs in each year) depends to a great extent on the rate of return employed. For a stream of net revenues of $-100, 0, 130$, the initial investment at the beginning of the first year is shown as a negative amount, and no additional receipts over costs are received until the $130 at the end of the second year. If a 10 per cent return is used in discounting, the NPV is $7.43:

$$NPV = -100 + 0 + \frac{130}{(1 + 0.10)^2} = -100 + 130(0.8264)$$

$$= -100 + 107.43 = 7.43$$

If a 20 per cent return is assumed, the NPV is $-\$9.73$:

$$NPV = -100 + 0 + 130(0.6944)$$

$$= -100 + 90.27 = -9.73$$

At $r = 10$ per cent the project is acceptable; but at 20 per cent it is not. The rate at which NPV is zero can be obtained by setting the expression for $NPV = 0$ and solving for r:

$$-100 + \frac{130}{(1 + r)^2} = 0$$

$$(1 + r)^2 = 1.30$$

$$1 + r = 1.14$$

$$r = 0.14, \text{ or } 14 \text{ per cent}$$

The relation between NPV and r is represented by the curve labeled project A in Figure 24-2.

Now consider an alternative project with a stream of net receipts of $-100, 120, 0$. This project is plotted as curve B in Figure 24-2. Intersection of the two curves is determined by the value of r obtained by equating the NPV equations:

$$-100 + \frac{130}{(1 + r)^2} = -100 + \frac{120}{1 + r}$$

$$\frac{(1 + r)^2}{1 + r} = \frac{130}{120}$$

$$1 + r = 1.0833$$

$$r = 0.0833, \text{ or } 8\tfrac{1}{3} \text{ per cent}$$

For values of r below $8\tfrac{1}{3}$ per cent, project A has higher NPV, but for those above $8\tfrac{1}{3}$ per cent, B has higher NPV. The decision as to which project is preferable thus depends upon the rate of return required. The firm that needs only a 7 per cent return will prefer project A; it has the patience to wait longer to recoup its initial outlay. The firm requiring a 10 per cent return is anxious to recoup its investment sooner. The choice thus depends upon time preference as well as on the fact that the two projects have different patterns (or profiles) of net revenues.

Suppose for the moment that the firm figures the NPV using a 7 per cent return. Project A, having the higher NPV, is preferred over project B. If it em-

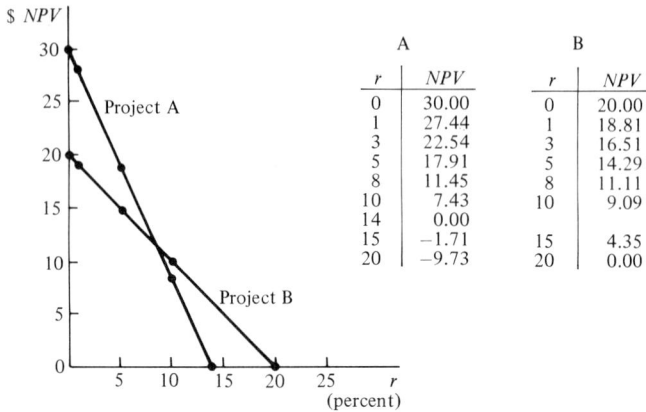

$ NPV

A		
r	NPV	
0	30.00	
1	27.44	
3	22.54	
5	17.91	
8	11.45	
10	7.43	
14	0.00	
15	−1.71	
20	−9.73	

B	
r	NPV
0	20.00
1	18.81
3	16.51
5	14.29
8	11.11
10	9.09
15	4.35
20	0.00

Figure 24-2

ployed the *IRR* technique also, it would observe only the points of intersection of the two curves with the horizontal axis; by this criterion, project B is preferred to project A, because 20 per cent is greater than 14 per cent. In the event of such conflicting advice, which project is best? The answer hinges upon the rate selected for discounting the streams of net revenues, which is not reflected by the *IRR* approach. The firm essentially makes its choice of projects when it selects the value of *r* that is appropriate for its goals and should therefore be guided only by the *NPV* comparison, other things being equal. The *IRR* comparison is irrelevant in this case.

Consider the two other alternative projects having the following patterns of annual net revenues: −100, 50, 160, and −100, 40, 150. In both projects the initial investment of 100 at the beginning of the first year is a negative net receipt; at the end of the first and second years, the first project has greater net returns than the second. When one project is superior in at least 1 year and is in no year inferior to the other, it is said to *dominate*. The first investment stream is dominant and therefore of higher priority than the second. If their curves were plotted in a graph similar to Figure 24-2, the curve for the first project would at all points lie above the curve for the second project. Since there is no intersection, there can be no conflict in recommendations obtained from the *NPV* and *IRR* techniques. In this case, either criterion suffices.

Consider now the annual stream of net revenues of −100, 500, −500. Losses are generated at the beginning and at the end of the project's anticipated life, which frequently occurs in extractive industries where the environment of the mine site must be restored to some satisfactory condition, and in other industries where financial obligations incurred over the span of the project are in excess of revenues in the past year. A plotting of the *NPV* and *r* reveals that the curve is not continuously downward-sloping, as is shown in Figure 24-3. Note that the curve has both positive and negative slopes; it is positive over a range in values of *r* from 38 per cent to 262 per cent and reaches a maximum at *r* = 100 per cent,

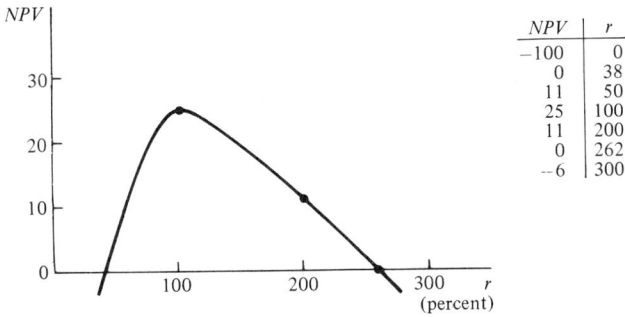

NPV	r
−100	0
0	38
11	50
25	100
11	200
0	262
−6	300

Figure 24-3

which is calculated by setting the first derivative of NPV with respect to r equal to zero and solving for r:

$$NPV = -100 + \frac{500}{1+r} - \frac{500}{(1+r)^2}$$

$$= \frac{-100(1+r)^2 + 500(1+r) - 500}{(1-r)^2}$$

$$= \frac{-100r^2 + 300r - 100}{(1+r)^2}$$

$$\frac{d(NPV)}{dr} = \frac{(1+r)^2(-200r + 300) - (-100r^2 + 300r - 100)2(1+r)}{(1+r)^4} = 0$$

$$= (1+r)(-200r + 300) - 2(-100r^2 + 300r - 100) = 0$$

$$= -200r + 300 - 200r^2 + 300r + 200r^2 - 600r + 200 = 0$$

$$= -500r + 500 = 0$$

$$r = 1.00, \text{ or } 100 \text{ per cent}$$

Note also that the IRR (values of r for which NPV = 0) has two values, which are calculated by setting the expression for NPV equal to zero and solving for r:

$$NPV = \frac{-100r^2 + 300r - 100}{(1+r)^2} = 0$$

$$= -100r^2 + 300r - 100 = 0$$

$$r = \frac{-300 \pm \sqrt{(300)^2 - 4(-100)(-100)}}{2(-100)}$$

$$= \frac{-300 \pm \sqrt{50,000}}{-200} = \frac{-300 \pm 224}{-200} = \frac{76}{200}, \frac{524}{200}$$

$$= 0.38, 2.62$$

Which *IRR* is correct? There is no way of justifying either, except by intuition. This is a major drawback of using the *IRR* criterion. Furthermore, it is possible to have three, four, or more *IRR* when there is more than one reversal of the curve relating *NPV* and *r*.

In comparing two projects, the analyst must be sure that the alternative projects being considered cover the same time periods. If one covers a shorter time span, it must be extended or renewed to the length of the other. It is also important to know if renewal can be made on the same terms. Comparison on the basis of *NPV* assumes the investment opportunities exist only for the stated period, but on the basis of the *IRR* it assumes the opportunity can be renewed on the same terms. Consider two projects, the first of which yields a 6 per cent *IRR* for two consecutive 5-year periods, after which the best obtainable investment is at the market rate of 3 per cent. The second project yields an 8 per cent return for the first 5-year period but cannot be renewed at the same rate and must revert to the market rate of 3 per cent in the sixth year. A comparison of the projects for only the first 5 years leads to acceptance of the second project, but when extended to cover 10 years, the second project is preferred. The higher return in the first 5 years is not sufficient to sustain the higher yield of the first project over the second 5 years in comparison with the second project. "Without information as to the opportunities for renewal, neither formula [*NPV* or *IRR*] can necessarily be expected to furnish a meaningful answer" [13, p. 973].

By the same token, it is possible under capital rationing that funds available in the early years should be placed in liquid investments yielding relatively low market rates of 3 per cent rather than invested immediately in nonliquid internal projects yielding 5 per cent. They might then be freed for use a year or two hence for a larger internal project that has promise of yielding a return in excess of 8 per cent. In this case, it would not pay the firm to be a short-run maximizer.

24-4 A Programming Formulation of Capital Budgeting

In the preceding examples, in which two investment projects were compared, it was assumed that they were mutually exclusive; that is, one but not both could be accepted [1, pp. 472–477]. This could be the case where the projects represent two ways of accomplishing the same end, such as the choice between two machines for embossing copper jewelry or two modes of transporting goods. Mutual exclusivity also comes into the picture where the investor has limited access to capital at the market rate and funds must be budgeted to the most important uses. Programming models are well suited for dealing with this and other problems involved in investment decisions.

Consider the following model. A construction firm with limited investment funds wishes to know how many trucks (x) of a given size it should purchase each year in order to maximize its total net discounted present value (P). The objective function is therefore

$$P = P_1 x_1 + P_2 x_2 + \cdots + P_n x_n \tag{30}$$

where P_i is the *NPV* of the x_i truck in which funds are invested, for instance, P_1 is the marginal contribution to the current value of profits expected to be generated by the first unit of investment in the form of the first truck, x_1, purchased. Marginal profitabilities of additional trucks must therefore be estimated and discounted to their present values to obtain the values for the P_i.

The firm is limited to M_t dollars, which can be invested in trucks in year t. If the cost of the ith truck in the period t is given by c_{it}, then the corresponding structural constraints may be represented by

$$c_{10} x_1 + c_{20} x_2 + \cdots + c_{n0} x_n \leq M_0$$
$$c_{11} x_1 + c_{21} x_2 + \cdots + c_{n1} x_n \leq M_1 \tag{31}$$
$$\cdots\cdots\cdots\cdots\cdots\cdots\cdots\cdots$$
$$c_{1m} x_1 + c_{2m} x_2 + \cdots + c_{nm} x_n \leq M_m$$

The time span extends from the present at $t = 0$ to some terminal date $t = m$. The first structural constraint states that the sum of the moneys paid in the initial period for all projects undertaken, $\sum_{i=1}^{n} c_{i0} x_i$, must not exceed the amount of money M_0 available to the firm during the period.

It is also necessary to stipulate that the trucks cannot be purchased in negative amounts:

$$x_1 \geq 0, x_2 \geq 0, \ldots, x_n \geq 0 \tag{32}$$

Negative investments in trucks could occur if one of the presently owned trucks is sold, in which case it could be represented by another variable, x_k, which must also be greater or equal to zero, since x_k represents an amount sold. In some cases the decision to sell depends upon another decision to purchase, which could add a nonlinearity to the model and require a nonlinear programming calculation.

Fractional values of x are meaningless in this problem, because trucks must be purchased in whole units. The linear programming model is transformed into an integer one by the following stipulation:

All x_i must be integers. $\tag{33}$

This requirement is present in problems where the decision is a matter of accepting or rejecting a particular project. This condition is imposed on the problem by additionally requiring that

$$x_i \leq 1 \tag{34}$$

where $x_i = 1$ means to accept and $x_i = 0$ to reject. Since under constraint (32), $x \geq 0$, and under constraint (33), x_i must be an integer, condition (34) leaves only two possibilities, that $x_i = 0$ or $x_i = 1$. The program is thereby modified to solve the all-or-none problem by adding constraint (34).

In problems where the acceptance or rejection of A, a project under consideration, such as a diesel engine, depends upon the adoption of another project, B, such as a building addition to house the engine, the programming approach is especially useful. All that is necessary to incorporate this condition into the problem is to add the constraint

$$x_a \leq x_b \tag{35}$$

Conditions (32), (33), and (34) require x_b to be either 0 or 1. Then under condition (35), rejection of project x_b (if $x_b = 0$) insures that project A must also be rejected

$(x_a = 0)$. Acceptance of B $(x_b = 1)$ permits $x_a = 0$ or $x_a = 1$, but A will not be approved without B.

In other cases, projects may be mutually exclusive. The adoption of project C may preclude the adoption of project D, and vice versa, owing to physical or budget limitations. This is easily accounted for in a programming model by adding the constraint

$$x_c + x_d \le 1 \tag{36}$$

This narrows the problem down to only three possibilities:

1. $x_c = 1, \quad x_d = 0$
2. $x_c = 0, \quad x_d = 1$
3. $x_c = 0, \quad x_d = 0$

The solution therefore permits the undertaking of only one of the two projects. A similar technique may be used with three or more mutually exclusive investments, that is, $x_c + x_d + x_e + \cdots + x_n \le 1$.

24-5   A Two-Period Model of Individual Investment Decisions

A person named Terry is assumed in this model [17, pp. 194–197] to have a constant annual income, y, which she can either spend on current consumption items or invest in financial instruments paying a constant rate of interest, r, compounded annually. A market exists for titles to future incomes that can be exchanged for current purchasing power. Current wealth is defined by the expression

$$W_0 = y_0 + \frac{y_1}{1+r} + \frac{y_2}{(1+r)^2} + \cdots + \frac{y_t}{(1+r)^t} + \cdots + \frac{y_n}{(1+r)^n} \tag{37}$$

$$= y_0 + K_0 \tag{38}$$

where K_0 denotes the amount of wealth, called capital, that is reserved for future consumption.

Consumption can be distributed in an optimal pattern over time by investment (lending), that is, by exchanging current claims on consumption (money income y_0) for future ones (financial instruments paying interest). Negative investment, called disinvestment (or borrowing), occurs when future claims on consumption are exchanged for present ones. In this model monetary savings from one period to the next are not possible, because only spending for current consumption or investing for future consumption are permitted.

The amount Terry decides to invest (or disinvest) is a function of her endowment of income over time, indicated by point Y in Figure 24-4a, with current and future period consumption coordinates (y_0, y_1), respectively; her time-preference pattern for consumption combinations, as indicated by the indifference map (curves labeled I_1, I_2, and I_3); and her opportunity set of attainable combinations, given by the triangular area OAB under the market line AB passing through point Y. The slope of the market line equals $-(1+r)$, indicating that a dollar's worth of current consumption, c_0, can be exchanged for $(1+r)$ dollars worth of c_1 by a movement upward along AB. There are other market lines

(a) Financial investments   (b) Productive investments

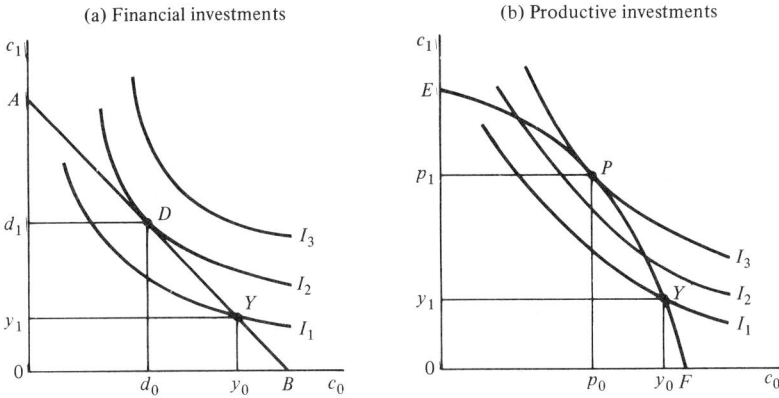

Figure 24-4

parallel to AB, one each for every possible Y endowment. She may move from point Y to a higher preference level (from I_1 to I_2) at point D by exchanging (lending) $d_0 y_0$ of short-term claims on consumption (money) for $d_1 y_1$ of longer-term claims (financial investments paying the constant interest rate r). The amount of repayment $d_1 y_1$ equals $(d_0 y_0)(1 + r)$. If point D were on the market line below point Y, Terry would have preferred instead to borrow, that is, to give up some future consumption (c_1) to get more present consumption (c_0).

Figure 24-4a showed how Terry could improve her position by investing in the financial market. Figure 24-4b shows how she might gain in another way by investing her money directly in a productive venture of her own, such as opening a machine shop or planting soybeans. Curve EF passing through point Y represents her productive investment (disinvestment) opportunities; its concave shape indicates an assumption of diminishing returns to such investment, that is, slope decreases when moving up the curve. The optimum investment of $p_0 y_0$ puts Terry on the highest indifference curve she can reach, I_3.

Figure 24-5a demonstrates how Terry might employ both productive and financial investment to her advantage. Beginning with her initial endowment at point Y, she invests an amount $y_0 q_0$ directly in some productive pursuit of her own, moving her to point Q on her productive investment-opportunities curve. This has the result of enlarging her opportunity set to the triangle bounded by GH. She does not stop at point P, which is on a higher personal preference curve, because she is aware of an opportunity in the financial market to sell claims on future consumption, perhaps in the form of shares in her own firm, equal to an amount $q_1 x_1$ in exchange for $q_0 x_0$ claims on present consumption in the form of cash or actual commodities. Terry has thereby increased her endowment from point Y to point X, where she has more of both present and future goods. The present value of her real and financial holdings is given by the distance OH, which is equal to

$$W_0 = 0q_0 + q_0 H$$

$$= q_0 + \frac{q_1}{1 + r} \tag{39}$$

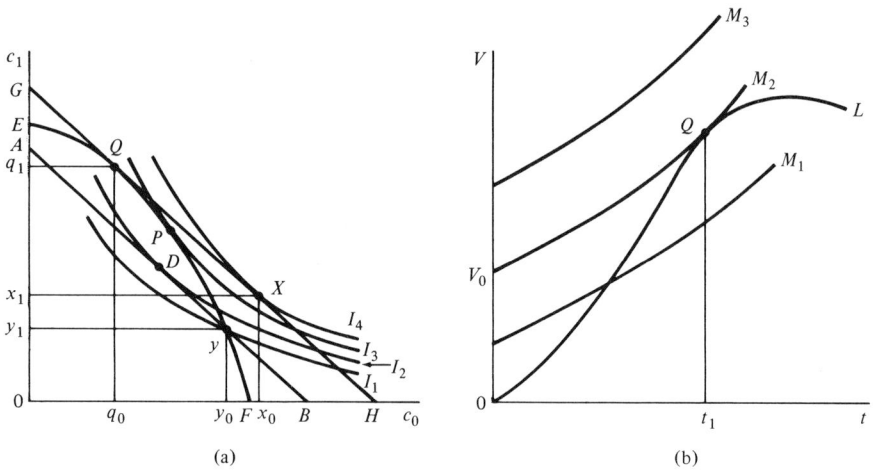

Figure 24-5

or in general terms for multiperiods,

$$W_0 = q_0 + \frac{q_1}{1+r} + \frac{q_2}{(1+r)^2} + \cdots + \frac{q_n}{(1+r)^n} \tag{40}$$

Note that the first shift, from point Y to point Q, involved real savings and investment for both Terry and society, while the second shift, from point Q to point X, was a financial one in which ownership of real goods and resources changed hands with no additional amounts produced.

24-6   Firm and Government Investment Decisions

A distinction can be made between the investment decision of an individual and that of a firm or government [7, pp. 200–201]. The essence of the firm is production and it consumes little, if any, final consumption goods. Income streams generated by the firm either flow through to owners or flow into capital, which generates future income to owners. The direction of flow is reversed when owners pour their assets back into the firm through purchase of the firm's financial assets. Decisions that maximize the firm's wealth also maximize the owners' wealth.

Government agencies are also instrumentalities of individuals and are like firms in that they provide productive services, such as education and postal services. In other ways, they are different from firms, because they may have an additional function of communal consumption, such as national defense. (Note that the decision to categorize defense expenditures as consumption rather than production rests largely on a value judgment.) They are owned collectively rather than individually and may undertake other than wealth maximization, such as income redistribution by taxes and subsidies. To the extent that pursuit of such goals diminishes community capital, they may be considered quasi-consumptive.

In the absence of an accepted criterion of social rationality telling us the relative importance of competing objectives, there can be no unique optimizing solution for government activities.

24-7   Capital Widening and Deepening

The two-period model above illustrates how greater investment in the current period can yield greater future consumption. This use of investment for more of the same processes (as mentioned in section 24-2) is referred to as *capital widening*. Another use of invested resources is for new processes with longer investment periods, called *capital deepening*. For example, more trenches for pipelines can be dug by investing in more hand shovels (capital widening) or by investing more time and effort in manufacturing a motorized trencher, which is probably much more productive than shovels (capital deepening). In the production of wood, more trees can be planted (widening) or existing trees can be permitted to grow for a longer time (deepening). In the latter case, the current sacrifice is assumed to be the same, but the output date is lengthened.

The decision to deepen capital involves determining the optimal length of investment, which can be examined with reference to Figure 24-5b, with time on the horizontal axis and present value on the vertical. Let the curve labeled L represent the various market values through time of standing timber, which is to be milled into lumber; it shows the productive growth of the asset. The "discount curves" designated M_1, M_2, and M_3 are alternative representations of the market curves like AB and GH of Figure 24-5a. They show the growing value of investments with interest compounded continuously over time according to the general equation $V_0 = V_t e^{-rt}$; they are also curves of equal wealth in that all points along a curve have the same discounted present value. The optimal investment period is t_1, where the L curve touches the highest attainable constant-wealth curve M_2; V_0 is therefore the maximum wealth or present value attainable along the L curve, which represents the relevant productive opportunity set. Solution at point Q corresponds to the production solution at point Q in Figure 24-5a. The financing solution cannot be shown on Figure 24-5b, because the preference function cannot be plotted on these axes.

Questions and Problems

24-1. Define and explain:
  a. investment
  b. capital
  c. net discounted present value
  d. marginal efficiency of investment
  e. internal rate of return
  f. capital widening
  g. capital deepening
  h. mutual exclusivity

24-2. Obtain answers for the following compound-interest problems.
  a. Find money value in 2 years of $1,000 invested at 10 per cent interest compounded annually.

    b. Find the answer to part *a* under quarterly compounding of interest.

    c. Find the answer to part *a* under daily compounding of interest.

    d. Find the answer to part *a* under continuous compounding of interest.

24-3. Calculate the constant annual amount that must be set aside, drawing interest at 7 per cent compounded annually, to accumulate $1 million in 30 years.

24-4. An investment of $40,000 is expected to yield receipts of $5,000 per year for 10 years. Calculate the annual compounded rate of return.

24-5. Calculate the present value of the following amounts, compounded annually at 7 per cent:

    a. $3,000 received 2 years hence

    b. $10,000 received 5 years hence

    c. $3,000 received at the end of the next 3 years

    d. $10,000 received at the end of the next 5 years

24-6. Show algebraically that

$$\frac{1 - D^{n+1}}{1 - D} = 1 + \frac{1 - (1 + i)^{-n}}{i}$$

24-7. How long should a tree grown to produce lumber be permitted to grow before being cut? Assume there are diminishing returns to investment of additional time in the lumber-production process.

24-8. The managers of a firm are considering investing in five projects having the *NPV* and first-, second-, and third-year costs shown in the table. Set up a programming formulation of the problem under the following assumptions:

    a. budget restrictions of $30 (million) in the first year, $20 in the second, and $10 in the third

    b. complementarity of projects 1 and 2, and also of 3 and 5

    c. mutual exclusivity of projects 1 and 3

Project	*1*	*2*	*3*	*4*	*5*
NPV	60	20	50	40	10
First-year cost	20	5	20	10	3
Second-year cost	10	10	20	5	2
Third-year cost	5	15	10	0	5

References

1. William J. Baumol. *Economic Theory and Operations Analysis*. 3d ed. (Englewood Cliffs, N.J.: Prentice-Hall, 1972), ch. 18–19.

2. Eugene L. Brigham and James L. Pappas. *Managerial Economics* (Hinsdale, Ill.: Dryden Press, 1972), ch. 13 and appendix A.

3. Herman Chernoff. "Decision Theory." In *International Encyclopedia of the Social Sciences*, IV, 62–66.

4. Irving Fisher. *The Theory of Interest* (New York: Kelley & Millman, 1954). First printed in 1930. The classic in decision theory and interest.

5. Floyd E. Gillis, Jr. *Managerial Economics—Decision Making Under Certainty for Business and Engineering* (Reading, Mass.: Addison-Wesley, 1969), ch. 1–5.

6. Eugene L. Grant and W. Grant Ireson. *Principles of Engineering Economy.* 4th ed. (New York: Ronald Press, 1960).

7. Jack Hirshleifer. "Investment: The Investment Decision." In *International Encyclopedia of the Social Sciences*, VIII, 194–202.

8. ————. "On the Theory of Optimal Investment Decision." *Journal of Political Economy* 66 (August 1958): 329–352. Reprinted in Ezra Solomon [14, pp. 205–228].

9. J. H. Lorie and L. J. Savage. "Three Problems in Capital Rationing." *Journal of Business* 28 (October 1955): 229–239. Reprinted in Ezra Solomon [14, pp. 56–66].

10. H. G. Manne. *Insider Trading and the Stock Market* (New York: Free Press, 1966).

11. Jacob Marschak. "Decision Theory." In *International Encyclopedia of the Social Sciences*, IV, 42–55.

12. E. J. Mishan. *Economics for Social Decisions—Elements of Cost-Benefit Analysis* (New York: Praeger, 1972), ch. 21–26.

13. Romney Robinson. "The Rate of Interest, Fisher's Rate of Return Over Costs and Keynes' Internal Rate of Return: Comment." *American Economic Review* 46 (December 1956): 972–973. Reprinted in Ezra Solomon [14, pp. 72–73].

14. Ezra Solomon (ed.). *The Management of Corporate Capital* (Chicago: Free Press of Glencoe, 1959).

15. H. Martin Weingartner. *Mathematical Programming and the Analysis of Capital Budgeting Problems* (Englewood Cliffs, N.J.: Prentice-Hall, 1963).

25 Knowledge, Risk, and Uncertainty

In all the preceding chapters of this text, analysis was based upon the assumption of certainty. The values of variables used were known in advance. In the real world the future is more accurately perceived as a distribution of eventualities; specific results have only limited probabilities of occuring. A large body of literature now exists for dealing with the entire distribution. Bayesian analysis and decision theory deserve more attention than they can be given in this chapter and are therefore left for consideration in other texts. This chapter provides a brief introduction to the theory of knowledge, information, investment decisions under risk and uncertainty, and portfolio choice.

25-1 The Economics of Knowledge

In the real world of economic events individuals who wish to maximize their preference functions first take stock of, and perhaps doubt the adequacy of, their first-hand knowledge of the environment and their opportunities for success. Although some minimum amount of knowledge is required for individuals to perceive, plan, pursue, and achieve their smallest objectives, they hesitate to take on ventures that might be outside their accustomed range of knowledge. At this point they may seek additional information to help avoid jeopardizing their resources and to increase their chances of realizing their goals.

In a very real sense, such knowledge is an intermediate good that may be produced by research, purchased from knowledge brokers (academic and business consultants), and obtained free of charge by monitoring the news media and research studies made available to the public [13, p. 32]. The first two involve explicit costs, and all three require additional expenses for search, evaluation, and dissemination. Search costs for a firm, for instance, may include the time and expense of a staff to write letters, telephone, look up references, stand in line at library checkout counters, duplicate printed matter, and read. Where information is incorrect or suspect, it must be evaluated, giving rise to additional costs of checking the accuracy of figures, comparison with other sources, and consultation among staff members concerning the nature of the materials. Once the information has been obtained and verified, it must be disseminated to interested members of the firm. This involves still more time and expense for preparing memos, telephoning, reading, conducting seminars, and scheduling training sessions.

Like a pickup truck, an airplane, or an electronic computer, knowledge can be a final good, yielding pleasure and satisfaction, as well as an intermediate good. Often it is not possible to discern when one is acquiring knowledge for knowledge's sake, because the human mind has the capacity to utilize eventually most kinds of knowledge. Pure research has a way of producing scientific breakthroughs that shape the technologies, consumption goods, and institutions of the future. The study of the humanities and religion can similarly produce a better understanding of personal and social needs, goals, and motivations. How often one hears it said, "The company is only as good as its people." Indeed, the human factor is what business is (or should be) all about. It is understandable that business people in the quest of short-run profits may disregard longer-run considerations. They may also be aware that it is not possible for everyone to concern themselves with society's policy decisions nor is everyone suited to do so. Economy dictates that each person pursue his or her comparative advantage. Still, most business executives support the idea that knowledge is worthwhile and encourage their employees to educate themselves—preferably on their own time.

Knowledge, like love and seeds, has the remarkable capacity of growing as it is distributed. The possessor of knowledge can give it to others and yet retain it [2, p. 3]. The benevolent disperser can enjoy seeing information put to good use and stands to gain materially as a member of an improved society. The disperser who charges for services gains more momentarily, but his or her psychic income may be thereby either enhanced or diminished, depending upon personal material needs and value standards.

Knowledge is sometimes categorized as being "good" or "bad." Good (truthful and enlightening) knowledge is generally acknowledged as being beneficial for the recipient and society; presumably one could not get too much of it, although bosses, parents, and politicians are sometimes not sure of this. Bad knowledge is that which is not in the best interests of society. Economics per se takes no position on the goodness or badness of knowledge or action. *Positive economics* observes behavior and studies its impact on persons and institutions, frequently with reference to some performance criterion or standard of efficiency. It is recognized, however, that the values of the researcher cannot be entirely excluded, since they implicitly influence the choice of data, tools of analysis, and criteria of economic studies. *Normative, or welfare, economics* applies value judgments explicitly. The distinction between positive and normative economics is fairly clear as a concept but difficult to apply in practice. Studies are usually confined to activities that are legal, or if illegal, those that have come to trial, because of the greater availability of data and the lack of stigma attached to such work.

The acquisition of knowledge is not always a cumulative, irreversible process, because men forget, lose their ability to communicate, and die [5, p. 183]. Writings become buried in libraries under the huge, continuous outpouring of new writings, and many may never be read by those who could most use the information; thus, inventions may be duplicated unknowingly by people who missed the descriptions of them in earlier literature. Consumer tastes and production techniques change, new products appear, and the relevance of information gained from the past fades with the passing of time.

Knowledge in economic analysis is also categorized according to its degree of perfection. In the absence of disclaimers, perfect knowledge is assumed with regard to prices, availabilities, and actions of competitors. In real-world situations, unlike theoretical ones, knowledge is usually less than perfect. Between perfect knowledge and no knowledge lies an awareness of possible outcomes whose relative probabilities of occurring are measurable (a condition of *risk*) or not measurable (a condition of *uncertainty*). The distinction between risk and uncertainty was made at least as early as the year 1921 by Frank H. Knight [14, pp. 19–21 and ch. 7]. Risk is uncertainty about events whose probabilities of occurring can be measured, but this definition cannot be pushed to the extreme, since outcomes with known probabilities can be insured against loss, which would have the effect of eliminating uncertainty. Where no uncertainty is present, some decisions need not be made and guesswork is eliminated. To cope with the problems of decision making, people always strive to increase their certainty about events, which ranges from no knowledge at all, through uncertainty and calculated risk, to the unattainable perfect state of omniscience.

25-2 Technological and Market Information

In the literature of economics there is a growing interest in an area of business knowledge and uncertainty called the *theory of information*. Only a sample of the many novel ideas developing in this exciting subject area can be given here. Jack Hirshleifer separates knowledge into two distinct branches [13, p. 33]— *technological uncertainty*, concerning resource endowments and productive opportunities, and *market uncertainty*, concerning supply and demand offers of others.

Under the first branch, production-function information is converted into legally recognized private property by means of *patents*. Other firms are legally permitted to use the patented information only upon payment of royalty fees to the patent holders. Such payments are viewed by some as hindering the optimal utilization of new information but are considered necessary compensation to reward inventors and encourage an optimal flow of investment into the research and development of more new ideas. However, patents are known to be less than perfect in guaranteeing inventors adequate compensation and in promoting optimal investment in new ideas, because patent laws are not sufficiently enforced to prevent pirating; all benefits are not captured for inventors by royalty schemes; and the inventions and exploitation of them are surrounded by discouraging uncertainties. Some inventors even try to safeguard their secrets by not applying for patents.

On the other hand, Hirshleifer has pointed out that the inventors with patents may be able to profit from advertising their information rather than selling it immediately, as the patent system facilitates. Being the first to know of the inventions and their possible uses, they can anticipate and profit from speculative rises and falls of resource prices and common-stock values. An example cited was the Hall process for raising values of bauxite ores [13, p. 34]. In a similar manner, the management of a firm with inside knowledge of the firm's activities can compensate itself further by buying and selling the firm's stock on the open market before the firm disseminates new information. H. G. Manne defends this insider trading as useful to society in compensating entrepreneurs for their innovations and therefore opposes its restriction by disclosure laws. Such activity is at least potentially in conflict with the interest of corporate owners, since insiders can gain from bad managerial performance by selling stock short on the basis of advanced knowledge of their own mistakes; also, they may be able to use company funds rather than their own to cover information costs. This mode of management remuneration is therefore believed to be an inefficient alternative to payment of higher salaries.

The most alert outsiders may gain from the use of information not yet widely disseminated by buying or selling resources, commodities, and stocks—still ahead of the crowd of other outsiders—and in the case of investment services and brokers, by selling the information to others. Distribution of this information by the owners without charge is probably not useful until after the truly undervalued property has been purchased and they wish to sell at prices driven higher by encouraged speculation. Evaluation and verification of information become especially critical for outsiders at this point. Authenticity may be obtained by simple inspection, made manifest at some cost, or guaranteed by the sellers.

Much of the literature dealing with market information excludes technological uncertainty by assuming that trading prices and terms are known. Information is sought here not to improve the individual's own demand and supply offers but to take advantage of those made by others. Buyers are predominantly the searchers for new information, and sellers are predominantly the "pushers" of information through the medium of advertising. Searchers investigate prices optimally according to a sequencing process and select items whose terms are superior to others that have been predetermined as acceptable. Returns to search efforts depend upon the commodity's importance in the budget and the information's durability. Search costs are influenced by the sellers' proximity, recognizability, and visibility of offers. On the other hand, sellers determine their optimum advertising based upon the number of buyers and their search activity, the commodity's distinctiveness, and communications media's efficiency. Movement toward an equilibrium might occur over time as sellers with high prices either reduce their prices or go out of business, as customers shift to other goods with lower prices. In the absence of changing conditions, there would eventually be no need for additional search and advertising expenses. But in the dynamic conditions of the real world, price dispersions are maintained not only by exogenous changes in demand and supply but also by endogenous mobility of buyers and sellers entering and leaving the market and by forgetting. The latter prevents participants from becoming perfectly informed.

Uncertainty about quality is more difficult to handle than uncertainty about price because of its multidimensionality, unquantifiability, subjectiveness, and asymmetry in informational endowments. When buyers are unable to detect differences in quality, sellers of superior products are discouraged from offering their products. They are encouraged to downgrade their quality in response to buyer ignorance, and inferior products become the rule in the market. This may bring about countervailing devices like brand names, guarantees, and informative advertising. Wary buyers can protect themselves to some extent by close inspection and by experience when purchases are repeated, thus classifying commodities as inspection goods or experience goods. The former tend to exist in a competitive market, while the latter, at least for the first unit, tend to have the very low elasticities characteristic of monopoly markets.

Most observers agree that greater availability of valid market information is desirable in promoting social efficiency. There is disagreement as to whether this should be encouraged by public policy, however, because of the potential for dissemination of misinformation and the fact that much of the alleged gain from better information is merely redistributive. In regard to the social desirability of advertising, the jury is still out.

25-3   Coping with Risk and Uncertainty in Investment Decisions

Several approaches for dealing with risk and uncertainty are reviewed in this section: (1) the cutoff period, (2) addition of a risk factor, (3) probability calculations, and (4) sensitivity analysis [1, pp. 477–484].

25-3-1   *Cutoff period*

Perhaps the crudest approach to dealing with risk and uncertainty is setting an arbitrary span of time over which an investment expenditure must be recovered. This is known as the *cutoff period, pay-back period,* or *finite-horizon technique.* Business managers who invest in projects located in foreign countries that have a history of unstable government and nationalization of externally owned firms will sometimes demand a sufficiently high rate of return to insure that their ventures will be recouped within, say, 3 years. They wish to get their money back before the next revolution comes. Such behavior throws them open to the criticism of exploiting the poor. The revolutionary can point to the obviously discriminatory investment practices of the firm compared to those made in its own country, using this information to fan the fires of revolution and consequently speeding up the date of nationalization. Also, the facilities built to last only for short periods of time may be inferior to those believed to be more permanent.

The same approach is applied to domestic projects but often with extended horizons of 10 to 50 years. Regardless of the time span selected, the approach is defective in that it ignores conditions following the cutoff date. Suppose two alternative buildings are being considered for a 15-year investment, one of which is designed to collapse in the sixteenth year and the other, slightly more expensive, is designed to last for more than 50 years. Under a 15-year horizon, the cheaper building would win out over the one with longer potential use. Considerations beyond the cutoff date are disregarded, although they may be known with some degree of certainty.

25-3-2   *Addition of a risk factor*

A more attractive device for dealing with risk is to add an appropriate percentage to the rate of interest used in discounting the values of future incomes and expenses. The discount rate $D = 1/(1 + i)$ used in calculating present values is reduced by the addition of a risk factor, j. Suppose a project merits a risk factor of, say, 4 per cent added to the cost of money, i, of 8 per cent. The discount rate becomes

$$D = \frac{1}{1 + i + j} = \frac{1}{1 + 0.08 + 0.04} = \frac{1}{1.12} = 0.893$$

The addition of a positive-valued risk factor always reduces the discount rate, since

$$\frac{1}{1 + i + j} < \frac{1}{1 + i}$$

A lower discount rate means that the present value of investments must also be lower. Also, projects with more distant returns are given less weight, because the smaller fractional value of D raised to greater powers becomes progressively smaller. Weightings given to events occuring in different years could, however, be changed by using different risk factors.

The major trouble with this approach is that the value assigned to the risk factor is somewhat arbitrary. This is especially so because investors' aversion to risk affects their judgment in deciding the percentage to use. The use of a constant risk factor also assumes that risk will not change over time, which is probably not true.

25-3-3 *Probability calculations*

The probability approach is based upon standard probability theory [1]. Harry Markowitz has shown how statistical probabilities can be assigned to various expected returns produced by combinations of stocks, bonds, and other widely held financial instruments [17]. His approach to optimal portfolio selection begins with a calculation of annual returns on selected common stocks for which there is a historical record covering a number of years (18, in his example). Annual per cent returns are defined by the formula

$$r = \frac{P_{ct} - P_{c(t-1)} + d}{P_{c(t-1)}} \tag{1}$$

where P_{ct} is the closing market price in the year t, $P_{c(t-1)}$ the closing price in the previous year, and d the dividends distributed during the year. In this way, both dividends and paper capital gains are included, but the equal weights given to dollars gained from each are appropriate only when such dollars are taxed equally. Next, an average return is calculated for each stock and annual deviations from the average are recorded for each year. These statistics are used, together with appropriate weightings given to relative amounts invested in each stock, to calculate two indexes for the portfolio: one for expected earnings and one for expected risk.

When expected earnings are based entirely upon past performance, average returns of the past are assumed to provide a best estimate of future returns. Sample calculations for a single security for only 5 years are given in Table 25-1. Expected earnings, r_e, are therefore 12.8 percent and variance is 0.093226.

Table 25-1

Year	Per cent return	Deviations from average	Squared deviations
1	−0.105	−0.233	0.054289
2	0.620	0.492	0.242064
3	0.050	−0.078	0.006084
4	−0.250	−0.378	0.142884
5	0.325	0.197	0.038809
Average	0.128	0.000	0.093226

The standard deviation, r_e, is obtained by taking the square root of the variance:

$$\sigma_e = \sqrt{(r - r_e)^2} = \sqrt{0.093226} = 0.30533 \tag{2}$$

If the past record of performance is absent or judged to be inappropriate for prediction of future values, then estimates depend upon subjective (belief) probabilities rather than upon those calculated from historical observations. One might take a poll of investment experts, asking them to assign probabilities to various categories of expected returns, such as a 25 per cent chance of no profits, a 50 per cent chance of a return of 10 per cent, and a 25 per cent chance of a 20 per cent return. From this information, the expected value can be calculated as a weighted average in which probabilities rather than frequencies are used as weights:

$$r_e = 0(0.25) + 0.10(0.50) + 0.20(0.25)$$
$$= 10 \text{ per cent}$$

The value of σ_e can also be calculated by use of the equation

$$\sigma_e = \sqrt{\sum (\gamma_i - \gamma_e)^2 P_i}$$
$$= \sqrt{(-0.10)^2(0.25) + (0)^2(0.50) + (0)^2(0.25)}$$
$$= \sqrt{(0.01)(0.25)} = \sqrt{0.0025} = 0.05, \text{ or 5 per cent risk}$$

Similar calculations could be made for other securities and the results plotted as shown in Figure 25-1. If one were to choose only one security, the one with the greatest return and least risk, security 1 would be clearly preferable to securities 2, 3, and 5, because it provides both a higher return and less risk. It is also preferred to security 6, since it has a higher return and the same risk, and to security 4, since the return is the same but with less risk. Of the remaining securities 7, 8, and 9, it cannot be said that any is inferior or superior to security 1, or to each other, in the absence of any knowledge of the investor's risk preference.

Assume for the moment that security 1 is preferred by the investor above all the rest. Does it follow that he or she should concentrate all his or her funds in

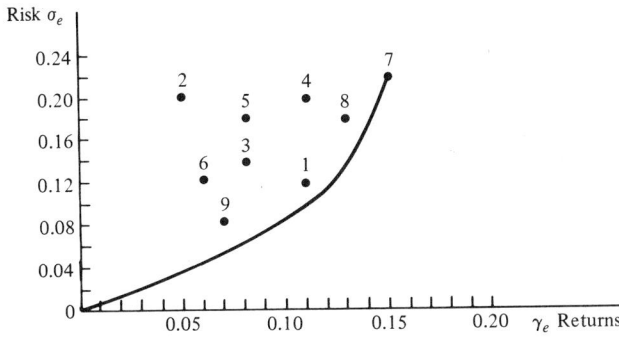

Figure 25-1

the shares of this single security? The answer is no, unless the returns and risks are perfectly correlated for all securities, which is highly unlikely. There are undoubtedly several different combinations of securities that will provide a greater expected return and with less risk. The solid line represents the smallest attainable standard deviation associated with each rate of return for portfolios selected from the nine securities. The curve lies below and to the right of all but security 7, because of risk reduction attributable to diversification. Diversification reduces risk, because the standard deviations of individual securities in the portfolios are different; that is, the standard deviation for the efficient portfolios on the curve are lower than the average of the sum of those for each security in the portfolios. In other words, the correlations between pairs of securities play a role in reducing the risk of portfolios. The better the risks offset each other in the portfolio (the lower the coefficient of correlation), the less the risk of the portfolio as a whole.

Since reference is made later to the coefficient of correlation, it should be discussed at this point. The coefficient of correlation, c, between any two securities (or other investments) x and y is defined by the ratio

$$c = \frac{\text{covariance between } x \text{ and } y}{\sigma_x \sigma_y} \tag{3}$$

where σ_x and σ_y are the standard deviations of x and y, respectively, and the covariance is simply the product of the variations of x and y:

$$\text{cov } xy = \frac{\sum (x - x_e) \sum (y - y_e)}{n} \tag{4}$$

The correlation coefficient can have values between -1 and $+1$, inclusive. If the variables are totally independent, $c = 0$ and the variables are said to be uncorrelated. If one variable is an exact positive multiple of the other, $c = +1$. If one is an exact negative multiple of the other, $c = -1$.

If the covariances are calculated on a two-by-two basis between all the securities of a portfolio, they can be used to demonstrate that the variance of a portfolio is generally lower than a weighted average of the variations (same as

Table 25-2 Variance of a Portfolio

	(1) Amount invested	(2) Covariance with security 1	(3) Amount × covariance	(4) Covariance with security 2	(5) Amount × covariance	(6) Covariance with security 3	(7) Amount × covariance	(8) Variance of portfolio
Security 1	0.50	0.092	0.0460	0.040	0.0200	0.062	0.0031	
Security 2	0.30	0.051	0.0153	0.035	0.0105	0.041	0.0123	
Security 3	0.20	0.037	0.0074	0.032	0.0064	0.050	0.0100	
Sum			0.0687		0.0369		0.0254	
Amount invested			× 0.50		× 0.30		× 0.20	
Amount sum			0.03435		0.01107		0.00508	0.0505

408

covariation of a security with itself) of individual securities. Table 25-2 provides an example of how the variance of a portfolio of three securities can be calculated. The value obtained, 0.0505, is less than the weighted average of variations of the three securities, 0.0665 ($= 0.0460 + 0.0105 + 0.0100$).

Markowitz uses programming methods for selecting a portfolio that minimizes the risk associated with expected earnings of a given level. The appropriate efficient portfolio depends, of course, upon the degree of risk aversion of the individual investor, as is discussed later in the chapter.

25-3-4 *Sensitivity analysis*

Sensitivity analysis (introduced in Chapter 14) is another method for taking into account risk in making investment decisions [1, pp. 482–483]. One simply selects the most crucial and uncertain variables used in calculating the estimated present value. By substituting a range of possible values into the programming model, the sensitivity of the present-value estimate to changes in key variables can be observed. For example, if a firm's plans for introducing a new product are based upon capturing 15 per cent of the market, estimated present values can be calculated first on the assumption that all expectations will be fulfilled, and second on the alternative that the next most likely expectations will be met; finally the net present value could be set equal to zero to determine the minimum market share required for the firm to break even on the project. Then if the firm does not achieve the minimum market share within a reasonable length of time, say a year or two, the new product can be dropped as unprofitable.

This approach enables the management to form some judgment of the magnitude of the risk involved. The calculation can be made quickly and inexpensively but gives results that are relatively crude compared to the Markowitz method based upon probabilistic information.

25-4 A Theory of Portfolio Choice Under Conditions of Risk

Traditional investment choice under risk [21], as employed by Irving Fisher [7] and Harry M. Markowitz [17], postulates individual preference for investments with high expected rates of return and low risk. Indifference curves reflecting these preferences, shown in Figure 25-2a, are upward-sloping to the right, reflecting positive utility of higher returns (wealth preference) and disutility of higher risk (risk aversion). They are typically curved to the right under the assumption of diminishing marginal rates of substitution, although this is not essential to the analysis. Curves that are lower and to the right represent higher levels of preference.

The investor's total utility function is given first by

$$U = f(W_e, \sigma_w) \tag{5}$$

where W_e indicates expected wealth and σ_w the forecasted standard deviation of W_e. Wealth preference implies $dU/dW_e = 0$ and risk aversion that $dU/d\sigma_w < 0$. The investor's utility can also be expressed more conveniently as a function of the expected rate of return r_e:

$$U = g(r_e, \sigma_e) \tag{6}$$

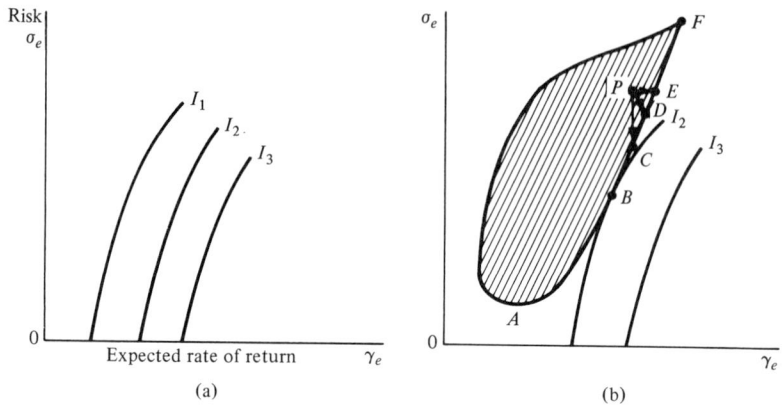

Figure 25-2

since the expected rate of return on a given commitment of wealth to investment is defined as

$$r_e = \frac{W_t - W_i}{W_i} \tag{7}$$

or

$$W_t = r_e W_i + W_i \tag{8}$$

where W_t is terminal wealth accumulated from invested wealth W_i and is shown to be directly related to r_e. The predicted standard deviation of r_e, denoted by σ_e, is the measure of risk.

All sets of available investment opportunities are represented by points within the shaded area shown in Figure 25-2b. All plans are assumed to involve some risk, otherwise the shaded area would touch the horizontal axis. In choosing the best plan consistent with their needs, investors will choose the one at point B that places them on their highest attainable indifference curves I_2. Their decisions can be made in two steps: first, determine which plans are *efficient* in the sense that no alternative plans have an equal rate of return with less risk, a higher return with equal risk, or a higher return with less risk; second, select a plan from among those that are efficient. Plans that lie along the lower right-hand boundary are the efficient ones, since any plan within the boundary at some point P is dominated by plans on the boundary, such as those at some points C, D, and E. The curve $ABCDEF$, representing all the efficient plans, is called the *investment-opportunity curve*.

The presence of any available riskless assets may be brought into the model by recognizing that risklessness implies zero standard deviation ($\sigma_e = 0$). A riskless asset must therefore exist at a point K on the horizontal axis shown in Figure 25-3a. The horizontal distance OK must (by definition) also be the pure rate of interest. If an investor divides his wealth between riskless (point K) and risky (point S) assets in the proportion α (alpha), his expected rate of return is

$$r_e = \alpha r_{eK} + (1 - \alpha) r_{eS} \tag{9}$$

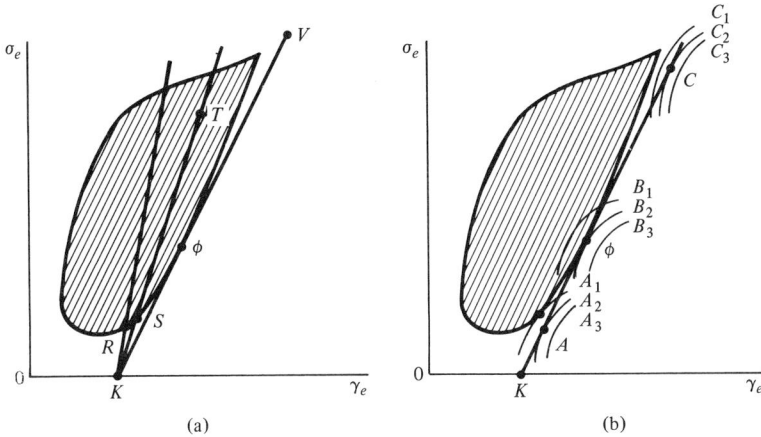

(a)   (b)

Figure 25-3

The standard deviation of this combination is

$$\sigma_e = \sqrt{\alpha^2\sigma_{eK} + (1 - \alpha)^2\sigma_{eS}^2 + 2r_{KS}\alpha(1 - \alpha)\sigma_{eK}\sigma_{eS}} \tag{10}$$

where r_{KS} is the correlation coefficient between the two plans. Since $\sigma_{eK} = 0$, expression (10) reduces to

$$\sigma_e = (1 - \alpha)\sigma_{eK} \tag{11}$$

From this it may be inferred that any combination of riskless and risky assets must have r_e and σ_e values that are on a straight line between the points K and S. All combinations of r_e and σ_e are attainable along line KS by lending some money at the pure rate of interest and investing the rest in some combination of risky assets. Similarly, combinations along line KR are attainable by lending some at the pure rate at point K and investing some at the risky rate at point R. Of all such possibilities, the investment plan at point ϕ, where the ray from point K is tangent to the investment-opportunity curve, will dominate.

An investor who borrows at the pure rate of interest K and invests the funds in more of plan S can obtain investment combinations at points, such as T, that lie along the extension of line KS. Borrowing at the pure rate is the equivalent to disinvesting in the riskless security K. The effect upon r_e and σ_e can be obtained by assigning negative values to α in equations (9) and (10). The investor who can borrow as much as desired at the lending rate would still purchase the investment combination at point ϕ, and the investment-opportunity curve now coincides with the line $K\phi V$. If the opportunity curve is not originally a straight line, the investor could first select the optimum combination at point ϕ and then lend or borrow to reach the precise point on KV where an indifference curve is tangent.

Two additional assumptions are necessary to derive the conditions under which equilibrium can exist in the capital market: All investors can borrow and lend on equal terms, and they agree upon the expected rates, standard deviations, and correlation coefficients of the various investments. These assumptions insure that each investor views investment alternatives in the same manner. Figure 25-3b illustrates the case for three different investors for some given set of asset prices. Investor A prefers point *A*, at which he or she lends some funds at the pure rate and invests the rest in the asset combination at point ϕ. Investor B puts all his or her funds in combination at ϕ. Investor C invests all his or her funds plus those he or she can borrow in order to reach the preferred point *C*. All three attempt to purchase only the risky assets contained in the combination at point ϕ.

Attempts by all the investors to purchase the same assets in combination ϕ would cause their prices to be bid up and their market yields to fall, thereby reducing the attractiveness of ϕ relative to other combinations. Point ϕ thus tends to move to the left of its original position. The falling prices of other combinations also cause these points to shift to the right. Revisions of prices and investors' actions tend to cause the investment-opportunity curve to become more linear and to coincide in part with the market line *KV*, as shown in Figure 25-4a. The process continues until every asset has a price low enough to cause it to be included in at least one combination on *KV*. Investors can hold alternative combinations of risky assets that are efficient, that is, those from points *A* to *C* along *KV*, which can be obtained by various combinations of borrowing and lending. For example, combination *A* can be obtained either by exclusive purchase of risky assets or by lending some funds at the pure rate and investing the rest in a combination *B* or *C* of risky assets.

This analysis, presented by William F. Sharpe, provides support for the presence of multiple portfolio choices distributed along the market line, depending upon individual risk preferences, rather than bunched at a single point ϕ, which would be the case if all investors had the same preferences. Support is given for the classical explanation of the pricing of capital assets associated with the capital market line in Figure 25-4b, whereby the *price of time* is measured by the pure interest rate at point *K* and the *price of risk* is given by the reciprocal of the slope of the line *KV* (the marginal expected return per unit of risk assumed). The positive linear market relation between the expected return and risk of an asset

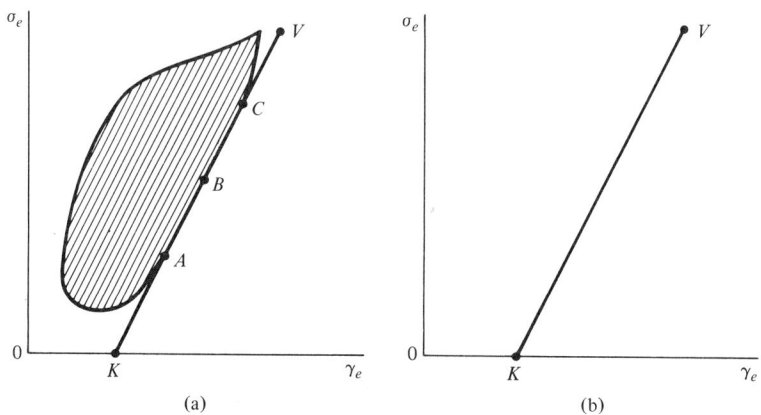

$$(a) \qquad\qquad (b)$$

Figure 25-4

appears to be consistent with the common practice of investment counselors of accepting lower expected returns from securities whose prices fluctuate less in response to changes in the economy.

25-5   The Theory of the Firm Under Conditions of Risk

Consideration of risk has important implications for the theory of the firm [20]. When risk is brought into the picture, it no longer follows that the firm will maximize its present market values by maximizing the net present value of its expected profits (net revenues). Both capital market theory and empirical evidence indicate that there is a trade-off between expected return and systematic risk. Market value can be enhanced either by increases in expected profits or by decreases in risk. The equilibrium market value of the firm is related to expected returns R_e and risk σ_e (standard deviation) according to the equation

$$V = \frac{R_e - \lambda c\sigma_e}{i} \tag{12}$$

where i is the opportunity cost of current consumption or the riskless rate of interest, λ is a constant value of risk set by the capital market on all firms, and c is the correlation coefficient between the returns of the firm and an average return of all firms in the market. (The fraction λ/σ_e for the capital market is referred to as the price of risk reduction.) The term $\lambda c\sigma_e$, called the risk premium, would equal zero if there were no risk. The $c\sigma_e$ component of risk is identified with the individual firm.

Equation (12) can also be expressed in terms of the firm's capitalization rate of earnings r by substituting the value of V into the definitional equation $r = R_e/V$:

$$r = i + \lambda c\left(\sigma_e \frac{R_e}{V}\right) \tag{13}$$

Richard Schramm and Rodger Sherman have noted that a firm taking actions to reduce the risk component σ_e rather than to increase net revenue R_e is also acting to maximize the firm's market value. Behavior attributed by some analysts to goals of sales or growth-rate maximization may, in fact, be nothing more than an attempt to smooth out fluctuations in reported profits. By increasing expenditures for advertising and research in times when current income is expected to be high, the firm can avoid reporting unsustainably high profit rates with the hope of enhancing profits in future years. Reduction of such expenditures in bad times also serves to reduce the standard deviation of reported profits by minimizing downward fluctuations. Firms behaving in this manner may actually be raising the expected value of the firm by significantly reducing the risk component. Risk management can be a viable alternative to current profit maximization in attempts to enhance the more encompassing objective of maximizing the expected market value of the firm. Schramm and Sherman have demonstrated that the firm practicing risk management departs from profit maximization in the same way as a firm attempting to maximize sales and growth rates. They argue that assumptions of risk management replace the need for those of sales and growth-rate maximization.

Profit risk management is not appropriate for all firms at all times. It is appropriate only where the firm's earnings are highly correlated with those of other firms, which is fact for most firms. This implies that the correlation coefficient, c, in the preceding equations relating the variation of the firm's earnings to those of all firms in the market has a value close to unity. The closer c is to unity, the stronger the influence on V will be of reductions in the standard deviation σ_e. The closer c is to zero, the less is to be gained from reductions in σ_e and the better it is for the firm to concentrate on maximizing expected profits.

The firm having a high value of c may practice risk management by seeking out those activities having the greatest returns to risk-reducing expenditures. Advertising may be more important to the firm whose customers are less well informed about its products. Such expenditures may also be helpful in smoothing out the demand for the product, which in turn permits efficient smoothing of production, employment, and inventories. Where they are already large, judicious cutbacks may be useful in reducing sudden large falls in profits.

Another firm may obtain better returns from varying research expenditures. In some industries, technical discoveries and new applications permit a more rapid growth, which in turn reduces labor costs associated with periodic layoffs and improves the firm's image with respect to present and potential employees, customers for its products, and investors in its debt and equity instruments.

Acceleration and postponement of investment expenditures may also be practical ways of reducing risk. This, of course, will depend upon the magnitude and urgency of the project. Plans for small replacements may be changed quickly with few disruptions to the rest of the firm, while major expansions requiring years of planning and coordination with other firms may be very costly to disrupt. Some installments may, however, be prepaid or deferred at year's end for tax purposes.

Questions and Problems

25-1. Define and discuss:

a. risk	*k.* coefficient of correlation
b. uncertainty	*l.* variance
c. knowledge	*m.* standard deviation
d. information	*n.* covariance
e. positive economics	*o.* an efficient portfolio
f. normative economics	*p.* investment-opportunity curve
g. cutoff period	*q.* price of time
h. risk factor	*r.* price of risk
i. probability calculations	*s.* risk management
j. sensitivity analysis	

25-2. Write one statement on the subject of knowledge.

25-3. Is knowledge exempt, as Kenneth Boulding claims, from "the iron laws of conservation and decay"?

25-4. How can one go about making information one's personal property?

25-5. How do business decision makers cope with risk and uncertainty in making investments?

25-6. Is it possible that a firm that takes actions to reduce its risks could produce short-run results that give the appearance of sales or growth-rate maximization?

References

1. William J. Baumol. *Economic Theory and Operations Analysis*. 3d ed. (Englewood Cliffs, N.J.: Prentice-Hall, 1972), pp. 477–498, ch. 24.
2. Kenneth E. Boulding. "The Economics of Knowledge and the Knowledge of Economics." *American Economic Review* 56 (May 1966): 1–13.
3. M. J. Brennan. "An Approach to the Valuation of Uncertain Income Streams." *Journal of Finance* 28 (June 1973): 661–672.
4. Herman Chernoff. "Decision Theory." In *International Encyclopedia of the Social Sciences*, IV, pp. 63–66.
5. Donald Dewey. *The Theory of Imperfect Competition: A Radical Reconstruction* (New York: Columbia University Press, 1969), ch. 8.
6. Donald E. Farrar and John R. Meyer. *Managerial Economics* (Englewood Cliffs, N.J.: Prentice-Hall, 1970), ch. 5.
7. Irving Fisher. *The Theory of Interest* (New York: Kelley & Millman, 1954). First printed in 1930.
8. Irvin Millman Grossack and David Dale Martin. *Managerial Economics— Microtheory and the Firm's Decision* (Boston: Little, Brown, 1973), ch. 13.
9. Albert N. Halter and Gerald W. Dean. *Decisions Under Uncertainty with Research Applications* (Cincinnati: South-Western Publishing Co., 1971).
10. W. W. Haynes. *Managerial Economics: Analysis and Cases*. Rev. ed. (Austin, Tex.: Business Publications, 1969), ch. 10.
11. David B. Hertz. "Risk Analysis in Capital Investment." *Harvard Business Review*, January–February 1964, pp. 95–106. Reprinted in Kristian S. Palda [18, pp. 209–222].
12. Jack Hirshleifer. "Investment: The Investment Decision." In *International Encyclopedia of the Social Sciences*, VIII, 194–202.
13. ———. "Where Are We in the Theory of Information?" *American Economic Review* 63 (May 1973): 31–39.
14. Frank H. Knight. *Risk, Uncertainty and Profit* (New York: Harper & Row, 1965). First published in 1921.
15. Henry G. Manne. *Insider Trading and the Stock Market* (New York: Free Press, 1966).
16. James C. T. Mao and John F. Helliwell. "Investment Decision Under Uncertainty: Theory and Practice." *Journal of Finance* 24 (May 1969): 323–338. Reprinted in Kristian Palda [18, pp. 234–246].
17. Harry M. Markowitz. *Portfolio Selection—Efficient Diversification of Investments* (New York: Wiley, 1959).
18. Kristian S. Palda. *Readings in Managerial Economics* (Englewood Cliffs, N.J.: Prentice-Hall, 1973), Pt. 5.
19. Howard Raiffa. *Decision Analysis: Introductory Lectures on Choices Under Uncertainty* (Reading, Mass.: Addison-Wesley, 1968).
20. Richard Schramm and Roger Sherman. "Profit Risk Management and the Theory of the Firm." *Southern Economic Journal* 40 (January 1974): 353–363.
21. William F. Sharpe. "Capital Asset Prices: A Theory of Market Equilibrium Under Conditions of Risk." *Journal of Finance* 19 (September 1964): 425–442.

PART FIVE

The Environment of Business

I *have a rule which says that a scientist should only say or write what he knows for sure, with one exception—when he is calling attention to a danger.*

Konrad Lorenz

26 Antitrust and Antimerger Constraints on American Industry

Government constraints upon the activities of businesses are a part of the legal environment of the firm. Firms are required by law to obtain corporate charters, pay taxes, fulfill contracts, submit to collective bargaining, meet minimum-wage standards, provide safe working conditions for employees, observe quality standards, restrict pollution, engage in ethical practices, and conform to antitrust rules. The purpose of this chapter is to introduce a portion of the subject matter of economics that is called *industrial organization*. Emphasis is given to the very important and interesting material on antitrust and antimerger philosophy, legislation, and cases. Students will quickly recognize some of the economic concepts, introduced in previous chapters, upon which legal judgments are based; on the other hand, they will also note occasions on which political and social goals are given priority over economic ones.

26-1 Economic Ideology and Antitrust Philosophy

American business executives, legislators, and economists generally profess strong allegiance to the free enterprise system, whereby, according to Adam Smith's "invisible hand" concept, each individual makes his greatest contribution to society by pursuing his own best interests. It is also generally accepted, however, that the invisible hand left uncontrolled will ultimately become the hand at the throat of society, concentrating wealth in the possession of a few people, eliminating competition in business affairs, and reducing the personal freedom of the citizenry. Excessive dependence on laissez faire is believed to lead inevitably to a system of state capitalism ruled by a rich and powerful elite—a system that eventually gives way to socialism.

It is important to recognize, however, that the corporation came into being in response to a technological need for large concentrations of capital. The emergence of this institution permitted the efficient organization of many people's efforts toward a dominant goal: the pursuit of private gain in the form of profits. Today, the corporation is probably our most important economic institution,

418

providing employment for a major portion of the population. Any proposals to radically change the corporate institution must be tempered by the awareness that such change would drastically alter the structure of society. Antitrust and antimerger policies are intended to preserve the competitive environment by preventing excessive corporate concentration.

The philosophy of antitrust legislation is summarized well in the words of Judge Charles Edward Wyzanski, Jr., written in 1953 in connection with the case of *United States* v. *United Shoe Machinery Corporation*:

> Concentrations of power, no matter how beneficently they appear to have acted, nor what advantages they seem to possess, are inherently dangerous. Their good behavior in the past may not be continued; and if their strength were hereafter grasped by presumptuous hands, there would be no automatic check and balance from equal forces in the industrial market. And in the absence of this protective mechanism, the demand for public regulation, public ownership, or other drastic measures would become irresistible in time of crisis. Dispersal of private economic power is thus one of the ways to preserve the system of private enterprise. Moreover, well as a monopoly may have behaved in the moral sense, its economic performance is inevitably suspect. The very absence of strong competitors implies that there cannot be an objective measuring rod of the monopolist's excellence, and the test of its performance must, therefore, be largely theoretical. What appears to the outsider to be a sensible, prudent, nay even a progressive policy of the monopolist, may in fact reflect a lower scale of adventurousness and less intelligent risk-taking than would be the case if the enterprise were forced to respond to a stronger industrial challenge. Some truth lurks in the cynical remark that not high profits but a quiet life is the chief reward of monopoly power. And even if a particular enterprise seeks growth and not repose, an increased rate in the growth of ideas does not follow from an increased concentration of power. Industrial advance may indeed be in proportion to economic power; for creativity in business as in other areas, is best nourished by multiple centers of activity, each following its unique pattern and developing its own esprit de corps to respond to the challenge of competition. The dominance of any one enterprise inevitably unduly accentuates that enterprise's experience and views as to what is possible, practical, and desirable with respect to technological development, research, relations with producers, employees, and customers. And the preservation of any unregulated monopoly is hostile to the industrial and political ideals of an open society founded on the faith that tomorrow will produce a better than the best [110 F Supp. 295 (1953), p. 347].

In short, antitrust laws are held to be necessary to remove concentrations of power that could prove dangerous to the private enterprise system should they fall into the wrong hands; to promote a system with strong competitors, so that other firms will be present to provide a measuring rod of economic performance; and to encourage creativity and superior economic performance by maintaining multiple centers of activity.

26-2 The Traditional Model of Industrial Organization

Most of the analysis in the field of industrial organization is conducted within the theoretical framework summarized in Figure 26-1, which was developed by Edward S. Mason in the late 1930s [21] and continued by modern economists Joe S. Bain [5], F. M. Scherer [29], and James V. Koch [14]. It is asserted that a chain of causation progresses from the basic conditions of demand and supply to market structure to the conduct of sellers to the performance of firms in society. Unfortunately, perhaps, the direction of causation is not only one-way, as the solid arrows imply; there is evidence that feedback relations also exist, as indicated by the dashed arrows.

Good production performance from the viewpoint of society embodies at least the following attributes or goals: Goods should be produced in response to consumer demand in appropriate quantities and qualities; scarce resources used in production should not be wasted; producers should be quick to adapt new, more efficient, technologies and to replace old products with superior new ones; producers should facilitate continuous full employment of human resources; and income should be distributed equitably, so that producers do not secure rewards greatly in excess of those necessary to call forth their services. Other standards may also be appropriate, but these are basic. As is true for the goals of individuals and firms, conflicts arise between competing social objectives, requiring choices and optimizing decisions. Because measurement is seldom exact, operational approximations are essential. Government and judicial bodies must often examine cases on an individual basis, making judgments on the degree to which the performance standards are being met and forming policies they believe are in the best interests of society.

The performance of firms, industries, and markets are believed to depend upon the *conduct of sellers* with regard to pricing behavior, cooperation and collusion among firms, product-line strategies, advertising and other promotional strategies, research and development commitments, and legal tactics like enforcing patent rights. If one is to change or modify the conduct of market participants,

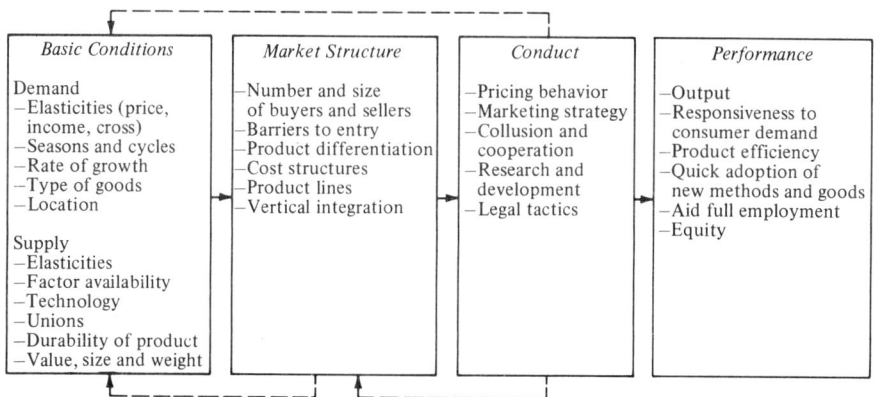

Basic Conditions	Market Structure	Conduct	Performance
Demand –Elasticities (price, income, cross) –Seasons and cycles –Rate of growth –Type of goods –Location Supply –Elasticities –Factor availability –Technology –Unions –Durability of product –Value, size and weight	–Number and size of buyers and sellers –Barriers to entry –Product differentiation –Cost structures –Product lines –Vertical integration	–Pricing behavior –Marketing strategy –Collusion and cooperation –Research and development –Legal tactics	–Output –Responsiveness to consumer demand –Product efficiency –Quick adoption of new methods and goods –Aid full employment –Equity

Figure 26-1

one must examine the structure of the relevant markets upon which that conduct depends.

The *structure of a market* is distinguished by features like the number and size of firms, product differentiation, barriers to entry of new firms, the relative amounts of initial capital outlays, the extent of vertical integration, the diversity of product lines, and the degree of geographical concentration of buyers and sellers. Conduct and market structure are, in turn, determined by the basic conditions of demand and supply.

Basic conditions are set by all the factors impinging upon demand and supply. On the demand side are the price, income, and cross-elasticities, the variations associated with seasons and business cycles, the rate of growth in demand over time, type of goods, and location of the market. Products are sometimes discussed with reference to three categories: *convenience goods*, which are small, inexpensive items (such as toothpaste and razor blades) purchased with little attention to relative prices; *shopping goods*, which are relatively expensive (such as furniture and mortgages) and purchased infrequently enough to merit comparisons of price and quality; and *specialty goods* of high value (such as high-priced cameras and electronic gear), which the consumer will go to great lengths to obtain.

On the supply side are included the availabilities and price of raw materials and the technological ease with which they may be substituted for each other as measured by their elasticities of input substitution, the presence and strength of unions, and the characteristics of the product with respect to size, weight, value, and durability.

In addition to the primary direction of causational flow indicated by the solid arrows in Figure 26-1, there are feedback effects denoted by the dashed arrows. For example, a sales promotion strategy may be successful in increasing demand conditions, as indicated by the top dashed line. Similarly, research efforts may modify the market structure by lowering the cost structure, augmenting the product line, and increasing product differentiation; new and different products, in turn, change the basic conditions. These adjustments are indicated by the lower dashed arrows.

According to the traditional model, it may be concluded that the profit-seeking behavior of private enterprise can be harmonized with the public interest by discouraging undesirable kinds of *business conduct* and by molding *market structure* along competitive lines. It is further hoped that an environment will be created in which desirable conduct and performance come about more or less automatically.

26-3 Antitrust Legislation

United States federal antitrust law is based predominantly upon three statutes: (1) the Sherman Act of 1890, (2) the Clayton Act of 1914, and (3) the Federal Trade Commission Act of 1914, and their subsequent amendments [29, pp. 422–425]. The purpose of the first was to forbid *all* contracts, combinations, and conspiracies in restraint of trade and by prohibiting the intended formation of monopolies in interstate and foreign commerce. The Attorney General was permitted to institute suits in equity and to enjoin illegal practices. Injured parties were permitted to sue offenders to recover treble the damages actually sustained. Enforcement was lax until Theodore Roosevelt became President in 1901. Judicial procedures were then streamlined, and a special antitrust enforcement division was established in the Department of Justice. Several important case decisions (discussed briefly later) followed, which established the rules for firms for decades to come.

The Clayton Act, supported by President Woodrow Wilson, outlawed some specific practices that were not covered under the Sherman Act and permitted monopolies to be nipped in the bud before they had progressed sufficiently to become Sherman Act violations. Other features prohibited price discrimination, tying clauses, exclusive-dealing agreements, certain mergers, and interlocking directorates; these features were generally held to be illegal when they served substantially to lessen competition, or tend to create a monopoly. The Clayton Act was amended in 1950 by the Celler-Kefauver Act, which is mentioned later in connection with merger legislation.

The Federal Trade Commission Act provided a much-needed panel of five full-time commissioners having the power to investigate and adjudicate cases. This commission was given a staff of professional personnel and the authority to judge the legality of "unfair methods of competition." Three arms of the Federal Trade Commission (FTC) are its Bureau of Industrial Economics, which investigates industry practices; its Bureau of Restraint of Trade, which prosecutes complaints; and its Office of Hearing Examiners, which adjudicates cases. The five-member FTC acts upon recommendations from its staff to issue cease-and-desist orders. Decisions in matters of law may be appealed to a federal appellate court and to the Supreme Court. Responsibility for enforcing antitrust laws is to this day shared by the Federal Trade Commission and the Department of Justice, but the latter has no poweres of adjudication, since its cases are held before a federal district court and appealed directly to the Supreme Court.

Over the years, exemptions from antitrust actions have been granted to labor unions, regulated industries, agricultural cooperatives, export associations, and retail price fixing (fair trade) by manufacturers. Comprehensive surveys are given by Wilcox [37, pp. 669–828] and the U.S. Department of Justice [35, pp. 261–314].

While Section 2 of the Sherman Act was specific in making it a misdemeanor to "attempt to monopolize," it was unclear as to what this meant in terms of a firm's share of the market and domination resulting from superior efficiency. This ambiguity undoubtedly reflected the mixed emotions of members of Congress who condemned the abuses by trusts but at the same time recognized the potential benefits to consumers to be derived from economies of large-scale production. It was left to the courts to decide when it was in the public interest to prevent monopoly control. Examination of some of the most prominent of the ensuing antitrust cases is helpful in showing how legal precedent has evolved.

26-4 Selected Antitrust Cases Involving Horizontal Monopolization

In 1911 the Supreme Court found the Standard Oil Company of New Jersey guilty of illegally monopolizing the petroleum refining industry [29, ch. 20].

From its inception in 1870 by the Rockefeller brothers, it appeared determined to dominate the market for petroleum products, mainly kerosene and lubricating oil in that pre-horseless carriage era. Its share of the market was maintained at 90 per cent in the 1880s and 1890s

> ... by acquiring more than 120 former rival firms, securing discriminatory rail freight rates and rebates, foreclosing crude oil supplies to competitors by buying up pipelines, conducting business espionage, and allegedly waging predatory price warfare to drive rivals out of business or soften them up for a takeover [29, p. 455].

The Court held that these acts went beyond reasonable business practice and therefore exhibited intent to monopolize. The Standard Oil holding company was dissolved by the Court, requiring that shares in the 33 subsidiaries be distributed to stockholders. This action did little to increase competition immediately because John D. Rockefeller and his associates retained controlling interest over the 33 fragments, but it was eventually successful as shares were distributed among numerous heirs and donated to nonvoting philanthropic institutions and as new stock was issued to other investors.

Following the same "rule of reason" that the monopolizing acts went beyond normal business practice, the Supreme Court only 2 weeks after its *Standard Oil* decision found the American Tobacco Company, a holding company known as the Tobacco Trust, guilty of cigarette trade monopolization. The trust had denied rival firms access to wholesalers, established "fighting brands" in local markets priced below cost, and bought out 250 rival plants, many of which were promptly closed down; these practices were found to be evidence of monopolistic intent. The Tobacco Trust was subsequently split into 16 pieces.

Similar verdicts were passed down against the Powder Trust in 1911, the Thread Trust in 1913, Eastman Kodak Company in 1915, the glucose and cornstarch trust in 1916, and a group of railroads that dominated the anthracite coal industry in 1920.

A new precedent was soon established, however, in a suit against the United States Steel Corporation. The company, formed by merger in 1901, produced over 65 per cent of the domestic output of iron and steel. Tennessee Coal and Iron Corporation was acquired in 1907 with President Roosevelt's express permission. Although periodic meetings were held with rivals to establish industry pricing policies, there was no cutthroat pricing or predatory practice. Prices were set high enough to encourage other steel makers to enter the industry and grow, resulting in a decline of market share to 52 per cent in 1915 and to progressively lower rates in succeeding years. In a 4-to-3 decision in 1920, the rule thus became established that firms behaving in a nonpredatory and nonaggressive manner toward rivals would not be subject to antitrust attack. Mere size and existence of unexerted power, in and of themselves, were not considered offenses. Similar decisions were made in three parallel cases: that of the United Shoe Machinery Corporation in 1918, where the company's 80 to 95 per cent market shares resulted largely from superior efficiency and legitimate exploitation of patent rights; the *American Can* case of 1916, where the firm's 90 per cent market share in 1901 eroded to 50 per cent in 1913 as competitors were sheltered under its umbrella of high prices; and the case of the International Harvester Company in 1927, where mere size in the absence of unlawful conduct was again judged to be legal.

The next important case was concerned with the Aluminum Company of America and was decided in 1945. Alcoa was formed in 1888 for the purpose of exploiting the Hall electrolytic reduction patents. Competing Bradley patents were purchased in 1903. Basic patents expired in 1909, but there were no successful rivals until 1940, largely because of Alcoa's cheap power sites, moderate pricing policies, and control of most of the conveniently accessible high-grade bauxite reserves. The firm was charged with illegal monopolization by the Justice Department in 1937. Eventually the case was decided by a court of last resort composed of three circuit court judges, constituted because a quorum of Supreme Court justices who had not previously participated in court litigation involving the defendant could not be obtained. The question of whether or not a monopoly existed hinged on the definition ascribed to the relevant market used to establish Alcoa's market share (obtained by dividing Alcoa's ingot output by that of the industry's, including imported ingots). The presiding judge, Learned Hand, rejected the lower court's inclusion of aluminum ingots used internally by Alcoa to fabricate its own panels, pots, and pans as a measure of the company's output. His reasoning was that aluminum ingots used in this manner served to reduce the external demand for ingots. This adjustment lifted the measured market share from 33 to 64 per cent for the 1930s. Furthermore, the judge preferred to remove reprocessed scrap metal from the denominator, which had the effect of raising the measure of Alcoa's market share of the aluminum ingot market to 90 per cent—sufficiently high to establish clearly evidence of a monopoly.

The court then turned to the question of intent to monopolize, a requirement for proving illegality under Section 2 of the Sherman Act. Such intent was held to be present because of the actions of Alcoa in expanding its ore reserves, electric power sources, and productive capacity well in advance of increased demand. Excess capacity effectively excluded the entry of competitors. This ruling, reinforced by a similar one in the *Tobacco* case a year later (1946), established the precedent—a "new" rule of reason—that illegal monopolization can be inferred without the presence of predatory pricing or other aggressive behavior.

After the war, when it came time to dispose of government-financed aluminum plants operated by Alcoa, the company was barred from the bidding. Reynolds Metals and Kaiser Aluminum were successful bidders, thereby transforming the primary ingot supply industry to a triopoly. Also, the Davis, Hunt, and Mellon families were required to divest themselves of joint stockholdings in Aluminum, Ltd., of Canada and in Alcoa to rule out the possibility of joint control of potential competitors.

The Alcoa precedent was strengthened by three following cases. The first involved several suits against motion-picture chains charged with monopolizing first-run film exhibitions. Some chains had threatened to refuse to exhibit certain films in towns with no competing theaters unless they were given first-run preference in cities with competing houses. The Supreme Court held that such chains were illegal even where no threats had been made; it was sufficient to judge illegality from the presence of monopoly without regard to the defendant's conduct. In effect, this overturned the *United States Steel* doctrine that bigness alone was no evidence of illegality.

The second case was against the A & P Company for conspiring to monopolize the retail food industry. Like Alcoa, A & P had competed too aggressively and successfully. Abusive practices included refusing to buy from suppliers who refused to give preferential discounts, threatening to extend its own manufacturing operations in competition with recalcitrant suppliers, and reducing grocery prices in cities where competition was greatest. A fine of $175,000 was imposed, and its food brokerage subsidiary was ordered dissolved in spite of the fact that A & P's share of the national market was under 10 per cent, and above 40 per cent in only 23 small cities. Conspiracy, rather than outright monopolization, was the controlling factor.

The third decision parallel to that of the *Alcoa* case involved the United Shoe Machinery Corporation, whose actions tended to prevent rival firms from entering the market. Machines were leased rather than sold to customers, lower prices and profits were accepted on machines unshielded by patents, and manufacturers were encouraged to use United's full line of machines by attractive pricing, service, and replacement provisions. The Supreme Court ordered compulsory licensing of patents and the divestiture of some minor subsidiary operations in 1954. Further divestitures were agreed upon by consent decree in 1968 and 1969, reducing United Shoe's share of the market to about 33 per cent.

26-5   Consent Decrees and Sherman's Ghost

Discussion up to now has dealt with cases in which the government was successful in obtaining a conviction, but there were others ruled in favor of the defendant [29, pp. 463–465]. One such prominent case, known as the *Cellophane* case, was in 1956 decided in favor of E. I. du Pont, although the company was recognized to have a patent-protected monopoly. The Supreme Court affirmed the Delaware district court's judgment that a broader definition of the product was appropriate—a definition including other flexible packaging materials with which cellophane had a high cross-elasticity of demand. Du Pont's 18 per cent share of the broader market represented no illegal monopoly.

Since 1956 there have been virtually no court decisions dealing exclusively with charges of horizontal market domination under Section 2 of the Sherman Act. Instead, there have been a number of cases settled out of court by *consent decrees*, whereby the question of guilt or innocence is left unresolved but the agreement between the government and the firm is binding upon approval by a federal court. A suit against Eastman Kodak Company for monopolizing the processing of color film was settled when Eastman agreed within 7 years to reduce its market share below 50 per cent, to license its patents, and to share its knowledge with new firms. A similar agreement was made by IBM in response to charges of monopolizing key punch and other mechanical processing equipment. RCA agreed to license its patents on a royalty-free basis after being charged with dominating television technology. Western Electric agreed to license its patents and give up minor subsidiary operations rather than sever its ties with AT & T. United Fruit Corporation spun off a firm for handling 35 per cent of

United States banana imports to reduce its banana barony. General Motors agreed in 1965 to reduce its 85 per cent market share for domestic intercity buses by helping competitors and by later divestiture if necessary. Such agreements were undoubtedly attributable in part to a reluctance on the part of both the prosecutors and defendants to assume the additional expense and risk of leaving the decisions in the hands of an unpredictable court, the partial success of a compromise being preferred by each to an uncertain outcome. A recognized disadvantage of the consent decree from a social standpoint, however, is that there is less opportunity for public evaluation and scrutiny.

In addition to being constrained by court decisions and consent decrees, the behavior of firms with sizable market shares is influenced to an unmeasurable degree by the *threat of antitrust action*. Any form of predation or legal harassment of weaker rivals opens the firm to the risk of having to pay treble damages and penalties. Unfortunately, competitive efforts may also be inhibited when firms approaching the threshold 60 to 64 per cent market share fear to reduce their prices when efficiencies permit. The antitrust environment is such that General Motors fears to reduce its automobile prices below competing brands, Xerox is inhibited from aggressive exploitation of its patents, and other large firms shift their energies to invading new markets rather than to improving their already dominant positions in old markets. General Electric and Westinghouse were punished for their participation in price-fixing agreements with other producers of electrical equipment in the 1950s—an agreement entered into for the major purpose of helping weaker rivals in order to ward off monopolization charges. Little wonder, then, that frequent reference is made to the ghost of Senator Sherman sitting on the board of every large corporation.

26-6 Proposed Reforms of the Sherman Act

In terms of producing a truly competitive business environment, Section 2 of the Sherman Act must be judged a failure [29, pp. 465–469]. Only the extreme cases are ever prosecuted, because of the limited budgets and staffs of the enforcement agencies. Some observers claim that concentration aided by the merger movement has become progressively greater in many basic industries, while antitrust officials and judges have been "policemen looking the other way" [1, p. vii]. Joe S. Bain's study of 20 manufacturing industries in 1947 concluded that

> ... concentration by firms is in every case but one greater than required by single-plant economies, and in more than half of the cases very substantially greater. Generally it is only within some of the industries with very important economies of large plant—e.g., fountain pens, copper, typewriters, autos, tractors, farm machines—that concentration by firms has not been much greater than required by single-plant economies. Even in these cases it may be two or three times as great as thus required. In the other cases concentration by firms tends to be a substantial or large multiple of that required by single-plant economies [4, p. 33].

The most influential of antitrust reform proposals has been put forth by Carl Kaysen and Donald F. Turner [13]. They would define unreasonable market power as being present where one firm has 50 per cent, or four firms 80 per cent, of the annual sales in a relevant market for 5 or more years. Such market power would be declared under law to be injurious to commerce and trade. To avoid fragmentation by the three D's of antitrust (dissolution, divestiture, or divorcement), a defendant would be required to prove that its power derived from scale economies, superior efficiency, innovativeness, or unabusive exploitation of valid patents.

Kaysen and Turner build their case for such legislation on three main propositions: the value judgment that a self-regulating competitive market is preferable to private market control and government bureaucracy; the analytical judgment that some minimum of structural competition must be sustained if there is to be market regulation rather than government regulation; and the analytical judgment that present antitrust policies cannot cope effectively with contemporary market power, especially with regard to joint action of oligopolists. They claim that oligopolies controlling the strategic half of manufacturing industry recognize their mutual interdependence and behave nonrivalously for mutual benefit. In short, monopoly pricing arises *in the absence* of explicit collusion or one firm serving as much as 65 per cent of the market—features required to provoke antitrust action under present law. In the view of Kaysen and Turner, the basic problem can be solved only by altering structural conditions, that is, by increasing the number of sellers where one or few dominate the relevant market.

In defense of the courts' reticence to apply antitrust laws ruthlessly, especially in more recent years, the courts are believed to fear that such action based upon incomplete knowledge of complex technologies and economies could impair industrial efficiency. Judicial fragmentation is much less likely where firms use complex production processes and engage in ambitious research and development programs. Courts and government prosecutors are more willing to alter the structure of firms distributing films and manufacturing railroad cars and shoe machinery by use of traditional techniques than companies producing digital computers, electronic circuits, cellophane, nylon, Teflon, and jet aircraft.

Structural fragmentation on an efficiency basis may also be limited by the nature of the physical facilities, as in the *Alcoa* case, where the firm owned only two plants. In the cases of the United Shoe Machinery Corporation and the General Motors intercity buses, production was concentrated in single plants because of scale economies and relatively small demand. On the other hand, Bain's research indicates that most oligopolistic industries could be fragmented without serious loss of production efficiency.

26-7 Prevention of Monopoly by Control of Mergers

The preceding discussion has considered government actions to remove monopoly interests when detected. One of the ways to help prevent the formation of monopolies is through the control of mergers [29, pp. 103–122, 469–473]. Many of these took place in multifirm consolidations at the turn of the century, during the years 1887 to 1904, permitting scores of firms to control more than half their relevant markets (see Markham [16], Nelson [25], and Stigler [32]). It was during this period that some of today's largest firms were formed and our basic industrial structure established. Two major but more modest waves of market concentration have occurred since then, generally coinciding with upward swings in the stock market, during the years 1916 to 1929 and during the extended period since World War II. The mergers of 1916–1929 were in the food products, chemicals, and metals industries rather than in oil, steel, rubber, glass, paper, fruit, and machinery, as in the first merger movement; merger was characterized by vertical rather than horizontal concentration, and according to Stigler, was more oligopolistic than monopolistic. The period since World War II has seen many mergers, but their significance in terms of increasing structural concentration has been relatively minor because most of the mergers involved small firms being absorbed by the very large and diversified corporations rather than being combinations of the largest.

The low number of mergers *having important structural consequences* in terms of market concentration in more recent times is attributed by Scherer to some strengthening of antimerger policy; exhaustion of most of the best opportunities in the first great wave; the many disappointing mergers undertaken by business people in the 1890s, when they attempted to manage the giant consolidations pushed upon them by unscrupulous promoters before the passage of the Securities Act of 1933 and the Securities Exchange Act of 1934; and greater awareness that monopoly through merger can be preserved only by erecting substantial barriers to entry by the new firms [29, p. 462].

The tendency for merger activity to increase when stock prices are high is not thoroughly understood but is believed to be influenced by the preference of owners wanting to liquidate their holdings to sell when the price of their stocks is high; the greater ease for the acquiring firm of obtaining funds to finance the merger; a tendency for the acquiring firm's price-earnings ratio to rise more quickly than the acquired firm's in a rising market; and greater optimism by the purchaser when stock prices are high [29, p. 112].

For a merger agreement to be reached, the seller and the buyer must come to terms. The price and other conditions must, of course, be right, but the threshold level is generally influenced by many factors. The owners may wish to abandon a hopelessly sinking ship or, less drastically, seek rescue from a firm having greater financial resources and more capable management; experience indicates that this factor seldom is of great significance for large firms. (See Leonard Weiss's study of mergers in six major industries from 1929 to 1958 [36].) The owners of small firms, because of advanced age, business pressures, and lack of suitable heirs or successors, will often select merger as the method of turning the wheel over to a respected competitor to perpetuate what they have built. The decision may be hastened by the impending necessity of making large capital investments to replace obsolete equipment. Also, the growth of the firm to a critical size, requiring new managerial philosophies and methods that the present owner-manager deems unattractive, may be a consideration. Tax considerations are very important; shares of stock can be sold at the lower capital-gains income-tax rate rather than recouping investments in the form of higher salaries and dividends taxed at much higher rates; inheritance tax considerations also enter since heirs may be forced to sell shares at distressing prices in a low market to pay their taxes ([8] and [15]). Finally, an owner may wish to reduce his risk by trading his stock for shares in a more diversified company [29, pp. 115–116].

On the buyers' side of the exchange, merger is desirable for a number of reasons (other than tax advantages), listed by F. M. Scherer [29, pp. 470–471]:
1. to reduce competition and gain monopoly power
2. to realize promotional profits
3. to utilize complementary resources more effectively
4. to secure production and physical distribution scale economies
5. to secure promotional and pecuniary economies of scale
6. to rationalize existing production operations
7. to spread risks or move from declining to expanding fields
8. to build an empire
9. to pick up a new capacity at bargain prices
10. to expand production without depressing prices

Only factors 3 and 4 (which can also be obtained by internal expansion) are believed to hold much promise of yielding social as well as private benefits. The others are largely competitive and of questionable social value, other than having possible incentive effects leading to greater and more efficient production.

An optimal merger policy ideally discourages social costs (in terms of stifling competition and all it connotes) in excess of social benefits (such as production efficiencies and higher real growth rates with minor depletions of exhaustible resources and few negative externalities). But in the real world it is often very difficult to predict with certainty the future impact of a given merger, regardless of the motives claimed or attributed to the interested parties. Because of such uncertainties and difficulties in culling out misinformation, a court in attempting to apply a rule of reason is more likely than not to err on the side of allowing doubtful acquisitions, resulting in a gradual decline in competition. The merging firms have an advantage over court attorneys and government economists, because they probably have information at their disposal that can be weighed and sifted before sharing it with outsiders. This means that as fish slip individually or in small numbers through the judicial net, competition must suffer a gradual decline. In recognition of this danger, reformers have argued for stronger rules that would place the burden of proof on the merging firms to show clearly how a merger will produce net social benefits. This rule could apply to certain mergers that would produce a share of the market above a given percentage. A stronger rule could declare such mergers illegal per se.

The case for stronger rules is supported by several arguments. First, even under stronger rules, only a small percentage of proposed mergers would be challenged. In recent years only 1 or 2 per cent of mergers have been questioned —about 10 per cent of those involving $10 million or more. Perhaps the greatest influence of stronger rules would be to deter attempts to merge. A second argument is that internal expansion is more beneficial to society than expansion by merger, except where capacity is already excessive; by attacking proposals with the highest estimated social costs, society can expect improved net benefits. Third, deterring concentration through strict merger policy is easier than later trying to police and fragment existing monopolies and oligopolies. A final argument is sometimes put forth in Congress on populist grounds—bigness is bad and social and political reasons dictate that competitive small businesses must survive regardless of some probable short-term inefficiencies.

Those who advocate soft rules for reasons other than self-interest argue that the costs and benefits must be carefully considered in each case. They claim that mergers leading to the formation of oligopolies have little, if any, deleterious effects on competition in a dynamic world of rapid technological change, where many substitute commodities are available. Competition may also be stimulated by supplanting a lethargic management with a more active one. In any case, the relative merit of a particular merger is largely an empirical and factual question for which evidence must be heard on both sides. Economists generally urge policy makers to err on the side of restraint when the implications of a merger are unclear and potentially harmful for competitive markets.

26-8   Antimerger Legislation

Mergers were first attacked under Section 1 of the Sherman Act, which proscribes "every contract, combination...or conspiracy in restraint of trade or commerce among the several states" [29, pp. 473–476]. The first government victory was in the *Northern Securities* decision in 1904, which struck down a merger proposed by J. P. Morgan, James Hill, and other tycoons of the Northern Pacific and Great Northern railroads. But after similar successes in preventing several other railroad consolidations, few suits were initiated under this provision in the 1920s and 1930s, perhaps reflecting the permissiveness of the 1920 *United States Steel* rule discussed earlier. It was not until 1964 that the law was given new life by its successful use in challenging the merger of two Kentucky banks having 40 and 13 per cent shares of the local market.

A weakness of the Sherman Act in attacking mergers is that the statute applies only to those cases where the firms are close to attaining substantial monopoly power, which may be too late to preserve competitive market structures. Recognizing this, Congress passed the Clayton Act in 1914 "to arrest the creation of trusts, conspiracies and monopolies in their incipiency and before consummation." Section 7 prohibited a corporation from acquiring the stock in another which would "substantially lessen competition," restrain commerce, or "tend to create a monopoly." A loophole was left open for the purchase of assets of another company without the corresponding purchase of its stock, a defect that inhibited the law's effectiveness until remedied by the Celler-Kefauver Act of 1950, which also brought nonhorizontal mergers under the law. By the end of 1967, some 173 new antimerger complaints were initiated by the Federal Trade Commission and the Department of Justice. Of the 133 that had been resolved by mid-1967, 82 per cent were successful in preventing or limiting mergers. Of the 12 substantive opinions written by the Supreme Court by March 1968 concerning Section 7 case appeals, 11 effectively prohibited mergers and the remaining one resulted from a 4-to-4 split decision failing to overturn a lower court's findings.

26-9   Selected Cases Involving Horizontal and Vertical Mergers

The first prominent case pursued successfully by the government under the new Section 7 of the Clayton Act involved the proposed merger of Bethlehem Steel Corporation and Youngstown Sheet and Tube Company [29, pp. 476–490].

Their respective shares of ingot capacity in the United States were 16.3 and 4.6 per cent. The firms pleaded that since most of Bethlehem's output was sold in the East and most of Youngstown's in the Midwest, only 10 per cent was sold in overlapping geographical territories. This defense was rejected by the district court in 1958; it held that the relevant market was nationwide rather than regional, because the transportation cost of shipping steel is small relative to the price of the product. Not only the combined national share of ingot capacity was found to lessen the competition substantially but also the shares in certain geographic submarkets and several narrowly defined product lines. A claim that the merger would permit greater competition with United States Steel was also rejected on the ground that there would be even less chance of preserving competition with smaller firms in the industry; to permit concentration-increasing mergers could open the door to a chain reaction of additional mergers of the same nature. Four years after the ruling, Bethlehem began to build a $500 million integrated facility at Burns Harbor, Indiana, which it claimed would be infeasible without the addition of the Youngstown market. Meanwhile, Youngstown committed $225 million for expansion and modernization of its Chicago plant.

One of the most substantive of recent merger cases involved a merger of Brown Shoe Company with G. R. Kinney Company (1962). Both were manufacturers and retailers of shoes. There was no real concern in this case of a threat to horizontal competition in manufacturing, since Brown and Kinney in 1955 were only the fourth and twelfth, respectively, in industry output, with shares of 4 and 0.5 per cent. It was the retailing market that was in question. Brown owned 470 of the nation's 22,000 specialized retail stores and 190 department-store outlets, while Kinney controlled more than 350 stores. There was concern with the nationwide trend toward shoe manufacturers obtaining control over retail outlets for pushing their own products, reducing available outlets for independent producers. Another observed trend was the closing of plants manufacturing shoes, which numbered about 10 per cent fewer in 1954 than in 1947. The courts rejected the contention by Brown that the relevant markets should be narrowly defined in terms of line of commerce (with regard to age and sex of intended customers as well as grade of material used, quality of workmanship, customer use, and price) and sections of the country (to as small an area as a business district in a large city). The three lines of commerce accepted by the courts were traditional—men's, women's, and children's shoes—and the relevant geographical sections of the country were defined as individual cities of population 10,000 or more and their environs. Since the combined sales in terms of units sold were in excess of 20 per cent for women's shoes sold in 32 cities and for children's shoes in 31 cities, the merger was held to lessen competition substantially. In regard to the vertical dimension, the evidence that Brown's shoes sold in Kinney's outlets rose from zero to 8 per cent in the 2 years after the merger was sufficient for the Supreme Court to agree with the lower court's decision against the merger.

The hard line taken in the *Brown Shoe* case was reinforced by several subsequent decisions, the most notable of which was the *Von's Grocery* case. In 1966 the Supreme Court reversed a lower court's approval of a merger of Von's Grocery Company with Shopping Bag Food Stores, both operators of retail food chains in Los Angeles. Ranking third and sixth, respectively, in sales within the local market, their combined share of market sales was 7.5 per cent, just under the dominant chain's (Safeway's) 8.0 per cent. From 1950 to 1961 the area had seen a decline in independent single-unit grocery stores from 5,365 to 3,818; from 1948 to 1958, the top 20 chains gained in market share from 44 to 57 per cent, a factor given more importance than the concomitant decline in the share of the top five. Holding the line against further concentration was the clear message for others to heed. The word went out immediately from the Attorney General's office that any future mergers between competitors each having a 4 per cent or more share of their markets would be challenged.

In regard to setting market definitions for measuring the impact of mergers on competition, we have seen in the *Bethlehem-Youngstown* case the acceptance of both single-state and national ones. In the *Brown Shoe–Kinney* case, the single-city definition was used in measuring horizontal impacts and a national one for measuring vertical facets. In the *Von's Grocery* case, a single-city definition was again used as the relevant market. What emerges from these and subsequent cases (see Scherer [29, pp. 478–482]) is rule whereby the observed practice is presumed illegal regardless of possible unique and favorable circumstances.

Horizontal mergers of firms having substantial (a combined 20 per cent) market shares and vertical ones believed to foreclose appreciable market shares (say 3 per cent) are automatically struck down, except where merger can avoid financial failure of one of the firms and where relevant market boundaries are especially difficult to delineate. Mergers with even smaller percentages are also struck down in the presence of an industrywide trend toward greater concentration, even where efficiencies can be shown. Furthermore, even conglomerate mergers with few functional links to prior operations are held to reduce *potential* competition by increasing the likelihood of predatory pricing and are ruled illegal under the Celler-Kefauver Act. (Supporting case decisions are discussed by Scherer [29, pp. 482–487]. The *P & G–Clorox* case in 1967 is one of the most important.)

26-10   Concluding Comments and Consideration of Structure Based Upon Chance

Emphasis was given in this chapter to policy, legislation, and cases dealing with industry structure and mergers. Because of lack of space, closely related legal topics, such as price discrimination, regulated industries, and international business, have not been considered in this text. Before closing this chapter the author wishes to share an interesting and somewhat perplexing thought concerning the determinants of market structure. Is it possible that market structure is the product of mere statistical *chance* rather than technology, demand elasticities, advertising, managerial effectiveness, merger decisions, and government policies, as assumed in this chapter? Such a view has been advanced.

Consider the hypothetical situation of a 50-firm industry being born at a point in time, with each firm having first-year sales of $100,000, representing a 2 per cent share of the market. Assume now that each firm is subject to the same average growth rate but that the average has a statistical variance, which means that in any given year some firms will grow more (and others less) rapidly than the average. Furthermore, assume that the annual rates of growth confronting each firm are distributed normally, with a 6 per cent mean and a 16 per cent standard deviation—parameters that Scherer associates with the actual performance of 369 of *Fortune's* 1959 list of the top 500 industrial corporations observed over the years 1954–1960. By the use of an electronic computer, each firm is assigned randomly selected growth rates having the same mean and standard deviation properties. Each firm's growth history and industry sales can then be tabulated for succeeding years. Scherer performed 16 consecutive simulation runs and obtained four-firm concentration ratios at 20-year intervals, which approximated the structures found in much of the United States manufacturing industry. After a century of growth the ratios ranged from 33.5 to 64.4 per cent and had a 46.7 per cent mean. Market shares of the leading firm ranged from 10 to 42 per cent, averaging 21 per cent [29, pp. 125–130].

Scherer's simulation demonstrates a tendency for concentration to develop over successive intervals even though each firm's growth is subject to the same random chance. Inevitably, some firms experience a run of luck over several successive years. Once a firm gets ahead, he explains, it is difficult for others to catch up, simply because both the large and the small continue to have equal chances of experiencing higher (as well as lower) future growth rates. Such growth experiments, conforming to Gibrat's law of proportional growth, generate a log-normal distribution—that is, a plotting of the frequencies of sales using an arithmetic scale is skewed, showing high sales by only a few firms and much lower sales for the majority, but a plotting of the same frequencies on a log scale traces a symmetrically bell-shaped curve. Log-normal distributions are often found in statistical studies to approximate the size data for actual firms.

For those with faith that the growth of firms is ruled by the knowledge, skill, and industriousness of their management, it is difficult to accept random chance as the principal determinant of success. Still, uncertainty admittedly plays a role in executive decisions to hire managers, conduct research, adopt new products, settle legal disputes, choose among promotional strategies, and in most other areas. Perhaps there is some comfort in the fact that correlations of performance of actual firms with the random-growth hypothesis are not precise. The deviations from chance expectations may indeed prove useful in measuring the success or failure of antitrust action, government policies, and managerial economies of scale. In any case, conventional explanations of market structure should not yet be rejected in favor of a "one decision is as good as any other" philosophy. The manager of the individual firm must continue to accept most of the dictates of the legal environment as one of the constraints imposed upon optimizing activity. Such knowledge is undoubtedly valuable in helping the managers to avoid many otherwise unconsidered pitfalls.

Questions and Problems

26-1. What exactly is the argument against monopoly as opposed to perfect competition?

26-2. Distinguish between a per se rule and a rule of reason in monopoly legislation and judicial rulings. Which dominates merger decisions today?

26-3. In your opinion, should the government give greater weight than it now does to efficiency rather than concentration in determining the legality of mergers?

26-4. Define the relevant market for consumer goods as used in antitrust legislation.

26-5. For what reasons might you suppose that exemptions from antitrust actions have been granted to
  a. labor unions
  b. regulated industries
  c. agricultural cooperatives
  d. export associations
  e. resale price maintenance by manufacturers

26-6. Why are most of the motives to merge considered in this chapter judged to be of little social benefit?

References

1. Walter Adams and Horace M. Gray. *Monopoly in America: The Government as Promoter* (New York: Macmillan, 1955).

2. Peter Asch. *Economic Theory and the Antitrust Dilemma* (New York: Wiley, 1970).

3. Joe S. Bain. *Barriers to New Competition: Their Character and Consequences in Manufacturing Industries* (Cambridge, Mass.: Harvard University Press, 1965). Copyrighted 1956.

4. ———. "Economies of Scale, Concentration, and the Condition of Entry in Twenty Manufacturing Industries." *American Economic Review* 44 (March 1954): 15–39.

5. ———. *Industrial Organization* (New York: Wiley, 1959).

6. John M. Blair. *Economic Concentration: Structure, Behavior and Public Policy* (New York: Harcourt Brace Jovanovich, 1972).

7. Eugene F. Brigham and James L. Pappas. *Managerial Economics* (Hinsdale, Ill.: Richard D. Irwin, 1964), ch. 11.

8. J. K. Butters, J. M. Lintner, and W. L. Cary. *Effects of Taxation on Corporate Mergers* (Boston: Harvard Business School, 1951).

9. John Chamberlain. *The Roots of Capitalism*. Rev. ed. (Van Nostrand, 1965).

10. John Maurice Clark. *Competition as a Dynamic Process* (Washington, D.C.: Brookings Institution, 1961).

11. John R. Commons. *Legal Foundations of Capitalism* (Madison: University of Wisconsin Press, 1957).

12. John Kenneth Galbraith. *American Capitalism: The Concept of Countervailing Power*. Rev. ed. (Boston: Houghton Mifflin, 1956).

13. Carl Kaysen and Donald F. Turner. *Antitrust Policy: An Economic and Legal Analysis* (Cambridge, Mass.: Harvard University Press, 1959).

14. James V. Koch. *Industrial Organization and Prices* (Englewood Cliffs, N.J.: Prentice-Hall, 1974).

15. John Lintner and J. K. Butters. "Effects of Taxes on Concentration." In National Bureau of Economic Research, *Business Concentration and Price Policy* (Princeton, N.J.: Princeton University Press, 1955), pp. 239–275.

16. Jesse W. Markham. "Survey of the Evidence and Findings on Mergers." In National Bureau of Economic Research, *Business Concentration and Price Policy*, pp. 141–212.

17. Edwin Mansfield. *Monopoly Power and Economic Performance: The Problem of Industrial Concentration*. Rev. ed. (New York: W. W. Norton, 1968).

18. Edward S. Mason (ed.). *The Corporation in Modern Society* (Cambridge, Mass.: Harvard University Press, 1959).

19. ———. "The Current State of the Monopoly Problem in the United States." *Harvard Law Review* 62 (June 1949): pp. 1265–1285.

20. ———. *Economic Concentration and the Monopoly Problem* (New York: Atheneum, 1964). Originally published by Harvard University Press in 1957.

21. ———. "Price and Production Policies of Large-Scale Enterprise." *American Economic Review* 24 (March 1939): 61–74.

22. John Moody. *The Truth About the Trusts: A Description and Analysis of the American Trust Movement* (New York: Greenwood Press, 1968). Originally published in 1904.

23. Willard F. Mueller. *A Primer on Monopoly and Competition* (New York: Random House, 1970).

24. Ralph Nader and Mark J. Green (eds.). *Corporate Power in America* (New York: Grossman Publishers, 1973).

25. Ralph L. Nelson. *Merger Movements in American Industry, 1895–1956* (Princeton, N.J.: Princeton University Press, 1959).

26. Warren G. Nutter and Henry Adler Einhorn. *Enterprise Monopoly in the United States 1899–1958* (New York: Columbia University Press, 1969).

27. Uwe E. Reinhardt. *Mergers and Consolidations: A Corporate Finance Approach* (Morristown, N. J.: General Learning Press, 1972).

28. *Report of the White House Task Force on Antitrust Policy*, July 5, 1968.

29. F. M. Scherer. *Industrial Market Structure and Economic Performance* (Chicago: Rand McNally, 1970).

30. Joseph A. Schumpeter. *Capitalism, Socialism, and Democracy* (New York: Harper, 1942).

31. Milton H. Spencer. *Managerial Economics*. 3d ed. (Homewood, Ill.: Richard D. Irwin, 1968), ch. 11.

32. George Stigler. "Monopoly and Oligopoly by Merger." *American Economic Review* 40 (May 1950): 23–24.

33. ———. *The Organization of Industry* (Homewood, Ill.: Richard D. Irwin, 1968).

34. G. W. Stocking and M. W. Watkins. *Monopoly and Free Enterprise* (New York: Twentieth Century Fund, 1951).

35. U.S., Department of Justice. *Report of the Attorney General's National Committee To Study the Antitrust Laws* (1955).

36. Leonard Weiss. "An Evaluation of Mergers in Six Industries." *Review of Economics and Statistics* 47 (May 1965): 172–181.

37. Clair Wilcox. *Public Policies Toward Business*. 4th ed. (Homewood, Ill.: Richard D. Irwin, 1971).

27 Ecology, Economics, and Ecoethics

Ecology is the study of how biological organisms relate to each other and to their environment. Sustainable life-support systems involve circular flows of food and energy. Cycles may occur very rapidly relative to the life of man, like those of microorganisms and insects, or they may proceed so slowly that they may appear to be one-way chains of events, which is certainly the way human beings view their evolution. The lives of many species are subject to a delicate balance of nature; if this is disturbed, they may be extinguished. Modern business people must be aware of the interrelations of the species of life so that they may better assess the impact of product design and production activities on the lives of their children and fellow human beings, now and in future generations. Ecology is also an important subject for students of economics for reasons beyond the efficient use of scarce material resources. In the end, the most expensive of all items, in an alternative-cost sense, is the life of the human species.

This chapter introduces the study of ecology and briefly examines the relation of human beings to their environment; American attitudes and values; recent federal environmental legislation; some implications of sustained economic growth; and the hasty approach of the spaceship economy.

27-1 An Ecosystem and Some Ecological Terminology

An ecosystem narrows an ecological study to a specific geographical area. Plants and animals are examined in relation to their physical environment—soil, water, climate, and energy. Resources are transferred in the form of food from one organism to another in a series of stages called a *food chain*. A network of such chains is called a *food web*; the more complex the web, the more stable the ecosystem is believed to be. At each stage, energy is lost in the form of heat; the greater the heat loss, the lower the *ecological efficiency* and the shorter the food chain. The energy loss explains why the volume of organisms is smaller at each successive stage in the food chain—a phenomenon described by ecological pyramids. (For example, a study of the ecosystem of Isle Royale in Lake Superior found that 762 pounds of plant food were required to produce 59 pounds of moose, which produced 1 pound of predatory wolves [23, p. E38].)

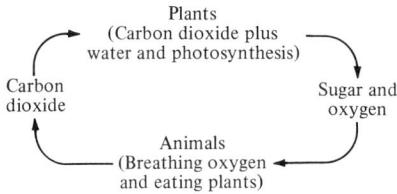

Figure 27-1

When chemical elements are regenerated in the cycle, such as carbon in the cycle shown in Figure 27-1, the cycle is said to be *perfect* or complete. Other chemicals produce an imperfect cycle, such as phosphorus, which passes from the soil to plants to animals but is not restored to the soil through the decomposition of biological matter. When ecosystems are maintained in terms of numbers and types of animals and resources, there is said to be stability or balance in nature. When systems change slowly from one type to another, *ecological succession* is said to occur.

27-2   The Balance of Nature

A balance of nature describes a state in which each species has an equilibrium population size depending upon those of the other species and the environment, including space, food, shelter, and chemicals. For instance, the number and kinds of fish, algae, plants, and minerals in a pond depend upon the abundance of each of the species present. If one of the species was reduced sufficiently, or removed altogether, the equilibrium might be so disturbed that others might die out until a new equilibrium developed.

The balance of nature may be better understood by briefly reviewing the roles played by some of the better-known species. Let us work from the ground up, so to speak, beginning with earthworms and proceeding to insects and birds. The role of worms in the balance of nature was unearthed as early as 1896 by Charles Darwin in *The Formation of Vegetable Mould, through the Action of Worms, with Observations on their Habits.* Earthworms are known to transport tons of soil per acre each year. Fine soil is carried to the surface in amounts of 1 to $1\frac{1}{2}$ inches deep in a decade, covering rocks and debris. On their downward trip, earthworms carry as much as 20 pounds of leaves and grass per square yard in 6 months. Their burrows, as well as those of other soil animals like mites, centipedes, and nematodes, aerate the soil, permitting proper drainage and helping the penetration of plant roots. The activities of earthworms, along with those of fungi and algae, increase the speed of decay of dead animals and plants. They enhance the nitrifying powers of soil bacteria and thereby reduce the putrifaction of the soil. Their excretion enriches the soil, which feeds the plants that feed the herbivores (plant eaters) and, indirectly, the carnivores (meat eaters). Finally, earthworms are a major food supply for robins and other birds [3, pp. 55–56].

The world of insects is bewildering in its complexity. More than 700,000 species have been described; this amounts to 70 to 80 per cent of all of Earth's creatures. Their ability to reproduce is staggering. The female aphid, for example, can reproduce without mating; Thomas Huxley a century ago calculated that the progeny of a single female in 1 year's time, if permitted to mature, would weigh as much as the inhabitants of China in his day. Populations are checked by the *resistance of the environment*, composed of food availability, weather and climate conditions, and the presence of competing and predatory species. Once environmental resistance is reduced, the reproductive powers of insects in general are truly explosive. Entomologist Robert Metcalf emphasizes the presence of predators as being the most important control: "The greatest single factor in preventing insects from overwhelming the rest of the world is the internecine warfare which they carry out among themselves." The ladybug is one of the most effective controls of aphids, scale insects, and other plant-eating insects; this accounts for their popularity with gardeners. Some parasitic insects kill their hosts outright, others indirectly by impregnating them with their own eggs or by depositing eggs among their victims' so that their offspring may feed upon those of their hosts [3, ch. 15, esp. pp. 247–250].

The role of birds in the balance of nature is also multifaceted. Birds have been found to influence the lives of human beings in other than the most obvious ways as providers of meat and eggs for food,[1] and song and beauty for recreation. Birds help control the insect population that preys upon man, his field crops, and trees. Birds specialize and divide the labor of controlling tree insects. For example:

> Nuthatches zigzag up and down tree trunks, searching for insects that live under the bark. Chickadees eat plant lice and scale insects that grow on the larger branches. Woodpeckers poke below the bark for wood-boring insects. Vireos and warblers eat insects that destroy leaves [23, p. B272].

Undigested seeds of wild fruits and plants pass through their bodies and fall on bare and remote ground, where they sprout into new trees and plants. (White oak forests in the eastern United States are thought to have been planted by bluejays.) Birds help scatter grass seeds, which when grown help to hold moisture in the ground. Sea birds produce the guano, rich with phosphorus and nitrogen, used by farmers as fertilizer. Birds also help the farmer by eating weed seeds, insects pests, and harmful rodents. Examples are numerous:

> In one year birds eat more than 300 weed seeds for every square foot of farm land in the United States. One bobwhite may eat 5,000 to 15,000 weed seeds in a day.
> Birds eat tussock moths, tent caterpillars, army worms, beetles, scale insects, plant lice, stinkbugs, and other insect pests that cause great damage during the growing season, and even destroy the farmer's crops in field and garden. The rose-breasted grosbeak finds potato beetles especially tasty. A pair of grosbeaks nesting near a potato patch may keep the potatoes free from beetles for an entire growing season while they are feeding their young. Two or three nests of sparrows, robins, or bluebirds near a garden will help to control the tomato worms, cabbage worms, and leaf beetles that harm the growing plants [23, pp. B252, B272].

---

[1] The sale of poultry and eggs each provide about $2.2 billion income in the United States; about 315 eggs are consumed per capita each year.

No farmer, aware of such facts, would foolishly claim to have produced a crop entirely by his own efforts. Lack of knowledge, however, has often led him to shoot hawks and owls caught killing his poultry, even though the greatest portion of these predators' diets may be harmful mice and rats. The farmer is not, however, helped by all birds. Some damage the fruit in his orchards and vineyards. Crows eat his corn. City dwellers as well are often annoyed by the unpleasant noise and waste of large flocks, which may also drive away the songbirds. This discussion of nature's balance could, of course, be continued indefinitely, but enough examples have been cited to set the stage for other topics.

27-3 The Exceptional Role of Human Beings in the Balance of Nature

Primitive man existed in nature much as did other animals, for the most part using only the biological organs with which he was born in his struggle to survive in his environment. Such organs are given the name *endosomatic instruments* by the biologist Alfred Lotka [12, p. 307]. Birds struggle generation after generation to catch their food supply of insects by using only their bodies—a tracking system, wings, and beak. Human beings, however, have the exceptional ability to use "organs" that are not components of their biological constitutions. Such components are called *exosomatic instruments* by Lotka, *artifacts* by Kenneth Boulding [1, p. 29], and *capital equipment* by economists in general. Human beings, having the physical attributes and intellect to devise exosomatic instruments, progressed, for example, from catching fish by hand, to using a pointed stick, then to a net, then to a boat, then to larger nets and fishing boats.

Kenneth Boulding draws an analogy between the case in nature of *mutual cooperation*, as exemplified by bees and clover, and the relation between human beings and artifacts. Figure 27-2a illustrates the interdependence of bees and clover. The bee curve, *B*, indicates by its positive intersection with the horizontal axis that there will be some bees without any clover and by its upward slope that

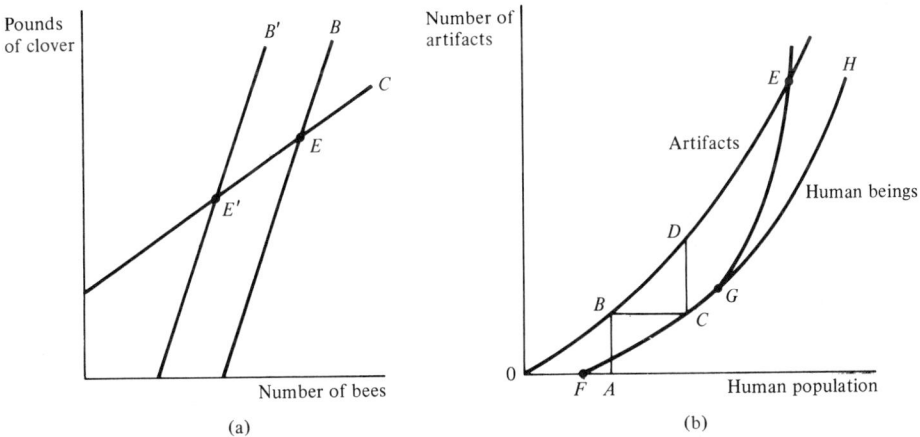

Figure 27-2

the bee population will be larger in the presence of more clover. Similarly, the clover curve, denoted by C, also indicates presence of some clover in the absence of bees but in greater abundance where there are more bees. Biological balance, or equilibrium, exists at the intersection of the two curves, at point E. A reduction of the bee population owing to some external cause such as the application of insecticide intended for other victims would be reflected by a shift of curve B toward the origin and a consequent reduction of equilibrium to point E'.

In the case of human beings and their artifacts, illustrated in Figure 27-2b, cooperation may be such that both may expand to very high levels, if not indefinitely, before reaching equilibrium. This situation, practically unknown in the biosphere, may account for the persistent expansion of the human population, which has not yet reached an equilibrium. The diagram suggests that a human population of OA creates AB artifacts, which in turn permit population to expand by an amount equal to BC, which produces CD additional artifacts. The population and artifacts continue to expand as long as the artifact curve lies above the population curve. The curves could converge to equilibrium because of the production of unfriendly artifacts like nuclear weapons and pollution or by a decline in the human capacity to make new artifacts.[2]

----

[2] Two other cases of two-species equilibrium in which he sees parallels for human society are also discussed by Boulding. The first is one of *mutual competition*, illustrated in Figure 27-3a. An increase in the number of lions in a given territory will mean a diminishing amount of resources for tigers and therefore a decrease in the tiger population. Also, the competitive position of lions is improved relative to tigers because of their greater numbers. The lion curve indicates the number of lions that will be in equilibrium with a given number of tigers in a territory. Similarly, the tiger curve shows how many tigers will be in equilibrium with a given number of lions. Ecological equilibrium exists at point E. If a disease affecting lions but not tigers reduces the lion population, shifting the lion curve toward the origin, equilibrium shifts to E' or perhaps so far to the left that lions become extinct.

The second case, illustrated in Figure 27-3b, is one of *parasitism*—one species is cooperative (dogs) but the other is competitive (fleas). The dog curve indicates there will be OA dogs when no fleas are present, but as the number of fleas increase, the number of dogs will decrease. The flea curve indicates there will be OB fleas even if no dogs are present, but the more dogs there are, the more fleas there will be. Equilibrium E is relatively insensitive to shifts in either curve compared to the cases of Figures 27-2a and 27-3a. Boulding claims "This [insensitivity] unquestionably accounts for the strong persistence of predation or parasitism in the natural world, and even in social systems" [1, p. 31].

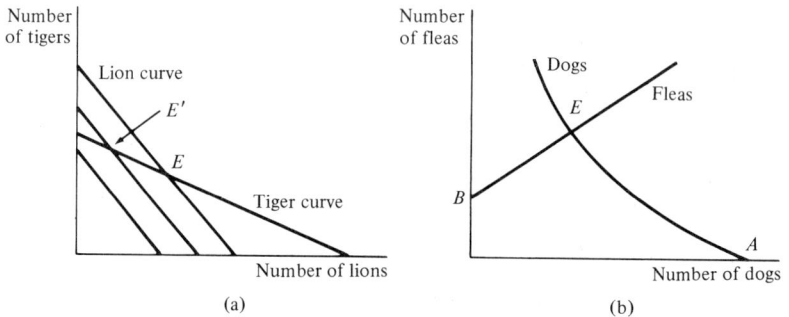

Figure 27-3

27-4   Ecosystems Changed by Human Beings

Ecosystems are being destroyed by diverse human activities like planting crops, logging forests, building dams, starting fires, draining swamps, constructing buildings, laying pavements, and using pesticides. The conversion of prairie to corn and wheat fields provides an interesting case study in which a stable, complex ecosystem was replaced by people with an unstable, relatively simple one. The tall grass prairies of the American Middle West and elsewhere in the world have largely been converted into farm or grazing land. Little remains today of the "sea of grass," which in moist eastern parts grew taller than people. Dark fertile topsoils were built up from the decay of deep and many-branched roots. The grassland also grew hundreds of species of flowers, a few trees, and numerous animals that fed on leaves, roots, and seeds. Jackrabbits, prairie dogs, and mice were fed upon by coyotes, foxes, and skunks, who in turn were the prey of badgers, hawks, owls, and some kinds of snakes. Grasshoppers, leafhoppers, and spiders were controlled by blackbirds, grouse, sparrows, meadow larks, and quail. Old-timers relate stories of multitudes of snakes and of large bison herds spanning several states up to the late 1800s.[3]

Forest ecosystems have been upset by wholesale logging. Many animals and plants disappear in an area when their food supplies and shade are removed. The topsoil erodes more quickly when directly exposed to the elements, reducing the area's water-retaining capacity, silting dams, and aggravating floods along rivers. The water cycle is changed in three ways by deforestation: water transferred from ground to air by trees, called *transpiration*, is reduced; the weather of downwind areas becomes arid and subject to wider fluctuations in temperature; and without reforestation, the area is invaded by weeds [7, p. 202].

Human activities are known to have increased the size of deserts and wastelands. Such land has reportedly increased from 9.4 per cent of the earth's surface in 1882 to 23.3 per cent in 1952, although some of the difference is undoubtedly due to better information in the latter year and to a redefinition of wasteland. Part of the Sahara Desert was man-made by overgrazing, faulty irrigation, and deforestation and is currently advancing southward several miles each year. The center of the Thar Desert of western India was a jungle 200 years ago; preservation of land for purposes of soil conservation is difficult to institute in poor areas in India, because the short-run needs for food have taken precedence over long-run requirements. In Cambodia the Khmer civilization of 800 to 1,000 years ago is thought to have been destroyed by a widespread process called *laterization*, whereby the soil of a defoliated tropical forest turns to rocklike laterite. This phenomenon also destroyed a farming project in the Amazon Basin of Brazil when, "in less than five years the cleared fields became virtually pavements of rock" [7, pp. 202–204].

In the colonial period in the United States it was common practice to abandon land when the soil was depleted by overworking or erosion. This was especially so in Virginia and North Carolina with regard to tobacco crops, which quickly

---

[3] It is estimated that about 20 million ill-tempered bison, ranging in weight up to 3,000 pounds, thundered over the western plains in 1850; by 1889 only 551 were found alive, but since then they have been sheltered from extinction [23, pp. 562–563].

strip nutrients from the ground in successive yearly plantings. The American myth of inexhaustibility of land as a resource generally prevailed until the later 1800s and the closing of the frontier.

27-5   Rachel Carson's *Silent Spring*

Rachel Carson's book *Silent Spring* (1962) [3] brought to the public's attention the dangers of inappropriate and excessive use of pesticides and played a large role in expediting needed legislation. She prophesied a day when, as a result of environmental contamination with chemicals and radiation, there would be no birds to sing on earth, no drone of bees pollinating fruit blossoms, no fish leaping from streams, no chattering and scurrying of creatures and farm animals; in short, where there used to be voices of spring, there would be only silence. While her prophecy could be pushed aside by her critics in government agencies and the chemical industry, the evidence of danger from overuse of chemicals, which she assembled from widespread and knowledgeable sources, could not.[4]

27-5-1   *Cases of death and destruction from misuse of chemicals*

Carson documented numerous ecologically unfortunate cases of spraying of chemicals. One was the spraying of elm trees on the Michigan State University campus at Lansing in 1954 for the intended purpose of killing bark beetles known on occasion to spread the Dutch elm disease [3, pp. 106–118]. The trees were sprayed in the spring with 2 to 5 pounds of DDT per 50-foot tree and sprayed again in July with one half this concentration. Succeeding events revealed what is now commonly known as the DDT-earthworm-robin cycle. When the leaves fell in autumn, they were still covered with the tenacious film of poison. Earthworms fed upon the elm leaf litter, one of their favorite foods, and the DDT became stored and concentrated in their bodies. When the robins returned in the spring and fed upon the worms, they began to die. While as few as 11 large worms contained a lethal dose, robins are known to eat that many in 10 minutes. The few surviving robins, and some other bird species, were found unable to reproduce themselves; some built nests, but laid no eggs; others laid and incubated eggs but did not hatch them.

In addition to 90 bird species, which suffered a heavy rate of mortality because of the poison, other animals eating the worms were affected, such as raccoons, opossums, shrews, and moles, which passed the poison along to their predators, hawks and owls. Furthermore, pollinating insects and predatory spiders and beetles were killed as well.

The saddest part of the story is that this killing of harmless and desirable creatures was later found of little use in controlling the Dutch elm disease, which spread as rapidly in treated areas as in those unsprayed. The best control was subsequently found to be simple sanitation—immediate removal and burning of

---

[4] Her credentials were more substantial than only literary skill and a respect for nature; she had earned a master's degree in biology from Johns Hopkins University, had taught biology there and at the University of Maryland, and eventually became editor-in-chief of the Fish and Wildlife Service's publications, where she had worked for about 15 years (1936–1951).

the affected trees, especially before the beetles emerge in the spring from the dead wood.

Another case of insecticide poisoning cited by Carson involved destruction of an age-old salmon breeding ground in the Miramichi River on the Atlantic coast of New Brunswick, Canada [3, pp. 129–135]. The yearly pattern was broken in June of 1954 as a result of the spraying of millions of acres of balsam forest by the Canadian government to combat an upsurge of budworms threatening the trees and indirectly the pulp and paper industries. Streams as well as forests were criss-crossed by planes spraying half a pound of DDT in oil solution per acre. Within 2 days, salmon and brook trout were found dead or dying along the stream banks. The stream insects, including larva of the caddis fly, stonefly, mayfly, and blackflies, were killed by the DDT, leaving nothing for the young fish to eat. By August it was evident the whole year's spawning had been wiped out. Only one in six remained from those spawned the previous year, and only one in three from two seasons before. This was revealed by a salmon study begun in 1950 by the Fisheries Research Board of Canada. Even after repeated applications, spraying for budworms proved in some areas to be only a stopgap measure, since populations resurged in following years.

In 1956 an all-out chemical war was declared on the gypsy moth in New Jersey, New York, Michigan, and Pennsylvania. Nearly a million acres were sprayed and plans for spraying three million more in 1957 were carried out in spite of strong opposition by conservationists and others. Even densely populated Nassau County in Long Island was showered by planes with the poisonous DDT mixed with fuel oil, in spite of the fact that the gypsy moth is a forest insect that does not inhabit cultivated fields, garden, meadows, and marshes—much less the metropolitan areas of New York City. Indiscriminate spraying covered truck gardens, fish ponds, dairy farms, and salt marshes. Carson wrote:

> They sprayed the quarter-acre lots of suburbia, drenching a housewife making a desperate effort to cover her garden before the roaring plane reached her, and showering insecticide over children at play and commuters at railway stations . . . . Birds, fish, crabs, and useful insects were killed [3, p. 158].

Property rights of private citizens were violated by the control agencies even after specific requests and protests were lodged against spraying their lands. Dairy farmers, truck gardeners, and beekeepers sustained losses and some were successful in collecting damages in legal suits. Some owners of apple orchards and bees, however, were unable to sue irresponsible, out-of-state contractors with no local addresses, who sprayed some areas several times, contrary to instructions. In spite of additional sprayings of some areas in following years, the gypsy moth continued to reappear. The attempted eradication had obviously been unsuccessful.

A similar campaign was undertaken against the fire ant in nine southern states, covering 20 million acres, where the major nuisance was the foot-high, rock-hard mounds built as nests, which hampered operation of farm machinery [3, pp. 161–172]. Rather than presenting a hazard to nesting birds, crops, livestock, and human beings, the fire ant was later found to feed chiefly on other insects, many of which are considered harmful to people's interests. It also picks boll weevil larvae off cotton and aerates the soil with its mound-building activities. The fire ant's sting was found to present no major problem, even in Alabama, where experience with this insect was the greatest; no human deaths from fire ant stings have ever been recorded over the 40 years since its entry from South America, while 33 deaths were recorded in the Office of Vital Statistics as being due to bee and wasp stings in 1959 alone. The agriculture department's control program was very costly— about $3.50 per acre compared to treatment of individual mounds at about $1.00 per acre and other methods costing as little as $0.23 per acre. Heavy doses of dieldren and heptachlor, many times more deadly than DDT, produced heavy losses of wildlife and farm animals, but the fire ant lives on and in larger numbers in some areas. Carson states:

> Never has any pesticide program been so thoroughly and deservedly damned by practically everyone except the beneficiaries of this "sales bonanza" [the chemical firms and private contractors]. It is an outstanding example of an ill-conceived, badly executed, and thoroughly detrimental experiment in the mass control of insects, an experiment . . . expensive in dollars, in destruction of animal life, and in loss of public confidence in the Agricultural Department . . . [3, p. 162].

27-5-2   *The threat of chemicals to human health*

With these and other cases as a background, Carson turned to the problem of assessing the human health cost of " the never-ending stream of chemicals of which pesticides are a part, chemicals now pervading the world in which we live, acting upon us directly and indirectly, separately and collectively" [3, p. 188]. Contemplation of their eventual, but as yet undetermined, effects was to Carson ominous and frightening. Her concern was shared by Dr. David Price of the United States Health Service, whom she quoted as saying:

> We all live under the haunting fear that something may corrupt the environment to the point where man joins the dinosaurs as an obsolete form of life, . . . And what makes these thoughts all the more disturbing is the knowledge that our fate could perhaps be sealed twenty or more years before the development of symptoms [3, p. 188].

She discussed the tragedy of soil, water, and food contamination so concentrated with pesticides that single exposures were sufficient to kill fish and birds and to bring sudden illness and death to farmers, spraymen, and pilots. But she expressed a greater concern about the accumulated poisons stored in fat tissue and sex organs in the body from small repeated doses over a period of time— buildups that may eventually reach levels sufficiently critical to cause illness, infertility, cancer, and disruption of energy production and genetic structures of the body.

Only we, among all life forms, can create cancer-producing substances, called carcinogens. While there are natural cancer-causing agents, such as ultraviolet radiation in sunlight and arsenic, living species have survived through selection of the most adaptable and resistant. Adjustment has taken place over millions of years to malignancy producers found in nature. Carcinogens introduced by man are quite recent in comparison, beginning perhaps with the industrial revolution producing soot containing arsenic and chromatic hydrocarbons. To these new threats we have little biological heritage of protection. It is now known that cancer results from repeated contact of certain chemicals with the skin; half a dozen sources were known by 1900, including arsenic fumes in early smelters and foundries, radiation in cobalt and uranium mines, hydrocarbons where there were exposures to tar and pitch. Countless new cancer-causing chemicals have been created since then. Exposure is no longer confined, however, to occupational contact. Even unborn children are exposed. Cancer is known to-day to kill more American school children than any other disease. The American Cancer Society predicts that two out of three families will be struck by cancer [3, pp. 219–221].

From animal experiments, several pesticides are known carcinogens: arsenic (sodium arsenite used in weed killer, calcium arsenate and other compounds in insecticides); DDT (insecticide); IPC and CIPC (herbicides); amino-triazole (weed killer). Some malignancies develop very slowly, requiring occupational exposures for a period of 15 to 30 years. An example of such harmful effects is provided by some women in the 1920s who hand-painted watch dials with radium; they developed bone cancer after 15 or more years. The tendency for symptoms of cancer to develop after long lapses of time is most unsettling to consider in the light of increasing use of new chemical products.

An exception to the rule of a long period of latency, however, is leukemia, a disease of the blood-forming tissue; Hiroshima survivors of the atomic bombing began developing leukemia after only 3 years. There is little doubt of the cause-and-effect relation between the presence of leukemia and exposure to toxic chemicals.

Human beings are exposed to cancer-producing chemicals in many ways: air pollution, water contamination, pesticide residue on food, medicines, cosmetics, wood preservatives, and coloring agents in paint and ink. All exposures may be safe in single doses but fatal in combination. Complicated interactions of small amounts of different chemicals could also produce cancer. Troublesome detergents that are not carcinogenic in themselves could possibly promote cancer by making the lining of the digestive tract more vulnerable. Viewed in this way, who can say what size dose of carcinogen is safe [3, pp. 237–239]?

27-5-3   *Insect immunity to insecticides and biological alternatives*

The use of insecticides for control purposes is fraught with pitfalls. Chemical spraying often leads to much greater resurgence of the target insect in following years because the natural predators prove to be more sensitive to the chemicals than the insects are. Also, the target insect may return with stronger immunity and less susceptibility to artificial control. In other cases, predators may be critically reduced in numbers because of the lapse in their food supply, rendering them unable to control the larger resurgence. In still other cases, killing one species may release their hosts from control, which previously were not numerous enough to be considered pests. A 1956 review cited 215 papers dealing with the effects of pesticides on insect populations [18].

While resistance of insects to chemical treatment is important in agriculture and forestry, it is of even greater concern in public health. Mosquitoes known to transmit malaria, yellow fever, encephalitis, and elephantiasis are becoming quite resistant. So, too, are house flies, which contaminate food with bacillus of dysentery; body lice, which transmit typhus; rat fleas, which cause plagues; tsetse flies, which cause African sleeping sickness; ticks, which cause various fevers; and innumerable others [3, ch. 16]. Experts now conclude that houseflies are no longer susceptible to insecticides and must once more be controlled by general sanitation [3, p. 268].

Today, spraying may only kill off the weak insects and even stimulate the growth of tougher, more resistant strains. Future control must rely more and more upon biological solutions contributed by biochemists, ecologists, entomologists, geneticists, pathologists, and physiologists. This is the developing science of biological control. From it have come proposals such as the production and release of strong but sterilized male insects to compete with wild ones, producing eventually only infertile eggs and dwindled population [3, p. 279]. This technique was successful in eradicating the screw-worm from the Dutch Caribbean island of Curaçao in 1954 and from the southeastern United States in 1959. This worm lays its eggs in the open wounds of warm-blooded animals, which upon hatching feed on the host's flesh. Livestock producers in Alabama and Georgia and other southeastern states were previously suffering annual losses of up to $20 million. Sterilization was accomplished by exposure of lab insects to X ray, and distribution was at weekly intervals by airplane. Further experiments with this technique are being made against the tsetse fly in Rhodesia, the melon and fruit flies in Hawaii and Rota, the housefly in Orlando, Florida, and others. Ways are being sought to produce sterilization other than by X ray.

Experiments are being made with chemicals and noises that attract and repel certain insects. These may eventually prove useful in insect control without the harmful effects of indiscriminate chemical spraying. A plea has more recently been made (1973) by entomologist Vernon M. Stern for more knowledge of "economic thresholds" (crop yields and pest density ratios) for more enlightened control measures [20].

27-6   The Consequences of *Silent Spring*

In the decade following the publication of *Silent Spring* in 1962, a much better understanding of the harmful effects of pesticides has been atatined. Much new information is summarized in "The Circle of Evidence," in Frank Graham, Jr.'s *Since Silent Spring* (1970) [13, pp. 91–160]. Space limitations here prohibit a review of the new evidence, controversy, and events, but it is fair to say that through the efforts of Rachel Carson and the Sierra Club, many environmentalists were called to action. Additional investigations took place and new federal legislation came into being. With the National Environmental Policy Act of 1969 (NEPA), signed by President Nixon on January 1, 1970, the federal government assumed responsibility for environmental legislation previously left up to individual states. A Council on Environmental Quality (CEQ) was set up in the Executive Office of the President to review and appraise government programs and activities concerning environmental problems. Adverse environmental impacts of *any* decision by federal officials and agencies must now be considered and included in a detailed statement when legislation or other major actions are proposed. When actions involve adverse environmental effects, alternative courses must be considered in the same depth as the proposed action, for compliance with the NEPA. Where only destructive courses of action are possible, they must be subjected to public scrutiny and can be approved only when anticipated long-term social benefits exceed long-term environmental costs. Relations between long-term and short-term uses must be spelled out. Where committed resources are irreversible and irretrievable, this must be revealed. Nonquantifiable values such as health, aesthetics, and diversity must be considered. The burden of proof now falls on those who would disturb the environment to show either that the action will not harm environmental quality or that social benefits outweigh social costs. Proposals for federal legislation must include analyses of environmental impact by "appropriate federal, state, and local agencies, which are authorized to develop and enforce environmental standards."

During the first 24 months under the NEPA one of the major problems of implementation was that virtually every filed statement contained "the engineering fallacy." This problem is present when the engineer evades the question of whether or not the project should be undertaken and proceeds to examine ways of accomplishing the proposed goal. It is easier for him to state a need, support it with growth projections, and focus his thinking on solutions.

> Point out to an engineer that the South Platte River in northeastern Colorado sometimes floods its lowlands, and he proposes building a dam—or in this case, one dam and three dikes. Point out to him that the dam will eliminate the fish run on the river and he proposes a fish ladder and artificial gravel spawning pits. Point out that one railroad and one state highway will be suddenly under water and he proposes relocating them. Point out that 15,000 acres of natural stream environment and 36,000 acres of good agricultural land, as well as 40 farms and three villages will be inundated, and he proposes calling in a planner to build a model city for the displaced persons. What he will *never* do is reconsider whether the Narrows Unit Dam of the Missouri River Basin Project should be built or not. Although NEPA may require him to consider the environmental implications of doing nothing, his whole background and training as an engineer distort his perspective [21, pp. 239–240].

A more ecologically sound approach, which can be termed the antigrowth thesis, begins questioning the real need for the project. What will happen if proposed construction does not take place on the Colorado dam, a fourth jetport in New York City, a new freeway through downtown Boston, or for the transportation of large amounts of fresh water from northern to southern California. The likely answer is that the projected statistical growth of people and use will not take place in that locality. Perhaps needs can be better served by moving people to where the resources are rather than vice versa. This approach is thought to be more consistent with the interests of the NEPA [21, pp. 238–239].

Other problems with statements filed during the first 2 years following the establishment of NEPA involve economic or technological impracticality. The first comes into play when the Tennessee Valley Authority claims it cannot afford to pay for reclaiming land damaged by strip mining for the coal it uses. In actuality, TVA is trying to pass increased power costs on to the public in the form of decreased environmental quality. The second arises when the claim is made that a project cannot wait for technological alternatives to be developed. Power shortages or changed habits of power consumption should be seriously considered as alternatives to rushed construction of nuclear plants with uncertain and serious environmental consequences left unanswered [21, pp. 240–241].

Further restriction on the use of chemical toxicants was authorized on February 8, 1973, by Executive Order No. 11643:

> It is the policy of the Federal Government to (1) restrict the use on Federal lands of chemical toxicants for the purpose of killing predatory mammals or birds; (2) restrict the use on such lands of chemical toxicants which cause any secondary poisoning effects for the purpose of killing other mammals, birds, or reptiles; and (3) restrict the use of both such types of toxicants in any Federal programs of mammal or bird damage control that may be authorized by law. All such mammal or bird damage control programs shall be conducted in a manner which contributes to the maintenance of environmental quality, and to the conservation and protection, to the greatest degree possible, of the Nation's wildlife resources, including predatory animals.

Rachel Carson's recommendations were thus, after a lag of one decade, formally accepted.

27-7   Ecoethics—Attitudes and Values Concerning the Environment

Attitudes of people toward their environment are categorized by Earl Cook, a geologist at Texas A & M University, under three ethics [4]: development, preservation, and equilibrium. He defines an ethic as "a self-imposed limitation on freedom of action in the struggle for existence," which "tells us what we *may* do, among all the things we *can* do."

The development ethic has its roots in the dominion, or conquest, ethic found in Judeo-Christian theology, which teaches man to "be fruitful and multiply," and to "have dominion over the fish of the sea and over the birds of the air and over every living thing that moves upon the earth." Good is thus produced by man's management and mastery of nature. This idea is reinforced by the work ethic, which urges man to use his energy to produce more and bigger goods at a faster pace and which implies the goodness of economic and population growth. In regard to nature, the development ethic directs the development of all perceived resources lest the perceiver be considered unpatriotic and probably sinful. The resource developer guided by this ethic can point with pride to his increased product with its associated economic multiplier effects and to his contribution to regional growth and national security.

The preservation ethic forbids man to alter natural areas thought to have aesthetic, ecological, recreational, therapeutic, or scientific value. The *moral* preservationist regards nature as good in itself, not to be "raped, desecrated, and despoiled" by roads, pipelines, dams, and mines. He would restrict the use of preserved areas to a limited number of visitors possessing certain qualities. The *nature-therapy* preservationist holds that man also is good and that he benefits physically and psychologically from getting close to and communing with nature. The *scientific* preservationist wishes to preserve some species in their native habitat, some diverse and undisturbed ecosystems, some unique geologic formations, for the information such preservation might provide. The *recreational* conservationist wants natural areas for hunting, hiking, and picnicking as well as for the peace and quiet they provide.

The equilibrium ethic recognizes the need for people to work toward obtaining a stable equilibrium between human beings and their environment. The modern version recognizes the actual and potential disruptions of nature of which human beings are capable. Cost-benefit analysis, including nonmarket costs and benefits, has been accepted in the United States under the National Environmental Policy Act of 1969, which requires public policy "to achieve a balance between population and resource use which will permit high standards of living and a wide sharing of life's amenities." The burden of proof has recently shifted to the developer to show that a proposed alteration of the environment has a positive net benefit to the nation. Environmental and ecological impacts must now be considered along with market values. This shift in the burden of proof promises to have a profound influence on economic and ecological change.

27-8   The Ecological Problem of Sustained Economic Growth

Turning now from careless, artificially created threats to our environment, let us direct our attention to the very important environmental questions, Can economic growth be sustained indefinitely? and Is such growth desirable [17]?

The answer to the first question requires an estimation of the supply of mineral resources available to fill projected needs. Current estimates may prove to be understated by a factor of 2, 4, or 8, but the fact is inescapable that their use at current rates will exhaust some of them within a few decades. The historical lesson economics provides is that as resources become scarce, their prices rise, encouraging more efficient use and replacement by substitutes. Concurrently, science comes to the rescue with new ways of meeting our needs. History fails to provide examples, however, of our ability to find substitutes for so large a group of important materials as copper, lead, platinum, silver, tin, and zinc— all of which could be used up within two decades (see [9]). Perhaps no good substitutes can be found. Optimistic forecasts are based upon faith and the presumption of scientific capability in technological innovation.

Technological advances of the past 200 years may have been due to especially favorable circumstances. Fossil fuels were abundant and cheap. The assimilative capacity of the biosphere presented no limitation. Scientific progress was aided by easy communication of scientists, whereas today research may be subject to diminishing returns to scale because of the problems of coordinating the work of many narrowly focused specialists. The problems of developing nuclear energy with safety limits on radiation and heat may not be solvable. Efficient and inexpensive recycling of materials and maintenance of the Green Revolution in food production may not keep pace with the expanding population.

The problems of sustaining an annual growth rate of 3 per cent are brought into focus by observing that average income must rise 100 times over the next 150 years and 10,000 times over 300 years. Contemplate the energy and material requirements. What kinds of expenditures will be made in reaching such fantastic standards? How can people possibly absorb them [17, p. 28]?

Turn now to the question of the desirability of sustained growth. First, there are dangers in pursuing an ever-increasing physical product. Public attitudes must change to produce the necessary political and economic institutions. Small inefficient units must yield to larger ones. International agreements on the use of the world's resources must be made and enforced; conflicts arising from the diverse judgments and the greed of nationalistic representatives may result in limited or terminal war. On the other hand, ecological catastrophe from new chemicals, increased radiation, interference in the biosphere, or other external diseconomies mentioned in Chapter 23 may come first. With the increasing motion of jet-age people around the globe, the possibility of a worldwide epidemic by a lethal virus for which there is insufficient vaccine also becomes greater.

Second, unthinking adaptation of our lives to the style and pace made possible by technology and the profitability of commercial ventures may cause us to lose irrevocably the sources of comfort and gratification of the past. Although the spill-overs of foul air, snarled traffic, noise, and fear of criminal violence cannot be measured objectively, any one of them could be large enough to counter the gains of prosperity. A family replete with material possessions may have little real enjoyment if it must take elaborate precautions against theft and if it fears to take an evening stroll lest a member be kidnapped for ransom, mutilated, or murdered. The diminishing marginal utility of goods must be considered in relation to the increasing marginal disutility of " bads." Choice among a growing variety of goods can also become tiresome and time-consuming, leaving less time for the use and appreciation of goods selected.

Third, people's satisfaction depends to some extent, as suggested by the Veblen dependence and keeping-up-with-the-Joneses effects mentioned in Chapter 6, upon their relative positions in the structure of incomes. The objective of increasing happiness or welfare through economic growth is futile, since *everyone* cannot become better off *relative to everyone else*. The unmeasured wealth-dissipative effects must, of course, be subtracted from measured income to determine economic welfare.

Fourth, discontent with existing levels of consumption is institutionalized by the advertising agencies of Madison Avenue, sanctioned by the business community, and hallowed by the system of higher education. Such discontent with prevailing conditions is referred to by Bernard Shaw as the " mainspring of progress." If continued discontent with existing status is required to maintain economic growth, there is doubt that people are really happier absorbing more goods. Induced obsessions may cut people off from full enjoyment of life, shrivel their generous impulses, shrink their capacities for friendship, and corrupt their character by encouraging them to use other people in unbenevolent ways for their own advancement.

Fifth, there is evidence that the " knowledge industry " that fuels the engine of economic growth advances the secular over the sacred.

One wonders if the loss of the great myths, the loss of belief in a benevolent deity, in reunion after death, has not contributed to a sense of desolation. One wonders also if a code of morality can be widely accepted in a society without belief in any god or in any hereafter.

As decisions are increasingly influenced by experts, democracy becomes more vunerable. As historical knowledge grows, and hawk-eyed scholars find a vocation in debunking national heroes and popular legend, the pride of peoples in their common past is eroded and, along with it, their morale as well.[5]

Sixth, the labor-saving inventions guided by computers in the factory, and recreation in the home ruled by television, promote estrangement between people. The older ideas of the good life—"a more settled way of natural beauty and architectural dignity, a rehabilitation of norms of propriety and taste"—may be lost to affluent societies promoting "ever more outlandish and expendable gadgetry and seeking eternally for faster economic growth."[6]

Professor Mishan summarizes these arguments and presents this disconcerting but unsurprising conclusion:

If it is conceded that, once subsistence levels have been passed, the sources of man's enduring satisfactions spring from mutual trust and affection, from sharing joy and sorrow, from giving and accepting love, from open-hearted companionship and laughter; if it is further conceded that in a civilized society the joy of living comes from the sense of wonder inspired by the unfolding of nature, from the renewal of faith and hope inspired by the heroic and the good—if this much is conceded, then is it possible to believe that unremitting attempts to harness the greater part of man's energies and ingenuity to the task of amassing an ever greater assortment of material possessions can add much to people's happiness? Can it add more than it subtracts? Can it add anything?

Recognizing the darker side of economic growth, we must conclude that the game is not worth the candle. And the answer to the question of whether continued economic growth in the West brings us any closer to the good life cannot be other than a resounding No.[7] [For a less pessimistic statement, see Wallich [22].]

27-9   Spaceship Earth

Kenneth Boulding refers to an aspect of ecological economics encompassing the problems of population, pollution, and exhaustion of resources. He points to the day when Earth's people will have removed all the easily extractable resources and will have filled all the earth's pollution reservoirs. In this state everything must be recycled, and human beings will have entered a spaceship economy. The present "through-put" economy of extracting ores and fossil fuels, processing commodities, and filling pollution reservoirs will have passed. This one-way economic system will have been superseded by a circular flow of the wastes of

[5] Quoted with permission of the publisher from E. J. Mishan, "Growth and Antigrowth: What Are the Issues?" *Challenge*, May–June 1973, p. 30.

[6] Ibid., p. 31.

[7] Ibid.

production and consumption. "We literally will have to eat our own excrement after it has been suitably processed and we have applied energy to the diminution of its entropy" [1, p. 43].

Thus, our through-puts of energy and materials yield costs to the system rather than returns or rewards, as GNP statistics often imply. The economic progress and standard of a country is typically measured by its GNP per capita. High production and consumption achieved by the exosomatic instruments of humans become national goals, although they may not be correlated with human welfare in the short or long run. In terms of exhausting irreplaceable resources and hastening the day of the spaceship economy, gross national product might better be called gross national cost. Welfare should be recognized as being improved when the same or better conditions are maintained with smaller through-put. Boulding prefers society's capital structure to GNP as a measure of welfare because GNP includes "unproductive" and maintenance items such as national defense and commuting to work [1, pp. 44–45].

Georgescu-Roegen has predicted a time in which even the limited passengers on Boulding's spaceship Earth must make their final voyage. Entropy, discussed in Chapter 19, prevails over all in the end. Dust returns to dust. Rachel Carson's *Silent Spring* becomes permanent. The implications may be recognized as Malthusian: the more people on Earth and the faster they pollute their environment and exhaust irreplaceable resources, the shorter will be the life of the human species. Decisions of business people in allocating scarce resources should be made with an awareness of such long-run effects.

Questions and Problems

27-1. Define and explain the following terms:

a. ecology	i. laterization
b. ecosystem	j. DDT-earthworm-robin cycle
c. balance of nature	k. pesticide
d. food web	l. carcinogens
e. ecological efficiency	m. through-put
f. ecological succession	n. consumption as a cost
g. endosomatic instruments	o. pollution reservoirs
h. exosomatic instruments, or artifacts	p. the three ecoethics
	q. spaceship Earth

27-2. a. Form a mathematical expression indicating that the population of a species x_i depends upon the populations of the remaining n species.

b. Form a system of n equations (species) of n populations that could be solved (in theory), producing ecological equilibrium.

27-3. Is there anything really wrong with economic growth as a goal of the firm? nation? world?

References

1. Kenneth E. Boulding. "Economics as an Ecological Science." In *Economics as a Science* (New York: McGraw-Hill, 1970), pp. 23–52.

2. David Brower. *The Meaning of Wilderness to Science: Proceedings, Sixth Biennial Wilderness Conference* (San Fransisco: Sierra Club, 1960).

3. Rachel Carson. *Silent Spring* (Boston: Houghton Mifflin, 1962).

4. Earl Cook. "Ecoethics and Environmental Politics." *EXXON USA* 12 (1973), pp. 16–19.

5. Robert Dorfman and Nancy S. Dorfman. *Economics of Environment: Selected Readings* (New York: W. W. Norton, 1972).

6. Daniel W. Ehrenfeld. *Conserving Life on Earth* (New York: Oxford University Press, 1972).

7. Paul R. Ehrlich and Anne H. Ehrlich. *Population, Resources, Environment: Issues in Human Ecology.* 2d ed. (San Fransisco: W. H. Freeman, 1972).

8. Edmund Faltermayer. "The Energy 'Joyride' Is Over." *Fortune*, September 1972, pp. 99ff.

9. ———. "Metals: The Warning Signals Are Up." *Fortune*, October 1972, pp. 109ff.

10. A. Myrick Freeman, III, Robert H. Haveman and Allen V. Kneese. *The Economics of Environmental Policy* (New York: Wiley, 1973).

11. Gerald Garvey. *Energy, Ecology, Economy: A Framework for Environmental Policy* (New York: W. W. Norton, 1972).

12. Nicholas Georgescu-Roegen. *The Entropy Law and the Economic Process* (Cambridge, Mass.: Harvard University Press, 1971).

13. Frank Graham, Jr. *Since Silent Spring* (Boston: Houghton Mifflin, 1970).

14. Dennis L. Meadows and Donnella H. Meadows. *Toward Global Equilibrium: Collected Papers* (Cambridge, Mass.: Wright-Allen Press, 1973).

15. Dennis L. Meadows et al. *The Dynamics of Growth in a Finite World* (Cambridge, Mass.: Wright-Allen Press, 1973).

16. Donnella H. Meadows et al. *The Limits to Growth* (Washington, D.C.: Potomac Associates, 1972).

17. E. J. Mishan. "Growth and Antigrowth: What Are the Issues?" *Challenge*, May-June 1973, pp. 26–36.

18. W. E. Ripper. "Effect of Pesticides on Balance of Arthropod Populations." *Annual Review of Entomology* 1 (1956): 403–438.

19. Robert Rudd. *Pesticides and the Living Landscape* (Madison: University of Wisconsin Press, 1964).

20. Vernon M. Stern. "Economic Thresholds." *Annual Review of Entomology* 18 (1973): 259–280.

21. Donald N. Thompson. *The Economics of Environmental Protection* (Cambridge, Mass.: Winthrop Publishers, 1973).

22. Henry C. Wallich. "How to Live with Economic Growth: Some Safety Devices to Ward Off Doomsday." *Fortune*, October 1972, pp. 114ff.

23. *World Book Encyclopedia*, 1973.

28 Econethics—Social Responsibility in Business

    The social responsibility of business is a controversial topic that has been debated by various groups: business, professional, religious, government, student, and consumer. Opinions range from the recommendations of the purely competitive economic model to the philanthropic ones of social activists, who would require corporate managers to pursue a wide range of social goals. This chapter examines a number of views on corporate social responsibility and considers the options open to managers in dealing with demands for a new social contract. In reference to the general programming model of the firm, such factors fall under the category of social and potentially legal constraints under which the firm pursues its objectives.

28-1 A Statement by the Committee for Economic Development

The June 1971 statement for the 50-member Research and Policy Committee of the Committee for Economic Development (CED) stated: " Business functions by public consent, and its basic purpose is to serve constructively the needs of society—to the satisfaction of society " [5, pp. 11–16, 26–29]. Should business fail to satisfactorily serve the needs of society, consent may be withdrawn and the legal constraints within which business must operate may be tightened.

    There is abundant evidence that, on the whole, business has served the American economy remarkably well. Since 1890 GNP has almost doubled every 20 years, real disposable income per capita has tripled, and the average work time per employee has declined by one third. Wealth generated by business has been shared by stockholders, employees, and consumers and has been used to sustain our government via increased tax revenues and our cultural, religious, and eleemosynary institutions via donations. Under the discipline of the private enterprise system, business people are spurred to improve their products, reduce their costs, and attract more customers. Our competitive market has served to allocate efficiently scarce resources for our ever-changing social requirements; this is especially evident when the performance of the United States economy is compared with those of most foreign countries.

    Notwithstanding these accomplishments, American expectations are now rising more rapidly than the country's economic and social performance. The economy has produced such affluence that many people believe attention can now be diverted from producing more products for a population, which is held to be to a large extent on the diminishing side of its average-utility function, to providing a better quality of life for the citizenry. The Research and Policy Committee lists the following goals for preventing further deterioration of our environment and community life:

Elimination of poverty and provision of good health care

Equal opportunity for each person to realize his or her full potential regardless of race, sex, or creed

Education and training for a fully productive and rewarding participation in modern society

Ample jobs and career opportunities in all parts of society

Livable communities with decent housing, safe streets, a clean and pleasant environment, efficient transportation, good cultural and educational opportunities, and a prevailing mood of civility among people

The status quo and "establishment" institutions are under assault by highly idealistic youth and numerous citizen groups crusading for conservation, consumerism, women's rights, black power, and freedom in the professional arts. In this age of accountability, all major institutions are being subjected to scrutiny and criticism, including government, the military, organized labor, schools, the church, and, of course, business—especially large business. Opinion Research Corporation found in 1970 that consumers were dissatisfied with information about products upon which to base wise choices; were not convinced companies were making any real progress toward pollution control; and believed business has a moral obligation to aid other institutions in achieving social progress even though profits must be reduced to do so.

The committee describes public expectations of business with reference to three concentric circles of responsibilities, as shown in Figure 28-1. The inner circle includes the fundamental responsibilities of efficiently providing products, jobs, and economic growth. The intermediate circle requires an additional awareness of changes in social values and priorities, say, of environmental impacts, employee relations, greater desire by customers for more product information, and protection from injury. The outer circle also encompasses the broader responsibilities of business to take an active part in improving the social environment, for example, by ameliorating poverty and urban blight—not necessarily because business has caused the problem, but because it possesses the resources and skills to make an improvement.

In short, the contractual terms between society and business are changing: Business is asked to assume broader responsibilities in serving a wider spectrum of human values. Management must voluntarily respond to changing public expectations if it is to avoid the imposition of mandatory institutionalized constraints. This, basically, is the view put forth by the Research and Policy Committee for the CED.

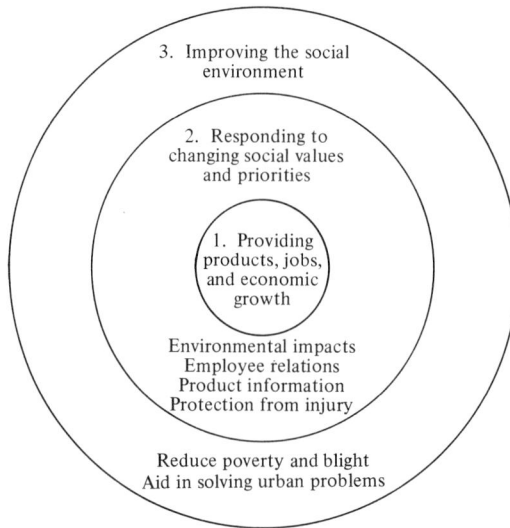

Figure 28-1

Why should business managers take an active role in improving the social environment, and how can they justify this activity to their stockholders? The answer provided by the CED is that advancement of the well-being of society is usually good for business. Companies look to society to provide their basic requirements—capital, labor, customers. Resources and good will are generally forthcoming only to enterprises that have worked for and developed them. The state explicitly recognized this *doctrine of enlightened self-interest* in 1935 by amending the Internal Revenue Code to permit corporations to deduct 5 per cent of their pretax income for charitable contributions. Subsequent corporate practice and court decisions have supported the concept that corporate contributions can legally be given for social purposes that provide no compensating direct benefits. In 1953 the New Jersey Superior Court upheld the legal right of a manufacturing company (A. P. Smith) to contribute funds to a university (Princeton), claiming it was a " duty of corporations to support higher education in the interest of the long-range well-being of their stockholders because the company could not hope to operate effectively in a society which is not functioning well." Corporate grants provide future trained personnel. Similarly, grants for health and cultural facilities can be justified in helping attract skilled people to the community, and grants to improve ghetto housing and recreational facilities contribute to a safer and more acceptable environment for employees and business operations. Indeed, the broadly defined corporate interest can support effort by management to solve social problems, because " people who have a good environment, education, and opportunity make better employees, customers, and neighbors for business than those who are poor, ignorant, and oppressed." Besides helping to enlarge markets and improve the work force, efforts to solve social problems help reduce costs of crime, disease, welfare, and waste of human potential.

Another aspect of the doctrine of self-interest is that the business that ignores its obligations to contribute to social improvement may eventually be subject to direct action by citizens in the form of petitions, picket lines, refusal to buy the firm's products and common stock, and sabotage. There may also be public hearings in which the firm's indiscretions and errors of judgment are aired, picked up by the media, and communicated to potential customers, investors, and employees. Finally, public pressures may result in government intervention and regulation. In view of these dismal prospects, it would appear to the advantage of the corporation to act voluntarily to forestall such confrontations. In this way, management is able to retain some flexibility in conducting its affairs in an efficient and adaptive manner. Rules imposed from the outside and in the heat of a crisis may be unduly restrictive. Obstinate opposition to social change by a single firm may also affect adversely the atmosphere in which all firms must function.

In summary, there are the "carrot and stick" aspects of the "positive appeal to the corporation's greater opportunities to grow and profit in a healthy, prosperous, and well-functioning society" and the "negative threat of increasingly onerous compulsion and harassment if it does not do its part in helping create such a society" [5, p. 29].

28-2   Six Views of Corporate Responsibility

Corporate responsibility is examined by Clarence C. Walton, Dean of the School of General Studies at Columbia University, with reference to six different points of view or, as he refers to them, models [36, ch. 5]. None alone is sufficient to provide an adequate framework for deciding if and when a given corporate act is, or is not, responsible and therefore in the public interest. Together, they provide a summary of the different philosophical positions supported by various interested groups.

First is the austere model, based on the proposition that owners of a firm are decision-making risk takers who rightly deserve all profits. In a competitive economy, where a large number of owners vie for scarce resources and rewards of profit, welfare is assumed to be largely automatic or appropriately provided by government. Profit-seeking business people are confronted with unions seeking better wage and working conditions, and business and unions are confronted with a consumer-protecting, equity-dispensing government. Under the concept of pluralism, each fights the other in a political arena where none can remain dominant for long. This view also echoes Emerson's warning to the philanthropist in his essay on "Self-Reliance" against putting "all poor men in good situations" by means of "miscellaneous popular charities; the education at college of fools; the building of meeting-houses to the vain end to which may now stand; alms to sots, and the thousandfold Relief Societies." Stockholders, being the self-reliant and deserving members of society, should therefore receive corporate benefits; to pay dividends rather than giving away the stockholders' money is the socially responsible function of management. The holders of this view firmly endorse free enterprise as the best way to assure economic vitality and personal freedom. (Discussion of this view is elaborated later in the chapter.)

Second is the household model, which might also be called the "big family" or "Good Shepherd" view. The company is seen as an extension of the family, having its warmth and intimacy. Employees are the most precious asset of the firm and therefore must be given the highest priority in business decisions. The sanctity of the individual is held in much higher esteem than the unfeeling machine culture. Obligatory legal rights of employees, such as collective bargaining, unemployment benefits, and seniority, are only part of the package. Exemplars of this view include Henry Ford, who initiated a "fifty-two paychecks a year" plan for employees with financial difficulties, and Procter and Gamble, which adopted a guaranteed annual wage at the turn of the twentieth century. Workers are viewed not as a commodity in the productive process, to be casually replaced by a new, more productive input. Obligations accrue to workers and the community that cannot be forgotten if the company contemplates a plant relocation. By placing social values above economic values, this view admittedly contravenes self-interest and tradition.

Third is the vendor model, which appears to be closely related to the modern dialogue of consumerism. The consumer is viewed as the forgotten man in terms of sharing the rewards of increased productivity. Big business, which pursues maximum profits, reaches an accommodation with big unions, which pursue better employment opportunities, incomes, and rights, with the result that the consumer is sqeezed out. As financial policy (profit maximization) benefits stockholders, and industrial policy (better wages and working conditions) benefits workers, a market policy is essential to promote consumers' rights, interests, and tastes. To this end, numerous institutions have come into being: the Federal Trade Commission, the Better Business Bureau, the Pure Food and Drug Administration, the Consumer Protection Agency, the Truth in Lending Act, and Ralph Nader's group. Presumably, a corporate management with commitment to the vendor model would be a likely target for attacks emanating from unsafe automobiles and drugs, withholding products from the market, and charging excessive rates and hidden fees in the granting of credit.

Fourth is the investment model, in which the company must justify its involvement in social problems on the basis of a cost-benefit comparison. This view encompasses the doctrine of enlightened self-interest discussed in section 28-1 and recognizes that if the corporation is to survive beyond the predictable tomorrow into the uncertain future, relations with institutional investors, industrial buyers, and the community at large must be viewed as more than transitory, Temptations to make the fast buck must be weighed against a possible loss of good will. Such considerations are relevant when considering contributions to higher education, which has recognized long-term indirect benefits. (See also David Novick's "Cost-Benefit Analysis in the Socially Responsible Corporation" in Anshen [1].)

Fifth is the civic model, which holds that the corporation must play the role of a good citizen who volunteers service to the community in advance of, and to avoid, being drafted. Serious consideration should therefore be given by managers to compliance with government requests for voluntary restraints to lower spending to reduce inflationary pressures and balance-of-payments problems. A commitment is given to support the political system of democracy by helping to alleviate unemployment during depressions and entering into discussions of social issues. An awareness of possible social costs of certain business activities is indispensable, along with an interest in reducing them and compensating the injured parties. (Recall the discussions of Chapter 23 and 27.)

Sixth is the artistic-cultural model, which gives recognition to the role of originality and creativity in business as well as in other human affairs. By supporting cultural and civic projects involving orchestras, dance companies, museums, libraries, and drama groups, business executives may be promoting a society that is more responsible and humane, and emphasizing the interdependence of business and community. Advocates of the artistic model claim corporations must help achieve this greater vision of man and society somewhat along the lines of God's message to man as heard by Pico della Mirandola:

> You alone are not bound by any restraint, unless you will adopt it by the will we have given you. I have placed you in the center of the world that you may the easier look about and behold all that is in it. I created you a creature, neither earthly nor heavenly, so that you could be your own creator and select whatever form you may choose for yourself [26, pp. 21–22].

28-3 The Views of Professors Baumol and Friedman on Corporate Social Responsibility

The views of Professors William J. Baumol and Milton Friedman on corporate social responsibility are important both because of their simplicity and soundness and because these men are effective spokesmen for a large number of economists from the time of Adam Smith to the present [1, ch. 4; 11].

Professor Baumol argues from a political standpoint that voluntary and direct pursuit of society's goals by powerful corporate managers presents a threat to effective democracy, and from an economic standpoint that such actions may adversely affect corporations' efficiency in specialized fields where they have been so strikingly successful. He believes that management should not be asked to assume the responsibility and the associated blame for allocating resources to achieve social and political goals. Neither should each firm individually attempt to select these goals and use its power to interfere with the lives of people while pursuing these goals. In international business, for example, American firms should not, under the influence of pressure groups, attempt to determine foreign policy by withholding foreign investments from countries practicing ethnic discrimination or expressing opposition to United States foreign policy. Where boycotts are necessary, this should be decided by the government rather than by corporate power.

It is widely accepted that a competitive system automatically rewards efficiency and punishes weak, ineffectual businesses. Accordingly, the consumers' best friend is the chiseler who undercuts the inefficient firm. While the competitive process prevents laziness and incompetence, it also precludes significant amounts of voluntarism. The business person who voluntarily contributes too great a portion of funds to improving the environment, training the handicapped, and supporting higher education is vulnerable to the chisler, who has no social conscience and can sell his goods more cheaply.

Economists have traditionally favored the use of taxes and subsidies to encourage businesses to work toward the solution of social goals. (Recall the discussion of externalities in Chapter 23, especially section 23-2-2.) By working within the system, little reliance is placed upon the benevolent action of managers. Gaseous wastes can be taxed by amounts sufficient to cover the social costs of production and consumption activity. Firms that are most efficient in reducing harmful emissions are thereby offered the largest rewards. No reliance is put upon enforcement agencies, whose vigor tends to wane rapidly over time. The market mechanism becomes an instrument of efficiency in promoting social goals. Businesses should favor this approach for four reasons: (1) support is given to the profit system, which they seek to preserve; (2) they are less likely to be accused of antisocial and criminal activity when wastes are unavoidably generated, because they must bear the full social costs of their actions; (3) they are protected against undercutting by competitors when their actions are consistent with social objectives, because potential chiselers must also abide by the same rules; and (4) they avoid the imposition of government controls dictating how they must be run. The last advantage should be of greatest long-run importance, since management retains flexibility in selecting the most efficient ways of, say, reducing emissions by installing taller smokestacks, recycling, or adopting a higher-grade fuel. As Professor Baumol explains,

> There need be no acceleration in the process of erosion of the freedom of enterprise. Changes in prices of inputs are a normal business phenomenon. Fuel can be expected to grow more expensive as its scarcity increases, and other inputs grow cheaper as innovation improves their productive technology, but neither of these changes undercuts the prerogatives of management. Similarly, the imposition of a charge corresponding to the social costs of the use of enviromental resources does not interfere with the managerial decision process. It merely changes the structure of the economy's rewards to the company, increasing the profitability of the behavior desired by the community [1, p. 65].

While a change in the rules under which all business firms must function requires no philanthropy or voluntarism, businesses must voluntarily cooperate in designing and implementing effective legislation to make appropriate changes in the rules—rules that apply equally to everyone and that support the final authority of government on matters of social policy.

Professor Friedman, perhaps the most widely known modern proponent of the classical libertarian philosophy, has expressed views similar to those of Baumol on numerous occasions. The following quotation from his classic book, *Capitalism and Freedom*, presents his position succinctly:

> The view has been gaining widespread acceptance that corporate officials and labor leaders have a "social responsibility" that goes beyond serving the interest of their stockholders or their members. This view shows a fundamental misconception of the character and nature of a free economy. In such an economy, there is one and only one social responsibility of business—to use its resources and engage in activities designed to increase its profits so long as it stays within the rules of the game, which is to say, engages in open and free competition, without deception or fraud. Similarly, the "social responsi-

bility" of labor leaders is to serve the interest of the members of their unions. It is the responsibility of the rest of us to establish a framework of law such that an individual in pursuing in his own interest is . . . [promoting the public interest].

Few trends could so thoroughly undermine the very foundations of our free society as the acceptance by corporate officials of a social responsibility other than to make as much money for their stockholders as possible. This is a fundamentally subversive doctrine. If business men do have a social responsibility other than making maximum profits for stockholders, how are they to know what it is? Can self-selected private individuals decide what the social interest is? Can they decide how great a burden they are justified in placing on themselves or their stockholders to serve that social interest [11, pp. 133–134]?

Under this doctrine, all profits would be passed on to stockholders, who could decide for themselves the amounts, if any, to be given to the charities of their choice. Needless to say, this position, as simply stated, has great appeal (see question 28-5 at end of this chapter). The issue is not closed, however, as exemplified by Robert Heilbroner in the next section.

28-4   Professor Heilbroner's Objections to Putting Profits First

Professor Robert L. Heilbroner lists several reasons why profits should not be the single goal of modern corporations [20]: (1) business people resent implications that they are only makers of money; (2) the consequences of maximizing profits would be price wars initiated by dominant firms, eventual takeovers of competitors, and an even greater concentration of economic power; (3) the rationale for permitting firms to maximize profits assumes that the government independently makes the rules that business must follow, but observation indicates that business has a hand in making the rules, that is, regulatory agencies are controlled by the industries they are supposed to control; and (4) it is assumed that stockholders are the rightful and sole claimants to corporate returns, which ignores the fact that most stockholders are merely passive certificate holders with little commitment or real knowledge of the firm's operations and performance beyond that generally available. Heilbroner believes that labor, management, and the public have a much more legitimate claim to corporate returns than stockholders. Furthermore, since only 2 per cent of the nation's families hold three fourths of the corporate stock, the decision to delegate corporate social responsibility exclusively to stockholders is to make the unsupportable assumption that the wealthiest group has greater social wisdom than the corporation's admittedly uncertain managers.

Heilbroner also questions the ability of the professional manager to administer corporate power for social progress in a superior manner:

Indeed, there is something hollow in the protestations of "professionalism" of a group of men who must meet no socially approved criteria for certification as managers, and who cannot be removed for failing to act in a "professional" manner [20, p. 242].

He is unwilling to subscribe to a "stewardship of wealth" doctrine, which leaves social change to the benevolence of an upper-class elite:

> I believe corporate executives if left to their own preferences would follow a path of least social change. Left to themselves, I have no doubt that business groups will address the problem of corporate responsibility with great seriousness, turning out admirable pamphlets such as that published by the Committee on Economic Development, but leaving matters thereafter to the "dynamic workings of the private enterprise system." If we are to go beyond such pieties to actual changes in corporate behavior, something more substantial than the present state of corporate conscience will have to provide the motivating influence [20, pp. 244–245].

What steps can be taken to promote corporate responsibility and humanize our economic organizations? This will be discussed in the next section.

28-5 Promotion of Corporate Responsibility

One proposal for promoting corporate responsibility is to break up the large monopoly firms into several small ones [20, pp. 223–264]. Such fragmentation is intended to reduce physical plants to their optimal production size while removing large concentrations of financial power. While such action is sometimes proposed in antitrust proceedings, it probably is not politically feasible because of widespread business opposition. Also, it is not clear that fragmented firms would be any more socially responsible than larger firms. They would be less visible and therefore less accountable and controllable. The solution, however, would be consistent with classical economic theory.

Another proposal sometimes made is to nationalize the offending companies. This might insure control, but experience has shown that it cannot insure efficiency or social performance. The Tennessee Valley Authority, although known for its efficiency, is also charged with devastation of the environment by strip mining. The New York City Transit Authority and the United States Post Office have been cited as examples of gross inefficiency. Nationalization of "war industries" might only wed them more closely to the Pentagon, causing an even greater interlocking of self-interest of the military-industrial complex. There would seem to be little to be gained by transferring ownership and control

> . . . from a group of private individuals mixing their desire to make money with a confused set of social "ideals," to a group of public officials mixing their desires to make careers together with *their* confused ideas as to social ideals [20, p. 249].

While the public-service motive may be preferable to the private profit-seeking motive, control over the latter may be superior because of the competitive discipline of free enterprise. In short, nationalized corporations also abuse authority, pollute the environment, create impenetrable bureaucracies, defy public opinion, exploit workers, and generally misbehave. Regardless of the type of organization or bureaucracy, the problem remains one of exerting effective political control where the authority is unresponsive to social needs.

Publicity, public outrage, and attempts to change the corporation structure through legal enactment appear to be the current approaches to influencing greater social responsibility in business. Suggested legal changes include requiring large corporations to have federal charters to increase accountability; forcing corporations to publish facts and figures concerning antipollution expenditures and their percentage of employees from minority groups; requiring boards of directors to have public representatives; increasing penalties for violation of consumer protection and pollution laws, including the suspension of guilty executives; making mandatory cumulative voting of shares to give minority stockholders a greater chance of electing directors; compelling public disclosure of corporate federal income-tax returns; forcing " social bankruptcy " for persistent violators of existing legislation; and protecting employees from corporate retaliation when they testify in public as to their corporations' violations of laws. Many of these proposals will undoubtedly become a part of the corporate structure in the same way that labor unions and collective bargaining did, which in an earlier day met with great objections from business people.

Even if a longer list of proposals were adopted, there would still be some doubt as to the extent to which they could be implemented. In the words of Ralph Nader,

> [The corporate system] has a greater absorptive capacity than Mandarin China, and more resiliance than the Vatican. Corporations, yielding when they were forced to, have in the end overwhelmed populism, organized labor, and the New Deal, the regulatory state, and they will so overwhelm the consumer movement. Any real reform will come from the disasters, not from the reforms [20, pp. 259–260].

Nevertheless, Heilbroner believes that the corporation, at best only half controlled, will prevail for many generations, because our needs and technology require it. Provision of the most basic products in industrial societies requires the coordinated efforts of a multitude of workers. Regardless of the system—socialistic, capitalistic, or other—a sizeable bureaucracy is necessary. Unfortunately, perhaps, we know of no better way to organize the immense numbers of people required to operate our technology. While people in small communities cooperate, those in large, more impersonal communities contend. Socialism under the nation-state with flags flying may prove preferable to a corporate system with insatiable wealth-seeking and dehumanizing calculus of net returns on private investments. Chances are that we will have to learn to live with both the corporation and the nation-state in order to survive.

Heilbroner therefore believes that the key social problem of our time may be the creation of a more responsive and responsible corporation to evolve a more responsive and responsible state. The task of humanizing our social organizations is to him difficult and challenging.

28-6 Optional Strategies Avaliable to Corporate Managers

Professor Melvin Anshen of Columbia University distinguishes four kinds of corporate strategy that are in current use but that he does not recommend [1, pp. 71–73]: (1) attempt to educate the general public as to the virtues and values inherent in the capitalistic system; (2) give a token response to social demands for change followed by much publicity about the firm's "socially responsible" actions; (3) passively accept pronouncements of government bodies, which are guided in their decisions by both well-intentioned and ill-intentioned activists; and (4) adopt an adversary position in opposition to all proposals by public bodies for specific changes.

The first option of extolling the virtues of the private enterprise system is totally unresponsive to social problems. The system itself is not under critical attack; what is being attacked is the impact of the system on the environment, consumer interests, and equal economic opportunities. Most reasonable people desire to retain the system while modifying some aspects of its behavior.

The second option, which deals cosmetically with social issues viewed as a problem to be handled appropriately by the public relations department, is based upon a deception that when uncovered destroys the firm's credibility, which it badly needs if it is to have a meaningful role in helping to shape the evolving American society.

The third option, passivity, prescribes economic decay and invites disaster by turning the issues to be contained in a new social contract over to enthusiasts for social betterment, who probably lack sufficient knowledge of modern technologies, costs, and motivations. Decisions made in ignorance by outsiders may prove to be impossible for insiders to follow in an efficient manner.

The fourth option, negativism, leads to defeat of specific business interests and to mistrust of the motives of all business leaders. To fight the desire of society to promote higher human values puts business managers in a difficult position when they wish to be heard on other matters, such as tariffs, subsidies, and tax relief.

What, then, is the recommended socially responsible behavior for the modern business manager in this time of emerging social expectations? The answer is clear. Management of an individual corporation should initiate those policies and programs that promise a rate of return equal to, or greater than, it receives on other long-term investments. Managers should avoid taking individual action where the associated expenses would endanger the firm's competitive position in the market. Cooperative efforts with other companies in the industry or geographical area should be undertaken on those projects where there is a common interest. Where cooperative efforts are not possible, the individual company should actively participate in government programs to deal with social ills caused in part by the company's activities. In all cases, an active and cooperative posture is preferred over a passive and refractory one. Good judgment is required in deciding the appropriate amount of effort to be expended in each case.

Questions and Problems

28-1. In what ways does the doctrine of enlightened self-interest apply to stockholders as well as to management?

28-2. What factors must be considered in deciding how much an individual corporation should contribute to ameliorating social problems?

28-3. Some 8,000 thalidomide children around the world are teenagers now. They were born with grotesque deformities, some having no arms or legs, three fingers projecting from each shoulder, feet attached directly to the thigh—all thought to have been caused when their pregnant mothers took the sedative thalidomide at a critical time. Some families have been broken by the financial and emotional strain of rearing the children. Suits by some 300 families in England against the now-defunct pharmaceutical subsidiary of Distillers Company, Ltd. have not as yet been settled, although another 52 suits filed early in the 1960s have been settled for $2.4 million [27, pp. 74–75].

a. What should be done for the thalidomide children?

b. If expense is involved, who should pay the bill?

c. What steps should be taken to prevent a similar problem from occurring in the future? Is federal law necessary?

28-4. In an effort to keep down the size of a regulatory bureaucracy, detection of violators of the law is sometimes left to voluntary actions by the citizens who are harmed by the violation [11]. Is this "rat on your neighbor" policy appropriate for dealing with price controls? with pollution problems?

28-5. In the January 8, 1973, issue of *Newsweek*, Milton Friedman discussed a study by Sam Peltzman of UCLA which indicated that the harm done by the stiffer standards imposed in 1962 on the Food and Drug Administration following the Kefauver hearings and thalidomide episode greatly outweighed the good. The 2-year delay in introducing new drugs was judged to have denied patients the needed treatment, resulting in longer suffering and premature death of many thousands of people, and to have caused prices of all drugs to be 5–10 per cent higher than they would have been. Friedman asked for a repeal of the 1962 amendments to the Food, Drug, and Cosmetic Act forcing FDA officials to "condemn innocent people to death" [12]. Does this information influence your judgment of Friedman's position? Why?

28-6. In March 1972 the activities and resources of Boys' Town, Nebraska, otherwise known as Father Flanagan's Boys' Home, were unveiled in local Omaha newspapers:

> While pleading poverty in direct-mail solicitations, the charity had piled up a net worth exceeding $200 million, most of which was invested in the stock market. In 1971, Boys' Farm took in almost $26 million, far more than it needed to care for some 700 boys, and increased its net worth by some $16 million [34, p. 3].

a. Was this social irresponsibility or just good business?

b. What, if anything, should be done? By whom?

28-7. Would you as a business executive submit a bid on a military contract if you knew you could not meet the production schedule [28]? even if there were no other way to get the contract? even if your job and the survival of your firm depended on it?

28-8. Should a professional engineer "blow the whistle" on a fellow-employee or his company

a. when a dam design is approved for construction with too small a safety factor?

b. when a defective or harmful product is being produced and promoted?

c. when a machine is designed, built, and sold that emits excessive pollution?

d. if he is given a job assignment involving a product that is not in keeping with ecological and social imperatives?

28-9. Evaluate and comment on the following statements:

a. Engineers must (1) view each project as a part of a system; (2) simultaneously serve and lead society; (3) offer alternatives and recommend what seems to be the best solution; (4) accept moral responsibility for their work.

b. "The need is for a broader approach, which will ensure that engineers consider the side effects of new developments and persuade people that these side effects are important and must be considered" (comment by Dr. Jerome Wiesner, provost and president-designate of M.I.T. and former presidential science adviser [17, p. 146].)

28-10. Is bribery or yielding to extortion justified in a case where (a) every day's delay of the project costs $40,000 per day in interest charges alone? or (b) delay is a threat to national security?

28-11. Is the distribution of drugs that mean life or death to sick people appropriately delegated to private pharmaceutical firms whose primary goal is making profits? Should the price of such drugs be left to the workings of supply and demand in the marketplace? Are drugs and medical services somehow different from any other goods and services people buy? If so, how?

References

1. Melvin Anshen (ed.). *Managing the Socially Responsible Corporation* (New York: Macmillan, 1974).

2. Neil W. Chamberlain. *The Limits of Corporate Responsibility* (New York: Basic Books, 1973).

3. ———. *The Place of Business in America's Future* (New York: Basic Books, 1973).

4. Stuart Chase et al. *The Social Responsibility of Management* (New York: New York University Press, 1950).

5. Committee on Economic Development. *Social Responsibilities of Business Corporations* (New York: Committee for Economic Development, 1971).

6. John J. Corson. *Business in the Humane Society* (New York: McGraw-Hill, 1971).

7. Keith Davis and Robert L. Blomstrom. *Business, Society, and Environment: Social Power and Social Response.* 2d ed. (New York: McGraw-Hill, 1971).

8. Meinolf Dierkes and Raymond A. Bauer (eds.). *Corporate Social Accounting* (New York: Praeger, 1973).

9. Alvar O. Elbing and Carol J. Elbing. *The Value Issues of Business* (New York: McGraw-Hill, 1967).

10. Henry Ford II. *The Human Environment and Business* (New York: Weybright and Talley, 1970).

11. Milton Friedman. *Capitalism and Freedom* (Chicago: University of Chicago Press, 1962).

12. ———. "Frustrating Drug Advancement." *Newsweek*, January 8, 1973, p. 49

13. ———. "The Social Responsibility of Business Is to Increase Profits." *New York Times Magazine*, September 13, 1970, pp. 32 ff.

14. Paul O. Gaddis. *Corporate Accountability: For What and to Whom Must the Manager Answer?* (New York: Harper & Row, 1964).

15. Thomas M. Garrett. *Business Ethics* (New York: Appleton-Century-Crofts, 1966).

16. "GM Calls Back 3.7 Million Cars in Steering Flaw." *Wall Street Journal*, January 23, 1973, pp. 1, 3.

17. Judson Gooding. "The Engineers Are Redesigning Their Own Profession." *Fortune*, June 1971, pp. 72ff.

18. Andrew Hacker (ed.). *The Corporation Take-Over* (New York: Harper & Row, 1964).

19. Marrell Heald. *The Social Responsibilities of Business: Company and Community, 1900–1960* (Cleveland: Press of Case Western Reserve University, 1970).

20. Robert L. Heilbroner et al. *In the Name of Profit* (Garden City, N.Y.: Doubleday, 1972).

21. Neil H. Jacoby. *Corporate Power and Social Responsibility: A Blueprint for the Future* (New York: Macmillan, 1973).

22. Abba P. Lerner. *The Economics of Control* (New York: Macmillan, 1944).

23. Henry G. Manne and Henry C. Wallich. *The Modern Corporation and Social Responsibility* (Washington, D.C.: American Enterprise Institute for Public Policy Research, 1972).

24. Ralph Nader and Mark J. Green (eds.). *Corporate Power in America* (New York: Grossman Publishers, 1973). Ralph Nader's report on Conference on Corporate Accountability.

25. Ralph Nader, Peter J. Pethas, and Kate Blockwell. *Whistle Blowing* (New York: Grossman Publishers, 1972). The report of the Conference on Professional Responsibility.

26. Reinhold Niebuhr. *The Nature and Destiny of Man* (New York: Scribner's, 1949).

27. *Newsweek*, December 4, 1972, pp. 74–75.

28. David Packard. "Notable & Quotable." *Wall Street Journal*, June 26, 1972, p. 10.

29. Thomas A. Petit. *The Moral Crisis in Management* (New York: McGraw-Hill, 1967).

30. "Rats." Editorial in *Wall Street Journal*, December 27, 1971, p. 4.

31. Prakash S. Sethi. *Up Against the Corporate Wall: Modern Corporations and Social Issues of the Seventies*. 2d ed. (Englewood Cliffs, N.J.: Prentice-Hall, 1974).

32. Andrew Shonfeld. *Modern Capatalism: The Changing Balance of Public and Private Power* (New York: Oxford University Press, 1965).

33. Henry Simons. *A Positive Program for Laissez Faire* (Chicago: University of Chicago Press, 1934).

34. Jeffrey A. Tannenbaum. "Home Town Press." *Wall Street Journal*, November 14, 1972, p. 1.

35. Clarence C. Walton (ed.). *Business and Social Progress: Views of Two Generations of Executives* (New York: Praeger, 1970).

36. ———. *Corporate Social Responsibility* (Belmont, Calif.: Wadsworth, 1967).

37. Jacob Weissman (ed.). *The Social Responsibilities of Corporate Management* (Hempstead, N.Y.: Hofstra University Press, 1966).

38. Joe Zalkind et al. *Guide to Corporations: A Social Perspective* (Chicago: Swallow Press, 1974).

29 The American Idea of Individual Success

Why have a chapter on the American idea of individual success in a book on managerial economics? One reason is that students who take a course in this field, perhaps more than nonbusiness students, are greatly concerned with being successful. What this means to each individual may be quite different, as are the motivating forces behind the success seeking. In any case, a business decision maker should have given some conscious thought to his or her life goals and the reasons for pursuing them. By understanding better their own thought processes, students should be in a better position to plot the course of their advancement as well as that of firms, employees, associates, customers, and competitors.

As an aid to students in thinking through their personal and professional objectives, this chapter reviews the major ideas discussed in the success literature of the United States during the past several decades. In addition, it examines a number of unsettling implications for society as a whole resulting from the transformation of the idea of success and the confusion stemming from several inherent paradoxes and ambivalences.[1]

29-1 Traditional Measures and Determinants of Success

Success in America has been defined as

1. holding a job of higher pay or prestige than one's father;
2. having a substantially better job or income at the end of one's working life than at the beginning;
3. being recognized as successful by others in terms of wealth, status, rank, fame, or public prominence;
4. bringing in more money than the wife can spend or, in the case of some women, marrying a man who brings home a lot of money;

---

[1] Much of the material in this chapter has been condensed and adapted from *The American Idea of Success*, written by American Studies scholar Richard M. Huber [10]. His study deserves to be read in its entirety. Used with permission of the author and McGraw-Hill Book Company.

5. possessing the "good" things money can buy, such as a fine home in a good neighborhood, expensive cars, status of school or college attended, prestigious circles of friends, distinctions of taste, manners, bearing, and speech (Veblen's conspicuous consumption) [10, pp. 1–9].

Ambition to strive for these measures of success was in the nineteenth-century United States a product of MERC—mother, education, religion, and capitalism.

Of course, not just any mother would do. The mother must be a *good* mother in developing ambition in her child, as described in the biographies of great men and discussed by the success writers. She was

> . . . a literate woman who set standards for her son, encouraged him to meet those standards, taught him to read and write, defended him against a father who might be oppressively dominant, and when the time came for him to get married, shoved him out of the nest to earn his own way and raise his own family. No doubt in many cases she projected her own secret ambitions onto his personality. This mother was not an illiterate, lower-class, peasant-oriented woman living in a stratified society where females were abundant. She was a literate, American, middle-class, Protestant mother in a mobile society where a shortage of women made her indispensable to a man because he could not survive as a civilized human being without a wife. There is just enough truth in the precept to make it interesting that "the hand that rocks the cradle rules the world" [10, pp. 120–121].

Or, in the words of the anthropologist Margaret Mead, "We can recognize that yearning for achievement which is planted in every American child's breast by his mother's conditional smile" [13, p. 113].

The educational system helped shape the competitive drive and taught that there were rewards for striving. While education of the seventeenth century served religion, by the nineteenth century it had become a religion itself. It was based upon the belief that democracy depends upon a literate citizenry capable of making decisions in the "American tradition." There was faith that schooling could lift one's children to a higher economic and social level. The child was taught that he could surpass the level of his parents. Competitive drive was aroused by the giving of marks, prizes, and degrees from the first grade onward, which instilled in the child competition with his schoolmates. Grades were given in academic, athletic, social, and other activities to prepare the student for a world of vigorous competition in which rewards are given for achievement [10, pp. 113–114].

The religion of Puritan Protestantism encouraged productivity. It taught entrepreneurial traits of self-reliance, initiative, and risk taking by stressing a direct, rather than indirect, relation between man and God. Man was his own priest, with personal responsibility between himself and God for his own destiny, but he had to answer to God for his indiscretions. Man as an individual was forced to seek his own answers. In Protestantism there was no intermediary between God and man, no authority to look to for guidance. This led the individual to seek no intermediate authority (religious counsel or otherwise) in the secular affairs of business, but to exercise his own judgment in business, to innovate, to improvise, to act with confidence. Emotionalism and sensuousness were suppressed because of the possible control they held over man, who should be in control in his striving-becoming. Worldly pleasures and laziness were struck with the stick 'of guilt [10, pp. 107–110].

Capitalistic values pronounced by Adam Smith taught that man could pursue his self-interest without having humanitarian scruples, since he would also be promoting public good. The businessman was assured that by promoting his own good, he was making his greatest contribution to society [10, pp. 110–111].

An additional factor was important in fanning the flames of ambition: an army of success writers and talkers, who provided the necessary information, inspiration, and encouragement for individuals to strike out on their own to seek their fortunes. The next two sections provide a sample of their writings and their contributions to the success ethic.

29-2 American Popularizers of the Character Ethic

Many American writers and lecturers attempted to answer the ancient but ever-present questions, What should be the goal of my life? How can I attain that goal? How can I be sure that this is the social, economic, and moral right thing to do? [10, p. 93]. These establishment philosophers and poets preached a gospel of success that undoubtedly served as a motivating force to many ambitious Americans. Their messages were particularly attuned to the material needs of a pioneering country. Throughout the early part of the twentieth century, their message was predominantly what has been called the Protestant Ethic,[2] or perhaps more accurately, the character ethic, because secular writers since the sixteenth century had also pointed out the obvious connection between working hard and making money. Before we discuss how the success ethic has changed in recent decades, some of the most important and colorful contributors to the character ethic and their works are briefly reviewed.

29-2-1 *Cotton Mather—religious interpreter of the character ethic*

Many early colonists were Calvinists, a religious group that had arisen in part because it objected to medieval Catholicism's disapproval of making a profit through the exchange of goods. Puritanism (Calvinism) made profits a virtue in an agrarian capitalistic society where mere survival demanded a large measure of frugality and toil. Economic behavior was encouraged and justified by religious values in guiding the individual toward his goal of material success. In the late seventeenth and early eighteenth centuries the greatest religious interpreter of what Huber calls the character ethic was Cotton Mather, a New England preacher. Speaking for God, he explained the Puritan concept that every Christian has two callings: (1) *a general calling* of being a good Christian by serving the Lord Jesus Christ and saving one's own soul by serving religion; and (2) *a personal calling* of having a job whereby one's usefulness in one's neighborhood could be distinguished. Without a job, the able man was judged to be "unright-

---

[2] The term *Protestant Ethic* was used because Catholicism during the Middle Ages taught that wealth acquisition was sinful.

eous" to his family, community, and country, and was apt to be tempted by the Devil [10, pp. 11–12].

Mather cautioned, however, that hard work motivated by greed or impious uses would lead to a greater sin than laziness—the personal calling must not "swallow up" the general calling. The two must be used as oars in rowing the man with a properly balanced life toward heaven. Too great a pull at either the spiritual or worldly oar would lead him away from the "Shoar of Eternal Blessedness" [10, p. 12].

Mather linked success to pleasing God. In his *Bonifacius*, he claimed "they who have conscientiously employed their *tenths* [tithes] in *pious uses*, have usually been blessed in their estates. . . ." He quoted the Bible: "Cast thy grain into the moist ground; for thou shalt find it after many days" (Ecclesiastes 11:1). and "Honor the Lord with thy substance; so shall thy barns be filled with plenty" (Proverbs 3:9, 10). And he also quoted from Thomas Gouge's *The Safest and Surest Way of Thriving* (London, 1673):

> I am verily persuaded, that there is seldom any man, who giveth to the poor proportionably to what God has bestowed on him, but he does observe the passages of God's Providence towards him, he shall find the same doubled and redoubled upon him in *temporal* blessings . . . even as the five loaves and few fishes did multiply in their breaking and distributing; and the widow's oil increased by the pouring it out [12, pp. 110–112].

In other writings (*Durable Riches*, 1695, and *Sober Sentiments*, 1722) Mather emphasized that God's blessing upon business is obtainable by those who say their prayers, obey the Sabbath, and stay honest, but not by those who are dishonest, unthankful, gluttonous, or full of pride. At the same time, he thought that material things are ephemeral and can corrupt the soul, while treasures stored in heaven yield our highest success [10, p. 13].

Some religious leaders denounced the Calvinist branch of Protestantism, but they endorsed Calvin's support of capitalism. This was especially true of William Penn and the Philadelphia Quakers. So, too, the Boston Congregationalists. The success prescriptions were neither new nor unique, since they drew upon a 200-year-old tradition of popular English writings on the subject [10, pp. 13–14].

29-2-2 Benjamin Franklin—secular interpreter of the character ethic

Many people in the United States in the eighteenth century felt that Benjamin Franklin was the greatest success writer who touched their lives.

> In America, it was the eighteenth century which produced the most influential success apostle in the history of the American experience. In his writings on success, which were to be handed down by Americans from generation to generation, Benjamin Franklin took the position that *wealth was the result of virtue* [10, p. 15; emphasis added].

In *The Way to Wealth*, a compilation of maxims from his *Poor Richard's Almanack*, and in his *Autobiography*, Franklin urged the ambitious youth to cultivate *industry* (" Early to bed, and early to rise, makes a man healthy, wealthy, and wise " " Then plough deep, while sluggards sleep, and you shall have corn to sell and to keep ") and *frugality* ("A fat kitchen makes a lean will " " Rather go to bed supperless than rise in debt ") [7, III, 407–418]. In *Advice to Young Tradesmen* he states: " In short, the way to wealth, if you desire it, is as plain as the way to market. It depends chiefly on two words, *industry* and *frugality*; that is, waste neither *time* nor *money*, but make the best use of both " [7, II, 372]. Eleven more virtues were added in his *Autobiography*: temperance, silence, order, resolution, sincerity, justice, moderation, cleanliness, tranquillity, chastity, and humility—virtues from which he selected a different one weekly for concentration and self-evaluation [7, I, 326–328; 10, p. 17].

Franklin's great impact upon his readers could be attributed at least in part to his personal success and to the image of himself that he promoted. As Harold Laski has maintained,

> The supreme symbol of the American spirit is Benjamin Franklin, for he made a success of all that he attempted. . . . In his shrewdness, his sagacity, his devotion to making this world the thing that a kindly and benevolent soul would wish it to be, Franklin seems to summarize in a remarkable way the American idea of a good citizen [11, p. 39].

Huber explains:

> He was a hard-driving businessman, sage philosopher, pioneer scientist, inventor of a stove and an arm for retrieving books from high shelves, founder of a college, sire of three children (one illegitimate), representative of his country to France, a steady hand at the Constitutional Convention—the list seems endless. His accomplishments were fantastic even for an age which could boast a considerable number of great men. The emperor by popular acclaim of the character ethic, so crafty a manipulator and so shrewd a self-promoter was Franklin that success writers have served him up as a model in our own age of persuasion. A man of action as well as ideas, it was typical of his versatility that towards the end of his life, when the gout and stone had him down, he longed for " A balloon sufficiently large to raise me from the ground . . . being led by a string held by a man walking on the ground [10, p. 16].

Franklin, unlike Cotton Mather, taught that wealth should be sought for utilitarian rather than religious reasons (" Poverty often deprives a man of all spirit and virtue: 'Tis hard for an empty bag to stand upright") [7, III, 416]. Success was justified because it benefited mankind and gave the individual the opportunity to be virtuous in his own way. For Franklin, money meant freedom and leisure. He may be said to have promoted the secular basis for the character ethic, while Cotton Mather promoted the religious basis.

> From a symbolic viewpoint, Benjamin Franklin's influence was immense. The *Autobiography* kindled the fires of ambition in countless numbers of young men. He was not only America's first famous self-made man, but has

remained, since the eighteenth century, the supreme symbol of the poor boy who made good. He represented the hope of rising in the world, the thrill of identification with the saga of rags to riches, the pride in a country where getting ahead was based on individual effort. Through the image of Benjamin Franklin, all America, by reason of hard work and diligence, not only stood before kings, but dined with one of them [10, pp. 20–21].

29-2-3 *The McGuffey Readers—the molding of children's minds*

The values of society are typically passed on to children through school books containing lessons that conform to adult mores. *Eclectic Readers*, written by William Holmes McGuffey, a Pennsylvania Presbyterian of Scottish descent and later a professor and university president, undoubtedly had a large impact on American values. It is estimated that over 122 million copies of its various editions were sold from 1836 through 1900, reaching at least half the school children of that time. The content of the stories was widely accepted and typical of that found in other school books and children's stories used across the country. McGuffey *Readers* extolled the theology of John Calvin and glorified the character ethic—hard work, industry, and thrift. They also commanded children to develop aggressive virtues along with those of kindness, gentleness, and good will. Defense of these opposite virtues was said to be a remarkable achievement of the McGuffey *Readers*. It was made clear that good boys who followed the character ethic won the prize, while bad boys won nothing. The making of money was held to be a moral duty supported by divine decree, since wealth could be used to do good after it had been made. It was stressed, however, that a higher goal than money making was the "true success" of having developed a noble character [10, pp. 23–35].

29-2-4 *Horatio Alger, William Makepeace Thayer, Russell Conwell—character, turning points, and opportunity*

From the 1860s through the 1890s three success spokesmen towered above a multitude of others. Each of the three was New England–born, Ivy League–educated, ordained to preach, and made wealthy by writing and talking about success.

Horatio Alger wrote approximately 100 novels on the subject of success. The Horatio Alger hero was typically a boy of lower-class origins but of sterling character who rose to the top by his own ingenuity and pluck. His successful transition, economically and socially, into the business world was often aided by luck. (In *Ragged Dick* a shoeshine boy rescued a child who tumbled from a ferryboat; the grateful father just happened to need an employee for the kind of job Dick wanted, and he was thus on his way to fame and fortune. In *Luck and Pluck* recovery of a will hidden by John's wicked stepmother restored him to his rightful inheritance.) The main intended point, however, was that the boy deserved the break because of his prior preparation through goodness, hard work, and perseverance to seize the impending opportunity. In this manner, Alger tutored a great migration of farm boys who sought their fortunes in the city. Every novel was a guidebook of minute descriptions about how to work and live in the nearest metropolis. Many youths were in this manner prepared for the shock of a new life that included city chiselers, urchins, loafers, and drunkards. The "baddies" were snobs, mortgage foreclosers, idlers, cheats, bullies, and oppressors of the poor. The "goodies" were the sacrificing mother, the son who aspired to do good and to make money, merchants, lawyers, and businessmen [10, pp. 43–50].

William Makepeace Thayer was a master of the biographical form. His anecdotes from the lives of famous men, along with Alger's novels, were the best known and most widely read of the success literature for youth. Biographical "facts" were used to support his moralizing advice that success begins with the development of character in the early years of life. The Christian life and the character ethic were extolled. Five of his life-of-a-great-man books were published in a Log Cabin to White House Series; while Washington, Garfield, Lincoln, and Grant all settled eventually in the White House, Franklin (who somehow qualified) simply went "From Boyhood to Manhood." Thayer explained in *Turning Points in Successful Careers* that famous and wealthy individuals had successfully negotiated the critical turning points in their lives that caused them to rise above mediocrity. He explained how 50 different individuals, by seizing the favorable opportunity, had transformed their lives. The turning points were boldly identified as changing a job, a new investment, or the accidental burning of law books as directed by a wise Providence. Anecdotes from great and famous lives were scattered throughout his *Ethics of Success: A Reader for the Higher Grades of Schools*. In it he held that success stemmed not from luck but from character, noble purpose, ability, courage, industry, perseverance, and patience. He urged, "religion demands success" and praised the wealthy as God's stewards to the community [10, pp. 50–55].

Russell Conwell's impact was through oratory. His "Acres of Diamonds" speech, delivered more than 6,000 times, "was the most popular speech ever given in America on the single theme of opportunity" [10, p. 55]. America's greatest salesman of opportunity multiplied his church's membership under the sporting offer of doubling his salary every time he doubled its membership. From the proceeds of his sermons, lectures, and 30 books, he was able to help found Temple University and three hospitals. The "Acres of Diamonds" lecture alone earned him several millions of dollars over a 30-year period. It began with a story about a wealthy and contented farmer in Persia who gave up his farm and possessions in a futile search for diamonds. After wandering through Asia and most of Europe, he drowned himself in despair in a great tidal wave. The man who purchased the farm, however, discovered on it the most magnificent diamond mine in the history of mankind. Had the farmer "remained at home and dug in his own cellar, or underneath his own wheat fields, or in his own garden, instead of wretchedness, starvation, and death of suicide in a strange land, he would have had 'acres of diamonds'" [6, p. 14]. This story was followed by others about poor fools who had sold their backyards in search of oil, gold, and silver. He explained that success could be made at home and that money should be sought because more could be done with it than without it. Furthermore, he believed that most poor people were made poor by their own shortcomings and therefore should not be given sympathy when God chose in this way to punish them for their sins [6, pp. 26–27; 10, pp. 56–61].

29-2-5 *Social Darwinism—survival of the fittest businessman*

Social Darwinism, an adaptation of Darwin's biological conclusions about the origin and survival of species to society and the economy, was used in the latter decades of the nineteenth century through the 1920s to argue against government intervention in the affairs of business. This was the period in which Andrew Mellon's "trickle-down" theory (more recently endorsed by President Richard Nixon) was invoked by the government in the form of tax relief for the wealthy under the assumption that money would be used more productively by the affluent than the poor. A popular stereotype of those who accepted Social Darwinism is superbly exemplified by Sinclair Lewis's leading character in the novel *Babbitt*. While often supported by entrepreneurs under the influence of Herbert Spencer and William Summer [see 5, pp. 201–203], Social Darwinism was rejected by some as a justification of their personal successes for several fundamental reasons. First, they preferred to view the real struggle as being with oneself rather than with other people. Second, it was not very flattering to replace altruistic motives by the totally selfish, amoral, negative philosophy of Social Darwinism. Third, this tack could not be used with dignity by businessmen in defending themselves against their critics. Fourth, businessmen who thought of themselves as Christians took little glory in being fittest if it meant doing unto their neighbor what they would not wish done unto them; they preferred to view the successful man as one who pulled countless others up with him. Finally, the implication of limited opportunity conflicted with the success idea of abundant opportunity. For these reasons, businessmen and success writers justified the getting of wealth by reference to the Bible and Christian ethics rather than by the *Origin of Species* and its associated law of the jungle [10, pp. 64–65, 71–74].

29-2-6 *Andrew Carnegie—gospel of wealth*

One of the most vocal supporters of Social Darwinism from the business community was Andrew Carnegie. He was a poor middle-class boy from Scotland who came to the United States and became a very wealthy industrialist and financier. He drove himself with compulsion in earning hundreds of millions of dollars, part of which he then proceeded to give away. He attempted to justify his wealth and fierce competitive drive in moral and humanitarian terms. In a widely debated article in the *North American Review* in 1889 he explained his famed "gospel of wealth." He held that in a highly competitive, individualistic, private-propertied economy, some men rise by superior talents to accumulate great fortunes.[3] While some individuals were hurt in the process, material development of the whole is better because the race insures the survival of the fittest in every department. This is Carnegie's recognition of Social Darwinism. The associated problem of unequal distribution of wealth was met by requiring the successful man to give away his money during his lifetime [10, pp. 66–69].

---

[3] Perhaps it should be noted here that the myth of the self-made man has come under attack. Twentieth-century historians point out that the majority of successful American businessmen were not poor lads who pulled themselves up by their own bootstraps but the sons of the advantaged, well-educated middle class. For example, see Taussig and Josyln [14].

This, then, is held to be the duty of the man of Wealth: First, to set an example of modest, unostentatious living, shunning display or extravagance; to provide moderately for the legitimate wants of those dependent upon him; and after doing so to consider all surplus revenues which come to him simply as trust funds, which he is called upon to administer, and strictly bound as a matter of duty to administer in the manner which, in his judgment, is best calculated to produce the most beneficial results for the community—the man of wealth thus becoming the mere agent and trustee for his poorer brethren, bringing to their service his superior wisdom, experience, and ability to administer, doing for them better than they would or could do for themselves [3, pp. 661–662]. . . . The man who dies thus rich dies disgraced [3, p. 664].

29-2-7   Elbert Hubbard—A Message to Garcia, or wake up and earn your pay

Elbert Hubbard's *A Message to Garcia* was second only to Benjamin Franklin's *The Way to Wealth* in effectiveness and wide distribution [10, ch. 6]. Some 40 million copies of the 1899 tract were printed in 40 to 50 languages and dialects. Only 1,500 words were used in honoring self-reliant perseverance and in attempting to defend propertied interests. The story began with a brief account of an army lieutenant's struggles across Cuba in the Spanish-American War to deliver a vital message from President McKinley to General Garcia, the head of the Cuban Insurgents, followed by a condemnation of the average man's inability to "carry the message"—that is, get the job done efficiently with a minimum of fuss and bother. Writing as a frustrated employer, he states:

> You, reader, put this matter to a test: You are sitting now in your office—six clerks are within call. Summon any one and make this request: "Please look in the encyclopedia and make a brief memorandum for me concerning the life of Correggio." Will the clerk quietly say, "Yes Sir," and go do the task? On your life he will not. He will look at you out of a fishy eye and ask one or more of the following questions: Who was he? Which encyclopedia? Where is the encyclopedia? Was I hired for that? Don't you mean Bismarck? What's the matter with Charlie doing it? Is he dead? Is there any hurry? Shan't I bring you the book and let you look it up yourself? What do you want to know for? And I will lay you ten to one that after you have answered the questions, and explained how to find the information, and why you want it, the clerk will go off and get one of the other clerks to help him try to find Garcia—and then come back and tell you there is no such man. Of course, I may lose my bet, but according to the Law of Average I will not.
>
> Now if you are wise you will not bother to explain to your "assistant" that Correggio is indexed under the C's, not in the K's, but you will smile sweetly and say, "Never mind," and go look it up yourself. And this incapacity for independent action, this moral stupidity, this infirmity of the will, this unwillingness to cheerfully catch hold and lift, are the things that put pure Socialism so far into the future. If men will not act for themselves, what will they do when the benefit of their effort is for all? . . . My heart goes out to the man who does his work when the "boss" is away, as well as when he is

at home. And the man, who, when given a letter for Garcia, quietly takes the missive, without asking any idiotic questions, and with no lurking intention of chucking it into the nearest sewer, or of doing aught else but deliver it, never gets "laid off," nor has to go on strike for higher wages. Civilization is one long anxious search for just such individuals. . . . The world cries out for such: he is needed, & needed badly—the man who can carry a message to Garcia [9, pp. 3–5, 10–11].

29-3 The Personality Ethic

Up to the 1930s the success literature predominantly supported the character ethic, in which character was thought to be the most important means to getting wealth. There was a parallel movement under way at the same time, however, that gave greater emphasis to personality, or how one *appeared to others*, as the way to wealth. Ironically, the personality ethic was also found in the writings of Ben Franklin, the most important success apostle of the character ethic. In his *Autobiography*, he made three confessions that gave support to the personality ethic: He turned an enemy into a friend by purposely asking him for a favor; he made a conscious effort in public conversations to appear humble; and he "sometimes pushed a paper-laden wheelbarrow through the streets to impress other businessmen with his industriousness" [10, p. 228]. While the trend from the character ethic to the personality ethic had been under way for several decades, the transition was symbolically marked by the publication in 1936 of Dale Carnegie's *How to Win Friends and Influence People* [10, pp. 226–228].[4]

29-3-1 Dale Carnegie—How to Win Friends and Influence People

More copies of this monumental work have been sold in America in the twentieth century than of any other nonfiction book, other than the Bible, textbooks, and manuals [10, ch. 16]. Sales of 8 million copies in English include 2.5 million hard-cover books and 5.5 million paperbacks. The message has been converted to more than 30 languages and dialects and supplemented by a public-speaking and human-relations course boasting more than a million graduates.[5] This "model success book of the personality ethic" provides a practical guide to manipulating others. Major points are hammered home in bold letters following each chapter. Biographical anecdotes from personal interviews, sometimes with well-known men and women, explaining how "little people" have become prosperous by application of a human-relations principle, add human interest and sustain the narrative. Carnegie relates personal incidents from his own experiences that help the reader relate to the author and his message. Above all, the book is optimistic and inspirational, spurring the reader to action. Qualities of character, however, are shoved aside as higher priority is given to calling people

---

[4] Huber discusses a number of other advocates of the personality ethic and also of another ethic called *new thought* or *mind power*.
    [5] The public-speaking course began at a YMCA in 1912 and grew over the decades to the extent that by the late 1960s enrollment numbers some 80,000 each year in 1,210 communities in the United States and 92 abroad.

by their first names [4, p. 73]. Business people and engineers are told that skills in human engineering, the leading of people, are about six times more important for financial success than technical knowledge [4, pp. 12–13]. Dale Carnegie's evaluation of man is not flattering. He tells us that people are illogical, emotional creatures bristling with prejudices and motivated by appeals to their pride and vanity [4, p. 27].

The only way to get anybody to do anything, Carnegie says, is to make the other person want to do it:

> When I go fishing, . . . I think about what they want . . . . I dangle a worm or grasshopper in front of the fish and say, "Wouldn't you like to have that?"
> Why not use the same common sense when fishing for men? [4, p. 39].

The fish is lured to the hook by Carnegie's "Six Ways to Make People Like You." Each rule ends a separate chapter containing examples of interpretations of the rules [4, p. 103]:

Rule 1: Become genuinely interested in other people.
Rule 2: Smile.
Rule 3: Remember that a man's name is to him the sweetest and most important sound in the English language.
Rule 4: Be a good listener. Encourage others to talk about themselves.
Rule 5: Talk in terms of the other man's interests.
Rule 6: Make the other person feel important—and do it sincerely.

The friendly fish is now induced to swallow the hook by "Twelve Ways to Win People to Your Way of Thinking [4, p. 171]:

Rule 1: The only way to get the best of an argument is to avoid it.
Rule 2: Show respect for the other man's opinions. Never tell a man he is wrong.
Rule 3: If you are wrong, admit it quickly and emphatically.
Rule 4: Begin in a friendly way.
Rule 5: Get the other person saying "Yes, yes" immediately.
Rule 6: Let the other man do a great deal of the talking.
Rule 7: Let the other fellow feel that the idea is his.
Rule 8: Try honestly to see things from the other person's point of view.
Rule 9: Be sympathetic to the other person's ideas and desires.
Rule 10: Appeal to the nobler motives.
Rule 11: Dramatize your ideas.
Rule 12: Throw down a challenge.

If the fish is not yet on the hook, he offers nine additional rules for changing people's minds without offending them [4, p. 200].

Carnegie's books, columns, courses, and speeches have helped thousands of troubled people to become happier in their relations with others and to gain promotions in their jobs. His customers are satisfied, as most of his devoted students will testify. There is even a Dale Carnegie Alumni Association for graduates of his course. His death in 1955 at the age of 66 marked the passing of the most important and influential success writer since the 1930s.

29-3-2   *Criticisms of the personality ethic relative to the character ethic*

1. Techniques may be superficial. The personality ethic requires not the qualities of character that one builds into oneself but only an easily learned cluster of psychological principles. No deep transformation of heart or mind is required [10, p. 259].
2. The temptation is to be insincere. Honesty between human beings is strained by a moral tug of war with hypocrisy, deception, insincerity, and fraud. Flattery and deceit may be effective, but the practitioner soon begins to dislike himself. How easy to fall into the habit of telling a lie for personal gain. Villains can also read books and learn to smile. Where success under the character ethic was through exploitation of natural resources, achievement under the personality ethic is through the exploitation of human beings—people are the raw material [10, pp. 259–261, 291].
3. Individuality is ignored. The rules do not fit every personality because people are different. According to James Bender and Lee Graham in *Your Way to Popularity and Personal Power*:

> If you were to follow the advice in these books, you'd become unnatural, irritating, and insincere. In your effort to conform to a pattern, your phoniness would break through. . . . If you don't think so, picture in your mind's eye the sort of person these books consider ideal. Do you see him clearly? He's constantly smiling. He praises everything. He lets the other fellow do the talking. He never expresses a contrary opinion. He wouldn't dream of criticising. He seldom gets angry and there's no one he dislikes. You can't say he isn't nice, but that's about all there is to it. And if you got to know him better, you'd have to admit that he was dull, mechanical, and not quite genuine [2, pp. 11–12].

The problem is "If you don't like yourself, you can't like other people; and if you don't like other people, they can't like you. No magic formula will help you" [2, p. 12]. Self-analysis and deep self-understanding are recommended.

> The personality ethic tarnishes all social relations. It is not easy to switch constantly from feigned regard for a person towards whom you feel indifference to an honest expression of feeling towards those whom you cherish as friends or loved ones. To smile so frequently with mercenary intent is to rape the smile with self-seeking. Though success writers kept protesting against flattery, mostly for the dubious reason that it wasn't effective, sincerity was an insoluble problem for the personality ethic. Sincerity without selection is hypocrisy [10, p. 291].

4. Conformity that is urged may be sterile. Subtle pressure is exerted to adjust one's thinking and mores to a particular pattern of living and thinking, a group-mindedness. The most effective rules of the game, however, might violate one's ethical principles and induce a sterility that can discourage advancements emanating from individuality and conflict.

> People . . . may well evolve a society so well adjusted that no one would be able—or willing—to give it the sort of hotfoot it regularly needs. We would all be too busy getting along with each other. In the personality ethic, intellectual timidity seems like sagacity; the sweet reasonableness of cliché-trading is safer than the sparkle of thoughtful, controversial conversation. Better to be cozy than controversial, wiser to use soft soap than the scrub brush, . . . and always be easy to get along with [10, pp. 290–291].

5. People may be alienated from themselves. When one shapes one's attitude and identity to control others, one is actually being controlled by others. Realization of this fact can be alarming.

> In a life of mirthless smiles and superficial relationships, one can feel a terrible sense of isolation and aloneness. It's a kind of emptiness which a gluttonous craving for companionship cannot fill. A feeling of emotional phoniness seeping into much of life can result in self-accusations of hypocrisy and lost integrity. It leads to an estrangement from one's fellow men, followed by a contempt for oneself as well as other people, and finally an inability to love or feel loved [10, p. 292].

6. Personality is preferred over mentality. Human relations are emphasized over formal education and intelligence, love of learning, the arts, things of the mind. Less attention is given to teaching youth the meaning of life [10, p. 266].

7. Relative indifference is shown to the dangers of materialism. No worry is shown about success destroying the very human qualities that produced success, such as hard work and sobriety, which under the character ethic were virtues in themselves. Sweet-talking and name memorizing were hardly moral virtues, and they did not threaten one's ability in handling people. There was less concern that greed might overcome the goodness of a balanced ambition [10, p. 267].

8. No mercy for those who failed. Those who failed to achieve material success under the character ethic could take refuge and comfort in the thought that they had achieved a goal higher than wealth or fame: "true success." This meant the individual could maintain his self-respect and stability in consolation that he could still lay claim to happiness, character, peace of mind, doing good, and having true friends [10, p. 268]. Would those who failed under the personality ethic be alienated from society and turn in frustration to disrupting the capitalistic system—toward socialism, or some other system with less competition?

29-3-3   *The inevitability of the transition to the personality ethic*

As the economy shifted over the years from one of scarcity and production to one of abundance and consumption, it was inevitable that the character ethic give way to the personality ethic [10, pp. 275–280]. The character ethic served well in a developing nation to inspire the population to feed, clothe, and house itself by physical toil. Ascetic qualities of thrift, stamina, and determination were necessary in the conflict of man with his physical environment. Because of the great scarcity of goods, material success was awarded to the man who could organize and produce.

With the introduction of mass production and continuous flow assembly in the 1920s, the scarcity barrier was broken. Economic growth came to depend upon the market to absorb goods that could be provided in greater quantities than were needed as basic necessities. The problem became one of selling what could be produced by machines. Service industries became relatively more important than goods-producing industries. New jobs and rewards shifted from those who were skilled in producing things to those with a knack for manipulating human beings, as in marketing, selling, advertising, promotion, and distribution. The competitive firm, in bidding for the consumer's discretionary dollar, was required to be more concerned with its public image and the molding of consumer preferences to its brand instead of a competitor's. The personality ethic became indispensable in an economy where there was a great variety of goods and services from which the consumer could choose. The fate of the producer has now come to depend upon the advertiser's effectiveness in controlling consumer choice.

Service competition increases as price competition decreases. "The Keynesian economy of the personality ethic is pumped by the glad hand," while the market economy of Adam Smith was pumped more "by the invisibile hand of supply and demand." Friendliness, courtesy, and smiles have become more important than previously for the clerk making the firm's sales.

> On the executive level, with bigger stakes riding on each sale, the glad hand is less calloused, but the grip is just as tight. In the office and on the links, at the conventions or in the most expensive restaurants, the glad hand, firm and sincere, reaches out for the contract while Adam Smith's invisible hand withers away. All these factors reinforced the habit of combining business and pleasure—spheres of interest which Europeans like to keep separate, but which Americans always try to unite [10, p. 277].

The glad-hand approach is encouraged by the federal government's permitting promotion expenses to be deducted from taxable profits. It becomes apparent that skill in handling a long-stemmed glass or a putter may be as important for a business person today as knowing how to produce or how to balance a ledger.

The virtues of frugality and thrift are ignored by the personality ethic, because they might be bad for business in a modern, Keynesian, aggregate-demand economy of installment buying, credit cards, and bountiful credit.

There is an additional factor that should not be overlooked. Americans, because of their nation's history of success, are susceptible to almost any success formula—whether given by Franklin, or by Carnegie, or by someone else. Whatever the United States set out to do—tame the frontier, defeat the Indians, bind the states together by a continental railroad system, lead the world in agricultural production, whip the British, the Mexicans, the Spaniards, the Germans—it succeeded magnificently. How could its people therefore be less than achievement oriented? How could they individually fail when collectively they had succeeded? Trapped by a kind of reverse fallacy of composition, they were receptive to the preachings of Mather, Alger, and Carnegie.[6]

29-4 Conflict Between Success and "True Success"—Six Dilemmas

The cultural measures of achievement, as described at the beginning of this chapter, were defined in material terms. Business success meant earning money, which was translated into fame or status. But, paradoxically, Americans have felt that success *ought* to be something other than money, defined in nonmaterialistic terms. Personal success, often called "true success" and representing the highest good in life, is to be found within oneself. Peace of mind or happiness was thought to flow from self-giving rather than self-seeking, from a happy family life, and from service to others [10, pp. 448–449].

Richard Huber questions whether the United States could function as a society if its people were not encouraged to hold conflicting feelings about success. Society may need the comfort of ambivalent attitudes to survive the anxiety-producing values. Most people agree with the bromide that "money won't buy happiness," but at the same time say, "I might be happier if I had a little more." Still, middle-class folks pity the "poor little rich girl," "the lonely wealthy widow," "the friendless crank living in the house on the hill." The affluent may be lonely people, who were happier in *becoming* successful than in *being* successful—the getting to the top being more fun than being there [10, pp. 449–451].

Six dilemmas emerge from Huber's study of the American experience with the success idea [10, pp. 453–457]:

1. Self-giving versus self-seeking. This is a moral issue the success idea strove to resolve. Is it possible to be a loving, kind-hearted Christian and a selfish, grasping capitalist, too? The character ethic met this dilemma by the "stewardship of wealth" doctrine, under which money making was justified by the religious interpretation of it as a means of getting resources for pious purposes and by the secular interpretation of it as providing humanitarian service. The degree of one's success indicated the amount of service given to the community. Moreover, pious Calvinists assumed that wealth was synonymous with being in God's favor, for He certainly would not, in his magnificent omniscience, allow an evil man to become affluent. The personality ethic provides no guidance for dealing with this dilemma.

2. Material success versus "true success." Everyone, according to the character ethic, should work hard for success but should also be aware that material success can become an end in itself and destroy the same virtues of character that made success possible. Happiness, noble character, and peace of mind should accordingly be the final goals in life. Honest money making was justified by contributions to the community under the stewardship doctrine and the concept of service. Tension between material success and "true success" was held in balance by the individual who was subjectively accountable for his own values and behavior. The personality ethic gives little thought to "true success."

---

[6] For the point made in this paragraph, the author is indebted to his business historian colleague and friend Dr. Jimmy Skaggs.

3. Hypocrisy versus sincerity. The personality ethic, which has been dominant in the self-help literature since the 1930s, provided a technique for *earning* a living, not a *philosophy* for living. The business person sells an image of himself, an idea, or a product. Manipulating other people has become a necessity for personal or corporate success in a consumption economy. "What happens to moral honesty when people become objects, when relationships are stained by the need to sell, when the self is soiled by the demand to sell the self?" Truth in business affairs comes to depend upon public opinion polls rather than moral principles. Ideals are confronted daily with the harsh realities of earning a living under the personality ethic.

4. Freedom versus equality. The freedom afforded by a free enterprise economic environment leads to unequal rewards and concentration of economic power. At least those with little or no success feel that unequal rewards for equal efforts are unfair. In a democratic society, with one vote per individual, majority rule can redistribute wealth in the interests of social justice. Conflict between freedom and equality becomes even greater where powerful vested interests control political decisions with flagrant disregard for the public good. Government must undertake the balancing act of sustaining the right to equal opportunity while safeguarding the right to unequal rewards.

5. Freedom versus authority. In a social democracy such as the United States, individuals do not have one powerful authority to whom to look for taste leadership. They tend to develop vulgarity, low taste, and anti-intellectualism. Under the rule of an authoritarian elite, taste leadership could be exerted by the government to exalt the arts and finer things in life by reordering the rewards to success. From the standpoint of European and American intellectual critics, there is a price to be paid for having a social democracy—the price being the American mode of materialism and anti-intellectualism. But the advantages of an authoritarian economic and social system are invariably countered by a reduction in individual freedom.

6. Individual self-fulfillment versus national power. National security and survival demands during the 1940s and later depended to a great extent upon achieving rapid material growth of the nation. These needs are not always synonymous with the individual goal of spiritual and aesthetic growth. The success idea promoted national strength, but at the cost of

> ... misrepresenting individual potential in relation to opportunity, sustaining anxiety-ridden pressures for success, provoking crime against person and property, increasing feelings of guilt and humiliation in failure-intensifying forces for unhappiness, and encouraging a vulgar grasping for success and status as a testimony to one's worth [10, p. 456].

These six dilemmas came about as a result of choice in a free society, where good can be accomplished only when there is freedom to do wrong.

29-5   Summary and Conclusions

Setting individual goals and deriving satisfaction from them have in the United States through the early part of the twentieth century been interwined with materialism, production, and the Protestant Ethic. Society judged that economic growth was good. Production, saving, and capital investment promoted individual and national strength. Great material rewards were given for personal austerity, self-denial, and increased productivity. Society followed the words of Cotton Mather and Benjamin Franklin.

> The way to wealth was by building within yourself specific personal virtues. The qualities of character which appear over and over again are industry or hard work, frugality or thrift, perseverance or resolution, initiative, sobriety, punctuality, courage, self-reliance, patient plodding and honesty [10, p. 95].

The young businessman was challenged by character-building obstacles to success. He could start an enterprise, expand it in competition with other businesses, and build it as best he could. Benjamin Franklin's virtues were thought to provide pride as well as profits. The entrepreneur who achieved success through dedication to the principles of the character ethic could be proud; he was a moral man; he had a healthy sense of identity with what he thought was good.

Then society began to change. An economy with many small businesses became dominated by large corporations. Big machines took over. Service industries increased. The man who could market the product became as important as the man who could produce it. Business success came to depend upon creating and expanding demand as well as satisfying it. The sales person or entrepreneur who could deal with people rather than with land and raw materials became more important, if not essential, to the success and profit of the enterprise. The new route to power and wealth was through controlling the responses of other people and manipulating their thinking in ways that would be profitable to the firm. Ambitious business people turned from Ben Franklin to Dale Carnegie, who showed people how to improve their personal relations. The healthy and moral character ethic gave way to a corrupt personality ethic. Hard work, perseverance, and honesty became less important than flattery, manipulating of others, and misrepresenting and hiding one's own true feelings from others to achieve business goals. The personality ethic stifled openness and honesty in daily relations with people in favor of conformity and group-mindedness—with the purpose of preventing alienation. Achievement became related less to inner qualities of character than to how one was viewed by other people. A life of mirthless smiles and superficial relationships somehow became a part of obtaining business success. Is it any wonder that a "successful" business person may feel an emptiness and ambivalence stemming from the contradictions between the character and personality ethics? At the end of his book, Huber writes:

> The game of life is to come up a winner, to be a success, or to achieve what we set out to do. Yet there is always the danger of failing as a human being. The lesson that most of us on this voyage never learn, but can never quite forget, is that to win is sometimes to lose [10, p. 457].

Perhaps a similar thought was expressed in the history recorded by Herodotus in the fifth century B.C., when the Egyptian Pharoah Amasis warned in a letter to his friend Polycrates of the dangers associated with perpetual good fortune:

It is a pleasure to hear of a friend and ally prospering but thy exceeding prosperity does not cause me joy, forasmuch as I know that the gods are envious. My wish for myself and for those whom I love is to be now successful, and now to meet with a check [restraint]; thus passing through life amid alternate good and ill, rather than with perpetual good fortune. For never yet did I hear tell of any one succeeding in all his undertakings, who did not meet with calamity at last, and come to utter ruin [8].

Personal Advice on Success From J. Paul Getty

In all my writing about the pursuit of business success—its joys, its challenges and its immense rewards—I have perhaps not emphasized strongly enough that the ultimate goal of the businessman, whether he be boss or trainee, middle manager or entrepreneur, is not primarily to forge a corporate empire but to fulfill himself. I speak from bitter experience and with deep regret at my own personal failures when I say that the narrow-minded pursuit of the "bitch-goddess success" frequently begets serious domestic dilemmas.

Burgeoning work loads and ever-increasing demands on time and energy are almost inevitable corollaries of business achievement—and they greatly reduce the time a man is able to devote to home and family. At ideal best, wife and children understand and adjust and the integrity of the family unit is maintained. At dismal worst—and with five marital disasters to my debit, I'm hardly unfamiliar with this extreme—there is no rapport. Marriage and family disintegrate. All too belatedly, I now appreciate that an ounce of domestic prevention is worth a courtroom full of cure. If I have any hindsight advice to offer, it is of a very humble nature: The businessman should take his wife and children into his confidence—explaining his work, his dreams and his hopes—and he should miss no opportunity to demonstrate that he is not only a businessman but a husband and a father, worthy and giving of love as well of substance (From "The Fine Art of Being the Boss," *Playboy*, June 1972, p. 200).

The dangers to an individual from success too quickly obtained may be related to his inability to adjust his life and thinking to his new-found freedom, power, and obligations obtained with material success. His success may puff him up to such an extent that he loses the sincere love and respect of his old friends. Some of his woe may come from an inability or unwillingness of members of his family to adapt to a new life and surroundings with each move that promotion entails. The problems faced by the wife may be even more demanding than those faced by her successful husband.

Moving on to broader issues, it may be disquieting to some people to note that America may have reached the limits of its national development in the traditional sense of producing more and more goods and services. There is growing sentiment that additional production of gadgets is not so important as dealing with problems of the environment and the using up of exhaustible resources necessary for human survival. Reflection on these problems has led more than one observer to the following conclusion:

> In an advanced, affluent, technically proficient democracy, the idea of success, the idea of universal productive endeavor as a national virtue, in a certain sense the idea of work itself, is fast growing obsolete [1].

If, indeed, the idea of work is itself growing obsolete, what is to replace it? It has been suggested that it might be replaced by the idea of the soul, where comforts of the spirit are regarded as important as material comforts [1]. This attitude, of course, is often associated with underdeveloped economies. A better solution for the United States appears to be to simply change its definition of work to include certain intellectual and artistic pursuits. Where we as individuals and business people will fit into such a scheme will require some thought. Achievement-oriented individuals in business will especially be required to deal with such problems. A better understanding of our heritage and our personal goals should help us to adapt to changing times.

Questions and Problems

29-1. What are your personal goals in life? Are you comfortable with them? Are they worthy of you and worth the sacrifices necessary for you to realize them?

29-2. What were the goals of your parents? In what ways are they different from yours? Why? Do you wish your children to have your goals? Why?

29-3. Do you believe the economic system of the United States is conducive to the achievement of your personal goals? In what ways? Do you know of a better system? How would you change the one you have?

29-4. In what ways do your goals conflict with those of other people? In what ways are they complementary? Would society be better off if everyone had your goals? Why?

29-5. Are your goals likely to become less feasible in future decades than they are now? For what reasons? Are scarce and exhaustible resources important factors?

References

1. David C. Anderson. "Is the Idea of Success Obsolete?" *Wall Street Journal*, January 5, 1972, p. 8.
2. James Bender and Lee Graham. *Your Way to Popularity and Personal Power* (New York: New American Library, 1950).
3. Andrew Carnegie. "Wealth." *North American Review* 148 (June 1889): 653–664.
4. Dale Carnegie. *How to Win Friends and Influence People* (New York: Simon and Schuster, 1948).
5. Henry Steele Commager. *The American Mind* (New Haven: Yale University Press, 1950).

6. Russell Conwell. *Acres of Diamonds* (Westwood, N.J.: Fleming H. Revell, 1960). First published in 1915.

7. Benjamin Franklin. *The Way to Wealth.* In Albert H. Smyth. *The Writings of Benjamin Franklin.* 10 vols. (New York: Macmillan, 1905).

8. *The History of Herodotus. Great Books of the Western World*, VI, 98.

9. Elbert Hubbard. *A Message to Garcia* (East Aurora, N.Y.: Roycroft Shop, 1899).

10. Richard M. Huber. *The American Idea of Success* (New York: McGraw-Hill, 1971).

11. Harold J. Laski. *The American Democracy* (New York: Viking Press, 1948).

12. Cotton Mather. *Bonificius: An Essay Upon the Good*, ed. David Levin (Cambridge, Mass.: Harvard University Press, 1966). First published in 1710.

13. Margaret Mead. *And Keep Your Powder Dry* (New York: Morrow, 1965).

14. F. W. Taussig and C. S. Joslyn. *American Business Leaders* (New York: Macmillan, 1932).

30 Summary and Conclusions

The purposes of this brief concluding chapter are to help readers bring together and solidify their knowledge of the text material and to point out some additional important areas of managerial economics in which readers may wish to continue their studies.

30-1 Synthesis

Managerial economics is basically the study of the firm and how it makes its economic decisions under constraints imposed by nature and society. Part One began with a review of basic mathematical tools, with an emphasis on linear programming. Mathematical programming is a useful tool in managerial economics, first, as a technique for optimizing the firm's internal operations, and second, as a way of conceptualizing the overall objectives and limitations of the firm. The objective function provides a statement of goals in terms of profits, sales, or other utility-giving variables. The structural equations define the limitations in terms of resources, technology, and rules of society.

The review of algebra, calculus, and programming presented in Part One was designed to convey an understanding of their usefulness and range of applications for business decisions rather than to allow classroom discussions to become bogged down in computer languages, techniques, and debugging exercises. Knowledge of the latter was judged to be less basic, more perishable, mechanical, and easily self-taught or delegated to computer assistants. The underlying philosophy was that an academic course at this level should deal with the scope and limitations of the tools, so that students would be less likely to misapply this new-found knowledge. It is better that students know what they are doing before they charge ahead to compute mechanically correct but conceptually meaningless answers. Perhaps the most frequently occurring example of this is in using linear programming techniques where the relations are significantly nonlinear. Careful preliminary investigation is indispensable for specifying a programming model. Examination of nonlinear programming problems is very helpful for understanding the pitfalls of blindly applying linear programming.

Part Two dealt with the demand constraints faced by the firm. The quantity of

488

a product the firm can sell was shown to be conceptually related to unit price, income of consumers, the demand for substitute and complementary goods, promotional activities, and a host of hitherto unquantified entities often subsumed under the category "tastes and preferences," such as knowledge of the product, expectations of future income, prices, scarcities, and interest rates, spending habits of friends and neighbors, association of price with quality, benevolence or malevolence toward the seller, and irrationality. Various demand elasticities, indifference curves, and statistical concepts were considered that are widely used by business researchers in studying and measuring demand phenomena. Some rather technical theoretical analysis was given to expose readers to traditional analysis, which is frequently adopted and applied in solving other business and economic problems. It is also useful for understanding why economists reason as they do.

Part Three was concerned with the analysis of production and cost. Traditional production theory was discussed in terms of the production function, returns to the variable factor, returns to scale, the expansion path, and several additional elasticity concepts. A linear programming model of production was considered to help relate the programming of Part One to traditional production theory; process rays, linear isoquants, equal-profit curves, and sensitivity analysis were considered. A survey of the various cost concepts used in economics and business analysis was followed by four chapters detailing contributions of modern economists to production analysis, including a reconstruction of the classical cost function, learning curves, technological forecasting, and an approach highlighting the partial process, entropy, the time element, and the factory system.

Part Four presented an analysis of price, output, and welfare. In addition to discussions of price determination with reference to the four standard economic models, other important pricing aspects were considered, including pricing under three degrees of discrimination, markup, multiple product, transfer, and new product. Welfare analysis included a brief review of some criteria used in theoretical analysis for judging if a change is an improvement, a model of welfare maximization, and some of the problems of group decisions. The chapter on externalities considered the numerous problems associated with spill-overs from production and consumption activities for which the price system provides insufficient rewards and penalties. Investment decisions were examined that take into account compound interest; a comparison was made between the net discounted present value and the internal rate of return approaches; a programming formulation of capital budgeting was given; and a two-period model of individual investment decisions was presented. The concluding chapter considered the problems of making valid decisions in the presence of imperfect knowledge, risk, and uncertainty; a model of portfolio choice under conditions of risk was also presented.

Part Five contained discussions of some of the broader and more topical aspects of managerial economics, including antitrust and antimerger laws, the ecological impacts of production and consumption activities, the necessity for conserving exhaustible natural resources, the impossibility of sustaining economic growth indefinitely, the role of ethics and social responsibility in business activities, and finally, a survey of the success literature that has served to motivate American entrepreneurs over the past several generations and, because of its shift in emphasis from the character to the personality ethic, has created a moral and motivational dilemma for business people and others.

The subjects covered in every chapter are related, in that each deals with some aspect of the firm's goals and constraints. Some are strictly mechanical problems that can be handled as an engineer designs an engine or a structure to meet given specifications. Others require estimation of future human behavior rather than the automatic application of well-known physical and biological properties of matter. Managerial judgments must today be consistent with, or made with an awareness of, trends and limitations imposed by nature and society. The decisions made by executives and other employees of large firms in a changing world of risk and uncertainty go far toward making life on this planet what it is and in determining how long it can last.

30-2 Limitations

The interdisciplinary study of managerial economics as presented in a single course to M.B.A. students is necessarily a survey course. The final word has not been said on a single subject, any one of which is in most cases an on-going area of study worthy of additional attention. For many students in previous semesters, the course has been an eye-opener in terms of discovering how the analytical tools of mathematics and economics studied in other courses are applied to aid the business executive in making decisions. Students with certain kinds of business and engineering experience have perceived many practical applications of the concepts covered in the course and have gained a better understanding of techniques and procedures they have observed on the job and been required by their employers to follow. For students with little or no practical business experience, the course has been both an extension of their previous academic work and a step toward gaining a better understanding of business problems. In no case did the author intend to foster the impression that knowledge gained from this single course is sufficient to qualify students immediately to give conclusive advice to the board of directors of any large corporation. Hopefully, however, students have attained sufficient information to encourage them to humbly present their information where it may prove enlightening, to continue their study of topics of interest, and to seek the help of specialists when they discover a problem to which one of the tools studied might be applicable. In some cases they may venture to apply the tools themselves, with an acute awareness of their limitations.

30-3 Suggestions for Continued Study

The ways in which students of managerial economics might extend the knowledge gained from this text are many and varied. A first step might be to select the topic that was most interesting and to check out the references provided at the end of the chapter. One reference has a way of leading to another until one comes abreast of the current state of published knowledge. Articles reprinted in books of readings are especially recommended, because they have survived an additional reviewing process; the ones by Palda [17] and Haynes, Coyne, and Osborne [11] are superb. At this point, students would then be ready to search for information on the narrow topic in recent periodicals and books. By this time, also, they are aware of the major questions still being asked in the field and are ready to write a thesis proposal to be submitted for approval by faculty advisors. Students would then be on their way to earning doctorates. Before they are through, however, they may find it necessary to take additional academic courses in economics, management science, mathematics, statistics, and computers.

For those who are not yet interested in knowing that much, but would like to increase their present understanding of how theoretical principles might be applied in real-world situations, there is value in considering case studies such as those given in Haynes [10], Christenson, Vancil, and Marshall [2], and Colberg, Forbush, and Whitaker [3]. Even those with possible longer-run academic interests (in some cases, especially so) may find a few years' employment in business and industry the best avenue for helping them to advance their knowledge. In many cases, personal financial considerations make this route a necessity.

Finally, mention should be given to some important work being conducted in the field of managerial economics that was not treated in this book. Several attempts are being made to combine interrelated decisions of the firm rather than to solve them separately, as in the case in operations analysis that deals separately with problems of inventory, finance, production, marketing, personnel, and research. One approach is through the use of econometric models of the firm utilizing environmental, control, and performance variables. Studies by Dennis C. Mueller [16], J. W. Elliot [6], and S. Saltzman [18] are summarized in Chapter 13 of Professor Elliot's text [5]. Other approaches include behavioral analysis pioneered by R. M. Cyert and J. G. March [4], industrial dynamics originated by J. W. Forrester [7], which he extended to problems of global resource allocation [8], and corporate simulations applied to corporations in over 100 models by 1970, summarized by George Gershefski [19, pp. 26–42]. Another approach that holds promise of usefulness in corporate forecasting is input-output analysis, developed originally in the 1930s by Nobel Prize winner Wassily Leontief [13] (see also [12] and [15]).

References

1. John E. Butterworth and Berndt A. Sigloch. "A Generalized Multistage Input-Output Model and Some Derived Equivalent Systems." *Accounting Review* 46 (October 1971): 700–716.

2. Charles J. Christenson, Richard F. Vancil, and Paul W. Marshall. *Managerial Economics: Text and Cases*. Rev. ed. (Homewood, Ill.: Richard D. Irwin, 1973).

3. Marshall R. Colberg, Dascomb R. Forbush, and Gilbert R. Whitaker, Jr. *Business Economics: Principles and Cases*. 4th ed. (Homewood, Ill.: Richard D. Irwin, 1970).

4. R. M. Cyert and J. G. March. *A Behavorial Theory of the Firm* (Englewood Cliffs, N.J.: Prentice-Hall, 1963).

5. J. Walter Elliot. *Economic Analysis for Management Decisions* (Homewood, Ill.: Richard D. Irwin, 1973).

6. ———. "Forecasting and Analysis of Corporate Financial Performance With an Econometric Model of the Firm." *Journal of Financial and Quantitative Analysis* 7 (March 1972): 1499–1526.

7. Jay W. Forrester. *Industrial Dynamics* (Cambridge, Mass.: M.I.T. Press, 1961).

8. ———. *World Dynamics* (Cambridge, Mass.: Wright-Allen Press, 1971).

9. Trenor E. Gambling and Ahmed Nour. "A Note on Input-Output Analysis: Its Use in Macro-economics and Micro-economics." *Accounting Review* 45 (January 1970): 98–102.

10. W. Warren Haynes. *Managerial Economics: Analysis and Cases.* Rev. ed. (Austin, Tex.: Business Publications, 1969).

11. W. Warren Haynes, Thomas J. Coyne, and Dale K. Osborne. *Readings in Managerial Economics* (Dallas, Tex.: Business Publications, 1973).

12. Wassily W. Leontief. "Input-Output Analysis." In *International Encyclopedia of the Social Sciences*, VII, 345–354.

13. ———. *The Structure of the American Economy, 1919–1939* (New York: Oxford University Press, 1951).

14. Dennis L. Meadows and Donella H. Meadows. *Toward Global Equilibrium: Collected Papers* (Cambridge, Mass.: Wright-Allen Press, 1973).

15. William H. Miernyk. *The Elements of Input-Output Analysis* (New York: Random House, 1965).

16. Dennis C. Mueller. "The Firm Decision Process: An Econometric Investigation." *Quarterly Journal of Economics* 81 (February 1967): 58–87.

17. Kristian S. Palda. *Readings in Managerial Economics* (Englewood Cliffs, N.J.: Prentice-Hall, 1973).

18. S. Saltzman. "An Econometric Model of a Firm." *Review of Economics and Statistics* 49 (August 1967): 332–342.

19. A. N. Schrieber (ed.). *Corporate Simulation Models* (Seattle, Wash.: University of Washington Press, 1970).

Appendix A
Determinants and Matrix Algebra

Programming models of firms and their operations typically require the solution of systems of many equations with many unknowns. They require more powerful and sophisticated techniques than were used in Chapter 2 for solving systems with up to three equations and three unknowns. Determinants and matrix algebra have become so important in reducing the effort of solving sizable systems, and in conceptualizing their solution in theoretical and applied studies appearing in professional journals, that it is well worth the time of students and business executives to gain a basic knowledge of them, especially so that they will not be overawed by the notations. Two- and three-equation systems are used as examples, not because they are necessarily the easiest ways of solving small problems, but because the steps are basically the same for large as they are for small problems, and in this way an understanding can be gained without unnecessary repetition of standard rules. Besides, large systems today are seldom solved by hand, since canned computer programs, usually based upon matrix methods, are readily available. In the spirit of providing readers with understanding rather than of making them technicians at this point, two of the most common approaches for solving large simultaneous equations are discussed.

A-1 Determinants

We begin discussion of determinants[1] by solving two equations with two unknowns; we then solve three equations with three unknowns, compute the inverse, and review the properties of determinants.

A-1-1 SOLVING TWO EQUATIONS WITH TWO UNKNOWNS BY USE OF DETERMINANTS

The determinant of a system of equations

---

[1]Determinants were invented before 1683 by the Japanese mathematician Seki-Kowa (1642–1708). Outside of isolated Japan the discovery took place in 1693, attributed to the German mathematician Gottfried Wilhelm Leibnitz (1646–1716).

$$a_{11}x_1 + a_{12}x_2 = b_1$$
$$a_{21}x_1 + a_{22}x_2 = b_2 \tag{1}$$

is defined as

$$D \equiv \begin{vmatrix} a_{11} & a_{12} \\ a_{21} & a_{22} \end{vmatrix} \tag{2}$$

The primary diagonal, $a_{11}a_{22}$, minus the secondary diagonal, $a_{21}a_{12}$, gives the value of the determinant. Values of x_1 and x_2 are simply the ratios of two determinants, given by *Cramer's rule*:

$$x_1 = \frac{\begin{vmatrix} b_1 & a_{12} \\ b_2 & a_{22} \end{vmatrix}}{D} \qquad x_2 = \frac{\begin{vmatrix} a_{11} & b_1 \\ a_{21} & b_2 \end{vmatrix}}{D} \tag{3}$$

where the numerators contain the coefficients of variables other than those whose value is sought. Equations (3) may also be put in the form

$$x_1 = \frac{a_{22}b_1 - a_{12}b_2}{a_{11}a_{22} - a_{21}a_{12}} \qquad x_2 = \frac{a_{11}b_2 - a_{21}b_1}{a_{11}a_{22} - a_{21}a_{12}} \tag{4}$$

In the case where the two linear equations have equal slopes, the curves have no intersection and $D = 0$. For example, if the equations are

$$2x_1 + 3x_2 = 500$$
$$4x_1 + 6x_2 = 1,500 \tag{5}$$

their slopes are $-(2/3)$ with x_1 on the horizontal axis and x_2 on the vertical axis, and they plot as parallel lines, shown in Figure A-1. The curves do not intersect for any value of x_1 and x_2. No point on one line can also lie on the other. If the first equation is multiplied by -2 and added to the second, both x_1 and x_2 disappear. The situation would change somewhat if the 1,500 were changed to 1,000; multiplying the first equation by -2 and adding to the second equation would result in both sides of the final equation being zero. The lines coincide; any point on one line lies on the other. In short, there will be a unique solution if $D \neq 0$; conversely, if $D = 0$, either no solution exists or an infinite number exist, depending upon the values on the right side of the equal signs.

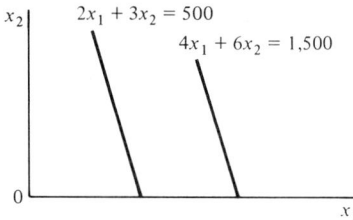

FIGURE A-1

A-1-2   SOLVING THREE EQUATIONS WITH THREE UNKNOWNS BY USE OF DETERMINANTS

Given a system of three equations and three unknowns

$$a_{11}x_1 + a_{12}x_2 + a_{13}x_3 = b_1$$
$$a_{21}x_1 + a_{22}x_2 + a_{23}x_3 = b_2$$
$$a_{31}x_1 + a_{32}x_2 + a_{33}x_3 = b_3 \tag{6}$$

solution may be obtained by Cramer's rule as the ratios of two third-order determinants:

$$x_1 = \frac{\begin{vmatrix} b_1 & a_{12} & a_{13} \\ b_2 & a_{22} & a_{23} \\ b_3 & a_{32} & a_{33} \end{vmatrix}}{D} \qquad x_2 = \frac{\begin{vmatrix} a_{11} & b_1 & a_{13} \\ a_{21} & b_2 & a_{23} \\ a_{31} & b_3 & a_{33} \end{vmatrix}}{D} \qquad x_3 = \frac{\begin{vmatrix} a_{11} & a_{12} & b_1 \\ a_{21} & a_{22} & b_2 \\ a_{31} & a_{32} & b_3 \end{vmatrix}}{D} \qquad (7)$$

where

$$D = \begin{vmatrix} a_{11} & a_{12} & a_{13} \\ a_{21} & a_{22} & a_{23} \\ a_{31} & a_{32} & a_{33} \end{vmatrix} \qquad\qquad\qquad (8)$$
$$= (a_{11}a_{22}a_{33} + a_{12}a_{23}a_{31} + a_{13}a_{21}a_{32}) - (a_{13}a_{22}a_{31} + a_{11}a_{23}a_{32} + a_{12}a_{21}a_{33})$$

For example, the determinant

$$D = \begin{vmatrix} 1 & 0 & 4 \\ 2 & 3 & 0 \\ 3 & 1 & 2 \end{vmatrix}$$

has the value

$$(1)(3)(2) + (0)(0)(3) + (4)(2)(1) - (4)(3)(3) - (1)(0)(1) - (0)(2)(2)$$
$$= 6 + 0 + 8 - 36 - 0 - 0 = -22$$

If $b_1 = 5$, $b_2 = 6$, and $b_3 = 7$, then

$$x_1 = \frac{\begin{vmatrix} 5 & 0 & 4 \\ 6 & 3 & 0 \\ 7 & 1 & 2 \end{vmatrix}}{D} = \frac{5 \cdot 3 \cdot 2 + 0 \cdot 0 \cdot 7 + 4 \cdot 6 \cdot 1 - 4 \cdot 3 \cdot 7 - 5 \cdot 0 \cdot 1 - 0 \cdot 6 \cdot 2}{-22}$$
$$= \frac{30 + 0 + 24 - 84 - 0 - 0}{-22}$$
$$= \frac{-30}{-22} = \frac{15}{11}$$

$$x_2 = \frac{\begin{vmatrix} 1 & 5 & 4 \\ 2 & 6 & 0 \\ 3 & 7 & 2 \end{vmatrix}}{-22} = \frac{12 + 0 + 56 - 72 - 0 - 20}{-22}$$
$$= \frac{-24}{-22} = \frac{12}{11}$$

$$x_3 = \frac{\begin{vmatrix} 1 & 0 & 5 \\ 2 & 3 & 6 \\ 3 & 1 & 7 \end{vmatrix}}{-22} = \frac{21 + 0 + 10 - 45 - 6 - 0}{-22}$$
$$= \frac{-20}{-22} = \frac{10}{11}$$

Equations (6) may also be written as

$$\sum_{j=1}^{3} a_{ij}x_j = b_i \qquad i = 1, 2, 3 \tag{9}$$

or, in the matrix notation discussed later,

$$\mathbf{D}\mathbf{X} = \mathbf{B} \tag{10}$$

where

$$\mathbf{D} = \begin{bmatrix} a_{11} & a_{12} & a_{13} \\ a_{21} & a_{22} & a_{23} \\ a_{31} & a_{32} & a_{33} \end{bmatrix} \qquad \mathbf{X} = \begin{bmatrix} x_1 \\ x_2 \\ x_3 \end{bmatrix} \qquad \mathbf{B} = \begin{bmatrix} b_1 \\ b_2 \\ b_3 \end{bmatrix}$$

and solution is given formally by

$$\mathbf{X} = \mathbf{D}^{-1}\mathbf{B} \tag{11}$$

Thus, if the inverse of $\mathbf{D}$ is determined, $\mathbf{X}$ may be obtained by multiplying two determinants. When determinants are greater than 3×3, matrix inversion facilitates computation.

A-1-3   *THE INVERSE COMPUTED BY DETERMINANTS*

For 2×2 and 3×3 matrices, the inverse may be computed by use of determinants as follows. If

$$\mathbf{A} = \begin{bmatrix} a_{11} & a_{12} \\ a_{21} & a_{22} \end{bmatrix} \tag{12}$$

then its inverse is

$$\mathbf{A}^{-1} = \begin{bmatrix} \dfrac{a_{22}}{D} & -\dfrac{a_{12}}{D} \\ -\dfrac{a_{21}}{D} & \dfrac{a_{11}}{D} \end{bmatrix} \tag{13}$$

If

$$\mathbf{A} = \begin{bmatrix} a_{11} & a_{12} & a_{13} \\ a_{21} & a_{22} & a_{23} \\ a_{31} & a_{32} & a_{33} \end{bmatrix} \tag{14}$$

computation of its inverse is more involved. Each element, c_{ik}, in the inverse matrix is calculated separately as the *cofactor* of a_{ki} divided by D. The cofactor is the *minor* of an element, a_{ik}, prefixed by its sign, where the minor of the a_{ik} element in the determinant like (13) is the 2×2 matrix obtained by deleting the row and column containing a_{ik}. For example, the minor of a_{22} is denoted by

$$|A_{22}| = \begin{vmatrix} a_{11} & a_{13} \\ a_{31} & a_{33} \end{vmatrix} \tag{15}$$

The sign prefixed to the minor to make it a cofactor is positive if the sum of the row and column subscripts are even and negative if subscripts are odd. For example, the sign of the cofactor of a_{13} is positive because $1 + 3$ is even. Thus,

$$\text{cofactor of } a_{ik} = (-1)^{i+k}\, |A_{ik}| \tag{16}$$

The cofactors of

$$A = \begin{bmatrix} 1 & 0 & 4 \\ 2 & 3 & 0 \\ 3 & 1 & 2 \end{bmatrix} \tag{17}$$

are

$$(-1)^2 \begin{vmatrix} 3 & 0 \\ 1 & 2 \end{vmatrix} = 6 \qquad (-1)^3 \begin{vmatrix} 2 & 0 \\ 3 & 2 \end{vmatrix} = -4 \qquad (-1)^4 \begin{vmatrix} 2 & 3 \\ 3 & 1 \end{vmatrix} = -7$$

$$(-1)^3 \begin{vmatrix} 0 & 4 \\ 1 & 2 \end{vmatrix} = 4 \qquad (-1)^4 \begin{vmatrix} 1 & 4 \\ 3 & 2 \end{vmatrix} = -10 \qquad (-1)^5 \begin{vmatrix} 1 & 0 \\ 3 & 1 \end{vmatrix} = -1 \tag{18}$$

$$(-1)^4 \begin{vmatrix} 0 & 4 \\ 3 & 0 \end{vmatrix} = -12 \qquad (-1)^5 \begin{vmatrix} 1 & 4 \\ 2 & 0 \end{vmatrix} = 8 \qquad (-1)^6 \begin{vmatrix} 1 & 0 \\ 2 & 3 \end{vmatrix} = 3$$

An element c_{ik} in the inverse matrix A^{-1} equals the cofactor of a_{ki} divided by $D\ (= -22$ from previous calculations):

$$A^{-1} = \begin{bmatrix} \dfrac{6}{-22} & \dfrac{4}{-22} & \dfrac{-12}{-22} \\[2mm] \dfrac{-4}{-22} & \dfrac{-10}{-22} & \dfrac{8}{-22} \\[2mm] \dfrac{-7}{-22} & \dfrac{-1}{-22} & \dfrac{3}{-22} \end{bmatrix} = \begin{bmatrix} \dfrac{-3}{11} & \dfrac{-2}{11} & \dfrac{6}{11} \\[2mm] \dfrac{2}{11} & \dfrac{5}{11} & \dfrac{-4}{11} \\[2mm] \dfrac{7}{22} & \dfrac{1}{22} & \dfrac{-3}{22} \end{bmatrix} \tag{19}$$

This result may be verified by checking to see (as will be explained later) if the product of A and its inverse is an identity matrix:

$$\begin{array}{ccc} A & \cdot & A^{-1} & = & I \end{array}$$

$$\begin{bmatrix} 1 & 0 & 4 \\ 2 & 3 & 0 \\ 3 & 1 & 2 \end{bmatrix} \cdot \begin{bmatrix} \dfrac{-3}{11} & \dfrac{-2}{11} & \dfrac{6}{11} \\[2mm] \dfrac{2}{11} & \dfrac{5}{11} & \dfrac{-4}{11} \\[2mm] \dfrac{7}{22} & \dfrac{1}{22} & \dfrac{-3}{22} \end{bmatrix} = \begin{bmatrix} 1 & 0 & 0 \\ 0 & 1 & 0 \\ 0 & 0 & 1 \end{bmatrix} \tag{20}$$

Determinant solution of three equations with three unknowns may be extended to n linear equations with n unknowns but is laborious when $n \geq 4$ and such computations are therefore usually made by electronic computers rather than by hand. While determinants are often inconvenient and inefficient for numerical calculation, they are most valuable in theoretical work for determining the existence of solutions.

A-1-4 *PROPERTIES OF DETERMINANTS*

Several properties of determinants used in reducing computations are given here for reference.

1. Two rows or columns can be interchanged if the sign is changed:

$$\begin{vmatrix} a_{11} & a_{12} & a_{13} \\ a_{21} & a_{22} & a_{23} \\ a_{31} & a_{32} & a_{33} \end{vmatrix} = (-1) \begin{vmatrix} a_{21} & a_{22} & a_{23} \\ a_{11} & a_{12} & a_{13} \\ a_{31} & a_{32} & a_{33} \end{vmatrix}$$

2. If any two rows or columns are equal, the determinant has a value of zero:

$$\begin{vmatrix} a_{11} & a_{12} & a_{11} \\ a_{21} & a_{22} & a_{21} \\ a_{31} & a_{32} & a_{31} \end{vmatrix} = 0$$

3. If the elements of any row or column are all zero, the determinant has a value of zero:

$$\begin{vmatrix} a_{11} & a_{12} & a_{13} \\ 0 & 0 & 0 \\ a_{31} & a_{32} & a_{33} \end{vmatrix} = 0$$

4. A multiple of one row may be added to another without changing the value of the determinant:

$$\begin{vmatrix} a_{11} & a_{12} & a_{13} \\ a_{21} & a_{22} & a_{23} \\ a_{31} + ca_{11} & a_{32} + ca_{12} & a_{33} + ca_{13} \end{vmatrix} = \begin{vmatrix} a_{11} & a_{12} & a_{13} \\ a_{21} & a_{22} & a_{23} \\ a_{31} & a_{32} & a_{33} \end{vmatrix}$$

5. Multiplication of all elements in a row or column by a constant, c, gives the same value as multiplication of the determinant by the same constant:

$$\begin{vmatrix} a_{11} & a_{12} & a_{13} \\ ca_{21} & ca_{22} & ca_{23} \\ a_{31} & a_{32} & a_{33} \end{vmatrix} = c \begin{vmatrix} a_{11} & a_{12} & a_{13} \\ a_{21} & a_{22} & a_{23} \\ a_{31} & a_{32} & a_{33} \end{vmatrix}$$

6. Corresponding rows and columns may be interchanged without changing the determinant's value:

$$\begin{vmatrix} a_{11} & a_{12} & a_{13} \\ a_{21} & a_{22} & a_{23} \\ a_{31} & a_{32} & a_{33} \end{vmatrix} = \begin{vmatrix} a_{11} & a_{21} & a_{31} \\ a_{12} & a_{22} & a_{32} \\ a_{13} & a_{23} & a_{33} \end{vmatrix}$$

A-2 Matrix Algebra

A mathematically nonrigorous explanation of matrix algebra is simply the erection of rules whereby sets of numbers may be manipulated and used to solve equations.

Matrix algebra is treated in this section under the categories of terminology, operations, and inversion.

A-2-1 *MATRIX TERMINOLOGY*

Comprehension of matrix algebra begins with an understanding of the jargon used to describe the different types of matrices. The most commonly used terms are listed and explained here:

1. *Matrix.* A rectangular array of numbers called *elements* or *scalars* arranged in rows and columns, enclosed in brackets or parentheses, and denoted by a boldface capital letter or a lower-case letter with two letter subscripts:

$$\mathbf{A} = \begin{bmatrix} a_{11} & a_{12} & \cdots & a_{1n} \\ a_{21} & a_{22} & \cdots & a_{2n} \\ & \cdots & & \\ a_{m1} & a_{m2} & \cdots & a_{mn} \end{bmatrix} = a_{ij}$$

One matrix can be said to be greater than another only if they have the same dimensions, for instance, 2×3 or 4×4, but a 2×3 matrix cannot be compared with one that is 4×4, and if every a_{ij} element is greater than the corresponding element in the other matrix:

$$\begin{bmatrix} 1 & 2 \\ 5 & 6 \end{bmatrix} > \begin{bmatrix} 0 & 1 \\ 4 & 5 \end{bmatrix}$$

but

$$\begin{bmatrix} 1 & 2 \\ 5 & 6 \end{bmatrix} \not> \begin{bmatrix} 0 & 1 \\ 6 & 5 \end{bmatrix}$$

2. *Square matrix.* A matrix with equal numbers of columns (n) and rows (m), that is, where $m = n$. If the matrix has only one row, it is called a *row vector;* if only one column, a *column vector.*

3. *Diagonal matrix.* A square matrix in which all elements other than where $i = j$ are equal to zero; for instance, a fourth-order diagonal matrix could be

$$\begin{bmatrix} 1 & 0 & 0 & 0 \\ 0 & 2 & 0 & 0 \\ 0 & 0 & 3 & 0 \\ 0 & 0 & 0 & 4 \end{bmatrix}$$

4. *Identity or unit matrix.* A diagonal matrix where all diagonal elements are equal to 1. A unit matrix of the third order is

$$\mathbf{I_3} = \begin{bmatrix} 1 & 0 & 0 \\ 0 & 1 & 0 \\ 0 & 0 & 1 \end{bmatrix}$$

5. *Transposed matrix.* A matrix in which the rows and columns are interchanged; that is, the transposed matrix of $\mathbf{A}$ in item (1) of this list is

$$\mathbf{A'} = \begin{bmatrix} a_{11} & a_{21} & \ldots & a_{m1} \\ a_{12} & a_{22} & \ldots & a_{m2} \\ \cdots & \cdots & \cdots & \cdots \\ a_{1n} & a_{2n} & \ldots & a_{mn} \end{bmatrix}$$

The transpose of

$$\mathbf{A} = \begin{bmatrix} 1 & 4 \\ 2 & 5 \\ 3 & 6 \end{bmatrix} \quad \text{is} \quad \mathbf{A'} = \begin{bmatrix} 1 & 2 & 3 \\ 4 & 5 & 6 \end{bmatrix}$$

Similarly, the transpose of a row vector is a column vector, and vice versa:

$$\mathbf{A} = [a_1 \quad a_2 \quad a_3] \qquad \mathbf{A'} = \begin{bmatrix} a_1 \\ a_2 \\ a_3 \end{bmatrix}$$

and

$$\mathbf{B} = \begin{bmatrix} a_1 \\ a_2 \\ a_3 \end{bmatrix} \qquad \mathbf{B'} = [a_1 \quad a_2 \quad a_3]$$

6. *Triangular matrix.* A square matrix in which $a_{ij} = 0$ for all elements for which $i > j$ or $i < j$:

$$\begin{bmatrix} a_{11} & a_{12} & a_{13} \\ 0 & a_{22} & a_{23} \\ 0 & 0 & a_{33} \end{bmatrix}$$

7. *Symmetric matrix.* A matrix in which $\mathbf{A} = \mathbf{A'}$, or $a_{ij} = a_{ji}$. A matrix is called *skew-symmetric* if $\mathbf{A} = -\mathbf{A'}$ and all $a_{ij} = 0$ for $i = j$.

8. *Null matrix.* A matrix in which all elements equal zero, denoted by 0.

9. *Scalar.* A matrix containing only one row and one column, that is, an ordinary number designated by lower-case numbers, say a_{12}.

10. *Singular matrix.* A square matrix having a determinate equal to zero: $|A| = 0$. A system of equations having a singular matrix has no unique solution; it will have either no solution or an infinite number of solutions.

11. *Adjoint matrix.* A matrix obtained by replacing the elements of a square matrix with their cofactors and then interchanging the rows and columns. The inverse matrix can be obtained by dividing the adjoint matrix by the determinant of the matrix:

$$\mathbf{A}^{-1} = \frac{\text{Adj } \mathbf{A}}{|A|}$$

A-2-2 MATRIX OPERATIONS

Matrix addition is accomplished by adding corresponding elements in two or more matrices of the same size to form a new matrix. For example,

$$\underset{\begin{bmatrix} a_{11} & a_{12} \\ a_{21} & a_{22} \end{bmatrix}}{\mathbf{A}} + \underset{\begin{bmatrix} b_{11} & b_{12} \\ b_{21} & b_{22} \end{bmatrix}}{\mathbf{B}} = \underset{\begin{bmatrix} a_{11} + b_{11} & a_{12} + b_{12} \\ a_{21} + b_{21} & a_{22} + b_{22} \end{bmatrix}}{\mathbf{C}} \tag{21}$$

Matrix subtraction is performed similarly:

$$\underset{\begin{bmatrix} a_{11} & a_{21} \\ a_{12} & a_{22} \\ a_{13} & a_{23} \end{bmatrix}}{\mathbf{A}} - \underset{\begin{bmatrix} b_{11} & b_{21} \\ b_{12} & b_{22} \\ b_{13} & b_{23} \end{bmatrix}}{\mathbf{B}} = \underset{\begin{bmatrix} a_{11} - b_{11} & a_{21} - b_{21} \\ a_{12} - b_{12} & a_{22} - b_{22} \\ a_{13} - b_{13} & a_{23} - b_{23} \end{bmatrix}}{\mathbf{D}} \tag{22}$$

Multiplication of a matrix $\mathbf{A}$ by a scalar, d, requires multiplying each element by d:

$$d \cdot \underset{\begin{bmatrix} a_{11} & a_{12} \\ a_{21} & a_{22} \end{bmatrix}}{\mathbf{A}} = \underset{\begin{bmatrix} da_{11} & da_{12} \\ da_{21} & da_{22} \end{bmatrix}}{\mathbf{E}} \tag{23}$$

A row vector, $\mathbf{A}$, can be multiplied by a column vector, $\mathbf{B}$, by summing the products of the corresponding elements:

$$\underset{[a_1 \quad a_2 \quad a_3]}{\mathbf{A}} \cdot \underset{\begin{bmatrix} b_1 \\ b_2 \\ b_3 \end{bmatrix}}{\mathbf{B}} = [a_1b_1 + a_2b_2 + a_3b_3] = \mathbf{C} \tag{24}$$

A matrix, $\mathbf{A}$, may be multiplied by a column vector, $\mathbf{B}$, if the number of columns in $\mathbf{A}$ equals the number of rows in $\mathbf{B}$, producing a new column vector $\mathbf{C}$. Each element in the product vector, $\mathbf{C}$, is obtained by multiplying the elements in each row of $\mathbf{A}$ by the corresponding elements in vector $\mathbf{B}$:

$$\underset{\begin{bmatrix} a_{11} & a_{12} & a_{13} \\ a_{21} & a_{22} & a_{23} \\ a_{31} & a_{32} & a_{33} \end{bmatrix}}{\mathbf{A}} \cdot \underset{\begin{bmatrix} b_1 \\ b_2 \\ b_3 \end{bmatrix}}{\mathbf{B}} = \underset{\begin{bmatrix} a_{11}b_1 + a_{12}b_2 + a_{13}b_3 \\ a_{21}b_1 + a_{22}b_2 + a_{23}b_3 \\ a_{31}b_1 + a_{32}b_2 + a_{33}b_3 \end{bmatrix}}{\mathbf{C}} \tag{25}$$

A matrix, $\mathbf{A}$, multiplied by matrix $\mathbf{B}$ gives a product matrix, $\mathbf{C}$, the elements within obtained by summing the products of the row elements and the corresponding column elements:

$$\underset{\begin{bmatrix} a_{11} & a_{12} & a_{13} \\ a_{21} & a_{22} & a_{23} \end{bmatrix}}{\mathbf{A}} \cdot \underset{\begin{bmatrix} b_{11} & b_{12} \\ b_{21} & b_{22} \\ b_{31} & b_{32} \end{bmatrix}}{\mathbf{B}} = \underset{\begin{bmatrix} a_{11}b_{11} + a_{12}b_{21} + a_{13}b_{31} & a_{11}b_{12} + \\ a_{21}b_{11} + a_{22}b_{21} + a_{23}b_{31} & a_{21}b_{12} + \end{bmatrix}}{\mathbf{C}} \tag{26}$$

$$\begin{bmatrix} a_{12}b_{22} + a_{13}b_{32} \\ a_{22}b_{22} + a_{23}b_{32} \end{bmatrix}$$

Matrix addition and scalar multiplication may be summarized as follows:

1. $(\mathbf{A} + \mathbf{B}) + \mathbf{C} = \mathbf{A} + (\mathbf{B} + \mathbf{C})$ (associative law)
2. $\mathbf{A} + \mathbf{B} = \mathbf{B} + \mathbf{A}$ (commutative law)

3. $\mathbf{A} + 0 = \mathbf{A}$
4. $(a + b)\mathbf{A} = a\mathbf{A} + b\mathbf{A}$ (distributive law)
   $a(\mathbf{A} + \mathbf{B}) = a\mathbf{A} + a\mathbf{B}$

Matrix multiplication may be summarized as follows:

5. $(\mathbf{AB})\mathbf{C} = \mathbf{A}(\mathbf{BC})$ (associative law)
6. $\mathbf{AI} = \mathbf{IA} = \mathbf{A}$
7. $a(\mathbf{AB}) = (a\mathbf{A})\mathbf{B} = \mathbf{A}(a\mathbf{B})$
8. $\mathbf{AB} \neq \mathbf{BA}$ (commutative law not satisfied)
9. $\mathbf{A}(\mathbf{B} + \mathbf{C}) = \mathbf{AB} + \mathbf{AC}$ (distributive law)
   $(\mathbf{B} + \mathbf{C})\mathbf{A} = \mathbf{BA} + \mathbf{CA}$

Note also that

10. $(\mathbf{AB})' = \mathbf{A}'\mathbf{B}'$

A-2-3 MATRIX INVERSION

To solve for the unknown variables of a system of equations, the coefficient matrix
$\mathbf{A}$ must be inverted (divided into 1) and multiplied by the column vector composed
of elements found on the right-hand side of the equal sign. For instance, equations

$$2x_1 + x_2 = 2,100$$
$$x_1 + 5x_2 = 3,000$$ (27)

may be represented by the matrix equation $\mathbf{AX} = \mathbf{B}$, where

$$\mathbf{A} = \begin{bmatrix} 2 & 1 \\ 1 & 5 \end{bmatrix} \qquad \mathbf{X} = \begin{bmatrix} x_1 \\ x_2 \end{bmatrix} \qquad \mathbf{B} = \begin{bmatrix} 2,100 \\ 3,000 \end{bmatrix} \qquad (28)$$

When both sides of $\mathbf{AX} = \mathbf{B}$ are multiplied by the inverse of $\mathbf{A}$, that is, by $\mathbf{A}^{-1}$,
we have

$$\mathbf{A}^{-1}\mathbf{AX} = \mathbf{A}^{-1}\mathbf{B} \qquad (29)$$

Since $\mathbf{A}^{-1}\mathbf{A} = \mathbf{I}$ and the identity matrix, $\mathbf{I}$, is equal to unity,

$$\mathbf{X} = \mathbf{A}^{-1}\mathbf{B} \qquad (30)$$

For example, given the preceding equations and the knowledge that the inverse
of $\mathbf{A}$ is

$$\mathbf{A}^{-1} = \begin{bmatrix} \dfrac{5}{9} & -\dfrac{1}{9} \\ -\dfrac{1}{9} & \dfrac{2}{9} \end{bmatrix} \qquad (31)$$

$\mathbf{X}$ may be found by multiplying $\mathbf{A}^{-1}\mathbf{B}$:

$$\mathbf{X} \quad = \quad \mathbf{A}^{-1} \quad \cdot \quad \mathbf{B}$$

$$\begin{bmatrix} x_1 \\ x_2 \end{bmatrix} = \begin{bmatrix} \dfrac{5}{9} & -\dfrac{1}{9} \\ -\dfrac{1}{9} & \dfrac{2}{9} \end{bmatrix} \cdot \begin{bmatrix} 2,100 \\ 3,000 \end{bmatrix} \qquad (32)$$

$$
= \begin{bmatrix} \frac{5}{9}(2,100) - \frac{1}{9}(3,000) \\ \\ -\frac{1}{9}(2,100) + \frac{2}{9}(3,000) \end{bmatrix}
$$

$$
= \begin{bmatrix} \dfrac{7,500}{9} \\ \\ \dfrac{3,900}{9} \end{bmatrix} = \begin{bmatrix} \dfrac{2,500}{3} \\ \\ \dfrac{1,300}{3} \end{bmatrix}
$$

Thus, $x_1 = 833\frac{1}{3}$ and $x_2 = 433\frac{1}{3}$. (Note that for a unique solution to be obtained, A had to be square and nonsingular.)

The principal task of the remainder of this section is to explain an easier way to obtain A^{-1}. Simply stated, the inverse is obtained by converting the coefficient matrix, A, to an identity matrix, I, while performing the same operations on an identity matrix. The identity matrix is thereby transformed into an inverse matrix. One or more of three row operations may be used: (1) interchange rows, (2) multiply each element in the row by a constant, and (3) add or subtract a multiple of one row to or from another. Arrange the elements in the partitioned matrix as follows:

$$
\begin{array}{ccc} \mathbf{A} & \mathbf{I} & Row \end{array}
$$
$$
\left[\begin{array}{cc|cc} 2 & 1 & 1 & 0 \\ 1 & 5 & 0 & 1 \end{array} \right] \begin{array}{c} \mathrm{I} \\ \mathrm{II} \end{array} \tag{33}
$$

To obtain a 1 in the upper left-hand corner of $\mathbf{A}$, interchange the rows:

$$
\left[\begin{array}{cc|cc} 1 & 5 & 0 & 1 \\ 2 & 1 & 1 & 0 \end{array} \right] \begin{array}{c} \mathrm{II} \\ \mathrm{I} \end{array} \tag{34}
$$

To convert the 2 in row I to zero, multiply each element in row I by $-\frac{1}{2}$ and add to the corresponding elements in row II:

$$
\left[\begin{array}{cc|cc} 1 & 5 & 0 & 1 \\ 0 & \frac{9}{2} & -\frac{1}{2} & 1 \end{array} \right] \begin{array}{c} \mathrm{II} \\ \mathrm{III} = \left(-\frac{1}{2} \right)\mathrm{I} + \mathrm{II} \end{array} \tag{35}
$$

To convert the 5 in row II to zero, multiply row III by $-\frac{10}{9}$ and add to II:

$$
\left[\begin{array}{cc|cc} 1 & 0 & \frac{5}{9} & -\frac{1}{9} \\ 0 & \frac{9}{2} & -\frac{1}{2} & 1 \end{array} \right] \begin{array}{c} \mathrm{IV} = \left(-\frac{10}{9} \right)\mathrm{III} + \mathrm{II} \\ \mathrm{III} \end{array} \tag{36}
$$

To convert the $\frac{9}{2}$ in row III to 1, divide each element in the row by $\frac{9}{2}$:

$$
\left[\begin{array}{cc|cc} 1 & 0 & \frac{5}{9} & -\frac{1}{9} \\ 0 & 1 & -\frac{1}{9} & \frac{2}{9} \end{array} \right] \begin{array}{c} \mathrm{IV} \\ \mathrm{V} = \mathrm{III} \div \left(\frac{9}{2} \right) \end{array} \tag{37}
$$

Thus,

$$A^{-1} = \begin{vmatrix} \dfrac{5}{9} & -\dfrac{1}{9} \\[2mm] -\dfrac{1}{9} & \dfrac{2}{9} \end{vmatrix}$$

Note that the conversion of the coefficient matrix to an identity matrix began with the upper left element, moved down the column, then shifted to the next column.

Consider the computation of the inverse for

$$A = \begin{bmatrix} 1 & 0 & 4 \\ 2 & 3 & 0 \\ 3 & 1 & 2 \end{bmatrix} \tag{38}$$

Begin with $[A \mid I]$:

$$\begin{bmatrix} 1 & 0 & 4 & 1 & 0 & 0 \\ 2 & 3 & 0 & 0 & 1 & 0 \\ 3 & 1 & 2 & 0 & 0 & 1 \end{bmatrix} \quad \begin{matrix} \text{I} \\ \text{II} \\ \text{III} \end{matrix} \tag{39}$$

Performing the elementary row operations to convert the matrix on the left side of the bar to an identity matrix,

$$\begin{bmatrix} 1 & 0 & 4 & 1 & 0 & 0 \\ 0 & -\dfrac{3}{2} & 4 & 1 & -\dfrac{1}{2} & 0 \\ 0 & -\dfrac{1}{3} & \dfrac{10}{3} & 1 & 0 & -\dfrac{1}{3} \end{bmatrix} \quad \begin{matrix} \text{I} \\ \text{IV} = \left(-\dfrac{1}{2}\right)\text{II} + \text{I} \\ \text{V} = \left(-\dfrac{1}{3}\right)\text{III} + \text{I} \end{matrix} \tag{40}$$

$$\begin{bmatrix} 1 & 0 & 4 & 1 & 0 & 0 \\ 0 & 1 & -\dfrac{8}{3} & -\dfrac{2}{3} & \dfrac{1}{3} & 0 \\ 0 & 0 & \dfrac{22}{9} & \dfrac{7}{9} & \dfrac{1}{9} & -\dfrac{1}{3} \end{bmatrix} \quad \begin{matrix} \text{I} \\ \text{VI} = \left(-\dfrac{2}{3}\right)\text{IV} \\ \text{VII} = \left(-\dfrac{2}{9}\right)\text{IV} + \text{V} \end{matrix} \tag{41}$$

$$\begin{bmatrix} 1 & 0 & 0 & -\dfrac{3}{11} & -\dfrac{2}{11} & \dfrac{6}{11} \\ 0 & 1 & 0 & \dfrac{2}{11} & \dfrac{5}{11} & -\dfrac{4}{11} \\ 0 & 0 & 1 & \dfrac{7}{22} & \dfrac{1}{22} & -\dfrac{3}{22} \end{bmatrix} \quad \begin{matrix} \text{VIII} = \left(-\dfrac{18}{11}\right)\text{VII} + \text{I} \\ \text{IX} = \left(\dfrac{12}{11}\right)\text{VII} + \text{VI} \\ \text{X} = \left(\dfrac{9}{22}\right)\text{VII} \end{matrix} \tag{42}$$

ending with $(I \mid A^{-1})$. Values for A^{-1} check with those obtained by use of determinants in section A-1-3.

The solution to the system of equations

$$\begin{aligned} x_1 + 0 + 4x_3 &= 5 \\ 2x_1 + 3x_2 + 0 &= 6 \\ 3x_1 + x_2 + 2x_3 &= 7 \end{aligned} \qquad \text{In matrix notation: } AX = B \tag{43}$$

is

$$\begin{bmatrix} x_1 \\ x_2 \\ x_3 \end{bmatrix} = \begin{bmatrix} -\dfrac{3}{11} & -\dfrac{2}{11} & \dfrac{6}{11} \\ \dfrac{2}{11} & \dfrac{5}{11} & -\dfrac{4}{11} \\ \dfrac{7}{22} & \dfrac{1}{22} & -\dfrac{3}{22} \end{bmatrix} \begin{bmatrix} 5 \\ 6 \\ 7 \end{bmatrix}$$

In matrix notation: $\mathbf{X} = \mathbf{A}^{-1}\mathbf{B}$

(44)

$$= \begin{bmatrix} -\dfrac{15}{11} - \dfrac{12}{11} + \dfrac{42}{11} \\ \dfrac{10}{11} + \dfrac{30}{11} - \dfrac{28}{11} \\ \dfrac{35}{22} + \dfrac{6}{22} - \dfrac{21}{22} \end{bmatrix}$$

$$= \begin{bmatrix} \dfrac{15}{11} \\ \dfrac{12}{11} \\ \dfrac{10}{11} \end{bmatrix}$$

Thus, $x_1 = \frac{15}{11}$, $x_2 = \frac{12}{11}$, and $x_3 = \frac{10}{11}$—the identical answers obtained in section A-1-2.

The values of $\mathbf{X}$ could have been obtained concomitant with the conversion of $\mathbf{A}$ to $\mathbf{I}$ and $\mathbf{I}$ to $\mathbf{A}^{-1}$ by adding another partition to the matrix and performing the same row operations on $\mathbf{B}$, that is, by solving $[\mathbf{A} \mid \mathbf{I} \mid \mathbf{B}]$

$$\begin{bmatrix} 1 & 0 & 4 & 1 & 0 & 0 & 5 \\ 2 & 3 & 0 & 0 & 1 & 0 & 6 \\ 3 & 1 & 2 & 0 & 0 & 1 & 7 \end{bmatrix}$$

(45)

to obtain $[\mathbf{I} \mid \mathbf{A}^{-1} \mid \mathbf{X}]$:

$$\begin{bmatrix} 1 & 0 & 0 & -\dfrac{3}{11} & -\dfrac{2}{11} & \dfrac{6}{11} & \dfrac{15}{11} \\ 0 & 1 & 0 & \dfrac{2}{11} & \dfrac{5}{11} & -\dfrac{4}{11} & \dfrac{12}{11} \\ 0 & 0 & 1 & \dfrac{7}{22} & \dfrac{1}{22} & -\dfrac{3}{22} & \dfrac{10}{11} \end{bmatrix}$$

(46)

Questions and Problems

A-1. Solve the following systems by use of determinants:

  a. $x + 2y = 3$
  $3x + 4y = 5$

b. $4x_1 + 2x_2 + 3x_3 = 2$
   $2x_1 + x_2 + 5x_3 = 3$
   $x_1 + 0 + x_3 = 1$
c. $0 + 4x_2 + x_3 = -2$
   $x_1 + 3x_2 + 0 = 1$
   $3x_1 + 5x_2 + 6x_3 = 3$
d. $x_1 + 2x_2 + 3x_3 = 3$
   $2x_1 + 5x_2 + 7x_3 = 7$
   $3x_1 + 7x_2 + 6x_3 = 6$

A-2. Perform the following exercises using matrix operations:

a. Given that $\mathbf{A} + \mathbf{B} = \mathbf{C}$, find $\mathbf{C}$:

1. $\mathbf{A} = \begin{bmatrix} 1 & 5 \\ 3 & 2 \end{bmatrix}$ and $\mathbf{B} = \begin{bmatrix} 3 & 4 \\ 7 & 6 \end{bmatrix}$

2. $\mathbf{A} = \begin{bmatrix} 7 & 3 \\ 1 & 2 \end{bmatrix}$ and $\mathbf{B} = \begin{bmatrix} 2 & 3 \\ 4 & 1 \end{bmatrix}$

3. $\mathbf{A} = \begin{bmatrix} 2 & 7 & 3 \\ 3 & 4 & 5 \\ 5 & 1 & 8 \end{bmatrix}$ and $\mathbf{B} = \begin{bmatrix} 4 & 5 & 2 \\ 1 & 7 & 3 \\ 2 & 1 & 1 \end{bmatrix}$

b. Given that $\mathbf{A} - \mathbf{B} = \mathbf{C}$, find $\mathbf{C}$:

1. $\mathbf{A} = \begin{bmatrix} 7 & 3 \\ 6 & 5 \end{bmatrix}$ and $\mathbf{B} = \begin{bmatrix} 2 & 1 \\ 3 & 6 \end{bmatrix}$

2. $\mathbf{A} = [8 \quad 5]$ and $\mathbf{B} = [3 \quad 1]$

3. $\mathbf{A} = \begin{bmatrix} 3 & 5 & 7 \\ 8 & 5 & 3 \end{bmatrix}$ and $\mathbf{B} = \begin{bmatrix} 5 & 4 & 7 \\ 6 & 3 & 2 \end{bmatrix}$

c. Given that $d \cdot \mathbf{A} = \mathbf{C}$, find $\mathbf{C}$:

1. $d = 3$ and $\mathbf{A} = \begin{bmatrix} 6 & 7 & 3 \\ 1 & 2 & 5 \end{bmatrix}$

2. $d = 4$ and $\mathbf{A} = \begin{bmatrix} 1 & 3 \\ 0 & 7 \\ 4 & 2 \end{bmatrix}$

3. $d = 2$ and $\mathbf{A} = \begin{bmatrix} 9 & 1 \\ -2 & 4 \end{bmatrix}$

d. Given that $\mathbf{A} \cdot \mathbf{B} = \mathbf{C}$, find $\mathbf{C}$:

1. $\mathbf{A} = [3 \quad 1 \quad 4]$ and $\mathbf{B} = \begin{bmatrix} 1 \\ 4 \\ 2 \end{bmatrix}$

2. $\mathbf{A} = \begin{bmatrix} 6 & 0 & 2 \end{bmatrix}$ and $\mathbf{B} = \begin{bmatrix} 1 \\ 9 \\ 3 \end{bmatrix}$

3. $\mathbf{A} = \begin{bmatrix} -3 & 1 & 7 \end{bmatrix}$ and $\mathbf{B} = \begin{bmatrix} -2 \\ -1 \\ 2 \end{bmatrix}$

e. Given that $\mathbf{A} \cdot \mathbf{B} = \mathbf{C}$, find $\mathbf{C}$:

1. $\mathbf{A} = \begin{bmatrix} 4 & 2 & 3 \\ 2 & 1 & 5 \\ 1 & 0 & -1 \end{bmatrix}$ and $\mathbf{B} = \begin{bmatrix} 2 \\ 3 \\ 1 \end{bmatrix}$

2. $\mathbf{A} = \begin{bmatrix} 0 & 4 & 1 \\ 1 & 3 & 0 \\ 3 & 5 & 6 \end{bmatrix}$ and $\mathbf{B} = \begin{bmatrix} -2 \\ 1 \\ 3 \end{bmatrix}$

3. $\mathbf{A} = \begin{bmatrix} 3 & 2 & 4 \\ 1 & 5 & 3 \end{bmatrix}$ and $\mathbf{B} = \begin{bmatrix} 3 & 1 \\ 4 & 2 \\ 2 & 5 \end{bmatrix}$

4. $\mathbf{A} = \begin{bmatrix} 1 & 0 & 0 \\ 0 & 1 & 0 \\ 0 & 0 & 1 \end{bmatrix}$ and $\mathbf{B} = \begin{bmatrix} 2 & 1 & 7 \\ 1 & 4 & 3 \\ 3 & 2 & 5 \end{bmatrix}$

5. $\mathbf{A} = \begin{bmatrix} 7 & 0 & 1 \\ -1 & 3 & 2 \end{bmatrix}$ and $\mathbf{B} = \begin{bmatrix} 1 & 3 \\ 0 & 2 \\ 1 & 4 \end{bmatrix}$

6. $\mathbf{A} = \begin{bmatrix} 1 & 1 & 1 \end{bmatrix}$ and $\mathbf{B} = \begin{bmatrix} 4 & 7 & 7 \\ 5 & 2 & 2 \\ 3 & 8 & 4 \end{bmatrix}$

7. $\mathbf{A} = \begin{bmatrix} 3 & 4 & 2 \\ 1 & 2 & 5 \end{bmatrix}$ and $\mathbf{B} = \begin{bmatrix} 3 & 1 \\ 2 & 5 \\ 4 & 3 \end{bmatrix}$

f. 1. Under what conditions will $\mathbf{AB} = \mathbf{BA}$ where

$$\mathbf{A} = \begin{bmatrix} a_{11} & a_{12} \\ a_{21} & a_{22} \end{bmatrix} \quad \text{and} \quad \mathbf{B} = \begin{bmatrix} b_{11} & b_{12} \\ b_{21} & b_{22} \end{bmatrix}$$

2. Calculate $\mathbf{AB}$ and $\mathbf{BA}$ where

$$\mathbf{A} = \begin{bmatrix} 7 & 3 \\ 1 & 2 \end{bmatrix} \quad \text{and} \quad \mathbf{B} = \begin{bmatrix} 2 & 3 \\ 4 & 1 \end{bmatrix}$$

3. Calculate **AB** and **BA** where

$$\mathbf{A} = \begin{bmatrix} 3 & 4 \\ 4 & 3 \end{bmatrix} \quad \text{and} \quad \mathbf{B} = \begin{bmatrix} 2 & 5 \\ 5 & 2 \end{bmatrix}$$

Note that both **A** and **B** are symmetrical, that is, $a_{ij} = a_{ji}$.

4. Calculate **AB** and **BA** where

$$\mathbf{A} = \begin{bmatrix} 1 & 2 & 3 \\ 2 & 5 & 7 \\ 3 & 7 & 6 \end{bmatrix} \quad \text{and} \quad \mathbf{B} = \begin{bmatrix} 2 & 3 & 4 \\ 3 & 7 & 6 \\ 4 & 6 & 8 \end{bmatrix}$$

Note that both **A** and **B** are symmetrical.

A-3. Solve the systems of problem A-1 by use of matrix operations.

References

1. R. G. D. Allen. *Mathematical Analysis for Economists* (New York: Macmillan, 1964), ch. 18.
2. Saul I. Gass. *Linear Programming.* 3d ed. (New York: McGraw-Hill, 1969), ch. 2.
3. F. B. Hildebrand. *Methods of Applied Mathematics* (Englewood Cliffs, N.J.: Prentice-Hall, 1958), ch. 1.
4. H. W. Kuhn. "Lectures on the Theory of Games." *Annals of Mathematical Studies 37.* (Princeton, N.J.: Princeton University Press, 1957).
5. Lyman C. Peck. *Basic Mathematics for Management and Economics* (Glenview, Ill.: Scott, Foresman, 1970), ch. 1.
6. Daniel Teichrow. *An Introduction to Management Science: Deterministic Models* (New York: Wiley, 1964), ch. 12–13.
7. Taro Yamane. *Mathematics for Economists: An Elementary Survey.* 2d ed. (Englewood Cliffs, N.J.: Prentice-Hall, 1968), ch. 10–11.

Appendix B
Experience Curve Tables—Unit Values

The values found in the tables of Appendix B are for y (say, man-hours) in hundreds of units required to produce the x_ith unit of product. They are calculated according to the equation

$$y = 100x_i^b \tag{1}$$

where b is the slope of the learning curve as related to the percentage of learning, P, by the equation

$$b = \frac{\log P - \log 100}{\log 2} = \frac{\log P - 2}{0.30103} \tag{2}$$

For example, to find y for $x_i = 30$ and $P = 80$ per cent, simply read from the table $y = 33.4599$. Without the table, the following calculations would be required:

$$y = 100(30)^b$$
$$= 100(30)^{-0.32193}$$
$$\log y = \log 100 - 0.32193 \log 30$$
$$= 2 - 0.32193(1.47712)$$
$$= 2 - 0.47553$$
$$= 1.52447$$
$$y = 33.46$$

$$b = \frac{\log 80 - 2}{0.30103}$$
$$= \frac{1.90309 - 2}{0.30103}$$
$$= -0.32193$$

Unit	55%	60%	65%	70%	75%	80%	85%	90%	95%
1	100.0000	100.0000	100.0000	100.0000	100.0000	100.0000	100.0000	100.0000	100.0000
2	55.0000	60.0000	65.0000	70.0000	75.0000	80.0000	85.0000	90.0000	95.0000
3	38.7690	44.5018	50.5213	56.8180	63.3836	70.2104	77.2915	84.6206	92.1919
4	30.2500	36.0000	42.2500	49.0000	56.2500	64.0000	72.2500	81.0000	90.2500
5	24.9540	30.5410	36.7789	43.6848	51.2745	59.5637	68.5671	78.2987	88.7720
6	21.3229	26.7011	32.8389	39.7726	47.5377	56.1683	65.6978	76.1585	87.5823
7	18.6683	23.8337	29.8388	36.7397	44.5916	53.4490	63.3657	74.3948	86.5889
8	16.6375	21.6000	27.4625	34.3000	42.1875	51.2000	61.4125	72.9000	85.7375
9	15.0304	19.8041	25.5240	32.2829	40.1748	49.2950	59.7397	71.6065	84.9935
10	13.7247	18.3246	23.9063	30.5792	38.4559	47.6510	58.2821	70.4688	84.3334
11	12.6416	17.0816	22.5313	29.1157	36.9643	46.2111	56.9941	69.4553	83.7406
12	11.7276	16.0207	21.3453	27.9408	35.6533	44.9346	55.8431	68.5427	83.2032
13	10.9463	15.1030	20.3094	26.7174	34.4883	43.7916	54.8049	67.7138	82.7118
14	10.2676	14.3002	19.3952	25.7178	33.4437	42.7592	53.8608	66.9553	82.2595
15	9.6744	13.5913	18.5812	24.8208	32.4996	41.8199	52.9965	66.2568	81.8406
16	9.1506	12.9600	17.8506	24.0100	31.6406	40.9600	52.2006	65.6100	81.4506
17	8.6844	12.3937	17.1906	23.2726	30.8544	40.1687	51.4639	65.0082	81.0860
18	8.2667	11.8825	16.5906	22.5980	30.1311	39.4360	50.7788	64.4458	80.7438
19	7.8900	11.4183	16.0424	21.9780	29.4625	38.7556	50.1391	63.9183	80.4214
20	7.5486	10.9948	15.5391	21.4055	28.8419	38.1208	49.5398	63.4219	80.1167
21	7.2375	10.6064	15.0750	20.8748	28.2637	37.5267	48.9763	62.9533	79.8280
22	6.9529	10.2490	14.6454	20.3810	27.7233	36.9689	48.4449	62.5097	79.5536
23	6.6914	9.9187	14.2463	19.9201	27.2165	36.4436	47.9425	62.0888	79.2924
24	6.4501	9.6124	13.8744	19.4886	26.7400	35.9477	47.4666	61.6884	79.0430

Unit	55%	60%	65%	70%	75%	80%	85%	90%	95%
25	6.2270	9.3275	13.5268	19.0835	26.2907	35.4784	47.0145	61.3068	78.8046
26	6.0199	9.0618	13.2011	18.7022	25.8662	35.0333	46.5841	60.9424	78.5762
27	5.8270	8.8132	12.8951	18.3425	25.4642	34.6102	46.1737	60.5938	78.3571
28	5.6471	8.5801	12.6069	18.0024	25.0827	34.2073	45.7817	60.2598	78.1465
29	5.4789	8.3611	12.3349	17.6803	24.7201	33.8231	45.4066	59.9392	77.9438
30	5.3210	8.1548	12.0778	17.3745	24.3747	33.4599	45.0471	59.6311	77.7485
31	5.1726	7.9601	11.8341	17.0838	24.0452	33.1046	44.7021	59.3347	77.5601
32	5.0328	7.7760	11.6029	16.8070	23.7305	32.7680	44.3705	59.0490	77.3701
33	4.9011	7.6016	11.3831	16.5430	23.4293	32.4450	44.0516	58.7735	77.2021
34	4.7764	7.4352	11.1739	16.2908	23.1408	32.1347	43.7443	58.5074	77.0317
35	4.6586	7.2791	10.9744	16.0496	22.8641	31.8362	43.4480	58.2501	76.8667
36	4.5467	7.1295	10.7839	15.8186	22.5983	31.5488	43.1620	58.0012	76.7066
37	4.4405	6.9870	10.6018	15.5972	22.3428	31.2717	42.8856	57.7602	76.5512
38	4.3395	6.8511	10.4276	15.3846	22.0969	31.0444	42.6182	57.5265	76.4003
39	4.2434	6.7211	10.2606	15.1803	21.8599	30.7462	42.3595	57.2998	76.2536
40	4.1517	6.5969	10.1004	14.9838	21.6314	30.4966	42.1088	57.0797	76.1109
41	4.0642	6.4779	9.9466	14.7947	21.4108	30.2551	41.8657	56.8699	75.9719
42	3.9806	6.3639	9.7987	14.6123	21.1978	30.0214	41.6298	56.6580	75.8366
43	3.9007	6.2545	9.6565	14.4365	20.9918	29.7948	41.4008	56.4557	75.7046
44	3.8241	6.1494	9.5195	14.2667	20.7925	29.5751	41.1782	56.2588	75.5799
45	3.7507	6.0484	9.3874	14.1027	20.5995	29.3619	40.9618	56.0669	75.4504
46	3.6803	5.9512	9.2601	13.9441	20.4124	29.1549	40.7513	55.8799	75.3278
47	3.6126	5.8576	9.1371	13.7906	20.2310	28.9537	40.5463	55.6975	75.2080
48	3.5476	5.7674	9.0184	13.6420	20.0549	28.7582	40.3466	55.5196	75.0909

Unit	55%	60%	65%	70%	75%	80%	85%	90%	95%
49	3.4581	5.6805	8.9035	13.4980	19.8841	28.5679	40.1520	55.3458	74.9764
50	3.4249	5.5965	8.7925	13.3584	19.7180	28.3827	39.9623	55.1761	74.8644
51		5.5154	8.6849	13.2230	19.5566	28.2023	39.7772	55.0103	74.7548
52		5.4371	8.5807	13.0915	19.3997	28.0266	39.5965	54.8482	74.6474
53		5.3613	8.4797	12.9638	19.2469	27.8553	39.4201	54.6896	74.5423
54		5.2879	8.3818	12.8397	19.0982	27.6881	39.2477	54.5344	74.4392
55		5.2169	8.2868	12.7191	18.9533	27.5251	39.0792	54.3825	74.3382
56		5.1481	8.1945	12.6017	18.8121	27.3699	38.9144	54.2338	74.2392
57		5.0814	8.1048	12.4875	18.6744	27.2104	38.7533	54.0881	74.1420
58		5.0167	8.0177	12.3762	18.5401	27.0585	38.5956	53.9453	74.0466
59		4.9539	7.9330	12.2678	18.4090	26.9100	38.4412	53.8053	73.9530
60	2.9265	4.8929	7.8505	12.1622	18.2810	26.7648	38.2900	53.6680	73.8611
61		4.8337	7.7703	12.0592	18.1560	26.6227	38.1419	53.5333	73.7708
62		4.7761	7.6922	11.9587	18.0339	26.4837	37.9967	53.4012	73.6821
63		4.7201	7.6161	11.8606	17.9146	26.3476	37.8545	53.2715	73.5949
64		4.6656	7.5419	11.7649	17.7979	26.2144	37.7149	53.1441	73.5092
65		4.6126	7.4696	11.6714	17.6837	26.0839	37.5781	53.0190	73.4249
66		4.5610	7.3990	11.5801	17.5720	25.9560	37.4438	52.8961	73.3420
67		4.5107	7.3302	11.4908	17.4627	25.8306	37.3120	52.7753	73.2604
68		4.4617	7.2630	11.4036	17.3556	25.7077	37.1826	52.6566	73.1802
69		4.4140	7.1974	11.3182	17.2508	25.5872	37.0556	52.5399	73.1011
70	2.5622	4.3674	7.1333	11.2347	17.1481	25.4690	36.9308	52.4251	73.0233
71		4.3220	7.0707	11.1530	17.0474	25.3529	26.8082	52.3122	72.9467
72		4.2777	7.0095	11.0730	16.9487	25.2390	36.6877	52.2011	72.8713

Unit	55%	60%	65%	70%	75%	80%	85%	90%	95%
73		4.2344	6.9497	10.9947	16.8519	25.1272	36.5692	52.0918	72.7969
74		4.1922	6.8912	10.9180	16.7571	25.0174	36.4527	51.9842	72.7237
75		4.1509	6.8339	10.8429	16.6640	24.9096	36.3382	51.8782	72.6515
76		4.1106	6.7779	10.7692	16.5727	24.8035	36.2255	51.7739	72.5803
77		4.0712	6.7231	10.6970	16.4829	24.6994	36.1147	51.6711	72.5101
78		4.0327	6.6694	10.6262	16.3949	24.5970	36.0056	51.5698	72.4409
79		3.9950	6.6168	10.5568	16.3085	24.4963	35.8982	51.4701	72.3727
80	2.2835	3.9581	6.5653	10.4887	16.2236	24.3973	35.7924	51.3718	72.3053
81		3.9220	6.5148	10.4218	16.1401	24.2999	35.6884	51.2748	72.2389
82		3.8867	6.4653	10.3563	16.0581	24.2041	35.5858	51.1793	72.1733
83		3.8522	6.4168	10.2919	15.9776	24.1099	35.4848	51.0851	72.1086
84		3.8183	6.3692	10.2286	15.8983	24.0171	35.3853	50.9922	72.0447
85		3.7852	6.3225	10.1665	15.8204	23.9258	35.2873	50.9005	71.9817
86		3.7527	6.2767	10.1055	15.7435	23.8358	35.1905	50.8101	71.9194
87		3.7208	6.2318	10.0456	15.6685	23.7473	35.0954	50.7209	71.8579
88		3.6896	6.1877	9.9867	15.5943	23.6601	35.0015	50.6329	71.7972
89		3.6590	6.1444	9.9288	15.5214	23.5742	34.9089	50.5460	71.7371
90	2.0629	3.6290	6.1018	9.8719	15.4496	23.4895	34.8175	50.4602	71.6778
91		3.5996	6.0601	9.8159	15.3678	23.4061	34.7274	50.3755	71.6193
92		3.5707	6.0191	9.7608	15.3093	23.3239	34.6386	50.2919	71.5614
93		3.5424	5.9788	9.7067	15.2407	23.2429	34.5509	50.2093	71.5041
94		3.5146	5.9391	9.6534	15.1732	23.1630	34.4643	50.1278	71.4476
95		3.4873	5.9002	9.6010	15.1067	23.0842	34.3789	50.0472	71.3916
96		3.4605	5.8619	9.5494	15.0412	23.0065	34.2947	49.9676	71.3363

Unit	55%	60%	65%	70%	75%	80%	85%	90%	95%
97		3.4341	5.8243	9.4986	14.9767	22.9299	34.2114	49.8890	71.2816
98		3.4083	5.7873	9.4486	14.9131	22.8543	34.1292	49.8113	71.2276
99		3.3829	5.7509	9.3994	14.8503	22.7798	34.0481	49.7344	71.1741
100	1.8837	3.3579	5.7151	9.3509	14.7885	22.7062	33.9680	49.6585	71.1211
101		3.3334	5.6799	9.3031	14.7276	22.6335	33.8888	49.5835	71.0688
102		3.3093	5.6452	9.2561	14.6675	22.5619	33.8106	49.5093	71.0170
103		3.2856	5.6111	9.2098	14.6082	22.4911	33.7334	49.4359	70.9658
104		3.2622	5.5775	9.1641	14.5497	22.4213	33.6570	49.3634	70.9150
105		3.2393	5.5444	9.1191	14.4921	22.3523	33.5816	49.2916	70.8648
106		3.2168	5.5118	9.0747	14.4352	22.2842	33.5071	49.2206	70.8151
107		3.1945	5.4798	9.0310	14.3790	22.2179	33.4334	49.1504	70.7660
108		3.1728	5.4482	8.9878	14.3236	22.1505	33.3605	49.0810	70.7173
109		3.1513	5.4171	8.9453	14.2689	22.0849	33.2885	49.0123	70.6691
110	1.7350	3.1301	5.3864	8.9034	14.2150	22.0201	33.2173	48.9443	70.6213
111		3.1093	5.3562	8.8620	14.1617	21.9560	33.1469	48.8770	70.5740
112		3.0889	5.3264	8.8212	14.1090	21.8927	33.0773	48.8104	70.5272
113		3.0687	5.2971	8.7809	14.0571	21.8301	33.0084	48.7445	70.4808
114		3.0488	5.2681	8.7412	14.0058	21.7683	32.9403	48.6793	70.4349
115		3.0293	5.2396	8.7020	13.9551	21.7072	32.8729	48.6147	70.3894
116		3.0100	5.2115	8.6633	13.9050	21.6468	32.8062	48.5508	70.3443
117		2.9910	5.1838	8.6252	13.8556	21.5870	32.7403	48.4875	70.2996
118		2.9723	5.1564	8.5875	13.8067	21.5280	32.6750	48.4248	70.2554
119		2.9539	5.1295	8.5503	13.7585	21.4696	32.6104	48.3627	70.2115
120	1.6096	2.9357	5.1029	8.5135	13.7108	21.4118	32.5465	48.3012	70.1680

Appendix C
Experience Curve Table—
Cumulative Values

The tables in Appendix C provide cumulative totals of values given in Appendix B.

Unit	55%	60%	65%	70%	75%	80%	85%	90%	95%
1		100.000	100.000	100.000	100.000	100.000	100.000	100.000	100.000
2		160.000	165.000	170.000	175.000	180.000	185.000	190.000	195.000
3		204.502	215.521	226.818	238.384	250.210	262.291	274.621	287.192
4		240.502	257.771	275.818	294.634	314.210	334.541	355.621	377.442
5		271.043	294.550	319.503	345.908	373.774	403.109	433.920	466.214
6		297.744	327.389	359.275	393.446	429.942	468.806	510.079	553.796
7		321.578	357.228	396.015	438.037	483.391	532.172	584.474	640.385
8		343.178	384.690	430.315	480.225	534.591	593.585	657.374	726.123
9		362.982	410.214	462.598	520.400	583.886	653.324	728.980	811.116
10		381.306	434.121	493.177	558.856	631.537	711.606	799.449	895.450
11		398.388	456.652	522.293	595.820	677.748	768.600	868.904	979.190
12		414.409	477.997	550.134	631.473	722.683	824.443	937.447	1062.393
13		429.512	498.307	576.851	665.962	766.474	879.248	1005.161	1145.105
14		443.812	517.702	602.569	699.405	809.234	933.109	1072.116	1227.365
15		457.403	536.283	627.390	731.905	851.054	986.106	1138.373	1309.205
16		470.363	554.134	651.400	763.545	892.014	1038.306	1203.983	1390.656
17		482.757	571.324	675.672	794.400	932.182	1089.770	1268.991	1471.742
18		494.639	587.915	697.270	824.531	971.618	1140.549	1333.437	1552.486
19		506.058	603.957	719.248	853.993	1010.374	1190.688	1397.355	1632.907
20		517.052	619.496	740.654	882.835	1048.495	1240.228	1460.777	1713.024
21		527.659	634.571	761.529	911.099	1086.021	1289.204	1523.730	1792.852
22		537.908	649.217	781.910	938.822	1122.990	1337.649	1586.240	1872.405
23		547.827	663.463	801.830	966.039	1159.434	1385.592	1648.329	1951.698
24		557.439	677.338	821.318	992.779	1195.382	1433.058	1710.017	2030.741

Unit	55%	60%	65%	70%	75%	80%	85%	90%	95%
25		566.766	690.864	840.402	1019.070	1230.860	1480.073	1771.324	2109.545
26		575.828	704.065	859.104	1044.936	1265.893	1526.657	1832.266	2188.122
27		584.641	716.961	877.447	1070.400	1300.503	1572.830	1892.860	2266.479
28		593.222	729.567	895.449	1095.483	1334.711	1618.612	1953.120	2344.625
29		601.583	741.902	913.129	1120.203	1368.534	1664.019	2013.059	2422.569
30		609.737	753.980	930.504	1144.578	1401.990	1709.066	2072.690	2500.317
31		617.698	765.814	947.588	1168.623	1435.094	1753.768	2132.025	2577.878
32		625.474	777.417	964.395	1192.353	1467.862	1798.138	2191.074	2655.256
33		633.075	788.800	980.938	1215.782	1500.307	1842.190	2249.847	2732.458
34		640.511	799.974	997.228	1238.991	1532.142	1885.934	2308.354	2809.489
35		647.790	810.949	1013.278	1271.787	1564.278	1929.382	2366.604	2886.356
36		654.920	821.732	1029.097	1284.386	1595.827	1972.544	2424.605	2963.063
37		661.907	832.334	1044.694	1306.728	1627.099	2015.430	2482.365	3039.614
38		668.758	842.761	1060.078	1328.825	1658.103	2058.048	2539.891	3116.014
39		675.479	853.022	1075.259	1350.685	1688.849	2100.408	2597.191	3192.268
40		682.076	863.123	1090.242	1372.317	1719.346	2142.516	2654.271	3268.379
41		688.554	873.069	1105.037	1393.727	1749.601	2184.382	2711.137	3344.351
42		694.918	882.868	1119.649	1414.925	1779.623	2226.012	2767.795	3420.187
43		701.172	892.525	1134.086	1435.917	1809.418	2267.413	2824.251	3495.892
44		707.322	902.044	1148.353	1456.710	1838.993	2308.591	2880.510	3571.468
45		713.370	911.432	1162.455	1477.309	1868.355	2349.553	2936.577	3646.918
46		719.321	920.692	1176.399	1497.721	1897.510	2390.304	2992.457	3722.246
47		725.179	929.829	1190.190	1517.952	1926.464	2430.850	2038.155	3797.454
48		730.946	938.847	1203.832	1538.007	1955.222	2471.197	3103.675	3872.545

Unit	55%	60%	65%	70%	75%	80%	85%	90%	95%
49		736.627	947.751	1217.330	1557.891	1983.790	2511.349	3159.021	3947.521
50		742.223	956.543	1230.688	1577.609	2012.173	2551.311	3214.197	4022.386
51		747.739	965.228	1243.911	1597.166	2040.376	2591.088	3269.207	4097.140
52		753.176	973.809	1257.003	1616.566	2068.403	2630.685	3324.055	4171.788
53		758.537	982.288	1269.967	1635.813	2096.259	2670.105	3378.745	4246.330
54		763.825	990.670	1282.806	1654.911	2123.947	2709.353	3433.279	4320.769
55		769.042	998.957	1295.526	1673.846	2151.472	2748.432	3487.661	4395.108
56		774.190	1007.152	1308.127	1692.676	2178.838	2787.346	3541.895	4469.347
57		779.271	1015.256	1320.615	1711.351	2206.049	2826.100	3595.983	4543.489
58		784.288	1023.274	1332.991	1729.891	2233.108	2864.695	3649.928	4617.535
59		789.242	1031.207	1345.259	1748.200	2260.018	2903.136	3703.733	4691.488
60		794.135	1039.058	1357.421	1766.581	2286.783	2941.426	3757.401	4765.349
61		798.969	1046.838	1369.480	1784.738	2313.406	2979.568	3810.934	4839.120
62		803.745	1054.520	1381.439	1802.771	2339.890	3017.565	3864.355	4912.802
63		808.465	1062.136	1393.299	1820.685	2366.238	3055.420	3917.606	4986.397
64		813.130	1069.678	1405.064	1838.483	2392.453	3093.134	3970.750	5059.906
65		817.743	1077.148	1416.736	1856.167	2418.537	3130.713	4023.769	5133.331
66		822.304	1084.547	1428.316	1873.739	2444.493	3168.156	4076.665	5206.673
67		826.815	1091.877	1439.807	1891.201	2470.324	3205.468	4129.440	5279.934
68		831.276	1099.140	1451.210	1908.557	2496.032	3242.651	4182.097	5353.114
69		835.690	1106.337	1462.528	1925.809	2521.619	3279.707	4234.637	5426.215
70		840.058	1113.471	1473.763	1942.956	2547.088	3316.637	4287.062	5499.238
71		844.380	1120.541	1484.916	1960.003	2572.441	3353.446	4339.374	5572.185
72		848.658	1127.551	1495.989	1976.952	2597.680	3390.133	4391.575	5645.056

Unit	55%	60%	65%	70%	75%	80%	85%	90%	95%
73		852.892	1134.500	1506.984	1993.804	2622.807	3426.702	4443.667	5717.853
74		857.084	1141.392	1517.902	2010.561	2647.825	3463.155	4495.651	5790.577
75		861.235	1148.226	1528.745	2027.225	2672.735	3499.493	4547.529	5863.228
76		865.346	1155.003	1539.514	2043.798	2697.539	3535.719	4599.303	5935.809
77		869.417	1161.727	1550.211	2060.281	2722.239	3571.834	4650.974	6008.319
78		873.450	1168.396	1560.837	2076.676	2746.836	3607.839	4702.544	6080.760
79		877.445	1175.013	1571.394	2092.984	2771.333	3643.737	4754.014	6153.132
80		881.403	1181.578	1581.883	2109.308	2795.730	3679.530	4805.386	6225.438
81		885.325	1188.093	1592.304	2125.348	2820.030	3715.218	4856.661	6297.677
82		889.211	1194.558	1602.661	2141.406	2844.234	3750.804	4907.840	6369.850
83		893.064	1200.975	1612.963	2157.383	2868.344	3786.289	4958.925	6441.959
84		896.882	1207.344	1623.181	2173.282	2892.361	3821.674	5009.918	6514.003
85		900.667	1213.667	1633.348	2189.102	2916.287	3856.961	5060.819	6585.985
86		904.420	1219.943	1643.453	2204.846	2940.123	3892.152	5111.629	6657.904
87		908.141	1226.175	1653.499	2220.514	2963.870	3927.247	5162.350	6729.762
88		911.830	1232.363	1663.486	2236.108	2987.530	3962.249	5212.983	6801.559
89		915.489	1238.507	1673.414	2251.630	3011.105	3997.158	5263.529	6873.297
90		919.118	1244.609	1683.286	2267.079	3034.594	4031.975	5313.989	6944.974
91		922.718	1250.669	1693.102	2282.458	3058.000	4066.703	5634.365	7016.594
92		926.288	1256.688	1702.863	2297.768	3081.324	4101.341	5414.657	7088.155
93		929.831	1262.667	1712.570	2313.008	3104.567	4135.892	5464.866	7159.659
94		933.345	1268.606	1722.223	2328.182	3127.730	4170.356	5514.994	7231.107
95		936.833	1274.506	1731.824	2343.288	3150.814	4204.735	5565.041	7302.498
96		940.293	1280.368	1741.373	2358.329	3173.821	4239.030	5615.009	7373.835

Unit	55%	60%	65%	70%	75%	80%	85%	90%	95%
97		943.727	1286.193	1750.872	2373.306	3196.751	4273.241	5664.898	7445.116
98		947.136	1291.980	1760.321	2388.219	3219.605	4307.371	5714.709	7516.344
99		950.519	1297.731	1769.720	2403.070	3242.385	4341.419	5764.443	7587.518
100	700.31	953.876	1303.446	1779.071	2417.858	3265.091	4375.387	5814.102	7658.639
101		957.210	1309.126	1788.374	2432.586	3287.724	4409.275	5863.686	7729.708
102		960.519	1314.771	1797.630	2447.253	3310.286	4443.086	5913.195	7800.725
103		963.805	1320.382	1806.840	2461.861	3332.777	4476.819	5962.631	7871.691
104		967.067	1325.960	1816.004	2476.411	3355.199	4510.476	6011.994	7942.606
105		970.306	1331.504	1825.123	2490.903	3377.551	4544.058	6061.286	8013.470
106		973.523	1337.016	1834.198	2505.338	3399.835	4577.565	6110.507	8084.286
107		976.718	1342.496	1843.229	2519.717	3422.053	4610.999	6159.657	8155.052
108		979.890	1347.944	1852.217	2534.041	3444.204	4644.359	6208.738	8225.769
109		983.042	1353.361	1861.162	2548.310	3466.288	4677.648	6257.750	8296.438
110	718.31	986.172	1358.747	1870.065	2562.525	3488.309	4710.865	6303.694	8367.059
111		989.281	1364.103	1878.927	2576.687	3510.265	4744.012	6355.571	8437.633
112		992.370	1369.430	1887.749	2590.796	3532.157	4777.089	6404.381	8508.160
113		995.439	1374.727	1896.529	2604.853	3553.987	4810.097	6453.126	8578.641
114		998.487	1379.995	1905.271	2618.858	3575.756	4843.038	6501.805	8649.076
115		1001.517	1385.235	1913.973	2632.814	3597.463	4875.911	6550.420	8719.466
116		1004.527	1390.446	1922.636	2646.719	3619.110	4908.717	6598.971	8789.810
117		1007.518	1395.630	1931.261	2660.574	3640.697	4941.457	6647.459	8860.109
118		1010.490	1400.786	1939.849	2674.381	3662.225	4974.132	6695.884	8930.365
119		1013.444	1405.916	1948.399	2688.139	3683.694	5006.743	6744.247	9000.576
120	734.95	1016.379	1411.019	1956.912	2701.850	3705.106	5039.289	6792.548	9070.744

Selected Answers to Questions and Problems

Chapter 1

1-1 The word discipline generally refers to a branch of knowledge or learning, such as English, mathematics, physics, biology, and economics. To the extent that managerial economics is the study of the behavior of the firm and its relation to the economy, it is a discipline—in the same sense that psychology studies the behavior of the individual person and sociology that of the group. At the same time, it is interdisciplinary in that it crosses the boundaries of several established disciplines, as do urban studies, Western civilization studies, engineering, and business administration. But one should not be too concerned with boundaries in one's search for knowledge.

1-3 The first requisite of continued employment is to please the boss. In this vein, the stockholders (board of directors or president) first must be satisfied; then please yourself.

1-6 Those who let opportunities to gain knowledge pass them by are most unlikely to be hired by one of the best firms, much less become boss. Detailed knowledge of problem-solving techniques can improve one's judgment and make one intellectually qualified to judge the quality of recommendations submitted for approval. The boss who knows less about decision-making than the employees and competitors is at their mercy. Also, the embarrassment of occupying a position with requirements obviously exceeding one's abilities can be very painful. Top executives tend to absorb uncommon amounts of knowledge from every experience, just as a sponge absorbs water.

1-8 One's conception of reality is a product of one's background and perception, which cannot be all-knowing. Our individual snapshots of reality do not provide us with adequate vision to permit perfectly accurate identification. Kenneth Boulding believes ". . . people tend to interpret the present in terms of the traumatic experiences of their youth" [4, p. 8].

Chapter 2

2-1 a. 3; c. 3/5.

2-2 a. 10; c. $16X^3 - 16$; e. $X^3(X - 4)/(X - 3)^2$; g. $-X/\sqrt{16 - X^2}$; i. $9X/4\sqrt{9X^2 - 25}$; k. $-18/X^2$; m. $4X + 1$; o. $2/3X^{1/3}$; q. $(16 - 9X)/2X(4 - 3X)$; s. $15^X \ln 15$; u. $-2e^{X-2/3}/3X^{5/2}$.

2-3 a. $\partial Y/\partial X = 3X^2 + 6ZX$, $\partial Y/\partial Z = 3X^2 + 2Z$; c. $\partial Y/\partial X = XZ^2e^{XZ} + Ze^{XZ}$, $\partial Y/\partial Z = (XZ + 1)Xe^{XZ}$.

2-4 a. $Y' = 9X^2 - 2$, $Y'' = 18X$; c. $Y' = 10X - 1$, $Y'' = 10$.

2-5 a. $X = 3.51/12, 20.49/12$; the latter value gives max. Y, since Y'' is negative for that value of X.

2-6 a. $X = 32.4$, $Z = 35.2$; c. $X = 41.3$, $Z = 17.6$.

2-7 a. $X = 3.83$.

2-9 b. $Q = 3.5$ units.

Chapter 3

3-1 $Z = 15$, $X_2 = 3$, $X_3 = 1$, $X_1 = S_1 = S_2 = 0$.
3-3 $Z = 18$, $X_2 = 3$, $S_1 = 1$, $S_2 = 5$, $X_1 = S_3 = 0$.
3-5 $Z = 710/31$, $X_2 = 20/31$, $X_4 = 130/31$, $X_1 = X_3 = S_1 = S_2 = 0$.

Chapter 4

4-2 $Y_1 = 5$, $Y_2 = 20$, $Z = 8{,}500$.
4-4 $Y_1 = 0$, $Y_2 = 5\frac{5}{11}$, $Y_3 = 6\frac{4}{11}$, $Z = 130\frac{10}{11}$.
4-6 a. $C = 37\frac{1}{7}$, $X_1 = 8\frac{4}{7}$, $X_2 = 5\frac{5}{7}$, $X_3 = 0$.
4-8 $Z = 80/3$, $Y_1 = 4\frac{2}{3}$. $W_3 = 97\frac{1}{3}$, $Y_2 = 2\frac{2}{3}$.

Chapter 5

5-1.
$$X^2 + Y^2 = 1$$
$$Y^2 = 1 - X^2$$
$$Y = (1 - X^2)^{1/2}$$
$$\frac{dY}{dX} = \tfrac{1}{2}(1 - X^2)^{-1/2}(-1)$$
$$= -\tfrac{1}{2}(1 - X^2)^{-1/2}$$
$$\frac{d^2Y}{dX^2} = \tfrac{1}{4}(1 - X^2)^{-1\frac{1}{2}}(-2X)$$
$$= -\frac{X}{2(1 - X^2)^{3/2}}$$

For $0 < X < 1$, d^2Y/dX^2 is negative. Therefore, curve is concave to the origin.

5-2a.
$$\Pi_\lambda = Q_1 - 3Q_1Q_2 + Q_2^2 + \lambda_1(300 - Q_1 - Q_2) + \lambda_2(Q_1Q_2 - 200)$$
$$\frac{\partial \Pi_\lambda}{\partial Q_1} = 1 - 3Q_2 - \lambda_1 + \lambda_2Q_2 \leq 0$$
$$Q_1\frac{\partial \Pi_\lambda}{\partial Q_1} = Q_1(1 - 3Q_2 - \lambda_1 + \lambda_2Q_2) = 0$$

$$\frac{\partial \Pi_\lambda}{\partial Q_2} = -3Q_1 + 2Q_2 - \lambda_1 Q_2 + \lambda_2 Q_1 \leq 0$$

$$Q_2 \frac{\partial \Pi_\lambda}{\partial Q_2} = Q_2(-3Q_1 + 2Q_2 - \lambda_1 Q_2 + \lambda_2 Q_1) = 0$$

$$\frac{\partial \Pi_\lambda}{\partial \lambda_1} = 300 - Q_1 - Q_2 \geq 0$$

$$\lambda_1 \frac{\partial \Pi_\lambda}{\partial \lambda_1} = \lambda_1(300 - Q_1 - Q_2) = 0$$

$$\frac{\partial \Pi_\lambda}{\partial \lambda_2} = Q_1 Q_2 - 200 \geq 0$$

$$\lambda_2 \frac{\partial \Pi_\lambda}{\partial \lambda_2} = \lambda_2(Q_1 Q_2 - 200) = 0$$

d. $$\Pi_\lambda = 5Q_1^2 Q_2 + \lambda_1(100 - 3Q_1 - Q_2^2) + \lambda_2(Q_1 - 15)$$

$$\frac{\partial \Pi_\lambda}{\partial Q_1} = 10Q_1 Q_2 - 3\lambda_1 + \lambda \geq 0$$

$$Q_1 \frac{\partial \Pi_\lambda}{\partial Q_1} = Q_1(10Q_1 Q_2 - 3\lambda_1 + \lambda_2) = 0$$

$$\frac{\partial \Pi_\lambda}{\partial Q_2} = 5Q_1^2 - 2\lambda_1 Q_2 \geq 0$$

$$Q_2 \frac{\partial \Pi_\lambda}{\partial Q_2} = Q_2(5Q_1^2 - 2\lambda_1 Q_2) = 0$$

$$\frac{\partial \Pi_\lambda}{\partial \lambda_1} = 100 - 3Q_1 - Q_2^2 \leq 0$$

5-3 a. Noninteger solution: $\Pi = 34\frac{2}{3}$, $X_1 = \frac{2}{3}$, $X_2 = 6\frac{1}{3}$, $S_1 = S_2 = 0$. Integer solution: $\Pi = 34$, $X_1 = 1$, $X_2 = 5$, $S_1 = 1$, $S_2 = 0$.

Chapter 6

6-2 Economists typically consider all of these items to be taken into account when using the concept of utility. This may be adequate for a theoretical concept, but the student should be aware of the assumptions being made. In practical life, it may be possible to approximate some of the factors a through j and use the knowledge profitably. This may be quite feasible for some commodities over certain periods of time when one factor is dominant and the others much less important.

6-4.

	I	II	III	IV	V	VI	VII	VIII	IX	X
GALLONS	4	3	2	1	0	0	0	0	0	0

Chapter 7

7-1. a. -0.005; c. 200; e. -3.0; g. $-1/3$; i. 0.20; k. 0.80.

7-3. Since DE and DB have a common y-intercept at point D, they will have the same elasticity at any given point. Therefore, the elasticity of DE at C is equal to the elasticity of DB at C. But AB and DB have the same x-intercept and therefore have the same elasticity at any given quantity. Thus, elasticity is the same at points C, C', and G.

7-5. $\dfrac{dQ}{dP} = -akP^{-a-1}$; $E_D \doteq \dfrac{dQ}{dP} \times \dfrac{P}{Q} = (-akP^{-a-1})\dfrac{P}{kP^{-a}} = -a$.

7-8. a. $E_D = -5.2$; c. $-16/17$.

Chapter 8

8-2. a. c; c. c; e. a, g; g. e.

8-3. b. $E_{A,A} = -9/51.7$, $E_{A,B} = 2.7/51.7$; d. $E_{A,A} = -2.5/5.7$, $E_{A,B} = 2.5/5.7$.

8-5. Elasticity of supply at any point B is

$$E_S = \frac{\triangle Q}{\triangle P} \cdot \frac{P}{Q} = \frac{CA}{AB} \cdot \frac{AB}{DA} = \frac{CA}{DA}$$

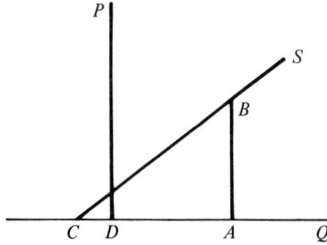

or by the use of calculus,

$$P = a + bQ$$
$$\frac{DP}{dQ} = b$$
$$E_S = \frac{dQ}{dP} \cdot \frac{P}{Q} = \frac{1}{b} \cdot \frac{a + bQ}{Q} = \frac{a + bQ}{bQ}$$

As long as a is positive, $E_S > 1$.

Chapter 9

9-2. When price of X falls, budget lines pivot counterclockwise from AB to AC to AD, and equilibrium points are 1, 2, 3, respectively. At P_1, AE will be spent on OH of commodity X. As price falls to P_2, AF is spent on OI, and for P_3, AG is spent on OJ.

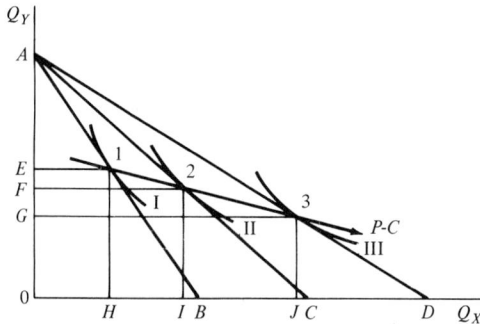

9-5. $U = Q_X^3 Q_Y^2$

$MU_X = \dfrac{\partial U}{\partial Q_X} = 3Q_X^2 Q_Y^3$

$MU_Y = \dfrac{\partial \Pi}{\partial Q_Y} = 3Q_X^3 Q_Y^2$

Note that MU depends on quantities of both X and Y, that is, their utilities are not independent.

In consumer equilibrium,

$$\frac{MU_X}{P_X} = \frac{MU_Y}{P_Y} \quad \text{or}$$

$$\frac{3Q_X^2 Q_Y^3}{P_X} = \frac{3Q_X^3 Q_Y^2}{P_Y} \quad \text{or}$$

$$\frac{Q_Y}{P_X} = \frac{Q_X}{P_Y} \quad \text{or}$$

$$P_Y Q_Y = P_X Q_X$$

Substituting in $R = P_X Q_X + P_Y Q_Y$,

$$R = 2P_X Q_X \quad \text{or} \quad Q_X = \frac{R}{2P_X}$$

which is the equation for a negatively sloped demand curve in the form of a rectangular hyperbola.

9-7b. As P_X rises, the budget line shifts from AB to AC. To restore the consumer to the original level, shift AC to DE tangent to III.

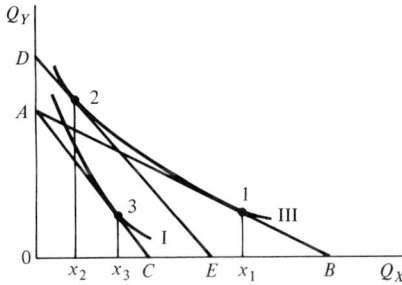

Total effect = substitution effect + income effect
$$X_1 X_3 = X_1 X_2 + X_3 X_2 \text{ (negative)}$$

Chapter 10

10-2 c. Given only the stated assumptions and no more information, the conclusions are valid for the individual. One can think of cases where some individuals might be better off economically and otherwise if they were not given the discretion to purchase whatever they thought for the moment only to be better, such as harmful drugs and gambling, or where receipt of cash might make them easier prey for muggers, thieves, and domineering relatives. But this requires a value judgment by officials of the state, whose judgments are inevitably suspect.

e. Yes. But this is not to say that all subsidies should be removed. Perhaps greater use of subsidies is desirable in creating jobs, reducing pollution, and so on.

10-3 b. Awareness of the upward bias of the CPI could influence his judgment in tying union wage agreements to movements in the CPI and in his assessment of the extent of inflation used in forecasting demand and planning investments.

Chapter 11

11-4. $b = 7,500$, $a = 4,354$.

11-6. $E_P = -3.9$, $E_Y = 0.35$.

Chapter 12

12-3. a. At point F' in Figure 13-2b if a is a free good. At E' if b is free.

c. Point B, since the slope of OB ($= AP_a$) equals the slope of TP at B ($= MP_a$).

e. Definitely not at point A. Point B if b is free or point C if a is free. Probably between B and C.

12-5. The same level of output can be produced by using less of both x and y, that is, the budget line can be shifted toward the origin until it becomes tangent to Q_1, the tangency point giving the least-cost input combination.

12-7. a. $x = (4M + 3)/18$, $y = (5M - 3)/9$; c. $x = (7P - 2)/2P$, $y = (16P - 5)/2P$.

12-8. b. $x^{1/2} = 3P$, $y^{1/2} = 2P$, $Q = 42P$.

Chapter 13

13-1. a. no; c. $E_x = \gamma^{-P} \delta(q/y)^P$, $E_y = \gamma^{-P}(1 - \delta) (q/y)^P$

Chapter 14

14-1. b. 400 man-hours of labor per week and no space left over.

d. Process 2 because it is more profitable.

2 units $\times$ \$120 = \$240
3 units $\times$ \$110 = \$330 = maximum profit
2 units $\times$ \$100 = \$200

14-3. No. Any use of process 2 is inefficient because both b_1 and b_2 are required to produce the same level of output as with process 1.

14-4. In Figure 14-4a, point A.

14-6. a. $\pi = 16$, $X_1 = 4\frac{2}{3}$, $X_2 = \frac{2}{3}$; c. $\pi = 1\frac{1}{7}$, $X_1 = 4\frac{2}{7}$, $X_2 = 1\frac{3}{7}$; e. $\pi = 22$, $X_1 = 4$, $X_2 = 2$.

Chapter 15

15-2. Historical costs are not relevant for replacement decisions. The only relevant costs are alternative costs. If unit costs, after taking into account all additional costs, can be lowered by substituting the new machine for the old one, then replacement should be made. Relevant considerations would include the relative efficiencies of the two machines, cost of the new machine, maintenance costs, scrap values, and tax considerations in addition to those associated with depreciation expenses such as investment tax credits.

15-3. a. $FC = 5$ at any Q; c. $TC = 44$; e. $Q = 0.839$; g. $Q = \frac{3}{10}$.

Chapter 17

17-1. $a = 59.62$, $b = -0.40957$, $P = 75.29\%$.

17-2. $\log Y = 117.14 - 0.28779 \log X$, or $Y = 117.14X^{-0.28779}$, σ est $Y = 0.03536$.

17-3. a. $P = 10$ per cent; c. $P = 90$ per cent; e. $P = 200$ per cent.

17-4. a. $b = -0.2345$; c. $b = -0.3959$.

17-5. a. $Y = 167$; c. $Y = 51$.

17-6. For unit 3, $Y = 73.01$, $Y_c = 255.01$.

17-7. a. $Y_c = 1,518$; c. $Y_c = 57,218$.

17-8. a. $a = \#1 = 237$; c. $a = 171$.

17-9. $\overline{Y} = 58$ man-hours.

17-10. Unit 32.

17-11. $Y_c = 27,555$ man-hours.

17-12. a. 17,497 man-hours; b. $173,528; c.

	Total	Average
year 1	$47,282	$3,152
2	59,941	1,998
3	50,190	1,673
4	16,115	1,612

17-13. First week, two units + work on third; second week, three units + work on sixth; . . . fifteenth week, eight units.

17-14. a. $300 per unit; c. unit 78.

17-15. a. Unit price $Y = \$2.45$; b. $P = 54.5$ per cent.

17-16. 12,000 man-hours.

17-17. a. Ye Olde, $31,687; Neue, $25,718; b. Neue has least total cost for 75 units.

17-18.	Unit	Assembly	Machine	Total
	#1	26	60	86
	5	19	53	72
	20	12	48	60

Chapter 18

18-2. a. Technological change refers to a shifting of an isoquant, while a change in technique may also refer to a movement from one point to another *along* the same isoquant.

c. A change in the relative costs of labor and capital is indicated by a change in the slope of the price line. The least cost combination of inputs will therefore move from one point to another along a given output, as from point 1 to point 2 in the figure.

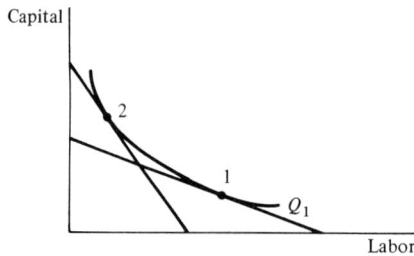

18-6. In the business of forecasting the guiding rule is "if it works, use it." One must be careful, however, if there are apparent reasons why the analogy may not work again.

Chapter 19

19-2. a. Description is not complete because some elements may have crossed the boundary and crossed back several times between the times observed.
  b. Some elements exist only as flows, such as time, electricity, and happiness.
  c. Tools and people are not embodied in any product. They provide services, but their fund remains intact (but with some wear and tear). The services may be used or not used, but they can not be accumulated for later use.
  d. This statement is accurate if it is recalled that it took time for the factory to be built and that it requires a process fund.

19-4. a. Requires sufficiently high demand for the product.
  b. Can't be used to produce everything man needs, for instance, new processes.
  c. Limited by the physical conditions of life on this planet: climate, seasons, energy resources. A process cannot be started at just any time desired if it depends on nature, as does farm production.

19-6. Different sources of energy: Agriculture depends more on solar radiation than mineral resources. Greater dependence of agriculture upon the workings of nature, which determines the timing.

Chapter 20

20-2. The upward-sloping portion of the firm's marginal-cost curve, which lies above its average variable cost.

20-5. $TR = PQ$

$$MR = \frac{d(TR)}{dQ} = \frac{d(PQ)}{dQ} = P\frac{dQ}{dQ} + Q\frac{dP}{dQ}$$

$$= P + Q\frac{dP}{dQ}$$

Since $E = -(P/Q) \cdot dQ/dP$, the value of dQ/dP can be substituted into the equation for MR:

$$\frac{dQ}{dP} = -\frac{EQ}{P}$$

$$MR = P + Q\frac{dP}{dQ} = P + \frac{Q}{dQ/dP} = P - \frac{PQ}{EQ}$$

$$= P - \frac{P}{E}$$

20-7. a. Profits obtained separately:

$$\frac{\partial \Pi_a}{\partial Q_a} = 6 - 2Q_a = 0, \text{ or } Q_a = 3$$

$$\frac{\partial \Pi_b}{\partial Q_b} = 8 - 2Q_b = 0, \text{ or } Q_b = 4$$

$$\Pi_a = 6(3) - (3)^2 - (4) = 5$$

$$\Pi_b = 8(4) - (4)^2 - 2(3) = 2$$

$$\Pi_s = 5 + 2 = 7$$

Profits obtained jointly:

$$\Pi_j = \Pi_a + \Pi_b$$

$$= 4Q_a - Q_a^2 + 7Q_b - Q_b^2$$

$$\frac{\partial \Pi}{\partial Q_a} = 4 - 2Q_a = 0, \text{ or } Q_a = 2$$

$$\frac{\partial \Pi}{\partial Q_b} = 7 - 2Q_b = 0, \text{ or } Q_b = 3.5$$

$$\Pi_j = 4(2) - (2)^2 + 7(3.5) - (3.5)^2$$

$$= 8 - 4 + 24.5 - \frac{49}{4} = 16.5$$

Profit difference $= \Pi_j - \Pi_s = 16.5 - 7 = 9.5$.

Chapter 21

21-2. Reference to overall elasticity typically means the slope of the demand curve. This can be misleading when comparing two markets, since the point on the curve is critical. The statement can be made precisely correct by substituting *elasticity coefficient* for *overall elasticity*.

21-3. Third-degree price discrimination: a. $\Pi = 69\frac{5}{12}$, $P_1 = 8\frac{1}{2}$, $P_2 = 12\frac{1}{2}$, $MR_1 = MR_2 = 1$; b. $\Pi_\lambda = 66$, $P_1 = 10.1$, $P_2 = 10.1$, $MR_1 = 3.2$, $MR_2 = -4.8$.

21-4. First-degree price discrimination: a. $Q = 6.33$, $P = 186.7$, $\Pi = 505.96$; b. $Q_1 = 6.32$, $P_1 = 156.8$, $Q_3 = 6.67$, $\Pi = 347$.

Chapter 22

22-2. This is an explicit value judgment, which is in accord with Bergson's recommendation for determining a social welfare function.

22-3. a. All points along O_AO_B between points 1 and 2 are superior to point 1, because one or both A and B can gain from exchange without loss to the others.
  b. A movement from point 1 to point 2 is an improvement for B, because he moves to a higher indifference curve (B_3 to B_4) but not for A, since he stays on his same curve (A_1)—this satisfies the Pareto criterion. A movement from 2 to 3 does not, because B is worse off in moving to a lower indifference curve (B_4 to B_3).
  c. No, because all points along O_AO_B are Pareto-efficient and a value judgment is required to determine which point is best.
  d. The point on or below the production-possibilities curve at which the community is producing determines the amounts of beans and machines in existence.

22-5. Unless one of the partners changes his mind, they cannot reach a decision, because a majority prefers each town and an equal number of points is given to each. The group decision is intransitive, since by majority vote Eureka is preferred to Emporia, Emporia is preferred to El Dorado, and El Dorado is preferred to Eureka.

Chapter 23

23-2. a. internalization; b. regulation; c. voluntary agreement; d. excise tax.
  e. The intended purpose of the excise subsidy may be what some would call a naive approach to reduce the consumption of what is thought to be an undersirable weed.

23-4. No. When the farmer moves his labor and capital to a less suitable location, the loss falls on the owners of land adjacent to the railway. Since all factors other than land are mobile enough to be used elsewhere at market prices, the economic loss is no more than the loss of rent suffered by the owners of the land. The loss may be even less to the extent that a switch can be made to more spark-resistant crops or devices be installed to prevent sparks at costs less than the value of the loss of rent [6, p. 7].

23-6. No. Partial equilibrium analysis assumes optimum conditions in all other sectors. If the conditions are not fully met, there is no certainty that optimal outputs in the examined sector will move the whole economy closer to the Pareto optimum [6, p. 8].

23-8. The cost of removing some of the wastes may not exceed the benefits derived. This means that resources may be better spent on other projects.

Chapter 24

24-2. a. $V = \$1,210$; c. $V = \$1,219.4$.

24-4. $i = 4.28$ per cent.

24-5. a. $P = \$2,620$; b. $P = \$7,130$; c. $P = \$7,872$; d. $P = \$40,100$.

Chapter 25

25-2. Possible answers:
1. Knowledge is the essence of human rationality.
2. Knowledge is capable of producing higher levels of knowledge and new ways of accomplishing goals that were not even perceived initially.
3. Knowledge can be given away and yet retained by the individual.
4. Knowledge is something one can never be sure one has enough of.

25-4. First he must obtain the information through research, purchase, or monitoring. If he is the sole possessor of the information, the surest way of preserving it as his personal property is to keep it secret. If secrecy is not preservable, he can apply for legal recognition of his property rights by seeking a patent or copyright.

Chapter 26

26-2. According to a per se law, bigness itself is conclusive evidence of illegal monopolization. Under a rule-of-reason interpretation, extenuating circumstances, such as an absence of any overt abusive acts, might permit the monopoly to be ruled legal. Recent court rulings in merger cases tend to be predominantly per se.

26-4. The relevant market is whatever the court says it is, ranging from a shopping center in a city to the nation. The government currently tends, in effect, to direct its attention to the market yielding the highest concentration ratio. The firm, of course, prefers to use market definitions yielding lower ratios.

Appendix A

A-1. a. $x = -1$, $y = 2$; c. $x_1 = 2\frac{2}{7}$, $x_2 = -\frac{3}{7}$, $x_3 = -\frac{2}{7}$.

A-2. a.1. $C = \begin{bmatrix} 4 & 9 \\ 10 & 8 \end{bmatrix}$; a.3. $C = \begin{bmatrix} 6 & 12 & 5 \\ 4 & 11 & 8 \\ 7 & 2 & 9 \end{bmatrix}$; b.3. $C = \begin{bmatrix} -2 & 1 & 0 \\ 2 & 2 & 1 \end{bmatrix}$;

c.3. $C = \begin{bmatrix} 18 & 2 \\ -4 & 8 \end{bmatrix}$; d.1. $C = 15$; d.3. $C = 19$; e.1. $C = \begin{bmatrix} 24 \\ 12 \\ 1 \end{bmatrix}$;

e.3. $C = \begin{bmatrix} 25 & 27 \\ 29 & 26 \end{bmatrix}$; e.5. $C = \begin{bmatrix} 8 & 25 \\ 1 & 9 \end{bmatrix}$; f.2. $AB = \begin{bmatrix} 28 & 24 \\ 10 & 5 \end{bmatrix}$;

$BA = \begin{bmatrix} 17 & 12 \\ 29 & 14 \end{bmatrix}$; f.4. $AB = BA = \begin{bmatrix} 20 & 35 & 40 \\ 47 & 83 & 94 \\ 51 & 94 & 102 \end{bmatrix}$.

A-3. a. $X = A^{-1}B = \begin{bmatrix} -1 \\ 2 \end{bmatrix}$ and therefore $x = -1$ and $y = 2$; c. $x_1 = 2\frac{2}{7}$, $x_2 = -\frac{3}{7}$, $x_3 = -\frac{2}{7}$.

Author Index

Subject Index